UNDERSTANDING ANTITRUST AND ITS ECONOMIC IMPLICATIONS

Fourth Edition

E. Thomas Sullivan
Irving Younger Professor of Law and Dean Emeritus
University of Minnesota Law School

Jeffrey L. Harrison
Stephen C. O'Connell Chair
University of Florida College of Law

™ LexisNexis™

Matthew Bender®

Library of Congress Control Number: 2002117759

ISBN#: 0-8205-5707-2

Editorial Offices
744 Broad Street, Newark, NJ 07102 (973) 820-2000
201 Mission St., San Francisco, CA 94105-1831 (415) 908-3200
701 East Water Street, Charlottesville, VA 22902-7587 (804) 972-7600
www.lexis.com

(Pub.0891)

For Susan and Sarah

PREFACE TO FOURTH EDITION

Fifteen years ago the first edition of this book appeared. At that time, lower courts were still in the process of recognizing the importance of two important shifts in antitrust law. The first was an increased emphasis on economic analysis as signaled by *Continental T.V. Inc. v. Sylvania*. The second was the application of the doctrines of antitrust standing and antitrust injury to narrow the scope of potential antitrust plaintiffs.

Subsequent editions of this book have treated further refinements with respect to these two crucial antitrust concerns. In addition, the intervening years witnessed progress toward a predictable standard for predatory prices, an effort by the Supreme Court to describe what a "quick look" analysis means, and much greater sophistication with respect to the analysis of market power. This fourth edition tracks further developments with respect to all of these traditional areas of analysis.

As with most areas of law, there always are new challenges as the world changes. In the case of antitrust, the new challenges stem from continued economic globalization and technological advances. Globalization requires consideration of the international reach of the United States' antitrust law. Technological change requires one to consider the intersection of antitrust law and intellectual property. This fourth edition includes greatly expanded treatment of these two important areas of analysis.

Since the last edition, clearly the most public display of antitrust came in the *Microsoft* case. The long-run impact of that case on antitrust law may not be felt for some time. In this volume we examine the possible implications of *Microsoft* for a variety of areas including monopolization, market power analysis, and tying doctrine.

As always this has been a joint undertaking. We have enjoyed our collaboration in producing what we hope will be a useful hornbook to students, practitioners and judges. Professor Harrison would like to thank

Margie Tyler for her help in preparing the manuscript. Professor Sullivan would like to thank David James and Matt Scheidt. Both of us greatly appreciate the work of Ally VonHockman whose diligence at LexisNexis made our work easier.

February 2003

E. THOMAS SULLIVAN
University of Minnesota
Law School

JEFFREY L. HARRISON
University of Florida
College of Law

PREFACE TO THIRD EDITION

Ten years have now passed since the first edition of this book. It has been a period during which antitrust law continues to be shaped by the judicial philosophy found in *Continental T.V. v. GTE Sylvania*. This perspective was played out most recently in *State Oil v. Khan*, in which the Supreme Court (finally, some would say) overruled *Albrecht v. Herald Co.*

More noteworthy, perhaps, has been lower court reaction to two Supreme Court decisions made just prior to the publication of our second edition. Thus, over the past five years, courts have begun applying the teachings of both *Eastman Kodak Co. v. Image Technical Services* and *Brooke Group Ltd. v. Brown & Williamson Tobacco Co.* This volume addresses *Khan* as well as judicial reaction to *Image Tech.* and *Brown & Williamson* and other antitrust "events" like the 1997 Merger Guidelines.

At the heart of the book, however, is a more expansive treatment of traditional antitrust matters. The theory of market power is considered in a more focused manner as is the continuing efforts by courts to make sense of the complexities of market power analysis. In addition, substantial new treatment of antitrust standing, of domestic and international "commerce" issues, and of conspiracy and its multiple permutations has been added.

In preparing this edition, the authors once again thank each other and report that the book is the result of a joint effort. Dean Sullivan would also like to thank Deidre McGrath and David Schlutz for their research assistance. Professor Harrison would like to thank Danny Payne for his secretarial efforts and Bill Shilling for his research assistance. Finally, the authors thank Kent Hanson, their editor at Matthew Bender, whose tireless work on the manuscript was of inestimable value.

May 1998

E. THOMAS SULLIVAN
University of Minnesota
Law School

JEFFREY L. HARRISON
University of Florida
College of Law

PREFACE TO SECOND EDITION

Six years have passed since the publication of the first edition of this book. The Sherman Act has closed its first 100 years and began its second. It would be misleading to suggest that the 100th anniversary was marked by landmark decisions or even by a significant change in emphasis. It is clear that the economic approach to antitrust announced in *Continental T.V., Inc. v. GTE Sylvania* and the judicial philosophy compatible with that approach remain dominant.

When the first edition was published, the teachings of *Sylvania* had already influenced the law of both vertical and horizontal restraints. In the past six years, those teachings have been applied even further afield. In its latest term, the Supreme Court announced tough standards for plaintiffs relying on a theory of predatory pricing. Additional hurdles have been erected for private parties attempting to enforce the Robinson-Patman Act. Recent decisions concerning such threshold issues of summary judgment, antitrust standing, and antitrust injury are also generally consistent with the view that antitrust should play a smaller role in modern society.

Antitrust law is, however, nothing if not complex. While its influence may be withering, there continue to be decisions that cannot be easily reconciled with a reduced role. In the past six years, the Supreme Court has indicated that there is a lasting and important role for *per se* rules in appropriate cases. It has given new hope to plaintiffs in tying cases. It has narrowed, or at least refined, the antitrust exemption for "the business of insurance." More importantly, the Court has, on more than one occasion, been critical of the use of economic theory in the absence of supporting empirical data. It is this complexity that makes antitrust an exciting and challenging field.

In preparing this edition, the authors would once again like to thank each other and report that this book is the result of a joint effort throughout. In addition to those acknowledged in the first edition, Dean Sullivan would like to thank Craig Marquiz for his able research assistance. Professor Harrison would like to thank Danny Payne and Gwen Reynolds.

December 1, 1993

E. THOMAS SULLIVAN
University of Arizona
College of Law

JEFFREY L. HARRISON
University of Florida
College of Law

PREFACE TO FIRST EDITION

This volume on federal antitrust laws is both timely and overdue. It is merely because we are on the eve of celebrating the 100th anniversary of the Sherman Act and the 75th anniversary of the Clayton Act and Federal Trade Commission Act. Accordingly, it is an appropriate time to reflect on the state of antitrust law and to consider its future. These two objectives informed the direction and content of this text. The effort is overdue, as we believe this is the most comprehensive and balanced treatment of antitrust law in a single volume since the United States Court's 1977 landmark decision in *Continental T.V., Inc. v. GTE Sylvania*, which signaled a new era of antitrust law.

As every antitrust practitioner and scholar knows, the changes in the wake of *Sylvania* have made antitrust one of the most challenging and exciting fields of contemporary law. At times, it is also bewildering. Business activities that were once subject to "bright line" tests of legality are increasingly judged under the elusive "rule of reason" standard. For example, it can no longer be stated with confidence that pricing agreements among competitors are *per se* violations of § 1 of the Sherman Act. Similarly, mergers that were readily condemned 15 years ago are now commonplace. Pervading these changes is an increased reliance by the courts and by public enforcement agencies on the sophisticated economic analysis.

We approached our task with several goals in mind. First, we have attempted to highlight and restate those areas of antitrust law where the law is relatively clear. At the same time, where the issues are especially difficult and the law remains unclear, we have endeavored to provide the reader with an appropriate analytical approach. Second, we have discussed fully the latest cases as well as their landmark forerunners. Third, we have identified what appear to be the trends and competing points of view which are likely to dictate the direction of antitrust law in the years to come. This treatise is specifically designed not to become obsolete with the release of the latest Supreme Court decision. Fourth, the book offers full coverage, including horizontal and vertical conduct, monopolies, mergers, price discrimination, private and public enforcement issues, and antitrust economics.

Finally, our intent is to present a balanced presentation which does not put forth the "Chicago School" approach or any doctrine as providing the "right" answers to the complex economic, political, and social issues that are woven throughout this area of law. We have made an effort to present a wide spectrum of ideas and opinions regarding the goals and economic underpinnings of antitrust law.

A number of individuals assisted in this project and deserve recognition. Professor Sullivan would like to acknowledge the able research assistance of Winston Smart, Gail Israelievitch, Tom Glassberg, and Gerald Bassett.

He also would like to give special recognition to Jane Bettlach for her indispensable secretarial skills. Professor Harrison would like to thank Warren Braums, Charles Carlson, Laurel Judd, and Tony Smith. In addition, we would like to thank each other and report that the book is, in every sense, a joint effort and the product of a rewarding collaboration.

We offer this treatise as a restatement and critical assessment of antitrust law in anticipation of the first of many anniversaries celebrating the antitrust laws. We hope it will stimulate discussion about the role antitrust has played in the twentieth century and, as we approach the twenty-first century, the role it should play in our society and economy in the next century.

January 1988

E. Thomas Sullivan
Washington University
School of Law

Jeffrey L. Harrison
University of Florida
College of Law

TABLE OF CONTENTS

Chapter 3
ANTITRUST COVERAGE: JURISDICTION, ENFORCEMENT, AND EXCEPTIONS

Chapter 4
HORIZONTAL RESTRAINTS AND CARTEL BEHAVIOR

**Chapter 6
MONOPOLIZATION AND RELATED OFFENSES**

Chapter 7
MERGERS AND ACQUISITIONS

Chapter 1

ANTITRUST POLICY: AN INTRODUCTION

§ 1.01 The Focus of Antitrust

Antitrust is the study of competition. It is a body of law that seeks to assure competitive markets through the interaction of sellers and buyers in the dynamic process of exchange. For example, as a consumer, you are motivated by a desire to purchase products at the highest quality and lowest price. Through purchases you seek to maximize your satisfaction. Sellers of products, in turn, attempt to determine what consumers will buy and how to supply products at the highest quality and best prices. They also attempt to produce those products by expending the least amount of resources.

When buyers and sellers react as these assumptions suggest, the market is competitive. The single most important feature of this competitive interaction is that buyers and sellers act independently, not in concert. For sellers this means that each searches for opportunities to respond to the demands of consumers. The search is intensified by knowledge that, if sellers do not respond to the needs of consumers with the desired product at a fair price, a competitor is likely to fill the void by offering the product and earning a profit by doing so. What this means for you as a consumer is an opportunity to pick and choose among alternatives in order to maximize your satisfaction from each dollar spent.

Contrast this independent action by sellers with a case in which they have agreed to act in concert. For example, suppose the presidents of all the textbook publishing companies gathered in the proverbial "smoke–filled room" and agreed that only one publisher would produce antitrust books or that no textbooks would be sold for less than a set price. This agreement not to compete would mean that each producer would be far less concerned about responding to your needs. As a result, the range of choices available to you would be severely restricted. It is very likely that the satisfaction derived by you per dollar spent would decline.

Antitrust law is centered on certain principles; the primary one is that society is better off if markets behave competitively. Thus to study antitrust is to examine the relationship between buyers and sellers in individual markets, how products and resources are allocated, and how quantities and prices are determined within those markets. Because every student of antitrust is a consumer and, as a lawyer, a seller of services, the study of antitrust should be intrinsically valuable. Each of us is directly affected by the operation of the antitrust laws.

As we study antitrust, we see that it attempts to regulate producers and suppliers of products and services when their conduct does not conform to

1

certain expectations. As a matter of policy, we have decided through Congressional enactment that markets should be competitive. When the market — the interaction of buyers and sellers — deviates from the competitive ideal, antitrust law has a role to play. Private parties or federal or state governments may invoke the antitrust laws in order to regulate or correct the market failure. We must be cautious, however, that the cost of antitrust intervention and regulation of markets does not exceed the cost associated with the identified market failure. If the cost of antitrust enforcement is greater than the costs of the breakdown of the market forces, another kind of failure exists; it too can result in higher prices and injury to consumers. The cost of excessive regulation, as in the case of market failure, is ultimately, of course, borne by each of us as consumers.

The development of antitrust law has been evolutionary, changing over time as we gain new knowledge about how exchanges occur between buyers and sellers. In studying antitrust, we are drawn into a lively debate not only on what the law is but what it ought to be. This implicates ideology and philosophy, as well as history, economics and public policy. In short, the study of antitrust, as told in this text, is an evolution of assumptions about production and exchange functions in society and how those activities are ordered and regulated by society when there is a breakdown of market forces. While the reader may be introduced to new terminology in this book, the conduct described here is familiar to all of us. We experience it each day as consumers. This book gives each of us an opportunity to reflect on the dynamics of marketplace and the kinds of laws that ought to govern it.

Each chapter of this book addresses separate problems that affect competition. Chapter 2 reviews the economic assumptions and implications of antitrust conduct. Chapter 3 introduces the reader to jurisdiction and enforcement requirements under each antitrust law. It also sets forth certain exceptions and defenses to antitrust coverage. Chapter 4 discusses the problems involved when competitors enter into agreements that have the effect of restraining competition. In contrast, Chapter 5 concerns competition issues raised by agreements between firms at different levels in the production or distribution of a product, firms which are not in competition with each other. For example, if a manufacturer of a product attempts to establish the price at which the product is sold by the retailer to the consumer, antitrust law is implicated. Chapter 6 analyzes monopolies and how their conduct can injure consumers. Mergers and acquisitions, which have been frequent topics in the popular press, are discussed in Chapter 7. Finally, Chapter 8 analyzes the law that prohibits a seller from discriminating in price when it sells a product.

What you are about to discover is that while antitrust law has a rich, diverse and interesting history, it has no less a critical role to play in contemporary society. Its rich fabric surrounds all of our lives, whether consumers or producers, and especially as students studying the market-place, where mergers, monopolies and contracts that rig public bids and agreements that restrict competition seem pervasive. Knowledge of antitrust is relevant whether we work on Wall Street or on Main Street.

§ 1.02 Legislative History and Antitrust Goals

Because antitrust is the study of competition, the central issue is how that term has been defined by courts. This is the core question which you will focus on as you move through the chapters of this text. As you will quickly discern, the answer is largely a question of policy. It varies depending on one's ideology and views of the legislative history and development of the antitrust laws and their underlying values. Policy choices confront the antitrust student at every turn and this is true whether one seeks a contemporary interpretation of antitrust or whether one starts by reviewing the legislative history of the antitrust laws.

A contemporary application of the antitrust laws has a certain *deja vu* quality. The central arguments heard today in antitrust are similar to those echoed in the early, formative years of this country. The genesis of the antitrust debate predates the first antitrust statute, the Sherman Act in 1890. The debate is as old as Jefferson's and Hamilton's view of government.[1]

Jefferson urged a deconcentrated society and government, one that valued independent decision–making and equality — enhancing opportunities for small, local businesses. Control of economic concentrations of industrial power was central to Jeffersonian populism. Hamilton, on the other hand, feared that decentralization might interfere with the goal of efficiency. He was an exponent of a strong national government, particularly central control over financial and economic issues and institutions.[2] In the main, these two themes were fundamental to the formation and shape of our government. As we will see in this text, they, likewise, are evident in the study of antitrust today.

Jeffersonianism found expression in the congressional debates culminating in the passage of the Sherman Act. The Congress that passed the Sherman Act was concerned with business concentration, acquisition of monopoly power, and cartels that might lead to increased prices and overcharges to consumers. Entrepreneurial independence and freedom for independent decision–making and contracting in the market were, in addition, themes expressed in the legislative debates by those favoring legislation. Dispersing economic power and stimulating access to free markets also were principal goals. Distributional effects and equity concerns were directed toward protecting consumers from a redistribution of

---

[1] *See generally, The Political Economy of the Sherman Act: The First One Hundred Years* (E. Thomas Sullivan, ed., 1991); Baker and Blumenthal, *Ideological Cycles and Unstable Antitrust Rules*, 31 Antitrust Bull. 323, 324–25 (1986); A. Schlesinger, Jr., *The Cycles of American History*, 220–23, 242 (1986); A.D. Neale and D.G. Goyder, *The Antitrust Laws of the U.S.A.*, 439–43, 470 (3d ed. 1980).

[2] A. Hamilton, J. Madison, J. Jay, *The Federalist Papers*, Nos. 9, 11, 16 (C. Rossiter ed. 1961).

wealth from consumers to monopolists, and toward protecting competitors from predatory practices.[3] Generally speaking, these goals are unrelated to the Hamiltonian goal of efficiency, or the efficient allocation of resources.

Rejecting this politically–centered, distributive–goal analysis, some scholars have concluded that the main, if not the sole, purpose behind the Sherman Act was the promotion of economic efficiency.[4] Grounded in a more Hamiltonian approach, this theory argues that antitrust policy should sanction business conduct that promotes efficient allocations of resources. For many students of antitrust the ultimate question is whether the challenged practice will produce a net gain or loss to the consumer. The resolution of the underlying policy rationale for antitrust is crucial to a contemporary study of antitrust.

An objective, balanced reading of the legislative history of the Sherman Act reveals that multiple goals and values were expressed by supporters as the legislation was debated.[5] There is agreement today, however, that the antitrust laws were written foremost to encourage competition.[6] Contemporary disagreement centers on how that is best achieved and what groups in society should benefit from this goal.[7] It is, of course, frequently the case that as the antitrust laws are applied, winners and losers, by definition, emerge.

How, you might ask, is this debate about policy relevant to today's economy and how we interpret antitrust law? Although disagreeing as to the primacy or hierarchy of the various goals and policies expressed in the congressional debates, most antitrust commentators agree that, at bottom, Congress was most concerned with monopoly and cartel conduct[8] that

[3] S.1 51st Cong., 1st Sess. (1889), *reprinted in 1 The Legislative History of the Federal Antitrust Laws and Related Statutes* 89 (E. Kintner ed. 1978), 21 Cong. Rec. 2460, 2457, 3146, 3152 (1890). *See also* Stephen Ross, *Principles of Antitrust Law* 6–11 (1993); Lande, *Wealth Transfers as the Original and Primary Concern of Antitrust: The Efficiency Interpretation Challenged,* 34 Hastings L.J. 67, 6870 (1982); Sullivan, *The Economic Jurisprudence of the Burger Court's Antitrust Policy: The First Thirteen Years,* 58 Notre Dame L. Rev. 1 (1982); Fox, *The Modernization of Antitrust: A New Equilibrium,* 66 Cornell L. Rev. 1140 (1981); Schwartz, *"Justice" and Other Non–Economic Goals of Antitrust,* 127 U. Pa. L. Rev. 1076 (1979); Flynn, *Antitrust Jurisprudence: A Symposium on the Economic, Political and Social Goals of Antitrust Policy,* 125 U. Pa. L. Rev. 1182 (1977); Blake and Jones, *In Defense of Antitrust,* 65 Colum. L. Rev. 377 (1965).

[4] Bok, *Legislative Intent and the Policy of the Sherman Act,* 9 J.L. & Econ. 1 (1966); Hovenkamp, *Distributive Justice and Antitrust Laws,* 51 Geo. Wash. L. Rev. 1–4 (1982); R. Posner, *Economic Analysis of Law* 10 (2d ed. 1977); R. Posner, *Antitrust Law: An Economic Perspective* 4, chap. 2 (1976).

[5] R. Hofstadter, *What Happened to the Antitrust Movement?, The Paranoid Style in American Politics and Other Essays* 199–200, 205, 209 (1965). *See also* Page, *Ideological Conflict and the Origins of Antitrust Policy,* 66 Tulane L. Rev. 1 (1991).

[6] Lande, *supra* note 3. *See also Standard Oil Co. v. FTC,* 340 U.S. 231, 248–49 (1951); W. Adams & J. Brock, *The Bigness Complex* 87-117 (1986).

[7] *See e.g.* Lande, Consumer Choice as the Ultimate Goal of Antitrust, 62 U. Pitt. L. Rev. 503, 525 (2001)(suggesting that the focus of antitrust should shift from price to consumer choice).

[8] *See* Chapters 4 and 6 for definitions of these terms.

restrict output, increase prices to consumers,[9] and result in monopoly profits. High output, low prices, and acceptable quality were and are popular goals. Indeed, they are the driving sources that define competition in the market.[10] Competitive pricing is central to the whole of the legislative debate. Beyond this statement, given the ambiguous state of the legislative record and the lack of expert testimony by economists before the Congress, the legislative intent is conflicting and thus unclear. The early debate and the subsequent evolution of the law suggest multiple values and policies. The continuing debate over whether the goal of promoting competition was rooted in concern over allocative efficiency or distribution of wealth is not likely to be resolved soon.[11] Notwithstanding the academic debate over congressional intent, the promotion of competition through restraints on monopoly and cartel behavior clearly emerges as the first principle of antitrust. Monopoly profits are condemned either because they are achieved through allocative inefficiency[12] or because they redistribute income and wealth from consumers to producers.

What is clear from the legislative history of the Sherman Act is that Congress intended to incorporate and federalize the common law antitrust

---

[9] *See, e.g.,* Hovenkamp, *supra* note 4, at 16–17; Arthur, *Farewell to the Sea of Doubt: Jettisoning the Constitutional Sherman Act,* 74 Calif. L. Rev. 263, 286–87 (1986).

[10] *See generally* Sullivan, *On Nonprice Competition: An Economic and Marketing Analysis,* 45 U. Pitt. L. Rev. 771 (1984); Hovenkamp, *supra* note 4, at 27–31; Bok, *supra* note 4, at 16–21; R. Bork, *The Antitrust Paradox* 20–21 (1978); R. Posner, *Antitrust Law: An Economic Perspective* 23 (1976).

[11] The legislative intent regarding the other antitrust statutes discussed in this book is clearer. For example, the dominant underpinning of the Robinson–Patman Act in 1936, 15 U.S.C. § 13, was the protection of small businesses from leveraged buying practices of larger businesses; the legislation plainly was designed to promote small business over larger firms. *See generally* R. Bork, *supra* note 10, at 383; Elman, *The Robinson–Patman Act and Antitrust Policy: A Time for Reappraisal,* 42 Wash. L. Rev. 1 (1966); Hansen, *Robinson–Patman Law: A Review and Analysis,* 51 Fordham L. Rev. 1113 (1983). *See* Chapter 8 *infra.*

The same is true for the Clayton Act in 1914, particularly with regard to the 1950 Celler–Kefauver Amendments. *See* Lande, *supra* note 3, at 126–40; Fox, *supra* note 3, at 1144 n.12; Bork, *Section 7 of the Clayton Act and the Merging of Law and Economics,* 74 Harv. L. Rev. 226, 233 (1960). Hovenkamp, *supra* note 4, at 24–26 ("Bork's description of the legislative history of the Celler–Kefauver amendment is so inconsistent with the legislative history itself that it is difficult to believe Bork had the correct book in his hands when he described its contents." *Id.* at 24.) *See also* 51 Cong. Rec. 9088 (1914) (remarks of Rep. Mitchell); 96 Cong. Rec. 11506 (1950) (remarks of Sen. Kefauver). *See* Chapters 5 and 7, *infra.*

The Federal Trade Commission Act in 1914 had efficiency, as well as wealth distribution, concerns. "Monopoly is the evil we wish to control. Competition is the thing we wish to maintain." 51 Cong. Rec. 8855 (1914) (remarks of Rep. Morgan). Most antitrust observers agree that the purpose of the FTC Act was the same as the Sherman Act but that expanded powers were needed. As Congressman Stevens, a sponsor of the bill, observed: the purpose of the FTC Act was to serve as "a method of enforcing [the Sherman Act] and making it more effective and preventing its misuse." *Report of the Senate Comm. on Interstate Commerce,* S. Rep. No. 597, 63d Cong., 2d Sess. 8 (1914); 51 Cong. Rec. 14,934 (1914) *quoted* in Lande, *supra* note 3, at 107. *See also* Averitt, *The Meaning of "Unfair Acts or Practices" in Section 5 of the Federal Trade Commission Act,* 70 Geo. L.J. 225 (1981). Here, too, the debate continues whether allocative efficiency or wealth distribution was the primary objective of the statute. See Lande, *supra* note 3, at 106–26. *See also* R. Bork, *supra* note 10, at 20–21, 51.

[12] *See infra* Chapter 2.

precedents.[13] A problem of interpretation arose, however, because no unified common law of trade restraints existed. The common law in 1890 included English as well as American judge–made decisions and statutes,[14] which during the eighteenth and nineteenth centuries reflected the economic philosophies espoused at the time.[15] As one authority explained:

> The congressmen who drafted and passed the Sherman Antitrust Law thought they were merely declaring the illegality of offenses that the common law had always prohibited. [Like others, they have too easily] accepted the mistaken view that the attitude of the common law towards freedom of trade was essentially the same throughout its history.[16]

§ 1.03 Early Interpretation

The initial interpretation of the Sherman Act by courts was difficult because, in the words of Senator Sherman, the sponsor of the legislation:

> [I]t is difficult to define in legal language the precise line between lawful and unlawful combinations. This must be left for the courts to determine in each particular case. All that we, as lawmakers, can do is to declare general principles, and we can be assured that the courts will apply them as to carry out the meaning of the law, as the courts of England and the United States have done for centuries. This bill is only an honest effort to declare a rule of action . . .[17]

Congress, therefore, delegated broadly to the courts the role of applying general principles and filling in the large gaps left by the open–ended text of the statute. Common law was to serve as the background for the "meaning of the law."[18] But, as noted above, this was no easy task. The early courts found elusive the operational standards and underpinnings.

Early decisions saw the Supreme Court rapidly change the course of its interpretation, thus permitting a more evolutionary process of decisionmaking. In the first Sherman Act case, *United States v. E.C. Knight Co.*,[19]

---

[13] 21 Cong. Rec. 2456, 3146, 3151–52 (1890). *See* Arthur, *supra* note 9, at 277, 279–80, 284.

[14] H. Thorelli, *The Federal Antitrust Policy* 10 (1954); Dewey, *The Common–Law Background of Antitrust Policy*, 41 Va. L. Rev. 759 (1955). *See also* May, *Historical Analysis in Antitrust Law*, 35 N.Y.L. Sch. L. Rev. 857 (1990).

[15] W. Letwin, *Law and Economic Policy in America* 18–32 (1965). *See generally* Hovenkamp, *The Sherman Act and the Classical Theory of Competition* 10–19 (1989).

[16] *Id.* at p. 18. Copyright 1965 by the University of Chicago Press. Reprinted with permission. *See generally* May, *Antitrust Practice and Procedure in the Formative Era: The Constitutional and Conceptual Reach of State Antitrust Law, 1880–1918*, 135 U. Pa. L. Rev. 495 (1987); May, *Antitrust in the Formative Era: Contemporary Theory and State and Federal Practice, 1880–1918* (1988).

[17] 21 Cong. Rec. 2460 (1890).

[18] *Compare* Arthur, *supra* note 9, at 290–300 *with* Baxter, *Separation of Powers, Prosecutorial Discretion, and the "Common Law" Nature of Antitrust Law*, 60 Tex. L. Rev. 661 (1982). See also May, *The Role of the States in the First Century of the Sherman Act and the Larger Picture of Antitrust History*, 59 Antitrust L.J. 93 (1990).

[19] 156 U.S. 1 (1895).

decided in 1895, the Court held that restraints affecting merely the manufacturing of commodities did not come within the jurisdiction reach of the Act. This narrow definition of commerce would not last as such an interpretation would make the Sherman Act illusory. When the Court decided its first Sherman Act case on the merits in *United States v. Trans–Missouri Freight Ass'n*,[20] it adopted an over–inclusive interpretation to § 1; every restraint, without exception, was declared illegal.

The next year the Court rejected its reasoning in *Trans–Missouri* by distinguishing common law restraints from those condemned by the Sherman Act. In *United States v. Joint–Traffic Assoc.*,[21] the Court made clear that market practices that affect competition directly are illegal without inquiry into their reasonableness. Indirect or incidental restraints, under the so–called common law "ancillary restraint" doctrine,[22] however, are not condemned under § 1. Thus the *Trans–Missouri* rule that *all* restraints were unlawful under the new Sherman Act was rejected. From *Joint–Traffic* to the present, courts and the antitrust academic community have debated the original intentions of the antitrust laws and this "characterization" process of determining whether the restraint is a direct or indirect interference with commerce.

---

[20] 166 U.S. 290 (1897).

[21] 171 U.S. 505 (1898).

[22] See § 4.04, *infra*.

Chapter 2

ANTITRUST ECONOMICS

§ 2.01 Introduction

Since the origins of antitrust, economic theory has become increasingly important in shaping antitrust law and policy.[1] Economists originally shunned or were indifferent towards antitrust development; they did not play a central role in the legislative debates of the Sherman Act. Only later did economists join the debate as to the economic implications of antitrust. More recently, courts have begun to use concepts and theories developed by economists. Courts often weave these concepts into decisions to support their results. In order to predict and understand court decisions, the antitrust student must have an adequate understanding of economic theory.

The premise of antitrust is that some industries contribute best to overall social welfare if they are competitive.[2] In a competitive market setting, consumers attempt to maximize their satisfaction by allocating expenditures among various goods and services. Producers, on the other hand, must direct resources into goods and services that consumers value the most (allocative efficiency) and produce these products at the lowest per unit cost (productive efficiency). Thus, the economic theory underlying antitrust centers on price theory or microeconomics: the study of individual markets, including how prices and quantities are determined and how products and resources are allocated.

In a market driven economic system, individual firms[3] decide what and how much to produce, and what prices to charge; individual consumers

---

[1] The discussion in this chapter is based on the following sources: A. Alchian and W. Allen, *Exchange and Production* (1983); R. Blair and D. Kaserman, *Antitrust Economics* (1985); J. Hirshleifer, *Price Theory and Applications* (3d ed. 1984); H. Hovenkamp, *Federal Antitrust Policy* (3d ed. 1999); F.M. Sherer, & D. Ross, *Industrial Market Structure and Economic Performance* (3d ed. 1991); G. Stigler, *The Theory of Price* (3d ed. 1966). *See also* Gellhorn, *An Introduction to Antitrust Economics*, 1975 Duke L.J.1.

[2] It is far from clear as a matter of economic theory that increasing the competitiveness of a particular industry, in the context of other industries that remain highly concentrated, actually increases overall welfare. Indeed, the "theory of second best" suggests the opposite may be true. *See* F.M. Scherer, *Industrial Market Structure and Economic Performance* 24–29 (2d ed. 1980).

[3] The firm is the principal target of antitrust regulation. In terms of economics, it is a unit of production that converts input factors (capital, labor, raw materials, etc.) into goods and services which in turn are traded with consumers or other firms. In short, firms are "productive agents of society, engaged in the conversion of resources into final goods. [They] constitute the supply side of the product market and individuals the demand side." J. Hirshleifer, *Price Theory and Application* 173 (3d ed. 1984). When several independent firms are engaged in the production of the same commodity, they comprise the "industry." A "market" is made up of the buyers and sellers in a given industry "who communicate and transact for a given good." W. Shepard, *The Economics of Industrial Organization* 5 (1979). As explained in Chapter 6, this market is defined further by cross–elasticity of demand.

decide how much to buy and what price to pay. The market is controlled
by individual decisions. In order to analyze and predict market behavior,
economists generalize about individual economic behavior from two basic
assumptions: (1) the individual makes market decisions based upon self–
interest; one buys and sells[4] to maximize one's own personal wealth, utility,
or satisfaction; and, (2) the aggregates of these individual decisions serve
to maximize the wealth of society. Throughout this book the various topics
discussed are introduced with an examination of economic considerations.

Here, however, some fundamental definitions are set out and central
theories examined. First, the economic consequences of competition are
compared with those of monopoly. This discussion provides the background
for an understanding of the most common justification for the existence of
the antitrust laws. Second, the concept of market power is examined in
some detail. In recent years, in particular, the determination of the degree
of market power has become a central focus of many antitrust cases ranging
from agreements among competitors to behavior by single firms to mergers.
For this reason it is important to view the market power material as critical
to a full understanding of the materials that follow in Chapters 4–8.

§ 2.02 Perfect Competition

Levels of competition can be described along a continuum, extending from
what is called "perfect competition" to "pure monopoly." In order for a
market to be perfectly competitive, several conditions must hold: there are
many buyers and sellers; no individual firm is large enough to affect price
by individual action; products in the market are homogeneous, with each
product capable of serving as a substitute for another; barriers to entry do
not exist; and ability to increase production is without restriction. In
addition, producers and consumers have complete information of all relevant market factors. Perfect competition is characterized by uncoordinated,
individual decision making by each producer and consumer.

[A] Demand and Supply

In order to understand how a perfectly competitive market functions, it
is necessary to master the concepts of demand and supply. Demand is a
schedule of prices and the quantities individuals are willing and able to
purchase at each price. One might determine demand by asking individuals
how many units of a good they would buy at one price. The amounts would
be added to get the total amount demanded at that price. Then the same
question could be asked about a series of higher and lower prices.[5] We

---

[4] The price of a good is the rate at which one unit can be exchanged for money or for other
goods. Such a rate, in the case of a consumer good, reflects the subjective utility and the value
of the good to the producer and, in the case of a resource, the productivity of the resource
and the price of the good it is used to produce.

[5] The process involves "horizontally summing" the demand curves of individual consumers.
The summation is horizontal because quantity demanded is typically plotted along the X or
horizontal axis of a graph.

would have a list of prices and the amounts that would be demanded at each price. Note that a consumer must be both willing and able to buy in order to be counted in the economist's definition of demand. A poor person who is hungry but who cannot afford food or shelter is not, according to the economist, included in the demand.

Customarily, demand is depicted on a graph. In Figure 2–1, the X or horizontal axis represents quantity. The Y or vertical axis represents price. The demand curve displays the amount of goods consumers attempt to purchase at any given price. At $10 per unit, consumers will demand 10 units. At $5 per unit, consumers will demand 50 units. At $1 per unit, consumers will demand 100 units. Demand curves almost always slope downward and to the right. As the price declines, consumers find the good increasingly attractive compared to other goods and that they are able to buy more of the good.[6]

Supply is the converse of demand. It is a schedule of prices and the amounts sellers are willing to make available to consumers at each price. To derive it one could ask all sellers how much they would make available at each price. By summing the amounts each would make available at that price, one would determine the total supply at that price. By repeating the process for a series of prices, one would get a total amount offered for sale at each price.

Obviously higher prices mean a greater opportunity for profit, and one would expect suppliers to offer more as prices increase. As shown in Figure 2–2, this results in an upward sloping supply curve. For example, at $10 per unit, producers will attempt to sell 100 units. At $5 per unit, producers will offer 50 units for sale. At $1 per unit, producers will offer only 10 units for sale.

[B] Elasticity

The "laws" of demand and supply tell us that quantity demanded is inversely related to price and quantity supplied is directly related to price. As important as these general economic relationships is information concerning exactly how sensitive buyers and sellers are to price changes. The measure of responsiveness is called "elasticity." Technically, it is the ratio of the percentage change in quantity to the percentage change in price leading to the quantity change. Or, stated differently, it is the percentage change in quantity divided by the percentage change in price (% change quantity % change in price).

In the case of demand, when the percentage change in quantity exceeds the percentage change in price — elasticity is greater than 1 — the demand

---

[6] There is both a "substitution" and an "income" effect. As price decreases, consumers substitute the good with the decreased price for other goods used for the same purpose. For example, if the price of champagne decreases, they might drink more champagne and less grape soda. In addition, as the price of any good decreases, the real income or "buying power" of consumers increases. This increase in "income" results in increased consumption of some goods and services.

FIGURE 2–1

DEMAND

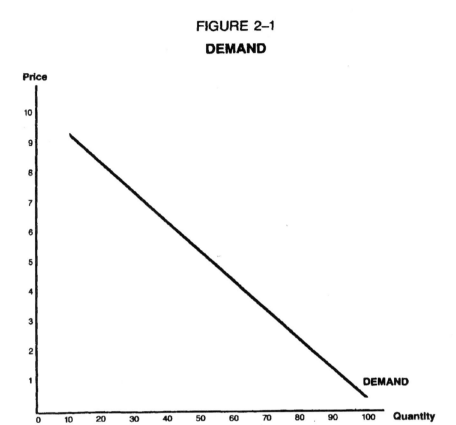

is elastic and amounts purchased will be greatly affected. Buyers are quite responsive to changes in price. When the percentage change in quantity is less than the percentage change in price, demand is said to be inelastic — buyers are not very responsive to price changes and purchases will not be drastically affected.

As will be discussed in greater detail below, elasticity of demand or "price elasticity," is critical in determining whether a firm possesses market power — that is, the ability to raise prices above what they would be in a competitive market. As a general matter, a firm facing an inelastic demand curve has greater market power than one facing an elastic demand.[7] The most important determinate of demand elasticity is the availability of substitute goods. If a firm attempts to raise price when there are good substitutes available, it will find its customers quite responsive and turning to the

---

[7] As a technical matter, all demand curves include an elastic and inelastic range. Sellers will always set prices in the elastic range.

FIGURE 2–2

SUPPLY

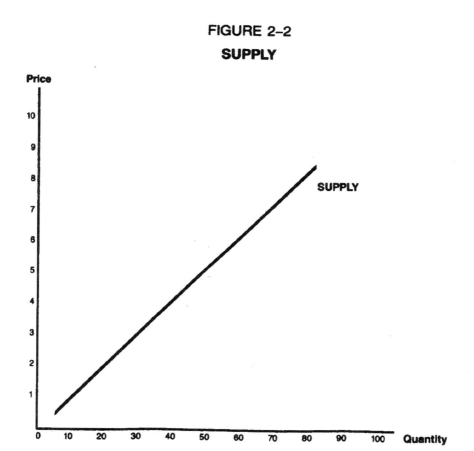

substitutes. On the other hand, if the seller is the sole seller of a necessary item, demand is likely to be relative inelastic.

The primary determinate of supply elasticity is the speed with which costs increase as production is increased. For example, if price increases and a firm is able to increase output at a relatively low additional cost, it will offer many more units for sale. This might be the case if the firm's plant is not operating at full capacity or if the good is produced with inexpensive inputs. Supply will also be elastic if new producers readily can enter the industry.[8] On the other hand, if it is quite costly to produce an additional unit, the firm will not respond to price increases by greatly increasing the quantity offered for sale.

---

[8] The reader who has a background in economics will note that the authors have studiously avoided making the distinction between "short run" and "long run" adjustments. We feel that the basic logic of microeconomics relevant to the study of antitrust can be understood without reference to this distinction. As a technical matter, though, the entrance of new producers is a "long run" phenomenon.

The term which is used to describe the way in which a firm's costs behave as it increases output is "marginal cost." Marginal cost is the additional cost to a firm of producing one more unit of output. In Figure 2–3, the marginal cost of unit 3 is $3. The marginal cost of unit 4 is $4 and so on.[9] When the marginal cost of each unit is displayed on the graph we have the firm's "marginal cost curve." The steeper the curve, the lower is the elasticity of supply for the firm. In other words, when costs increase rapidly as output increases, producers tend not to be very responsive to price changes.

[C]   Market Equilibrium

In a competitive market, the market price of a good or service and the quantity sold are determined by the interaction of demand and supply. In Figure 2–4, the demand curve from Figure 2–1 is superimposed over the supply curve from Figure 2–3. The price in the market will gravitate towards $5 — the equilibrium price — and the quantity bought and sold with gravitate towards 50 — the equilibrium quantity.[10] At any price other than $5 there will be a "surplus" or "shortage" in the market and forces will be set in motion to bring the price back to $5.

For example, at a price of $3, consumers will seek to purchase 70 units but suppliers will offer only 30 units for sale. The shortage of 40 units will mean that consumers will bid the price up and that suppliers will offer more for sale as price increases. The price will increase until the quantity supplied is equal to the quantity demanded. At a price of $7 producers will offer 70 units for sale but consumers will be willing to buy only 30 units. There will be a surplus of 40 units and prices will tend to fall. Only at a price of $5 and a quantity of 50 — where the demand and supply curves intersect — will quantity demanded equal quantity supplied. This is the point of competitive equilibrium.

Figure 2–4 illustrates two additional important concepts in antitrust economics: consumer surplus and producer surplus.

Although the price determined in the market is $5, the demand curve indicates that there were some consumers willing and able to pay more than $5 for the product. In other words, they placed a higher value on the good than the amount they were required to pay. The difference between the amount paid and the maximum a buyer would have been willing to pay is consumer surplus. There is consumer surplus associated with every unit sold.[11] This is because rational consumers will not buy items that are not

---

[9] The complete marginal cost curve would be U–shaped with the curve first sloping downward at low levels of output and then back up. The relevant portion of the curve, however, is the upward sloping segment.

[10] This is not to say that the price will be $5 or the quantity 50 units all the time. These are equilibrium points that the market will gravitate toward.

[11] The 50th unit is sold for exactly the maximum price the consumer is willing to pay. Thus, as a technical matter, the consumer is actually indifferent with respect to the purchase of this unit.

FIGURE 2–3

THE FIRM'S MARGINAL COST CURVE

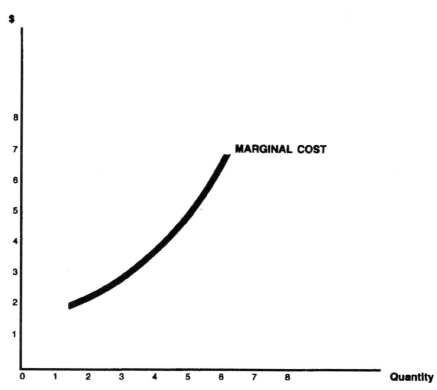

at least as valuable to them as the price they are required to pay.[12] The total consumer surplus in the market is the area of triangle PAC. It is the summation of all the consumer surplus accruing to buyers in the market.

From the supply curve, we know that some sellers were willing to offer units for sale at prices less than $5. When a producer sells an item for more than the least that would have been acceptable, it receives producer's surplus. There is producer's surplus associated with every unit sold out to unit 50. This is because, at every level of production out to 50 units, producers would have been willing to sell the unit for less than $5. The triangle PCO approximates the total producer's surplus in the market.[13] It is the sum of all of the producer surplus accruing to sellers.

---

[12] The price they are "required to pay" is in reality the goods and services that cannot be purchased if this item is purchased.

[13] It is unlikely that a supply curve would extend to the origin in the manner depicted in the graph. Instead, it will intersect the Y axis at a price above 0. Thus, PCO overstates producer's surplus.

FIGURE 2–4

SUPPLY AND DEMAND

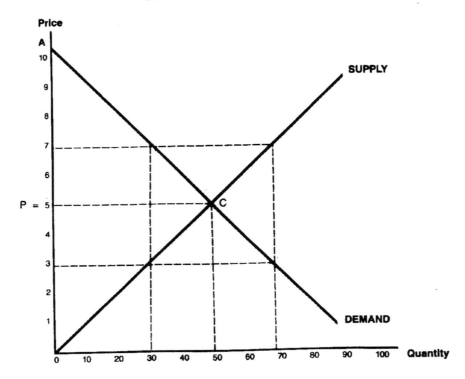

The total surplus created by the exchanges in this market is equal to the area of triangle OAC — the sum of consumer and producers' surplus. The market, by establishing a price and quantity, determines the size of this total surplus and how it is to be divided between consumers and producers.

[D] The Individual Firm Under Perfect Competition: The Marginal Revenue = Marginal Cost Rule

So far the discussion has focused on the perfectly competitive industry. It is important, however, to examine the behavior of the individual firm under perfectly competitive conditions. Remember that under perfect competition no single firm is large enough to affect the market price. In other words, no firm can cause prices to rise by withholding its output from the market or cause prices to fall by offering all of its output for sale. In effect, the market price is set by the interaction of market supply and demand, and the individual firm simply responds to this impersonally determined price. The firm is a "price taker."

The individual firm faces a horizontal demand curve at the market price as shown in Figure 2–5. A horizontal demand curve is perfectly elastic; the firm can sell all it wishes at the market price but if it raises price above the market price its sales will drop to zero. The horizontal demand curve also indicates what is called "marginal revenue." Marginal revenue is the amount of increase in a firm's total revenue resulting from the sale of an additional unit. In this case, the firm receives an additional $5 each time it sells a unit. Thus, the price it charges and its marginal revenue are $5. As we will see in the examination of monopoly,[14] price and marginal revenue are the same only when the demand curve is horizontal.

On the supply side of the analysis, the firm's supply curve is the same as its marginal cost curve. The reasoning is that the number of units a firm offers at a particular price depends on a comparison of the price offered with the marginal cost of producing an additional item. It will offer a

FIGURE 2–5

Supply and Demand for the
Perfectly Competitive Firm

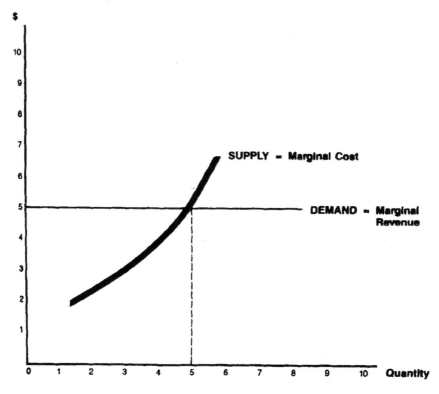

---

particular unit as long as the addition to total cost (marginal cost) does not exceed the price offered. Thus, the firm's marginal cost curve also indicates the number of units that will be offered for sale at each price.

The firm's output is determined in the same manner as output was determined for the industry as a whole; it settles on the quantity where demand and supply intersect. In Figure 2–5 the firm's demand curve — set at the market price — intersects its supply curve at 5 units. But something even more fundamental is illustrated in the graph. Remember, in the case of a horizontal demand curve, price and marginal revenue are the same. The firm has, therefore, decided on the output where marginal cost and marginal revenue intersect. This is its profit maximizing output. As long as the marginal revenue — the addition to total revenue from selling a unit — exceeds the marginal cost of its production, the sale of that unit adds to the firm's profits. In Figure 2–5, this is true out to unit 5. Beyond unit 5, marginal cost exceeds marginal revenue and the firm will not offer additional units for sale. Profit maximization occurs where marginal cost and marginal revenue intersect. Although explained here in the context of monopoly, this fundamental rule holds true regardless of how competitive the market is.

[E] Equilibrium Under Perfect Competition

Further understanding of competitive equilibrium requires the introduction of a few additional economic concepts. Costs of production are generally classified as being fixed or variable. Fixed costs do not vary with the level of output. Examples are rent on a parcel of land or executives' salaries. Variable costs do change as output changes — increasing as output increases and decreasing as it falls. Labor and raw materials are good examples. Total cost is the sum of fixed and variable costs. To economists a "normal" or fair return to investors is regarded as a cost of production like any other. Thus, total cost includes a profit for shareholders.

A better indication of the firm's efficiency can be had by calculating the average per unit cost of production. The most relevant calculations are average variable cost (variable cost divided by the number of units produced) and average total cost (total cost divided by the number of units produced). Less useful is average fixed cost, which is the fixed cost divided by the number of units produced.

The way in which these three measures of average cost behave is illustrated in Figure 2–6. The horizontal axis is quantity of output; the vertical axis is dollars. Average fixed cost (AFC) steadily declines as output increases; it is the same amount divided by higher levels of output. Average total cost (ATC) and average variable cost (AVC) tend to be U–shaped. This is because a firm generally operates more efficiently as output increases thereby lowering the average cost per unit of production. After some point though, a firm begins to strain against its designed capacity and average cost is likely to begin increasing. The optimal level of output is where average total cost reaches its minimum point — quantity 5 in the graph. Average total cost and average variable cost converge because the difference between them is average fixed cost, which steadily declines as output increases.

The graph also includes the firm's marginal cost curve (MC). Note that it intersects average variable cost (AVC) and average total cost (ATC) at their lowest points. The reason for this can be understood by considering the relationship of marginal to average cost. Marginal cost is the additional cost of producing another unit. As long as it is less than average cost — either variable or total — one would expect those curves to decline. It would be like calculating the average height of a basketball team and then recalculating after a player is added who is shorter than the previous average. The new team member is the marginal member and he or she lowers the team's average height.

On the other hand, if the marginal unit of output is more expensive to produce than the average, one would expect it to cause the average to increase. Thus, as long as marginal cost is above average cost, the average cost curve is upward sloping. Technically, at their minimum points, average variable cost and average total cost are sloping neither upward nor downward; they are flat for a very short interval. At this point, marginal cost equals average cost.

Figure 2–6 also includes the demand curve faced by the firm under competitive conditions. Remember that this is a flat or perfectly elastic demand curve as the individual firm in perfect competition is a "price taker." In the graph, the firm will sell the quantity where marginal revenue (MRl) equals marginal cost — 5 units — at the market price of $5. (Ignore for the moment the line drawn at the price of $6.) The graph has been drawn so that this also happens to be the level of output where the firm produces at its lowest average total cost. Thus, the firm is selling for a price equal to its marginal cost and is producing at its lowest possible average total cost. From consumers' standpoint this is ideal. And, since average total cost includes a fair return on investment, this outcome is satisfactory to investors as well. Of course, any firm that is unable to produce the good at a minimum average cost of $5 will not earn a satisfactory profit and eventually will exit the industry.[15]

How likely is this ideal outcome? Under the assumptions set forth at the beginning of this discussion of perfect competition, market forces will work to produce exactly this result. For example, if industry demand and supply interacted to produce a higher price of $6 (MR2 in the graph), the firm would expand output to 6 units and its price would exceed its average total cost. It would receive above normal or supracompetitive profits. Under the assumptions about perfect competition, however, entry into the market is easy and information readily available. Thus, the supracompetitive profits will attract new entrants into the market. Their competition will drive prices back down to minimum average total cost.

---

[15] This is another "long run" adjustment. *See* note 8, *supra*.

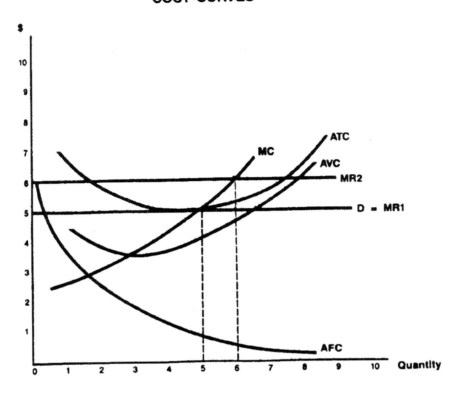

FIGURE 2-6

THE INDIVIDUAL FIRM'S
COST CURVES

   In sum, under conditions of perfect competition, price is set by large
numbers of buyers and sellers interacting in impersonal markets. Perhaps
the closest real life examples are the stock market and markets for some
agricultural commodities. Individual firms operate where this price —
which is also marginal revenue — is equal to marginal cost. Because of the
competitive pressure caused by the large number of firms in the industry,
each firm will tend to produce at a level where average total cost is
minimized. They earn "normal" but not supracompetitive profits. If the
market changes to enable existing firms to charge prices in excess of
average total cost, new firms will enter the market, driving the price back
to average total cost.[16]

---

[16] After this adjustment, the average total cost may not be the same as it was prior to entry
by the new firms. Their entry could cause some of the resources used in the industry to become
more or less costly and, consequently, the new average total cost to be higher or lower.

§ 2.03 Monopoly

Perfect competition forms one end of a continuum which describes the level of competition. At the other end of that continuum is monopoly. In reality, just as perfect competition is a theoretical construct, pure monopolies rarely exist. The discussion that follows, however, is true of any firm that, although not a true monopolist, possesses some degree of monopoly power. Under conditions of monopoly, there is one seller of a good for which there is an absence of acceptable substitutes. Although the basic process of determining price and output under conditions of monopoly are the same as they are in perfect competition, the result is significantly different.

Since the monopolist is the only producer in the market, the industry demand is the demand faced by the monopolist. Thus, unlike the firm in perfect competition, the monopolist faces a downward sloping demand curve. Because of this, the marginal revenue curve is also downward sloping. However, it does not coincide with the demand curve. For example,

FIGURE 2–7

PRICE AND OUTPUT DETERMINATION BY A MONOPOLIST

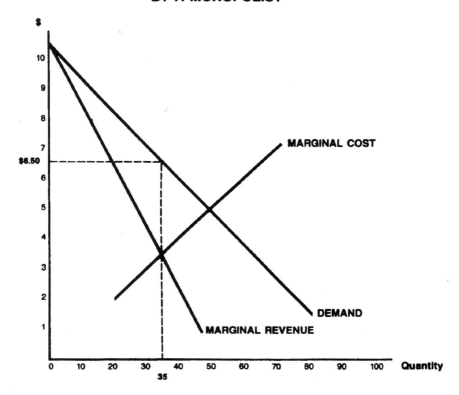

suppose on the demand curve faced by the monopolist, 20 units would be demanded at a price of $8. If the monopolist wished to sell one more unit it might have to lower the price to $7.90. Before the price change the total revenue was $160 ($8 x 20). After the price change and sale of 21 units, total revenue is $165.90 ($7.90 x 21). The increase in total revenue from selling one more unit — marginal revenue — is $5.90. Marginal revenue is less than the price charged for the additional unit because, in order to increase sales to 21 units, the monopolist had to lower the price for all units sold from $8 to $7.90. Thus, as depicted in Figure 2–7, the marginal revenue curve for the monopolist lies below the demand curve.

In order to ascertain its profit maximizing level of output, the monopolist applies the marginal revenue equals marginal cost rule. It will sell each unit where the increase in total revenue from selling that unit exceeds the addition to total cost resulting from its production. In the graph, this means it will produce 35 units. It will then set the price at the highest level consistent with selling 35 units. In the graph this is $6.50. Note that under conditions of monopoly there is no supply curve or series of prices and quantities that would be offered for sale at each price. Instead, the monopolist simply sets a price that is consistent with its profit maximizing level of output.

§ 2.04   Monopoly v. Competition: A Synthesis

One way of comparing perfect competition and monopoly is to assume that a once perfectly competitive industry becomes a monopoly when all the individual producers merge. The comparison is depicted in Figure 2–8. D and S are the demand and supply curves under competitive conditions. The competitive price is Pc and Qc units would be sold. When the firms are united, the single firm now faces a downward sloping demand curve and a corresponding marginal revenue curve (MR). Since the supply curve was once the sum of all the individual firms' marginal cost curves, it is now the monopolist's marginal cost curve.[17] The monopolist's profit maximizing level of output is Qm and its profit maximizing price is Pm.

The monopolist produces less than is the case under competitive conditions. In addition, it charges a higher price. It may not charge a price equal to marginal cost nor are there competitive forces at work in the market that would force its price down to average total cost.[18] Thus, it may "earn" indefinitely a supracompetitive profit. In addition, consumer surplus, which was triangle PcAE has been reduced to triangle PmAF under monopoly. Some of the consumer surplus has been transferred from consumers to the monopolistic producer. Some of it — triangle GFE — has been eliminated. This "deadweight" loss is a decrease in consumer surplus or welfare that is not offset by a gain to anyone else

---

[17] This assumes that the monopolist is unable to increase efficiency.

[18] Ultimately it may charge a price equal to average total cost but this would be the result of the relative levels of demand and cost, not the result of competition with other firms.

FIGURE 2–8

PERFECT COMPETITION AND MONOPOLY COMPARED

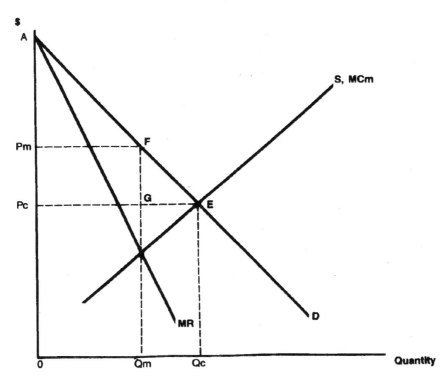

The deadweight loss actually flows from a misallocation of resources caused by the monopolist. The price individuals are willing and able to pay for a commodity is a measure of how much they value it. The marginal cost of producing a commodity is the measure of the value society attributes to the resources that must be used to produce an additional unit of the commodity.[19] Society's resources are allocated most efficiently when used to produce units of output that consumers say — through the prices they offer — are more valuable than the resources used in their production.

If resources were allocated efficiently in the market illustrated in Figure 2–8, Qc units would be produced. There would not be a deadweight loss. The monopolist's profit maximizing level of output, however, is lower than the allocatively efficient level. Unlike the competitive market, resources are

---

[19] Resources are demanded for other uses and their value in those uses is reflected in their price. Thus, the marginal cost — the price paid to attract those resources — indicates their value in the production of other goods or services.

not automatically funneled into the production of goods consumers find most valuable.

Another loss associated with monopoly flows from the lure of supracompetitive profits. From a cost/benefit point of view, if monopoly status results in $1,000,000 in supracompetitive profit, it would make sense for a firm to invest up to that amount to maintain its monopoly position or to achieve monopoly status. Thus, it may invest money in entry deterring practices designed to exclude potential competitors, or predatory practices aimed at injuring present competitors. Expenditures devoted solely to these purposes can hardly be regarded as producing anything that enhances social welfare.[20]

Another cost associated with monopoly cannot be depicted on a graph nor is it readily quantifiable. It lies in the political clout that may flow from concentrated economic power. Certainly large firms have disproportionate access to media and can make their self– serving messages heard more readily than small firms or individuals. Greater resources are also available for lobbying activities and appearances before regulatory agencies. In many instances, the efforts that serve the interests of the monopolist are inconsistent with overall social welfare.

The discussion so far has noted the clear advantages of competitive markets over monopolistic ones. The reasons for favoring an antitrust policy designed to promote markets characterized by large numbers of competitors have been highlighted. This does not necessarily mean, however, that every market with monopolistic tendencies should be divided into firms so small that they all would be price takers. To do so could mean sacrificing "productive efficiency."

Productive efficiency concerns the production of goods or services at the lowest cost per unit. Economies associated with large scale production can result in lower per unit costs as a firm expands. These "economies of scale" can flow from factors ranging from the specialization of labor to the use of highly advanced (and typically expensive) equipment.[21] Breaking large firms up into smaller firms could mean that these sources of efficient production would not longer be usable. For example, if the automobile industry were broken up into 100,000 small producers, it is unlikely that the smaller producers would be able to take advantage of robotics and assembly techniques to the extent current producers do. This would mean higher costs of production and higher prices.

The existence of economies of scale does not mean that every market must be dominated by a few large producers. Certainly there are instances in which many firms can take full advantage of all available economies of scale. That is, they can all operate at the "minimum optimal size." In these industries, allocative efficiency caused by intense competition can be achieved along with productive efficiency resulting from use of the best production techniques.

---

[20] The expenditures do not "create" income or welfare, they merely redistribute it.

[21] *See* P. Samuelson & W. Nordhaus, *Economics* 323 (15th ed. 1991).

In other instances, in order to achieve productive efficiency, a firm must serve a large share of the market. The most extreme example of this is a "natural monopoly" — a condition under which a single firm can serve the entire market at the lowest per unit cost. When this is the case, policy makers typically forego antitrust altogether and directly regulate the firm's prices.

When the market is left to antitrust enforcement, there is a dilemma. For example, suppose that a natural monopoly is left unregulated. The firm can be expected to charge a profit maximizing price which exceeds its marginal cost, thereby deviating from the allocatively efficient output. On the other hand, by producing the good at the lowest possible average total cost, productive efficiency is achieved. One might consider breaking the industry up into 100 firms. They might be intensely competitive and force price down to a level approaching their marginal and average total costs, which could be lower than that charged by the monopolist. At the same time, though, the firms will produce the good in an inefficient manner.

In short, when the minimum optimal size of a firm requires serving a substantial portion of a market, there is a trade-off between productive efficiency and allocative efficiency; seeking one means losing some of the other. One solution is to attempt to maximize the total of allocative and productive efficiency. That is, one might give up allocative efficiency and permit industrial concentration as long as it is offset by gains in productive efficiency.[22] Of course, this requires one to accept the view that efficiency is the sole concern of antitrust — a notion that is far from unanimous. Clearly, though, concern with productive efficiency means that antitrust policy is a much more complicated matter than it once was. Moreover, scholarly and judicial attention to productive efficiency underlies much of the change antitrust law has undergone in recent years.

§ 2.05 Oligopoly

Oligopoly is a market structure characterized by few producers. It is very common in the American economy. Because their numbers are small, sellers in an oligopoly perceive that their interdependent action will be more profitable than independent action. Interdependence suggests that each seller takes into account the actual or potential market reactions of competitors before output or price decisions are made.

If one seller were to increase output and reduce price in order to capture more sales, other producers in the oligopoly would follow suit and, if the first price change is not concealed, the reaction would be swift. A price cutter would gain little. Accordingly, the incentive to price compete is reduced. Likewise, unless a price increase were coordinated among all members of the oligopoly, there would be no rational incentive to undertake it, since consumers would buy from the sellers that did not increase price.

---

[22] *See generally* R. Bork, *The Antitrust Paradox* 107–10 (1978).

Reaction, coordination, and strategic behavior are, therefore, important elements of oligopoly behavior.

Even if interdependence results in price rigidity in oligopoly markets, nonprice competition in the form of advertising, quality improvements or pre– or post–point of sale service may take place. Each form of nonprice competition, however, may be subject to the same limits as price competition. For example, quality improvements may be quickly duplicated, giving the innovator only a temporary advantage. Moreover, each form of nonprice competition has a cost which will be a restraining force on its use or on the minimum price of the product.

From an antitrust perspective, oligopoly pricing is a concern because it may not be based on competitive factors but on coordinated pricing actions, whether following from tacit or explicit understandings. The antitrust laws, however, prohibit agreements among firms and some types of single firm behavior. As a consequence, a great deal of oligopoly behaviors, even though anticompetitive, falls through the cracks. The more interdependence that exists among firms in an oligopoly, the more the market may result in conduct similar to a monopoly without violating the law.

§ 2.06 Market Power

The question of market power is pervasive in antitrust; it arises the analysis of agreements between and among firms under § 2 in monopolization and attempt to monopolize cases, in § 1 cases, in cases involving tying under § 3 the Clayton Act, and in merger cases under § 7 of the Clayton Act. Market power has been defined by the Supreme Court as "the power to control prices or exclude competition."[23] The logical interpretation of the Court's language is that market power is a measure of a firm's ability to raise prices above competitive levels without incurring a loss in sales that more than outweighs the benefits of the higher price.

This section begins with an examination of the economic theory of market power. Most important is consideration of the limitations of market share, the proxy courts have historically used for market power. Next, market power analysis in practice is discussed.

[A] The Economic Theory of Market Power

A firm's market power can be measured by the *Lerner Index* which is expressed mathematically as follows:

$$L = (P - C)/P.$$

L is the *Lerner Index*, P is the firm's profit maximizing price and C is the marginal cost at the profit maximizing output.[24] Since the price charged

---

[23] *U.S. v. E.I. Du Pont de Nemours & Co.*, 351 U.S. 377, 391–92 (1956).

[24] The original discussion of the Lerner Index can be found in Lerner, *The Concept of Monopoly and the Measurement of Monopoly Power*, 1 Rev. Econ. Stud. 157 (1934). *See also*, Landes & Posner, *Market Power in Antitrust Cases* 94 Harv. L. Rev. 937 (1981).

under competitive conditions is equal to marginal cost, the formula measures the difference between the firm's profit maximizing price and the competitive price divided by the profit maximizing price.[25] The higher the index the greater the firm's market power.

Obviously a firm's ability to charge a price above competitive levels is related to the elasticity of demand it faces. Thus the *Lerner Index* also is equal to the reciprocal of the elasticity of the firm's demand curve, 1/Ed.[26] Predictably, a lower elasticity means a higher index and greater market power, and a higher elasticity means a lower index and less market power.

Although the *Lerner Index* makes a great deal of theoretical sense, the data required to make the actual calculation are often unavailable. Instead courts have traditionally started from the premise that marker share – the firm's sales in the market divided by total sales (or industry capacity) — is typically used as a proxy for market power. Strict reliance on market share as a measure of market power is problematic, however, for two reasons. First, market share is only one of the determinants of power. Second, the determination of market share requires defining the relevant product and geographic market, a far from exacting process.

[1]   **Market Share and Market Power**

The problem of relying too heavily on market share as a measure of market power can be illustrated by expanding on the mathematical relationships in the *Lerner Index*. There the ability to raise price above competitive levels was shown to be related to the elasticity of the demand curve faced by the individual firm. The elasticity of the firm's demand is in turn a function of the elasticity of demand for the industry, the firm's market share, and the elasticity of supply of competing firms. Combining these elements, the *Lerner Index* can be formally expressed as:

$$L \; = \; S \, / \, (Em \, + \, Es(1\text{--}S))$$

where S is the firm's market share, Em is the elasticity of the demand faced by the industry, and Es is the elasticity of supply of competing firms.

The formula reveals that market power is positively related to market share. After all, one would hardly expect a firm with only 10% of the market to increases prices without a rapid decline in sales. For a firm with 90% of the market the story could be quite different as there may not be alternatives for disaffected customers.[27] In addition, market power is

---

[25] The monopolist's cost at its profit maximizing level of output may differ from the costs that would exist under conditions of perfect competition. Thus, it may not be entirely accurate to say that the ratio is based on the difference between the monopolist's price and costs under competitive conditions. Still, the Index stands as a measure of the monopolist's power to raise prices above its own costs. *Id.* at 941.

[26] *Id.* at 940.

[27] *See* R. Posner & F. Easterbrook, *Antitrust* 351–52 (2d ed. 1981).

inversely related to the industry demand elasticity. Again, this is what one would expect. If the product sold is one that consumers regard as interchangeable with others, the individual firm is likely to find that its customers are responsive to its own price changes. The elasticity of supply measures how readily competing firms can increase their supply if the individual firm raises price. Again, the more responsive competitors can be, the less power the individual firm has to raise price above competitive levels. In general, if everything else remains constant, three general propositions can be stated:

(1)   Market power varies directly with market share;

(2)   Market power varies inversely with the elasticity of the industry demand; and,

(3)   Market power varies inversely with supply elasticity.

As an example of the potentially misleading consequences of relying on market share alone as a proxy for market power and as an illustration of how the three variables interact, consider two hypothetical firms, each with a market share of 75%. Firm A is part of an industry that faces, collectively, a generally elastic demand. In short, consumers turn to substitutes when prices increase. In addition, suppose that firm A's competitors have excess capacity and that the costs of entering the industry are relatively modest.

On the other hand, suppose firm B's industry faces a demand curve that is relatively inelastic — consumers are likely to continue purchasing the product regardless of price. Here the principal question is from whom. Further suppose that all firms are operating near capacity and that the industry is relatively costly to enter. Obviously, the two firms, although having identical market shares, do not have the same degree of market power. Firm A is, in fact, relatively powerless and unlikely to be able to raise prices without suffering a great loss in sales. Conversely, Firm B is in a good position to raise prices without suffering as great a loss in sales.[28]

The above propositions are important reminders of the dangers of relying solely on market share as the determinant of market power. On the other hand, the fact that some fairly convincing mathematical relationships can be stated should not create the impression that the determination of market power is a matter of simply adding a few numbers. From a practical standpoint, one is unlikely to find sufficiently reliable market share, industry elasticity, and supply elasticity data to permit a precise estimate of market power. Indeed, if these data were available, it seems likely that a direct computation of the *Lerner Index* would be possible from the individual firm's elasticity.

The equations presented thus far to some extent beg the issue. Certainly market share data should be qualified by examination of the elasticity of

---

[28] To some extent the full equation has a self–correcting character. For example, a high market share as a consequence of not including all of the possible substitutes in the market will be off–set by high elasticities of demand for the industry and high supply elasticities. *See* Landes & Posner, *supra* note 24, at 962–63.

demand for the industry and the elasticity of supply. The problem is that these two measures themselves depend on estimates of the relevant market. For example, to derive the demand elasticity for the industry one must initially decide what is to be included in the industry. Similarly, the calculation of supply elasticity requires one to determine which firms are included in the group of suppliers or potential suppliers.

Examination of the factors influencing firm elasticity and the *Lerner Index* is an important step in market power analysis. Insights about market power can shield courts from the hazards that have plagued their efforts to determine a firm's market power from market share. In recent years, although market share remains the starting point for a market power analysis, courts have shown an increased receptivity to a more refined analysis. This usually take the form of examining data that tend to qualify the accuracy of market share as a proxy for market power.

[2] Market Definition and Cross–Elasticity of Demand

A defendant's market share is its sales divided by total sales in the relevant market, including items that consumers regard as reasonable substitutes. The economic tool most commonly referred to in determining what should be included in the market from which one then determines the defendant's market share is cross–elasticity of demand. Cross–elasticity of demand is a measure of the substitutability of products from the point of view of buyers. More technically, it measures the responsiveness of the demand for one product to changes in the price of a different product. It can be expressed as:

$$\% \text{ change Qx} / \% \text{ change in Py}$$

where Qx is the quantity of product X and Py is the price of product Y. A high cross–elasticity indicates that the products are good substitutes and should be included in the same market.

Cross–elasticity of demand is probably more useful in theory than in practice. There can be a number of problems which limit its utility, one of which is illustrated by *United States v. E.I. Du Pont de Nemours & Co. (Cellophane)*,[29] a leading Supreme Court monopolization decision. The defendant's market share was critical and hinged on whether the market was defined as cellophane, in which case the market share would have been 75%, or flexible wrapping paper, in which case the share would have been 20%.[30] The Court described the question as whether flexible wrappings were reasonably interchangeable. It relied on the high cross–elasticity between cellophane and other flexible wrapping materials as the basis for settling on the broader market definition.[31]

---

[29] 351 U.S. 377 (1956).

[30] *Id.* at 394–404.

[31] *Id.* at 400.

The primary criticism of the *Cellophane* Court's analysis is that a high cross–elasticity is what one would expect if a firm with market power were pricing at its profit maximizing level. In other words, the firm will raise price just short of the point of experiencing a substantial drop in sales. A finding of a high cross–elasticity at this price merely tells us that buyers will only go so far. It really does not give one an accurate reflection of the degree of substitutability between products. Cross–elasticity based on prices closer to marginal cost is a better test of reasonable interchangeability.[32] Of course, the overall problem lies in the schism between market reality and the economist's ideal: the data for fully satisfactory calculations of cross–elasticity and determinations of market boundaries are frequently unavailable.

Another distortion in cross–elasticity can occur if the products involved are sold in greatly differing quantities.[33] For example, the producer of product Y may raise price substantially and discover that all or most of its relatively modest number of customers switch to product X. Product X, however, can be used for a number of purposes, including those product Y was used for, and its total sales are so large that the addition of former product Y users results in a very small percentage increase in sales. Clearly, product X is a good substitute for product Y. On the other hand, the actual measure of cross–elasticity — % change in Qx / % change in Py — may indicate that they are poor substitutes.

Further caution is in order in understanding the limitations of cross–elasticity: the actual numerical cross–elasticity may differ depending on the time period examined. For example, if the price of a home heating fuel increases, one may not, in the short run, find a significant increase in the demand for other fuels. The reasons are fairly clear; most home or business owners are committed to a particular method of heating and cannot easily convert to one requiring a different fuel. Over a longer period of time, however, conversion is more likely and cross–elasticity higher.

[3] Elasticity of Supply

The measure of the responsiveness of producers to price increases is called supply elasticity. Here the primary focus is on the behavior of competitors and potential competitors and the costs of production. If costs increase slowly with increases in production, competitors are in position to add their output relatively easily to that already in the market. The best example is firms with existing excess capacity that could be used to produce the same good as the defendant or one that is regarded as an acceptable substitute. The elasticity of supply of these firms may be high enough to warrant including their capacity in the defendant's market.

If the denominator of the market share fraction is limited to the productive capacity of all manufacturers who currently produce the good sold by

---

[32] R. Blair & D. Kaserman, *supra* note 1, at 110.

[33] R. Posner & F. Easterbrook, *supra* note 27, at 359.

the defendant and the capacity of all manufacturers selling a reasonable substitute, it may understate the size of the market and, consequently, overstate the market power of the defendant. In particular, there may be firms that produce goods that are not reasonable substitutes but employ labor and capital that are easily adaptable to the production of the defendant's good. If so, the elasticity of supply with respect to these firms may be high enough for them to be regarded as competitors and their potential output should be added to the denominator of the market share equation. Similar reasoning may be applied to firms that sell in different geographic regions. If slight increases in the defendant's price make it worthwhile for outsiders to ship into the defendant's market, their responsiveness may be high enough to warrant including their productive capacity in that market. Indeed, if entry costs are low it may make sense to include the output of even nonexistent firms. After all, the possibility of entry by others limits the defendant's pricing discretion.

Obviously, the analysis of potential supply for the purpose of determining what is to be included in the denominator of the market share fraction is far from a simple matter. Two complications arise. First, there are data problems that preclude accurate assessment of the responsiveness of competitors or potential competitors to price increases by the defendant. Second, one must make a judgment about how elastic the supply of a particular competitor must be in order to be included in the market. In a sense every self–interested entrepreneur in the world is a potential competitor. The key is to include those firms that may actually have an influence of reasonable magnitude on the defendant's decision–making.

[4] Geographic Markets

Typically the process of determining market share includes defining the relevant product and geographic markets. [34] The emphasis courts have placed on this distinction obscures the point that a full definition of "product market" includes a geographic component. Thus, cement in San Diego from the point of view of building contractors in San Diego is not the same product as cement in Chicago. Despite this, courts have been consistent in attributing independent importance to the geographic market issue.

For the most part, a definition of the geographic market requires the same general analysis described above. From the point of view of demand, the issue is whether buyers of the defendant's output have a tendency to increase purchases from more distant suppliers as the defendant's price increases. If this tendency is great — the cross–elasticity is high — the distant suppliers should be counted as part of the defendant's market. On the supply side, if distant sellers already make sales in competition with the defendant and can relatively easily expand their sales to these customers, their capacity should be included as part of the defendant's market. Just how responsive distant suppliers are, and whether their entire

---

[34] *See, e.g., United States v. Grinnell Corp.*, 384 U.S. 563 (1966).

capacity should be counted, are the primary points of dispute in geographic market definition considerations.[35]

As one would expect, the most important factor influencing the scope of a geographic market is transportation costs.[36] Transportation costs shelter local producers and allow them a range within which prices can be raised without suffering unacceptable losses in sales. If transportation costs are low absolutely, or low relative to the total price of the product, the sheltering effect is not as great and the market power enjoyed by the defendant is less.

[5] Further Refining the Importance of Market Share

A number of reasons why market share data alone may be unreliable already have been described. Two additional matters relating to the use or usefulness of market share data should be noted. First, the standard view in antitrust is that a high market share, without more, is something to be avoided. In recent years, particularly in the wake of *United States v. Microsoft Corp.*,[37] the problem of reconciling traditional antitrust economics with the existence of network effects has been discussed. When there are "network effects" the actual attractiveness and usefulness of a product increases as the number of people using the product increases. In a manner analogous to a natural monopoly, one might expect the market to evolve eventually to a monopolistic state. The standard example might be a computer operating system in which a user would like to be compatible with other users and available software. Greater compatibility may follow from one firm having a dominant market share. To put it in economic terms, consumer surplus may be positively related to dominance by one producer. Here it is important to distinguish between having a large market share and the use of market power. The consumer's interest may be advanced by the possession by one producer of a large market share. There is little to suggest, however, that the consumer is better off by efforts to use that market power to exact higher prices or to otherwise stifle the innovation of others.

A further word of caution is in order for the purpose of putting the role of market analysis in perspective. As already noted, market power is an important part of a case under § 1 or § 2 of the Sherman Act and §§ 3 and 7 of the Clayton Act. Under § 2, the plaintiff will generally be required to show that a single firm either is a monopolist or that there is a dangerous probability that the firm will become a monopolist. In other cases, and especially those in which the charge is that firms have conspired to reduce competition, a showing of monopoly is not required. Furthermore, the Supreme Court has noted that in these cases, the purpose of the market

---

[35] Compare Landes & Posner, *supra* note 24, at 966–67 with Brennan, *Mistaken Elasticities and Misleading Rules*, 95 Harv. L. Rev. 1849 (1982).

[36] *See generally* Elzinga & Hogarty, *The Problem of Geographic Market Delineation in Antimerger Suits*, 18 Antitrust Bull. 45 (1973).

[37] 253 F.3d 34 (D.C. Cir. 2001).

definition is to assess whether the agreement will have anticompetitive effects. In other words, market analysis is a means to an end of determining the likely impact. If the impact can be assessed without a complete market analysis, a court may not require the plaintiff to go through the market analysis.[38] As the Court reasoned, proof of detrimental effect "can obivate the need for an inquiry into market power."[39]

[B]   Market Power in the Courts

The application of sound economic principles to market power analysis has had an uneven history in the courts. It is not uncommon for a court to approach the market power issue with a methodology that is consistent with economic theory. Sometimes, these sound instincts break down at the point of application. The classic example of this the Supreme Court's reasoning in *Cellophane*. On the other hand, there is a trend toward greater sophistication among the courts when it comes to market analysis.

As the following cases and guidelines indicate, the analysis of power frequently involves three questions. First, what is the relevant market for ascertaining the defendant's market share? What is the defendant's market share within that market. Finally, what does that market share indicate about market power when all relevant factors are considered? This analysis begins with an examination of two important and older cases, *United States v. Aluminum Company of American (Alcoa)*[40] and *United States v. Grinnell Corp.*,[41] in which the courts did not apply the current understanding of the variety of factors influencing market power. The remainder of the cases illustrate more recent interpretations.

[1]   *United States v. Aluminum Company of America (Alcoa)*

One of the best know and most frequently discussed efforts to determine market share is found in Judge Hand's opinion in *Alcoa*. The issue was what was Alcoa's market share in the virgin ingot market. Several facts complicated the analysis. First, some ingot was imported. Second, some ingot was manufactured by Alcoa and then fabricated by Alcoa into shapes that were sold. Third, to some extent, ingot could be made from aluminum that was recaptured. This is secondary ingot. In determining that Alcoa's market share was 90%, Judge Hand took a number of controversial steps. First, he excluded from the market, or the denominator of the market share fraction, all foreign produced ingot except that sold within the United States. He implicitly recognized the concept of supply elasticity and the impact foreign production could have on Alcoa's pricing decisions. In fact,

---

[38] *FTC v. Indiana Federation of Dentists*, 476 U.S. 447 (1986).

[39] *Id.* at 461. *See also National Athletic Ass'n v. Board of Regents of the University of Oklahoma*, 468 U.S. 85 (1984).

[40] 148 F.2d at 426.

[41] 384 U.S. at 566–67.

he observed that foreign producers could "immediately . . . divert to the American market what they have been selling elsewhere."[42] He evidently felt that this supply elasticity was too low to warrant including the capacity of foreign producers in the United States market due to barriers created from "the tariff and the cost of transportation."[43] Precisely why these costs would limit foreign competition as thoroughly as Judge Hand indicated is not clear from the opinion, and it is likely that the market was drawn too narrowly.[44]

Second, Judge Hand also excluded from the market all secondary ingot. His reasoning was that Alcoa was ultimately in control of the secondary market. In addition, there were users who found secondary ingot unacceptable regardless of the price of virgin ingot. In all likelihood, the cost of recycling may have been high enough to result in a low elasticity of supply. Still, it is unlikely that Alcoa's pricing was unaffected by the availability of secondary aluminum. The fact that Alcoa was ultimately in control of the amount of "secondary" available does not mean that it could control the amount recycled in any one year. Complete exclusion of the secondary market, may have resulted in an inappropriately narrow market.[45]

[2] *United States v. Grinnell Corp.*

The Supreme Court's market power analysis in *Grinnell* is typically noted because of its geographic market designation. Both the product and geographic market analyses are, however, worthy of review. *Grinnell* owned controlling interest of three firms which in combination provided 87% of accredited central station protective services. Accredited central station services include the installation of detection devices on the premises that transmit an electronic signal to a central location in the event of a break–in or fire. From the central station, the proper officials are notified. Accreditation is a result of approval by insurance underwriters; it means lower insurance premiums for subscribers.[46]

Even though the central station service could be designed to provide burglary protection or fire protection separately, the Court designated the market as all central services. It reasoned that the market was actually the central service protection of property.[47] To compete effectively, according to the Court, a seller had to offer all central services. Moreover, it found that other forms of property protection were not reasonably interchangeable under the standards of *Cellophane*.[48] Although the Court recognized that

---

[42] 148 F.2d at 426.

[43] *Id.*

[44] *See* R. Posner & F. Easterbrook, 626–27 (2d ed. 1981).

[45] Professor Landes and Judge Posner suggest that the narrow market definition may have influenced Judge Hand's decision to require high market shares in order for Alcoa to be characterized as a monopoly. Landes & Posner, *supra* note 25, at 978–79.

[46] 384 U.S. at 566–67.

[47] *Id.* at 572.

[48] *Id.* at 574.

the firms did not have "unfettered power to control the price of their services," it explained that many customers would "be unwilling to consider anything but central service protection."[49] Whether the actual product market definition was correct, the Court's rationale is not compelling: virtually every seller is able to engender enough loyalty among some of its customers to make it appear that "nothing else will do."

Even more enigmatic was the Court's geographic market definition. An individual central station was able to serve an area within a 25 mile radius. Although central stations outside a local area were literally useless to residents of that area, the Court defined the market as national in scope. The justification offered was that the business was "operated on a national schedule of prices, rates, and terms."[50] Justices Fortas and Stewart dissented, noting the lack of a connection between the scope of the seller's planning and its power to raise prices and restrict output.[51] More recently it has been suggested that the geographic market definition in *Grinnell* can be understood by reference to supply elasticity and the possibility of national firms entering local markets with relative ease.[52] This may have been the case, but it is not an explanation that can be gleaned easily from the Court's opinion.

[3] *Telex Corp. v. IBM Corp.*

A relatively early case recognizing the importance of attention to supply side factors is *Telex Corp. v. IBM Corp.*,[53] in which the Tenth Circuit Court of Appeals addressed the market definition issue. The case arose as a challenge by producers wishing to sell peripheral equipment for IBM computers. Plaintiffs charged that IBM had monopolized the market of equipment that was "plug compatible" with its central processing units. The issue was whether the proper market was peripheral equipment that was "plug compatible" with IBM central units or all peripheral equipment including some that was not "plug compatible" with IBM central units.

The trial court judge settled on the narrower definition, reasoning that for owners of IBM central units, non–plug compatible peripheral equipment was not reasonably interchangeable with "plug compatible" equipment. In other words, the cross–elasticity between types of peripherals was low. The Court of Appeals reversed, focusing on the supply rather than demand side of the market.[54] It noted the lower court's finding that "suppliers of peripherals plug compatible with non–IBM systems could in various instances shift to the production of IBM plug compatible peripherals, . . . should the economic rewards in the realities of the market become

---

[49] *Id.*

[50] *Id.* at 575.

[51] *Id.* at 588–9 (Harlan, J., dissenting).

[52] *See* H. Hovenkamp, *supra* note 1, at 116.

[53] 510 F.2d 894 (10th Cir.), *cert. dismissed*, 423 U.S 802 (1975).

[54] 510 F.2d at 916–19.

sufficiently attractive."[55] In particular, the court found compelling the ease of developing interfaces that would permit the use of the IBM central units with peripherals manufactured by others.

[4] *United Parcel Service* and *Dimmit Agri Industries*

Two lower court opinions are representative of attempts to respond to the complexities inherent in considerations of market power. In *Broadway Delivery Corp. v. United Parcel Service* (UPS),[56] UPS was charged with monopolizing and attempting to monopolize the pickup and delivery of small packages sent by wholesalers in the New York City garment district. The trial court instructed the jury that a finding that plaintiff possessed less than a 50% share of the relevant market was sufficient to establish an absence of the required market power for a monopolization claim.

The Second Circuit Court of Appeals found the instruction erroneous and emphasized that an instruction on market power should not "deflect the jury's attention from the indicia of monopoly power other than market share."[57] The court implied, however, that market shares in the range of 50% would require additional evidence of market power to provide a basis for a finding that § 2 had been violated. The court noted the importance of supply and demand elasticities, in addition to market share, in assessing power. It also recognized the difficulty a jury may encounter in comprehending a complicated economic market power model. It concluded, however, that:

> a jury can usefully be given some explanation concerning the relationship between market share and market structure to make it clear that, although a particular share might enable a company to have monopoly power in one market, the same share might not enable another company to have monopoly power in a different market with different market characteristics.[58]

A different emphasis is found in *Dimmitt Agri Industries Inc. v. CPC International Inc.*,[59] in which the defendant's market shares were 25% and 17% in the national cornstarch and national corn syrup markets, respectively. The jury found for the plaintiff; Fifth Circuit Court of Appeals reversed the lower court denial of *judgment non obstante verdicto*. The defendant's basis for requesting a j.n.o.v. was the claim that "as a matter of law" market shares as low as it had could not establish the market power required for a monopolization offense.[60] The Fifth Circuit found that

---

[55] *Id.* at 916.

[56] 651 F.2d 122 (2d. Cir.), *cert. denied*, 454 U.S. 968 (1981).

[57] 651 F.2d at 130.

[58] *Id.* at 129.

[59] 679 F.2d 516 (5th Cir. 1982), *cert. denied*, 460 U.S. 1082 (1983). *See also Ball Memorial Hospital Inc. v. Mutual Hospital Insurance*, 784 F.2d 1325 (7th Cir. 1986); *United States v. Waste Water Management Inc.*, 743 F.2d 976 (2d Cir. 1984).

[60] 679 F.2d at 521.

market shares in the range of the defendants's "are insufficient — at least absent other compelling structural evidence — as a matter of law to support monopolization."[61] The court held that the evidence of the defendant's ability to control price was, in this instance, insufficient to overcome the strong presumption that it did not possess sufficient market power. In particular, the court noted the ease with which the remainder of the industry could meet the demand of disaffected buyers if the defendant attempted to lower its output and raise prices. It stopped short, if ever so slightly, of ruling that market shares in the 25% range always would be indicative of insufficient market power.

[5] *Eastman Kodak v. Image Technical Services* and the Lock–in Issue

More recently, courts have been concerned with issue of market power when buyers are arguable locked into a market by virtue of a prior purchase in a market in which the defendant did not have market power. The Supreme Court addressed the issue in *Eastman Kodak v. Image Technical Services.* [62] Kodak sold office equipment for which it also sold parts and service. Parts manufactured for office equipment manufactured for non Kodak machinery was not interchangeable with Kodak replacement parts. In essence, buyers of Kodak equipment were dependent on Kodak for replacement parts. In addition, Kodak embarked on a strategy of supplying replacement parts only to owners of Kodak equipment who repaired their own machines or used Kodak service. The alleged impact was to make it difficult if not impossible for independent service organizations to compete effectively with Kodak for the business of repairing Kodak equipment. Independent service organizations claimed that Kodak had monopolized or attempted to monopolize the markets for Kodak replacement parts and service. There was evidence that Kodak controlled nearly 100% of the replacement parts market and 80% to 95% of the service market. [63] Procedurally, the issue before the Court was whether Kodak's lack of market power in the market for the original equipment foreclosed, as a matter of law, the possibility of violating § 2 with respect to the markets of parts and service.

The Court first noted that a single brand of a product can be a relevant market for antitrust purposes. It reasoned that, for owners of Kodak equipment, the only relevant choices were suppliers of Kodak replacement parts and Kodak service. The Court then responded to the theory, put forth by the defendants, the dissenting Justices, and the Department of Justice, that any effort by Kodak to exercise monopoly power in the aftermarket would undermine Kodak's position in the market for original equipment. In effect, the defendants argued that aftermarket consumers could not be treated as though they were part of a "captive market" as long as there were readily

---

[61] *Id.* at 529 (emphasis added).

[62] 504 U.S. 451 (1992).

[63] *Id.* at 457.

available substitutes for the original equipment. The theory was that potential buyers of original equipment would not buy from manufacturers who charged supracompetitive prices in aftermarket and those who already had purchased Kodak equipment would purchase substitutes when the opportunity arose. In economic terms, the argument was that Kodak's high market share in the replacement parts and service markets overstated Kodak's actual market power due to the high cross elasticity of demand in the market for original equipment.

In holding that the existence of market power in the aftermarket was a question of fact, the Court relied on the cost of information for potential purchasers and the difficulty of switching brands for those who already had purchased Kodak equipment. For supracompetitive pricing in the aftermarket to have an impact on the original equipment markets, potential buyers would have to have accurate and possibly expensive to obtain information about the cost of the product over its entire lifecycle. In addition, those who already had purchased original equipment could not switch costlessly even if aftermarket prices were supracompetitive. Thus, depending on information and switching costs, it was, according to the majority, possible to have monopoly power in the aftermarket without market power in the original equipment market.[64]

The most interesting facet of the Court's opinion with respect to market power analysis is its discussion of information costs and switching cost as sources of market power. Actually, although discussed separately by the Court, these two types of costs are in essence quite similar. Both are a type of investment required of a buyer in order to avoid supracompetitive prices. Obviously, the higher this investment, whether in the form of a search among alternatives before making the initial purchase or buying new original equipment, the more insulated from price competition a seller can be. In other words, when cost of this investment is high enough, it makes economic sense for buyers to opt for the choice that may entail paying supracompetitive prices.

Whether *Kodak* signals a change to a more expansive view of the sources of market power to which § 2 should respond remains to be seen. Typically one thinks of the market power enjoyed by a firm guilty of violating § 2 as being a consequence of its efforts. This view is reflected in Justice Scalia's admonition in dissent that "[w]e have never suggested that the principal players in a market with such commonplace informational deficiencies (and, thus, bands of apparent consumer pricing indifference) exercise market power in any sense relevant to the antitrust laws."[65] Justice Scalia's position seems consistent with the that expressed by Judge Hand in *Alcoa* that power possessed by natural monopolies as well as any power "thrust upon" a firm fell outside § 2 of Sherman Act. Indeed as recently as 1984,

---

[64] *Id.* at 472–479.

[65] *Id.* at 496–497. Justice Scalia cited *Jefferson Parish Hospital v. Hyde. See* Chapter 5, § 5.02[B][2][c]. *See also* Hovenkamp, *Market Power in Aftermarkets: Antitrust Policy and the Kodak Case*, 40 UCLA 1447 (1993).

in *Jefferson Parish Hospital v. Hyde,*[66] the Supreme Court rejected the view that the price insensitivity of consumers in medical care markets due to the presence of third party payors could be viewed as a source of market power for antitrust purposes. That logic, arguably, would seem to carry forward to power resulting from natural market imperfections such as information and switching costs. Consequently, any extreme application of *Kodak* would be difficult to square with *Aloca*, as well as *Jefferson Parish*.

One thing that does seem clear in the aftermath of *Kodak* is that courts are not receptive to claims by those who have agreed contractually to be "locked in." For example in *Queen City Pizza, Inc. v. Domino's Pizza, Inc.,*[67] plaintiffs sought to describe the relevant market as "the $500 million aftermarket for sale of supplies to Domino's franchisees." This was based on a requirement, under the franchise agreement, that franchisees buy these aftermarket supplies from Domino's or approved suppliers. The plaintiffs relied on the contact for the proposition that they where locked into the purchases of Domino's aftermarket supplies. The Third Circuit Court of Appeal rejected this argument. First, it noted that there were aftermarket supplies that were reasonably interchangeable with those offered by Domino's. The fact that the plaintiffs had agreed contractually to buy only from Domino's did not warrant creating a market of buyers who had opted to deal with a single supplier. In addition, the court noted that Kodak concerned an instance in which there were unilateral changes in conditions of sale after the purchase was made of the original equipment. In the case of these franchisees, however, the terms of the exchange, including aftermarket purchases was know at the time of the original contract. In short, one is not locked in, at least for market definition and antitrust purposes, if one voluntarily consents to the arrangement.

Much the same reasoning is found in *SMS Systems Maintenance Services, Inc. v. Digital Equipment Corp.,*[68] which dealt with the sales of computer systems that included warranties. Plaintiff claimed that by locking in computer buyers to the manufacturer's warranty, independent service organizations were kept out of the market. At one level, the court applied the same reasoning as the court in *Queen City Pizza*, observing that the warranty was know about at the outset of the transaction and that any consumer aversion to the warranty would be felt in the market for computers — a market in which the defendant did not possess power.[69] The court also responded to an argument that buyers were locked–in by virtue of having invested in software and personnel training consistent with using defendant's equipment. Plaintiff's reasoning appeared to be that switching costs were high and, as a consequence, defendant did have market power with respect to those who had devoted significant resources to defendants computers. The court rejected this argument and distinguished the

---

[66] *See* discussion in Chapter 5, § 5.02[B][2][c].

[67] 125 F.3d 439 (3rd Cir. 1997).

[68] 188 F.3d 11 (1st Cir. 1999).

[69] *Id.* at 19.

switching costs in *Kodak* from those at hand. In *Kodak*, attempting to use independent service organizations would have meant actually buying new equipment. In the case at hand, plaintiffs were free to use independent service organization if they were willing to write off that portion of the selling price that represented the warranty.[70]

[6] Market Definition and Methods of Distribution: *FTC v. Staples, Inc.*

In some instances, market power is not addressed adequately by focusing on products alone. This was made clear in *FTC v. Staples*[71] in which the Commission challenged the merger of Staples and Office Depot, two retailers of office supplies. The problem is that office supply retailers sell a multitude of products almost all of which have substitutes and, if not substitutes then multiple sources. The defendants, therefore, sought to have the market defined as "office products."[72] If so defined, the merging firms would have a 5.5% market share. The Commission defined the relevant market as "the sale of consumable office supplies through office super-stores." The Commission argued that, although office supplies purchased from a superstore were functionally interchangeable with those purchased from other retailers, this was a different matter than whether there was high cross elasticity.

The Court noted that within markets, submarkets could exist. In this instance, it was faced with evidence that there was a low cross elasticity between consumable office supplies sold by superstores and those same items when offered by other retailers. In particular, the FTC was able to demonstrate that in the market in which the three office supply superstores — Staples, OfficeMax and Office Depot — competed, Staples' prices were 13% lower than in markets in which it faced no superstore competition.[73] In effect, this and other data tended to support the position that the cross elasticity between an item sold by a superstore and the very same item sold elsewhere was low. Thus, the court upheld the market definition based on the type of retailer. The result was to encourage acceptance of submarkets as an appropriate measure of market power.

[7] *Lucas Automotive Engineering, Inc. v. Bridgestone/ Firestone, Inc.:*[74] **The Matter of Submarkets**

An appeal to something other than pure functional interchangeability is also found in *Lucas Automotive*. Here the issue was whether "original equipment major brand vintage tires" could constitute a relevant market for antitrust purposes. The alternative definition was "all tire manufactur-ing capacity that could be used to produce replacement tires for vintage

---

[70] *Id.* at 21.

[71] 970 F. Supp. 1066 (D.C. 1997).

[72] *Id.* at 1073.

[73] *Id.* at 1075–76.

[74] 275 F.3d 762 (9th Cir. 2001).

automobiles."[75] Like office supplies in *Staple*'s, tires would seem to be functionally interchangeable as long as the technical specifications are the same. Thus, the issue was one of the cross–elasticity between major brand and private brand vintage tires. The court reversed a lower court decision granting summary judgment to the party arguing for the broader market definition. The court relied primarily on assertions that, for some uses — principally, automobile show competitions — branded tires were essential in the interest of authenticity.

In both *Lucas Automotive* and *Staples*, the courts discussed the concept of submarkets. These are economic markets that exist within broader economic markets. For example, there could be a market for tires, a submarket for vintage tires and, evidently, even a sub submarket for major brand vintage tires. The analysis of submarkets can be traced generally to *Brown Shoe Co. v. United States*,[76] a merger case that is discussed at length in Chapter Seven. In most instances, the notion of a submarket refers to the fact that one or more sellers of a functionally interchangeable product are deemed to be preferable, by some segment of consumers, to other sellers. The labeling of something as a submarket is probably an unnecessary step since there is little indication that the requirements for identifying a submarket are any different from those for identifying a market. The issue does lead to an interesting and, so far unanswered question. Since, submarket analysis seems to focus on specific groups of customers within a market, how does one decide that the group is economically significant. For example, could devotees of a specific rock group or brand of soft drink ever be viewed as a submarket? If not, how would one distinguish the buyer of branded vintage tires?

[8] *Microsoft* and the Relevance of Net–Work Effects

The most analyzed antitrust opinion in recent years is *United States v. Microsoft*[77] in which the government's principal claim was that Microsoft had violated § 2 by monopolizing Intel–compatible computer operating systems. In appealing the district court holding, Microsoft made a number of arguments contesting this market definition and the inference that it was indicative of market power. The first was that the market was defined too narrowly by virtue of excluding the Apple Computer operating system Mac OS, operating systems for non–PC devices like handheld units, and middleware.[78] The Court of Appeals for the District of Columbia rejected these arguments[79] noting that none of these options was currently reasonably interchangeable.

---

[75] *Id.* at 766.

[76] 370 U.S. 294 (1962).

[77] 253 F.3d 34 (D.C. Cir. 2002).

[78] Middleware is software that contains some of the general protocols (application programming interfaces) found in an operating system.

[79] Microsoft was required to show that the lower courts findings of fact were clearly erroneous.

Second, Microsoft argued that there were low entry barriers to the market, meaning that even a high market share overstated Microsoft's capacity to raise price and restrict entry. This argument also was rejected due to "the 'applications barrier to entry.' "[80] The court noted a chicken and egg problem within the market. For new operating systems to emerge, new software for those systems would have to be available. On the other hand, those who write and produce software have an obvious preference for writing and producing for existing operating systems. In short, Microsoft's position was protected. On this point, Microsoft also argued that whatever barrier existed was the result of its popularity and efficiency and, consequently, it would be inappropriate to weight this as a factor in favor of antitrust liability. The court reasoned that, once established, an applications barrier was not a function of popularity but would exist regardless of the quality of the dominant operating system.

Finally, and perhaps more interesting, is Microsoft's argument that "dynamic technological markets" require direct proof — by examination of actual behavior — of monopoly power as opposed to that inferred from market share.[81] Essentially the argument was that rapid changes in technology make static market analysis inappropriate and likely to overstate current power. The court rejected this indicating that, as a matter of case–law, direct evidence was not required. On a more substantive economic basis, the court reasoned that the issue in any market was whether substitutes were likely to materialize sufficiently soon that would restrict the monopolist's ability to raise prices. It found that there was no indication that the standard market definition applied by the district court had excluded substitutes that would have a "relatively near future" impact.[82]

A substantial amount of the interest in Microsoft stemmed from the fact that it was expected to raise the issue of network effects. In short, was a "new economy" antitrust analysis warranted in markets in which monopoly was likely to be consistent with increased consumer welfare. Microsoft's argument that entry barriers were a function of its popularity can be seen as an argument that market dominance resulting from network effects should be treated differently. In effect, high "entry barriers" owing to consumer preference for a highly "networked" product might be consistent with higher consumer surplus. The court expressly addressed the concept of network effects but generally avoided suggesting that their existence would affect its analysis.[83] First, it noted that there appeared to be no consensus on the importance of network effects to antitrust policy. Second, the existence of network effects would seem to be irrelevant in the analysis of the conduct of a firm that already had achieved market dominance.

---

[80] *Id.* at 55.

[81] *Id.* at 56.

[82] *Id.* at 57. The court indicated that Microsoft would likely fail a direct proof test.

[83] *Id.* at 49.

[9] Market Definition in the Context of Monopsony

Although it is not as common as addressing anticompetitive conduct by sellers, a number of antitrust cases arise when buyers combine to set prices or the terms of exchange.[84] When this occurs, the defendants are said to be using monopsony power. Monopsony power can be the result of an agreement, unlawful under § 1 of the Sherman Act or the result of single firm behavior under § 2.

Regarding market power, the key in a monopsony case is to assess the market from the point of view of sellers attempting to sell their goods or services. In the monopsony context influences exist that are comparable to demand and supply substitutability. For example, when the focus is on sellers, we ask whether buyers can find substitute products or whether new suppliers might enter the market to lower the ability of sellers to raise prices above competitive levels. In the case of monopsony, we ask whether sellers could find alternative buyers for their goods or services or whether prices might be forced so low by the monopsonist that new buyers would enter the market.

A recent monopsony case in which the proper perspective was applied is *Todd v. Exxon Corporation,*[85] in which professional workers claimed that several employers had, in effect, conspired to suppress wages. The court correctly noted that the approach to take in assessing the market power of buyers was the "mirror image" of that involved in the case of sellers.[86] Thus, the issue in terms of the relevant market was whether there were substitute buyers for the employees that would have an impact on the ability of the defendants to lower wages. If so, these buyers would be included in the relevant market.

[10] Department of Justice and Federal Trade Commission Guidelines

In 1992 the Department of Justice and the Federal Trade Commission released *Guidelines* pertaining to enforcement policy with respect to mergers.[87] The same *Guidelines* are not necessarily applicable to enforcement of § 2 of the Sherman Act. Nor does the issuance of the *Guidelines* mean that they will be applied by courts considering § 2 offenses. The *Guidelines* are noteworthy, however, because the actual process of arriving at the relevant market helps illuminate the economic relationships that influence market power.

With respect to product market definition, the objective is to determine "a group of products such that a hypothetical firm that was the only present

---

[84] *See e.g., Fraser v. Major League Soccer,* 284 F.3d 47 (1st Cir. 2002); *Todd v. Exxon Corp.,* 275 F.3d 191 (2d Cir. 2001); *Kartell v. Blue Shield of Massachusetts,* 749 F.2d 922 (1st Cir. 1984), *cert. denied,* 471 U.S. 1029 (1985).

[85] 275 F.3d 191 (2d Cir. 2001).

[86] *Id.* at 202.

[87] With respect to the materials that follow, the Guidelines are similar to those issues by the Department of Justice in 1984. For a more detailed discussion *see* Chapter 7.

and future seller of those products" could profitably impose a "small but significant and non–transitory" increase in price. With respect to geographic market definition, the goal is also to identify the geographic boundaries of a hypothetical firm selling the relevant products that could profitably raise prices.

In both instances the agency starts with the product and geographic market of the firm under question and assumes a small price increase in order to determine if other firms would respond. If the response, in terms of substitute products or shifting of products from other locations, is great enough to make the price increase unprofitable, those producers or locations are added to the market in ascertaining the defendant's market share. The process goes through successive iterations until the smallest product and geographic market is identified that, if it were served by a single firm, the firm could profitably impose a small but nontransitory price increase. On the supply side of the analysis, firms that are not selling substitutes but which could convert relatively easily within one year are included in the defendant's market.

Although it may vary from market to market, the basic definition of a "small but significant and nontransitory" price increase is a 5% increase lasting a year. The change in price is seen as made at "prevailing prices." Since the *Guidelines* are designed for merger analysis, there is no indication of what market share would be sufficiently high to lead to an inference that the defendant possessed the required monopoly power in a § 2 case. The general market definition methodology is, however, relatively liberal with respect to the inclusion of the productive capacity of competitors or potential competitors in the defendant's market. If all other factors remain constant, when applied to § 2 cases, the approach would result in relatively few instances in which firms are found to possess monopoly power.

Chapter 3

ANTITRUST COVERAGE: JURISDICTION, ENFORCEMENT, AND EXCEPTIONS

§ 3.01 Introduction

Antitrust law can be enforced on several levels.[1] Public enforcement is pursued on the federal level by the Department of Justice Antitrust Division and the Federal Trade Commission (FTC). The two agencies have concurrent jurisdiction over several sections of the Clayton Act and the Robinson–Patman Act. Only the Department of Justice has criminal jurisdiction, however. The Department also has authority over the Sherman Act, while the FTC exercises additional authority over the Federal Trade Commission Act. On the state level, state attorneys general have authority to file Sherman Act suits for damages or equitable relief as *parens patriae* on behalf of individuals (consumers) residing within the state.[2] Private civil enforcement can be commenced by "any person who [is] injured in his business or property"[3] by reason of a violation of "anything forbidden in the antitrust laws." The action can be for either treble damages[4] or injunctive relief.[5] Reasonable attorney's fees and costs are permitted under either a damage award or injunctive relief.

§ 3.02 Private Enforcement

Section 4 of the Clayton Act[6] has been interpreted to require that a plaintiff bringing a civil action for damages must demonstrate that she has suffered an actual injury to her property or business and that the injury

---

[1] 15 U.S.C. § 15. Subject matter jurisdiction rests exclusively in the federal district court. No minimum amount in controversy is required. For a Sherman Act violation, the conduct need only have a substantial "effect" on commerce, *Summit Health, Ltd. v. Pinhas*, 111 U.S. 1842 (1991); *McLain v. Real Estate Bd. of New Orleans*, 444 U.S. 232 (1980). The Clayton Act, however, is only triggered if the alleged practices are "in" interstate commerce. An exception is made for § 7 of the Act (mergers); jurisdiction is present if the "effects" test is met. The Robinson–Patman Act's jurisdictional reach requires antitrust conduct "in" interstate commerce. The FTC's jurisdiction extends to practices which affect interstate commerce. Both the Sherman Act and the FTC Act also have an extraterritorial reach extending to foreign commerce. But the "effects" on foreign commerce must be direct, foreseeable and substantial.

[2] 15 U.S.C. §§ 15C, 15h.

[3] 15 U.S.C. § 15.

[4] *Id.*

[5] 15 U.S.C. § 26.

[6] 15 U.S.C. § 15.

was caused by defendant's conduct that violated the antitrust law.[7] Section 4, with its provision for treble damages, has been the principal force for deterring anticompetitive conduct, penalizing antitrust defendants, compensating victims, retrieving the fruits of illicit gains, creating an incentive for private suits, and supplementing public enforcement. The treble damage remedy, however, has not been without challenge or controversy.[8]

Some economists and antitrust commentators have criticized treble damages as inefficient and unfair. Others argue that they produce over-deterrence and encourage nuisance or strike suits.[9] Section 4 is inefficient, the argument goes, because it gives consumers an incentive to purchase from overcharging sellers "in order to benefit . . . threefold the amount of damages actually sustained."[10] The statute does not encourage consumers to mitigate damages.

Second, because the proscribed antitrust conduct is sometimes vague, treble damages may create a disincentive for competitors to compete aggressively on the merits for fear that their conduct may overstep the bounds of legality. Thus, the competitor avoids the risk of illegality and forgoes the conduct. An optimal sanction might be somewhere between actual damages and treble damages, but this remains only a theoretical proposition.[11]

Third, meritless suits[12] are encouraged by the possibility of treble damages because defendants cannot afford to risk an outcome that may award damages three times actual injury; hence, the antitrust defendant will settle with plaintiff without a trial determination. Attorney fees add to the incentive to settle. The antitrust suit also may be used as a predatory, strategic tactic against a rival for the purpose of either extracting a commercial concession or discouraging vigorous competition.[13] It can serve

---

[7] *Brunswick Corp. v. Pueblo Bowl–O–Mat, Inc.*, 429 U.S. 477 (1977). The antitrust laws incorporated by reference into § 4 include the Sherman and Clayton Acts and certain portions of the Wilson Tariff Act, but not § 5 of the FTC Act or § 3 of the Robinson–Patman Act.

[8] *See, e.g., Blue Shield of Virginia v. McCready*, 457 U.S. 465, 472 (1982); *American Society of Mechanical Eng'rs, Inc. v. Hydrolevel Corp.*, 456 U.S. 556, 572 (1982); Lande, *Are Antitrust "Treble" Damages Single Damages?*, 54 Ohio S.L.J. 115 (1993); Cavanagh, *Detrebling Antitrust Damages: An Idea Whose Time Has Come?*, 61 Tul. L. Rev. 777 (1987); Easterbrook, *Detrebling Antitrust Damages*, 28 J.L. & Econ. 445 (1985); G. Garvey, *Report of the Commission on the Judiciary, U.S. House of Representatives–Study of the Antitrust Treble Damage Remedy*, 98th Cong., 2d Sess. (1984); K. Elzinga and W. Breit, *The Antitrust Penalties* 65 (1976).

[9] *See* Cavanagh, *supra* note 8 at 781–820, where the author sets out an excellent review of the competing theories, which, in turn, are outlined here.

[10] K. Elzinga and W. Breit, *supra* note 8 at 430. *Contra* Easterbrook *supra* note 8 at 451 (1951).

[11] *See generally* Breit and Elzinga, *Private Antitrust Enforcement: The New Learning*, 28 J.L. & Econ. 405 (1985); Easterbrook, *supra* note 8; Landis, *Optimal Sanctions for Antitrust Violations*, 50 U. Chi. L. Rev. 652, 678 (1983).

[12] *See* Rules 11 and 16 of Federal Rules of Civil Procedure.

[13] *See, e.g.,* Krattenmaker and Salop, *Anticompetitive Exclusion: Raising Rival's Costs to Achieve Power over Price*, 96 Yale L.J. 209 (1986); Austin, *Negative Effects of Treble Damage Actions: Reflections on the New Antitrust Strategy*, 1978 Duke L.J. 1353.

as a form of protectionism for the antitrust plaintiff.[14]

Finally, treble damages have been called unfair because the amount awarded overcompensates a plaintiff in excess of the gains from actual injury ("windfall") and penalizes a defendant (or the stockholders of the corporate defendant rather than management) in excess of the gains from actual misconduct. Unfairness may be evident particularly if a violation is based on the frequently ambiguous rule of reason.[15] This standard rarely admits bright/line tests of predictability. In addition, unfairness is compounded by the fact that contribution and claim reduction among antitrust defendants are not permitted, while joint and several liability are the norm.[16]

The debate continues on each of these challenges to treble damages. Some commentators urge a discretionary use of treble damages. This has the advantage of reducing the inherent unfairness of treble damages, but it also decreases deterrence, reduces incentives for private causes of action, reduces business predictability, and increases litigation complexity and costs. Others suggest a modified trebling rule which would reserve trebling for *per se* offenses or when anticompetitive intent is demonstrated, leaving actual damages recoverable for rule of reason cases.[17]

Civil damage actions under § 4 of the Clayton Act require an allegation of injury to plaintiff's "business or property." In *Hawaii v. Standard Oil Co.*[18] the Supreme Court invoked a standing doctrine to deny a state the right to sue under the antitrust laws for injuries to the state's general economy. Distinguishing between the "business or property" requirement of § 4, the Court held that personal injuries alone were not sufficient to grant standing. The Court observed that the language of § 4 refers to "commercial interests or enterprise."

In contrast, the Court cautioned that the pleading rules governing § 4 differs from those under § 16. Because the "business or property" requirement is lacking in § 16, pleading and proof requirements are less severe. One need not establish that an injury already has been sustained but rather that there is a threatened loss or damage. Further, injunctive relief has

---

[14] Baumol and Ordover, *Use of Antitrust Laws to Subvert Competition*, 28 J.L. & Econ. 247 (1985).

[15] *See* Chapter 4 on horizontal restraints and cartel behavior, and Chapter 5 on vertical restraints.

[16] *See generally* Polden and Sullivan, *Contribution and Claim Reduction in Antitrust Litigation: A Legislative Analysis*, 20 Harv. J. Leg. 397 (1987); Sullivan, *New Perspectives In Antitrust Litigation: Towards A Right of Comparative Contribution*, 1980 U. Ill. L.F. 389. For an excellent review and analysis see Cavanagh, *Contribution, Claim Reduction, and Individual Treble Damage Responsibility: Which Path to Reform of Antitrust Remedies?* 40 Vand. L. Rev. 1277 (1987).

[17] *See generally* Cavanagh, *supra* note 8 at 820–48. As the *per se* categories are narrowed and the rule of reason classification expanded, as the present Supreme Court is inclined to do (*see* Chapters 4 and 5 on horizontal and vertical restraints), the application of treble damages is significantly decreased.

[18] 405 U.S. 251 (1972).

not been limited to injuries to business or property under § 16; non–commercial interests also have been protected.[19]

A more liberal interpretation was given subsequently to the "business or property" requirement of § 4 for damage suits. In *Reiter v. Sonotone Corp.,*[20] the Court, in referring to its decision in *Hawaii,* said "[u]se of the phrase 'commercial interests or enterprise,' read in context, in no sense suggests that only injuries to a business entity are within the ambit of § 4."[21] It held that a consumer can maintain a treble damage action, although no commercial or profit interest is at stake, as long as a monetary injury is alleged. If a price–fixing overcharge is asserted, the consumer is injured in her "property" to the extent that the value of her money is diminished.[22] Thus the Court gave the words "any person" and "property" in § 4 broad and inclusive meaning. "Any person" was defined to include consumers, without distinguishing between personal or commercial interest. The result of *Reiter* encouraged antitrust enforcement through private causes of action by consumer suits. It was anticipated that deterrence would increase accordingly. But the statute is not without its limitations or further judicial restrictions.

When the Court speaks of "standing," it generally is referring to the directness or remoteness of plaintiff's injury to the antitrust conduct. But the Court has invoked "antitrust injury" as a limitation on § 4 as well. Under this theory the Court inquires whether the alleged injury is the kind that Congress intended to redress. In addition, in price–fixing actions where a plaintiff alleges overcharges by reason of an illegal conspiracy, the Court requires that the plaintiff be a direct purchaser from the alleged conspirator.

[A] Standing

Under this judicially created limitation, the class of persons capable of filing an antitrust damage action is significantly reduced. In *Blue Shield of Virginia v. McCready*[23] the question presented was whether a policyholder of a group insurance plan, who employed a psychologist had standing to sue the insurance company that had engaged in a concerted refusal to deal with the psychologist for payment of treatment. The defendant's policy limited reimbursement to treatment by psychiatrists. Plaintiff alleged that she was injured when the group health plan refused to reimburse her for the costs of psychologist's services.

Holding that plaintiff had standing to sue Blue Shield, the Supreme Court reasoned that plaintiff's injury was directly integral to the conduct

---

[19] *See, e.g., Midwest Paper Prods. v. Continental Group,* 596 F.2d 573 (3d Cir. 1979). *See generally Cargill, Inc. v. Monfort of Colorado, Inc.,* 479 U.S. 104 (1986).

[20] 442 U.S. 330 (1979).

[21] *Id.* at 341–42. "The phrase 'commercial interest' was used there as a generic reference to the interests of the State of Hawaii as a party to a commercial transaction."

[22] *See also Chattanooga Foundry and Pipe Works v. Atlanta,* 203 U.S. 390, 396 (1906).

[23] 457 U.S. 465 (1982).

of the insurance company because psychologists were the target of a boycott and the patients were the means through which defendant achieved the boycott. McCready was "within the area of the economy . . . endangered by the break down of competitive conditions, resulting from Blue Shield's selective refusal to reimburse,"[24] because she was a "consumer of psychotherapy services entitled to financial benefits under the . . . plan."[25] Her injury "was inextricably intertwined with the injury the conspirators sought to inflict on the market."[26]

From an economic viewpoint, the refusal to reimburse psychologists reduced the demand for their services, and resulted in a decrease in competition and increased prices for the services of psychiatrists. The overcharge would be passed on to the users of the services of psychiatrists.

Setting forth the test of standing, the Court said: "It is reasonable to assume that Congress did not intend to allow every person tangentially affected by an antitrust violation to maintain an action to recover threefold damages for the injury to his business or property . . . ;"[27] a court should look "to the physical and economic nexus between the alleged violation and the harm to the plaintiff,"[28] and whether the injury is the type that Congress was concerned with when it made the alleged conduct unlawful. This latter inquiry generally is referred to as the "antitrust injury" test, while the former standard is the standing rationale. Standing focuses on the relationship or closeness (or remoteness) of the injury to the antitrust conduct.

In the term after *McCready*, the Court seemed to tighten its interpretation of standing in *Associated General Contractors, Inc. v. California State Council of Carpenters.*[29] In an opinion written by Justice Stevens, who had

---

[24] *Id.* at 480, *citing In Re Multidistrict Vehicle Air Pollution M.D.L. No. 31*, 48 F.2d 122, 129 (9th Cir. 1973).

[25] *Id.*

[26] *Id.* at 484.

[27] *Id.* at 477.

[28] *Id.* at 478. For instance, the inquiry might be how fortuitous or incidental is the harm to the plaintiff from the actual challenged conduct.

See also Id. at 476–77, where the McCready Court readily admitted to the difficulty of setting out a concrete test for the abstract concept of "standing." The Court stated that, without Congressional guidance, "courts are forced to resort to an analysis no less elusive than that employed traditionally by courts at common law with respect to the matter of 'proximate cause.' " The Court suggested that much of this elusiveness can be attributed to the broad language and remedial objectives of § 4. Clearly, the potential problems associated with determining standing and defining its parameters have been apparent from the beginning.

[29] 459 U.S. 519 (1983). *See generally* Note, *More Trouble with Treble: The Effects of McCready and Associated General on Antitrust Standing*, 10 J. Corp. L. 463 (1985); Note, *Private Antitrust Standing: A Survey and Analysis of the Law After Associated General*, 61 Wash. U. L.Q. 1069 (1984); Note, *Antitrust Standing, Antitrust Injury, and the Per Se Standard*, 93 Yale L.J. 1309 (1984); Comment, *Segregation of Antitrust Damages: An Excessive Burden on Private Plaintiffs*, 72 Cal. L. Rev. 403 (1984); Comment, *A Farewell to Arms: The Implementation of a Policy–Based Standing Analysis in Antitrust Treble Damage Action*, 72 Cal. L. Rev. 437 (1984).

dissented in *McCready*, the Court held that a union lacked standing to sue a multiemployer association which allegedly coerced certain third parties not to enter business relationships with union firms. As a matter of law, the union was held not to be a "person" injured within the meaning of § 4 because it was not a consumer or competitor in the market in which trade was restrained. It was unclear whether the union's "interests would be served or disserved by enhanced competition in the market."[30] Said the Court with regard to "antitrust injury:"

> [A] union's primary goal is to enhance the earnings and improve the working conditions of its membership; that goal is not necessarily served, and indeed may actually be harmed, by uninhibited competition among employers striving to reduce costs in order to obtain a competitive advantage over their rivals. Set against this background, a union, in its capacity as bargaining representative, will frequently not be part of the class the Sherman Act was designed to protect, especially in disputes with employers with whom it bargains. In this case, particularly in light of the longstanding collective bargaining relationship between the parties, the Union's labor–market interests seem to predominate.[31]

With regard to "standing," the Court observed that the chain of causation between the union and the restraint on construction subcontracts was vague, indirect, and speculative. The union failed to allege (1) that any collective bargaining agreement was terminated as a result of the coercion; (2) that the aggregate share of the contracting market controlled by union firms had diminished; (3) that the number of employed union members had declined; (4) that union revenues in the form of dues or initiation fees had decreased; or (5) that any firm was prevented from doing business with a union.[32] In short, the plaintiff union did not satisfy the standing requirement because it did not demonstrate a *direct* link between the alleged injury and a decrease in competition.

In *Holmes v. Securities Investor Protection Corp.*,[33] the Court perpetuated the holding in *Associated General* by interpreting RICO's provision for civil actions, which was actually a near carbon copy of § 4, to incorporate the concept of proximate cause. The Court denied standing to SIPC in its attempt to recover funds paid to discharge brokerage debts to customers which were lost through alleged fraudulent handling of stock held by the brokerages. The Court found SIPC's injuries too indirect.

> [T]he notion of proximate cause reflects ideas of what justice demands, or of what is administratively possible and convenient. (Citation omitted). Accordingly, among the many shapes this concept took at common law. . .was a demand for some direct relation between the injury asserted

---

[30] *Id.* at 539.

[31] *Id.* at 539–40.

[32] *Id.* at 542. Lower federal courts subsequent to *Associated General* have required that plaintiff demonstrate that it was a "participant in the same market as the alleged malefactors." *See, e.g., Bhan v. NME Hosps., Inc.*, 772 F.2d 1467 (9th Cir. 1985).

[33] 503 U.S. 258 (1992).

and the injurious conduct alleged. Although such directness of relationship is not the sole requirement of Clayton Act causation, it has been one of its central elements, . . .for a variety of reasons. First, the less direct an injury is, the more difficult it becomes to ascertain the amount of a plaintiff's damages attributable to the violation, as distinct from other, independent factors. . . . Second, quite apart from problems of proving factual causation, recognizing claims of the indirectly injured would force courts to adopt complicated rules apportioning damages among plaintiffs removed at different levels of injury from the violative acts, to obviate the risk of multiple recoveries. . . . And, finally, the need to grapple with these problems is simply unjustified by the general interest in deterring injurious conduct, since directly injured victims can generally be counted on to vindicate the law as private attorneys general, without any of the problems attendant upon suits by plaintiffs injured more remotely. . . .[34]

At bottom, *Associated General* seems to hold that only consumers or competitors have standing under § 4. That conclusion may distinguish the results of *McCready* and *Associated General*. Both cases, in addition to standing, address the "antitrust injury" test and seem to incorporate it into the standing inquiry. Consequently, under modern antitrust analysis, the plaintiff must satisfy the antitrust injury requirement *and* otherwise be an "appropriate" party to bring the action.

[B] Antitrust Injury

"Antitrust injury," as a judicially created exception, focuses on the "by reason of" language of § 4. The doctrine had its genesis in a challenge to an acquisition under § 7, the Clayton Act antimerger provision.

In *Brunswick Corp. v. Pueblo Bowl–O–Mat*,[35] plaintiffs, owners of bowling centers, alleged that Brunswick's acquisition of a competitor injured them because, had there been no acquisition by Brunswick, the competitors would have gone out of business and plaintiffs would have received greater profits and increased market share. Noting that the alleged injury — the loss of income — had "no relationship to the size of either the acquiring company or its competitors,"[36] the Court found that plaintiff would have "suffered the identical loss — but no compensable injury — had the acquired centers instead obtained refinancing or been purchased by [a] "shallow pocket."[37] And because the antitrust laws were enacted for the "protection of *competition* not competitors,"[38] the Court concluded that plaintiff's injury

---

[34] *Id.* at 268–269.

[35] 429 U.S. 477 (1977). *See generally* R. Blair & J. Harrison, *Rethinking Antitrust Injury*, 42 Vand. L. Rev. 1539 (1989).

[36] *Id.* at 487.

[37] *Id.*

[38] *Id.* at 488, *citing Brown Shoe Co. v. United States*, 370 U.S. 294, 320 (1962).

was due to an increase of competition and was not "the type the statute was intended to forestall."[39]

> Plaintiffs to recover treble damages . . . must prove more than injury causally linked to an illegal presence in the market. Plaintiffs must prove *antitrust* injury, which is to say injury of the type the antitrust laws were intended to prevent and that flows from that which makes defendants' acts unlawful. The injury should reflect the anticompetitive effect either of the violation or of anticompetitive acts made possible by the violation. It should, in short, be the " type of loss that the claimed violations . . . would be likely to cause."[40]

Brunswick, therefore, requires that an antitrust plaintiff under § 4 must plead and prove that its injury was caused by illegal conduct and that the injury is the type the antitrust laws were intended to prevent. Specifically, the injury must flow from the violation that was the result of anticompetitive conduct — a diminution in competition in the field of commerce in which plaintiff is engaged.[41] Lost profits or reduced market share by reason of an *increase* in competition is not actionable under the *Brunswick* doctrine. The antitrust loss must occur "by reason of" that which makes the conduct unlawful.

Unlike "standing," which looks to the directness or remoteness of the injury from the antitrust violation, the doctrine of "antitrust injury" centers on the nature of plaintiff's injury.[42] Each requirement is a separate pleading and proof burden on the plaintiff; the Court must be sure each is satisfied. In *Associated General*, the Court joined the two tests — standing and antitrust injury — into a single broad–based inquiry.

Courts also have applied the antitrust injury standard to substantive provisions of the Sherman Act as well as the Clayton Act, and to injunction requirements under § 16 of the Clayton Act. In *Cargill, Inc. v. Monfort of Colorado, Inc.*,[43] the Court applied *Brunswick's* antitrust injury test to a

---

[39] *Id*. at 487–88, *citing Wyandotte Co. v. United States*, 389 U.S. 191, 202 (1967).

[40] *Id*. at 489.

[41] *See National Association of Review Appraisers & Mortgage Underwriters, Inc. v. Appraisal Foundation*, 64 F.3d 1130, 1134–35 (8th Cir. 1995) (holding plaintiff responsible for own injuries through incidents evidencing poor management and development of reputation as a "diploma mill.")

[42] *See generally* Page, *Antitrust Damages and Economic Efficiency: An Approach to Antitrust Injury*, 47 U. Chi. L. Rev. 467 (1980). The standing inquiry also will consider, secondarily, the risk of multiple liability, damage allocation complexity, and the presence of other more directly affected plaintiffs. *See* Blair & Harrison, *supra* note 35, at 1551.

[43] 479 U.S. 104, and n.6 (1986). *See, e.g., J. Truett Payne Co. v. Chrysler Motors Corp.*, 451 U.S. 557 (1981); *Berkey Photo, Inc. v. Eastman Kodak Co.*, 603 F.2d 263 (2d Cir. 1979), *cert. denied*, 444 U.S. 1093 (1980); *Schoenfopf v. Brown & Williamson Tobacco Corp.*, 637 F.2d 205, 210–11 (3d Cir. 1980). *See also* P. Areeda & H. Hovenkamp, *Antitrust Law* § 334.2 (1993 Supp.).

Recently, the Court applied the antitrust injury test to the substantive antitrust law governing a vertical, maximum price–fixing scheme. In *Atlantic Richfield Co. v. USA Petroleum Co.*, 495 U.S. 328 (1990), the Court held that a plaintiff who loses sales to a competitor charging nonpredatory prices within a vertical, maximum price–fixing scheme did not suffer antitrust

private action for equitable relief. Holding that a plaintiff, who seeks injunctive relief, must show more than a casual connection between the injury and the antitrust violation, the Court held that even under § 16 of the Clayton Act the plaintiff must demonstrate a *threat* of antitrust injury.

The Court in *Cargill* explained that standing may take on different meanings under § 16 or § 4, and the remedy sought may dictate the analysis. Because § 4 provides for damage recovery, the Court, under the standing rubric, is concerned also with multiple lawsuits, duplicative recoveries and complexity of damage apportionment. These concerns are not present, however, if the remedy sought is an injunction under § 16. Thus, standing under § 16 may be easier to prove than under § 4. To satisfy the antitrust injury test, a plaintiff, under either section, must plead and prove that the injury (or threat of injury under § 16) was in fact caused by a decrease in competition through defendant's conduct, and not merely that plaintiff's injury (or the threat of injury) was caused by procompetitive conduct of the defendant. A casual connection between plaintiff's injury and defendant's conduct is insufficient: the injury or threat of injury must be by reason of defendants' violation of antitrust law, the result of which is a decrease in market competition.

The Court in *Atlantic Richfield Co. v USA Petroleum Co.*[44] found that an independent gas merchant was not unduly injured by an alleged vertical conspiracy between Atlantic Richfield and its dealers which fixed maximum resale prices for Atlantic Richfield gas. The Court admitted that maximum price fixing is a per se illegal activity because it inhibits competition in the same manner as minimum price fixing.[45] But the plaintiff's ability to compete as an independent dealer was not affected by the activity, nor was the plaintiff a consumer directly affected by the activity. The Court stated that the plaintiff might have lost sales due to the newly lowered prices, but that is "the very essence of competition" and not an antitrust violation.[46] As long as pricing is not predatory, nor determined by collusion, it is lawful. The purpose of the antitrust injury requirement is to make sure

---

injury and thus was precluded from bringing a claim under § 4 of the Clayton Act. As long as the competitor's prices were not predatory — below marginal cost — the plaintiff was not injured by reason of the defendant's conduct because the pricing was not anticompetitive, but rather procompetitive, reasoned the Court. "[U]ntil a private party is adversely affected by an anticompetitive aspect of the defendant's conduct . . . in the context of pricing practices, only predatory pricing has the requisite anticompetitive effect." *Id.* at 339. Plainly, then, before a plaintiff can recover from a federal antitrust violation, it must first demonstrate that it was the kind of person sought to be protected by the antitrust laws and one who suffered by reason of a decrease in competition brought about by defendants' behavior. *See* further discussion of *Atlantic Richfield* in Chapter 5.

[44] 495 U.S. 328 (1990).

[45] *Id.* at 335. But *see State Oil v. Khan*, 522 U.S. 3 (1997) (holding that maximum vertical price–fixing agreements are not *per se* illegal), discussed *infra* § 5.02[B](5). Maximum price fixing inhibits competition because it can act as an effective minimum resale price. *See* C. Douglas Floyd & E. Thomas Sullivan, *Private Antitrust Actions: The Structure and Process of Civil Antitrust Litigation* § 6.4 (1996 & 2001 Supp.)

[46] *Id.* at 338.

the plaintiff is injured by competition–reducing activity, and merely because the activity is *per se* unlawful, that doesn't mean the plaintiff was injured by it. The Court in *Atlantic Richfield* held "proof of a *per se* violation and of antitrust injury are distinct matters that must be shown independently."[47]

Antitrust injury can occur in other seemingly anomalous situations besides that presented in *Atlantic Richfield*. For example, in *Board of Regents of University of Oklahoma v. NCAA*[48] and *Volvo North America Corp. v Men's Intnat'l Professional Tennis Council*,[49] the Tenth and Second Circuits dealt with suits between co–conspirators. The Tenth Circuit held that, even though the University of Oklahoma participated in NCAA activities which were found to be anticompetitive, they had suffered a restriction in "revenues, market share, and output" which "restrain[ed] their ability to sell in accordance with their own judgment."[50] The Second Circuit also found the plaintiff to have standing, despite its membership in MIPTC. The court stated that it would not "adopt a rule precluding cartel members from raising antitrust challenges against the cartel."[51]

[T]o the extent a cartel member credibly asserts that it would be better off it if were free to compete — such that the member's interest coincides with the public interest in vigorous competition — we believe that the individual cartel member satisfies the antitrust injury requirement. . .We therefore hold that a cartel member has antitrust standing to challenge the cartel to which it belongs, to the extent that the member can demonstrate antitrust injury and subject to the "other reasons" set forth in *Associated General Contractors*.[52]

Thus, these two cases make clear that antitrust injury can happen to members of a group engaged in anticompetitive activities who have since decided to compete.[53]

There is uncertainty among the circuits with respect to how the standing and antitrust injury requirements affect plaintiffs who are not customers or competitors of defendants. In *Sullivan v. Tagliabue,*[54] the First Circuit said *McCready* extended recovery rights to some plaintiffs who were neither competitors nor direct victims of the violation, but instead stood in a "vertical relation" to the direct victim.[55] The plaintiff was denied relief in

---

[47] *Id.* at 344, *citing* P. Areeda and H. Hovenkamp, *Antitrust Law* ¶ 334.20, p. 330 (1989 Supp.).

[48] 707 F.2d 1147 (10th Cir. 1983), *aff'd on other grounds*, 468 U.S. 85 (1984).

[49] 857 F.2d 55 (2d Cir. 1988).

[50] *Id.* at 1151. (Citation omitted).

[51] *Id.* at 67.

[52] *Id.* at 67–68.

[53] *See also* § 3.04 *supra* for discussion on *in pari delicto* and the impact of that doctrine on cases such as these.

[54] 25 F.3d 43 (1st Cir. 1994).

[55] *Id.* at 48.

that case, however, because he was not a "necessary instrument to effectu-ate the alleged conspiracy."[56] In contrast, the First Circuit held, one year later, that "presumptively proper" plaintiffs are consumers or competitors, and the "inextricable intertwining" of injury and antitrust violation may not be enough if the plaintiff does not fit into one of the two proper categories.[57]

In *Crimpers Promotions, Inc. v. Home Box Office, Inc,*[58] the Second Circuit allowed recovery for a plaintiff who was neither a consumer or competitor. The plaintiff was a trade show organizer whose activities had been banned by the defendants, as they considered it a threat to their business of assembling programming for sales to local stations. The purpose of the show was to promote communications and dealing between local cable TV stations and program producers. The court held the plaintiff had suffered antitrust injury which was "inextricably intertwined" with the injury the defendants sought to inflict on producers and TV stations in the cable television programming market.[59] As such, plaintiff's injury was directly related enough to satisfy § 4. Similarly, the Tenth Circuit in *Reazin v. Blue Cross Blue Shield of Kansas, Inc.*[60] allowed the plaintiff hospital to sue Blue Cross & Blue Shield for discontinuing its contracting provider agreement, even though the hospital was not involved in the market for health care financing which was said to be affected by Blue Cross conspiring with two other hospitals. The court felt that the hospital's affiliation with another provider of health care financing was a direct enough relation to the injurious actions by Blue Cross to accord the plaintiff standing.[61]

In contrast, those courts which apply the *Brunswick* formula for antitrust injury are not as quick to grant standing to noncompetitors and noncon-sumers.[62] The Eighth Circuit denied the plaintiff standing in *South Dakota v. Kansas City Southern Industries, Inc.,*[63] stating that "suppliers of competitors in the relevant market [as was the plaintiff] have been denied standing because any injury is considered derivative of the harm sustained by the competitor."[64] Similarly, the Ninth Circuit concluded that the lessor of geothermal land who claimed his competitors had worked together to inhibit his plans to develop geothermal steam was denied standing partially because the plaintiff was "neither a competitor nor a consumer in the steam market."[65] Finally, in *Henke Enterprises, Inc. v. Hy–Vee Food Stores,*[66] the

---

[56] *Id.* at 49.

[57] *SAS of Puerto Rico, Inc. v. Puerto Rico Tel. Co.*, 48 F.3d 44 (1st Cir. 1995).

[58] 724 F.2d 290 (2d Cir.) 1983), *cert denied*, 467 U.S. 1252 (1995).

[59] *Id.* at 294.

[60] 899 F.2d 951 (10th Cir.) *cert. denied*, 497 U.S. 1005 (1990).

[61] *Id.* at 962–63.

[62] *See infra* 3.02[B].

[63] 880 F.2d (8th Cir. 1989), *cert denied* 493 U.S. 1023 (1990).

[64] *Id.* at 47.

[65] *R.C. Dick Geothermal Corp. v. Thermogenics, Inc.*, 890 F.2d 139 (9th Cir. 1989). *Mr. Furniture Warehouse, Inc. v. Barclays American/ Commercial Inc.*, 919 F.2d 1517, 1523 (11th Cir. 1990).

[66] 749 F.2d 488 (8th Cir. 1984).

Eighth Circuit, again, denied standing to a plaintiff attempting to challenge a covenant not to compete between the grocery store owner who had leased space previously in the same shopping center as the plaintiff and the subsequent owner of the space.[67] The plaintiff argued that since another grocery store could not lease the space the volume of business in the mall, including his own hardware store, had decreased greatly. The court rejected this argument:

> Henke's hardware store was neither a competitor, participant, nor consumer within the retail grocery market . . . . Further, although the harm suffered by Henke may have been an incidental by–product of the conspirators' claimed anticompetitive action, it was neither a "necessary step" nor an "integral . . . aspect" of a conspiracy to restrain the retail grocery market . . . . Hence, Henke's injury was not inextricably intertwined with the injury on the retail grocery market. We conclude that the injury suffered by Henke, although arguably caused by defendants' actions, is not linked sufficiently to the procompetitive policy underlying the antitrust laws and is not antitrust–type injury.[68]

These cases demonstrate that there is a fair amount of controversy and disagreement surrounding whether noncompetitors and noncomsumers can actually suffer "antitrust injury" as traditionally understood and whether the courts can accord such plaintiffs standing without completely disregarding *Brunswick*. There does not seem to be a strong trend in either direction.

[C] Direct Purchaser Requirement

Another requirement running throughout *Associated General* and *Mc-Cready* is the issue of "identifying damages and apportioning them . . . directly"[69] or determining whether they were passed on to others. *McCready* made clear that this inquiry is analytically distinct from standing and antitrust injury.[70] The roots of the "direct purchaser" requirement are found in *Illinois Brick Co. v. Illinois*.[71]

In *Illinois Brick*, the Court ruled that a plaintiff does not state a claim for relief for an illegal overcharge due to a price–fixing agreement if the plaintiff did not purchase directly from a member of the price–fixing conspiracy. Indirect purchasers, in other words, are not "persons" injured in their "business or property" under § 4 of the Clayton Act. In order to bring a treble damage claim under a price–fixing theory, the plaintiff must have been a direct purchaser from an alleged wrongdoer. The fact that the

---

[67] *Id.*

[68] *Id.* at 489–490.

[69] *Associated General*, 459 U.S. at 545; *McCready*, 457 U.S. at 473–75; *Cargill*, 479 U.S. 109.

[70] *McCready*, 457 U.S. at 476. *See also* Page, *The Scope of Liability of Antitrust Violations*, 37 Stan. L. Rev. 1445, 1483–85 (1985).

[71] 431 U.S. 720 (1977).

overcharge was "passed–on" through the distribution chain to the ultimate consumer is not enough.

The Court feared, as a matter of policy, that if indirect purchasers were permitted to sue under the pass–on theory: (1) the process costs of litigation would increase because of the tracing complexities and uncertainty; (2) defendants would be exposed to multiple liability from direct purchasers to middlemen, as well as from the ultimate consumer; (3) that plaintiffs as a class would recover duplicative recoveries; and (4) that inconsistent judgments would result.

The *Illinois Brick* Court also was concerned that damages would be too speculative, injuries too remote, and tracing too difficult if indirect purchasers were given a cause of action, reasoning that the litigation costs of tracing outweighed the benefits of deterrence and compensation. Antitrust policy, the Court opined, is better served by permitting the direct purchaser to recover the full amount of the overcharge than apportionment of damages among all parties in the distribution process.[72] Deterrence is greater because of the magnitude of the loss to the direct purchaser compared to multiple suits by indirect purchasers:

> The apportionment of the recovery throughout the distribution chain would increase the overall costs of recovery by injecting extremely complex issues into the case; at the same time such an apportionment would reduce the benefits to each plaintiff by dividing the potential recovery among a much larger group. Added to the uncertainty of how much of an overcharge could be established at trial would be the uncertainty of how that overcharge would be apportioned among the various plaintiffs. This additional uncertainty would further reduce the incentive to sue. The combination of increasing the costs and diffusing the benefits of bringing a treble–damages action could seriously impair this important weapon of antitrust enforcement.[73]

The Court did suggest some exceptions to the rule that only direct purchasers state a claim for relief under § 4: First, the rule does not apply if there is a preexisting, fixed quantity, cost–plus contract between the first purchaser and the indirect buyer which automatically passes on the overcharge to the indirect buyer who is committed to buying the fixed quantity regardless of price.[74] But the pass–on cannot be discretionary. If these conditions are met, the problems of tracing and duplicative recovery are minimized.

Second, where the first purchaser is "controlled or owned" by the wrongdoer, an indirect buyer may state a claim for relief and show that the

---

[72] *Id*. at 730.

[73] *Id*. at 745. The Court also reaffirmed the *Hanover Shoe, Inc. v. United Shoe Mach. Co.*, 392 U.S. 481 (1968) doctrine that prohibited defensive use of pass–on: defendant is not permitted to show that the plaintiff passed the overcharge on down the distribution chain and thus was not injured by the overcharge.

[74] *Id*. at n.2, *citing Hanover Shoe*, 392 U.S. at 494.

overcharge was passed–on. The relevant inquiry is whether defendants may suffer multiple liability[75] and whether more than one transaction occurred.

Third, if a vertical price–fixing conspiracy is alleged, *Illinois Brick* does not apply because the plaintiff (consumer) becomes a direct purchaser from a co–conspirator.[76] However, in order to foreclose the possibility of multiple liability, the co–conspirator middleman may have to be joined in the suit.[77]

Finally, lower courts have held that indirect purchasers are not barred from filing injunction actions, as long as they establish "that equity principles entitle them to injunctive relief."[78] The specter of windfall recovery, speculative damages, multiple litigation and intricate tracing problems is avoided when injunctive relief is sought, unlike in damages actions. Like the standing requirement, courts have liberalized the "direct purchaser" rule for injunction actions under § 16.[79]

An issue on which courts are divided is the application of *Illinois Brick* to direct purchases made from nonconspirators whose prices have increased as a result of the conspiracy. The leading case is *Mid–West Paper Products Co. v. Continental Group, Inc.,*[80] where the Third Circuit Court held that *Illinois Brick* would prevent suit in cases where the plaintiff has purchased goods or services from a nonconspirator. The court based its decision on the belief that applying *Illinois Brick* to such cases would lead inevitably to "speculative" evidence surrounding damages and complex economic inquiries that *Illinois Brick* forbids. It would be unduly difficult to determine whether direct purchases actually led to injury, and, if so, how much.[81] The court also noted that it would be "at the very least highly conjectural" to determine what the price would have been had no conspiracy existed, especially given the various and subjective considerations that go into setting product price.[82] Finally, the court feared that if such suits were permitted under *Illinois Brick*, it could lead to those who directly purchased from nonconspirators recovering even though they may not have been injured, while indirect purchasers who actually were injured would be denied recovery.

The Third Circuit later adopted a narrower interpretation of *Mid–West Paper.* In *In re Lower Lake Erie Iron Ore Antitrust Litigation* (MDL 587),[83]

---

[75] *Illinois Brick*, 431 U.S. at 730.

[76] *See, e.g., Arizona v. Shamrock Foods Co.*, 729 F.2d 1208 (9th Cir. 1984); *Jewish Hospital Ass'n. v. Stewart Mechanical Enters., Inc.*, 628 F.2d 971, 975 (6th Cir. 1980).

[77] *See, e.g., In re Beef Indus. Antitrust Litigation*, 600 F.2d 1148 (5th Cir. 1979). *See also* Floyd & Sullivan, *supra* note 45, § 6.3.4 n.35.

[78] *Midwest Paper Products Co. v. Continental Group*, 596 F.2d 573, 594 (3d Cir. 1979). *See also* Floyd & Sullivan, *supra* note 45, § 6.31.

[79] *See also* § 3.04 *supra* for discussion on *in pari delecto* and the impact of that doctrine on cases such as these.

[80] 596 F.2d 573 (3d Cir. 1979).

[81] *Id.* at 585.

[82] *Id.* at 584.

[83] 998 F. 2d 1144 (3d Cir. 1993), *cert denied*, 114 S.Ct 921 (1994).

a suit was brought against railroad companies by steel producers, private docking companies, and trucking companies. The plaintiffs were challenging an alleged conspiracy to block the implementation of new vessels intended to increase efficiency and decrease the need for manpower in hauling iron ore. The docking and trucking companies were found to have been directly injured by the railroads' activities and, hence, to have met the requirements for standing and antitrust injury.[84] The claim by the steel companies, however, was a bit more questionable. Nonetheless, the court found them to have standing on two separate theories. First, the steel companies claimed that they were forced to pay more to haul ore to nonconspiring companies. The court accepted the argument that this "directly impacted the steel companies" even though the claim basically revolved around nonconspiring third parties, which was held to be insufficient for standing in *Mid–West Paper*.[85] The court stated that just because other victims also suffered directly from the activity, that did not mean the steel companies did not have standing. The injuries of the third parties were "tangential" to those of the steel companies, not the duplicative type that *Illinois Brick* sought to prevent.[86] However, to avoid duplicative recovery issues, as mandated by *Illinois Brick and Mid–West Paper*, the steel companies had to show "meticulously" that their damages would not overlap with those claimed by the trucking and docking companies.[87]

The second theory on which the court found the steel companies to have standing was through their claims for damages from the increased dock handling charges paid to the railroads. Standing existed here, the court reasoned, because the steel companies were acting as direct purchasers.[88]

Hence, the court in *Iron Ore* seemed to disregard the "speculative damages" argument of *Mid–West Paper* out of a belief that duplicative damages could be avoided through careful proof of damages by all parties involved.[89] While this may be advantageous for those sincerely injured but more than one step removed from the alleged conspiracy, it could also lead courts to become mired in subjective analysis when ruling on standing issues, further confusing an already ambiguous concept.[90]

---

[84] Id. at 1164 n.14, 1171.

[85] *Id.* at 1168.

[86] *Id.* at 1168–69.

[87] *Id.* at 1169. *See also* § 3.02[B] for further discussion on *in pari delicto* as applied to antitrust suits between conspirators and their former co–conspirators.

[88] *Id.* at 1169-70.

[89] *But see Steamfitters Local Union No. 420 Welfare Fund v. Phillip Morris Inc.*, 171 F. 3d 921, 932 (3d Cir. 1999), *cert. denied*, 528 U.S. 1105 (2000) (distinguishing *Iron Ore* and rejecting its application to union health and welfare funds that sought to recover damages for the funds 'costs of treating their participants' smoking–related illnesses because the injuries they "allegedly suffered are simply too remote from that wrongdoing to be cognizable under the antitrust laws"). *See also Campos v. Ticketmaster Corp.*, 140 F.3d 1166, 1169 (8th Cir. 1998) (ticket purchasers are indirect purchasers "by virtue of an antecedent transaction between the monopolist and another, independent producer").

[90] *See generally* R. Blair & J. Harrison, *Reexamining the Rule of Illinois Brick in Modern Antitrust Standing Analysis,* 68 Geo. Wash. L. Rev. 1 (1999).

The Supreme Court has stated that when the purchase is made from an intermediary in a vertical situation who is a nonconspirator, the indirect purchaser does not have standing to sue. This is true even if one hundred percent of the price overcharge was passed on to the indirect purchaser. In *Kansas v. Utilicorp United, Inc.,*[91] the defendant originally brought suit against the pipeline company and five natural gas companies under a price inflation conspiracy theory. The states of Missouri and Kansas brought separate suits against the defendant as *parens partriae* for all citizens of the respective states who actually had paid the increased prices after the defendant passed them on. After consolidating the actions, the district court rejected the states' claims for lack of standing, stating that the utility company, and not the citizens at large, suffered direct injury from the conspiracy. The Court of Appeals affirmed, as did the Supreme Court. The plaintiffs attempted to formulate an exception to *Illinois* by suggesting that, since the pass–on was one hundred percent of the price inflation, the problems associated with apportioning damages between direct and indirect purchasers did not exist.[92] The Court rejected this line of reasoning and found that, in order for the indirect purchaser to prove that the utility company was not at all damaged by the overcharge, "the indirect purchaser would have to prove, among other things, that the direct purchaser could not have raised its rates prior to the overcharge."[93] Thus, courts would have to find that "the State's regulatory schemes would have barred any rate increase except for the amount reflected by cost increases."[94] This is exactly the speculative sort of proof the Court sought to avoid. The Court also voiced concerns about issues of timing related to the various factors which might delay the passing–on of a price increase and lead to damages for the utility.[95]

Second, the plaintiffs asserted an exception would be proper in this case because the states and the utility company would be seeking completely different, and, therefore, not multiple, damages. The Court rebutted this argument with the simple assertion that this case was complicated enough, with the states representing indirectly affected citizens and directly affected agencies, so that trying to guarantee no damages overlapped would add an unnecessary level of complexity to the analysis.[96] Finally, the Court refused to apply an industry–wide exception for indirect purchasers where utility companies are involved, stating that "[t]he possibility of allowing an exception, even in rather meritorious circumstances, would undermine the rule."[97] The Court also refused to find in the case the "cost–plus contract" exception to *Illinois Brick*.

---

[91] *Id.* at 585–86.

[92] 497 U.S. 199 (1990).

[93] 497 U.S. at 208.

[94] *Id.* at 209.

[95] *Id.* at 210.

[96] *Id.* at 210–11.

[97] *Id.* at 213.

The respondent did not sell gas to its customers under a pre–existing cost–plus contract. Even if we were to create an exception for situations that merely resemble those governed by such a contract, we would not apply the exception here. Our statements above show that we might allow indirect purchasers to sue only when, by hypothesis, the direct purchaser will bear no portion of the overcharge and otherwise suffer no injury. That certainly does not exist here.[98]

Clearly, the Supreme Court is serious about evenly applying the direct purchaser rule, even in cases where the indirect purchaser is bearing what appears to be all the costs of the price–fixing scheme.

A possible exception to the direct purchaser rule deals with an assignment of the antitrust claim. In *Gulfstream III Associates, Inc. v. Gulfstream Aerospace Corp.,*[99] Judge Greenberg noted in his concurring opinion that an antitrust claim can be assigned, and, thus, an exception can be made to the direct purchaser rule, but only if the assignment is express. A general assignment that includes a potential antitrust claim "would be disfavored under the direct purchaser rule."[100] Therefore, "general assignments, without specific reference to antitrust claims, cannot validly transfer the right to pursue those claims."[101] Express assignments, on the other hand, are not victim to the problem of duplicative recovery.[102]

The policy implications are sweeping for *Illinois Brick'*s direct purchaser requirement. For example, although the plaintiff in *Reiter* was declared a "party" within the meaning of § 4 and one injured, in her "property" by reason of a manufacturers' price–fixing agreement, she was not a "direct purchaser" and could not state an antitrust claim unless one of the exceptions applied.[103] Thus, while *Reiter* grants consumers standing to bring an antitrust claim, *Illinois Brick* limits that rule, in price–fixing damage suits, to consumers that are direct purchasers. Similarly, if the consumer lacks a claim for relief under § 4, the attorney general of the consumer's state cannot bring a *parens patriae* action (on behalf of consumers) under § 4c of the Clayton Act.[104]

Benston, *Indirect Purchasers' Standing*, 55 Antitrust L.J. 213 (1986); Snyder, *Efficient Assignment of Right to Sue for Antitrust Damages*, 28 J.L. & Econ. 469 (1985).

The holding in *Illinois Brick* raises the question whether states could permit, under state antitrust law, damage actions for indirect

---

[98] *Id.* at 215.

[99] 798 F.2d 1144 1167 n.20 (3d Cir. 1993), *cert. denied*, 114 S.Ct. 921 (1994).

[100] 995 F.2d 425, 438–39 (3d Cir. 1993) (Greenberg, J. Concurring).

[101] *Id.* at 439.

[102] *Id.* at 440.

[103] *Reiter v. Sonotone Corp., supra,* note 20. It should be noted that on remand, the lower court in *Reiter* found that the direct purchaser rule did not apply because of the allegations of vertical price fixing and because injunctive relief also was requested under other theories.

[104] *Illinois Brick*, 431 U.S. at 758, n.14.

purchasers.[105] The question implicates the preemption doctrine under the federal constitution: Does the federal antitrust law, as interpreted by *Illinois Brick*, preempt states from creating a claim for relief on behalf of indirect purchasers? The Supreme Court in *California v. ARC America Corp.*,[106] held that state antitrust laws permitting indirect purchasers to sue to recover illegal overcharges were not preempted by the federal statute.

Under *ARC America*, downstream antitrust victims retain a remedy, if provided by state law, although such damage recovery is precluded in federal court. The Court concluded that the two decisions are not in conflict because: (1) such state statutes will not affect unnecessarily federal proceedings since there is no federal remedy provided for the indirect purchasers, (2) the state remedy will not decrease the direct purchaser's incentives to bring a federal suit because the state action might exhaust defendant's assets, and (3) by permitting an indirect purchaser's suit in state court, no federal policy condemning multiple liability is contravened because *Illinois Brick* construed only federal policy under § 4 of the Clayton Act, not state law or state policy.

The Court observed that this dual enforcement approach might have an effect on reducing the direct purchaser's recovery in federal court but that this is a "function of the fact and form of settlement rather than the impermissible operation of state indirect purchaser statutes."[107] Moreover, the Court was unpersuaded that dual enforcement would expose antitrust defendants to multiple liability, contrary to the dictates of *Illinois Brick*, *McCready* and *Associated General*. The policy of preventing multiple liability is one limited to multiple liability *in the federal courts*, the Court reasoned, since state claims are not generally preempted by federal law merely because a defendant may be exposed to additional liability. "Ordinarily, state causes of action are not preempted solely because they impose liability over and above that authorized by federal law."[108]

In short, the Court held that *Illinois Brick* "was a [narrower] decision construing [only] the federal antitrust laws," unlike *ARC America* which

---

[105] Benston, *Indirect Purchasers' Standing*, 55 Antitrust L.J. 213 (1986); Snyder, *Efficient Assignment of Right to Sue for Antitrust Damages*, 28 J.L. & Econ. 469 (1985).

[106] 490 U.S. 93 (1989). Sixteen states had enacted such laws in response to the *Illinois Brick* decision. *Illinois Brick* had not addressed the issue of federal preemption. *See Id.* at 102. *But see* William H. Page, *The Limits of State Indirect Purchaser Suits: Class Certification in the Shadow of Illinois Brick*, Antitrust L.J. 1 (1999) (discussing that in practice *ARC America* has not led to successful indirect purchaser suits under the so-called repealer laws in state courts because class certification often acts as a barrier).

[107] *Id.* at 105.

[108] *Id.* Consider what effect this dual enforcement approach might have on a defendants' incentive to enter pretrial settlements, and whether the twin claims for relief might create over-deterrence of the underlying legal policies. *See Paper Sys., Inc. v. Nippon Paper Indus. Co.*, 281 F.3d 629 (7th Cir. 2002) (*Illinois Brick* does not preclude application of joint and several liability); *Free v. Abbot Labs.*, 176 F.3d 298, 301 & n.7 (5th Cir. 1999), *aff'd by an equally divided court*, 529 U.S. 333 (2000) (listing state appellate decisions that follow *Illinois Brick*).

rests on important federalism grounds "defining the interrelationships between the federal and state antitrust laws."[109]

In sum, the Supreme Court has rejected a literal interpretation of § 4 of the Clayton Act. In order to plead and establish a private antitrust damage action, plaintiffs must demonstrate that the injury suffered is directly related to the proscribed antitrust conduct and that the injury is of the kind intended by Congress to be redressed. When a price–fixing overcharge is alleged, indirect purchasers are generally without a claim for relief in federal court for treble damages.

§ 3.03   "Domestic and International Antitrust 'Commerce' Jurisdiction."

[A]   Sherman Act requirements

The basis for Sherman Act or Clayton Act jurisdiction is the commerce clause of the United States Constitution, which gives Congress the ability to "regulate commerce with foreign nations, and among the several states."[110] Practices which are "in" interstate commerce or which have an "effect" on interstate commerce are included under the purview of either the Sherman or Clayton Act.

The primary Supreme Court case to rule on the proper jurisdiction of the Sherman Act was *Mandeville Island Farms, Inc. v. American Crystal Sugar Co.*,[111] in which the Court found certain sugar refiners to have conspired to restrain trade. Because the refiners' activities had an effect on commerce, the Sherman Act applied.[112] This holding was affirmed more recently in *McLain v. Real Estate Board*,[113] where the Court held that the Sherman Act applied to activities "in commerce" or having an "effect on commerce."[114] The jurisdictional element was easily fulfilled by showing the defendant's activities had a substantial effect on interstate commerce.

---

[109] *Id. See* Roger D. Blair and Jeffrey L. Harrison, *Reexamining the Role of Illinois Brick in Modern Antitrust Standing Analysis*, 68 Geo. Wash. L. Rev. 1, 2 (1999) (arguing that the Court or Congress needs to revisit *Illinois Brick* to reconcile it with "more general principles of antitrust standing" in part because state statutes that allow indirect purchasers to recover antitrust damages expose defendants to liability based on geography, not the level of antitcompetitive conduct). *See generally* Hovenkamp, *The Indirect Purchaser Rule and Cost–Plus Sales*, 103 Harv. L. Rev. 1717 (1990); S. Breyer, Regulation and Its Reform (1982). *See also Kansas and Missouri v. Utilicorp United, Inc.*, 497 U.S. 199 (1990) where the Court, subsequent to *ARC America*, held that only a utility has a claim for relief under § 4 when a supplier overcharges a public utility for natural gas and the utility passes the overcharge on to its customers.

[110] U.S. Const., Art. III, § 2.

[111] 334 U.S. 219 (1948).

[112] *Id.* at 234.

[113] 444 U.S. 232 (1980).

[114] *Id.* at 242.

In *Summit Health, Ltd. v. Pinhas*,[115] the Court clarified *Maudeville* and *McLain*. The Court rejected the defense that there did not exist a natural connection between the alleged trade–restricting activity, which was a conspiracy to drive the plaintiff ophthalmologist out business, and interstate commerce. Instead, the Court found that one need not prove an *actual* effect on interstate commerce in order to prove Sherman Act jurisdiction.[116] Rather, the judiciary is to concentrate on "the potential harm that would ensue if the conspiracy were successful," and the plaintiff need only allege an anticompetitive effect on the market (defined in the case as the ophthalmologist market), suggesting an effect on interstate commerce.[117]

Most lower courts have followed the *Summit Health* Court's "effects test."[118] Recently, in *Hammes v. AAMCO Transmissions, Inc.*,[119] the Seventh Circuit held that allegations of a "restraint on commerce" would be sufficient for fulfilling the Sherman Act jurisdictional requirement.[120] The court added that the allegation does not have to be that the restraint is "substantial."[121] At issue was the refusal of the members in a call–forwarding network for a transmission repair center to include the plaintiffs in their group, leading to a marked decrease in business for the plaintiffs and eventual bankruptcy. The court decided that the jurisdictional requirement would be fulfilled as long as "the complaint alleges that the plaintiff was engaged in interstate commerce and was injured by the alleged antitrust violation."[122]

Hammes leaves unanswered, however, the question of the necessity of a "substantial" effect on interstate commerce in proving jurisdictional requirements. Although the Seventh Circuit found that no such requirement existed under the *Hammes* facts, the court decided to the contrary in *BCB Anesthesia Care, Ltd. v. Passavant Memorial Area Hosp. Assn.*,[123] decided in the same year.

---

[115] 500 U.S. 322 (1991).

[116] *Id.* at 331 (emphasis added).

[117] *Id.* The Court's recent narrowing of the commerce clause in *United States v. Lopez*, 514 U.S. 549 (1995), and *United States v. Morrison*, 529 U.S. 598 (2000), is unlikely to affect antitrust enforcement. By definition federal antitrust laws apply to interstate commerce and a plaintiff must prove that a defendant's conduct had or would have the requisite anticompetitive effect.

[118] *See generally Fuentes v. South Hills Cardiology*, 946 F.2d 196 (3d Cir. 1991) (finding jurisdiction to be legitimate in plaintiff's allegations that a hospital that revoked certain of his staff privileges had entered a conspiracy with five doctors in order to restrain interstate commerce).

[119] 33 F.3d 774 (7th Cir. 1994).

[120] *Id.* at 779.

[121] *Id.*

[122] *Id.* at 782.

[123] 36 F.3d 664 (7th Cir. 1994).

[B]   Clayton Act requirements

The jurisdictional reach of the Clayton Act is not, for the most part, as extensive as that of the Sherman Act. This fact was set out in *Gulf Oil Corp. v. Copp Paving Co.*,[124] in which the Court found the Clayton Act to apply only to those activities constituting a part of the flow of commerce between states.[125] Hence, the "effects" test does not apply to Clayton Act claims, with the exception of Section 7, which governs mergers.[126]

Section 7 of the Clayton Act, which deals with mergers and acquisitions, is considered to have the same jurisdictional requirements as the Sherman Act.[127] The text of Section 7 suggests the similarities between it and the Sherman Act. It prohibits any corporation acting within the realm of commerce or engaging in an activity affecting commerce from merging with or acquiring another firm when the merger or acquisition will have the *effect* of lessening competition or creating a monopoly.[128]

[C]   International Application of U.S. Antitrust Laws

The issue of international antitrust enforcement has become increasingly important and controversial over the past decade with the increases in technology and trade interdependence between countries. Although the reach and application of the Sherman and Clayton Acts to anticompetitive conduct abroad is controversial, it is clear that American antitrust laws apply equally to activities in interstate and foreign commerce.[129] Since the Clayton Act has a more limited reach than the Sherman Act, its extra–territorial scope is correspondingly more limited. In general, three situations have necessitated application and domestic antitrust law to activity in foreign markets. "(1) activities of foreign firms within the United States which have an effect in this country, (2) activities of foreign firms outside United States boundaries which have an adverse effect on the United States economy, and (3) activities of United States firms located outside of the country which have adverse effects on the economy of the United States."[130]

Traditionally, courts have utilized two approaches to define the proper extraterritorial scope of the Sherman Act. The first is the "effects" test, which was established in *United States v. Aluminum Co. of America*

---

[124] 419 U.S. 186 (1974).

[125] *Id*. at 195.

[126] *Id*.

[127] Floyd & Sullivan, *supra* note 45, § 1.13, at 13 (1996).

[128] 15 U.S.C. 18 (1996) (emphasis added).

[129] Areeda & Hovenkamp, *supra* note 43, ¶ 2706. Both civil and criminal actions may be brought against defendants who intend that their foreign activities have a substantial effect on United Sates commerce. *United States v. Nippon Paper*, 109 F.3d 1 (1st Cir. 1997).

[130] Floyd & Sullivan, *supra* note 45, § 1.1.4, at 14 (1996). *See also* P. Areeda and H. Hovenkamp, *supra* note 47, ¶ 2706. Both civil and criminal actions may be brought against defendants who intend that their foreign activities have a substantial effect on United States commerce.

(Alcoa).[131] At issue was Alcoa's alleged monopoly, both domestically and internationally, of aluminum ingot. The government suggested that the defendant had become a part of a foreign aluminum cartel which lent itself to artificial price increases.[132] The Second Circuit upheld the application of the Sherman Act to the foreign activity because the extraterritorial conduct was intended to and, in fact, did effect the United States market for aluminum.[133] The effects test has since been described as having its basis in "the notion that if a regulating nation or its citizens are hurt, and hurt rather directly, the nation has a stake in regulating the conduct and ought to be able to do so."[134]

This approach was criticized and transformed into a balancing test in *Timberlane Lumber Co. v. Bank of America National Trust & Saving Ass'n.*[135] The Ninth Circuit determined that the *Alcoa* test neglected to consider the interests of foreign parties when considering antitrust claims. Hence, the court set out various elements which every court should weigh in deciding to apply the Sherman Act abroad:

[1] the degree of conflict with foreign law or policy, [2] the nationality or allegiance of the parties and the locations or principal places of business or corporations, [3] the extent to which enforcement by either state can be expected to achieve compliance, [4] the relative significance of effects on the United States as compared with those elsewhere, [5] the extent to which there is explicit purpose to harm or affect American commerce, [6] the foreseeability of such effect, and [7] the relative importance to the violations charged of conduct within the United States as compared with conduct abroad.[136]

The Ninth Circuit remanded the case; the district court determined that the extension of the Sherman Act abroad was inappropriate, since subject matter jurisdiction did not exist.[137]

Timberlane suggests a one–step analysis, in which comity and subject matter jurisdiction are considered simultaneously. This approach was split into a two–step inquiry in *Mannington Mills, Inc. v. Congoleum Corp.*,[138] where the Third Circuit listed a new set of comity considerations while incorporating those suggested by the Ninth Circuit:

---

[131] 148 F.2d 416 (2d Cir. 1945) (The Second Circuit heard what was essentially a Supreme Court case because four Justices had removed themselves from the decision). The Supreme Court subsequently validated Judge Hand's test in *Steele v. Bulova Watch Co.,* 334 U.S. 280 (1952).

[132] *Id.* at 422.

[133] *Id.* at 443–4.

[134] Eleanor M. Fox, *U.S. Law and Global Competition and Trade — Jurisdiction and Comity*, Antitrust Report 3, 4 (October 1993).

[135] 549 F.2d 597 (9th Cir. 1976).

[136] *Id.* at 614.

[137] *Timberlane Lumber Co. v. Bank of Am. Nat'l Trust & Sav. Ass'n,* 574 F.Supp. 1453, 1465 (N.D. Cal. 1983).

[138] 595 F.2d 1287, 1297–98 (3d Cir. 1979).

(1)   Degree of conflict with foreign law or policy;

(2)   Nationality of the parties;

(3)   Relative importance of the alleged violation of conduct within the United States compared to that abroad;

(4)   Availability of a remedy abroad and the pendancy of litigation there;

(5)   Existence of intent to harm or affect American commerce and its foreseeability;

(6)   Possible effect upon foreign relations if the court exercises jurisdiction and grants relief;

(7)   If relief is granted, whether a party will be placed in the position of being forced to perform an act illegal in either country or be under conflicting requirements by both countries;

(8)   Whether the court can make its order effective;

(9)   Whether an order for relief would be acceptable in this country if made by the foreign nation under similar circumstances, and;

(10)   Whether a treaty with the affected nations has addressed the issue.[139]

Once a negative effect on commerce has been determined, one must then turn to these ten factors in deciding whether to extend the existing jurisdiction.[140]

These two approaches to international application of the domestic anti-trust laws have been codified several times in various federal legislation and agency actions. For instance, in 1982, Congress passed the Foreign Trade Antitrust Improvement Act (FTAIA),[141] which prohibited Sherman Act claims dealing with export or nonimport foreign commerce without a "direct, substantial and reasonably foreseeable effect" on commerce.[142]

The Department of Justice officially adopted the FTAIA in 1988 with the issuance of the Antitrust Enforcement Guidelines for International Operations. The Department enunciated that the Sherman Act should be applied only to conduct that presented a "direct anticompetitive harm to users *in the United States.*"[143] The Department eliminated this requirement in

---

[139] *Id.*

[140] Floyd & Sullivan, *supra* note 45, § 1.14, at 22–23.

[141] 15 U.S.C. § 6a (1982).

[142] *Id. See Den Norske Stats v. HeereMac V.O.F*, 241 F.3d 420, *cert. denied sub. nom. Statoil ASA v. HeereMac V.O.F.*, 122 S.Ct. 1059 (2002) (holding that the plaintiff's claim must arise directly out of the domestic effect of the challenged conduct in order for § 1 to apply to foreign conduct); *Caribbean Broadcasting System, Ltd. v. Cable and Wireless PLC*, 148 F.3d 1080, 1087 (D.C. Cir. 1998) (holding that alleged monopolization of foreign companies, their fraudulent misrepresentations about their broadcast capabilities, and their sham opposition to plaintiff's broadcast application, constitute a direct, substantial, and reasonably foreseeable effect on United States commerce).

[143] C. Douglas Floyd & E. Thomas Sullivan, *Private Antitrust Actions* 25 (1996), *citing* E.

1992, however, making claims actionable under the Sherman Act in which no domestic entities have been harmed.[144] The Guidelines adopted the *Mannington Mills* approach to international comity, as well.

The first suit to be brought and settled under the revised 1988 Guidelines was *United States v. Pilkington PLC*,[145] which had been brought against a British manufacturer of flat glass, charging the company with closing off the flat glass production market from all foreign competition in violation of the Sherman Act. The suit was settled in favor of the plaintiff, enabling the United States to compete for business in newly developed flat glass plants and leading to potentially hundreds of millions of dollars in increased export revenue.[146]

The *Mannington Mills* two–part approach was implicitly called into question by *Hartford Fire Insurance Co. v. California*, when the Court affirmed the Ninth Circuit's contention that international comity did not act as a restraint on the extension of Sherman Act subject matter jurisdiction to a complaint against London–based reinsurers.[147] The Supreme Court affirmed the Ninth Circuit's contention that international comity did not act as a restraint on the extension of Sherman Act subject matter jurisdiction.[148] Instead of undertaking a two part analysis, the Court assumed that the defendant's activities had an adverse effect on interstate commerce. Working from that assumption, the Court could not find a legitimate conflict between the foreign and domestic laws at issue.[149] As such, international comity was not a concern. The decision suggests a new doctrine in international antitrust that requires a finding of subject matter jurisdiction and an application of the Sherman Act unless a conflict exists.[150]

Thomas Sullivan and Herbert Hovenkamp, *Antitrust Law, Policy and Procedure* 13 (3d ed. 1994) (emphasis added). This view is referred to as "Footnote 159." 66 ANTITRUST & TRADE REG. REP. (BNA) 617 (June 2, 1994).

[144] *Id.*

[145] 1994–2 Trade Cas. (CCH) 70,842 (D.Ariz. Dec. 22, 1994).

[146] 66 ANTITRUST & TRADE REG. REP.(BNA) 617, 618 (June 2, 1994).

[147] 113 S.Ct. 2891 (1993). *See* discussion Section 3.06[D], *infra.*

[148] *Id.* at 2910.

[149] *Id.* at 2911.

[150] Accord *Metro Indus., Inc. v. Sammi Corp.*, 82 F3d 839, 843 (9th Cir. 1996) (stating that "when alleged illegal conduct occurred in a foreign country, we must first examine the impact on commerce in the United States before we can determine we have subject matter jurisdiction over the claim"). *But see Filetech S.A.R.L. v. France Telecom*, 978 F. Supp. 464, 476 (S.D.N.Y. 1997), *vacated on other grounds*, *Filetech v. France Telecom S.A.*, 157 F.3d 922 (2d Cir. 1998) (asserting that *Hartford* requires threshold inquiry of conflict with foreign law before other factors of *Timberlane* test apply and that comity considerations govern regardless of lack of conflict).

Academic commentary on *Hartford* has varied. *See, e.g.*, Eleanor Fox, *National Law, Global Markets, and Hartford: Eyes Wide Shut*, 68 Antitrust L.J. 73 (2000); James P. Rhatican, *Hartford Fire Ins. Co. v. California: A Mixed Blessing for Insurance Antitrust Defendants*, 47 Rutgers L. Rev. 905 (1995); Varun Gupta, Note, *After Hartford Fire: Antitrust & Comity*, 84 Geo. L.J. 2287 (1996).

This approach was explicitly adopted by the Department of Justice in the new Antitrust Enforcement Guidelines for International Operations of 1995.[151] In addition to adopting a strict effects doctrine, the Department also adopted the "substantial" test in assessing the required effect on commerce, adding fire to the same old debate about how substantial is substantial enough.

As the United States' policies of international antitrust enforcement have developed, so have its efforts to enter into cooperative agreements with other nations.[152] The Guidelines do recognize, however, that substantiality will vary with the facts of each case.[153] Similarly, the relative weight of the comity factors will depend on the individual circumstances involved in each claim.[154] In short, under the 1995 Guidelines, "jurisdiction exists when conduct has a direct, substantial, and reasonably foreseeable effect on U.S. domestic commerce, U.S. import commerce, or the commerce of U.S. exporters."[155] Although the Ninth Circuit and the Department of Justice have made clear their preference for the effects test, the debate over the doctrines is still very much alive.

The 1995 Guidelines also set out the four exceptions in which a foreign country can escape United States jurisdiction over antitrust matters. The first is foreign sovereign immunity, which is governed by the Foreign Sovereign Immunities Act of 1976 (FSIA).[156] Some activities are "the type that only sovereign government can perform" and, as such, are immune from the Sherman Act.[157] Second, conduct which is compelled by the foreign sovereign because of an inherent conflict of laws between the two countries may be immune.[158] Nonetheless, if the compelled activity takes place within United States borders, the exception does not apply.[159] Third, acts of state on "matters pertaining to its governmental sovereignty" are immune.[160] Finally, foreign lobbying of the United States government is protected from Sherman Act jurisdiction, even if it is done with the intent of restraining trade within the United States.[161]

---

[151] U.S. DEP'T OF JUSTICE, ANTITRUST ENFORCEMENT GUIDELINES FOR INTERNATIONAL OPERATIONS (1995) (hereinafter 1995 Guidelines). In addition to adopting the *Hartford Fire* test, the Department of Justice noted that the FTAIA continues to apply to foreign commerce other than imports.

[152] The United States has entered into formal bilateral agreements with Australia, Canada, Germany, and Japan, as well as "positive comity" agreements with the European Union. *See* 1995 Guidelines § 2.91; U.S./European Union Antitrust Cooperation Agreement, 74 Antitrust Trade and Reg. Rep. (BNA) No. 1864, at 592 (July 11, 1998).

[153] 67 ANTITRUST & TRADE REG. REP. 488 (Oct. 20, 1995).

[154] *Id.*

[155] Diane P. Wood, Address to Business Development Associates, Inc. in Washington D.C. (March 15, 1995) (transcript available with authors).

[156] 28 U.S.C. 1602 *et seq.*

[157] 1995 Guidelines, Draft for Public Comment, at 24.

[158] *Id.* at 25.

[159] *Id.* at 26.

[160] *Id.* at 27.

[161] *Id.* at 28. This exemption is based on the Noerr–Pennington doctrine, which is covered more fully *infra*.

Also in 1995, Congress passed the International Antitrust Enforcement Assistance Act (IAEAA). This law calls for the creation of assistance treaties which mandate the sharing of evidence of antitrust violations between countries.[162] Under the Act, the FTC or the Attorney General will provide foreign antitrust enforcement agencies with information to be used in determining whether an antitrust violation has occurred or is about to occur, and vice versa.[163] Confidential information, however, is still protected in the usual manner.[164] The evidence will prove useful for a number of reasons, especially for generating enforcement effectiveness and the magnifying the need for countries to form cooperative alliances to prevent illegal infringements on interstate commerce.[165] This is a positive step towards antitrust cooperation on an international scale.

Another similar agreement is the Mutual Legal Assistance Treaty (MLAT) between Canada and the United States. In place since 1990, this treaty has allowed the countries to gain evidence from each other to be used in criminal antitrust cases.[166] The act was put to the test in 1994, when the United States and Canada "broke up a $120 million dollar a year international cartel in the fax paper market" whose members included "a Japanese corporation, two American subsidiaries of Japanese companies, and the former president of one of the U.S. subsidiaries . . . ."[167] The defendants pleaded guilty to criminal charges in both countries, culminating in fines of approximately $7 million dollars.[168]

An important development in the extraterritorial enforcement of United States antitrust law in a criminal context occurred in 1997, when the First Circuit affirmed that the Sherman Act applies to anticompetitive conduct that takes place entirely in another country, but which is intended to have, and does have, substantial effects on the United States economy. In *United States v. Nippon Paper*,[169] the Department of Justice brought a criminal action against a Japanese manufacturer of facsimile paper, alleging that defendants had colluded to fix the price of thermal fax paper throughout North America. The Japanese manufacturer moved to dismiss, stating that United States antitrust laws do not reach conduct that occurs wholly

---

[162] C. Douglas Floyd & E. Thomas Sullivan, *Private Antitrust Actions* 30 (1996).

[163] *Id.*

[164] Diane P. Wood, Address to Business Development Associates, Inc. in Washington D.C. (March 15, 1995) (transcript available with authors).

[165] *See* Anne K. Bingaman, Statement before the Subcommittee on Economic and Commercial Law, U.S. House of Representatives (Aug. 8, 1994), at 4 ("In some of these cases, only the U.S. is targeted and only U.S. antitrust laws are involved. Others of these cartels are aimed at both U.S. and foreign markets, and could be far more effectively investigated and prosecuted by joint action between U.S. and foreign antitrust authorities").

[166] Anne K. Bingaman & Joel I. Klein, *Cooperating on Antitrust*, 18 LEGAL TIMES 27 (Jan. 1, 1996).

[167] Anne K. Bingaman, Statement before the Committee on the Judiciary, U.S. Senate (Aug. 4, 1994), at 5.

[168] *Id.*

[169] 109 F.3d 1 (1st Cir. 1997).

outside the United States. The district court agreed and dismissed the indictment.[170]

The First Circuit reversed, stating that the extraterritorial application of the Sherman Act was well established in the civil context. "Common sense" dictated that the same statute should be read the same way in both civil and criminal actions.[171] Although its decision appeared unprecedented, the court stated that "absence of earlier criminal actions is probably more a demonstration of the increasingly global nature of our economy than proof that Section One cannot cover wholly foreign conduct in the criminal milieu."[172] The court rejected the defendant's comity–based argument, which would have defeated the court's jurisdiction, because the charged conduct was illegal under Japanese and American laws. Furthermore, to dismiss on the basis of lack of subject matter jurisdiction would create a safe harbor for future cartels or price–fixers, who could simply erect territorial barriers between them and the United States, even while targeting the United States economy.[173]

In short, international enforcement and cooperative measures have gained great importance in the antitrust arena over the past years. As the market becomes more globally integrated, internationally acceptable antitrust policies will become even more crucial for adequately protecting the flow of commerce.[174]

§ 3.04   First Amendment Defenses

[A]   *Noerr–Pennington* Doctrine

If competitors join in combination for the purpose of influencing government decision making, their action is protected from antitrust challenge. This is true even if their underlying intention is to restrain competition or gain an advantage over competitors. This defense is grounded in the First Amendment constitutional theory of the right to petition government. The theory is named after two leading Supreme Court decisions.

In the first case, *Eastern R.R. Presidents Conference v. Noerr Motor Freight, Inc.,*[175] the Supreme Court held that antitrust law does not apply to restraints which are the result of valid government actions. Only private

---

[170] *United States v. Nippon Paper Indus. Co,* 944 F. Supp. 55 (D. Mass 1996).

[171] 109 F.3d at 4.

[172] *Id.*

[173] *Id.* at 8–9.

[174] *See* Spencer Weber Waller, *Can U.S. Antitrust Laws Open International Markets?*, 20 Nw. J. Int'l L. & Bus. 207, for a discussion of the positive role that U.S. antitrust law plays in ensuring an open market globally. *But see* Andrew T. Guzman, *Is International Antitrust Possible?*, 73 N.Y.U. L. Rev. 1501 (1998) (arguing that as efforts begin to focus on substantive, and not procedural, agreement on antitrust policy the more difficult agreement becomes, resulting in "losers" whose specific antitrust policies are trumped).

[175] 365 U.S. 127 (1961).

restraints are regulated under the antitrust laws. In *Noerr*, railroads influenced legislation restricting competition from the trucking industry. The Court found this activity protected[176] as it did in *UMW v. Pennington*,[177] where mine operators and workers lobbied the executive branch to induce the Tennessee Valley Authority, a government agency, to curtail spot market purchases and to increase minimum wages. The Court remarked that "[j]oint efforts to influence public officials do not violate the antitrust laws even though intended to eliminate competition. Such conduct is not illegal, either standing alone or as a part of a broader scheme itself violative of the Sherman Act."[178] Later, the Court extended its protection for lobbying activities to include judicial and adjudicatory agencies, and it made clear that the defense was grounded on the First Amendment right to petition for government action.[179] *Noerr* protection also has been extended to include activities not necessarily a part of the petitioning process, but reasonably incident or "normally attendant" to it.[180]

McGuire Oil Co. v. Mapco, Inc., 958 F.2d 1552, 1560 (11th Cir. 1992). *Noerr and Pennington* circumscribes the complex litigation process. *See, e.g. A.D. Bedell Wholesale Company, Inc. v. Phillip Morris, Inc.* 263 F.3d 239 (2001)(stating that through the tobacco multistate settlement agreement negotiations defendants agreed to enter into an output cartel and this violated sections 1 and 2 of the Sherman Act; but that *Noerr–Pennington* immunity applied because the settlement negotiations were "akin to petitioning the government"). An example of this might be the threat of instituting a lawsuit which does not fall under the sham exception to *Noerr*.[181] However, the defense is not absolute.

If efforts by competitors to influence government are a "sham,"[182] the defense is inapplicable. In *California Motor Transport*,[183] the Court held that concerted activities resulting in a "pattern of baseless repetitive

---

[176] *See generally* Kintner and Bauer, *Antitrust Exemptions for Private Requests for Government Action: A Critical Analysis of The Noerr–Pennington Doctrine*, 17 U.C. Davis L. Rev. 549 (1984); Handler and De Sevo, *The Noerr Doctrine and Its Shame Exception*, 6 Cardozo L. Rev. 1 (1984).

[177] 381 U.S. 657 (1965).

[178] *Id.* at 670.

[179] *California Motor Transport Co. v. Trucking Unlimited*, 404 U.S. 508 (1972); *United States v. Otter Tail Power Co.*, 410 U.S. 366 (1973). *But see Sessions Tank Liners, Inc. v. Joor Mfg. Inc.*, 53 Antitrust Trade Reg. Rep. (BNA) 449 (9th Cir. Sept. 17, 1987) where the Ninth Circuit held that a manufacturer is protected under *Noerr–Pennington* in efforts to persuade a private code–setting organization. Said the Court, the *Noerr–Pennington* doctrine covers "appeals to some who are not government actors but who are nevertheless in the political process." The question of protection for lobbying activities directed at private or "quasi–legislative" bodies was before the Supreme Court in *Allied Tube & Conduit Corp. v. Indiana Head, Inc.*, 486 U.S. 492 (1988), where the court held that no immunity existed for private standard–setting. *Noerr–Pennington* circumscribes the complex litigation process.

[180] *Id.* at 440.

[181] *See infra* n.175 and accompanying text.

[182] 365 U.S. at 149.

[183] *California Motor Transport Co. v. Trucking Unlimited*, 404 U.S. 508 (1972).

claims"[184] which attempted to bar a party from government access were, in reality, a "sham" to conceal an attempt to interfere with the commercial interest of the competition. Trucking companies through administrative and judicial harassment had attempted to prevent competitors from obtaining operating privileges. The Court also commented that the defense would be unavailable if there were evidence of perjury, bribery, fraud or a conspiracy where a government official participated.[185]

The sham and conspiracy exceptions have undergone recent clarifications, however. In *City of Columbia v. Omni Outdoor Advertising, Inc.*,[186] the Supreme Court held that the sham exception only "encompass[es] situations in which persons use the governmental *process* — as opposed to the *outcome* — as an anticompetitive weapon."[187] The Court distinguished *California Motor Transport* as "a classic example [of] the filing of frivolous objections" for the sole purpose of using the government process "simply in order to impose expense and delay."[188] On the other hand, legitimate or genuine attempts to achieve a *result* which is anticompetitive, through the governmental process, is protected behavior.

Omni broadens *Noerr–Pennington's* protection to apply whenever the defendant genuinely seeks favorable government action, and blocks that defense from being accepted if the defendant only attempts to delay or abuse the *process* of government decision making. The sham test, then, focuses on whether there is a genuine attempt to gain a favorable result as opposed to merely an attempt to misuse the government process.

By drawing the distinction between a genuine attempt to influence the *process* or to affect the *result* of government decision making, the Court created an issue of how "intent" should be interpreted in applying the sham exception. This question was answered in *Professional Real Estate Investors Inc. v. Columbia Pictures Industries, Inc.*,[189] where the Court held that the "genuine attempt" test must be based on an objective reasonableness standard. The *Noerr–Pennington* immunity applies, the Court held, unless the defendants' conduct is "objectively baseless."

The issue presented in *Professional Real Estate* was whether a copyright infringement action was a sham, and thus without *Noerr–Pennington* protection, merely because a subjective expectation of success did not motivate the litigation. In rejecting a subjective definition of sham conduct, the Court reasoned that neither indifference to the governmental outcome nor failure to prove that a petition for redress of grievances would have been brought but for a predatory motive was enough to trigger the sham exception. Evidence of subjective expectation or intent of success on the

---

[184] *Id.* at 513.

[185] Compare *Affiliated Capital Corp. v. City of Houston*, 735 F.2d 1555 (5th Cir. 1984), with *Metro Cable Co. v. CATV of Rockford, Inc.*, 516 F.2d 220, 229 (7th Cir. 1975).

[186] 499 U.S. 375 (1991).

[187] *Id.* at 380 (emphasis in original).

[188] *Id.*

[189] 508 U.S. 49 (1993).

merits, then, is not, according to the Court, the standard. Rather, a sham will be determined by whether the petitioning was "objectively reasonable." A purely subjective definition of sham would chill, the Court opined, first amendment rights protected under *Noerr–Pennington*.

Professional Real Estate established a two–tier definition for determining the "objectively baseless" test for sham conduct. First, the court will ask whether a reasonable participant could realistically expect success or a favorable outcome on the merits. Second, if the challenged government petition is found to be meritless, then the court will inquire where the baseless petition conceals "an attempt to interfere *directly* with the business relationships of a competitor . . . through the use of government *process* — as opposed to the *outcome* of that process."[190] The second test is more subjective in nature, but this requisite anticompetitive intent evidence can not play a role in determining the objective, first tier requirement of a realistic expectation of a favorable outcome.

In short, the Court's reformulation of the sham exception will protect a petition for government action if there is evidence of an objectively reasonable effort to affect the government's decision making, regardless of the subjective intent of the petitioner. Only if the Court finds an objectively meritless petition *and* anticompetitive intent to injure a competitor will it conclude that the petition was a sham and, consequently, unworthy of *Noerr–Pennington* protection.

The majority holding in *Professional Real Estate* indicates that any claim that has some reasonable possibility of success on the merits fall under *Noerr* protection, even if it is clear that the plaintiff is manipulating the process of legislation. Justice Steven's concurrence in *Professional Real Estate*, however, suggests that this should not be the case in some complex situations. Justice Stevens opined that the plaintiff in some cases might harbor a collateral purpose for the litigation, such as imposing burdensome costs on the defendant in an attempt to weaken his financial position. Such would most likely be the case in instances where litigation needlessly has become repetitive or drawn out. In these cases, Justice Stevens believes that even those arguments should not be given *Noerr* protection.

The Ninth Circuit has adopted this position in *USS–Posco Indus. v. Contra Costa County Building Trades Council.*[191] The Court of Appeals found the two tier Professional Real Estate test did not apply to a pattern of claims which had been undertaken without prior consideration of merit, regardless of whether some of them showed promise of success. This is clearly contrary to the position taken in *Professional Real Estate*, and it is too early to forecast whether other courts will adopt the approach of the Ninth Circuit. Nevertheless, a suit that is ultimately adjudicated as successful will *never* be found to be a sham, since, by definition, it was brought with "probable cause."[192]

---

[190] *Id.* at 60–61.

[191] 31 F.3d 800 (9th Cir. 1994).

[192] 508 U.S. at 49.

Taken together, *Omni* and *Professional Real Estate* expand *Noerr–Pennington's* first amendment protections and limit significantly the application of the sham exception. In addition, the Court has broadened *Noerr–Pennington's* immunity also by narrowing the conspiracy exception.

In *Omni*, the Court rejected earlier case precedent that created an exception to *Noerr–Pennington* immunity when government officials participated in the antitrust conspiracy with private parties seeking government action. The so–called conspiracy exception fell because:

> [s]ince it is both inevitable and desirable that public officials often agree to do what one or another group of private citizens urges upon them such an exception would virtually swallow up the [purpose underlying the immunity]: All anticompetitive regulation would be vulnerable to a 'conspiracy' charge. [193]

The Court observed, in addition, that [f]ew government actions are immune from the charge that they are "not in the public interest" or in some sense "corrupt." [194] Moreover, "virtually all regulation benefits some segments of society and harms others." [195] Thus, the Court concluded, it would be impractical "to allow plaintiffs to look behind the actions of state sovereigns to base their claims on 'perceived conspiracies to restrain trade.' " [196]

On a related issue to the conspiracy exception, the Court in *Omni* commented on whether private petitions to government, which are accompanied by illegal or fraudulent actions, enjoy *Noerr–Pennington* protection. It implied that the illegal conduct exception, also, is no longer available since the key inquiry is whether the government action is in the "public interest." Said the Court in *Omni*:

> To use unlawful political influence as the test of legality of state regulation undoubtedly vindicates (in a rather blunt way) principles of good government. But the statute we are construing is not directed to than end. Congress has passed other laws aimed at combatting corruption in state and local governments. [197]

Thus, the Court directs that those who engage in illegal or fraudulent actions should be prosecuted under the criminal laws, without a judicially created exception to the immunity. The outcome is that if the political conduct is aimed at political decision making and outcomes, and not merely the process of government, it remains protected political activity under *Noerr–Pennington*.

Finally, several courts have refused to apply *Noerr–Pennington* protection when the attempt to influence was not directed at the government's

---

[193] 499 U.S. at 375.

[194] *Id.* at 377.

[195] *Id.*

[196] *Id.* at 379 (quoting *Hoover v. Ronwin*, 446 U.S. 558, 580 (1984)).

[197] *Id.* at 378–79. *See, e.g.* 18 U.S.C. § 1951 (The Hobbs Act).

sovereign authority but rather at a purely commercial or proprietary venture of the government.[198] Governments frequently act in commercial capacities, such as a purchaser of goods in a commercial market, and when they do they are not acting as a deliberative political body.[199] The circuit courts, however, are split on whether there should be a "commercial enterprise" exception to the *Noerr–Pennington* doctrine. The Ninth Circuit, for example, has reasoned that "the nature of the government activity is [but] one factor in determining the type of public input acceptable to the particular decision making process."[200] It has rejected the "commercial enterprise" exception as an airtight defense. But in *Omni* the Supreme Court implied that it might entertain a commercial dealing or market participant exception.[201]

Other courts have confronted the issue whether conduct which goes beyond mere lobbying and includes an economic boycott directed at private parties in order to achieve political ends, such as new legislation, ought to be protected by the *Noerr–Pennington* immunity. Although the courts are split on this issue, the weight of authority seems to protect "an economic boycott, politically motivated, to achieve a legislative goal."[202] Courts have been willing to examine the purpose behind the means, and if the overriding purpose, in fact, is to influence government action, the fact that economic rather than political means were employed has not destroyed the defense.[203]

The Supreme Court addressed this question directly in *FTC v. Superior Court Trial Lawyers Ass'n*[204] where criminal defense lawyers engaged in a collective boycott by refusing to take more court appointed indigent clients in an attempt to influence the city government to raise the lawyers' compensation. The economic boycott was used as the means, together with lobbying the city council, to achieve an economic advantage for the lawyers.

In distinguishing the *Noerr* case, the Court said, "in the *Noerr* case the alleged restraint of trade was the intended consequence of legislation; in this case the boycott was the *means* by which [the lawyers] sought to obtain favorable legislation."[205] The Court observed that "the undenied objective

---

[198] *See, e.g., Federal Prescription Serv. v. American Pharmaceutical Ass'n.*, 663 F.2d 253 (D.C. Cir. 1981), *cert. denied*, 455 U.S. 928 (1982).

[199] *George R. Whitten Jr., Inc. v. Paddock Pool Builders, Inc.*, 424 F.2d 25 (1st Cir. 1970), *cert. denied*, 400 U.S. 850 (1970).

[200] *See In re Airport Car Rental Antitrust Litigation*, 693 F.2d 84 (9th Cir. 1982), *cert. denied*, 462 U.S. 1133 (1983); *see also Greenwood Utilities Comm'n v. Mississippi Power Co.*, 751 F.2d 1484 (5th Cir. 1985).

[201] 111 S.Ct. at 1353.

[202] *See, e.g., NAACP v. Claiborne Hardware Co.*, 458 U.S. 886 (1982); *Missouri v. National Organization for Women, Inc.*, 620 F.2d 1301 (8th Cir. 1980), *cert. denied*, 449 U.S. 842 (1980).

[203] *See, e.g., Borough of Lansdale v. Philadelphia Electric Co.*, 692 F.2d 307 (3d Cir. 1982); *Feminist Women's Health Center v. Mohammed*, 586 F.2d 530, 543 n.7 (5th Cir. 1978). *See also* D. Mandelker, J. Gerard, E.T. Sullivan, *Federal Land Use Law* § 13.06[2] (2001).

[204] 493 U.S. 411 (1990).

[205] *Id.* at 424–25.

of the boycott was an economic advantage for those who agreed to participate," the result of which would be an increase in the price of lawyers services.

Thus, in finding that the lawyers' boycott was not protected under the First Amendment, even though there was a component of political petitioning to the local government, the Court held that when the immediate and ultimate objective of the restraint is economic, as is the principal means through a boycott, the conduct is not protected under *Noerr* or under broader first amendment principles.

Noerr's protection, after *Trial Lawyers*, therefore turns on motivation and means employed. It matters whether the economic boycott was the means by which the challenged party petitioned the government or rather the consequence of the petitioning conduct.[206] Because the lawyers who had an economic motive used principally economic means to achieve an economic objective, even though they sought to influence the local government, their antitrust conduct was not protected from challenge.[207]

Most recently, the Third Circuit granted *Noerr* immunity to the American Bar Association in *Massachusetts School of Law at Andover v. American Bar Association,*[208] where the plaintiff brought a challenge to the defendant's accreditation requirements after being denied ABA accredited status. The court held that the ABA was protected from liability because, among other things, it had lobbied the states to convince them to adopt ABA accreditation decisions as their own.[209] Since there was no proof of a sham and the ABA had not directly attempted to dissuade others from dealing with the plaintiff, no exceptions to Noerr applied.[210] Thus, the injury complained of by the plaintiff was the indirect product of state lobbying and, as such, constituted protected activity.

[B] Overbroad Remedial Orders

The First Amendment also is implicated when antitrust remedial orders regulate conduct. Behavior–oriented administrative or judicial decrees can infringe on the commercial speech rights of the defendant. First recognized by the Supreme Court in *Virginia Pharmacy,*[211] the commercial speech

---

[206] *Id.* at 425. The Court found the unprotected conduct to be a *per se* violation of the antitrust laws.

[207] In *Sande River Nursing Care v. Aetna Casualty*, 985 F.2d 1138 (1st Cir. 1993), *cert. denied*, 114 S.Ct. 70 (1993), the court rejected the argument that *Trial Lawyers* is limited to cases where the government is a purchaser or market participant. "What was significant about the concerted activity in *Trial Lawyers* was that the defendants sought to influence the government through an economic boycott that directly affected the marketplace.

[208] 107 F.3d 1026 (3d Cir. 1997).

[209] *Id.* at 1038.

[210] *Id. But see* Marina Lao, *Discrediting Accreditation?: Antitrust and Legal Education,* 79 Wash. U. L. Q. 1035 (2001).

[211] *Virginia State Bd. of Pharmacy v. Virginia Citizens Consumer Council, Inc.*, 425 U.S. 748 (1976).

doctrine now is analyzed under a four–tiered evaluation established in *Central Hudson Gas & Elec. Corp. v. Public Serv. Comm'n.*[212] To be protected, the speech must involve a lawful activity and not be related to illegal conduct. To be constitutional the regulation must serve a substantial government interest, directly advance the asserted government interest and be no more extensive than necessary to serve that interest. Thus, if the challenged conduct violates the antitrust laws, or is integral to or facilitates part of the antitrust conduct, it can be prohibited as long as the order prohibiting it does not deter other, competitive conduct.[213] If the decree extends beyond the interests it serves, it may be held to be impermissibly broad and offensive to constitutional sensitivities.

§ 3.05 Common Law Defenses

In equity, the unclean hands doctrine is recognized as a defense. In essence, it blocks a plaintiff from recovery if the plaintiff has violated some other antitrust provision unrelated to the alleged violation in plaintiff's complaint. In antitrust litigation, it has lost much of its force and application.[214] In *Kiefer–Stewart Co. v. Joseph E. Seagram & Sons, Inc.*[215] the Court said:

> If [plaintiff] and others were guilty of [violations] of the antitrust laws, they could be held responsible in appropriate proceedings brought against them by the Government or by injured private persons. The alleged illegal conduct of [plaintiff], however, could not legalize the unlawful combination by respondents nor immunize them against liability to those they injured.[216]

Kiefer–Stewart, however, was a treble damage action. Lower federal courts are divided on the doctrine's application in antitrust injunction suits.[217] To the extent the doctrine finds application in antitrust actions

---

[212] 447 U.S. 557, 566 (1980).

[213] Sullivan, *First Amendment Defenses in Antitrust Litigation*, 46 Mo. L. Rev. 517 (1981). *See also* E. Thomas Sullivan, Comparing Antitrust Remedies in the U.S. and E.U.: Advancing a Standard of Proportionality, __ Antitrust Bull. __ (2003).

[214] Conversely, in the patent or copyright infringement suit context, patent and copyright misuse defenses, which also have their origin in the unclean hands doctrine, have gained currency. The misuse defense overlaps proscribed monopoly conduct that comes under the scrutiny of the antitrust laws. *See Morton Salt Co. v. Suppiger Co.*, 313 U.S. 555 (1942); *Alcatel USA, Inc. v. DGI Technologies, Inc.,* 166 F.3d 772, 793 (5th Cir. 1999); *Lasercomb America, Inc. v. Reynolds,* 911 F.2d 970 (4th Cir. 1990); *see also* David McGowan, *Innovation, Uncertainty, and Stability in Antitrust Law*, 16 Berkeley Tech. L.J. 729, 811 (2001); E. Thomas Sullivan, *The Confluence of Antitrust and Intellectual Property at the New Century*, 1 Minn. Intell. Prop. Rev. 1 (2000); Note, *Clarifying the Copyright Misuse Defense: The Role of Antitrust Standards and First Amendment Values*, 104 Harv. L. Rev. 1289 (1991).

[215] 340 U.S. 211 (1951).

[216] *Id*. at 214.

[217] *See, e.g., Memorex Corp. v. IBM*, 555 F.2d 1379 (9th Cir. 1977); *Singer v. A. Hollander & Son*, 202 F.2d 55 (3d Cir. 1953).

for equitable relief, the incentive to sue and the deterrent effect of the laws are reduced.[218]

At common law, a related defense, *in pari delicto* was recognized when the plaintiff was involved in the alleged illegality set forth in the complaint.[219] The term literally means that if the plaintiff is "of equal fault," the action is barred. In *Perma Life Mufflers, Inc. v. International Parts Corp.*[220] the Court required a showing that plaintiff was truly of equal fault before it recognized the defense and barred the action. As a matter of policy, the Court rejected the defense, absent clear evidence of equal fault because:

> The plaintiff who reaps the reward of treble damages may be no less morally reprehensible than the defendant, but the law encourages his suit to further the overriding public policy in favor of competition. A more fastidious regard for the relative moral worth of the parties would only result in seriously undermining the usefulness of the private action as a bulwark of antitrust enforcement. And permitting the plaintiff to recover a windfall gain does not encourage continued violations by those in his position since they remain fully subject to civil and criminal penalties for their own illegal conduct.[221]

In *Perma Life* the Court found that although plaintiffs sought the franchises with defendant, they did not seek each provision of the agreement. Some were in fact detrimental to their interests. Moreover, the Court found that plaintiffs lacked relative bargaining power and had unequal economic leverage. Acquiescence seemed necessary to achieve the business opportunity. The Court observed.

> The possible beneficial byproducts of a restriction from a plaintiff's point of view can of course be taken into consideration in computing damages, but once it is shown that the plaintiff did not aggressively support and further the monopolistic scheme as a necessary part and parcel of it, [plaintiff's] understandable attempts to make the best of a bad situation should not be a ground for completely denying [defendant] the right to recover which the antitrust acts give him.[222]

And in a broad sweep, the Court concluded that "the doctrine of *in pari delicto* . . . is not to be recognized as a defense to an antitrust action."[223]

---

[218] *Chrysler Corp. v. General Motors Corp.*, 596 F. Supp. 416, 419 (D.D.C. 1984) (where the court, striking the unclean hands defense by General Motors, said "lower courts have almost uniformly declined to permit the unclean hands defense in antitrust suits where injunctive relief is sought"). *See also Polk Bros. v. Forest City Enterprises, Inc.*, 776 F.2d 185 (7th Cir. 1985) (rejecting the unclean hands defense).

[219] The doctrine had its early origins, as applied in antitrust actions, in *Eastman Kodak Co. v. Blackmore*, 277 F. 694 (2d Cir. 1921). *See also Simpson v. Union Oil Co.*, 377 U.S. 13 (1964). *See also* § 3.02[B] for further discussion *pari dilecto* as applied to antitrust suits between conspirators and their former coconspirators.

[220] 392 U.S. 134 (1968), *overruled on other grounds, Copperweld Corp. v. Independence Tube Corp.*, 467 U.S. 752 (1984).

[221] *Id.* at 139.

[222] *Id.* at 140.

[223] *Id.*

The lower federal courts have largely ignored the sweeping admonition of the Court and have attempted to weigh the relative degrees of fault among the antitrust violators. [224] The defense, under these decisions, turns on the nature and degree of involvement. Before applying the defense, courts have required that the plaintiff be a co–initiator, or possess equal bargaining strength, or be a perpetrator. They have inquired also whether an arm's length transaction was involved. In concurring opinions in *Perma Life*, Justices White and Fortas noted that, even if the doctrine is not applicable, a plaintiff may have difficulty establishing causation of the injury when its conduct is equal or greater than defendant's.

More recently, the Court seemed to recede from its absolute ban on the use of the *in pari delicto* defense. In *Eichler v. Berner*, a securities case, the Court concluded that "a private action for damages . . . may be barred on the grounds of the plaintiff's own culpability only where: (1) as a direct result of his own actions, the plaintiff bears at least substantially equal responsibility for the violations he seeks to redress, and (2) preclusion of suit would not significantly interfere with the effective enforcement of the . . . laws . . . ." [225]

§ 3.06 Antitrust Enforcement in Regulated Industries

[A] Introduction

The antitrust laws are a means to regulate firms competing under free market forces. Firms may be subject to antitrust review when the market is not operating according to our accepted models of competition [226] or when externalities are present. Antitrust is supposed to assure competitive markets and to make corrections for market failures and externalities that artificially interfere with commerce. Cartel behavior and monopolies are examples. The Court did mention, however, that this immunity does not apply when a state pardons "those who violate the Sherman Act by authorizing them to violate it, or by declaring that their action is lawful. . ." [227] In other words, the state cannot simply authorize a party to break the law under the Sherman Act. The actions of the party must further public policy in order to qualify for immunity.

---

[224] *Moecker v. Honeywell Intern., Inc.*, 144 F. Supp. 2d 1291, 1312–13 (M.D. Fla. 2001) (asserting that the defense is available but that "application of the defense is to be made on a case by case basis and is limited to the situation where the plaintiff's responsibility is 'essentially indistinguishable' from or 'clearly greater' than the responsibility of the defendant."). *See, e.g., Thi–Hawaii, Inc. v. First Commerce Financial Corp.*, 627 F.2d 991, 995–96 (9th Cir. 1980).

[225] 472 U.S. 299, 311–12 (1985). *See also General Leaseways, Inc. v. National Truck Leasing Assn*, 1987–2 Trade Cases (CCH) ¶ 67,706, at 58,667 (7th Cir. 1987) (antitrust damages denied because plaintiff initially supported challenged restraints).

[226] *See* Chapter 2 on antitrust economics.

[227] *Id*. at 351 (citations omitted).

There are many industries, however, where competition has been replaced with regulation. Federal and state agencies have been established to regulate some or all of the market behavior within a given industry. The regulated behavior might include market entry, price, output or exit. [228] Thus regulation or government intervention can take many forms. It generally is considered, on a continuum, as the opposite of antitrust.

According to the First Circuit in *Town of Concord v. Boston Edison Co.,* [229] "regulation and antitrust typically aim at similar goals — i.e., low and economically efficient prices, innovation, and efficient production methods — but they seek to achieve these goals in very different ways." [230]

Economic regulators seek to achieve them *directly* by controlling prices through rules and regulation; antitrust seeks to achieve them *indirectly* by promoting and preserving a process that tends to bring them about. An antitrust rule that seeks to promote competition but nonetheless interferes with regulatory controls could undercut the very objectives the antitrust laws are designed to serve. [231]

Therefore, the question in any regulatory scheme should be whether the intent of Congress was to repeal the antitrust laws through enacting the regulation. [232]

Industry behavior may be controlled by an agency or commission through statutory or rulemaking directives, rather than free market forces. [233] Economic or other policy reasons drive the decision whether to formally regulate an industry through agency action or to permit regulation through antitrust enforcement and market forces. Economic justifications for regulation include (1) market failures that suggest noncompetitive conditions or that competition is not workable; (2) inadequate or scarce resources; (3) inadequate market information; or (4) the existence of a natural monopoly. Noneconomic justifications include political reasons that attempt to *protect* certain industries from competition. [234]

[B] Regulation of Natural Monopoly

The economic justification for regulation over a natural monopoly is illustrative of when regulation may be preferable to market competition. A natural monopoly is a market that can be served at the lowest per unit cost by one firm satisfying the entire demand. [235] In theory it is a market

---

[228] S. Breyer, *Regulation and Its Reform* (1982).

[229] 915 F.2d 17 (1st Cir. 1990).

[230] *Id.* at 22.

[231] *Id.*

[232] *National Gerimedical Hosp. & Gerontology Ctr. v. Blue Cross*, 452 U.S. 378, 389, (1981).

[233] J. Harrison, T. Morgan, and P. Verkuil, *Regulation and Deregulation* (1995). If an industry is exempt from antitrust coverage, there may or may not be a regulatory agency that controls it.

[234] *See* Wiley, *A Capture Theory of Antitrust Federalism*, 99 Harv. L. Rev. 713 (1986).

[235] A. Kahn, *The Economics of Regulation* 65–70 (1970); Posner, *Natural Monopoly and Its Regulation*, 21 Stan. L. Rev. 548, 550–53 (1969).

that is most efficient and can be run more cheaply when there is only one seller. But we know that a monopolist does not price at marginal costs, as one would expect if there were perfect competition. Rather a profit–maximizing monopoly will price where marginal cost equals marginal revenue.[236] We can expect the monopolist "to capture much of the extra value that would otherwise accrue to consumers,"[237] the so–called consumer surplus, thus facilitating a redistribution of income from the consumer to the monopolist. Regulation, by an agency charged with monitoring price and restricting monopoly pricing, is a means to recapture the consumer surplus that otherwise would be lost. The regulator optimally wants to restrict the natural monopolist so that price is set at the most efficient level — at average cost. In this way supracompetitive profits are minimized.

Regulation over a natural monopoly results in a single producer occupying the entire market subject to government control. Numerous industries, including most utilities, are regulated in this way by federal, state and local agencies. But not all economists agree that natural monopolies lack competition and therefore should be regulated in this manner. For instance the theory of "contestable markets" argues that the appropriate economic model for viewing a natural monopoly is one which recognizes that, while competitors will not compete *in* the market because it is inefficient to do so, they will compete *for* the market.[238] The theory asserts that the effect that potential competitors might have on the market has been ignored under the traditional theory of natural monopoly. The theory of contestable market views pricing in the market as dependent on potential as well as actual competition; potential competition can create a restraining influence on the incumbent's pricing[239] and can inhibit monopoly pricing.

Regarding natural monopolies, the theory of contestable markets holds that it is the level of sunk costs (costs which are expended and not retrievable) and not the existence of economics of scale and the high level of fixed costs, that is the major deterrent to potential entrants. Low sunk costs decrease barriers to entry and increase the level of potential competition. However, it is the inability of the would–be newcomer to bear the high level of sunk costs that keeps it out of the market. If the regulator can control the sunk costs through competitive bidding for the market, more competitors may be in competition *for* the market. The presence of potential competitors for that market will cause the monopolist to price, during the time it is the sole producer in the market, closer to marginal costs which, of course, is in the interest of consumers. If the incumbent monopolist

---

[236] *See* Chapter 2 on antitrust economics and Chapter 6 on monopolization.

[237] Posner, *supra* note 235 at 550.

[238] *See, e.g.*, W. Baumol, J. Panzar & R. Willig, *Contestable Markets and the Theory of Industry Structure* (1982); Bailey and Baumol, *Deregulation and the Theory of Contestable Markets*, 1 Yale J. Reg. 111 (1984). Bailey, *Contestability and the Design of Regulatory and Antitrust Policy*, 71 Am. Econ. Rev. 178 (1981); Demsetz, *Why Regulate Utilities?*, 11 J.L. & Econ. 55 (1968); Morrison and Winston, *Empirical Implications and Tests of the Contestability Hypothesis*, 30 J.L. & Econ. 53 (1987).

[239] *See* Chapter 7 on mergers.

knows there are potential competitors for the market when the bidding process is renewed, it is likely not to exact monopoly profits but rather price more competitively. The bidding process should produce more competitive bids.

The degree of competition, therefore, is directly related to the level and transferability of sunk costs. The higher the sunk costs, the fewer potential competitors and the greater the likelihood that the natural monopolist will price above marginal costs. The more contestable the market, the more it will resemble a competitive market with entry occurring when prices rise above average costs. Accordingly, the more contestable the market, the more one can argue for deregulation of the market. Competitive markets rarely justify regulation. To be sure, the theory of contestable markets has served as one of the principal bases for deregulation that has occurred since the late 1970's. But the theory and the resulting decisions to deregulate have been confined largely to industries where sunk costs are low.[240] As industries are deregulated, we return to the idea that the public interest is best served by free and open competition. And that is the role played by the enforcement of the antitrust laws. Deregulation, then, normally increases antitrust scrutiny.

[C]   Antitrust or Regulation?

Not all formal regulation displaces competition. Regulation and competition sometimes co–exist.[241] Some regulated industries face scrutiny under both agency review and traditional antitrust. Numerous legal and policy issues may be in conflict when antitrust and regulation interact.

A frequent inquiry is: When is antitrust displaced by regulation? Explicit and implicit exemptions from antitrust coverage occur. The "pervasiveness" of the regulatory scheme may dictate whether antitrust enforcement has any role to play. Exemptions can be absolute or qualified.[242] If only qualified, the industry may be subject to both "regimes of government control."[243] This may raise tensions between antitrust enforcement and the economic regulation.

Questions of primary jurisdiction arise whether the antitrust court or the regulatory agency should determine the exemption issue in the first instance. In turn, we ask: When should an antitrust court defer to the agency on antitrust issues?[244] Generally, if the antitrust resolution would frustrate a specific regulatory provision or frustrate agency approval, the

---

[240] *See supra* note 238.

[241] J. Harrison, T. Morgan, and P. Verkuil, *supra* note 233.

[242] *See generally United States v. AT&T*, 461 F. Supp. 1314 (D.D.C. 1978).

[243] J. Harrison, T. Morgan, and P. Verkuil, *supra* note 233, at 527.

[244] *See Keogh v. Chicago & Northwestern Railway Co.*, 260 U.S. 156 (1922); *Far East Conference v. United States*, 342 U.S. 930 (1960); *Pan American World Airways v. United States*, 371 U.S. 570 (1952); *MCI Communications Corp. v. American Telephone & Telegraph Co.*, 708 F.2d 1081 (7th Cir. 1983), *cert. denied*, 464 U.S. 891 (1983).

federal regulatory scheme will control over antitrust,[245] and that agency initially will review the issues. But if primary jurisdiction is invoked the antitrust court, where the issue was first brought, will refer the issue but retain ultimate authority to decide.

Federal regulation, either explicitly or implicitly, may preempt the antitrust law's application.[246] The intent of Congress and specific language of the regulatory scheme will have to be consulted. The more pervasive the regulation the more likely antitrust principles may have been displaced. But regulated industries are not necessarily exempt from antitrust. Where the enabling legislation does not confer express immunity nor indicate a "plain repugnancy" or inconsistency between antitrust enforcement and the administration of the regulatory system, courts are reluctant to immunize an industry from antitrust liability.[247] In fact, the Supreme Court has clearly stated that "[e]ven when an industry is regulated substantially, this does not necessarily evidence an intent to repeal the antitrust laws with respect to every action taken within the industry . . . Intent to repeal the antitrust laws is much clearer when a regulatory agency has been empowered to authorize or require the type of conduct under antitrust challenge."[248] Thus, we must consider explicit statutory exemptions, where the expressed intent was to displace competition, and implied exemptions allowed by the courts. Implied exemptions require two conditions:

1) When a regulatory agency has, with Congressional approval, exercised explicit authority over the challenged practice itself (as distinguished from the general subject matter) in such a way that antitrust enforcement would interfere with regulation . . . and

2) when regulation by an agency over an industry or some of its components or practices is so pervasive that Congress is assumed to have determined competition to be an inadequate means of vindicating the public interest.[249]

This second requirement is somewhat elusive, however. In *Gordon v New York Stock Exchange*,[250] the Court plainly rejected the argument that *only* a pervasive regulatory scheme can trump the antitrust laws.[251] The Court found that, although the SEC's authority over the stock exchange was not all–encompassing, the agency did have some power to approve or prohibit

---

[245] *Id. See also Hughes Tool Co. v. Trans World Airlines*, 409 U.S. 363 (1973); Convissor, *Primary Jurisdiction: The Rule and Its Rationalization*, 65 Yale L.J. 315 (1956).

[246] *See, e.g., United States v. Philadelphia National Bank*, 374 U.S. 321, 350 (1963); *Pan American World Airways v. United States*, 371 U.S. 296 (1962); *Gordon v. New York Stock Exchange*, 422 U.S. 659 (1975); *California v. Federal Power Comm'n*, 369 U.S. 482 (1962).

[247] *Otter Tail Power Co. v. United States*, 410 U.S. 366, 372 (1973), *quoting United States v. Philadelphia National Bank*, 374 U.S. 321 (1963); *see also Georgia v. Pennsylvania R.R. Co.*, 324 U.S. 439 (1945).

[248] *National Gerimedical Hosp. & Gerontology Cir. v. Blue Cross*, 452 U.S. 378, 389 (1981).

[249] *United States v. AT&T*, 461 F. Supp. 1314, 1322 (D.D.C. 1978).

[250] 422 U.S. 659 (1975).

[251] *Id.* at 688.

behavior, and, in that situation, it was sufficient to protect the exchange members from antitrust liability.[252] This finding certainly puts the necessity of the second prong of the implied exemption test in a questionable state. On the other hand, the Second Circuit has found the first prong of the test to be a seemingly essential element to any implied exemption case, stating that an implied repeal is available only if the antitrust laws and regulatory provisions conflict.[253] These two cases together suggest that a heavier emphasis is put on the first inquiry of the dual–pronged test.[254] This is not to say, however, that both are not given serious consideration when the argument of implied immunity is raised.[255]

[D] Expressed Federal Exceptions

On numerous occasions Congress has explicitly granted antitrust exemptions to certain industries.[256] Several reasons suggest why enforcement of the antitrust laws may not be ideal in every instance. First, the promotion of competition may produce some undesirable results which we may wish to minimize from a policy perspective. Second, there may be other policy objectives which are equal to, or more important than, the promotion of competition through market forces. Regulation assumes that the "judgment of expert agencies may produce results superior to those of the marketplace, and that for this reason competition . . . will necessarily not serve the public interest."[257]

Conscious choices are made to relax or minimize enforcement in certain industries where market competition would lead to diminished social welfare. The expressed exemptions are of two kinds: (1) those that further broad national policy, and, (2) those that apply to specific industries. Among the former are the promotion of the right of workers to organize, combine and bargain collectively; the promotion of export activity; the encouragement and promotion of research, development and technological change; the need to minimize restrictions on national defense capabilities in times of emergency; and the need to promote small business development. Industry's specific exemptions include insurance, railroads, agriculture, fisheries and professional baseball.

[1] Exemptions Furthering National Policy

Two examples are illustrative of specific exceptions that further national policy.

---

[252] *Id.* at 667, 672, 679, 684.

[253] *Finnegan v. Campeau Corp.*, 915 F.2d 824 (2nd Cir. 1990), *cert. denied*, 499 U.S. 976 (1991).

[254] *See also Pan American World Airways, Inc. v. United States*, 371 U.S. 296 (1963).

[255] *See American Agric. Movement, Inc. v. Bd. of Trade*, 977 F.2d 1147 (7th Cir. 1992).

[256] States, cities and other political subdivisions have done so also. The question of preemption, whether a state or local regulation is in conflict with the federal antitrust law, will be discussed later in § 3.06b.

[257] *United States v. AT&T*, 461 F. Supp. 1314, 1321 (D.D.C. 1978).

[a] Labor Organizations

Section 6 of the Clayton Act states that the antitrust laws do not apply to union organizations or to union members acting within the legitimate objective of the union.[258] This exemption was designed to further the Congressional policy favoring collective bargaining. In order to qualify for the exemption, the union must act in its own self–interest and not in combination with non–labor groups or third parties. As the Supreme Court said in *United States v. Hutcheson*,[259] "[s]o long as a union acts in its self–interest and does not combine with non–labor groups, the licit and illicit under § 20 [of the Clayton Act] are not to be distinguished by any judgment regarding the wisdom or unwisdom, the rightness or wrongness, the selfishness or unselfishness of the end of which the particular union activities are the means."[260]

The Ninth Circuit has held recently that both of the *Hutcheson* requirements must be met in order for the exemption to apply.[261] The Court applied stringent meaning to the words "legitimate union purpose," broadly stating that whether the ends are legitimate depends on whether the "ends to be achieved are among the traditional objectives of labor organizations" *and* whether the means adopted are "activities normally associated with labor disputes."[262] The court remanded the case, suggesting that activities like pressing baseless lawsuits and mechanically objecting to the plaintiff's application for assorted permits are "troublesome" due to their "nontraditional" nature.[263] This opinion is considerably more constricting for unions than is *Hutchenson*; however, it is not without some textual support.[264] Section 20 of the Clayton Act provides that specified labor activities are not to be considered "violations of any law of the United States."[265] The statutory exemption on its face, however, protects conduct by a union or its members; it does not speak to a union agreement with an employer,[266] which normally would be outside the statutory exemption. For employer–union agreements, the Court has created a further exemption.[267]

The nonstatutory exemption for employer–union agreements was first set out in *United Mine Workers v. Pennington*.[268] Pennington claimed that the

---

[258] 15 U.S.C. § 17. *See generally* Roberts, *Reconciling Federal and Antitrust Policy*, 75 Geo. L.J. 19 (1986).

[259] 312 U.S. 219 (1941).

[260] *Id.* at 232.

[261] *USS POSCO Indus. v. Contra Costa County Bldge. & Constr. Trades Council*, 31 F.3d 800 (9th Cir. 1994).

[262] *Id.* at 808–809.

[263] *Id.* at 809.

[264] The Norris–LaGuardia Act 29 U.S. Sec. 101 *et seq.*, which was passed by Congress to largely prohibit the issuance of injunctions in labor dispute cases, contains broad language which can be read to support *USS–Posco*'s holding.

[265] 29 U.S.C. § 52.

[266] *United Mine Workers v. Pennington*, 381 U.S. 657, 662 (1965).

[267] *Connell Construction Co. v. Plumbers Local 100*, 421 U.S. 616, 622 (1975).

[268] 381 U.S. 657 (1965).

union engaged in unfair trade and labor practices by entering assorted agreements with larger coal operations for the purpose of eliminating competition from smaller mining companies. These agreements had the effect of increasing wages in the larger companies, necessitating that the smaller companies do the same, despite their lack of funds, in order to remain competitive. The defendant used this argument in his cross–claim and cited other steps that had been undertaken by the union to "exclude the marketing, production, and sale of nonunion coal."[269]

The Supreme Court found that "[n]either the Clayton nor the Norris–LaGuardia Acts deal with arrangements between employers and unions" nor do they "tell us whether such agreements are barred or permitted by antitrust laws."[270] The Court also clearly found that the alleged activity did not constitute a direct restraint on the product market, which would deny the union the protections of the labor exemption.[271] Therefore, the Court was faced with the formidable task of determining whether this type of wage bargaining fell under the nonstatutory labor exemption.

Although the Court admitted that the determination of wage levels is an integral part of the bargaining process, it refused to hold that *any* agreement dealing with or impacting wages is immediately exempt from the antitrust laws.[272] Rather, the Court held that not all labor market restraints integrated in collective bargaining agreements are covered by the exemption. As such, wage bargaining was said to have its limitations. The dissent, however, did not share in this point of view. Instead, Justices Goldberg, Harlan, and Stewart felt that wage bargaining should be exempt throughout. Justice Goldberg opined that "[t]he Court should hold that, in order to effectuate congressional intent, collective bargaining activity concerning mandatory subjects of bargaining under the Labor Act is not subject to the antitrust laws."[273]

The Eighth Circuit extended *Pennington* in *Powell v. NFL*.[274] The plaintiffs challenged the NFL's "Right of First Refusal/Compensation" system, which had been adopted into the collective bargaining agreement between the league and the players' union and which put restrictions on the rights of players to sign with other teams once their contract was up. After the agreement between the union and NFL expired, the union attempted to revise the provision to no avail. An impasse followed, and the players attempted unsuccessfully to strike. The Court of Appeals found that, even though an impasse had occurred, the exemption still applied. The court stated that the point of impasse could not be the point of expiration of the exemption, given the fact that impasses were often temporary

---

[269] *Id*. at 660.

[270] *Id*. at 662.

[271] *Id*. at 663.

[272] *Id*. at 665. (Emphasis added).

[273] *Id*. at 710. The reference is to the National Labor Relations Act, which required unions and employers to engage in wage bargaining, among other types.

[274] 930 F.2d 1293 (1989), *cert. denied*, 498 U.S. 1040 (1991).

in nature, leading to a final agreement between the bargaining parties.[275] The court also suggested that making impasse the endpoint for the exemption would lead to problems with employers intentionally driving impossible bargains in order to gain access to antitrust protections. Impasse is a "lawful stage of the collective bargaining process" and, as such, should not be treated as "misconduct by the defendants."[276]

The Eighth Circuit suggested that the exemption would terminate only when the parties no longer share an "ongoing collective bargaining relationship."[277] The court concluded that "[a]s long as there is a possibility that proceedings may be commenced before the Board, or until final resolution of Board proceedings and appeals therefrom, the labor relation continues and the labor exemption applies."[278]

The Second Circuit faced a similar question in *National Basketball Assn. v. Williams*,[279] where the NBA sought to continue the terms of an expired collective bargaining agreement. The court found that the NBA could not be prevented from doing so, as the activity was consistent with hard bargaining and the use of economic force in the employment arena.

Most recently, the Supreme Court addressed the issue of collective bargaining and the nonstatutory exemption in *Brown v. Pro Football, Inc.*[280] Petitioners challenged the NFL's implementation of a salary cap and requirement of $1000 for all members of the developmental squads which scrimmaged with players during practices and substituted for them in cases of injury. This cap had been the subject of much controversy between the union and the NFL, and, eventually, the parties had bargained to an impasse on the issue, with the union feeling that all players should have the ability to bargain individually for salary. Despite the impasse, the NFL implemented the fixed salary requirement.

The Supreme Court found the NFL exempt from antitrust liability. In adhering to the limited power accorded the judiciary under the nonstatutory exemption, the Court held that the collective bargaining engaged in by the NFL was a reasonable practice deserving antitrust exemption. The Court tersely rejected the three arguments offered by the plaintiffs. The first theory suggested that the exemption applies only to labor–management agreements, as opposed to labor–management negotiations.[281] The Court said this argument simply reflects the fact that agreements usually have been the focus of previous similar cases, and the argument says nothing about the rationale behind the exemption.[282] The purpose behind the

---

[275] *Id.* at 1299. (Citation omitted).

[276] *Id.* at 1302.

[277] *Id.* at 1303 and n.12.

[278] *Id.* at 1303–1304.

[279] 45 F.3d 684 (2d Cir. 1995).

[280] 518 U.S. 231 (1996).

[281] *Id.* at 243.

[282] *Id.*

exemption is a policy favoring the association of employees to prevent excess competition for jobs, leading to wage depression and poor working conditions.[283] As such, the process of the bargaining arrangement is just as important as the agreement eventually reached. This was a new stretch in terms of the nonstatutory exemption because now the entire process of collective bargaining is exempt from antitrust law, unless the agreement eventually decided upon is "sufficiently distant in time and circumstances from the bargaining process."[284]

This finding doomed the plaintiff's second theory, as well. The Solicitor General attempted to argue, once again, that the exemption should terminate at the point of impasse. The *Brown* Court adopted the same point of view as the *Powell* court, saying that impasses are often temporary, with effective collective bargaining continuing afterwards.[285] The Court found that "[i]mpasse and an accompanying implementation of proposals constitute an integral part of the bargaining process," necessitating exemption.[286] The Court also rejected the Solicitor General's alternate suggestion that the exemption should only be "reasonably extended" in such cases, stating that "even so modified, the impasse–related rule creates an exemption that can evaporate in the middle of the bargaining process, leaving later antitrust courts free to second–guess the parties' bargaining decisions and consequently forcing them to choose their collective–bargaining responses in light of what they predict or fear that antitrust courts will eventually decide."[287]

Finally, the Court dismissed the suggestion that the exemption for post–impasse agreements should only apply to bargaining tactics, but not to substantive terms. The Court found this unacceptable, as it would require courts to look into employers purposes and motives, which is both "amorphous" and outside the regular concerns of the labor exemption.[288] In sum, the Court applied the nonstatutory exemption in this case because

> [the] conduct took place during and immediately after a collective–bargaining negotiation. It grew out of, and was directly related to, the lawful operation of the bargaining process. It involved a matter that the parties were required to negotiate collectively. And it concerned only the parties to the collective–bargaining relationship.[289]

---

[283] *See Richards v. Neilsen Freight Lines*, 810 F.2d 898, 905 (9th Cir. 1987) (explaining *Connell Construction Co. v. Plumbers & Steamfitters Local Union No. 100* in terms of the policy driving the decision).

[284] *Brown*, 518 U.S. at 250.

[285] *Id.* at 244–46.

[286] *Id.* at 239.

[287] *Id.* at 246–47.

[288] *Id.* at 247.

[289] *Id.* at 250.

The Court was adamant in its position that the decision did not insulate completely from antitrust law every multi–employer imposition of terms couched in a collective bargaining agreement, however.[290]

Justice Stevens' dissent strongly discouraged the majority's broad application of legality to any activity implemented during the collective bargaining process. He feared that the majority opinion would effectively allow employers to be protected in denying employees the opportunity to negotiate their salaries individually through an exemption designed to protect collective action by employees.[291] Nonetheless, it cannot be denied that the *Brown* decision, while broad, does clarify the nonstatutory labor exemption and is certainly in accord with current trends in interpreting the exemption, as demonstrated in *Powell* and *Williams*.

The only issue the *Brown* Court left untouched is whether a labor law violation should immediately destroy the exemption. The lower courts are largely split on this issue.[292] Some critics feel that this is a moot point in the case of *Brown*, since "[a]s long as the collective bargaining relationship remains intact and the negotiations do not substantially affect outside parties, violations of labor laws should not extinguish the antitrust exemption."[293]

Four points are worth noting regarding the modern interpretation of the labor exemption. First, in order for it to apply, the union must act in its own self–interest.[294] Second, the union can only use means that are the least restrictive necessary to achieve the goals.[295] Third, there must be a specific employer–employee relationship, as opposed to, for example, an independent contractor relationship.[296] Fourth, the exemption applies only when the union is acting in its official capacity as a representative of workers.[297] If the union engages in its own commercial or productive activity, its activity is covered under the Sherman Act and is not exempt.

---

[290] *Id.* ("Distance in time and circumstances from the collective–bargaining process" may overcome the exemption).

[291] 518 U.S. at 251–66.

[292] Compare *Consolidated Express v. New York Shipping Ass'n (Conex)*, 602 F.2d 494 (3d. Cir. 1979) (holding that a labor law violation can destroy the nonstatutory labor exemption) with *Richards v. Neilsen Freight Lines*, 810 F.2d 898 (9th Cir. 1987) (finding that a possibly illegal bargaining agreement is still exempt from antitrust enforcement).

[293] *The Supreme Court, 1995 Term–Leading Case*, 110 HARV. L. REV. 227, 337 (Nov. 1996).

[294] *United Mine Workers v. Pennington*, 381 U.S. 657, 665–66 (1965) (wages are included, but not an agreement between a union and an employer to impose a certain wage on another employer).

[295] *H.A. Artists & Assocs. v. Actors' Equity Ass'n*, 451 U.S. 704, 722 (1981); *Allen Bradley Co. v. Local Union No. 3*, 325 U.S. 797, 809 (1945) (agreements that bar entry of new employers not exempt).

[296] *Columbia River Packers Ass'n v. Hinton*, 315 U.S. 143 (1942) (question of fact in determining whether relationship is with employee or independent contractor); *Burlington Northern Santa Fe Ry. Co. v. Int'l Bhd. of Teamsters, Local 174*, 203 F.3d 703, (9th Cir. 2000)(union members who are subcontractors are employees).

[297] *Streiffer v. Seafares Sea Chest Corp.*, 162 F. Supp. 602 (E.D. La. 1958) (business subsidiary owned by union not exempt).

[b] Export Associations

Most foreign countries, including advanced capitalist economies, do not proscribe and punish cartel organizations as does the United States. The role of competition in economic life varies with different philosophies and ideologies. As a result, American firms selling in export markets face severe competition from foreign cartels. Congress has attempted to reduce the disadvantages to United States exporting companies through the adoption of two statutes.

The Webb–Pomerence Act was first enacted in 1918 to encourage American exports through joint export associations. Export associations are exempt from the antitrust laws if their "sole purpose" is to engage in export trade and if their actions (1) do not interfere with or restrain trade in the United States or (2) restrain the export trade of domestic competitors.[298] Congress passed the Webb–Pomerene Act largely as an attempt to remedy the competitive disadvantage that firms in the United States suffered due to their inability to form joint associations.[299]

The Federal Trade Commission is charged with the responsibility of investigating export associations. This is the federal agency with which an association must file reports on its export activities. If conduct outside the exemption occurs, the FTC may refer the matter to the Department of Justice for prosecution.[300] Nonexempt conduct includes the export association: (1) joining with a foreign cartel,[301] (2) establishing a foreign subsidiary,[302] or (3) joining with non–members to restrict competition and price.[303]

The Third Circuit further clarified the reach of Webb–Pomerene protections in *Intnat'l Raw Materials v. Stauffer Chemical Co.*[304] One of the defendants in the case was the American National Soda Ash Corporation (ANSAC), which constituted an association of soda ash producers. All members of the corporation were domestic corporations with their principal place of business in the United States. All but one was owned by or affiliated with a major foreign corporation. ANSAC bargained with IRM to obtain a set rate for terminal services and, eventually, they reached an agreement. After the contract expired, however, ANSAC took its business to Hall–Buck Marine, a competitor of IRM, because Hall–Buck offered ANSAC a better price. The deal between Hall–Buck and ANSAC included a five year renewal option for ANSAC for ten years on the same terms. If ANSAC rejected the option after the first five years, it had to pay Hall–Buck a

---

[298] 15 U.S.C. § 62.

[299] *Id.* at 2130–31.

[300] *See generally United States Alkali Export Ass'n v. United States*, 325 U.S. 196 (1945); *United States v. Concentrated Phosphate Export Ass'n*, 393 U.S. 199 (1968).

[301] *United States v. United States Alkali Export Ass'n*, 86 F. Supp. 59 (S.D.N.Y. 1949).

[302] *United States v. Minnesota Mining & Mfg. Co.*, 92 F. Supp. 947 (D. Mass. 1950).

[303] *Export Screw Ass'n*, 43 F.T.C. 980 (1947).

[304] 978 F.2d 1318 (3d Cir. 1992), *cert. denied*, 507 U.S. 988 (1993).

portion of the costs for construction of the new terminal. ANSAC was to have a 50% ownership interest in the operation. IRM sued ANSAC, among others, under a price–fixing theory, saying that ANSAC did not qualify for Webb–Pomerene protection because 1) many members of ANSAC were foreign owned and 2) ANSAC had acted outside its "sole purpose" requirement by engaging in terminalling.

The court rejected both arguments and found ANSAC's actions fully protected by the Act. As for the IRM's first theory, the court stated that "[n]othing in the language of the statute or its legislative history explicitly restricts membership in Webb–Pomerene associations to American–owned firms."[305] In fact, the legislative history suggests otherwise, as the House of Representatives firmly rejected the suggested addition of such limiting language.[306] The court found that a Congressional intent to so limit the Act could not be inferred from individual statements or debates, either.[307]

IRM's second theory was based on ANSAC's part ownership and somewhat integrated business activity with Hall–Buck Marine. The plaintiff suggested that this association brought ANSAC outside the "sole purpose" requirement because ANSAC was effectively in the business of terminalling, as well as soda ash producing. The court found that, in order for this assertion to hold true, Hall–Buck and ANSAC would have to be in either a joint venture or partnership arrangement, which they were not. The court held that, even though ANSAC may receive some economic benefit from Hall–Buck's dealings with other customers, as the terminal could not be built without that extra revenue, this did not constitute a joint venture.[308] Additionally, there was no agreement between Hall–Buck and ANSAC to apportion losses, further proving that no partnership or joint venture existed.[309] As such, both arguments failed.

In 1982 Congress passed another statute to encourage export activity and to reduce trade deficits. The Export Trading Company Act[310] provides for a "certification" issued by the Department of Commerce with the concurrence of the Department of Justice. When it is issued, the certification immunizes an export trading company from federal and state antitrust enforcement. Several conditions must first exist, however, before the certification will issue. The export activity: (1) cannot result in a "substantial lessening of competition" in the United States or with an export competitor; (2) cannot "unreasonably" affect prices in the United States; (3) cannot amount to an "unfair method of competition" against competitors in the export market; and (4) cannot engage in the sale or resale of goods in the

---

[305] *Id*. at 1323.

[306] *Id*.

[307] *Id*. at 1324.

[308] *Id*. at 1332.

[309] *Id*.

[310] 15 U.S.C. §§ 4001–4021. *See generally*, Areeda & Hovenkamp, *Antitrust, supra* note 43, ¶ 251a.

domestic market.[311] Once the certificate issues, there is a presumption of legality that attaches to the export activity.[312] But a private right of action for injunctive relief and actual (not treble) damages exists if the exporter goes outside the conditions stated in the certificate.[313]

A further restriction was added in 1982. Before a court has jurisdiction to entertain an enforcement action against exporting companies, the plaintiff must show that the conduct had a "direct, substantial, and reasonably foreseeable effect" on commerce in the United States, or on the export commerce of a United States resident.[314]

[2]   Exemptions For Specific Industries

[a]   Insurance

Although there are several congressional exemptions which are industry specific, our discussion is limited to one central exemption—the insurance industry. Prior to 1944, insurance was exclusively regulated by the states because it was believed that it was not "commerce" within the meaning of Congress' regulatory powers. In *United States v. South–Eastern Underwriters Ass'n*,[315] the Supreme Court held that insurance was within the regulatory ambit of the commerce clause and thus subject to antitrust. Several challenges were addressed to this expanded antitrust coverage.

First, there was fear that this would restrict the power of the states to regulate the business of insurance; second, a preemption issue was raised when there was tension between the state regulation and the Sherman Act; and third, there was fear of loss of "efficiency–enhancing joint insurer activities."[316]

In response, Congress, in 1945, enacted the McCarran–Ferguson Act.[317] Congress decided that the federal antitrust laws shall not cover "the business of insurance" as long as it is "regulated by state law." If the conduct engaged in by the insurance company is not regulated and authorized by

---

[311] 15 U.S.C. § 4013(a).

[312] Areeda & Hovenkamp, *supra* note 43, ¶ 251a.

[313] *Id.*

[314] 15 U.S.C. § 6a. *See* discussion of the Foreign Trade Antitrust Improvement Act, § 3.03[C], *infra*.

[315] 322 U.S. 533 (1944). *See generally* Kinter, Bauer and Allen, *Application of the Antitrust Laws to Activities of Insurance Companies*, 63 N.C. L. Rev. 431 (1985).

[316] Statement of Charles Rule, Acting Asst. Atty. Gen. before the Committee on Small Business, House of Representatives (Apr. 29, 1987). Note also that the "state action doctrine," discussed *infra* § 3.06(A), is a basis for a state to regulate and immunize conduct subject to the federal antitrust laws. *See Southern Motor Carriers Rate Conference, Inc. v. United States*, 471 U.S. 48 (1985). In light of the developments of this doctrine, perhaps no other exemption is warranted. Apparently, the recent trend in state regulation is to permit freer competition among insurers. *See* 133 *Cong. Rec.* S. 342–44 (daily ed. Jan. 6, 1987) (statement of Senator Metzenbaum).

[317] 15 U.S.C. §§ 1011–15.

state law, or is not a part of the business of insurance, it is not exempt from the federal antitrust laws.[318]

Several definitions have been advanced for what is meant by the "business of insurance." Certainly underwriting and the spreading of risk are the core of the insurance business. A broader definition also includes the relationship between the insurer and the insured. In *Union Labor Life Ins. Co. v. Pireno*,[319] the Supreme Court set forth the test for determining exemptions: "First, whether the practice has the effect of transferring or spreading a policyholder's risk; second, whether the practice is an integral part of the policy relationship between the insurer and the insured; and third, whether the practice is limited to entities within the insurance industry."[320]

The *Pireno* three–part test for the "business of insurance" was questioned by the Supreme Court. In *U.S. Dept. of Treasury v. Fabe*,[321] the Court was faced with a challenge to an Ohio statute which gave the federal government fifth priority in liquidation proceedings for insolvent companies. The United States argued that it should be given first priority under the corresponding federal statute and that the McCaran–Ferguson Act did not apply to this situation because the state statute did not regulate the "business of insurance."[322] The Supreme Court held that the Ohio statute fell under the first clause of § 2(b) and, hence, was protected from federal preemption.

The Court relied largely on its previous decision in *Securities & Exchange Commn. v. National Securities, Inc.*,[323] where it had said that a state law intended to protect policyholders and their interests would be decidedly engaged in the business of insurance.[324] As such, the Ohio statute's purpose was to ensure the performance of insurance agreements, thereby protecting policyholders and regulating the "business of insurance." The Court stated that *Pireno* should not be read to say that the "business of insurance" deals only with the writing, as opposed to the performance, of contacts, as both activities are integral to the business.[325] In fact, "without performance of the terms of the insurance policy, there is no risk transfer at all."[326] The Court expanded *Pireno* to include protection of activities that are directly related to the performance of an insurance contract, even if the activities

---

[318] *See, e.g., Group Life & Health Insurance Co. v. Royal Drug Co.*, 440 U.S. 205 (1979).

[319] 458 U.S. 119 (1982).

[320] *Id.* at 129. (summarizing factors identified by the Court in *Group Life & Health Ins. Co. v. Royal Drug Co.*, 440 U.S. 205 (1979)).

[321] 508 U.S. 491, 113 S.Ct. 2202 (1993).

[322] The first clause of section 2(b) of the McCarran–Ferguson Act provides that no federal statute shall preempt a state statute enacted for the purpose of regulating the business of insurance.

[323] 393 U.S. 453 (1969).

[324] *Id.* at 460.

[325] 508 U.S. at 504.

[326] *Id.*

do not necessarily spread risk by themselves. The Court also found that the fact that only part of the statute was enacted for the purpose of regulating the business of insurance did not prevent it from enjoying at least partial protection under the McCarran Act.

The unusual aspect of *Fabe* lies in the Court's comment that *Pireno* does not apply as precedent for the case. The Court supported this suggestion by differentiating between the first and second clauses of § 2(b). The second clause, upon which *Pireno* was decided, states that antitrust law "shall be applicable to the business of insurance to the extent that such business is not regulated by State law."[327] The first clause, upon which the *Fabe* holding rests, states that "[n]o Act of Congress shall be construed to invalidate, impair, or supersede any law enacted by any State for the purpose of regulating the business of insurance, . . . unless such Act specifically relates to the business of insurance."[328] The Court distinguished the two clauses by defining the first clause much more broadly than the second. Accordingly, the Court found the first clause to deal with "laws that possess the end, intention, or aim of adjusting, managing, or controlling the business of insurance" and makes up the Act's "primary objectives."[329] Upon applying this analysis, the performance of a contract becomes the "business of insurance." This was an unprecedented step in the interpretation of the McCarran–Ferguson Act, and one which was criticized by the dissent.

The challenge continues today in defining certain activities as part of the "business of insurance" and certain others as outside the realm of the McCarran–Ferguson Act. The most recent decision has been handed down by the Third Circuit in *Ticor Title Insurance Co. v. FTC,*[330] in which the court held that fixing fees for title search and examination services is not within the "business of insurance" contemplated by § 2(b). The court found that rate fixing of this sort does not spread risk for the policyholder, and that the activity was better characterized as "ancillary" to insurance contracting and performance.[331] This effectively overruled prior Third Circuit decisions which had held otherwise.[332] However, this view about title search and examination and price fixing is not held by all circuits. The Tenth Circuit in *Commander Leasing Co. v. Transamerica Title Ins. Co.*[333] held that, in deciding what is in the business of title insurance, one can not fragment insurance from searches and examinations.[334]

---

[327] 15 U.S.C. § 1012(b)(1988).

[328] *Id.*

[329] 508 U.S. 504–505.

[330] 998 F.2d 1129 (3d Cir. 1993), *cert denied,* 114 S.Ct. 1292 (1994).

[331] Id. at 1134, 1136.

[332] In *In re Real Estate Title & Settlement Serv. Antitrust Litig.* 1686–1 Trade Cas. (CCH) Paragraph 67, 149, 62,933 (E.D. Pa. 1986), *aff'd,* 815 F.2d 695 (3d Cir. 1987), *cert denied* 485 U.S. 909 (1988), the court found such activities to be protected by the McCarran–Ferguson Act because of their close relation to the issuance of title insurance and the fact that they had been historically performed by title insurance companies.

[333] 477 F.2d 77 (10th Cir, 1973).

[334] *Id.* at 82.

Notwithstanding the broad exemptions, Congress provided for specific limitations on the scope of the exemption. If the insurance company engages in agreements to boycott, coerce or intimidate, the exemption does not apply.[335] For example, a refusal to deal except at a fixed price is a boycott and subject to antitrust challenge.[336] According to the Supreme Court in *St. Paul Fire & Marine v. Barry,*[337] the victim of the boycott does not have to be a competitor of the boycotting parties in order for the exception to apply.[338] "Boycott," as used in the McCarran–Ferguson Act, should be defined in its usual way. Plainly, it is "a method of pressuring a party with whom one has a dispute by withholding or enlisting others to withhold, patronage or services from the target."[339] According to the Supreme Court in *St. Paul Fire & Marine v. Barry,*[340] the victim of the boycott does not have to be a competitor of the boycotting parties in order for the exception to apply.[341] "Boycott," as used in the McCarran–Ferguson Act, should be defined in its usual way. Plainly, it is "a method of pressuring a party with whom one has a dispute by withholding or enlisting others to withhold, patronage or services from the target."[342] In addition, where transactions are so interstate in nature that the state cannot effectively regulate the activity, the exemption is not "regulated by state law," hence the exempt may not apply.[343]

In *Hartford Fire Insurance Co. v. California,*[344] nineteen states and various private plaintiffs alleged that the defendants, both domestic and foreign insurance carriers, conspired to restrict the terms of coverage for commercial general liability (CGL) insurance within the United States. In their complaint, the plaintiffs alleged that the purpose behind the conspiracy was to force certain primary insurers (those insurers who sell insurance directly to consumers) to change the terms of their standard CGL insurance policies to conform with the policies the defendant insurers wanted to sell. While the foreign defendant's raised international comity as a bar to extension of extraterritorial jurisdiction, the domestic defendants argued that the alleged conduct fell within the grant of antitrust immunity for insurance contained in § 2(b) of the McCarran–Ferguson Act,[345] since it amounted to 'the business of insurance' and was 'regulated by State law.'

After all actions were consolidated, the district court granted defendants motions to dismiss believing the alleged conduct fell within the grant of

---

[335] Sections 2(b) and 3(b) of the Act, 15 U.S.C. §§ 1013(b), 1014.

[336] *California League of Independent Ins. Procedures v. Aetna Casualty & Surety Co.*, 179 F. Supp. 65 (N.D. Cal. 1959).

[337] 438 U.S. 531 (1978).

[338] 438 U.S. 531 (1978).

[339] *Id.* at 541.

[340] 438 U.S. 531 (1978).

[341] 438 U.S. at 543, 550.

[342] *Id.* at 541.

[343] *See FTC v. Travelers Health Ass'n*, 362 U.S. 293 (1960).

[344] 477 F.2d 77 (10th Cir, 1973).

[345] 15 U.S.C. § 1011 et seq.

antitrust immunity contained in § 2(b) of the McCarran–Ferguson Act and that the conduct did not constitute an unprotected "boycott" within § 3(b) of the Act.[346] On appeal, however, the Ninth Circuit Court of Appeals reversed and held that "although the conduct involved the 'business of insurance,' the domestic defendants could not claim antitrust immunity since: (1) they forfeited their § 2(b) exemption when they conspired with the nonexempt foreign reinsurers, and (2) the conduct fell within the § 3(b) exemption for 'acts of boycott, coercion, or intimidation.'"[347]

The Supreme Court affirmed the Ninth Circuit's holding regarding the inapplicability of antitrust immunity for the alleged conduct in question and specified four propositions concerning 'boycotts' under § 3(b) of the McCarran–Ferguson Act. Specifically, conduct among insurers will not qualify for antitrust immunity if it represents a refusal to deal involving the coordinated action of multiple actors. This refusal to deal need not be absolute in nature nor must the boycott entail unequal treatment between the targets and the instigators. Finally, "concerted activity," although a necessary element, is not, by itself, sufficient to justify a finding of "boycott" under § 3(b) of the McCarran–Ferguson Act.

§ 3.07 Federalism

[A] The State Action Doctrine

The antitrust laws regulate private agreements and conduct that restrain trade; they are not directed at regulating "state action or official action directed by the state."[348] State action immunity was first expressed by the Supreme Court in the seminal case of *Parker v. Brown*,[349] where the concept of federalism was applied in upholding a state statute that created a commission to set prices and restrict output among raisin growers. Federalism is a policy that emphasizes a return of certain decision making functions to state and local governments. Noting that "[i]n a dual system of government in which, under the Constitution, the states are sovereign, save only as Congress may constitutionally subtract from their authority,"[350] the Supreme Court reasoned that as long as there is no direct conflict with federal policy, the two schemes of regulation, federal and state, may co–exist.

The Court did mention, however, that this immunity does not apply when a state pardons "those who violate the Sherman Act by authorizing them

---

[346] *In re Insurance Antitrust Litigation*, 723 F. Supp. 464 (1989).

[347] *In re Insurance Antitrust Litigation*, 938 F.2d 919 (9th Cir. 1991).

[348] *Parker v. Brown*, 317 U.S. 341 (1943). *See generally* Lopatka, *The State of "State Action" Antitrust Immunity: A Progress Report*, 46 La. L. Rev. 941 (1986). For a discussion of how antitrust regulation has fostered a theme of federalism over competition the last 50 years in local government issues *see* E. Thomas Sullivan, *Antitrust Regulation of Land Use: Federalism's Triumph Over Competition, The Last Fifty Years,* 3 Wash. U. J. Law & Policy 473 (2000).

[349] *Id.*

[350] *Id.* at 351.

to violate it, or by declaring that their action is lawful . . ."[351] In other words, the state cannot simply authorize a party to break the law under the Sherman Act. The actions of the party must further public policy in order to qualify for immunity.

In the absence of federal preemption, action by a state (or a subdivision thereof whose authority comes from the state), through legislation or regulation is immune, irrespective of the anticompetitive effect. The state may, in short, replace the federal scheme with its own judgment.[352] But the requisite degree of state authorization was an issue that would be frequently litigated. Subsequent courts were asked to decide the degree of state involvement needed to immunize an anticompetitive practice. A central question was whether implicit sanctioning by the state would suffice.

That issue was raised in *Goldfarb v. Virginia State Bar*.[353] Plaintiff successfully challenged a minimum fee schedule established by the state bar association that had not been mandated, compelled or supervised by the state supreme court, although it was implicitly sanctioned. *Goldfarb* implied that antitrust conduct is only immunized when the state through its sovereign power *requires* the practice under question and actually supervises it.[354] Not every act of the state or its subdivisions therefore automatically comes within the state action immunity.[355] In *Goldfarb* the price–fixing agreement was not immunized because the state did not require the practice. Soon the focus turned to the degree of the initial authorization and on the degree of supervision by the state.

In *Cantor v. Detroit Edison Co.*,[356] plaintiff challenged as anticompetitive the utility company's practice of tying the sale of light bulbs to electricity sales. The state utility commission had approved a tariff which included the costs of the bulbs. Cantor alleged that through this tying defendant utility used its monopoly power in one market (electricity) to suppress competition in another market (light bulbs). The Court declined to apply the state action doctrine once it concluded that passive approval by the state was not enough to trigger the immunity. A policy of "state neutrality" regarding the challenged practice was insufficient as a matter of law.[357] The Court required both a clear articulation of state policy to displace

---

[351] *Id.* at 82.

[352] *See generally* Mather, *Antitrust Implications of Municipal Land Use Planning*, 33 Wayne L. Rev. 965, 985, 987 (1987); Hovenkamp & MacKerron, *Municipal Regulation and Federal Antitrust Policy*, 32 U.C.L.A. L. Rev. 719 (1985).

[353] 421 U.S. 773 (1975).

[354] *Id.* at 791.

[355] *See California Retail Liquor Dealers Ass'n v. Midcal Aluminum, Inc.*, 445 U.S. 97 (1980) (state failed to establish or review prices required to be filed under state statute); *Cantor v. Detroit Edison*, 428 U.S. 579 (1976) (in absence of state requirement, state utility commission approved light bulb sale by utility).

[356] 428 U.S. 579 (1976).

[357] *Id.* at 585.

competition with the challenged practice, rather than a mere tolerance for the practice, and state supervision of the practice. [358]

Those two conditions were satisfied the following year in *Bates v. State Bar of Arizona*, [359] in which the Court applied the immunity once it found that the restrictions on lawyer advertising were compelled by the state supreme court and actively supervised by it. Thus the Court extended *Parker's* federalism rationale, with its deference to state regulation, to private parties regulated by the state.

Most recently, in *Massachusetts School of Law at Andover v. American Bar Assoc.,* the Third Circuit rejected an antitrust injury contention by a law school which was predicated on the ABA's accreditation standards. One theory upon which the law school claimed injury was the fact that, since it was not ABA accredited, graduates from the plaintiff school were unable to take the bar exam in most states. The court held that, although the ABA sets its own accreditation requirements, the states are ultimately responsible for determining who is eligible to take the bar. Thus, "[without state action the ABA's accreditation decisions would not affect state bar admissions requirements. [360] Therefore, the court found that the ABA was protected from antitrust liability.

Local regulation, however, did not enjoy the same favoritism. In *City of Lafayette v. Louisiana Power and Light Co.*, [361] the Court curtailed, at the local government level, the concept of federalism. The question presented was whether state action immunity applied to a political subdivision of the state, such as a city when it attempts to regulate commercial activities. Drawing the boundaries of federalism and local authority to regulate commerce, the Court held that cities are not automatically treated the same as states:

> Cities are not themselves sovereign; they do not receive all the federal deference of the States that create them . . . . *Parker's* limitation of the exemption to "official action directed by a state," . . . is consistent with the fact that the States' subdivisions generally have not been treated as equivalents of the States themselves. In light of the serious economic dislocation which could result if cities were free to place their own parochial interests above the Nation's economic goals reflected in the antitrust laws, . . . we are especially unwilling to presume that Congress intended to exclude anticompetitive municipal action from their reach. [362]

At issue was the question whether a city–owned utility enjoyed state action immunity. It is not enough, the Court reasoned, that the city is an agent of the state. There must be a clear, intentional displacement of

---

[358] *See* Areeda, *Antitrust Immunity for "State Action" after Lafayette*, 95 Harv. L. Rev. 435, 438 (1981).

[359] 433 U.S. 350 (1977).

[360] *Id.* at 1036.

[361] 435 U.S. 389 (1978).

[362] *Id.* at 412–13.

competition by regulation on the part of the state before the local regulation will be covered under the doctrine. Two requirements remain: first, there must be evidence that "the legislature contemplated the kind of action complained of" and second, the challenged practice must be rationally necessary to carry out the legislative intent.[363] The first condition called for a "clearly articulated and affirmatively expressed" state policy, although explicit authorization was not required.[364]

Two years later the Court again suggested, as it had in *Goldfarb* and *Bates*, that active state supervision of the challenged practice was required.[365] Before later calling this requirement into question, the Court directed its attention again to local government regulation, this time in the context of home/rule charters.

Plaintiffs in *Community Communications Co. v. City of Boulder*[366] challenged a city ordinance that temporarily restricted its local cable television operation from extending service while the city surveyed the market in order to enact a systematic cable television ordinance. The city of Boulder argued that it was immune from suit under the state action doctrine because of Colorado's home–rule charter, which conferred and guaranteed local autonomy. It asserted that the home–rule provision constituted a "clearly articulated and affirmatively expressed" approval.

The Supreme Court disagreed. It ruled that home–rule charters which merely express a "neutral" state policy on the challenged practice are insufficient to warrant the state action immunity: "A state that allows its municipalities to do as they please can hardly be said to have 'contemplated' the specific anticompetitive actions for which municipal liability is sought . . . ."[367] Colorado's provision entitled each city to independently choose competition or monopoly service. Given this open–ended discretion, the state could not have "clearly articulated and affirmatively expressed" a policy in favor of regulation over competition. Federalism, the sharing of government power and responsibility, between the states and the federal government, "has no place for sovereign cities,"[368] the Court remarked.

Boulder created many tensions between states and their cities and at least one irony. Larger cities generally enjoy home–rule authority to govern, while smaller cities regulate under specific grants of authority from the state such as local zoning authorizations. Under *Boulder* the smaller city, with its subject–matter specific authority, may enjoy state action immunity from antitrust challenge, while the larger city, with its general home–rule charter, would be subject to antitrust scrutiny.[369] *Boulder* and *Lafayette*

---

[363] Areeda, *supra* note 358, at 446.

[364] 435 U.S. at 410.

[365] *California Retail Liquor Dealers Ass'n v. Midcal Aluminum, Inc.*, 445 U.S. 97 (1980).

[366] 455 U.S. 40 (1982).

[367] *Id.* at 55.

[368] *Id.* at 53.

[369] Mather, *supra* note 352, at 986–88.

seemed to retreat significantly from *Parker's* drive to return market regulation from the federal level to a more decentralized control. *Boulder* did not reach, however, the question whether there must be "active state supervision" over the local regulation. That issue was answered by the Court in 1985.

In *Town of Hallie v. City of Eau Claire* [370] a city's monopoly in sewage treatment services was challenged by four unincorporated townships. The townships alleged that they were potential competitors of the city in the collection and transportation of sewage and that the city had engaged in tying arrangements and refusals to deal in order "to gain an unlawful monopoly." [371] The Court extended state action immunity for the alleged conduct, however.

Clarifying the immunity standard applied to local regulations, the Court said that local governments "need not 'be able to point to a specific, detailed legislative authorization' in order to assert a successful *Parker* defense to an antitrust suit." [372] Wisconsin's home–rule statute met the "clearly expressed policy . . . to displace competition" standard because it granted cities authority to "construct, add to, alter, and repair sewerage systems [including the power to] describe with reasonable particularity the district to be [served]." [373] The Court found that this language "clearly contemplat[ed] that a city may engage in anticompetitive conduct," since it is a "foreseeable result of empowering the city to refuse to serve unannexed areas." [374] The Court was able to easily distinguish its earlier holding in *Boulder*:

> [In *Boulder*] . . . the municipality was . . . free to decide every aspect of policy relating to cable television, as well as policy relating to any other field of regulation of local concern. Here, in contrast, the State has specifically authorized Wisconsin cities to provide sewage services and has delegated to the cities the express authority to take action that foreseeably will result in anticompetitive effects. [375]

The Ninth Circuit has set out three conditions under which the *Parker* immunity may apply. [376] First, where the circumstances point to a state policy to replace competition with regulation in a certain industry or activity, the entity claiming immunity only needs to show that it is authorized by the state to "do business", since the decrease in competition is a forseeable result in those cases. However, in the second case, where there are "abundant indications that a state's policy is to support competition, a subordinate state entity must do more than merely produce an

---

[370] 471 U.S. 34 (1985).

[371] *Id.* at 38.

[372] *Id.* at 39.

[373] *Id.* at 40.

[374] *Id.* at 41.

[375] *Id.* at 43.

[376] *Lancaster Community Hosp. v. Antelope Valley Hospital District,* 940 F.2d 397 (9th Cir. 1991), *cert denied,* 502 U.S. 1094 (1992).

authorization to 'do business' to show that the state's policy is to displace competition."[377] Finally, a third situation exists where the state has a general policy of increasing competition, yet it allows for a specific anticompetitive activity. In those cases, the exemption would apply. The court seemed to focus on equating a "clear articulation" of state policy with a state policy of substituting regulation for competition.

The court took this idea to the extreme in *Brown v. Ticor Title Insurance Co.*[378] In that case, the Ninth Circuit applied a reformulation of the "clear articulation" test, which required a determination of 1) whether the state legislature authorized the challenged action and 2) whether the legislature intended to displace competition with regulation.[379] The court found the statute authorizing collective rate fixing among insurers passed part one but failed part two of the new test and, therefore, immunity did not apply.[380] This outcome is easily criticized, however, since it can be assumed that the legislature knew that, by adopting and enforcing the statute, some competition would be destroyed.

In short, as long as the state has specifically authorized local government to occupy or regulate a particular field and the challenged conduct is "foreseeable," state authorization is established. All specific conduct that may be subject to challenge need not be mentioned in the state authorization for immunity to attach.[381] It is important to remember, however, that it is the *specific conduct* engaged in by the defendant that must be foreseeable, not anticompetitive conduct in general.

Moreover, the *Hallie* court disclaimed the requirements, set forth in *Cantor* and *Goldfarb*, that state compulsion and state supervision were preconditions to immunity when the antitrust defendant is a local government. In a companion case,[382] the Court held that the "active state

---

[377] 940 F.2d at 403.

[378] 982 F.2d 386 (9th Cir. 1992), *cert dismissed*, 114 S.Ct. 1359 (1994).

[379] The Tenth Circuit also has adopted this reformulation.

[380] *Id.* at 392–93.

[381] Floyd & Sullivan, *supra* note 45, at § 4.1.7.7n.135. D. Mandelker, J. Gerard, E.T. Sullivan, *supra* note 203, at § 11.06 (2001).

See e.g., Columbia Steel Casting Co. v. Portland Gen. Elec. Co., 60 F.3d 1390 (9th Cir. 1995); *Askew v. DCH Regional Health Care Auth.*, 995 F.3d 1033 (11th Cir.)(anticompetitve acquisition of private hospital immune due to authority of health care entity to acquire health care facilities), *cert. denied*, 114 S.Ct. 603 (1993); *Porter Testing Lab. v. Bd. of Regents for the Okla. Agric. & Mechanical Colleges*, 993 F.2d 768 (10th Cir.) (authority of educational institution to conduct agriculture extension services led to foreseeability of displaced competition), *cert. denied*, 114 S.Ct. 344 (1993).

[382] *Southern Motor Carriers Rate Conference, Inc. v. United States*, 471 U.S. 48 (1985). Defendants were private rate bureaus of motor common carriers which submitted *joint* rate proposals to state public service commissions. State laws permitted but did not require a joint submission. The Department of Justice alleged that the rate bureaus were engaged in price fixing when joint proposals were submitted. It argued that "collective ratemaking [was] not compelled by any of the states." 471 U.S. at 51. *See also 324 Liquor Corp. v. Duffy*, 479 U.S. 335 (1987), where the Supreme Court held that New York's Alcoholic Beverage Control Law, which required retailers to charge at least 112% of the "posted" wholesale price, but permitted

supervision" requirement was a precondition to immunize a private party engaged in conduct regulated by a state or local law. Compulsion by the state, however, is not a requirement. Addressing the rationale for this distinction, the earlier *Hallie* Court had observed:

> Where a private party is engaged in anticompetitive activity, there is a real danger that he is acting to further his own interests, rather than the governmental interests of the state. Where the actor is a municipality there is little or no danger that it is involved in a *private* price–fixing arrangement. The only real danger is that it will seek to further purely parochial public interests at the expense of more overriding state goals. This danger is minimal, however, because of the requirement that the municipality act pursuant to a clearly articulated state policy. Once it is clear that state authorization exists, there is no need to require the State to supervise actively the municipality's execution of what is a properly delegated function. [383]

Likewise, in *Southern Motors*, the Court concluded that the compulsion requirement would be inconsistent with the "principles of federalism and the goal of the antitrust laws" [384] because it "reduces the range of regulatory alternatives available to the state." [385] On the other hand, evidence of compulsion directed to the private party is strong evidence that the state has clearly articulated a policy to displace competition. Although such evidence is relevant, it is not a requirement for invoking the state action doctrine.

In *City of Columbia & Columbia Outdoor Advertising, Inc., v. Omni Outdoor Advertising, Inc.,* [386] the Supreme Court reaffirmed *Hallie's* and *Midcal's* two–tier test to determine the existence of state action immunity. For the *Parker* defense to apply, "authority to regulate" and a "clear articulation of a state policy to authorize anticompetitive conduct" must exist. [387] In *Omni*, an outdoor advertising company sued its principal competitor [388] and the City of Columbia for an alleged conspiracy to maintain Columbia's monopoly position through billboard advertising zoning restrictions. [389]

---

wholesalers to sell to retailers at less than the "posted" price, was "clearly articulated and affirmatively expressed as state policy," but was not "actively supervised," because the statute did not provide for a system of state regulation nor did it monitor market conditions. Thus the state statute did not cloak the wholesalers and retailers with state action immunity. Said the Court, "[t]he national policy in favor of competition cannot be thwarted by casting such a gauzy cloak of state involvement over what is essentially a private price–fixing arrangement." *Id.* at 345, *citing Midcal*, 445 U.S. at 106.

[383] 471 U.S. at 47.

[384] *Id.*

[385] *Id.*

[386] 111 S.Ct. 1344 (1991).

[387] *Id.* at 1350.

[388] Columbia Outdoor Advertising "controlled more than 95 percent of the market and enjoyed close relations with city officials, lobbied these officials to enact zoning ordinances restricting billboard construction." *Id.* at 1347.

[389] The ordinance restricted the "size, location, and spacing of billboards within downtown

Following a jury verdict in favor of Omni, Columbia successfully moved the trial court for a judgment notwithstanding the verdict. On appeal, however, the U.S. Court of Appeals for the Fourth Circuit reversed the judgment n.o.v. and reinstated the jury verdict. Specifically, the Fourth Circuit invoked a "conspiracy" exception and declared that *Parker* immunity does not apply where politicians or political entities are involved as conspirators with private actors in restraint of trade."[390] The Supreme Court reversed.

Commenting that South Carolina's zoning statutes authorized the City of Columbia to regulate the size, location, and spacing of billboards,[391] the Court held that the city council possessed the "authority to regulate" for purposes of state action immunity.[392] It rejected the idea, again, that the statute must explicitly authorize displacement of competition. The Court, though, specifically overruled the "conspiracy" exception to state action immunity. In particular, the Court commented that:

"the general language of the Sherman Act should not be interpreted to prohibit anticompetitive actions by the States in their governmental capacities as sovereign regulators. Rather, it is enough if the supervision of competition is a "foreseeable result" of the state authorization. [This] immunity, [however, may] not obtain where the State acts as a commercial participant in a given market."[393]

Consequently, "with the possible market exception, any action that qualifies as state action is ipso facto . . . exempt from the operation of the antitrust laws."[394]

The "active supervision" requirement, by comparison, was clarified by the Court in *FTC v. Ticor Title Insurance Co.*[395] In *Ticor Title*, the Federal Trade Commission filed an administrative complaint against six of the nation's largest title insurance companies alleging a horizontal price–fixing agreement in their fees for title searches and examinations.[396] Within each

---

Columbia." *Id.* at 1348. Since Columbia already had its billboards in place, its monopoly power was significantly strengthened by the ordinance, whereas Omni, as a new competitor to the market, was unable to freely construct new billboards.

[390] *Id.* at 1351 *citing* 891 F.2d, at 1134.

[391] "S.C.Code § 5–23–10 (1976) (Building and Zoning Regulations Authorized) provides that [f]or the purpose of promoting health, safety, morals or the general welfare of the community, the legislative bodies of cities and incorporated towns may by ordinance regulate and restrict the height, number of stories and size of buildings and other structures." *Id.* at 1349.

[392] "The city's restriction of billboard construction was *prima facie* entitled to *Parker* immunity." *Id.* at 1350–51.

[393] *Id.* at 1351.

[394] *Id.* at 1353.

[395] 112 S.Ct. 2170 (1992).

[396] "Title insurance is the business of insuring the record title of real property for persons with some interest in the estate, including owners, occupiers, and lenders. A title insurance policy insures against certain losses or damages sustained by reason of a defect in title not shown on the policy or title report to which it refers. Before issuing a title insurance policy, the insurance company or one of its agents performs a title search and examination. The search produces a chronological list of the public documents in the chain of title to the real property. The examination is a critical analysis or interpretation of the condition of title revealed by the documents disclosed through this search." *Id.* at 2173.

state, "uniform rates were established by a rating bureau licensed by the State and authorized to establish joint rates for its members. Rate filings were made to the state insurance office and became effective unless the State rejected them within a specified period."[397] In each of these states, however a "negative option" system was used to approve rate filings by the bureaus. Under this system, "the rating bureau filed rates with the state insurance office which became effective unless the state rejected them within a specified period of time, such as 30 days."[398] In their defense, the defendants claimed that the insurance practices in question were actively supervised by state officials and thereby warranted state–action immunity.[399]

In addressing whether the states "actively supervised" the fee setting practices in question, the Supreme Court commented that:

> our decisions make clear that the purpose of the active supervision inquiry is not to determine whether the State has some normative standard, such as efficiency, in its regulatory practices. Its purpose is to determine whether the State has exercised sufficient independent judgment and control so that the details of the rates or prices have been established as a product of deliberate state intervention, not simply by agreement among private parties.[400]

Consequently, the Court held that in the absence of *active* supervision in fact, the negative option procedure was inadequate to trigger the state action immunity.[401]

The First Circuit recently clarified the "active supervision" requirement in *New England Motor Rate Bureau, Inc. v. FTC*.[402] The court rejected the FTC's contention that the state must actively review private activities in order to determine their "anticompetitive consequences."[403]

> There is nothing in the state action doctrine, as formulated, that turns on the economic philosophy of a state's regulatory program, the mind–set of its administrators or the degree its goals mesh with the FTC's view of good regulatory policy. Rather, the state immunity is based on the Supreme Court's determination that Congress, in enacting the federal antitrust laws, meant not to preempt state programs and policies that are genuine products of state governmental action. It is immaterial whether the policies guiding the state's actions are or are not consistent with federal antitrust aims.[404]

---

[397] *Id.* at 2172.

[398] *Id.*

[399] *Id.* at 2174.

[400] *Id.* at 2177.

[401] Cf. *Snake River Valley Electric Assn. v. Pacificorp*, 228 F.3d 972 (9th Cir. 2000)(finding that state and regulatory scheme gave authorization for, but not adequate supervision of, utility's refusal to wheel power for plaintiff.

[402] 908 F.2d 1064 (1st Cir. 1990).

[403] *Id.* at 1074.

[404] *Id.*

As such, it is important to remember that the reasoning behind state supervision is not to ensure that the private action is not anticompetitive. Rather, it is to keep the private action in line with chosen state policy, whatever that may be.

Another interesting question surrounding the active supervision requirement is that of who exactly can legally engage in supervising private conduct. *Parker* suggested that an agency can practice active supervision over anticompetitive activities in order to immunize them, as the supervising body in that case was a state agricultural commission. However, the Supreme Court has never dealt directly with the question of whether a city can actively supervise, as well. The Ninth Circuit has extended supervisory powers to cities. [405]

In sum, state action immunity applies to private conduct as long as there is a clearly expressed state policy *and* active state supervision of the private conduct. The immunity is applicable to local governments if there is a clear state policy to displace competition and the challenged conduct is foreseeable within that authorization; state supervision is not required to immunize local government conduct, as it is for private parties acting pursuant to state or local regulation.

It is interesting to note that state agencies are treated more like municipalities than private actors with state action; rather, when the agency is implementing state policy, that policy should be clearly articulated by the state's legislature. [406] Several recent circuit court decisions have held that active supervision by the state is not required for agency actions to be immune. [407]

In fact, the Supreme Court in *Hallie* alluded to this treatment of agencies without directly ruling on it. "In cases in which the actor is a state agency, it is likely that active state supervision would also not be required, although we do not here decide that issue." [408] This treatment of state agencies like municipalities is sensible given the substantial control by the state legislature over both entities. However, there may be times where the state agency is actually formulating policy instead of applying it. In those cases, the agency is to be given the immunity of the state itself.

Because of the disparity in treatment between state and municipality under the *Parker* doctrine, the way the agency is classified can have a bearing on the permissible scope of its activities. Needless to say, this has been the focus of much litigation. For example, *Bolt v. Halifax Hospital*

---

[405] *Tim Hudson & Assocs. v. City of Chula Vista*, 746 F.2d 1370 (9th Cir. 1984), *cert. denied*, 472 U.S. 1028 (1985).

[406] *See. e.g. Cine 42nd Street Theater Corp. v. Nederlander Organization Inc.*, 790 F.2d 1032 (2d Cir. 1986).

[407] *See e.g. Porter Testing Lab. v. Bd. of Regents for the Okla. Agric. & Mechanical College*, 998 F.2d 768 (19th Cir), *cert denied*, 495 U.S. 924 (1990) *vacated on other grounds* 980 F.2d 1381 (11th Cir. 1993); *Neo Gen Screening, Inc. v. New England Newborn Screening Program*, 187 F.3d 24 (1st Cir. 1999).

[408] 471 U.S. at 46 n.10.

Medical Center, [409] the Eleventh Circuit admitted that some circumstances may allow extending immunity to state agencies. Nevertheless, the case was not one of those situations, as the defendant resembled a municipality rather than an agency. Largely because there was no proof that the agency was acting "pursuant to authority delegated by the legislature or state supreme court" [410] the court found this logic persuasive. Often the key to differentiating between the agency as municipality and the agency as the state is the level of authority the agency has secured in the arena of policymaking.

Courts also have had some difficulty distinguishing public behavior from private for purposes of state action immunity. The distinction is important because private actions are subject to the "active supervision" requirement while public actions are not. In *Riverview Investments, Inc. v. Ottawa Community Improvement, Corp.,* [411] the Sixth Circuit was faced with the question of whether to characterize the nonstock, nonprofit corporate defendant as public or private. Although the court had previously determined that such companies were to be treated as public, [412] the defendant was found to be private. The court drew a difference, stating that it was not created by the government, its members were not government–appointed, and the municipality had no control over its decisions or processes. [413] The court also rejected the idea that the city controlled Community Improvement Corporation because it could discontinue its operations. [414] Finally, after applying a "functional" analysis to determine whether the Community Improvement Corporation could be immune as a private entity acting as a public one, or hybrid, through furthering public interests, the court found the defendant failed under that test, as well. [415]

Similarly, in *Washington State Elec. Contractors Assn. v. Forrest,* [416] the Ninth Circuit found that the Washington State Apprenticeship Council, which worked to get minimum wage rates for apprentices performing electrical services for the state, was not a state agency. It required that the council be subjected to the "active supervision" test because "[t]he council has both public and private members, and the private members have their own agenda which may or may not be responsive to state labor policy." [417]

Finally, in *R. Ernest Cohn, D.A.B.C.O. v. Bond,* [418] the Fourth Circuit found that certain members of a hospital staff who had denied staff

---

[409] 891 F.2d 810 (11th Cir. *cert denied,* 495 U.S. 924 (1990), *vacated on other grounds,* 980 F.2d 1381 (11th Cir. 1993).

[410] *Id.* at 824.

[411] 899 F.2d 474 (6th Cir.) *cert denied,* 498 U.S. 855 (1990).

[412] *See Consolidated Television Cable Service, Inc. v. City of Frankfort,* 857 F.2d 354 (6th Cir. 1988), *cert denied,* 489 U.S. 1082 (1989).

[413] *Id.* at 479–80.

[414] *Id.* at 480.

[415] *Id.* at 481–82.

[416] 930 F.2d 736, *cert denied,* 498 U.S. 439 (1991).

[417] 930 F.2d at 737.

[418] 953 F.2d 154 (4th Cir. 1992).

privileges to a chiropractor were to be treated as agents of the hospital and, hence, public entities. This holding is in tension with other circuits, which have treated members of hospital peer review committees, like the one in *Bond*, as private entities.[419]

While determination of whether activities are public or private will be largely case specific, there are a few factors which reoccur in the analysis: 1) whether the entity being challenged has been publicly or privately created, 2) whether members of the entity are privately or publicly appointed, 3) whether members are subject to the usual constraints and regulations applicable to public employees, 4) the extent to which the entity undertakes activities and functions specifically given it by the state law, and 5) the extent to which the state controls and reviews the entity's activities (keeping in mind that active supervision is not a requirement for state agencies).[420]

In both *Hallie* and *Southern Motor Carriers*, the Court returned to a bolder federalism theme, first articulated in *Parker*, giving greater deference to state and local sovereignty over regulation at the expense of the national policy in favor of competition.[421] As long as there is evidence that the state is acting as sovereign, the state or local action will enjoy immunity from antitrust prosecution. Whether the sovereign acted wisely or in an anticompetitive fashion is not relevant to the Court's inquiry.[422] The state's

---

[419] *See e.g. El Shahany v. Harrison*, 875 F.2d 1529 (11th Cir. 1989); *Patrick v. Berget*, 486 U.S. 94 (1988).

[420] Floyd & Sullivan, *supra* note 45 at 429.

[421] *See generally* Wiley, *A Capture Theory of Antitrust Federalism*, 99 Harv. L. Rev. 713 (1986); Garland, *Antitrust and State Action: Economic Efficiency and the Political Process*, 96 Yale L.J. 486 (1986); Wiley, *Revision and Apology in Antitrust Federalism*, 96 Yale L.J. 1277 (1987); and, Garland, *Antitrust and Federalism: A Response To Professor Wiley*, 96 Yale L.J. 1291 (1987). The authors debate whether a state regulation which is anticompetitive and at odds with the goals of federal antitrust policy should be immunized under the state action doctrine or struck down as merely another example of regulation designed, not to aid consumers but, to protect firms in the industry from competition at the expense of consumers. The so–called "capture" theory of regulation advanced by Professor Wiley argues that courts should be suspicious of regulations which seek to protect certain groups in an industry from competition, and, in the context of state or local regulation, should favor the federal antitrust policy of competition when there is evidence that producers in the industry have been successful in obtaining advantageous regulations that reduce competition and free market forces:

> *Parker* reflected a New Deal confidence in market regulation . . . . A growing suspicion that procedures have "captured" the political bodies regulating them has inclined people to view regulation as the product and protector of producer interests . . . . Thus, it is hardly surprising that courts have, under the guise of the very state action doctrine that was meant to protect state sovereignty, intruded more and more on state and local regulatory policy.

99 Harv. L. Rev. at 714. But the Court has never cited the capture theory of regulation as the basis for its occasional retreat from *Parker*'s federalism theme, and its three most recent decisions, *Hallie, Southern Motors* and *324 Liquor*, belie a major threat of interfering with state regulation. *See* Jorde, *Antitrust and the New State Action Doctrine: A Return to Deferential Economic Federalism*, 75 Cal. L. Rev. 227 (1987).

[422] *Hoover v. Ronwin*, 466 U.S. 558 (1984).

motives in undertaking or authorizing the challenged conduct are not an issue. Rather the analytical focus centers on whether the challenged practice is that of the state sovereign.[423]

[1] Local Government Antitrust Act

Before *Hallie* and *Southern Motor Carriers* were decided, Congress passed a statute in response to *Boulder* to ease the tension created between the federal antitrust policy of promoting competition and potential municipal antitrust liability. In fact, the Supreme Court has clearly stated that "[e]ven when an industry is regulated substantially, this does not necessarily evidence an intent to repeal the antitrust laws with respect to every action taken within the industry . . . Intent to repeal the antitrust laws is much clearer when a regulatory agency has been empowered to authorize or require the type of conduct under antitrust challenge."[424] Congress broadly defined "local government," to include any "city, county, parish, town, township, village, or any other general function governmental unit, established by state law,"[425] and any "school district, sanitary district, or any other special function governmental unit established by State law in one or more States."[426] Many believed that judgments rendered against cities could bankrupt local governments, given the provisions for treble damages and attorney's fees.

The Local Government Act of 1984[427] precludes damage actions under the federal antitrust laws against local governments or officials of local governments. Congress broadly defined "local government," to include any "city, county, parish, town, township, village, or any other general function governmental unit, established by state law,"[428] Injunction actions[429] are still permitted, however. And attorney's fees[430] for equitable relief are retained. Immunity from damage suits also is extended to third parties who

---

[423] *Hallie* states that "[i]n cases in which the actor is a state agency, it is likely that active state supervision would also not be required, although we do not decide that issue." 471 U.S. at 46, n.10. *But see 324 Liquor Corp. v. Duffy*, 479 U.S. 335 (1987), where the Court insisted on State supervision by the New York State Liquor Authority.

[424] 915 F.2d 17 (1st Cir. 1990).

[425] Act Sec. 2(1)(A), 15 U.S.C. Sec. 34(1)(A) (1988).

[426] Act Sec. 2(1)(B), 34 U.S.C. Sec. 34(1)(B) (1988).

[427] 15 U.S.C. §§ 35, 36. Ordinarily when we think of potential antitrust violations by a local government, we consider violations of § 1 (price fixing, market division, concerted refusal to deal, or exclusive dealing arrangements) or § 2 (monopolization). But in *Cine 42nd Street Theater Corp. v. Nederlander Org.*, 790 F.2d 1032 (2d Cir. 1986), the Second Circuit held that the state action doctrine applied to § 7 of the Clayton Act (mergers). New York City had acquired several independent theaters for a rehabilitation project which eventually were leased back to the same firm.

[428] Act Sec. 2(a)(A), 15 U.S.C. Sec. 34(a)(A)(1988).

[429] Section 16 of the Clayton Act, 15 U.S.C. § 26.

[430] 15 U.S.C. § 16.

are "expressly required" by local governments to engage in anticompetitive conduct.[431]

The Tenth Circuit, in *Tarabishi v. McAlester Regional Hospital*,[432] narrowed the Act's broad definition of "local government," where it broke with tradition and held that a hospital district did not fall under the Act's immunity. The hospital was a "public trust" hospital, and even though it was formed to further public functions, had public officers as trustees, and was created for the benefit of the city of McAlester, the court denied it immunity. Behind the court's unusual decision was the fact that, under Oklahoma law, public trust hospitals are considered separate from their beneficiary cities for legal purposes, and the city could not be held liable for any judgment rendered against the hospital.[433] Since determining whether an entity has the necessary characteristics to fall under the federal definition of "local government" is "a question of state law,"[434] the court acted within its realm of authority in denying the hospital an immune status.

Explicit in the Act is the congressional intention, expressed for the first time, that local governments come within the jurisdiction of the federal antitrust law, although the scope of the Act is limited to injunctive relief. To this extent, the federal antitrust goal of promoting competition is emphasized, but the burden of treble damages is eased. Thus, if the state action doctrine does not immunize completely the local conduct, an antitrust plaintiff may sue a local government or its officials, when acting in their official capacity, for injunctive relief for conduct which is anticompetitive. If *Hallie* applies, however, the "official action directed by the local government" is immune from all antitrust suits, since the intent of the Act was to codify the state action doctrine.

[B] The Doctrine of Preemption

A preemption analysis is invoked, under the Supremacy Clause of the Constitution, when there are conflicting enactments between "two different sovereigns—one federal and the other state."[435] It also applies when there

---

[431] *See Communications, Inc. v. City of Detroit*, 650 F. Supp. 1570, 1578–79 (E.D. Mich. 1987) (once it is determined that the municipality is entitled to immunity from the antitrust laws, the private parties who are regulated by the municipality, are also entitled to immunity as long as the effective decision maker is the municipality rather than the private parties).

[432] 951 F.2d 1558 (10th Cir. 1991) *cert denied,* 505 U.S. 1206 (1992).

[433] *Id.* At 1565–66, n.6.

[434] *Id.* at 1565–66 and n. 6.

[435] *Community Communications Co. v. City of Boulder*, 455 U.S. 40, 61 (1982) (Rehnquist, J., dissenting) *quoting* Handler, *Antitrust 1978*, 78 Colum. L. Rev. 1363, 1379 (1978). Article VI, § 2 of the United States Constitution mandates that federal statutes and treaties are the supreme law of the land and supersede any state law or rule to the contrary. *See also California Liquor Dealers v. Midcal Aluminum, Inc.*, 445 U.S. 97 (1980); Note, *Preemption and Anticompetitive State Statutes*, 54 Ford. L. Rev. 247 (1985); Comment, *Municipal Antitrust Liability*, 73 Cal. L. Rev. 1829 (1985).

is a clear federal intention to occupy a field and where there is an irreconcilable conflict between the federal and nonfederal scheme. The doctrine requires that when the conflict exists the state statute or regulation must fall "without any effort to accommodate the State's purposes or interests."[436]

Preemption was raised in the antitrust–state action context in Justice Rehnquist's dissent in *Boulder*. He concluded that the state action doctrine was not a question of antitrust exemption, but rather of federal preemption. A majority of the Court declined to accept his invitation to treat the *Parker* rationale as a preemption issue. However, in *Rice v. Norman Williams Co.*,[437] decided the same year as *Boulder*, the Court decided an antitrust challenge to a state statute by invoking the preemption analysis.

In *Rice*, a California statute provided that a liquor importer could purchase liquor from outside the state "*only* if the beverages [were] consigned to a licensed importer."[438] In a suit that sought injunctive relief against the enforcement of the statute, the Supreme Court held that the proper inquiry was whether there was an irreconcilable conflict between the federal antitrust law and the state regulatory scheme. A mere hypothetical or potential conflict was not enough to trigger the preemption analysis. The state statute on its face must irreconcilably conflict with the federal antitrust policy before there is preemption.[439] Only if the state statute or regulation "necessarily constitutes a violation of the antitrust laws *in all cases*, or if it places irresistible pressure on a private party to violate the antitrust laws in order to comply with the [state] statute"[440] is it preempted by the federal antitrust laws.

This condition is satisfied if the challenged conduct is a *per se* violation of the antitrust laws. Conversely, if the conduct is analyzed under the rule of reason standard, preemption is not applicable — a facial inconsistency is lacking. Since the state statute at issue did not fall under the *per se* ban of conduct proscribed by the Sherman Act, a preemption analysis was inappropriate. The state statute could co–exist with the antitrust law.

The Court's strongest statement on the interaction of preemption and state action is found in *Fisher v. City of Berkeley*,[441] where a city had enacted by popular initiative a rent control ordinance. The ordinance was challenged by landlords. The question was whether the ordinance was preempted by § 1 of the Sherman Act.

The *Fisher* Court held that preemption was not present because the local ordinance did not necessarily violate § 1 "in all cases," nor did it force

---

[436] *Id.*

[437] 458 U.S. 654 (1982).

[438] *Id.* at 656.

[439] *Id.* at 659.

[440] *Id.* at 661 (emphasis added).

[441] 475 U.S. 260 (1980). *See generally* Gifford, *The Antitrust State–Action Doctrine after Fisher*, 39 Vand. L. Rev. 1257 (1986).

private parties to violate the Sherman Act. An antitrust violation did not "necessarily" flow from the ordinance because concerted action was not present; the ordinance was unilaterally imposed by the city.[442] Absent an agreement between separate entities, there was no illegal agreement, hence no direct, irreconcilable conflict with § 1. Facial inconsistency was lacking. Therefore, since the ordinance was challenged on its face and preemption was inappropriate, that was the end of the inquiry. Both the antitrust law and the local ordinance could stand together.

Fisher is instructive for a number of reasons. First, the Court, for the first time, held that a city, acting through its officials, may be immune from a § 1 challenge because it is a single entity incapable of conspiring with itself.[443] That is a distinct principle and one easier to establish than either preemption or state action. It is an absolute defense regardless of the degree of anticompetitiveness flowing from a local ordinance. If there is only unilateral action by the local government, there is no need to reach questions of preemption or state action. Unilateral decision making is not actionable under § 1. Further inquiry is not necessary.[444]

Second, like *Rice* which analyzed a state statute under a preemption analysis, *Fisher* applied the same analysis to a local ordinance. No distinction is made when there are different sources of the restraint or the level of government involved.[445] The preemption analysis was identical.

Third, *Fisher*, like *Hallie*, suggests that the Court is more inclined today to rely on federalism with its deference to state and local sovereignty over national policy to promote competition. The result is that state and local governments have a greater range of regulation and flexibility to control local economies. Implicit in *Parker* was the idea that state regulation should not be preempted by federal antitrust law.[446] That is a concept with which the present Court is comfortable.

How then are we to reconcile, analyze and apply the doctrines of preemption and state action? *Fisher* teaches that the following tests should be applied to the interaction of these doctrines. First, determine whether there is, on the face of the state or local regulation, a direct conflict with the

---

[442] Compare *Hertz v. City of New York*, 1 F.3d 121, 126–27 (2d. Cir. 1993), where the court distinguished a New York City ordinance regulating prices for car rentals from the statute in *Fisher* by finding there to be no "unilateral restraint" in the ordinance at bar. The court stated that the ordinance failed the *Fisher* test because "the law [was] not a 'pure regulatory scheme. . .' [it lacked] the independent, quasi–judicial board that in *Berkeley* could adjust rates and provide relief in individual circumstances," and the City of New York was not "operating in an area vital to its municipal authority" like the City of Berkeley.

[443] *See* Chapter 4 on horizontal restraints.

[444] D. Mandelker, J. Gerard, E.T. Sullivan *supra* note 203, at § 1108. If the allegation is that city officials entered into an agreement with third parties or if a § 2 monopolization charge is made, the Court will turn to a preemption analysis or state action discussion. *See, e.g., Westborough Mall, Inc. v. City of Cape Girardeau*, 693 F.2d 733 (8th Cir. 1983) (concerted action allegation); *Town of Hallie v. City of Eau Claire*, 471 U.S. 34 (1985) (§ 2 allegation).

[445] 475 U.S. at 264–65.

[446] *See Wiley, supra* note 421.

federal antitrust law so that action under the regulation conflicts with the federal policy. If so, there is federal preemption. Second, if preemption exists, inquire if the state or local regulation is protected under the state action doctrine.[447] Third, if state action immunity is lacking, turn to the challenged conduct and determine whether there is a substantive violation under the antitrust law. This was the analysis employed by the Court in *324 Liquor Co. v. Duffy*[448] where it found preemption but not state action because there was no active supervision by the state over the private wholesalers' and retailers' resale price maintenance system.

If federal preemption does not exist because there is no irreconcilable conflict in each case, two approaches are evident from *Fisher* and *Rice*. First, if the challenge to the state or local regulation is to the face of the regulation, then the court's inquiry is ended. Both the federal and state regulatory schemes can co–exist. Further inquiry into the antitrust violation is not warranted. This was the result in both *Fisher* and *Rice*. Second, if the challenge is not to the face of the local regulation but rather how it is applied,[449] the Court, after finding no preemption, should determine whether the challenged conduct is immune by reason of the "state action" doctrine, and if not, whether it violates the antitrust law. These analyses are set forth in the following chart.

---

[447] "Legislation that would otherwise be preempted under *Rice* may nonetheless survive if it is found to be state action immune from antitrust scrutiny under *Parker*." *Fisher*, 475 U.S. at 265–66. Even if the action is protected under the state action immunity, the state's regulation cannot burden interstate commerce or offend First Amendment rights of commercial speech. *See* Sullivan, *First Amendment Defenses In Antitrust Litigation*, 46 Mo. L. Rev. 517 (1981).

[448] 479 U.S. 335 (1987).

[449] For example, a city may lawfully have *authority* to establish zoning restrictions, but *how* it exercises that authority (the manner in which the restriction is applied) — by granting one competitor an exclusive commercial zone but not another — may be challenged as anticompetitive. Likewise, Boulder's *authority* to grant a cable television franchise may not have been challenged; the challenge may have been to the conditions under which it was *exercised* — an exclusive franchise was given to one firm, but all others were denied access.

PREEMPTION-EXEMPTION ANALYSIS

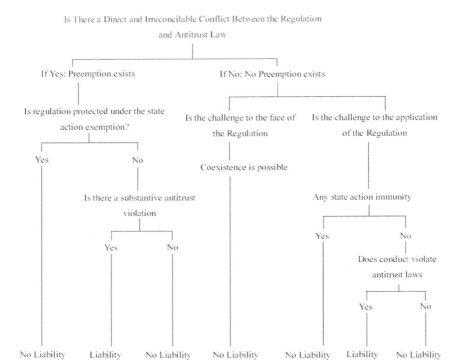

Chapter 4

HORIZONTAL RESTRAINTS AND CARTEL BEHAVIOR

§ 4.01 Introduction

Section 1 of the Sherman Act is concerned with concerted conduct which has an effect on trade or commerce. When competitors enter into an agreement which interferes with interstate commerce, the conduct is classified as a horizontal restraint. Such conduct can take many forms, including price fixing, market divisions or concerted refusals to deal. The concern of § 1 is cartel behavior: agreements among competitors that restrict output, increase price and otherwise exclude competition. If the concerted action restricts "consumers choice by impeding the 'ordinary give and take of the market place' "[1] § 1 is triggered. A cartel can not "pre–empt the working of the market by deciding for itself that its customers do not need that which they demand."[2]

§ 4.02 Policy Introduction

From the early days to the present, Supreme Court antitrust jurisprudence has undergone several distinct changes. Generally, over the years the Court has focused on one of two major themes underlying its antitrust policy. These themes, developed in greater detail below, are: (1) controlling economic concentrations of industrial power and (2) enhancing efficiency. The first emphasizes protection of the small competitor; the second is regarded as protecting competition rather than competitors. At times the Court has had difficulty reconciling these two often conflicting antitrust policies. A brief overview of the Court's changing antitrust theories is helpful in understanding how prior case law affects the Court's current interpretation. The Court's analytical shifts are particularly evident in the context of horizontal price–fixing cases.

[A] Populism

A populist theme focusing on concern for small business was evident in the first Sherman Act cases. In *United States v. Trans–Missouri Freight Ass'n*,[3] the Court focused on the effects of defendants' conduct on "worthy

---

[1] *FTC v. Indiana Fed'n of Dentists*, 476 U.S. 447, 459 (1986), *citing National Soc'y of Prof'l Eng'rs v. United States*, 435 U.S. 679, 692 (1978).

[2] 476 U.S. at 462.

[3] 166 U.S. 290 (1897).

men whose lives have been spent [in trade or commerce], and who might be unable to readjust themselves to their altered surroundings. Mere reduction in the price of the commodity dealt in might be dearly paid for by the ruin of such a class and the absorption of control over one commodity by an all–powerful combination of capital."[4] *Chicago Board of Trade v. United States*[5] showed the Court's interest in promoting competitive equality. The Court considered the legality of an agreement by members of the Board of Trade that regulated the price that any member could pay for grain purchased after the Board's normal closing hour. The Court announced the test of legality as "whether the restraint imposed is such as merely regulates and perhaps thereby promotes competition or whether it is such as may suppress or even destroy competition."[6] This balancing approach was necessarily broad enough to weigh the various competing interests. In applying this test, the Court upheld the challenged conduct because it "helped to improve market conditions."[7] *Chicago Board of Trade*, like *Trans–Missouri*, reflected the Court's populist concern over the fate of small competitors as they faced increasing competition from large, perhaps more efficient firms.

[B] Structuralism and the Warren Court

The Warren Court rejected the earlier balancing approach in favor of a structuralist approach. It focused on the structure of markets, reasoning that normal market structures will yield competitive environments, at least in the absence of explicit horizontal price fixing. This approach enabled the Warren Court to avoid balancing social and economic policy concerns. Market structure was viewed as a means to predict market behavior.

For example, in *United States v. Container Corp.*,[8] the Warren Court, in an opinion by Justice Douglas, held that the exchange of current price information among competitors selling a fungible product in an oligopolistic

---

[4] *Id.* at 323.

[5] 246 U.S. 231 (1918).

[6] *Id.* at 238.

[7] *Id.* at 240; *see also* Carstensen, *The Content of the Hollow Core of Antitrust: The Chicago Board of Trade Case and the Meaning of the "Rule of Reason" in Restraint of Trade Analysis*, 1992 Res. in Law & Econ. 1. Some scholars and judges continue to espouse this populist viewpoint. *See, e.g., MCI Communications Corp. v. Amer. Tel & Tel. Co.*, 708 F.2d 1081 (7th Cir. 1983) (Wood, J., concurring and dissenting). Judge Harlington Wood Jr. observed,

> There is a persistent strain running through creation and political endurance of the antitrust laws which reveals them to be instruments to ensure the disaggregation of concerted economic power and to assure fairness among competitors and not just instruments to assure neoclassical economic efficiency, as worthy and beneficial a goal as that may be.

Id. at 1177–78. After quoting Senator Sherman as suggesting that large, aggregate economic powers should be subject to " 'strong resistance of the state and national authorities,' " *id.* at 1178 (*citing Trans–Missouri* as proof of the Supreme Court adoption of this point of view), Judge Wood closed by questioning the "enthusiasm with which many embrace the theory that these laws stand only for economic efficiency." *Id.* at 1179.

[8] 393 U.S. 333 (1969).

market — one that is highly concentrated — is a violation of § 1 of the Sherman Act, even when the price exchange yields lower, rather than higher, prices. The Court focused on the price stabilizing effect of defendants' conduct, which, it found, resulted from horizontal price exchanges.

The Court in *Container* focused on preservation of natural market forces as the underlying concern of antitrust. "The limitation or reduction of price competition brings the case within the ban [of § 1], for . . . interference with the setting of price by free market forces is unlawful *per se*."[9] The *Container* Court's principal concern was to assure that the natural market structure would neither be interfered with by cooperation among market participants, nor that independent decisionmaking by competitors would be compromised. The limited focus on preservation of natural market structure obviated the necessity of balancing competing social and economic policy concerns or dealing with economic efficiency arguments. The Court favored the *per se* rule of illegality over the broader rule of reason analysis.

[C] Economic Efficiency and the Burger Court

Numerous Burger Court decisions evidence a rejection of the Warren Court's *per se* antitrust analysis in favor of an efficiency–oriented rule of reason. The efficiency analysis derives from the Chicago school's reliance on price theory and its preference for the rule of reason. The rule of reason permits weighing competitive harm against economic benefit even when the allegedly unlawful conduct directly affects price competition.[10] As applied, the rule frequently permits a market solution rather than antitrust intervention.

In *United States v. United States Gypsum Co.*,[11] a criminal case, the Burger Court flatly rejected *Container*'s limited analysis. The Court reviewed the legality of price exchanges among wallboard manufacturers competing in an oligopolistic market.[12] The Court held that exchange of price information is not *per se* unlawful but that the antitrust plaintiff must prove general intent by showing that defendants acted with knowledge of their consequences. The Court reasoned that exchange of price information does not necessarily have anticompetitive effects and "can in certain circumstances increase economic efficiency and render markets more, rather than less, competitive."[13] In effect, the Court discarded *Container*'s pure structural analysis in favor of reversion to the broad–based *Chicago*

---

[9] *Id.* at 337, *citing United States v. Socony–Vacuum*, 310 U.S. 150, 224, n.59 (1940).

[10] *See generally*, E. Thomas Sullivan, *The Political Economy of the Sherman Act: The First One Hundred Years* (1991); E. Thomas Sullivan, *The Economic Jurisprudence of the Burger Court's Antitrust Policy: The First Thirteen Years*, 58 Notre Dame L. Rev. 1, 20 (1982), *citing Broadcast Music, Inc. v. Columbia Broad. Sys.*, 441 U.S. 1 (1979).

[11] 438 U.S. 422 (1978).

[12] The gypsum board industry was highly concentrated, with only 9 to 15 competitors, the eighth largest of which accounted for 94% of national gypsum board sales. *Id.* at 426.

[13] *Id.* at 441, n.16.

Board of Trade rule of reason where the Court weighs the nature and effect of the exchange within the given structure of the industry.

The Burger Court's predisposition for economic efficiency underlies many of its decisions. For example, in *National Society of Professional Engineers v. United States*,[14] the Court stated that the competitive effect of certain agreements "can only be evaluated by analyzing the facts peculiar to the business, the history of the restraint, and the reasons why it was imposed."[15] Similarly, in *Broadcast Music, Inc. v. Columbia Broadcasting System, Inc.*[16] the Court, in rejecting a *per se* unlawful label for defendants' conduct, reasoned that the search for "redeeming competitive virtues [of the challenged practice] . . . is not almost sure to be in vain."[17] And in *National Collegiate Athletic Association v. Board of Regents*,[18] the Court applied a rule of reason analysis for a joint venture in the face of both a price–fixing agreement and an output restriction.

Focusing on the underlying policy of the Burger Court's analysis is helpful both to an understanding of the analytical framework and in order to predict the future course of Supreme Court antitrust jurisprudence. At this point it is useful to consider the core concerns of horizontal behavior and the economic implications.

[D]   Guidelines for Collaboration Among Competitors

On April 7, 2000, the Federal Trade Commission and the Department of Justice issued Guidelines for Collaborations Among Competitors. These set forth an enforcement framework that allows businesses to understand the current governmental view of horizontal agreement, enabling them to determine the likelihood of an antitrust action.

The Guidelines distinguish between *per se* and rule of reason analysis, treating conduct that raises prices or reduces output as illegal *per se*. Agreements that do not fall into this category will be analyzed under rule of reason, and market factors will be considered. Moreover, the Guidelines establish "safe zones" for specified collaborations that are unlikely to have anticompetitive effects.

§ 4.03   Economic Analysis, Market Power and Horizontal Restraints

Many of the Supreme Court opinions discussed in the next sections contain an analysis of the economic ramifications of an array of conduct. A general review of the economic models discussed in Chapter 2 informs our understanding of the cases considered in this Part.

---

[14] 435 U.S. 679 (1978).

[15] *Id.* at 692.

[16] 441 U.S. 1 (1979).

[17] *Id.* at 13.

[18] 468 U.S. 85 (1984).

[A] Price Fixing Effectiveness

In *United States v. Trenton Potteries Co.*,[19] the Court reviewed the conduct of members of a trade association that controlled 82% of the domestic vitreous bathroom fixture production. Members of the association were charged with combining to fix and maintain uniform sanitary pottery prices. In ruling that defendants' conduct was *per se* illegal, the Court limited its holding to "those controlling in any substantial manner a trade or business in interstate commerce."[20] This language suggests that *per se* treatment is applicable only when price fixing is effective; it is also the forerunner of the Court's later full–blown market analysis. The Court subsequently rejected, in *United States v. Socony–Vacuum Oil Co.*,[21] the requisite that a price fix is only *per se* unlawful if it is effective, stating that "a conspiracy to fix prices violates § 1 of the [Sherman] Act . . . though it is not established that the conspirators had the means available for the accomplishment of their objective . . . ."[22] Indeed, the Court found, "Any combination which tampers with price structures is engaged in an unlawful activity."[23]

Further support for the notion that a defendant need not have market power before a price–fixing scheme is unlawful is found in *NCAA* and *FTC v. Indiana Federation of Dentists*.[24] "[A]s a matter of law, the absence of proof of market power does not justify a naked restriction on price or output . . . . '[P]roof of actual detrimental effects, such as a reduction of output' can obviate the need for an inquiry into market power."[25]

[B] Output Analysis

Several landmark antitrust cases illustrate the Court's use of output analysis to determine the effect of alleged unlawful conduct on competition. For example, in *Chicago Board of Trade v. United States*,[26] the Court announced its classic rule of reason.[27] In doing so, the Court alluded to an output analysis when it observed that the plaintiff "made no attempt to show that the [defendant's allegedly unlawful] rule was designed to or that it has the effect of limiting the amount of grain shipped to Chicago;

---

[19] 273 U.S. 392 (1927).

[20] *Id.* at 398.

[21] 310 U.S. 150 (1940).

[22] *Id.* at 224, n.59.

[23] *Id.* at 225, n.59.

[24] 476 U.S. 447 (1986). *See also Superior Court Trial Lawyers Association v. Federal Trade Commission*, 493 U.S. 411 (1990).

[25] *FTC v. Indiana Fed'n of Dentists,* 476 U.S. 447, 460–61 (1986) (*citing* VII P. Areeda, *Antitrust Law* § 1511, at 429 (1986). The Court actually found that the Federation had market power in two Indiana cities, thus it did not have to rest its holding on whether the boycott could be condemned regardless of market power. *Id. See also FTC v. Superior Ct. Trial Lawyers Ass'n,* 493 U.S. 411 (1990).

[26] 246 U.S. 231 (1918).

[27] *See supra* note 6 and accompanying text.

or of retarding or accelerating shipment; or of raising or depressing prices
. . . ."[28] Because the Government failed to allege either an output restriction or an effect on prices, the Court refused to characterize the defendants' conduct as price fixing. Thus a *per se* analysis was inappropriate and the rule of reason test was applied. Similarly, the Court in *NCAA*[29] held that "[a]s a matter of law, the absence of proof of market power does not justify a naked restriction on price or output. To the contrary, when there is an agreement not to compete in terms of price or output,'no elaborate industry analysis is required to demonstrate the anticompetitive character of such an agreement.'"[30] *Indiana Federation* is consistent with this output analysis.[31] The clear trend is toward output analysis as the key determinative of whether there is a price–fixing restraint.[32]

[C] Market Power Analysis

The Court also has turned to an analysis of antitrust defendants' market power or the structure of the market in order to determine the likely consequences of the allegedly unlawful conduct. In *Sugar Institute, Inc. v. United States*,[33] the Court considered the legality of an agreement among competitors to make advance announcements of price changes. Defendants were sugar refiners with a self–imposed code of ethics that prohibited secret price concessions and discriminatory rebates. The Court held that an agreement to make advance announcements of price changes is lawful but that agreeing to abide by previously announced prices, coupled with an enforcement mechanism among competitors, is illegal.

In reaching this conclusion, the Court focused on the defendants' role in the sugar market. Fifteen members of the Sugar Institute refined practically all the imported raw sugar processed domestically; they supplied 70 to 80 percent of the sugar consumed. Sugar was a fungible product sold in a market where the only competition was on price. The Court was concerned that defendants' conduct occurred in an oligopolistic market for a fungible product. Although defendants had not literally agreed to fix prices, because of the nature of the sugar market their agreement was found to affect prices. The early beginnings of the Court's market power analysis

---

[28] 246 U.S. at 238.

[29] 468 U.S. 85 (1984).

[30] *Id.* at 109, *quoting National Society of Professional Engineers v. United States*, 435 U.S. 679, 692 (1978).

[31] 476 U.S. at 458–59.

[32] *See generally* Easterbrook, *The Limits of Antitrust*, 63 Texas L. Rev. 1 (1984); Sullivan, *On Nonprice Competition: An Economic and Marketing Analysis*, 45 U. Pitt. L. Rev. 771 (1984); Easterbrook, *The Limits of Antitrust*, 63 Texas L. Rev. (1984). *See also In re Detroit Auto Dealers Association, Inc.*, 955 F.2d 457, 472 (6th Cir. 1992) (holding that a concerted effort between car dealers to limit showroom hours served as an unreasonable restraint of trade, even though it was not necessarily a price–fixing scheme); *Chicago Prof'l Sports Ltd. P'ship v. NBA*, 95 F.3d 593, 597 (7th Cir. 1996) (stating that "[t]he core question in antitrust is output").

[33] 297 U.S. 553 (1936).

in *Sugar Institute* were developed more fully in *United States v. Container Corp. America*.[34]

In *Container* the Court employed a full–blown market power/structural analysis. The Court concluded that the mere exchange of current price information among competitors in an oligopolistic market for a fungible product is unlawful. The Container Court first characterized the allegedly unlawful conduct as the exchange of current prices among competitors, inferred an agreement to exchange prices from the fact that price exchanges occurred regularly, and finally reviewed the structure of the market in which this conduct occurred. It found that defendants controlled a 90% market share; the product was non–differentiated and fungible; demand for corrugated containers was inelastic because buyers placed orders for only short run needs; and the market was dominated by relatively few sellers. Based upon these market factors, the Court concluded that the price exchange agreement, even though informal, "had an anticompetitive effect in the industry, chilling the vigor of price competition."[35]

The Court employed a similar analysis, although it reached a different conclusion, in *United States v. United States Gypsum Co.*[36] *Gypsum*, like *Container*, involved defendants selling a fungible product, gypsum wall board, and facing an inelastic demand curve. The industry was highly concentrated, with the eight largest producers accounting for 94% of all sales nationwide. The basis of the government's criminal charge was that defendants fixed prices by regularly exchanging price information among competitors.

In discussing the antitrust implications of the price data exchange, the Court focused on the effect of the exchanges on the competitiveness of the industry. In doing so the Court utilized a modified market structure analysis, stating that "[a] number of factors including most prominently the structure of the industry involved and the nature of the information exchanged are generally considered in divining the procompetitive or anticompetitive effects of this type of interseller communication."[37]

These cases illustrate that market power and structure may embrace a number of industry and product characteristics. An industry dominated by a small group of producers which have a large market share is indicative of market power. Likewise, a product that is undifferentiated, or fungible, that faces an inelastic demand, is indicative of market power. When both industry and product characteristics converge, as in *Gypsum* and *Container*, the Court is likely to find the existence of market power. However, recent Supreme Court decisions suggest that market power is not necessarily a

---

[34] 393 U.S. 333 (1969).

[35] *Id.* at 337.

[36] 438 U.S. 422 (1978).

[37] *Id.* at 441, n.16 (1978), *citing United States v. Container Corp. of America*, 393 U.S. 333 at 338 (Fortas, J., concurring) (1969); *Bhan v. NME Hospitals, Inc.*, 929 F.2d 1404, 1413 (9th Cir. 1991).

precondition to finding a Sherman violation,[38] although this point is still contested as a normative proposition by antitrust proponents of the Chicago school.

§ 4.04   Ancillary Restraint Doctrine

The Sherman Act was enacted in 1890 and on its face made unlawful "[e]very contract, combination . . . or conspiracy in restraint of trade."[39] Five years later the Supreme Court decided *United States v. E.C. Knight*,[40] its first case under the Act. In *Knight* defendant sugar trust was charged with acquiring the stock of four sugar refiners and thereby "acquir[ing] nearly complete control of the manufacture of refined sugar within the United States,"[41] an alleged restraint of trade in violation of the Sherman Act. In holding that the Sherman Act did not apply to restraints of trade affecting only the manufacture of commodities, because "[c]ommerce succeeds to manufacture, and is not a part of it,"[42] the Court bespoke of the early beginnings of the ancillary restraint doctrine:

> [c]ontracts, combinations, or conspiracies to control domestic enterprise in manufacture, agriculture, mining, production in all its forms, or to raise or lower prices or wages, might unquestionably tend to restrain external as well as domestic trade, but the restraint would be an *indirect* result, however inevitable, and whatever its extent, and such result would not necessarily determine the object of the contract, combination or conspiracy.[43]

Thus, the *Knight* Court reasoned that mere manufacturing is not commerce and, therefore, is not within the reach of the Sherman Act, a result unlikely to be reached today.

Although *Knight* severely narrowed the reach of the Sherman Act, the next case considered by the Court concluded that the scope of the Act was not limited to the confines of common law antitrust. In *United States v. Trans–Missouri Freight Ass'n*.[44] defendants were a group of railroad companies controlling rail service west of the Mississippi. They were members of an association that established uniform freight rates in an attempt to eliminate price wars that allegedly were devastating to the

---

[38] *See, e.g., FTC v. Indiana Fed'n of Dentists*, 476 U.S. 447 (1986); *National Collegiate Athletic Association v. Board of Regents of the Univ. of Oklahoma*, 468 U.S. 85 (1984). This is true with regard to price–fixing agreements but market power is playing an increasingly important role in cases involving non–price restraints. The absence of market power is a central defense frequently advanced by antitrust defendants. Briggs & Calkins, *Antitrust 1986–1987: Power and Access (Part I)*, 32 Antitrust Bull. 275 (1987).

[39] 15 U.S.C. § 1.

[40] 156 U.S. 1 (1895).

[41] *Id.* at 9.

[42] *Id.* at 12.

[43] *Id.* at 16.

[44] 166 U.S. 290 (1897).

railroad industry. Defendants argued that the rates, as fixed, were reasonable in amount and would have been legal under the common law. The Court applied the literal language of the Sherman Act in rejecting an argument that the Act only makes unlawful unreasonable restraints of trade. The Court held that every restraint of trade violates § 1 of the Sherman Act, even those restraints deemed reasonable and lawful under the pre–Sherman Act common law. In dissent Justice White argued that such a strict statutory interpretation would condemn every contract, however reasonable, would "work an enormous injustice, and operate to the undue restraint of the liberties of the citizen."[45]

Trans–Missouri condemned the setting of railroad rates by a cartel of eighteen railroads. In *United States v. Joint–Traffic Ass'n*,[46] a year later, the Court found no substantial difference between the alleged conduct and the conduct found unlawful in *Trans–Missouri* and refused to overrule the earlier *Trans–Missouri* case. In condemning railroad rate fixing in *Joint–Traffic*, however, the Court suggested that perhaps not every restraint violates § 1, and that those restraints with only an incidental effect on competition may be lawful under the Sherman Act. The Court was concerned that the "natural and *direct* effect [of the rate–fixing agreements in *Trans-Missouri* and *Joint-Traffic*] is . . . to maintain rates at a higher level than would otherwise prevail . . . ."[47] This language suggested permissiveness with respect to indirect restraints of trade; it foreshadowed the establishment of the "ancillary restraint" doctrine announced the same year by the Sixth Circuit in *United States v. Addyston Pipe.*[48]

The Court also suggested, in *Hopkins v. United States,*[49] a difference in applicability of the Sherman Act depending upon whether the restraint imposed was direct or indirect. In *Hopkins* the Court reasoned that "[t]he contract condemned by the [Sherman Act] is one whose *direct and immediate* effect is a restraint . . . . There must be some *direct and immediate* effect upon interstate commerce, in order to come within the [Sherman] Act."[50]

In *United States v. Addyston Pipe,*[51] defendants were six competing cast–iron pipe producers who allocated territories among themselves and jointly fixed prices in each territory. The apparent purpose of the combination was to create an artificial barrier to entry by establishing prices low enough to discourage new entrants, albeit higher than prices that would have occurred from natural market conditions. Defendants argued that the arrangement had the benign purpose of preventing ruinous competition and

---

[45] *Id.* at 354.

[46] 171 U.S. 505 (1898).

[47] *Id.* at 565 (emphasis added).

[48] 85 F. 271 (6th Cir. 1898), *aff'd.*, 175 U.S. 211 (1899).

[49] 171 U.S. 578 (1898).

[50] *Id.* at 592 (emphasis added).

[51] 85 F. 271.

that their association would have been valid at common law because the prices they fixed were reasonable.

The Sixth Circuit rejected both arguments. In an opinion by Judge, later Chief Justice, Taft, the court reasoned that even under the common law all such agreements were unlawful unless they were ancillary. "[N]o conventional restraint of trade can be enforced unless the covenant embodying it is merely ancillary to the main purpose of a lawful contract . . . ."[52] Having found that the defendants' territorial and price–fixing contract was not ancillary to a main lawful purpose, the court rejected defendants' "reasonable" argument by stating that "we do not think that at common law there is any question of reasonableness open to the courts with reference to such a contract."[53]

Addyston Pipe established the ancillary restraint doctrine. It provides that all direct restraints are *ipso facto* unlawful, even when the outcome is reasonable; ancillary restraints which are unreasonable are unlawful; and ancillary restraints that are reasonable are lawful. The Supreme Court affirmed the Sixth Circuit's holding in *Addyston Pipe*.[54] The Court, however, emphasized Judge Taft's finding that the prices fixed were not reasonable, thus at least temporarily diluting the importance of Judge Taft's ancillary restraint doctrine. The doctrine is depicted graphically as follows:

	Direct Restraint	Ancillary Restraint
Restraint Reasonable	Unlawful	Lawful
Restraint Unreasonable	Unlawful	Unlawful

In *Standard Oil Co. v. United States*,[55] the Supreme Court modified a portion of the *Addyston Pipe* ancillary restraint doctrine. *Addyston Pipe* had concluded that a direct restraint is *per se* unlawful and that no inquiry into reasonableness of the restraint is justified. The *Standard Oil* defendants, a group of thirty–seven oil companies managed by a single holding company, were charged with predatory conduct — conduct designed to destroy a competitor — and anticompetitive abuses. Although the Court found Sherman Act violations and ordered dissolution of the holding company, it softened the impact of the ancillary restraint doctrine by ruling that even direct restraints of trade may be lawful if reasonable. Thus a rule of reason analysis may apply to both direct and ancillary restraints. Once applied, the rule examines the contents and nature of the entire agreement to decide if it is reasonable, and, under *Standard Oil*, the Court will assess reasonableness whether the restraint is direct or ancillary.[56] If, however, the

---

[52] *Id*. at 282.

[53] *Id*. at 293.

[54] 175 U.S. 211 (1899).

[55] 221 U.S. 1 (1911).

[56] *See infra*, § 4.05 for fuller explanation and development of the rule of reason analysis.

agreement encompasses rate fixing among competitors, then the restraint will be characterized as a presumptively illegal 'naked' restraint; and reasonableness will not be a defense.

The origins of the ancillary restraint doctrine discussed above still maintain validity today and indeed the doctrine is being expanded. In *Polk Bros., Inc. v. Forest City Enterprises, Inc.*,[57] the Seventh Circuit reviewed a challenge to a horizontal agreement not to compete on both a territorial and a product line basis. Plaintiff and defendant entered into an agreement requiring the plaintiff to erect a building in which plaintiff and defendant would operate retail stores within a single building but separated by a partition. Each party agreed not to stock or sell certain products which the other would have the exclusive right to sell within the building. Due to declining profits and a change in management, defendant sought to be relieved of its covenant not to compete with the plaintiff. When the defendant informed the plaintiff that it considered the noncompete covenant to be invalid, plaintiff sued for an injunction.

The core of the Seventh Circuit's reasoning in *Polk Bros.* was a determination of whether the allegedly unlawful covenant was a naked or an ancillary restraint. In an opinion by Judge Easterbrook, the court observed that, if ancillary, the restraint would be evaluated under a rule of reason analysis, but that "the *per se* rule is designed for 'naked' restraints."[58]

First, the court ruled that to determine if a restraint should be characterized as ancillary or naked it is appropriate to "ask whether an agreement promoted enterprise and productivity *at the time it was adopted*."[59] By this the court meant whether "it may contribute to the success of a cooperative venture that promises greater productivity and output . . . . Only when a quick look reveals that the practice facially appears to be one that would always or almost always tend to restrict competition and decrease output should a court cut off further inquiry."[60] The court concluded that the principal purpose of the agreement between the parties was to embark on a new venture to build a joint facility. The parties "were cooperating to produce, not to curtail output; the cooperation increased the amount of retail space available and was at least potentially beneficial to consumers . . . ".[61] Thus the covenant not to compete within that building was ancillary, even though the covenant was an essential part of the arrangement. The agreement was not *per se* unlawful. Judge Easterbrook's opinion is worth review at least for the broad and expansive interpretation placed on the definition of ancillary restraint.

In *National Ass'n of Review Appraisers & Mortgage Underwriters, Inc. v. Appraisal Foundation*,[62] the Eighth Circuit found that the defendant's

---

[57] 776 F.2d 185 (7th Cir. 1985).

[58] *Id.* at 188.

[59] *Id.* at 189 (emphasis added).

[60] *Id.* at 189 *quoting Broadcast Music, Inc. v. Columbia Broad. Sys.*, 441 U.S. 1, 19–20 (1979).

[61] *Id.* at 190. *See also SCFC ILC, Inc. v. Visa USA, Inc.*, 36 F.3d 958 (10th Cir. 1994).

[62] 64 F.3d 1130 (8th Cir. 1995).

refusal to admit the plaintiff as a member of its association was best characterized as an ancillary restraint on trade. The Foundation was created to promote educational and ethical standards for appraisal services, and its membership criteria appeared to be designed to accomplish those goals by establishing such standards and requiring non–profit status for appraisal organizations. Such requirements generally pose merely incidental market restraints and are necessary to successful industry self–regulation.[63] As such, the activities were not presumptively illegal. In fact, the court affirmed summary judgment in favor of the defendants, holding their actions to be legal and actually procompetitive.[64]

The Seventh Circuit refused to apply the ancillary restraint doctrine to a dissolution agreement which divided the market for attorney services geographically by permanently delineating certain areas in which each of the former partners could advertise.[65] The agreement was neither necessary to the dissolution of the partnership nor legitimate as a temporary covenant not to compete.[66] Hence, the Seventh Circuit held the agreement to be a *per se* violation of § 1.[67]

One must be careful not to take the protections of the ancillary restraint doctrine too far, however. In *Sullivan v. NFL*,[68] the First Circuit had to determine whether the NFL's restraints on public ownership of teams was ancillary to its overall purpose of facilitating effective and efficient sports team management. The court readily admitted that the NFL's policy exemplified an ancillary restraint in the form of a joint venture policy restricting membership and that the policy "contributes to the ability of the NFL to function as an effective sports team, and that the NFL's functioning would be impaired if publicly owned teams were permitted. . ."[69] The court, however, refused to find, however, that these factors alone established, "as a matter of law, that the NFL's policy [did] not unreasonably restrain trade."[70] "The holdings in *BMI*, *Rothery Storage*,[71] and *Northwest Stationers*[72] do not throw the rule of reason out the window merely because one establishes that a given practice among joint venture participants is ancillary to legitimate and efficient activity — the injury to competition must still be weighed against the purported benefits under the rule of reason."[73]

---

[63] *Id.* at 1133.

[64] *Id.*

[65] *Blackburn v. Sweeney*, 53 F.3d 825 (7th Cir. 1995).

[66] *Id.* at 828–29.

[67] The court maintained its holding without questioning *Polk Bros.* by admitting that, if the partnership dissolution could have been characterized as a temporary covenant not to compete, *Polk Bros.* would have applied.

[68] 34 F.3d 1091 (1st Cir. 1994).

[69] *Id.* at 1102.

[70] *Id.*

[71] 792 F.2d 210 (D.C. Cir. 1986).

[72] 472 U.S. 284 (1985).

[73] *Sullivan*, 34 F.3d at 1102. The case was reversed and remanded in the defendant's favor due to a series of prejudicial errors at the trial court level.

§ 4.05 Rule of Reason Development

The open–ended text of § 1 of the Sherman Act gives courts broad discretion in interpretation. The statute sets forth only general principles, giving reviewing courts authority to engage in diverse interpretation, if not expansion. The pre–Sherman Act common law precedents served as benchmarks throughout the development of the law.

Early cases struggled with the breadth of the statutory language. In *Standard Oil Co. v. United States*,[74] the Supreme Court began to chart the range of discretion available to courts in interpreting § 1. The Court advanced the rule of reason standard, permitting courts to weigh competitive factors and determine whether the restraint is reasonable: whether there has been a significant interference with or impact on competition.

Under this standard, only *unreasonable* restraints are illegal. But *Standard Oil* also recognized that certain conduct is, by its very nature or character, inherently anticompetitive and thus unreasonable.[75] Such conduct, therefore, does not need to be evaluated under the broad rule of reason standard to determine the actual effects of the challenged conduct. This observation foreshadowed the development of the competing *per se* rule of illegality and its application to price–fixing agreements.

The distinction is not always clear when the rule of reason or the *per se* standard should be employed. Not all restrictive conduct is inherently anticompetitive. Courts are called upon to draw fine line distinctions on a case by case basis. At times it is difficult to reconcile all the precedents. Inconsistencies frequently result because antitrust laws are largely judge–made, derived from statutory interpretations.

As the following discussion reveals, the case law trend is away from a cursory analysis under the *per se* approach, especially if the court has had little experience with the challenged practice. A more detailed factual inquiry, which scrutinizes the purpose and effect of the challenged conduct, is used more frequently today. As we will see, the characterization process, whether rule of reason or *per se*, is critical to the court's analysis, and in many respects determinative of the result.

The classic case illustrating the rule of reason methodology is *Chicago Board of Trade v. United States*.[76] Members of the Board of Trade entered an agreement requiring all members who purchased grain after closing hours to purchase at a price set at the close of the day's business. Even though this agreement could be characterized as one that foreclosed price competition during the nonregular trading hours, thus subject to a *per se* condemnation, Justice Brandeis, writing for the court, outlined instead a broad rule of reason test:

---

[74] 221 U.S. 1 (1911).

[75] In *United States v. Joint Traffic Ass'n*, 171 U.S. 505, 568 (1898), the Court held that price fixing was such an illegal agreement because its effects are "direct and immediate."

[76] 246 U.S. 231 (1918).

The true test of legality is whether the restraint imposed is such as merely regulates and perhaps promotes competition or whether it is such as may suppress or even destroy competition. To determine that question the court must ordinarily consider the facts peculiar to the business . . . ; its conditions before and after the restraint was imposed; the nature of the restraint and its effect, actual or probable. The history of the restraint, the evil believed to exist, the reason for adopting the particular remedy, the purpose or end sought to be attained are all relevant facts.[77]

This standard was then used to determine the reasonableness of the restraint. The Court upheld the challenged conduct on the theory that this price restraint actually promoted competition by "perfecting market conditions," by regulating the Exchange's business hours, by breaking up a monopoly previously held by a limited number of warehouses that purchased grain during nonregular hours, and by increasing the number of possible transactions.[78] In using a wide–open rule of reason analysis, Justice Brandeis was able to further those values he perceived essential under § 1 — the protection of small business in a pluralistic society increasingly dominated by large business.[79]

Like *Chicago Board of Trade*, the Supreme Court in *Appalachian Coals, Inc. v. United States*,[80] sanctioned a rule of reason standard in another case characterized by a price–fixing cartel. Producers of bituminous coal in the Appalachian area entered into an agreement to establish an exclusive selling agent. Appalachian Coals, Inc., the selling agent, was to sell, at the highest prices, the entire production for all 137 producers. The producers held 12% of the bituminous production east of the Mississippi and 74% of the Appalachian territory.

Upholding the exclusive selling agreement, the Court reasoned that the arrangement was justified because of the realities of "deplorable economic conditions in the industry." The opinion was issued during the depression and perhaps this explains the Court's broadly–based weighing analysis:

> The question of the application of the statute is one of intent and effect, and is not to be determined by arbitrary assumptions. It is therefore necessary in this instance to consider the economic conditions peculiar to the coal industry, the practices which obtained, the nature of defendant's plan of making sales, the reasons which led to its adoption, and the probable consequences of the carrying out of that plan in relation to market prices and other matters affecting the public interest in interstate commerce in bituminous coal.[81]

Appalachian Coals advance a rule of broad discretion in favor of courts weighing competitive, market factors before reaching antitrust conclusions.

---

[77] *Id.* at 238.

[78] *Id.* at 240–41. *See also* Sullivan, *The Economic Jurisprudence of the Burger Court's Antitrust Policy: The First Thirteen Years*, 58 Notre Dame L. Rev. 1, 12–13 (1982).

[79] Sullivan, *supra* note 78, at 13.

[80] 288 U.S. 344 (1933).

[81] *Id.* at 361.

These cases also are important for introducing the role of efficiency and integration of productive capacity as acceptable antitrust inquiries and defenses. As the subsequent discussion indicates, agreements designed to facilitate the operation of a market and efficiency within markets are increasingly being evaluated under the rule of reason standard. *Chicago Board of Trade* portended this development.[82]

§ 4.06 *Per Se* Rule of Illegality and Price Fixing

Although the *Standard Oil* decision introduced the distinction between the rule of reason and *per se* illegality, the summary analysis implicit in the *per se* conclusive presumption was not developed in any detail until *United States v. Trenton Potteries Co.*[83] Twenty–three corporations and twenty individuals were indicted and charged with fixing the price of pottery for bathrooms. The trial court instructed the jury that if it found "the agreements or combination complained of, it might return a verdict of guilty without regard to the reasonableness of the price fixed, or the good intentions of the combining units. Whether prices were actually lowered or raised . . . since [such] agreements . . . were unreasonable restraints." Defendants argued that the instruction was erroneous on the theory that the established prices were reasonable and noninjurious to the public. The Supreme Court upheld the jury instruction, rejecting the defense that fixed prices may nevertheless be reasonable.

> The aim and result of every price–fixing agreement, if effective, is the elimination of one form of competition. The power to fix prices, whether reasonably exercised or not, involves power to control the market and to fix arbitrary and unreasonable prices. The reasonable price fixed today may through economic and business changes become the unreasonable price of tomorrow . . . . Agreements which create such potential power may well be held to be in themselves unreasonable or unlawful restraints, without the necessity of minute inquiry whether a particular price is reasonable or unreasonable as fixed and without placing on the government in enforcing the Sherman Law the burden of ascertaining from day to day whether it has become unreasonable through the mere variation of economic conditions.[84]

---

[82] The trend is obvious in a number of cases, but the Eleventh Circuit may have best embodied this general affinity for the rule of reason when it said, "We apply the *per se* rule 'only when history and analysis have shown that in sufficient similar circumstances the rule of reason unequivocally results in a finding of liability,' i.e. when the conduct involved 'always or almost always tend[s] to restrict competition and decrease output.' " *Levine v. Central Fla. Med. Affiliates, Inc.*, 72 F.3d 1538, 1549 (11th Cir. 1996) (citations omitted). *See also* Thomas C. Arthur, *A Workable Rule of Reason: A Less Ambitious Antitrust Role for the Federal Courts*, 68 ANTITRUST L.J. 337, 389 (2000) (suggesting that "the Supreme Court get out of the competition regulation business," leaving that to the FTC and instead focusing on the Sherman Act's prescription of "cartels, monopolistic mergers, and nakedly predatory practices").

[83] 273 U.S. 392 (1927).

[84] *Id.* at 397–98.

Implicit in *Trenton Potteries* is the idea that the range of judicial discretion is narrower in price–fixing cases. One conclusion that follows is that in price–fixing cases the only inquiry is whether an agreement to fix the price can be established. If found, the agreement is illegal and further inquiry (including the reasonableness of the price) is irrelevant. Illegal purpose will be inferred from the agreement.

Trenton Potteries implies that by definition a price–fixing agreement is *per se* unlawful. But the Court used the limited terms, "if effective," to couch its reasoning. This raised the additional question whether price fixing was *per se* illegal only if the conspirators had market power to achieve the object of the conspiracy. The issue was decided 13 years later in *United States v. Socony–Vacuum Oil Co.* [85] It was clear, however, in *Trenton Potteries* that the Court believed that price competition was at the core of § 1.

In *Socony* the Court was confronted with whether an agreement among competitors to reduce the supply of petroleum products from the market was a *per se* price–fixing agreement. The Court held unequivocally that a conspiracy that "tampers with the price structure" is *per se* unlawful, thereby foreclosing possible defenses that attempt to weigh competing interests or policies. The *per se* classification was applied, with its conclusive presumption of illegality, even though the agreement did not set or peg the exact price of gasoline. Conduct which directly *affects* price, said the Court, has by its nature and necessary effect no social utility and should be condemned without further consideration. [86] The Court's conclusion was grounded in the theory that an agreement which interferes with independent market decisions is contrary to § 1 of the Sherman Act.

In its now famous footnote 59, the *Socony* Court made clear that market power is not a precondition to finding a *per se* violation:

> [I]t is well established that a person "may be guilty of conspiring although incapable of committing the objective offense." . . . It is the "contract, combination . . . or conspiracy in restraint of trade or commerce" which § 1 of the Act strikes down, whether the concerted activity be wholly nascent or abortive on the one hand, or successful on the other . . . .
>
> . . . .
>
> . . . Only a confusion between the nature of the offenses [under § 1 and § 2] . . . would lead to the conclusion that power to fix prices was necessary for proof of a price–fixing conspiracy under § 1. [87]

Socony is perhaps the strongest Supreme Court decision in support of a *per se* condemnation for price–fixing agreements. Its classic definition of price fixing, "tampering with the price structure" is a broad standard capable of sweeping in various market conduct, some of which may not *directly* affect price. The conduct challenged in *Socony*, however, was clearly

---

[85] 310 U.S. 150 (1940).

[86] *Id.* at 224.

[87] *Id.* at n.59.

pernicious and the most effective method of affecting price — an agreement to reduce output or supply in the market. Under *Socony*'s *per se* characterization process, the judicial inquiry is limited to whether the challenged agreement, once established, comes within the price–fixing category.[88]

The *per se* rule of illegality, as a policy matter, furthers the goals of clarifying the law, promoting certainty for business planning and promoting judicial economy. As the Supreme Court noted in *Northern Pac. Ry. v. United States*:[89]

> [T]here are certain agreements or practices which because of their pernicious effect on competition and lack of any redeeming virtue are conclusively presumed to be unreasonable and therefore illegal without elaborate inquiry as to the precise harm they have caused or the business excuse for their use. This principle of *per se* unreasonableness not only makes the type of restraints which are proscribed by the Sherman Act more certain to the benefit of everyone concerned, but it also avoids the necessity for an incredibly complicated and prolonged economic investigation into the entire history of the industry involved, as well as related industries, in an effort to determine at large whether a particular restraint has been unreasonable — an inquiry so often wholly fruitless when undertaken.[90]

Many economists disagree with the sweeping rule announced in *Socony* and the premises on which it rests. First, they question whether it make sense or is good public policy to condemn an agreement by competitors when they lack market power. In this regard it is important to remember that cartels are condemned because they reduce output below competitive levels and increase price above marginal costs. Market power is one test for determining whether competitors have the ability to achieve these results. If market power is lacking, industry output will not fall even if the members of the cartel restrict their own output, because other firms in the market will increase output as a response to the cartel action. Thus, absent market power to enforce the output limitation, prices will not rise. Many economists conclude that without the requisite market power the agreement is not price fixing. Therefore, it would not be classified as *per se* illegal.

Stated somewhat differently, if market power is lacking, any agreement to raise price will cause consumers to buy elsewhere, and higher prices will serve as an incentive for potential competitors to enter the market, or for present competitors to increase supply in order to fill the gap caused by the output restriction. When this occurs, price will not increase because output will remain constant. If increased supply creates a surplus, the competitors will lower price to clear the market and consumers will benefit.

---

[88] *See e.g. United States v. Alston*, 974 F.2d 1206, 1208 (9th Cir. 1992) (vigorously upholding *Socony*'s characterization of price fixing as per se illegal).

[89] 356 U.S. 1, 5 (1958).

[90] *See* Ayres, *How Cartels Punish: A Structural Theory of Self–Enforcement Collusion*, 87 Colum. L. Rev. 295 (1987); *see also* F. Scherer & D. Ross, Industrial Market Structure and Economic Performance 509–513 (3d ed. 1990).

Moreover, if an agreement has the effect of lowering price, this too will benefit consumers because other competitors will be forced to lower their prices in order to compete for customers.[91]

Second, although the *per se* classification has the benefit of creating a "bright line" standard as to specific illegal conduct, it prevents defendants from introducing evidence that may establish a business justification for the conduct or from showing that the conduct may yield procompetitive benefits. In some instances, then, the *per se* rule may create overdeterrence which may stifle creative competition.

§ 4.07 Modern Treatment of the *Per Se* Rule

Questions also arose after *Socony* whether agreements that were attenuated from direct price fixing, or those that only had indirect effects on price should be treated under the narrow *Socony* approach. The Court has been far from clear on this issue, but in *Catalano, Inc. v. Target Sales, Inc.*[92] it addressed the subject.

In *Catalano* the Court held that a horizontal agreement among competitors to eliminate credit was the equivalent of a discount and thus an inseparable part of the price. The agreement was condemned as *per se* unlawful; the Court noted, "[W]e have held agreements to be unlawful *per se* that had substantially less direct impact on price than the agreement alleged in this case."[93] The Court concluded that if the challenged conduct has an effect on an inseparable component of the price, the only question open for consideration is whether the conduct occurred. In doing so, the Court rejected the Ninth Circuit's approach that weighed the procompetitive benefits of lowered entry barriers and increased price visibility against the increase in price. Once the agreement to eliminate credit was established, the judicial inquiry ended, the Court reasoned. "It is no excuse that the prices fixed are themselves reasonable."[94]

The *per se* rule was next applied in *Arizona v. Maricopa County Medical Society*[95] where the Court struck down a maximum fee schedule agreed upon by doctors for reimbursement for health services provided to policyholders of certain insurance plans. Concluding that a maximum price was just as anticompetitive as a minimum price, the Court observed that:

> The *per se* rule "is grounded on faith in price competition as a market force [and not] on a policy of low selling prices at the price of eliminating competition." In this case the rule is violated by a price restraint that tends to provide the same economic rewards to all practitioners regardless of their skill, their experience, their training, or their willingness

---

[91] For a more detailed analysis of the economic discussion, *see supra* Chapter 2.

[92] 446 U.S. 643 (1980).

[93] *Id.* at 647.

[94] 457 U.S. at 647.

[95] 457 U.S. 332 (1982).

to employ innovative and different procedures in individual cases. Such a restraint also may discourage entry into the market and may deter experimentation and new developments by individual entrepreneurs. It may be a masquerade for an agreement to fix uniform prices, or it may in the future take on that character.[96]

At bottom, the *Maricopa* Court held that maximum fees as well as minimum fees are illegal *per se* regardless of their potential procompetitive features. In addition, the Court did not hesitate to apply, although for the first time, the *per se* rule to professionals.[97] Notwithstanding the clear resolution in Maricopa, the Court failed to articulate any systematic criteria for reviewing horizontal price–affecting cases.

Perhaps it was critical to the Courts' holding that the competing doctors were the source of and participated in the pricing scheme, when the insurance company could have implemented the cost containment efficiencies. The result seems to turn, although it is not free from doubt, on whether the agreement among the doctors was necessary to achieve the desired efficiencies or whether less restrictive means were available. The Court seemed to conclude that the doctors' participation was not necessary for this integration to be effective, that the doctors' agreement was "not a 'necessary consequence' of [the] arrangement with the insurer,"[98] and that a less restrictive alternative was available.

Also, because the challenged conduct directly fixed the price of the medical reimbursement, the ancillary restraint doctrine, at least as traditionally formulated, was inapplicable as a defense.[99] Interestingly, if the Court had applied an output restriction analysis,[100] it would have found that this plan did not restrict physicians from charging a competitive price to patients not insured under the approved plan. Hence, although a maximum fee may have been established, it did not restrict the doctors' ability to recoup any loss by charging higher prices to others.

More recently, the Supreme Court in *Palmer v. BRG of Georgia, Inc.*,[101] reaffirmed a rule of *per se* illegality for horizontal market divisions. In a per curiam opinion, the Court, citing *Socony–Vacuum* and *United States v. Topco Associates, Inc.*,[102] held that an allocation of markets or

---

[96] *Id.* at 348.

[97] *See Goldfarb v. Virginia State Bar*, 421 U.S. 773 (1975), and *National Soc'y of Prof'l Eng'rs v. United States*, 435 U.S. 679 (1978), where the Court implied that a rule of reason balancing analysis would be employed if the restraint were premised on noncommercial objectives such as public service or ethical norms or if the restraint enhanced professional services. But to weigh noncommercial objectives against competitive harms would conflict directly with the central holding of *Professional Engineers* and *Broadcast Music, Inc. v. Columbia Broad. Sys.*, 441 U.S. 1 (1979). *See also*, Harrison, *Price Fixing, the Professions, and Ancillary Restraints: Coping with Maricopa County*, 1982 U. Ill. L. Rev. 925.

[98] 457 U.S. at 356–57 & n.33.

[99] *See supra* at 12.

[100] *See supra* at 8.

[101] 498 U.S. 46 (1990).

[102] 405 U.S. 596 (1972).

submarkets by competitors is unlawful whether or not the competitors had previously competed amongst themselves in the same market.[103]

In *Palmer*, a former law student alleged that the price of his bar review course with BRG was "enhanced [due to] an unlawful market allocation agreement [entered into by] the defendant and another provider, (HBJ)."[104] In his complaint, Palmer alleged that prior to 1980, both BRG and HBJ directly competed within Georgia for bar review business. In 1980, however, both parties "entered into an agreement that gave BRG an exclusive license to market HBJ's material in Georgia and to use its tradename 'Bar/Bri'."[105] Pursuant to this agreement, both parties "agreed that HBJ would not compete with BRG in Georgia and that BRG would not compete with HBJ outside of Georgia."[106]

The Supreme Court held the agreement unlawful on its face. With respect to the price–fixing component present in the 1980 agreement, the Court commented that:

> [t]he revenue–sharing formula in the 1980 agreement between BRG and HBJ, coupled with the price increase that took place immediately after the parties agreed to cease competing with each other in 1980, indicates that this agreement was formed for the purpose and with the effect of raising the price of bar review course.[107] . . . [U]nder the Sherman Act a combination formed for the purpose and with the effect of raising, depressing, fixing, pegging, or stabilizing the price of a commodity in interstate or foreign commerce is illegal per se.[108]

Furthermore, the Court reiterated that "horizontal territorial limitations . . . are naked restraints of trade with no purpose except stifling competition. Such limitations are *per se* violations of the Sherman Act."[109] Said the Court: "agreements among competitors not to compete within the other's territories are anticompetitive regardless of whether the parties split a market within which both do business or whether they merely reserve one market for one and another for the other".[110]

Palmer, thus clarifies that market allocations between competitors are *per se* unlawful even (1) in the absence of an agreement on price or evidence that one party has the right to be consulted about the other's prices, and (2) when the parties had not competed previously in the same market.[111]

---

[103] *Id.* at 49–50.

[104] 498 U.S. at 46.

[105] *Id.* at 47. "Under the agreement, HBJ received $100 per student enrolled by BRG and 40% of all revenues over $350. Immediately after the 1980 agreement, the price of BRG's course was increased from $150 to over $400." *Id.*

[106] *Id.*

[107] *Id.* at 49.

[108] *Id.* at 48 *citing United States v. Socony–Vacuum Oil Co.*, 310 U.S. 150, 223 (1940).

[109] *Id.* at 49 *citing United States v. Topco Associates, Inc.*, 405 U.S. 596, 608 (1972).

[110] *Id.* at 49–50.

[111] E. Thomas Sullivan & H. Hovenkamp, *Antitrust Law, Policy and Procedure* Ch. 2 (4d ed. 1994).

Another activity that has been held to be *per se* unlawful is bid rigging between competitors. In *United States v. Reicher*,[112] the defendant convinced a fellow engineering company (Giolas) to submit a bid higher than the defendant's on a contract with Los Alamos National Laboratory in order to secure that the defendant would get the job. The defendant's partner in the bid rigging had neither the financial capacity nor the desire to engage in the project; however, the court still labeled him a "competitor," thereby making the defendant guilty of a *per se* violation of the Sherman Act.

Despite its ultimate inability to perform the contract, Giolas held itself out as a competitor for the purposes of rigging what was supposed to be a competitive bidding process. This is exactly the sort of "threat to the central nervous system of the economy" that the antitrust laws are meant to address.[113]

This opinion is consistent with the holdings of other circuits on bid rigging.[114] In *Denny's Marina, Inc. v. Renfro Productions, Inc.*,[115] the Seventh Circuit reversed the district court's refusal to apply the *per se* rule to a horizontal conspiracy among various defendants engaged in the production of boat shows to exclude the plaintiff from participating in the shows. The lower court based its refusal on the fact that the plaintiff regularly undersold its competitors and that the plaintiff had not shown a "potential market–wide impact" from the defendant's actions.[116] The Court of Appeals readily asserted that the defendant's actions warranted a *per se* analysis, as they constituted illegal price fixing and an unreasonable restraint of trade.[117] Also, since one of the justifications for the *per se* rule is to destroy the need for individualized showings, no potential market impact needed to be proved by the plaintiff.[118]

Bid rigging can be the product of lawful activity in a few limited cases, however. As Professor Areeda has indicated, bids that are based on a "standard and uniform market price" and are, therefore, identical, are not a product of illegal per se price fixing.[119] Also, "pricing. . .based upon traditional applications of common cost factors" can serve as exceptions to the per se illegal treatment of bid rigging.

---

[112] 983 F.2d 168 (10th Cir. 1992). *See also U.S. v. All–Star Industries*, 962 F.2d 465 (5th Cir. 1992).

[113] *Id.* at 170 (citation omitted).

[114] *See United States v. MMR Corp.*, 907 F.2d 489 (5th Cir. 1990), *cert. denied*, 499 U.S. 936, (1991); *United States v. WF Brinkley & Son Constr. Co.*, 783 F.2d 1157 (4th Cir. 1986). *United States v. Finis P. Ernest, Inc.*, 509 F.2d 1256 (7th Cir.) *cert. denied*, 423 U.S. 893 (1975). The opinion is also consistent with the well–respected rule that one need not have market power in order to violate antitrust laws. *See* § 4.06.

[115] 8 F.3d 1217 (7th Cir. 1993).

[116] *Id.* at 1219.

[117] *Id.* at 1220–21. *See also ES Dev., Inc. v. RWM Enters., Inc.*, 939 F.2d 547, 556 (8th Cir. 1991) (holding horizontal agreement between car dealerships to prevent plaintiff from building car mall subject to *per se* analysis as an unreasonable restraint of trade).

[118] *Id.* at 1222.

[119] VI P.E. Areeda, *Antitrust Law*, ¶ 1420 (1986).

Although *Maricopa*, *Catalano* and *Palmer* are consistent with *Socony*, except for the output analysis, another standard of review, embracing a focused rule of reason, was being advanced simultaneously in the Supreme Court. The clash between these analyses has left us with no easy guide for evaluating horizontal price fixing.[120]

§ 4.08 Trend Towards a Structured Rule of Reason for Price Fixing

The process by which certain concerted conduct is characterized as price fixing, is not always easy to predict. A trend has developed which suggests that the Supreme Court is less willing to merely take a "quick look" at the restraint before it is prepared to label it price fixing and thus *per se* illegal.[121] As the following discussion indicates, not all concerted action that affects price is classified as price fixing.

National Society of Professional Engineers v. United States[122] illustrates the Supreme Court's changing analysis of horizontal restraints. The government charged that the professional association's canon of ethics prohibiting competitive bidding by its members violated § 1 of the Sherman Act. The issue was "whether the canon [was] justified under the Sherman Act, . . . because it was adopted by members of a learned profession for the purpose of minimizing the risk that competition would produce inferior engineering work endangering the public safety."[123] Defendant urged the Court to apply a rule of reason in order to weigh the public safety against the restraint imposed by the canon. In declining to adopt a broad–based rule of reason, the Court did concede that a summary analysis was too narrow a focus. The standard adopted was a balancing test that determined the "competitive significance" of the restraint:[124]

> There are . . . two complementary categories of antitrust analysis. In the first category are agreements whose nature and necessary effect are so plainly anticompetitive that no elaborate study of the industry is needed to establish their illegality — they are "illegal *per se*." In the second category are agreements whose competitive effect can only be evaluated by analyzing the facts peculiar to the business, the history of

---

[120] *See American Ad Management, Inc. v. GTE*, 92 F.3d 781, 785 (9th Cir. 1996) (holding the rule of reason to be the proper level of analysis, despite *Socony* and *Catalano*, because the relationship involved was "one of agency, not wholesale retail.")

[121] Some circuit courts are just as unwilling as the Supreme Court. *See e.g. United States Healthcare, Inc v. Healthsource, Inc.*, 986 F.2d 589, 595, 597 (1st Cir. 1993) (refusing to apply a "quick look" analysis to an exclusivity clause in a contract between a HMO and a doctor, even though such clauses "might in some situations constitute the wrongful act that is an ingredient in monopolization claims under § 2"); *Chicago Prof'l Sports Ltd P'ship v. NBA*, 95 F.3d 593, 600 (7th Cir. 1996) (holding the NBA is "sufficiently integrated that its [televising] rules may not be condemned without analysis under the full Rule of Reason").

[122] 435 U.S. 679 (1978).

[123] *Id.*

[124] *Id.* at 692.

the restraint, and the reasons why it was imposed. In either event, the purpose of the analysis is to form a judgment about the competitive significance of the restraint; it is not to decide whether a policy favoring competition is in the public interest, or in the interest of the members of an industry.[125]

The test of "competitive significance" was limited to an economic analysis of the agreement's competitive impact. The safety or "quality product" defense was excluded from the balancing process because defendants did not argue that it would increase efficiency or promote competition. The underlying assumption of the Sherman Act, the Court reasoned, was that "competition will produce not only lower prices, but also better goods and services."[126] To weigh public interest, including public safety, would be beyond the discretion of the Court.

Specifically, the analysis employed by Justice Stevens, writing for the Court, was to examine the business justification for the canon. Once he found that it actually restricted competition, he rejected the practice as illegal. In short, *Professional Engineers* teaches that the rule of reason in price–affecting cases is focused on an examination whether the challenged practice promotes or suppresses competition. Here, the Court found that the ban on bidding, which resulted in an output restriction, would, by definition, increase price with no offsetting procompetitive feature. By its nature, the ban on competitive bidding resulted in maintenance of price levels; it also prevented customers from making price comparisons. As *Socony* instructed, an agreement to maintain price levels is illegal.

Professional Engineers also made clear that the Sherman Act does not permit competitors to agree on one form of competition over another. To do so would interfere with free and open markets. Consumers, the Court noted, should be able to decide whether they want higher quality or lower priced buildings:

"The heart of our national economic policy long has been faith in the value of competition." . . . The assumption that competition is the best method of allocating resources in a free market recognizes that all elements of a bargain — quality, service, safety, and durability — and not just the immediate cost, are favorably affected by the free opportunity to select among alternative offers.[127]

Thus, under *Professional Engineers* a structured or focused rule of reason is adopted. It is, however, far narrower than that recognized in *Chicago Board of Trade*. The parameters of the antitrust analysis are defined by the nature of the competition. The range of decisional options includes only whether the challenged agreement promotes or restrains competition. No room is left for an evaluation of noneconomic factors such as social or political benefits.[128] But certainly the Court was more willing to permit

---

[125] *Id.*

[126] *Id.* at 695.

[127] *Id.*

[128] *See also Reiter v. Sonotone Corp.*, 442 U.S. 330, 344–45 (1979), where the Court refused

an examination that went beyond a quick *per se* classification to the extent that it weighed the net economic, competitive consequences of the challenged practice. A retreat from the high point of *per se* analysis, illustrated in *Socony* and *Container*, was evident.

Professional Engineers' analytical style raised numerous questions: whether the Court would apply a focused rule of reason to commercial conduct outside a profession and whether the defenses would be limited to economic justifications. A partial answer was forthcoming the next Supreme Court term.

In *Broadcast Music, Inc. v. Columbia Broadcasting System (BMI)*,[129] the Supreme Court extended the focused rule of reason beyond professionals to a commercial blanket licensing arrangement.[130] CBS, a licensee, challenged the arrangement as a price–fixing agreement. Invoking the *Professional Engineers* balancing test, defendants urged that the blanket license agreement was procompetitive because it facilitated the orderly and efficient operation of the market by reducing the transaction costs between players in the market. By providing a blanket license covering all members of the defendants' association, a purchaser of musical or artistic works would only have to negotiate and contract with one entity for the right to use all products represented by the licensor rather than individual contracting. The cost of transacting would be reduced accordingly.

Because the Court had not had substantial experience with blanket licensing arrangements, it rejected the quick characterization process of the *per se* rule, even though it conceded that a price–fixing agreement was "literally" at stake.[131] The Court stressed that the review standard is limited to whether the conduct is "designed to 'increase economic efficiency and render markets more, rather than less, competitive.'"[132]

Applying the efficiency test, the Court concluded that the blanket license arrangement produced cost efficiencies in the monitoring and integration of sales and in enforcement against unauthorized copyright use that could not have been achieved by individual composers. Even though the arrangement foreclosed "competitive pricing as a free market's means of allocating resources," the Court remanded the issue to the Second Circuit for determination, under the rule of reason standard, whether individual transaction costs were too high for individual licensing to work competitively. The lower court found that they were and the license arrangement was upheld.[133]

---

to weigh under the Clayton Act, the interests and policies involved in the issue whether "the cost of defending consumer class actions will have a potentially ruinous effect on small businesses . . . and will ultimately be paid by consumers . . . ."

[129] 441 U.S. 1 (1979).

[130] Membership in BMI included composers, authors, and publishing houses. The association issued blanket licenses of copyrighted musical composition for fees set by the individual member competitors. *Id.*

[131] *Id.* at 19.

[132] *Id.* at 20, *citing United States v. United States Gypsum Co.*, 438 U.S. 422, 441 (1978).

[133] *CBS v. American Soc'y of Composers and Publishers*, 620 F.2d 930 (2d Cir. 1980).

Another factor important to the analysis in *BMI* was the finding that the individual copyright owners were free to sell compositions separately from the blanket license.[134] Thus, supply and output were not restricted by the license. Moreover, unlike the doctors in *Maricopa*, participation of the individual composers in *BMI* was essential to the plan.[135] With this distinction in mind, *BMI*'s admonition established a turning point in price–fixing cases:"[n]ot all arrangements among . . . competitors that have an impact on price are *per se* violations of the Sherman Act or even unreasonable restraints."[136] *BMI* takes *Professional Engineers'* "competitive significance" standard and defines it in the context of an efficiency analysis: (1) whether the challenged conduct (the market integration) is reasonably necessary to achieve the cost–reducing efficiencies; (2) whether the restraint that follows is actually necessary to the integration; and (3) whether the efficiency achieved by integration outweighs the adverse effect of the restraint.[137] The net effect determines the outcome under the new rule of reason.

BMI also suggests that the price–fixing label is applied or rejected after the Court makes this harm–benefit analysis. At this point, the Court is able to reach a conclusion whether the conduct is a naked restraint or whether it has redeeming virtues. When the *per se* classification is accepted, it now seems more like a substantive law conclusion at the end of the balancing analysis that the net effect of the practice is not procompetitive. Thus, the initial summary analysis under the *per se* rule is on the decline, although at times the Court vacillates on where the line should be drawn in classifying price fixing.

Quite clearly, the focused rule of reason represents a significant analytical shift. The Supreme Court now values economic efficiency as a means of defining competition. Competitive harms will be weighed against economic benefits, even when the challenged conduct directly affects price competition.[138] The Court's inquiry is whether economic efficiency is achieved without sacrificing output. This point was central to the Court's most recent price–fixing case.

---

[134] 441 U.S. at 29 (Stevens, J., dissenting).

[135] This "essentialness" aspect has been the basis for distinguishing other horizontal market arrangements subjected to *per se* analysis. *See United States v. Alston*, 974 F.2d 1206 (9th Cir. 1992).

[136] 441 U.S. at 23.

[137] *See Gerhart, The Supreme Court and Antitrust Analysis: The (Near) Triumph of the Chicago School*, 1982 Sup. Ct. Rev. 319.

[138] Compare *BMI*, 441 U.S. at 20 with *National Soc'y of Prof'l Eng'rs* 435 U.S. at 692–93. The procompetitive justifications offered by the defendant "should generally [be given] a measure of latitude . . . ; however, courts should also maintain some vigilance by excluding justifications that are so unrelated to the challenged practice that they amount to a collateral attempt to salvage a practice that is decidedly in restraint of trade." *Sullivan v. NFL*, 34 F.3d 1091, 1112 (1st Cir. 1994). 513 U.S. 1190 (1995). *See also All–Care Nursing Serv., Inc. v. High Tech Staffing Servs.*, 135 F.3d 740 (11th Cir. 1998) (applying the rule of reason and upholding an agreement by hospitals to create a preferred provider program), *cert. denied*, 526 U.S. 1016 (1999).

In *NCAA v. Board of Regents*,[139] the Court rejected a *per se* analysis even though it found horizontal price and output restrictions. The rule of reason was again accepted, this time on the belief that in certain markets "horizontal restraints on competition are essential if the product is to be available at all."[140] The context was a joint venture among college sports teams and their conference leagues that entered into contracts with television networks for broadcast rights to football games. The contracts restricted the total number of games that could be broadcast, specified the number of times any one team could appear on a broadcast, required the networks to carry different schools a minimum number of times,[141] and set the price of the telecasts. Two schools sued the NCAA on theories that the restrictions restrained trade and amounted to price fixing.

Agreeing with the plaintiff schools, the Supreme Court found that the contracts did restrict output (the number of times a school could appear on the network) and did fix the price for each telecast by establishing the total compensation paid to member schools.[142] But the Court rejected the *per se* approach because this was a market, the Court reasoned, that required cooperation or interdependence among competitors before a product could be produced. Accordingly, the Court went beyond its findings of price and output restrictions and asked whether, under the *BMI* analysis, there were offsetting procompetitive features that could take this case out of the "naked restraint" category.

The NCAA offered three procompetitive justifications in defense of its contract. First, the television restrictions minimized loss of game attendance; second they minimized loss of athletic program revenues; and third they spread the television income among many schools, thus increasing competition among more schools. The Court rejected each defense.

As to the first, the Court found that the restrictions could not minimize game attendance losses because the games were shown on television at the same time the games were being played, thus potentially drawing viewers out of the stands. Moreover, the Court said competitors could not choose one form of competition over another. Second, the restrictions would not minimize loss of athletic program revenue because, by definition, the restrictions reduced revenue by mandating fewer games. Finally, although the Court found the third defense laudable and legal in purpose, it found that it was flawed in execution because with fewer opportunities to appear on television schools had less chance to share the proceeds. Concluding that the NCAA plan lacked procompetitive justifications, the Court declared the scheme illegal. Unlike *BMI*, the price and output restrictions remained without offsetting efficiencies. Moreover, in *BMI* there were not output restrictions.

---

[139] 468 U.S. 85 (1984).

[140] *Id.* at 101.

[141] *Id.* at 92–93.

[142] *Id.* at 93 n.11.

In finding that the NCAA television plan was illegal, the Court rejected a market power analysis as a part of plaintiff's burden of proof.[143] As long as defendant is unable to demonstrate an offsetting procompetitive rationale for the restraint,[144] the conduct is deemed a naked restriction, and therefore illegal, when price and output limitations are established.[145] Hence, plaintiffs need only show price and output restrictions and the lack of procompetitive justification for a conclusion of illegality to follow. If price or output limitations cannot be shown, then plaintiff may need to establish that defendant does have market power[146] — ability to set price above competitive levels without a drop in demand. This condition is evident when price and supply are not responsive to consumer demand.[147] However, "[a]s a matter of law, the absence of proof of market power does not justify a naked restriction on price or output."[148]

Along the same vein, a simple showing of market power alone may not be enough to prove adverse effect. As the Second Circuit stated in *KMB Warehouse Distributors, Inc. v. Walker Manufacturing Co.*,[149] "[t]here must be other grounds to believe that the defendant's behavior will harm competition market–wide, such as the inherent anticompetitive nature of the defendant's behavior or the structure of the interbrand market."[150] According to the Second Circuit, the same can be said for the anticompetitive intent requirement, since "[w]ithout some evidence of an adverse impact on competition in either the interbrand or interbrand market, the fact that customers induce a seller to refrain from dealing with another

---

[143] *Id.* at 111. The Court went on to find market power by the NCAA, nevertheless. *See also FTC v. Indiana Fed'n of Dentists*, 476 U.S. 447, 460–461 (1985) ("proof of actual detrimental effects, such as a reduction of output, can obviate the need for an inquiry into market power").

[144] Courts are in disagreement as to whether the procompetitive effects and the anticompetitive injury must be felt in the same market. Some courts argue that different effects in different markets lead to factors which cannot be compared because they do not correlate, while others see no problem with using benefits and burdens in separate markets as a reference point. *See Sullivan v. NFL,* 34 F.3d 1091, 1111–12 (1st Cir. 1994) for a listing of cases and circuits that have dealt with this issue and a brief discussion of the implications.

[145] *See also Big Apple BMW v. BMW North America*, 974 F.2d 1358, 1375–80 (3d Cir. 1992) (holding that defendant's justifications for stifling competition must be more than "pretextual" to be valid).

[146] *Lie v. St. Joseph Hosp. of Mt. Clemens, Michigan*, 964 F.2d 567, 569 (6th Cir. 1992) (holding that since the plaintiff could not prove "actual detrimental effects," he was obliged to prove market power

[147] *See Levine v. Central Fla. Med. Affiliates, Inc.*, 72 F.3d 1538, 1553, 1555 (11th Cir. 1996), where the court refused to find antitrust violations in either the defendant medical organization's refusal to extend an invitation for membership to the plaintiff doctor or the defendant hospital's temporary suspension of staff privileges for the plaintiff. The court ruled that the plaintiff had failed to establish either anticompetitive effects on the market or market power in both cases.

[148] 468 U.S. at 109.

[149] 61 F.3d 123, 129 (2d Cir. 1995).

[150] *Id.*

potential customer in order to limit competition does not satisfy a plaintiff's initial burden under § 1."[151]

The Supreme Court in *Summit Health Ltd. v. Pinhas*.[152] expanded on the idea behind proof of market power as a partial substitute for proof of price and output restrictions. The Court held,

> [B]ecause the essence of any violation of § 1 is the illegal agreement itself — rather than the overt acts performed in furtherance of it — proper analysis focuses, not upon actual consequences, but rather upon the potential harm that would ensue if the conspiracy were successful. . . . If establishing jurisdiction required a showing that the unlawful conduct itself had an effect on interstate commerce, jurisdiction would be defeated by a demonstration that the alleged restraint failed to have its intended anticompetitive effect. This is not the rule of our cases. A violation may still be found in such circumstances because, in a civil action under the Sherman Act, liability may be established by proof of either an unlawful purpose or an anticompetitive effect. Thus, respondent need not allege, or prove, an actual effect on interstate commerce to support federal jurisdiction.[153]

Market power represents the potential for anticompetitive effects on the market under the rule of reason analysis. As such, if actual effects are not proved or provable, market power serves as a viable alternative basis or proxy for finding an antitrust violation.

Further modification of the abbreviated rule of reason analysis is evident in the Third Circuit's opinion in *United States v. Brown University*.[154] The defendants (eight Ivy League colleges and the Massachusetts Institute of Technology) had formed an agreement as the "Ivy Overlap Group" which effectively set the price at which each would offer needy students financial assistance as an inducement to enroll. The agreement was challenged under a price–fixing theory. After applying the truncated rule of reason analysis to the situation, the district court found for the plaintiffs. Defendants appealed, and the Third Circuit remanded the case, ordering the lower court to apply the extended rule of reason. Although the court agreed that the scheme was "anticompetitive on its face,"[155] and that MIT needed to put forth a procompetitive justification for the agreement,[156] regardless of actual or possible adverse effects to the plaintiffs,[157] the Court of Appeals felt that the case deserved a more extensive consideration.

MIT claimed that the scheme "enhanced the consumer appeal of an overlap education" through increased diversity within the schools, as well

---

[151] *Id.* at 130.

[152] 500 U.S. 322 (1991).

[153] *Id.* at 330–31 (citations omitted).

[154] 5 F.3d 658 (3d Cir. 1993).

[155] *Id.* at 672 (*citing Prof'l Eng'rs*, 435 U.S. at 693, 698). Unquestionably, the overlap agreement restricted the output of the financial assistance available to the admitted students.

[156] *Id.*

[157] *Id.* at 674.

as enhanced the educational choices for many students who previously could not have afforded an Ivy League education.[158] Similarly, MIT argued that the plan "promoted the social ideal of equality of educational access and opportunity,"[159] much like the federal government had been attempting to do for years. The Third Circuit considered these to be potentially meritorious justifications for the Group.

> It is most desirable that schools achieve equality of educational access and opportunity in order that more people enjoy the benefits of a worthy higher education. There is no doubt, too, that enhancing the quality of our educational system redounds to the general good. To the extent that higher education endeavors foster vitality of the mind, to promote free exchange between bodies of thought and truths, and better communication among a broad spectrum of individuals, as well as prepares individuals for the intellectual demands of responsible citizenship, it is a common good that should be extended to as wide a range of individuals from as broad a range of socio–economic backgrounds as possible. It is with this in mind that the Overlap Agreement should be submitted to the rule of reason scrutiny under the Sherman Act.[160]

Although the overlap agreement admittedly bore striking similarities to those in *Professional Engineers* and *Indiana Dentists*, the court suggested it could be distinguished in that it was an attempt to broaden the spectrum of possibilities for the average consumer through market self–regulation. Unlike *Professional Engineers* and *Indiana Dentists*, it was not based on the "faulty premise" that consumers will make "unwise or dangerous" choices in a fully competitive market.[161] The court pointed out that extensive rule of reason analysis could show that no goods were being withheld from consumers, bringing both social benefit and increased consumer participation in the market.[162] The court remanded for consideration of these issues, plus others like whether the overlap agreement was "necessary" to achieve its proffered goal of educational equality and whether a less–restrictive alternative existed.[163] The case was settled after remand.

In sum, if one attempts to reconcile the Supreme Court's jurisprudence on price–fixing from *Standard Oil* through *Socony* to *NCAA*, a synthesis might result in the following principles: direct agreements that fix price and restrict output are illegal unless cooperation, interdependence, or integration is required to produce procompetitive efficiencies that offset the resulting restraint, such as a reduction of transaction costs or externalities (a cost external to private decisionmaking), and unless less restrictive means to achieve the net economies are not available.

---

[158] *Id.*

[159] *Id.* at 675.

[160] *Id.* at 678.

[161] *Id.* at 676.

[162] *Id.*

[163] *Id.* at 674.

In *BMI* that balance was struck in finding no illegal price–fixing agreement because the restriction did not contain output limitations and the procompetitive consequences outweighed the harm. In *NCAA* and *Professional Engineers*, defendants failed to demonstrate offsetting procompetitive benefits, leaving the price and output restrictions standing as naked restraints. And in *Maricopa* the price agreements were found overbroad, not the least restrictive means available to achieve the cost economies. Finally in *Socony* and *Catalano* the agreements were hard core price–affecting schemes among competitors that required no cooperation or integration for an effective market to perform competitively, nor were procompetitive motives advanced for the collusion. The schemes were designed to derail "overly" robust competition.[164]

In 1999, the Supreme Court decided *California Dental Ass'n v. FTC*, which addressed advertising restrictions that the professional association placed on its members.[165] The Court found that quick look analysis was inappropriate because "any anticompetitive effects of given restraints [were] far from intuitively obvious."[166] The Court, in an opinion by Justice Souter, explained that quick look analysis is appropriate when "the great likelihood of anticompetitive effects can easily be ascertained."[167] Because this was not the case here, the Ninth Circuit incorrectly analyzed the restriction under a quick look.[168] Moreover, the Court suggested that there is no bright line test for the depth of analysis that must be taken, indicating instead that it should be determined case–by–case.[169] Justice Breyer, in dissent, would have affirmed the Ninth Circuit's adjudication, because he determined that even under traditional rule of reason analysis, the restrictions violated the antitrust laws.[170]

§ 4.09   The Rule of Reason and Anticompetitive Conduct by Professionals

On several occasions, the Supreme Court has ruled on the legality of concerted conduct by professionals. The analysis employed by the Court has varied between a rule of reason and *per se* illegality.

---

[164] Of course, the ancillary restraint doctrine also may serve as a legal standard which insulates an agreement from illegality.

[165] 526 U.S. 756, 759 (1999).

[166] *Id.*

[167] *Id.* at 770.

[168] *Id.* at 769.

[169] *Id.* at 779–80.

[170] *Id.* at 781 (Breyer, J., dissenting). Several journal articles address the implications of *Calif. Dental Ass'n. See, e.g.,* Thomas A. Piraino, Jr., *A Proposed Antitrust Approach to Collaborations Among Competitors*, 86 Iowa L. Rev. 1137, 1207 (2001) (suggesting that *California Dental Ass'n* illustrates the federal judiciary's failure to develop a unified approach to § 1 of the Sherman Act, and proposing a continuum–based approach to resolve the confusion); Sam Stanton, *Burden Shifting and Presumptions Under Section One of the Sherman Act After* California Dental Ass'n v. FTC, 53 Rutgers L. Rev. 247, 275 (2000) (arguing that *California Dental Ass'n* is limited to advertising self–regulation by professional associations).

In *Goldfarb v. Virginia State Bar* [171] a minimum fee schedule for lawyers enforced by the state bar association was challenged as a price–fixing agreement in violation of § 1. Chief Justice Burger, writing for the Court, held that professional services come within the Sherman Act and that the minimum fee schedule was an illegal price–fixing scheme:

> The nature of an occupation, standing alone, does not provide sanctuary from the Sherman Act, nor is the public service aspect of professional practice controlling in determining whether § 1 includes professions . . . . Congress intended to strike as broadly as it could in § 1 of the Sherman Act, and to read into it so wide an exception as that urged on us would be at odds with that purpose. [172]

But the Court added a statement that foreshadowed a rule of reason analysis for professional organizations when the restraint was in the public interest:

> [T]he fact that a restraint operates upon a profession as distinguished from a business is, of course, relevant in determining whether that particular restraint violates the Sherman Act. It would be unrealistic to view the practice of professions as interchangeable with other business activities, and automatically to apply to the professions antitrust concepts which originated in other areas. The public service aspect, and other features of the professions, may require that a particular practice, which could properly be viewed as a violation of the Sherman Act in another context, be treated differently. [173]

Implicitly, the Court seemed to say that it would balance and perhaps accommodate noneconomic interests and policies when professional conduct was under scrutiny. But the Court also concluded that the minimum fee schedule was a "naked agreement," language generally used to connote *per se* illegality.

The next case to address the issue was *National Society of Professional Engineers v. United States*, [174] in which the Court rejected a broad reading of the *Goldfarb* dictum. While sharing *Goldfarb*'s differential tone for professional conduct, including a statement that "professional services may differ significantly from other business services, and, accordingly the nature of the competition in such services may vary," [175] the Court nevertheless found the ban–on–bidding practice by engineers to be anticompetitive. The Court, however, observed that "[e]thical norms may serve to regulate and promote . . . competition and thus fall within the Rule of Reason." [176] But

---

[171] 421 U.S. 773 (1975).

[172] *Id.* at 787.

[173] *Id.* at n.17.

[174] 435 U.S. 679 (1978).

[175] *Id.* at 696.

[176] *Id. See also Tripoli Co. v. Wella Corp.*, 425 F.2d 932 (3d Cir. 1970) (*en banc*), where the court upheld restraints on marketing related to product safety, provided they were ancillary to the seller's main purpose of protecting the public from harm or itself from product liability.

because the ban on competitive bidding reduced competition and increased price, the Court was unwilling to accept the defense that the competition itself was unreasonable. Thus, the Court applied a focused rule of reason that balanced market factors as means to determine the competitive consequences. But the Court found no offsetting competitive features since the canon of ethics actually suppressed competition rather than promoted it. Hence the practice was declared illegal.

Professional Engineers portended a more willing acceptance of the rule of reason approach when professional conduct is challenged. However, judicial discretion is limited to weighing the competitive effects; the net consequences must be procompetitive before the practice will be declared legal.

Professional Engineers raised the question whether *per se* condemnations might ever be applied to professional conduct. The answer was forthcoming in *Arizona v. Maricopa County Medical Society*[177] in which doctors were charged with establishing a maximum fee schedule on insurance reimbursement plans. In applying a *per se* test, the Supreme Court reasoned that the doctors did not argue that the quality of the public service they provided would be enhanced by reason of the price restraint, or that the restraint was necessary because of ethical considerations. Thus the conduct fell out of rule of reason protection. The economic investigation of weighing the competitive benefits and harms, which was central to *Professional Engineers*, ends once inferences are drawn that the challenged practice is a price–fixing agreement.

In *FTC v. Indiana Federation of Dentists*,[178] the Court, under § 5 of the FTC Act, held that a concerted refusal by dentists to provide X–rays to insurance companies for reimbursement approval should be examined under the rule of reason because the dentists had argued that the refusal to deal (group boycott) was based on an ethical and moral policy designed to enhance the patients' welfare through quality dental care. But once the Court began to weigh the competitive factors, it concluded, that the boycott was no more than a scheme to protect the price the dentists charged to the patient — precisely the justification rejected in *Professional Engineers*. The insurance requirement of submitting X–rays was designed to reduce the marginal costs of providing insurance in the dental services market. The effect of the boycott was to impair this mechanism.[179]

Similarly, in *Superior Court Trial Lawyers Association v. Federal Trade Commission*,[180] the Court held that a horizontal arrangement among lawyers to withhold the supply of legal services and thereby increase hourly wage rates represented a "naked restraint" on price and output. In *Superior Court Trial Lawyers*, a group of private–practice lawyers, pursuant to a

[177] 457 U.S. 332 (1982).

[178] 476 U.S. 447, 458–59 (1986).

[179] *Id.* at 457.

[180] 493 U.S. 411 (1990).

well–publicized plan, agreed not to represent indigent criminal defendants in the District of Columbia Superior Court until the city government increased the lawyers' hourly compensation.[181]

The lawyers refusal to accept new appointments until their hourly wages increased had dramatic effects on the criminal justice system. Convinced that the system was on the brink of collapse, key figures within the District of Columbia's criminal justice system advocated a temporary increase in hourly wages — an increase that was subsequently authorized by the city council. The FTC, however, filed suit against the lawyers, alleging that the boycott constituted an unfair method of competition in violation of § 5 of the Federal Trade Commission Act.

In evaluating the requisite conduct, the Court commented that although there was a political impact, the means employed (the boycott) to obtain the more favorable legislation was economic, rather than political in nature. In the end, it was clear that the goal of the lawyers was to raise the price of legal services to indigent clients. Thus the means employed, as well as the objective of the agreement, was economic in nature. Said the Court:

> The effectiveness of price–fixing agreements is dependent upon many factors, such as competitive tactics, position in the industry, the formula underlying pricing policies. Whatever economic justification particular price–fixing agreements may be thought to have, the law does not permit an inquiry into their reasonableness.[182] Because the lawyers' only goal was a salary increase, and they failed to also advance an ethical norm or compelling public interest, the Court found the boycott conduct illegal on its face.

Finally, in *Massachusetts School of Law at Andover v. American Bar Assoc.*,[183] the Third Circuit quickly rejected the plaintiff's argument for a *per se* analysis. At issue was certain provisions in the ABA's standards for accreditation, particularly the provision calling for a consideration of faculty salaries before granting accreditation. The court felt that, although the practice somewhat resembled price–affecting conduct, a rule of reason analysis was still appropriate. Citing *Indiana Federation of Dentists*, the court explained that the Supreme Court is " 'slow to condemn rules adopted by professional societies as unreasonable *per se*,' even when the behavior resembles conduct usually subject to a *per se* approach."[184] Thus, the Third Circuit chose to follow the Supreme Court's lead in this regard and apply a rule of reason analysis.

An attempt to reconcile the six professional conduct cases leads to the following rules. If a defense is asserted that the challenged practice

---

[181] *Id.* at 413. "Although over 1,200 lawyers [were] registered for District of Columbia Criminal Justice Act Appointments, relatively few applied for such work on a regular basis. In 1982, most appointments went to approximately 100 lawyers who derive almost all of their income from representing indigents." *Id.* at 415.

[182] *Id.* at 435 *citing United States v. Socony–Vacuum Oil Co.*, 310 U.S. 150 (1940).

[183] 107 F.3d 1026 (3d. Cir. 1997).

[184] *Id.* at 1033 (*citing Indiana Fed'n.*, 476 U.S. 447, 458 (1986)).

promotes a public interest (quality) or an ethical norm, the Court will apply a structured rule of reason.[185] The second step is to determine whether it also promotes competition. If the result is procompetitive, the conduct is legal. But if the conduct interferes directly with price and no public interest or ethical norm is asserted in its defense the practice may be condemned unlawful under the *per se* classification. Of course, even in the absence of a public interest or ethical justification, the conduct can be legal if its net result enhances the competitive forces in the market.

Note also that the Court now employs the *per se* terminology it is usually a conclusion at the end of the analysis rather than an initial presumption. Only if it is clear from the record that the agreement among professionals is "so plainly anticompetitive that no elaborate study of [its effects] is needed to establish [its] illegality" may a court properly make a *per se* judgment. The *per se* label should not be assigned without carefully considering substantial benefits and procompetitive justifications."[186]

§ 4.10   Trade Association and Data Dissemination Activity

Horizontal restraints can be created by exchanges of commercial information among competitors. The clearinghouse for such industry data is generally a trade association, but the exchange also can occur between individual firms within an industry. The mere exchange of data concerning prices, output, inventories, production quotas and supply levels may have effects on price. The competitive consequences will depend on the structure of industry, the nature of the information exchanged and how the firms respond to the data exchanged. The mere exchange of price information, however, is not unlawful.[187]

In fact, price sharing can be a logical and helpful activity to stimulate competiton. In *Wallace v. Bank of Bartlett,*[188] the defendant argued, and

---

[185] For an example of a circuit court applying the rule of reason to a case in which the "quality control" defense was implicit, *see Sanjuan v. American Bd. of Psychiatry & Neurology, Inc.*, 40 F.3d 247 (7th Cir. 1995).

See also National Assoc. of Review Appraisers & Mortgage Underwriters, Inc. v. Appraisal Foundation, 64 F.3d 1130, 1134 n.2 (8th Cir. 1995) (holding that the defendant's behavior should be examined under a rule of reason analysis after the court considered "relevant economic structures and market forces").

[186] *Prof'l Eng'rs*, 435 U.S. at 692. In *Palmer v. BRG of Georgia, Inc.*, 498 U.S. 46 (1990), however, a case involving the professional training of lawyers, the Supreme Court reaffirmed a rule of *per se* illegality for horizontal market divisions between competitors irrespective of whether the competitors had previously competed in the same market. In addition, the Court reaffirmed that a combination formed for the purpose and with the effect of raising, depressing, fixing, pegging, or stabilizing the price of a commodity in interstate or foreign commerce is illegal per se. Reference *supra* notes 85–94 and accompanying text; *see also National Ass'n of Review Appraisers & Mortgage Underwriters, Inc., v. Apprisal Found.*, 64 F.3d 1130, 1134 n.2 (8th Cir. 1985).

[187] *Sugar Inst., Inc. v. United States*, 297 U.S. 553 (1936). *Sugar Institute* indicates that the relationship between the communication and a price–fixing agreement must be more than merely incidental before the price exchange can be enjoined. *See* Sullivan, *First Amendment Defenses In Antitrust Litigation*, 46 Mo. L. Rev. 517 (1981).

[188] 55 F.3d 1166 (6th Cir. 1995).

the court agreed, that it is natural for banks to survey the rates charged by their competitors for overdrawn accounts "in order to make strategic competitive decisions."[189] Hence, although price sharing can lead to a violation of § 1, plaintiffs must do more than simply present evidence of price evaluation among competitors.

Professor Areeda emphasizes that one must always find a motive to conspire before speculating on the potential § 1 implications of shared information.[190] This helps answer the core question in any price–sharing inquiry —"whether a conspiracy to deal concertedly with the plaintiff can be inferred from the price–exchange."[191]

The forming of a trade association, of course, is a "combination" within the meaning of § 1 of Sherman Act.[192] The remaining question is whether the activities of the trade association unreasonably restrain trade. Trade associations do engage in lawful and productive activities that can enhance competition as, for example: exchange of information on the availability of raw materials, advancement of technology through the sharing of product innovation, promotion of the industry through institutional advertising and promotion of the standardization of certain products. But when the exchange affects price, even indirectly, antitrust laws are implicated.

Because of the ambiguous or uncertain consequences of an exchange, courts generally apply a rule of reason analysis. They analyze the structure of the industry, including market power of the firms engaged in the exchange, the effect of the exchange and the purpose underlying the exchange.

In *American Column Lumber Co. v. United States*[193] the Supreme Court was unsympathetic to a trade association that required its members to make daily reports, subject to audits, on sales, purchases, production, and to require immediate reporting on any price changes. Speeches and memoranda were circulated among the members stressing the danger of overproduction. Discussions followed regarding restrictions on output and price maintenance. Even though the association membership represented only 33% of the industry production, there was evidence of actual increases in price. The Court found that the "purpose and effect were to restrict production and to encourage members to unite in pressing for higher and higher prices."[194] It observed that the extensive interchange of reports, supplemented by monthly meetings, certainly constituted a combination

---

[189] *Id.* at 1169.

[190] VI P.E. Areeda *Antitrust Law*, ¶ 1423 (1986).

[191] *Id.*

[192] However, *see Alvord–Polk, Inc. v. F. Schumacher & Co.*, 37 F.3d 996, 1007–08 (3d Cir. 1994), where the court held that a trade association is capable of conspiring within itself, but only if it acts as an "entity." The court added that a full examination of the facts and circumstances may be necessary in such an instance, since "concerted action does not exist every time a trade association member speaks or acts." *Id.*

[193] 257 U.S. 377 (1921).

[194] *Id.* at 407.

through which agreements, actual or implied, could readily be arrived at and maintained.

Specifically, the Court in *American Column* disapproved of a trade association soliciting views of members as to future market conditions, including production estimates and analyses which suggested price levels and production limits. But the exchange of past, closed transaction prices was sanctioned.

Several years later, in *Maple Flooring Manufacturing Ass'n v. United States*,[195] the Court upheld a data exchange plan where the exchange of statistical data included only past prices and other data in summary, average or aggregate form and which did not identify individual customers. The information also was fully available to customers of the trade association members, the public, and all buyers and sellers in the industry. Defendants controlled 70% of total production, but the Court reasoned that it was important that there be a free exchange of ideas and knowledge of the competitive factors. The Court observed that information exchanges increase the likelihood of rational competition, even though this market fell short of perfect competition. No evidence of price stabilization was found, even though the dissemination of market data could lead to this result.

More recently, in *Stephen Jay Photography, Ltd. v. Olan Mills, Inc.*,[196] the Fourth Circuit rejected the plaintiff photographer's claim of an illegal price sharing agreement between two other high school yearbook photographers who had one hundred percent of the market combined. The court held, "The fact that the price information about one company is found in a competitor's files or an employee reports a competitor's pricing policy to his home office and the two companies charge similar prices for their products, without more, cannot support an inference that the two competitors entered into an agreement to share prices."[197] The court found the plaintiff's price sharing theory to have no merit because he offered no proof which suggested the defendants had not acted independently.[198] In fact, the evidence showed that one had secured the information without the knowledge of the other.

A review of the important Supreme Court cases on data dissemination indicates that the Court is inclined to approve an exchange of *past* data in summary or aggregate form which do not disclose individual transactions or customers, (1) where there is no disclosure of present or future information, (2) where there are no enforcement or coercive mechanisms that pressure the membership, (3) where the data are available to nonmembers for reasonable fees, or at least to those that have a "commercial need to know" or would be at a competitive disadvantage without the information,

---

[195] 268 U.S. 563 (1925). *See also United States v. American Linseed Oil Co., 262 U.S. 371 (1923)*.

[196] 903 F.2d 988 (4th Cir. 1990).

[197] *Id*. at 996.

[198] *Id*.

and (4) where the market structure of the industry suggests that it is not highly concentrated or tending towards collusion.[199]

As discussed above, the structure of the industry can inform our thinking about the competitive significance of an exchange among competitors of commercial information. The less concentrated the market, the more the exchange can be procompetitive. The more market information that is available to competitors the greater the chance that allocative efficiency (sellers producing products desired by consumers in appropriate quantities) will be enhanced. When buyers and sellers have a wide variety of available market information they buy and sell at the lowest prices, thereby promoting efficiency and competition in the market. Conversely, as *United States v. Container Corp. of America*[200] teaches, the more concentrated a market is, the more predisposed it is toward collusive stabilization of prices when there is a price exchange. In both *Container* and *United States v. U.S. Gypsum Co.*[201] the Supreme Court's analytical focus shifted from a review of the purpose of the exchange to a prediction of the probable price consequences of the exchange given a certain market structure.

Container was the Court's first explicit recognition that market structure may effect price exchanges. Economic theory suggests that the vigor of competition in a market is related positively to the number of firms in the relevant industry. In a market dominated by a few sellers, with a product which is homogeneous and fungible, price exchanges may tend to stabilize prices.[202] A highly concentrated market, or oligopoly, may exhibit interdependence among the firms in the market — sellers taking into account pricing and output decisions of each competitor before any price changes are undertaken.[203]

Container accepted the theory that coordinated behavior may facilitate anticompetitive consequences, and it inferred anticompetitive conduct from the market structure. Market structure was thus critical to predicting market behavior. In *Container* there was only a moderate degree of concentration, cross–elasticity of demand existed among products, market entry was easy, and the market was characterized by over–capacity.[204] The

---

[199] The Ninth Circuit noted two situations where the exchange of price information would help to establish whether an antitrust violation had occurred. *In re Coordinated Pretrial Proceedings in Petroleum Prods Antitrust Litig.*, 906 F.2d 432 (9th Cir. 1990). Where "the exchange indicates the existence of an express or tacit agreement to fix or stabilize prices, or the exchange is made pursuant to an express or tacit agreement that is itself a violation of § 1 under a rule of reason analysis," price sharing becomes a more valuable piece of evidence for the plaintiff. *Id.* at 447 n.13.

[200] 393 U.S. 333 (1969). *But see Cement Mfrs. Protective Ass'n. v. United States*, 268 U.S. 588 (1925).

[201] 438 U.S. 422 (1978).

[202] 393 U.S. at 337.

[203] Turner, *The Definition of Agreement Under the Sherman Act: Conscious Parallelism and Refusal to Deal*, 75 Harv. L. Rev. 655 (1962). As the Court said in *Container*: "Price information exchanged in some markets may have no effect on a truly competitive price . . . . The exchange of price data tends toward price uniformity" in oligopolistic markets. 393 U.S. at 337.

[204] 393 U.S. at 336–37; *see generally* L. Sullivan, *Handbook of the Law of Antitrust* 272

Court, nevertheless, found the conclusion "irresistible that the exchange of price information . . . had an anticompetitive effect."[205] A *per se* rule of illegality was suggested.

In two subsequent cases,[206] including *Gypsum*, the Court explicitly rejected a *per se* approach when employing a market structure analysis: "[t]he exchange of price data and other information among competitors does not invariably have anticompetitive effects; indeed such practices can in certain circumstances increase economic efficiency and render markets more, rather than less, competitive."[207] Interseller price communications, therefore, are regulated on a rule of reason basis.

§ 4.11   Joint Ventures

Similar in many respects to a trade association is a joint venture. The leading cases[208] on point have been discussed above, but at this point a brief overview of the major antitrust issues is in order.

By definition, a joint venture is the formation of a single entity by two or more independent firms for the purpose of engaging in research, production or marketing activities. The joint conduct may be of the type that either firm is capable of carrying out individually or, because of its nature, could not be undertaken if the firms acted separately.

Firms engage in joint ventures for numerous reasons — some lawful, some not. Benefits that may flow from joint ventures include increased productivity and competition. By joining skills, spreading risks, achieving certain economics of scale, and reducing transaction costs, the joint firm may be more efficient and willing to undertake research or production. "The combined capital, assets, or know–how of two companies may facilitate entry into new markets and thereby enhance competition, or may create efficiencies or new productive capacity unachievable by either alone."[209]

However, the costs associated with joint ventures include the potential for price fixing, output restrictions, market divisions, and increased monopoly power. The venture may include as members competitors, potential

---

(1977). Eighteen defendants accounted for 90% of the corrugated container production in the particular geographical region. Defendants agreed to exchange current price information on request; no other conduct was challenged.

205 393 U.S. at 337.

206 *United States v. Citizens & Southern National Bank*, 422 U.S. 86 (1975); *United States v. United States Gypsum Co.*, 438 U.S. 422 (1978).

207 438 U.S. at 441 n.16.

208 A joint venture may be challenged under either § 1 of the Sherman Act or § 7 of the Clayton Act. *United States v. Addyston Pipe*, 85 F. 271 (6th Cir. 1898), *aff'd*, 175 U.S. 211 (1899); *Chicago Bd. of Trade v. United States*, 256 U.S. 231 (1918); *Appalachian Coals, Inc. v. United States*, 288 U.S. 344 (1933); *Associated Press v. United States*, 326 U.S. 1 (1945); *Broadcast Music, Inc. v. Columbia Broad. Sys.*, 441 U.S. 1 (1979); *National Collegiate Athletic Association v. Board of Regents*, 468 U.S. 85 (1984); *Polk Bros., Inc. v. Forest City Enters., Inc.*, 776 F.2d 185 (7th Cir. 1986).

209 *In re Brunswick Corp.* 94 F.T.C. 1174, 1265 (1979), *aff'd sub. nom., Yamaha Motor Co. v. FTC*, 657 F.2d 971 (2d Cir. 1981).

competitors, or those in a vertical relationship. The potential is substantial that competition may be reduced if such firms are permitted to join as a single entity. But the benefits may be great as well. Thus we are concerned, from an antitrust perspective, with not only the creation[210] but also with the continuing nature of the venture: Will it reduce competition between the members? To what extent does the venture control the competitive activities of its members? Will they remain significant competitors in the market? The purpose and effect of the venture are the core of our analysis.

Because joint ventures have the potential of producing benefits as well as costs, courts analyze them under the rule of reason. They attempt to weigh the economic efficiencies against the actual costs of the venture. The cases reveal a spectrum of antitrust scrutiny. The more "pure" research oriented the venture the more likely it is lawful. Research and development are key to productivity and competition, and in most industries both can be expensive and risky if undertaken individually. As the venture moves toward production, and certainly into marketing, more serious antitrust concerns are implicated. Joint price and output decisions may be undertaken. Collusion and cartel behavior may result. Restraints involving the use of the results may be more than ancillary or benign.

Courts begin their analysis with an inquiry into the nature (whether research, production or marketing) of the joint venture and whether the actual creation was lawful, especially in purpose. They consider, in addition, the joint venturers and the competitive relationship, or lack thereof, of the members of the venture. Direct competitors who join together in a joint venture have a greater potential for anticompetitive conduct than other relationships. The industry is surveyed with a view towards how much market power is held by the members of the venture. Joint ventures within concentrated markets are scrutinized more carefully.

Finally, courts analyze the restraints imposed on the joint venturers in scope and duration, and determine whether they are reasonably necessary to achieve the benefits of the venture or whether they are overbroad. A venture which is broad in scope and lengthy in time is more problematic.[211]

If the collateral restrictions include price agreements, output limitations, market divisions, customer allocations or refusals to deal, they probably will be declared *per se* unlawful. But if the restraints are merely ancillary to an otherwise lawful agreement,[212] and limited in scope and duration to that reasonably necessary to achieve the goals of the project, they will be held lawful. The Department of Justice has stated, as an enforcement

---

[210] *Citizen Publ'g Co. v. United States*, 394 U.S. 131 (1969) (when formation found illegal); *United States v. Sealy, Inc.* 388 U.S. 350 (1967); *Hawaii Newspaper Agency v. Bronster*, 103 F.3d 742 (9th Cir. 1996).

[211] *See generally, U.S. Department of Justice Antitrust Guide Concerning Joint Ventures* (Dec. 4, 1980). *See also* Brodley, *The Legal Status of Joint Ventures Under the Antitrust Laws: A Summary Assessment*, 21 Antitrust Bull. 453 (1976); Brodley, *Joint Ventures and Antitrust Policy*, 95 Harv. L. Rev. 1521 (1982).

[212] *See Polk Bros., Inc. v. Forest City Enters., Inc.*, 776 F.2d 185 (7th Cir. 1986).

policy, that the following collateral restrictions generally are lawful: "the obligation to exchange any results from research undertaken previously in the field of the joint venture, the duty not to disclose results of the joint research to outside parties until patents are obtained, and the division of particular aspects of the research between the venturers."[213]

In short, antitrust is concerned with the joint venture's purpose, effect, restrictions and access. Specifically, the venture should not eliminate competition, at least to the extent that procompetitive benefits are not realized; the collateral restrictions placed on the members and outsiders must be closely related to the venture's essential purpose, limited in scope and duration; and access to the results of the undertaking must be reasonable so as not to raise questions of a concerted refusal to deal.[214]

Recently, the Third Circuit in *International Raw Materials, Ltd. (IRM) v. Stauffer Chemical Co.*,[215] identified four factors which courts generally analyze in determining the existence of a joint venture. Specifically:

(1) whether there is an express or implied agreement that demonstrates the parties' intent to form a partnership or joint venture; (2) whether the parties share a common interest in the subject matter of the joint venture; (3) whether the parties share profits and losses from the venture; and (4) whether the parties have joint control or the joint right of control over the venture.[216]

In *International Raw Materials*, IRM, a terminal operator who loaded products including soda ash[217] into ocean–going vessels, alleged that an association of soda ash producers ("ANSAC")[218] and its members[219] conspired to fix the rates of domestic services for the export of soda ash.[220] In its complaint, IRM alleged that "prior ANSAC's formation, each soda ash producer bargained separately for terminal services" and after its formation, ANSAC negotiated a common rate for all association members.[221] Shortly thereafter, ANSAC entered into a service agreement with

---

[213] *U.S. Department of Justice Antitrust Guide Concerning Joint Ventures* 5 (Dec. 4, 1980).

[214] *United States v. Topco Assoc.*, 405 U.S. 596 (1972). *See generally*, T. Jorde & D. Teece, *Antitrust, Innovation, and Competitiveness* (1992); T. Jorde & D. Teece, *Innovation and Cooperation Implications for Competition and Antitrust*, 4 J. Econ. Persp. 75 (1990); Kattan, *Antitrust Analysis of Technology Joint Ventures: Allocative Efficiency and the Rewards of Innovation*, 61 Antitrust L.J. 937 (1993).

[215] 978 F.2d 1318 (3d. Cir. 1992).

[216] *Id.* at 1332 *citing* Harry G. Henn & John R. Alexander, *Laws of Corporations* 106 (3d ed. 1983).

[217] Soda ash is primarily used in making glass. *Id.* at 1320 n.1.

[218] All but one of the soda ash producers who comprise the American National Soda Ash Corporation (ANSAC) is either owned, in full or part, or affiliated with a major foreign corporation." *Id.* at 1320.

[219] Association members include the Stauffer Chemical Co., TG Soda Ash, Chemical General Partners, Tenneco Minerals, Kerr–McGee, and the FMC Wyoming Corp. *Id.* at n.2.

[220] *Id.* at 1320.

[221] *Id.*

IRM's competitor, Hall–Buck, Inc. The agreement provided for a specified shipping quantity at rates substantially lower than IRM's in exchange for an option to acquire a 50% share of a newly constructed terminal. This arrangement, IRM alleged, "restrained trade and depressed competition in the business of terminal services."[222] In response, ANSAC petitioned the district court for summary judgment claiming antitrust immunity under the Webb–Pomerene Act.[223]

On appeal,[224] the Third Circuit held that the Webb–Pomerene Act did, in fact, authorize such an arrangement. "Even assuming ANSAC [receives] subsidized rates, it [did] not enter into a risk sharing agreement in relation to the losses or potential losses of the terminal". Absent an agreement to apportion losses or potential losses, the relationship does not amount to a joint venture" and, therefore, is not beyond the scope of the Webb–Pomerene Act.[225]

The Tenth Circuit reversed a finding of a violation of § 1 by a joint venture in *SCFC ILC, Inc. v. Visa USA, Inc.*[226] The court began by admitting that the line between conduct necessitating *per se* analysis and that requiring rule of reason analysis "especially blur[s]" when joint venture's are involved, since, in those cases, "competitive incentives between independent firms are intentionally restrained and their functions and operations integrated to achieve efficiencies and increase output."[227] Visa USA is a joint venture between Visa and MasterCard. The facts of the case dealt with Visa USA's refusal to accept the plaintiff Sears and its Discover Card's application for membership. The court did not read Supreme Court precedent as requiring anything but the usual application of rule of reason analysis to joint ventures.[228] Hence, upon review of the facts under the rule of reason, the court found the defendants did not violate the Sherman or Clayton Acts.

The court first inquired into whether Visa USA had the requisite level of market power to "facilitate the determination that the practice harms competition and not simply a single competitor."[229] The court divided the

---

[222] *Id.* at 1322.

[223] "[T]he Webb–Pomerene Act permits associations to form export cartels without fear of suit under the Sherman Act, provided they do not restrain domestic trade in the good or product they export, or hinder the export trade of domestic competitors that are not members of the association." *Id.* at 1323 *citing* 15 U.S.C. § 62 (1988). For a further discussion of the Webb–Pomerene Act and export association immunity, reference *supra*, § 3.05.

[224] Following the district court's approval of defendants motion, IRM appealed to the U.S. Court of Appeals for the Third Circuit. Commenting that "a more complete factual record" was required before a determination of Webb–Pomerene immunity could be made, the Third Circuit reversed and remanded. After additional discovery was conducted and IRM filed an amended complaint, the association renewed its motion for summary judgment which was subsequently granted by the trial court.

[225] *Id.* at 1332.

[226] 36 F.3d 958 (10th Cir. 1994). One of the authors served as counsel in this case.

[227] *Id.* at 963.

[228] *Id.* at 964–65.

[229] *Id.* at 965.

relevant market into intra–and intersystem subparts. Discover ranked second in intrasystem competition.[230] It is defined as the market in which individual card issuers, whether they be members of Visa USA or not, compete for customers.[231] The intersystem market, on the other hand, is defined as "the competition among the manufacturers of the same generic product."[232] The court held there to be 5 relevant competitors in this market, with Visa USA holding 45.6%, MasterCard (Visa USA's joint venture partner) at 26.4%, American Express at 20.5%, Discover with 5.5%, and Diner's Club with 2%.[233] Although it appeared that Visa USA had market power in the intersystem market, the relevant market in the case was the issuer or intrasystem market, where Visa USA did not have market power.

The court then rejected the contention that Visa USA's ability to make rules calling for collective activity between Visa USA and MasterCard suggested market power and the possibility for a § 1 violation. "A joint venture made more efficient by ancillary restraints is a fusion of the productive capabilities of the members of the venture."[234] The court stated that the effect of the rules, not the simple act of making them, was the relevant inquiry when delving into issues of market power.[235] As such, upon reviewing the facts, Visa USA could not be said to possess the requisite market power. The exclusion of Sears, the parent corporation of Discover Card, from the joint venture also "did not alter the character of the general purpose credit card market or change any present pattern of distribution," thus showing that there were no anticompetitive effects on the market, either.[236]

The common law principles discussed here have their roots in the 1918 *Chicago Board of Trade*[237] opinion written by Justice Brandeis. There a broad rule of reason was sanctioned for joint ventures. It was continued through the depression period in *Appalachian Coals*.[238] That same approach continues today, although perhaps more focused or limited, as illustrated in the recent *BMI*[239] and *NCAA*[240] cases. Even in the face of

---

[230] Discover Card was found to be the second largest in terms of charge volume or amount owed on cards. "Citicorp's [charge volume] is 21.9% in the relevant market, while that of Sears Discover Card is 5%." *Id.* at 967. These figures are not indicative of market power for either Citicorp or Discover Card in the intra–system/issuer market.

[231] *Id.* at 967.

[232] *Id.* at 966 (citation omitted).

[233] *Id.* at 967.

[234] *Id.* at 968 (*quoting Rothery Storage v. Atlas Van Lines*, 792 F.2d 210, 230 (D.C. Cir. 1986)).

[235] *Id.*

[236] *Id.* at 971.

[237] 246 U.S. 231 (1918).

[238] 288 U.S. 344 (1933).

[239] 441 U.S. 1 (1979).

[240] 468 U.S. 85 (1984).

price restraints and output limitations, the Court has been willing to weigh the anticompetitive costs against the procompetitive benefits in determining whether the net consequences are procompetitive. If procompetitive justifications are outweighed by the restraints imposed, the joint venture will be declared illegal. The ancillary restraint doctrine also has played a major analytical role in determining the legality of joint ventures. From *Addyston Pipe* in 1898[241] to *Polk Brothers* in 1986,[242] courts have been receptive to restraints which are only ancillary to an otherwise lawful objective, as long as they are limited in scope and duration.

In 1984 Congress passed the National Cooperative Research Act (NCRA) which was intended to encourage procompetitive joint research. Among other provisions, the statute detrebles antitrust liability, and allows prevailing defendants to recover attorney's fees and costs attributable to frivolous suits. In order to come within the Act, parties must give notification to the Department of Justice and the FTC of the intended venture by identifying the parties and the nature and goals of the undertaking. Moreover, a "reasonableness" standard is incorporated into the Act.[243]

In 1993, the NCRA was significantly expanded with the enactment of the National Cooperative Production Amendments Act (NCPA).[244] Similar to the 1984 Act, the new law limits antitrust damage exposure to actual, single damages for qualifying production joint ventures, requires a voluntary notification procedure, and employs a rule of reason analysis to assess the alleged restraint. Contrary to the 1984 Act, however, the new statute requires that a qualifying production joint venture must locate its principal production facilities in the United States or its territories. Furthermore, except for the product manufactured by the joint venture, marketing and distribution agreements are excluded from the immunity.

§ 4.12   Maximum Price–Fixing Schemes

Until recently, the Supreme Court has not drawn distinctions between agreements that fix maximum or minimum prices; both are illegal. In *Kiefer–Stewart Co. v. Joseph E. Seagram & Sons, Inc.*,[245] Justice Black, writing for the Court, said that maximum prices "no less than those to fix minimum prices, cripple the freedom of traders and thereby restrain their ability to sell in accordance with their own judgment . . . . 'Under the Sherman Act a combination formed for the purpose and with the effect of raising, fixing, pegging, or stabilizing the price of a commodity . . . is illegal *per se*.' "[246]

---

[241] 85 F. 271 (6th Cir. 1898), *aff'd*, 175 U.S. 211 (1899).

[242] 776 F.2d 185 (7th Cir. 1986).

[243] *See* Pub. L. 98–462, 15 U.S.C. §§ 4301–05.

[244] *See* Pub. L. 103–42, 107 Stat 117.

[245] 340 U.S. 211 (1951).

[246] *Id.* at 213 (*quoting United States v. Socony–Vacuum Oil Co.*, 310 U.S. 150, 223 (1940)).

Faithful to this *per se* approach, the Court more recently in *Maricopa* [247] held that the *per se* rule "is grounded on faith in price competition as a market force [and not] on a policy of low selling prices at the price of eliminating competition." [248] The Court found that the evils inherent in maximum price agreements include the fact that such conduct might discourage market entry and deter research and development by entrepreneurs because the maximum price may be too low to create incentives for entry or product development or service. Further, the Court was concerned that a maximum price might masquerade for an agreement to fix uniform or minimum prices.

The Court in *Maricopa* and in *Albrecht v. Herald Co.* [249] rejected procompetitive justifications for the restraint. Said the *Maricopa* Court,

> The anticompetitive potential inherent in all price–fixing agreements justifies their facial invalidation even if procompetitive justifications are offered for some. Those claims of enhanced competition are so unlikely to prove significant in any particular case that we adhere to the rule of law that is justified in its general application. [250]

Not all antitrust commentators agree, however, that maximum price fixing should be characterized under the *per se* label. [251] If one accepts Justice Black's rationale, that it is *per se* illegal because it interferes with free and independent decisionmaking in the market thereby restraining traders' freedom, then the *per se* characterization is complete once the "agreement" is established. But if one views more broadly the purposes underlying the Sherman Act, such as whether the agreement benefits consumers and enhances overall competition, then a rule of reason is necessary to undertake a harm–benefit analysis. Several examples inform our thinking on this point.

What the Court in fact did in *Maricopa* was to undertake a structured rule of reason analysis; it weighed the purpose and effect of the maximum price fixing agreement (to reduce costs of medical services) before it reached its conclusion that the arrangement lacked offsetting procompetitive effects. It was declared *per se* illegal. Second, the economic learning suggests that the maximum price fixing in *Maricopa* probably was not, as the Court surmised, really nothing more than a disguised agreement "to fix minimum or uniform price." [252] If it were a price (fee) below which the subscribing doctors could not go, why would the insurance company, really the buyer of the services (the proxy for the patient), agree? Insurance companies generally want to reduce transaction costs and prices of services to their

---

[247] 457 U.S. 332 (1982); *see supra* § 4.07. *See also Albrecht v. Herald Co.*, 390 U.S. 145 (1968), *overruled by State Oil Co. v. Khan*, 522 U.S. 3 (1997).

[248] 457 U.S. at 146, *quoting* Rahl, *Price Competition and the Price–Fixing Rule — Preface and Perspective*, 57 Nw. U. L. Rev. 137, 142 (1962).

[249] 390 U.S. 145 (1968).

[250] 457 U.S. at 351.

[251] *See generally* Easterbrook, *Maximum Price Fixing*, 48 U. Chi. L. Rev. 886 (1981).

[252] 457 U.S. at 348.

customers. An agreement to enter such an arrangement would make little economic or business sense from the standpoint of the insurance company (the buyer of the service). A strict *per se* rule would foreclose this kind of searching analysis.

In *Albrecht*, a vertical price–fixing case, a newspaper wanted to restrict the price at which the home delivery service could distribute newspapers for fear that the dealers were charging a monopoly price given their market power in the home delivery market. The maximum price restriction would have benefitted both the newspaper (increased output due to increased demand) and customers (lower prices) at the expense of the monopoly dealer (lower profits). The *Albrecht* Court adhered to the *Kiefer–Stewart* rationale:

> Maximum and minimum price fixing may have different consequences in many situations. But schemes to fix maximum prices, by substituting the perhaps erroneous judgment of a seller for the forces of the competitive market, may severely intrude upon the ability of buyers to compete and survive in that market . . . . Maximum prices may be fixed too low for the dealer to furnish services and conveniences which consumers desire and for which they are willing to pay. Maximum price fixing may channel distribution through a few large or specifically advantaged dealers who otherwise would be subject to significant nonprice competition.[253]

The Court in *Maricopa* recognized, however, that while the legal rule for maximum price fixing should be on the same "legal footing" as for minimum price fixing, the economic rationale is different.[254]

In *Atlantic Richfield v. USA Petoleum Co.*,[255] the Court excused a vertical maximum price–fixing scheme from punishment under the Sherman Act. The Court admitted the maximum price fixing was *per se* illegal in the same manner as minimum price fixing because of its tendency to inhibit competition.[256] However the Court remanded the case because the plaintiff could not prove any adverse direct effects upon itself or the market due to defendant's activities. In effect, the Court reasoned that the plaintiff was only damaged to the extent it could not *raise* prices. Because the plaintiff had neither proof of antitrust injury nor proof that the pricing scheme set up by the defendants was either predatory or determined by collusion, the defendants were allowed to continue setting the maximum price for Atlantic Richfield gasoline.

In 1997, the Supreme Court overturned *Albrecht* when it ruled in *State Oil v. Kahn*[257] that vertical maximum price–fixing schemes are no longer *per se* illegal, but rather should be analyzed under a rule of reason because by their nature they are not always anticompetitive and are frequently

---

[253] *Id*. at 347.

[254] *Id*. at 348.

[255] 495 U.S. 328 (1990).

[256] *Id*. at 335.

[257] 522 U.S. 3 (1997).

procompetitive. The *Khan* Court questioned the logic, particularly the economic reasoning, that had supported a *per se* approach to price–fixing agreements.[258]

In contrast to maximum price fixing, few doubt that an agreement to fix a minimum price is the most pernicious and anticompetitive trade restraint. It repeatedly has been declared *per se* illegal because it interferes with the lowering of price by normal market forces of supply and demand. Indeed, the minimum price may be set too high (*i.e.*, above marginal costs) thus preventing competitive forces from driving it down. The Court's reasoning in both *Trenton Potteries*[259] and *Socony*[260] seems to have settled this issue. *Goldfarb*[261] reached the same conclusion, although the fact that professionals engaged in the restraint caused the Court to be more circumspect in its analysis.[262]

§ 4.13   Concerted Refusals to Deal

Arrangements through which firms refuse to deal with or isolate another firm can be anticompetitive. Collective agreements may be designed to limit competition either by creating entry barriers or facilitating market exits. When the agreement is between competitors, it is a horizontal restraint known as a group boycott or a concerted refusal to deal.

Several examples are illustrative. Firms at one level of competition may refuse to deal with a supplier or customer that deals with a competitor of the agreeing firms. The trade pressure may force the vertical partner to cease doing business with the target in order to retain the business of the target's competitor. Or a firm at one level (retailer) may enter an agreement with a firm at another level (supplier) to refuse to deal with a competitor of the retailer.[263]

The first example is a horizontal agreement (between competitors) aimed at a competitor or a potential competitor; it is known as a secondary boycott and is classified as a concerted refusal to deal. The second arrangement is between noncompeting firms in a vertical relationship aimed at a target in competition with at least one of the conspirators; the effect is horizontal, although the agreement is not. Courts generally analyze the objectives and effects of the agreement and the market power of the firms engaged in the concerted conduct before drawing a conclusion whether the agreement is reasonable or *per se* illegal. It is important to remember that, even if an

---

[258] This is discussed more fully in Chapter 5 on Vertical Restraints.

[259] *United States v. Trenton Potteries Co.*, 273 U.S. 392 (1927).

[260] *United States v. Socony–Vacuum Oil Co.*, 310 U.S. 150 (1940).

[261] *Goldfarb v. Virginia State Bar*, 421 U.S. 773 (1975).

[262] *See supra* § 4.09.

[263] For an example of an antritrust claim that as brought under the first theory but decided upon the second, *see Discon, Inc. v. Nynex Corp.* 93 F.3d 1055, (2d Cir. 1996), *vacated by* 525 U.S. 128 (1998). *See also Center Video Indus. Co., Inc. v. United Media, inc.*, 995 F.2d 735, 736–37 (7th Cir. 1993).

activity is determined to be *per se* illegal, the plaintiff still must prove that the group boycott or anticompetitive behavior led to the plaintiff's specific injury.[264]

The purpose of a boycott may be to punish a maverick price cutter or others not adhering to certain industry standards. It also may be designed to gain market power at the expense of other competitors. Some concerted refusals to deal, however, especially those where the firms are engaged in a joint venture, may enhance efficiency, thus making the market more competitive. Other agreements may be designed to avoid free riders. Once again, the Court's characterization process of the refusal to deal is at the core of the analysis and may preordain the legal conclusion.

Numerous labels or classifications have been assigned to refusals to deal as an attempt to predict or judge the competitive consequence: exclusionary, regulatory or commercial. The standard of analysis and legal conclusions have varied, depending on the court's approach.

In *Eastern State Retail Lumber Dealers' Assn v. United States*[265] the Supreme Court held that a retail lumber trade association violated § 1 of the Sherman Act when it circulated to its members a list of maverick wholesalers who also attempted to sell at retail in competition with the members of the trade association. "The particular thing which this case concerns is the retailers' efforts . . . by the *circulation* of the reports in question, to keep the wholesalers from selling directly to the local trade."[266] The "blacklisting" was a means to insulate the membership from increased price competition at the retail level by new entrants. The aim of the boycott was to affect price and protect the market power of member retailers.

If an individual retailer ceased doing business with a maverick wholesaler, such unilateral conduct would not be violative of § 1, but here the concerted agreement, inferred from the circulation, was unlawful. "An act harmless when done by one may become a public wrong when done by many acting in concert, for it then takes on the form of conspiracy, and may be prohibited or punished, if the result be hurtful to the public or to the individual against whom the concerted action is directed."[267] The natural effect of the circulation would be to cause retailers to boycott the wholesalers engaged in retail businesses.

Eastern States is an example of an exclusionary, commercial, nonregulatory boycott. It established the rule that an agreement by firms at one level of competition (retail) not to deal with firms at another level (suppliers), that also compete on the first level, is an illegal concerted refusal to deal.

---

[264] *Balaklaw v. Lovell*, 14 F.3d 793, 800–01 (2d Cir. 1994). *See also Rebel Oil Co. v. Atlantic Richfield Co.*, 51 F.3d 1421, 1443–44 (9th Cir. 1995). ("*Per se* rules relieve plaintiffs of the burden of proving anticompetitive effects, which are assumed, but they do not excuse plaintiffs from showing that their injury was caused by the anticompetitive aspects of the illegal act.").

[265] 234 U.S. 600 (1914).

[266] *Id*. at 606.

[267] *Id*. at 614, *quoting Grenada Lumber Co. v. Mississippi*, 217 U.S. 433, 440 (1910).

The same conclusion was reached in *Fashion Originators' Guild of America, Inc. v. Federal Trade Commission*[268] under § 5 of the Federal Trade Commission Act. Members of trade association that designed and manufactured women's dresses sought to prevent "style piracy" through an agreement to refuse to deal with retailers who had purchased from the targeted manufacturers that sold copies. As a result of the Guild's collective action, 12,000 retailers signed agreements to cooperate with the Guild's boycott.

The Guild's action limited competition, reducing the number of outlets to which the member manufacturers could sell and the sources from which the retailers could buy. Freedom of choice was affected in the market. The Court came close to declaring a *per se* standard for such conduct when it upheld the FTC's refusal to consider evidence of the "reasonableness" of the methods pursued. But the Court did evaluate the purpose behind the conduct and the market power (60% for higher priced garments) of the member firms. The Court also noted that less restrictive alternatives were available such as state, civil tort actions against the piracy, rather than the creation of an "extra governmental agency" to punish the price discounters.

FOGA is a model boycott case in which the parties engaged in industry self–regulation by putting pressure on buyers to refuse to deal with competing suppliers in competition with defendants. The Court found no public interest protected by the refusal to deal; only the self–interest and protection from commercial competition was at stake. In a similar case today, defendants would interpose as a defense the theory that the Guild's boycott was an effective method of avoiding "free rider" problems[269] and would ask the court to balance these externalities against the effect of the refusal to deal on price and the protection of market power.

It was not until 1959 that the Court again addressed concerted refusals to deal. In *Klor's Inc. v. Broadway–Hale Stores, Inc.*[270] the Court was more explicit, concluding that a concerted refusal to deal by competitors was *per se* unlawful. A retailer, Broadway, entered into an agreement with suppliers of appliances "either not to sell to Klor's or to sell to it only at discriminatory prices and highly unfavorable terms."[271] Broadway was alleged to have monopolistic buying power. Broadway did not dispute the allegation but moved for summary judgment, asserting a failure to state a cause of action because there was no public injury: "there were hundreds of other household appliance retailers, some within a few blocks of Klor's who sold many competing brands of appliances, including those the defendants refused to

---

[268] 312 U.S. 457 (1941).

[269] *See supra* at § 4.14[A][3]. *But see United States v. General Motors Corp.*, 384 U.S. 127 (1966) (boycotts are unlawful even when they are effective methods of controlling free riding.) *Contra United States v. Realty Multi–List*, 629 F.2d 1351 (5th Cir. 1980); *Phil Tolkan Datsun, Inc. v. Greater Milwaukee Datsun Dealers' Adver. Ass'n, Inc.*, 672 F.2d 1280 (7th Cir. 1982).

[270] 359 U.S. 207 (1959).

[271] *Id.* at 209.

sell to Klor's."[272] In short, defendant argued that because consumers and other competitors had access to supply, the public was not injured.

Klor's per se finding is implied in the following statement of the Court:

[g]roup boycotts or concerted refusals by traders to deal with other traders, have long been held to be in the forbidden category. They have not been saved by allegations that they were reasonable in the specific circumstances, nor by a failure to show that they "fixed or regulated prices, parcelled out or limited production, or brought about a deterioration in quality.' "[273]

The competitive harm included Klor's inability to buy in an open, competitive market, its inability to be a dealer in defendants' products, and the manufacturers' inability to sell to Klor's. The conduct had a "monopolistic tendency," the Court concluded. Summary judgment for defendants was reversed.

Unclear from the Court's logic in *Klor's* is how Broadway, a local appliance store with numerous local competitors, could have used monopolistic buying power to force major suppliers like RCA and General Electric from dealing with Klor's. The Court seemed concerned that if this conduct went unchecked there could be a "tendency toward monopoly," with the result that small competitors, like Klor's, would be driven out of the market only to have prices then increase. This was not the case where a retailer was denied access to one product or brand with other suppliers or brands available. The concerted refusal to deal included numerous major brands. The implication was that the makers of these brands all agreed with Broadway (and perhaps among themselves) to withhold supply from Klor's. This conduct went beyond "a manufacturer and dealer agreeing to an exclusive distributorship [thereby tying up one product] . . . . [A] wide combination consisting of manufacturers, distributors and a retailer" was alleged.[274]

In *Silver v. New York Stock Exchange*,[275] the Court made clear that an agreement by firms at one level of competition to deny a market through a group boycott by themselves or through others to competing firms is illegal *per se* without more. Through the New York Stock Exchange, securities brokers denied access to facilities to nonmember broker–dealers. Although finding that the exchange enjoyed a qualified immunity from antitrust coverage under the federal securities law,[276] the Court observed that, but for this fact, the concerted refusal to deal was *per se* unlawful. The Court concluded that defendants violated the law because they failed

---

[272] *Id.* at 209–10.

[273] *Id.* at 212, *citing Fashion Originators' Guild v. Federal Trade Comm'n*, 312 U.S. 457, 466 (1941). *See also Radiant Burners, Inc. v. People's Gas Light & Coke Co.*, 364 U.S. 656 (1961); *United States v. General Motors Corp.*, 384 U.S. 127 (1966).

[274] 359 U.S. at 212–13.

[275] 373 U.S. 341 (1963).

[276] SEC Act of 1934, 15 U.S.C. § 78(b). *See generally* § 3.05, *supra*.

to give plaintiff sufficient regulatory notice and hearing as to the grounds for the refusal to deal and the exclusion. The Court rejected an inquiry into the reasons underlying the boycott, implying an unqualified *per se* rule of illegality.

In sum, *Eastern States, FOGA, Klor's* and *Silver* teach that concerted refusals to deal aimed at a competitor to deny access or supply at that level of competition, either through vertical or horizontal agreements, are illegal. However, the extent of the analysis varied; at times the focus was on purpose, at other times it was on market power and effect. But, the Court, notwithstanding its *per se* predilections and broad language, seemed not to foreclose completely all justifications for a boycott.[277] This became evident in 1985 when the Court receded from its sweeping *per se* language. Only a narrow window remains through which the Court will apply its *per se* presumption of illegality to concerted refusals to deal. Otherwise, the rule of reason is the standard benchmark.

In *Northwest Wholesale Stationers v. Pacific Stationary and Printing Co.*[278] the Court, in a unanimous decision, rejected, except for a narrow category of cases, the *per se* characterization for concerted refusals to deal. A cooperative purchasing agency expelled a member without a *Silver* due process hearing which would have provided an opportunity for a hearing before termination. The cooperative was made up of 100 office supply retailers acting as a wholesaler to member retailers. Nonmember retailers could purchase at the same price as members, but they were not permitted to share in the cooperatives' profits. Members received their profits in the form of a rebate percentage on the purchase price. The cooperative also provided warehousing facilities.

The plaintiff was denied membership after it changed its policy and began dealing as a wholesaler as well as retailer. Prior to the refusal to deal, plaintiff received $10,000 annually in rebates on purchases as a member of the retail cooperative. The expulsion allegedly created a competitive disadvantage as a nonmember. Defendant cooperative urged that the purpose and effect were to achieve economies of scale and to reduce transaction costs in purchasing and warehousing.

In addressing *Silver*'s due process requirement, the Court held

[T]he absence of procedural safeguards can in no sense determine the antitrust analysis. If the challenged concerted activity of Northwest's members would amount to a *per se* violation of § 1 of the Sherman Act, no amount of procedural protection would save it. If the challenged action would not amount to a violation of § 1, no lack of procedural protections would convert it into a *per se* violation because the antitrust laws do not themselves impose on joint ventures a requirement of due process.[279]

---

[277] *See* P. Areeda, *Antitrust Analysis* § 376, at 514 (1981); L. Sullivan, *Handbook on the Law of Antitrust* 236 (1977).

[278] 472 U.S. 284 (1985).

[279] *Id*. at 293.

In effect, *Silver*'s process requirements apply only when the challenged conduct had a qualified antitrust immunity.

The Court surveyed its prior concerted refusal to deal cases and found that the *per se* approach had been applied when there were "joint efforts by a firm or firms to disadvantage competitors by 'either directly denying or persuading or coercing suppliers or customers to deny relationships the competitors need in the competitive struggle.' "[280] The Court noted that frequently the boycotting firms also had market power or a dominant position and that the challenged practices did not enhance overall efficiency.

Here, however, the Court concluded that Northwest was designed to increase economic efficiency by achieving "economies of scale in both the purchase and warehousing of wholesale supplies, and also [that the plan] ensure[d] ready access to a stock of goods" that otherwise might not be available.[281] Reversing the *per se* approach of the court of appeals, the Supreme Court held that the *per se* standard is only acceptable when the boycotting cooperative possesses market power or has exclusive access to supply or an essential element so that competition is effected. Otherwise, the refusal to deal is to be judged under the rule of reason analysis.

Thus, the Court raised the plaintiff's burden of proof in refusal to deal cases. The threshold test is either a showing of (1) market power, or (2) exclusive or unique accesses to supply (an essential element of competition), or (3) a lack of an efficiency rationale when the boycott is aimed at a competitor. No longer are "all concerted refusals to deal . . . predominantly anticompetitive." Except in this narrow range of cases, the Court abandoned the *per se* rule for group boycotts.

Once again the Court embraced an economic analysis that focused on reduced transaction costs and enhanced efficiency as a means of promoting competition — an approach entirely consistent with the Court's price–fixing cases in *BMI* and *NCAA*. The benefits of the bright line *per se* test were waning. This was proven even more so the next Supreme Court term.

In 1986 the Court refused to apply the *per se* classification to an agreement by competitors, dentists, to deny patient X–rays to the insurance companies.[282] The X–rays in *Indiana Federation of Dentists* were used to serve as a peer review check on the appropriateness of the dentists' charges and as a cost containment mechanism. The dentists were found to have monopoly power. Yet the Court held, in this exclusionary, commercial boycott, where detrimental effects were clearly established, that the rule of reason should govern the outcome:

> [W]e decline to resolve this case by forcing the [defendant's] policy into the "boycott" pigeonhole and invoking the *per se* rule . . . . [T]he category of restraints classed as group boycotts is not to be expanded indiscriminately, and the *per se* approach has generally been limited to cases in

---

[280] *Id.* (*quoting* Sullivan, *supra* note 204, at 261–62).

[281] 472 U.S. at 295.

[282] *FTC v. Indiana Fed'n of Dentists*, 476 U.S. 447 (1986).

which firms with market power boycott suppliers or customers in order to discourage them from doing business with a competitor — a situation obviously not present here. Moreover, we have been slow to condemn rules adopted by professional associations as unreasonable *per se* . . . .[283]

The Court proceeded to find that the conduct of withholding the X–rays was indeed illegal, because, as the Court opined, "[a] refusal to compete with respect to the package of services offered to customers, no less than a refusal to compete with respect to the price term of an agreement impairs the ability of the market to advance social welfare by ensuring the provision of desired goals and services to consumers at a price approximately the marginal cost . . . ."[284]

While continuing, and perhaps, expanding its frame of reference to include the deprivation of goods or services to consumers[285] for § 1 violations, the Court's reference to this not being a *per se* case can be reconciled with other cases. The target of the boycott was not a competitor, but rather a customer (here the insurance company, that is the "buyer" since it reimburses the actual patient). But the Court's suggestion that conduct engaged in by professionals is generally treated under the rule of reason is not consistent with its 1982 decision in *Maricopa*.[286] This overstatement is indicative of the Court's drift to embrace a rule of reason approach, except in the narrowest of cases. Recall here that competitors, with market power, engaged in a refusal to deal without any efficiency justification. Competition among the dentists to compete with each other with respect to policies dealing with insurers was decreased. The probable result was higher dental bills to patients. But the target was the insurance companies, a customer in a vertical relationship, not one in competition with defendant. Accordingly, no *per se* conclusion or presumption was reached.[287]

---

[283] *Id.* at 458. Note the Court's limitation on the use of the *per se* test: "firms with market power boycott suppliers or customers in order to discourage them from doing business with a competitor." *id.*

[284] *Id.* at 459.

[285] *See* discussion of *Aspen Skiing Co., infra* § 6.05[E].

[286] It is inconsistent except to the extent that the dentists argued ostensibly that the refusal to deal promoted an ethical and moral policy based on the patient's welfare.

[287] The rule of reason test was again used by the Sixth Circuit in *Chiropractic Coop. Ass'n of Mich. (CCAM) v. American Med. Ass'n (AMA)*, 867 F.2d 270 (6th Cir. 1989). In 1963, the AMA formed a committee on "quackery" headed by the three individual defendants. The committee eventually adopted an official position making it unethical for doctors to voluntarily associate with chiropractors on a professional basis. The four other defendant health care providers gradually adopted this position, as well, leading to a concerted refusal to deal with chiropractors.

In response to a lawsuit brought against the defendants in the mid–1970's, all parties officially renounced their former refusal to deal with chiropractors. The AMA, however, took a slightly different stance. It held to its conviction that it is "wrong to engage in or aid and abet any treatment which has no scientific basis and is dangerous," which was the same viewpoint it had espoused upon adopting its original position against chiropractors. *Id.* at 274.

In the second lawsuit against the defendants, the district court granted summary judgment

Northwest and *Indiana Federation of Dentists* together suggest, at the least, that *Klor's* announced *per se* test [288] is subject to reexamination. In many respects, *Indiana Federation of Dentists* was a better candidate for the *per se* classification than *Klor's*, particularly in light of the market power held by the dentists and the horizontal agreements.

Additional insight is provided by the Supreme Court's decision in *Superior Court Trial Lawyers Association v. Federal Trade Commission,*[289] where the Court held that a horizontal arrangement among lawyers to withhold the supply of legal services and thereby increase hourly wage rates represented a "naked restraint" on price and output. In *Superior Court Trial Lawyers*, a group of private–practice lawyers, pursuant to a well–publicized plan, agreed not to represent indigent criminal defendants in the District of Columbia Superior Court until the city government increased the lawyers' hourly compensation.[290]

In evaluating the requisite conduct, the Court commented that although there was a political impact, the means employed (the boycott) to obtain the more favorable legislation was economic, rather than political in nature. Therefore, irrespective of "whatever economic justification particular price–fixing agreements may be thought to have, the law does not permit an inquiry into their reasonableness."[291]

Thus in a concerted refusal to deal context, the facts of the given case will likely dictate whether the Court applies a *per se* or rule of reason approach to assess the alleged restraint. As Justice Brandeis noted in

---

to all defendants, stating that there had been no overt activity continuing the conspiracy after the late 1970's. The Sixth Circuit upheld this ruling for all defendants but the AMA, finding that "the AMA's activities in the late 1970's. . .were ambiguous and equivocal at best with respect to chiropractors." *Id*. The plaintiffs had presented some evidence of loss of reputation and denial of staff privileges in certain Michigan hospitals. The court found that the mere fact of increased earnings did not equate to lack of antitrust injury. *Id*. at 275. The court reminded the defendants that chiropractors "might have earned much more had the AMA not taken the actions in dispute. . ." *Id*. This case serves as another example of professionals being subjected to the rule of reason.

[288] *See, e.g., Valley Liquors, Inc. v. Renfield Imps., Ltd.*, 678 F.2d 742 (7th Cir. 1982); *Diaz v. Farley*, 215 F.3d 1175 (10th Cir. 2000) (not finding an alleged boycott of three anesthesiologists to be *per se* illegal).

[289] 493 U.S. 411 (1990).

[290] *Id*. at 413.

[291] *Id*. at 435 *quoting United States v. Socony–Vacuum Oil Co.*, 310 U.S. 150 (1940). In *Betkerur v. Aultman Hospital Association*, 78 F.3d 1079 (6th Cir. 1996), the Sixth Circuit rejected the plaintiff's claim of *per se* illegality under a group boycott theory. Defendants had terminated a program at the hospital which allowed for blind referrals of neonatologists (like the plaintiff by OB/GYN physicians to their patients). The plaintiff claimed among other things, that this constituted a group boycott. The court quickly disposed of this claim, since the plaintiff still practiced at the defendant hospital and received referrals from those allegedly boycotting her. *Id*. at 1090. More importantly, the court found most of the defendants to have no incentive to try to freeze out the plaintiff, meaning that there was no danger of the defendants acting in concert to harm consumers through boycotting the plaintiff's services. *Id*. Finally, the court could not discern any negative economic effect originating out of the defendant's decision to terminate the blind referral program. *Id*. at 1091.

Chicago Board of Trade v. United States,[292] "[t]he true test of legality is whether the restraint imposed is such as merely regulates and perhaps promotes competition or whether it is such as may suppress or even destroy competition."[293] Consequently, when a particular restraint more closely parallels a promotion of competition a *Northwest Wholesale Stationers* holding may result. When a restraint suppresses competition, by comparison, a *Superior Court Trial Lawyers* approach will be applied.

§ 4.14   Horizontal Market Divisions

Section 1 of the Sherman Act targets restraints of trade. Although the most obvious horizontal restraint of trade is price fixing among competitors, price fixing is not the only anticompetitive behavior condemned under § 1. A horizontal market division is created when competitors agree not to compete in a designated market. Such an agreement may divide a market in various ways.[294]

(1) Territorial market divisions are created when competitors allocate markets along geographic lines. For example, one conspirator may be assigned the western region and another the eastern region of an area. Territorial market divisions are often combined with price–fixing agreements, as in *Timken Roller Bearing Co. v. United States*.[295] The unlawful conduct in two other cases illustrate market allocations affected by exclusive licenses for assigned areas. In *United States v. Sealy*,[296] licenses were combined with price fixing;[297] 1). and in *United States v. Topco Associates, Inc.*[298] there was an exclusive license but no price–fixing arrangement.[299]

(2) Customer market divisions are created when competitors allocate specific customers among themselves, agreeing not to solicit business from customers allocated to designated competitors.

---

[292] 246 U.S. 231 (1918).

[293] *Id.* at 238.

[294] It should be noted that market divisions that involve domestic firms but occur in foreign countries are not subject to *per se* analysis under the Sherman Act. *Metro Industries, Inc. v. Sammi Corp.*, 82 F.3d 839, 844–45 (9th Cir. 1996). However, "it is well established. . .that the Sherman Act applies to foreign conduct that was meant to produce and. . .produc[ed] some substantial effect in the United States." *Hartford Fire Insurance Co. v. California*, 509 US 764, 795 (1993).

[295] 341 U.S. 593 (1951).

[296] 388 U.S. 350 (1967).

[297] *See also Columbia Steel Casting Co. v. Portland Gen. Elec. Co.*, 103 F.3d 1446, 1455 n.7 (9th Cir. 1996) (holding that agreement between competing power companies to exclusively service certain areas in Portland amounted to horizontal territorial allocation agreement, and, although no explicit price–fixing activity occurred, the fact that the agreement prevented the plaintiff from buying electricity from a competitor company at a lower price made the agreement a per se violation of §1).

[298] 405 U.S. 596 (1972).

[299] *See also Smalley & Co. v. Emerson & Cuming, Inc.*, 13 F.3d 366, 368 (10th Cir. 1993) (holding that dual distribution systems where the manufacturer sells the product itself in some areas and sells to distributors to resell in other areas constitute vertical restrictions and, since no price fixing was involved, should be analyzed under the rule of reason).

(3) Functional market divisions are created when competitors allocate, for example, the wholesale market to selected members of a conspiracy and the retail market to other members.

(4) Product market divisions are created when competitors agree not to compete along certain product lines. For example, conspirators may agree that one will market only small appliances while the other will market only large appliances in a defined area.

Many horizontal market agreements constitute a combination of one or more of the above market division arrangements, often together with price-fixing agreements.

For example, in *Polk Bros., Inc. v. Forest City Enterprises, Inc.,*[300] two firms agreed to occupy a physically divided common retail establishment in which the firms would sell only non–competing, yet complementary, products. The agreement thus called for both product and territorial allocations.

Horizontal nonprice agreements are aimed at limiting and controlling participation in designated markets. These agreements have the effect of reducing competition. When competition is reduced, participants in the market no longer need to compete on price to the extent that price competition would exist in the absence of a horizontal market division. If the market division is sufficiently pervasive, a small number of firms may effectively enjoy a monopoly in a designated territory, for a certain product line, or with a selected group of customers. When this occurs the market division may be as anticompetitive as direct price fixing.

In addition, when conspirators agree to fix prices there is always the possibility that one or more of the conspirators may be tempted to "cheat" on the co–conspirators by lowering selected prices in anticipation that competitors will not detect the price deviation. When this occurs, detection is difficult, at least in nonretail markets, because wholesale price information is customarily not available to competitors, and customers suspicious of being victimized by an illegal price–fixing scheme are unlikely to report a supplier who "cheats" on the cartel by lowering its price. When, however, competitors agree to divide markets and one member of the conspiracy deviates from the agreement, detection, by other members of the conspiracy, is much easier than in price fixing because of the greater visibility of sales in markets or customers allocated to others. Horizontal market divisions, then, may be more easily monitored and enforced by the conspirators, and in this sense may be even more anticompetitive than price–fixing agreements. Moreover, in an air tight market division no competition exists, but where the only restraint is price fixing other nonprice competition (on quality, service, or inventory) may exist and even be robust. Consequently, a

---

[300] 776 F.2d 185 (7th Cir. 1985).

market division in some circumstances may be more pernicious than price fixing. [301]

[A] Dividing Territories and Fixing Price

[1] Introductory Cases

One of the earliest territorial division cases decided under the Sherman Act was *United States v. Addyston Pipe & Steel Co.* [302] Defendants in *Addyston Pipe* were competing cast iron pipe producers who allocated territories among themselves and jointly fixed prices in each territory. The apparent purpose of the combination was to create an artificial barrier to entry by establishing prices low enough to discourage new entrants, albeit higher than prices that would have resulted from competitive forces. Defendants argued that the arrangement had the benign purpose of preventing ruinous competition and that their association would have been valid at common law because the prices fixed were reasonable.

The Sixth Circuit rejected both arguments. In an opinion by Judge, later Chief Justice, Taft the court reasoned that even under the common law all such agreements were unlawful unless they were ancillary. "No conventional restraint of trade can be enforced unless the covenant embodying it is merely ancillary to the main purpose of a lawful contract . . . ." [303] Having found that the defendants' territorial and price–fixing contract was not ancillary to a main lawful purpose, the court rejected defendants' reasonableness argument, stating that "we do not think that at common law there is any question of reasonableness open to the courts with reference to such a contract." [304] Because the *Addyston Pipe* court focused most of its analysis on defendants' price–fixing conduct, the case does not provide meaningful guidance as to the legality of territorial allocations.

In another early case, *United States v. National Lead Co.*, [305] the Supreme Court upheld the lower court's finding of a § 1 violation by defendants who pooled their numerous patents and allocated markets for the manufacture and sale of titanium. The pooling of the multiple patents by agreement

---

[301] A claim of *per se* illegality based on a horizontal restraint failed in *Betkerur v. Aultman Hosp. Ass'n*, 78 F.3d 1079 (6th Cir. 1996). The Sixth Circuit refused to find that an agreement between a neonatologist, her employer hospital, and several OB/GYN's to discontinue a blind referral system of neonatologists (including the plaintiff) by OB/GYN's constituted a *per se* illegal horizontal restraint. Because the OB/GYN's were not competitors with the plaintiff neonatologist and because the one defendant who was in direct competition with the plaintiff did not "secure an exclusive referral arrangement in order to increase her prices and undermine a competitor's prices," no *per se* violation of § 1 had occurred. *Id.* at 1092. Hence, the rule of reason analysis applied by the district court did not constitute an error; the judgment was upheld.

[302] 85 F. 271 (6th Cir. 1898), *aff'd*, 175 U.S. 211 (1899).

[303] *Id.* at 282.

[304] *Id.* at 293.

[305] 332 U.S. 319 (1947).

among defendants resulted in "domination of an entire industry."[306] The territorial division was unlawful even though competition was vigorous between selected plants operated by the defendants.[307]

Four years after it decided *National Lead*, the Court reviewed the legality of a territorial restriction combined with price fixing. In *Timken Roller Bearing Co. v. United States*,[308] defendants were a corporate parent and its partially owned subsidiaries who were producers of antifriction bearings sold in the international market. Defendants were parties to agreements which licensed the trademark "Timken," allocated territories in which each of the parties would market "Timken" bearings, and established prices to be charged when one defendant sold bearings in a territory assigned to another.

Defendants argued that their agreements were ancillary to the otherwise lawful purposes of protecting the "Timken" trademark and effectuating the relationship among the defendants.[309] They characterized this as a joint venture. The Court rejected defendants' argument, holding that an agreement that divided territorial markets among competitors and fixes prices violates § 1 if the dominant purpose of the market divisions is to avoid competition among the conspirators.

Reasoning that the agreement to divide territories was broader than necessary to protect the "Timken" trademark, the Court found that the market division was the dominant purpose, not trademark protection. This suggests "a least restrictive alternative" test to determine if certain restraints are valid. For example, the restraint in *Timken* affected competition in the interbrand market because the agreements "went far beyound the protection of the name 'Timkin,' and provided for control of the manufacture and sale of antifriction bearings whether carrying the ['Timken' trade]mark or not."[310] Because the restraint operated in the interbrand market, it was more likely to be overbroad, the Court reasoned. If, however, the restraint applied only to products bearing the "Timken" trademark, affecting only the intrabrand market, then defendants might have argued that such effects were less restrictive and accordingly less anticompetitive.

The *Timken* Court did not specifically state whether defendants' conduct was unlawful *per se* or subject to a rule of reason analysis. A *per se* conclusion would seem to be inconsistent with the Court's consideration of defendant's market power. The issue was clarified in *United States v. Sealy, Inc.*,[311] however, when the Court, citing *Timken*, condemned market divisions in combination with price fixing. The Court said that "they are

---

[306] *Id.* at 328.

[307] *Id.* at 352.

[308] 341 U.S. 593 (1951).

[309] *See* § 4.06, *supra.*

[310] 341 U.S. at 598–99.

[311] 388 U.S. 350 (1967).

unlawful under § 1 of the Sherman Act without the necessity for an inquiry in each particular case as to their business or economic justification, their impact in the marketplace, or their reasonableness."[312] Clearly, this language rejects a rule of reason analysis in favor of a *per se* conclusion, but subsequent cases call into question such a broad generalization.

[2]   Exclusive License for an Assigned Area

Like *Timken, United States v. Sealy, Inc.*[313] involved both territorial allocations and price fixing.[314] Defendants were mattress manufacturers who combined to form Sealy, Inc. Sealy licensed thirty mattress manufacturers who owned substantially all the stock of Sealy, Inc. Each licensee was assigned an exclusive geographic territory in which it alone was licensed to sell mattresses with the Sealy label; however, each licensee was free under the licensing agreement to manufacture and sell mattresses under non–Sealy private labels both within its assigned Sealy territory and anywhere else it chose. The licensing agreements also stipulated the minimum retail prices for the advertising and retail sale of Sealy–labelled mattresses. It provided, in addition, for Sealy, Inc. to police the enforcement of the price minimums.

The defendants first argued that the territorial allocations were merely vertical arrangements between Sealy, Inc. and the various licensees. The Court, however, "look[ing] at substance rather than form, found them to be horizontal restraints. These must be classified as *horizontal* restraints."[315] The Court reasoned that the licensees, as shareholders and directors of Sealy, Inc., were in charge of Sealy's operations and because they were competitors the restraints were horizontal rather than vertical limitations imposed by a separate entity upon independent manufacturers. The Court held that territorial market divisions, in combination with price fixing by competitors in the interbrand market, constitute a *per se* violation. The Court did not clarify whether territorial allocations, standing alone without price–fixing, are similarly condemned; rather, it merely attached the *per se* label to the "aggregation of trade restraints," which, of course, included both market divisions and price–fixing.[316]

In *dictum* the *Sealy* Court opined that territorial allocations in the intrabrand market may be subject to a rule of reason analysis. It gave as an example a small number of grocers using a common name and sharing advertising, combined with exclusive territorial allocations.[317] Five years later the Court reconsidered its hypothetical in *United States v. Topco Associates, Inc.*[318]

---

[312] *Id.* at 357–58.

[313] *Id.* at 351.

[314] 388 U.S. 350 (1967).

[315] *Id.* at 352.

[316] *Id.* at 357, *citing Timken Roller Bearing Co. v. United States*, 341 U.S. 593, 598 (1951).

[317] *Id.* at 357, n.4, citing *Northern Pacific R. Co. v. United States*, 356 U.S. 1, 6–7 (1958).

[318] 405 U.S. 596 (1972).

In *Topco* the Supreme Court finally clarified the ambiguous "aggregation of trade restraints" language of *Sealy* and *Timken*. Topco Associates was comprised of several dozen regional supermarket chains that operated as a purchasing agent for its members. Topco was organized by the regional chains in order to compete with national chains that marketed private–label grocery products. By taking advantage of their combined size and purchasing power, the regional members were able, through Topco, to advertise and purchase in volume their own private–label products. The Topco chains had an average 6% market share; thus it did not have substantial market power.

The alleged unlawful conduct in *Topco* consisted of territorial allocations, together with Topco members' effective veto power over the membership application of competitors. Each Topco member was licensed to sell the private–labelled Topco products only in a designated area. Members were prohibited from selling the products outside the assigned areas. Most licenses were exclusive; no other member could sell Topco private label products in another members' assigned territory.

The *Topco* defendants argued that their association actually increased competition because it enabled its members to increase efficiency in competing with the larger national chains. The Court rejected this argument, however, holding that geographic market divisions among competitors, standing alone, are *per se* violations of § 1. Even though the Court unambiguously attached the *per se* label once it concluded that the territorial allocation was horizontal in nature,[319] Topco's market power discussion[320] indicates at least some limited rule of reason analysis, and it belies a pure *per se* conclusion.

Subsequent Supreme Court precedent makes clear that not all horizontal restraints are *per se* illegal. The Court's price–fixing cases, *National Collegiate Athletic Association v. Board of Regents, (NCAA)*[321] and *Broadcast Music, Inc. v. CBS*,[322] suggest that *Topco* and *Sealy* may have been weakened. These cases discussed more fully at § 4.08 *supra* reasoned that "cooperation is necessary if the type of competition that [defendant] and its member institutions seek to market is to be preserved."[323] The *NCAA* Court ruled that if cooperation is necessary to preservation of competition, then horizontal cooperation will not be *per se* unlawful; rather a rule of reason analysis will apply. Although *NCAA* did not specifically overrule *Timken*, *Sealy*, or *Topco*, its rationale arguably cast doubt on the continued validity of a broad *per se* conclusion when *intrabrand* cooperation is necessary to preserve and promote competition in the *interbrand* market.[324]

---

[319] *Id.* at 608.

[320] *Id.* at 600.

[321] 468 U.S. 85 (1984).

[322] 441 U.S. 1 (1979).

[323] 468 U.S. at 117. *See generally* Louis, *Restraints Ancillary to Joint Ventures and Licensing Agreements: Do Sealy and Topco Logically Survive Sylvania and Broadcast Music?* 66 Va. L. Rev. 879 (1980).

[324] For a thorough explanation of the intrabrand/interbrand distinction *see SCFC ILC, Inc. v. Visa USA*, 36 F.3d 958, 966–67 (10th Cir. 1994).

Caution is in order, however, when applying a standard of analysis to market division cases. For example, the Supreme Court's decision in *Palmer v. BRG of Georgia, Inc.*,[325] declaring a price fixing and horizontal market allocation agreement *per se* unlawful raises doubt as to a broad application of a rule of reason approach, and revives *Topco* and *Sealy* as vigors precedent.[326]

In *Palmer*, a former law student alleged that the price of his bar review course with BRG was enhanced due to an unlawful market allocation agreement entered into by the defendant and another provider, (HBJ).[327] Palmer alleged that prior to 1980, both BRG and HBJ directly competed within Georgia for bar review business. In 1980, however, both parties "entered into an agreement that gave BRG an exclusive license to market HBJ's material in Georgia and to use its tradename 'Bar/Bri'."[328] Pursuant to this agreement, both parties "agreed that HBJ would not compete with BRG in Georgia and that BRG would not compete with HBJ outside of Georgia."[329]

The Supreme Court found the agreement unlawful on its face, commenting that the "agreement was formed for the purpose and with the effect of raising the price of bar review courses"[330] and that "horizontal territorial limitations . . . are naked restraints of trade with no purpose except stifling competition." Both practices, said the Court, "are per se violations of the Sherman Act."[331]

---

[325] 498 U.S. 46 (1990).

[326] *See also Blue Cross & Blue Shield of Wisc. v. Marshfield Clinic*, 65 F.3d 1406, 1415 (7th Cir. 1995) (holding that the defendant had engaged in market dividing by territory, a practice that violates § 1 of the Sherman Act.)

[327] 498 U.S. at 46–47.

[328] *Id.* at 46.

[329] *Id.* at 47.

[330] *Id.* at 49.

[331] This treatment of horizontal market divisions as *per se* violations of § 1 recently was affirmed by the Seventh Circuit in *Blackburn v. Sweeney*, 53 F.3d 825 (7th Cir. 1995). The issue in this case involved a partnership dissolution agreement which provided that half of the partners would have the exclusive right to advertise within a specific geographical area and half would advertise in a separate area. The Seventh Circuit reversed the district court, holding that the agreement constituted a *per se* illegal horizontal market division. Even though all parties to the agreement could still practice law throughout the state, the court still struck down the agreement, stating that "[t]o fit under the per se rule, an agreement need not foreclose all possible avenues of competition." *Id.* at 827.

The court also refused to apply the ancillary restraint doctrine. The agreement "was not necessary for the dissolution of the partnership and the resulting increase in competition." *Id.* at 828. Also, because of its "infinite duration," the agreement could not be characterized as an ancillary covenant not to compete. *Id.*

The court did deny the plaintiff treble damages and attorneys fees, however, because the parties were deemed to be equally at fault for the materialization of the agreement.

[3] Externalities and the Free Rider Defense

An externality is a cost or a benefit associated with a decision which is not taken into account by a decisionmaker, but which nevertheless results from the decision. The externality is thus outside to the decision–making process. The cost of the externality may be borne by society. For example, prior to government regulation of the environment, when an electrical utility generated power by fossil fuel rather than hydroelectric means, the decision may not have accounted for the detrimental downstream thermal affect of the power generating plant's condenser water discharge. Such detrimental effect is a negative externality. More common examples of externalities occur daily, as when homeowners decide to fertilize their lawns or paint the exterior of their homes. The decisionmaking process ordinarily does not consider the beneficial effects on the surrounding neighborhood that result in the expenditure; those beneficial effects are externalities.

Expressed in economic terms, "[e]xternalities or spillovers are . . . examples of market failure that may justify government intervention. Externalities are effects on third parties that are not transmitted through the price system and that arise as an incidental by–product of another person's or firm's activity."[332] Externalities may cause market failure, or market imperfections, which "prevent the allocation of resources in accord with consumer valuations."[333]

A "free–rider" is also an externality. When an individual builds a levee that protects both his or her property as well as a neighbors' property, the neighbor gets a free–ride on the builder's expenditure. The neighbors of the homeowner whose home is freshly painted or lawn is recently fertilized similarly "ride free" because they made no expenditure, yet gained a benefit from the decision and expenditure of another. Indeed, the benefit may be economic, for when the free–rider sells his or her home, its value may be increased by the enhanced attraction of the neighborhood.

An understanding of externalities and free–riders is important to application of the antitrust laws. A form of government regulation or intervention that may be justified by an externality, market failure, or free–rider is enforcement of the antitrust laws. Parties may have a legitimate interest in eliminating free riders. If the manufacturer of a new product wishes to induce a retailer to advertise and promote the manufacturer's product, the manufacturer must create an incentive for the retailer to do so. If, however, the retailer knows that if it makes advertising and promotion expenditures that its competitors do not make, then its cost of doing business will be higher than those of its competitors. Competitors will be free–riders because they will be able to take advantage of the greater consumer awareness of the new product as a result of the retailer's advertising and promotional expenditures. Thus the manufacturer and retailer may agree on contractual restrictions to prevent or control this free–rider problem.

---

[332] S.E. Rhoads, *The Economist's View of the World, Government, Markets, & Public Policy* 67 (1985). *See also* discussion in § 5.01[B][4], *infra*.

[333] *Id.* at 66.

The manufacturer may, for example, agree that the retailer will have an exclusive right to sell the manufacturer's product within a designated geographic area. This is known as an output contract which binds the manufacturer. In return the retailer may agree to sell only the manufacturer's product, and no other competing products. This is a requirements contract which binds the retailer. Ultimately one of the parties may attempt to void the contractual restriction on the grounds that it is anticompetitive and violative of the antitrust laws. The legal question then becomes whether avoidance of free–riders is sufficient grounds for upholding the restraint even though it is facially anticompetitive.

The manufacturer–retailer hypothetical is an example of the free–rider defense in the context of a vertical constraint. The free rider defense also has applicability to horizontal market divisions as the next cases illustrate.[334]

[4] *Polk Brothers* and the Trend Towards a Rule of Reason

Polk Bros., Inc. v. Forest City Enterprises, Inc.[335] illustrates the free rider defense in a horizontal market division case. The plaintiff, Polk Bros., was in the retail appliance and home furnishing business. The defendant, Forest City Enterprises, sold building materials, lumber, tools, and other related products. Because of the complementary nature of their products, the two firms decided to occupy a common building with their respective sales areas divided by a partition. Pursuant to an agreement between them, Polk Brothers built the common building and leased space to Forest City, with an option to buy. In order to maximize the benefits of their joint undertaking and to prevent competition between themselves, the agreement also contained a restrictive covenant that identified specific product lines that each party agreed not to sell in the new building. When Forest City subsequently exercised its option to buy, the restrictive provisions of the lease became covenants running with the land for fifty years.

---

[334] In *SCFC ILC, Inc. v. Visa USA, Inc.*, 36 F.3d 958 (10th Cir. 1994), the Tenth Circuit reversed an antitrust violation against Visa USA for denying plaintiff Sears Company membership in its credit card issuer association. Besides finding that no violation could exist because there was no anticompetitive effect on the relevant market and Visa USA did not have market power, the court also accepted Visa USA's argument that the exclusion was based on free rider concerns. As Sears and Visa USA were viable competitors in the brand and operating systems market for credit cards, Visa USA sought to avoid the extra costs of taking Sears under its wing and producing for it a new credit card, when Sears had done nothing to contribute to Visa USA and had spent a considerable amount of time competing against it. *Id.* at 970. Visa USA contended, and the Tenth Circuit agreed, that Sears was trying to get a free ride off Visa USA's success as a credit card company when "it [did] not need Visa USA to compete in the relevant market and [could not] demonstrate it [could] only issue a low–cost card with Visa USA's help." *Id.* at 970–71.

See also Alvord–Polk, Inc. v. F. Schumacher Co., 37 F.3d 996, 1012 (3d Cir. 1994) (where the court rejected a summary judgment motion to a horizontal restraint claim based on a free rider defense because it was a possible pretext for the defendant's true motives behind its alleged trade restraining actions).

[335] 776 F.2d 185 (7th Cir. 1985).

About seven years after the two stores opened for business, Forest City decided to sell products that were covered by the restrictive covenant. Polk Bros. sought an injunction to enforce the restrictive covenant and to prevent Forest City from selling the prohibited products.[336]

The restraint in *Polk Bros.* contained two kinds of horizontal market divisions. First, the agreement restricted sales of designated products, and was thus a product division. Second, because the agreement limited what each party could sell from a specified location, it also served as a geographic division. Forest City argued that the market division was unenforceable as a *per se* restraint of trade in violation of § 1.

In rejecting Forest City's argument, the Seventh Circuit held that a horizontal agreement not to compete is *per se* unlawful only if it is a "naked" restraint, but if ancillary to an otherwise lawful purpose it is subject to a rule of reason analysis. The court relied on the *Addyston Pipe*[337] ancillary restraint doctrine in distinguishing between naked and ancillary restraints. Reasoning that the restrictive covenant facilitated "productive cooperation" between *Polk Bros.* and *Forest City,* the court found that the restraint was ancillary and subject to rule of reason analysis.[338]

The court's rule of reason analysis recognized the free rider defense as "a legitimate objective of a system of distribution."[339] When it entered into the build/lease contract, Polk Bros. was legitimately concerned that it might spend substantial sums advertising appliances to attract customers into its store only to have them lured away by Forest City. As long as Forest City did not advertise and promote appliances to the same extent as did Polk Bros., its costs would be less and hence its prices might be lower. The restrictive covenant reflected Polk Bros.' legitimate attempt to eliminate the possibility that Forest City would become a free-rider.

Reasoning that but for the restrictive covenant Polk Bros. would have neither constructed the new building nor permitted Forest City to become its lessee, the court found that "the cooperation increased the amount of retail space available and was at least potentially beneficial to consumers;

---

[336] Polk Bros. filed suit for injunctive relief in state court. "Forest City removed the action to the district court under 28 U.S.C. § 1441, where it could have been filed initially under the diversity jurisdiction." *Id.* at 188. Under the *Erie* doctrine, the federal court analyzed the case under the antitrust law of Illinois. Illinois antitrust law, however, "refers courts to federal antitrust law as a guide to questions of interpretation." *Id.* Thus the *Polk* Court held that "[i]n order to find out what Illinois law forbids, we inquire into what federal antitrust law forbids." *Id.*

[337] *United States v. Addyston Pipe & Steel Co.*, 85 F. 271, 280–83 (6th Cir. 1898), *aff'd.*, 172 U.S. 211 (1899). *See* ancillary restraint doctrine, *supra*, § 4.04.

[338] 776 F.2d at 190. Polk Bros. "would not have entered into this arrangement . . . unless it had received assurances that [Forest City] would not compete with it in the sale of products that are the 'foundation of [Polk's] business'... The agreement not to compete was an integral part of the lease and land sale." *Id., quoting* the district court opinion. *See also* Louis, *supra* note 236.

[339] 776 F.2d at 190 (*citing, inter alia, Monsanto Co. v. Spray-Rite Service Corp.*, 465 U.S. 752, 760–61 (1984)).

the restrictive covenant made the cooperation possible."[340] Because Forest City's arguments were directed toward a *per se* condemnation of the restrictive covenant, it had not presented evidence of substantial market power. Due to the lack of market power evidence, and the reasoning that an assessment of market power is the first step of any rule of reason analysis, the court concluded that Forest City could "prevail under the *per se* rule or not at all. 'Not at all' it must be."[341]

Other Circuits agree. The District of Columbia Circuit has held that the recent Supreme Court cases seem to effectively overrule *Topco* and *Sealy*, at least if those cases stand for the proposition that horizontal restraints are illegal *per se*. Judge Bork, writing for the court, reasoned that horizontal restraints that reduce free–rider problems and promote efficiency are legal, absent market power. The issue was addressed in *Rothery Storage & Van Co. v. Atlas Van Lines, Inc.*[342] in which a van line company adopted, as a result of deregulation, a policy, of terminating independent, local agents who competed against the national van line, Atlas, or who dealt with another national carrier while using the Atlas name. The Supreme Court denied without dissent the petition for certiorari.

The question arises whether *Polk Bros.* and *Rothery* are reconcilable with *Topco* or whether they are mere examples of judicial activism by lower federal court judges. None of the defendants in *Topco, Polk Bros.* or *Rothery* had substantial market power, yet *Topco* held that territorial market divisions among competitors are *per se* violations of § 1, while *Polk Bros.* and *Rothery* applied a rule of reason analysis.

The cornerstone of the Seventh Circuit's analysis in *Polk Bros.* is the ancillary restraint doctrine of *Addyston Pipe*. Judge Easterbrook opined in *Polk Bros.* that

> The reason for distinguishing between "ancillary" and "naked" restraints is to determine whether the agreement is part of a cooperative venture with prospects for increasing output. If it is, it should not be condemned *per se* . . . . The benefits of cooperation may be greatest when launching a new venture.[343]

Because the arrangement to build and lease the new building would not have been consummated without a contractually guaranteed resolution of the potential free rider problem, the *Polk Bros.* restriction was not a naked restraint. Similarly, in *Topco* it could be argued that the restraint was ancillary to the otherwise lawful purpose of increasing defendants' ability to compete with major supermarket chains in the private label market. Arguably both restraints inured to the benefit of consumers. But the Supreme Court's discussion in *Palmer* suggests a return to the more rigid *per*

---

[340] *Id.*

[341] *Id.* at 191.

[342] 792 F.2d 210 (D.C. Cir. 1986).

[343] 776 F.2d at 190. *But see General Leaseways v. Nat'l Truck Leasing Ass'n*, 744 F.2d 588 (7th Cir. 1984) (applying *Topco* after finding that market division was not efficient). *See also* Louis, *supra* note 323.

se approach for market division agreements, even in the absence of a price agreement and even when the parties have not previously competed in the market.

§ 4.15   The Conspiracy Doctrine

Section 1 of the Sherman Act makes unlawful "[e]very contract, combination . . . or conspiracy in restraint of trade."[344] Section 3 of the Clayton Act makes unlawful leases, sales, or contracts "on the condition, agreement, or understanding that the lessee or purchaser thereof shall not use or deal in the goods . . . of . . . competitors of the lessor or seller."[345] Thus both § 1 of Sherman and § 3 of Clayton require some form of combination, agreement, condition, or understanding, commonly referred to as "concerted action" or a "meeting of the minds."[346] As a minimum, concerted action means something more than unilateral action. "For most kinds of anticompetitive business conduct, condemnation has depended and continues to depend on finding two or more parties who may be said to have 'agreed' to do what was done, since 'agreement' is an essential ingredient of 'contract, combination, or conspiracy.'"[347]

The prevailing view suggests that it is unnecessary to distinguish between "contract," "combination," and "conspiracy."[348] Courts "usually use these terms interchangeably, and the use of one term does not imply any distinction between them."[349] A distinction should be made, however, between "motive" and "objective" when searching for concerted activity. It

---

[344] 15 U.S.C. § 1.

[345] 15 U.S.C. § 14.

[346] This "meeting of the minds" requirement does not have to arise out of a fully voluntary relationship. *See MCM Partners, Inc. v. Andrews–Bartlett & Associates, Inc.*, 62 F.3d 967, 973, 975 (7th Cir. 1995) ("[A]cquiescence in an illegal scheme is as much a violation of the Sherman Act as the creation and promotion of one . . . So long as defendants knew that they were acquiescing in conduct that was in all likelihood unlawful. . .they thereby joined a combination or conspiracy. . ." (quoting *United States v. Paramout Pictures, Inc.*, 334 U.S. 131 (1948)). A coerced party can be considered a co–conspirator whether the plaintiff is demanding relief from the coercer or the coerced. *Id.* at 974–75.

However, the alternatives available to the coerced party may determine whether that party is definitely considered a conspirator. As Professor Areeda stated, "To impose liability on one who acts in fear of another is necessarily to rule that he should have acted differently. Certainly, we would prefer that the firm threatened by a cartel complain to the antitrust authorities rather than join in price fixing. But how much protection results depends on what those officials choose or are able to do."

VI P.E. Areeda, *Antitrust Law*, ¶ 1408 (1986).

[347] Turner, *The Definition of Agreement Under the Sherman Act: Conscious Parallelism and Refusals to Deal*, 75 Harv. L. Rev. 655, 655–56 (1962). For an example of the essential role the conspiracy doctrine plays in the determination of whether an antitrust violation occurred, *see Wigod v. Chicago Mercantile Exch.*, 981 F.2d 1510 (7th Cir. 1992), where the court denied the plaintiff's *per se* antitrust claim because no conspiracy existed.

[348] *Bogosian v. Gulf Oil Corp.*, 561 F.2d 434, 445 (3d Cir.)(1977).

[349] VI P. Areeda, *Antitrust Law* 17 (1986); L. Sullivan, *supra* note 204, at 312 (1977). *See also Harold Friedman, Inc. v. Kroger Co.*, 581 F.2d 1066, 1072, n.3 (3d Cir. 1978).

is the latter with which § 1 is concerned. As the Third Circuit stated in *Fineman v. Armstrong World Industries, Inc.*,[350] "the emphasis is upon the participant's 'commitment to [the] scheme [which is] designed to achieve an unlawful purpose,'" and whether one can find an "agreement with the objective from knowledge of [it] and action calculated to achieve the objective despite differing motives."[351] The court did suggest that motives may become relevant if there is absolutely no other proof of unity of purpose available.[352]

Various rationales have been offered to explain the concerted action requirement. In general, the requirement of an agreement is useful in distinguishing joint conduct that is harmful from unilateral conduct that is harmless or unavoidable.[353] More specifically, joint conduct "(1) increases the risk of anticompetitive action *and* results, (2) expands market power, (3) creates an anticompetitive restraint not otherwise possible, or (4) surrenders important decisionmaking autonomy on a matter of competitive significance."[354]

[A] Proof of an Agreement

[1] Express Agreements

Antitrust defendants rarely are found to have agreed expressly to fix prices or engage in other anticompetitive behavior. Accordingly, most § 1 cases require evidence from which an agreement may be inferred. Sometimes, however, the evidence demonstrates an express agreement.

For example, in *United States v. Socony–Vacuum Oil Co., Inc.*,[355] defendants, several major Midwestern oil producers, were concerned about the declining tank car and retail prices of gasoline which resulted from crude oil overproduction and retail gasoline price wars. The producers entered into an "informal gentlemen's agreement or understanding whereby each undertook to perform his share of the joint undertaking"[356] and thereby effectuate a rise in spot and retail gasoline prices. Specifically, defendants agreed to purchase the depressed (excess) gasoline, thereby reducing the supply in the market and increasing prices. The defendants even attempted to "keep [themselves] informed as to the current prices of gasoline and to use [their] persuasion and influence to see to it that the [major refiners] paid a fair going market price and did not 'chisel' on the small refiners."[357]

---

[350] 980 F.2d 171 (3d Cir. 1992).

[351] *Id.* at 212 (*quoting Edward J. Sweeney & Sons, Inc. v. Texaco, Inc.*, 637 F.2d 105 (3d Cir. 1980)). The defendants in *Fineman* were vertically, not horizontally, aligned.

[352] *Id.* at 214–15.

[353] E. Gellhorn, *Antitrust Law and Economics* 257–59 (3d ed. 1986).

[354] VI P. Areeda, *Antitrust Law* ¶ 1402, at 10 (1986).

[355] 310 U.S. 150 (1940).

[356] *Id.* at 179.

[357] *Id.* at 182–83.

The Supreme Court upheld a jury instruction which stated that an agreement to raise or tamper with a price structure was illegal regardless of whether the prices produced were reasonable or not.[358]

Similarly, in *United States v. Trenton Potteries Co.*,[359] defendants, members of a trade association known as the Sanitary Potters' Association, controlling 82% of the domestic vitreous bathroom fixture production, were charged with combining to fix and maintain uniform prices for the sale of sanitary pottery. Although the principle issue in *Trenton Potteries* concerned reasonableness of the price fixed and application of the *per se* rule of illegality, there was no material dispute over existence of the "combination" requisite under § 1 of the Sherman Act.

Although *Socony–Vacuum* and *Trenton Potteries* may be typical of many trade associations and other cases where evidence of an agreement, combination, or conspiracy is not a principle matter of dispute,[360] most § 1 cases permit less direct evidence to satisfy the conspiracy doctrine.

[2] Implied Agreements

When direct evidence of an agreement does not exist, and existence of the agreement is disputed, it is often necessary to utilize indirect or circumstantial evidence in order to infer the requisite agreement, combination, or conspiracy.[361]

[3] Procedural Matters

Existence of the requisite agreement is an issue to be resolved by the trier of fact. The antitrust plaintiff must adduce sufficient evidence of an "agreement" so as to defeat both a directed verdict motion and post–trial motions directed to the sufficiency of the evidence. The Federal Rules of Civil Procedure provide that a directed verdict will be granted only when "a review of the evidence demonstrates conclusively that reasonable minds could not differ about the controlling issue of fact."[362] On a motion for directed verdict, the court views the evidence in the light most favorable to the party opposing the motion. Thus, in order to make a case that can be submitted to the jury, a plaintiff must, at a minimum, present sufficient evidence that "permits the conclusion that the existence of a conspiracy is more likely than not,"[363] otherwise, the plaintiff has not satisfied its burden

---

[358] *Id.* at 210.

[359] 273 U.S. 392 (1927).

[360] *See United States v. Hayter Oil Co.*, 51 F.3d 1265 (6th Cir. 1995), where the defendants admitted that a conspiracy existed at one point, but denied it existed within the relevant statute of limitations.

[361] *See Lovett v. General Motors Corporation*, 998 F.2d 575, 580–81 (8th Cir. 1993) (refusing to imply a conspiracy from GM's decision to quit supplying cars to the plaintiff because of his price–cutting techniques which were becoming detrimental to other GM dealerships).

[362] Fed. R. Civ. P. 50(a).

[363] VI P. Areeda, *Antitrust Law* ¶ 1405, at 21 (1986).

of proof. Such evidence may include admissions which would otherwise be hearsay statements, if the admission is from an alleged coconspirator, made "during the course and in furtherance of the conspiracy."[364]

In *American Tobacco Co. v. United States*[365] the Court stated that "[w]here the circumstances are such as to warrant a jury in finding that the conspirators had a unity of purpose or a common design and understanding, or a meeting of minds in an unlawful arrangement, the conclusion that a conspiracy is established is justified." In *Monsanto Co. v. Spray–Rite Service Corp.*[366] the Court deemed it "of considerable importance" that independent activity by a single entity be distinguished from a concerted effort by more than one entity. Evidence, which establishes an agreement, requires a showing of "a conscious commitment to a common scheme designed to achieve an unlawful objective."[367] Thus, "there must be [direct or circumstantial] evidence that tends to exclude the possibility that [defendants] were acting independently."[368]

It is important to remember that the mere capacity to conspire does not immediately warrant a finding of actual conspiracy in violation of § 1. As the Second Circuit stated in *Capital Imaging Associates, P.C. v. Mohawk Valley Medical Associates*,[369] "[t]he mere opportunity to conspire does not by itself support the inference that such an illegal combination actually occurred." In order to prove the defendants illegally conspired and avoid defendant's summary judgment motion, the plaintiffs in *Mohawk* needed to "present evidence that casts doubt on inferences of independent action or proper conduct by defendants."[370] This does not mean, however, that plaintiffs faced with convincing the court to deny the summary judgment motion must prove the defendants specifically meant to restrain trade.[371] Although the plaintiffs in *Mohawk* were successful in proving a conspiracy, summary judgment was still granted because they could not prove that the defendants had market power or that their conduct substantially harmed competition.

Traditionally, a motion for summary judgment was disfavored as a means of terminating an antitrust action.[372] The reason advanced was that antitrust litigation is often a fact–bound controversy with issues of intent and effect in dispute. More recently, the use of summary judgment as a

---

[364] Fed. R. Evid. 801(d)(2)(E).

[365] 328 U.S. 781, 810 (1946).

[366] 465 U.S. 752, 763 (1984).

[367] *Id.* at 764, *citing Edward J. Sweeney & Sons, Inc. v. Texaco, Inc.*, 637 F.2d 105, 111 (3d Cir. 1980). The Eighth Circuit has stated that "lay testimony," i.e., testimony by witnesses outside the conspiracy, can be sufficient evidence of an agreement or conspiracy. *United States v. Misle Bus Equipment Co.*, 967 F.2d 1227, 1234 (8th Cir. 1992).

[368] 465 U.S. at 764.

[369] 996 F.2d 537, 544 (2d Cir. 1993).

[370] *Id.*

[371] *Id.*

[372] *Poller v. CBS*, 368 U.S. 464 (1962).

means of preliminary disposition of the action has become more accepted, if not favored.[373] Indeed, the Supreme Court in *Matsushita Elec. Indus. Co. v. Zenith Radio Corp.*,[374] refused to infer a conspiracy among Japanese television manufacturers to charge below cost prices in the United States from plaintiff's theory and evidence that the Japanese manufacturers were charging high prices in Japan to support their cross–subsidization in the United States market. The Court affirmed a summary judgment disposition against a plaintiff because after prolonged discovery of the alleged conspiracy, the evidence was speculative and equally consistent with defendants' theory.[375] Said the Court, "conduct that is as consistent with permissible competition as with illegal conspiracy does not, without more, support even an inference of conspiracy."[376] The announced standard for granting summary judgment is evidence produced by the plaintiff "that tends to exclude the possibility" that defendants acted independently of each other.[377]

Courts also have stated that the conspiracy claim should have an economically rational motive. In *Johnson v. Hospital Corp. of America*,[378] the court refused to reverse the lower court's finding of no conspiracy to exclude because, among other reasons, the defendants did not stand to benefit economically through excluding the plaintiffs from practicing at the defendant hospital. The Fifth Circuit, in quoting *Matsushita Elec. Industrial Co. v. Zenith Radio Corp.*,[379] stated that if the parties "had no rational economic motive to conspire, and if their conduct is consistent with other, equally plausible explanations, the conduct does not give rise to an inference of conspiracy."[380]

Another issue surrounding the conspiracy doctrine is determining the type of behavior sufficient to suggest a subsequent withdrawal from the

---

[373] For a good discussion on the required showings for a summary judgment motion to succeed, including the good faith requirement, *see Reserve Supply Corp. v. Owens–Corning Fiberglass Corp.*, 971 F.2d 37, 49 (7th Cir. 1992).

The court in *Ideal Dairy Farms, Inc. v. John Labatt, Ltd.*, 90 F.3d 737, 747 (3d Cir. 1996), attributes this gradual acceptance of summary judgment as a means of efficiently adjudicating some antitrust claims to the abandonment of the "special standard" that the Supreme Court used to apply to summary judgment motions when trade restraints were involved.

[374] 475 U.S. 574 (1986).

[375] Cf. *Eastman Kodak Co, v. Image Tech. Servs., Inc.*, 504 U.S. 451 (1992).

[376] *Id*. at 597 n.21.

[377] *Id*. at 597–98, *citing Monsanto Co. v. Spray–Rite Serv. Corp.*, 465 U.S. 752, 764 (1984). *See also Blomkest Fertilizer, Inc. v. Potash Corp. of Saskatchewan, Inc.*, 203 F.3d 1028 (8th Cir. 2000) (holding that parallel pricing followed by price verification does not meet the burdens on plaintiff imposed by *Matsushita* and *Monsanto*), *cert. denied*, 531 U.S. 815 (2000).

[378] 95 F.3d 383, 392 (5th Cir. 1996).

[379] 475 U.S. 574, 587 (1986).

[380] *Id*. at 393. *See also Amerinet, Inc. v. Xerox, Corp.*, 972 F.2d 1483, 1494 (8th Cir. 1992) ("[I]f the factual context renders respondents' claim implausible — and if the claim. . . simply makes no economic sense — respondents must come forward with more persuasive evidence to support their claim than would otherwise be necessary" (*quoting Matsushita*, 475 U.S. at 587)).

conspiracy. [381] *CCAM v. AMA* [382] is an instructive example of effective and ineffective withdrawals from a conspiracy. Courts recognize that evidence of withdrawal depends largely on the context and facts of each case. The court in *CCAM* felt that the actions of all three defendants except the AMA constituted a verifiable withdrawal from the concerted refusal to deal, thereby excusing them from liability for any alleged antitrust violation.

In *United States v. Antar,* [383] the Third Circuit heard an appeal from two defendants convicted of RICO violations for fraudulent book keeping activities. The defendants were the former president and a member of the "Office of President" for Crazy Eddie's Inc., an electronics chain in the New York area. One defendant appealed his conviction on the theory that he had withdrawn from the conspiracy when he resigned from his position in 1987. The court rejected his contention. The court first delineated its two part standard for establishing withdrawal.

> First, the defendant must come forward with evidence evincing a prima facie showing of withdrawal. If the defendant makes this prima facie showing, the burden then shifts to the [plaintiff] to rebut the prima facie case, "either by impeaching the defendant's proof or by going forward with evidence of some conduct in furtherance of the conspiracy subsequent to the act of withdrawing. . ." [384] When seen through the lens of a two stage burden of proof, we believe the cases establish that if the defendant completely severs his or her relationship with the enterprise, he or she has established a prima facie showing of withdrawal without showing any other affirmative act inconsistent with the conspiracy and without giving any further notice to his or her co–conspirators. [385]

The court set out principles for cases dealing with withdrawal.

> (1) [R]esignation from the enterprise does not, in and of itself, constitute withdrawal from a conspiracy as a matter of law, (2) total severing of ties with the enterprise may constitute withdrawal from the conspiracy; however, (3) even if the defendant completely severs ties with the enterprise, the defendant still may remain a part of the conspiracy if he continues to do acts in furtherance of the conspiracy and continues to receive benefits from the conspiracy operations. [386]

The court determined that the defendant fell under the third principle. Since he had maintained stock in the corporation after resigning, he had continued to receive benefits from the illegal activity. Also, even though the defendant claimed he attempted to take over the company, the court

---

[381] For an example of an effective withdrawal, *see In re Potash Antitrust Litigation,* 954 F.Supp. 1334 (D. Minn. 1997).

[382] 867 F.2d 270 (6th Cir. 1989).

[383] 53 F.3d 568 (3d Cir. 1995). *See also United States v. Stouffer,* 986 F.2d 916, 922 (5th Cir. 1993) (holding that forcible removal from a work position does not constitute withdrawal from a conspiracy, since there is no proof of affirmative action inconsistent with the scheme.)

[384] *Id.* at 582 (*citing United States v. Local 560,* 974 F.2d 315, 338 (3d Cir. 1992).

[385] 53 F.3d at 582–83 (*quoting United States v. Local 560,* 974 F.2d 315, 338 (3d Cir. 1992)).

[386] *Id.*

did not equate this with an attempt to expose the fraud, as he could have been acting in a manner calculated to further the wrongful activity. [387] As such, the defendant in *Antar* failed to establish his burden of proof concerning the alleged withdrawal.

The Seventh Circuit explained the extraordinary precautions and general reluctance surrounding the withdrawal defense from a policy standpoint in *United States v. Schweihs*. [388]

" '[A] conspirator will not be permitted by the law to limit his responsibility for [the conspiracy's] consequences by ceasing, however definitively, to participate. . .You do not absolve yourself of guilt of bombing by walking away from the ticking bomb. And similarly, the law will not let you wash your hands of a dangerous scheme that you have set in motion and that can continue to operate and cause great harm without your continued participation.' " [389]

The court clarified its position by stating that "withdrawal requires more than a mere cessation of activity on the part of the defendant; it requires some affirmative action which disavows or defeats the purpose of the conspiracy." [390]

[4] Conscious Parallelism

In *Interstate Circuit v. United States* [391] the Supreme Court faced the question whether a trial court finding of an inference of an agreement could be upheld. The standard of review dictates that the trial court could not be reversed unless the finding of fact is clearly erroneous.

Interstate Circuit was a movie exhibitor with a complete monopoly of first run theatres and a significant share of the subsequent–run theatre market in several cities. Interstate, together with Consolidated Theatres, Inc., another defendant that was affiliated with Interstate, contributed over 74% of the license fees paid in their areas to certain motion picture distributors, who represented a second group of defendants. The distributor defendants had approximately 75% market share of all first–class feature films exhibited domestically.

The Government alleged that the distributor defendants had violated § 1 of the Sherman Act by combining to control theatre admission prices and exhibition of double–features. The evidence demonstrated that Interstate sent a letter to the distributors naming their representatives and asking them to agree to impose controls over admission prices and double–features as a condition of Interstate's continued patronage of the distributors' films. There was no direct testimony that the distributors agreed with each other

---

[387] *Id.* at 584.

[388] 971 F.2d 1302 (7th Cir. 1992). This is actually a criminal case involving extortion, but it serves our purposes as well.

[389] *Id.* at 1323 (*quoting United States v. Patel*, 879 F.2d 292, 294 (7th Cir. 1989).

[390] *Id.* at 1323.

[391] 306 U.S. 208 (1939).

to comply with Interstate's demand; however, each distributor did subsequently agree with at least some of Interstate's requested conditions. Thus the government was "compelled to rely on inferences drawn from the course of conduct of the alleged conspirators" in order to prove the requisite § 1 agreement.[392]

The Supreme Court upheld the trial court's inference of an agreement. The Court identified several "plus factors" from which such an inference properly could be made.[393] These "plus factors" remain the benchmark from which an agreement can be inferred:[394]

    * Whether defendant's actions were a *radical departure* from prior practice.

    * Whether defendant was *aware* that its co–defendants had been solicited to conduct themselves similarly.

    * Whether defendant had been *invited* to engage in the alleged conspiracy when it was solicited.

    * Whether each defendant had a substantial *profit motive* for concerted action.

    * Whether defendant *actually participated* in the scheme and engaged in substantial *unanimity of action*, or uniform conduct.

    * Whether defendant's conduct represented *interdependent action* in the sense that compliance would not profit any single defendant unless all the other defendants similarly complied.

Interstate Circuit shows that although mere evidence of parallel conduct by competitors is not enough for an antitrust plaintiff to obtain a directed verdict, an agreement is properly inferred from conscious parallelism when these so–called "plus factors" exist.[395] *Interstate Circuit* also shows, however, that such an inference, even if based on sufficient "plus factors," may be rebutted by defendants' evidence. "When the proof supported . . . the inference of such concert[ed] [action], the burden rested on [defendants] of going forward with the evidence to explain away or contradict it."[396]

Defendants in *Interstate Circuit* failed to carry this burden when they called as witnesses only lower level local managers, with questionable authority to act, to testify that they had acted independently. Defendants did not "call as witnesses those officers who did have authority to act for

---

[392] *Id.* at 221.

[393] *Id.* at 222–23.

[394] The Third Circuit in *Petruzzi's IGA Supermarkets, Inc. v. Darling–Delaware Co.*, 998 F.2d 1224, 1244 (3d. Cir. 1993), warned that courts must use caution in applying the "plus" factors in order to avoid overapplication. As Professor Areeda explained, in some cases such as oligopoly pricing, the existence of "plus" factors may reflect the interdependence of the industry rather than the intent to conspire and restrain trade. IV P. Areeda, *Antitrust Law*, ¶ 1434c, at 214–15. This, of course, raises structural antitrust concerns.

[395] 306 U.S. at 225–27. *See also Toys "R" Us v. FTC*, 221 F.3d 928 (7th Cir. 2000) (inferring a horizontal agreement from evidence of a series of vertical agreements, per *Interstate Circuit*).

[396] 306 U.S. at 225–6.

[them] and who were in a position to know whether they had acted in pursuance of agreement . . . ."[397] From this absence, the Court inferred that testimony of such officers would have been adverse to the defendants, noting that "[t]he production of weak evidence when strong is available can only lead to the conclusion that the strong would have been adverse."[398] *Interstate Circuit* shows that when the burden shifts to the defendant to rebut an inference of conscious parallelism, a threshold requirement is the use of the defendant's strongest available evidence.

In *United States v. Masonite Corp.*,[399] defendant had a unique patent for manufacturing wallboard. Masonite entered into separate agreements with numerous competitors whereby each competitor would market Masonite manufactured wallboard as Masonite's agent, utilizing the competitor's own name on the product and selling at prices set by Masonite. The agreements also specified classes of persons to whom each agent was authorized to sell the patented wallboard product. The various competitors who made such separate agreements with Masonite were each aware of the other similar agency agreements.

The Court, faced with the question whether the defendants, Masonite and its agents, had combined to restrain trade in violation of §§ 1 and 2 of the Sherman Act, stated that "[i]t was enough that, knowing that concerted action was contemplated and invited, the distributors gave their adherence to the scheme and participated in it. "[400] The Court was not troubled by the fact that the district court found that each of the defendants who entered into an agreement with Masonite acted independently and, unlike the *Interstate Circuit* defendants, "desired the agreement regardless of the action that might be taken by any of the others [and] did not require as a condition of its acceptance that Masonite make such an agreement with any of the others."[401] The absence of plus factors that were present in *Interstate Circuit* was not fatal to the government's case in *Masonite*. Also, even though the defendants in *Masonite* argued "that they did not intend to join a combination or to fix prices," the Court determined that they " 'must be held to have intended the necessary consequences of their acts . . . .' "[402]

In *Theatre Enterprises, Inc. v. Paramount Film Distributing Corp.*,[403] the Supreme Court considered parallel conduct in a different procedural context than it did in *Interstate Circuit*.[404] In a treble damage civil action tried

---

[397] *Id.* at 226.

[398] *Id.*

[399] 316 U.S. 265 (1942).

[400] *Id.* at 275, *citing Interstate Circuit, Inc. v. United States*, 306 U.S. 208, 226 (1939).

[401] *Id.*

[402] *Id.* citing *United States v. Patten*, 226 U.S. 525, 543 (1913).

[403] 346 U.S. 537 (1954).

[404] In *Interstate Circuit* the Supreme Court reviewed the factual finding of the trial court that defendants' agreement could be inferred from their conduct. The applicable standard of review was that the lower court's finding was not reversible unless clearly erroneous. In

before a jury, the trial judge denied the plaintiff's motion for directed verdict, and the jury inferred an antitrust agreement based upon defendants' parallel conduct, even though defendants offered some evidence of independent business judgment to rebut the inference of an agreement.

In affirming, Justice Clark reiterated that "this Court has never held that proof of parallel business behavior conclusively establishes agreement or . . . that such behavior itself" is sufficient to warrant a directed verdict for a plaintiff in a civil antitrust suit.[405] Although there was some evidence of an agreement, many of the *Interstate Circuit* plus factors were absent. For example, defendants in *Theatre Enterprises* were able to argue plausible profit maximizing business justifications that could make each of the defendants' actions independently rational and thereby negate the charge of interdependency. Additionally, plaintiff failed to show that all the defendants knew of their co–defendants' conduct, thus negating knowledge. Furthermore, defendants introduced testimony of their responsible corporate officers as strong evidence to rebut the inference of an agreement. The Court affirmed the jury verdict in favor of defendant.

[a] Interpretation

Lower courts have interpreted the Supreme Court's cases on conscious parallelism to mean that the requisite agreement or combination can be shown by evidence of consciously parallel conduct in combination with at least some of the plus factors discussed above. Evidence of conscious parallelism or interdependence alone is not enough to warrant a finding of an agreement.[406] The next section discusses a specific industry practice which implicates the problems of proof associated with finding an agreement.

[b] Base Point Delivered Pricing

In *Federal Trade Commission v. Cement Institute*,[407] the Supreme Court provided a cogent explanation of base point delivered pricing, a mechanism sometimes used to determine the price of delivered industrial goods:

Theatre Enterprises the jury returned a general verdict for defendants. The Supreme Court reviewed the lower court's denial of plaintiff's motion for a directed verdict. The applicable standard of review of denial of plaintiff's motion was that a directed verdict should issue only if the evidence "raised [no] fact issues requiring the trial judge to submit the issue of conspiracy to the jury." *Id*. at 542.

405 *Id*. at 541.

406 *See, e.g., Michelman v. Clark–Schwebel Fiber Glass Corp.*, 534 F.2d 1036 (2d Cir.)(1976); R. Bork, *The Antitrust Paradox* 178–97 (1978); 1 M. Handler, *Twenty–Five Years of Antitrust* 531 (1973); C. Kaysen & D. Turner, *Antitrust Policy* 106–09 (1959); Nye, *Can Conduct Oriented Enforcement Inhibit Conscious Parallelism?*, 44 Antitrust L.J. 206, 222 (1975); and L. Sullivan, *supra* note 196, at 317 (1977); *Wallace v. Bank of Bartlett*, 55 F.3d 1166, 1168–69 (6th Cir. 1995), *rehearing denied*, ("[P]arallel pricing, without more, does not itself establish a violation of the Sherman Act."); *Petruzzi's IGA Supermarkets, Inc. v. Darling–Delaware Co.*, 998 F.2d 1224, 1232–1233, 1242–43 (3d Cir. 1993).

407 333 U.S. 683 (1948).

Goods may be sold and delivered to customers at the seller's mill or warehouse door or may be sold free on board (f.o.b.) trucks or railroad cars immediately adjacent to the seller's mill or warehouse. In either event the actual cost of the goods to the purchaser is, broadly speaking, the seller's "mill price" plus the purchaser's cost of transportation. However, if the seller fixes a price at which [it] undertakes to deliver goods to the purchaser where they are to be used, the cost to the purchaser is the "delivered price." A seller who makes the mill price identical for all purchasers of like amount and quality simply delivers [its] goods at the same place ([its] mill) and for the same price (price at the mill). [It] thus receives for all f.o.b. mill sales an identical net amount of money for like goods from all customers. But a "delivered price" system creates complications which may result in a seller's receiving different net returns from the sale of like goods. The cost of transporting 500 miles is almost always more than the cost of transporting 100 miles. [408]

Base point pricing establishes the purchaser's cost predicated upon delivery costs from a standard shipping location which may not be the actual place from which the goods for a particular order are shipped. [409]

In *Cement Institute*, [410] the Supreme Court reviewed a cease and desist order issued by the Federal Trade Commission against the 74 corporate members of a trade association, the Cement Institute, and 21 individuals associated with the Institute. The corporations manufactured, sold, and distributed cement employing a multiple base point pricing system that resulted in identical pricing by all competing corporations at any point in the United States, allegedly interfering with competition by means of an unlawful combination. The cement industry was highly concentrated, with 10 of its 80 domestic manufacturers controlling over half of the mills. The Federal Trade Commission charged that this conduct constituted an unfair method of competition in violation of § 5 of the Federal Trade Commission Act. [411]

The Court ruled first that the "[Federal Trade] Commission has jurisdiction to declare that conduct tending to restrain trade is an unfair method of competition even though the selfsame conduct may also violate the Sherman Act." [412] The Court then questioned whether there was sufficient evidence to warrant the Commission's finding of concerted conduct based upon defendants' parallel base point delivered pricing.

The defendants attempted to rebut an inference of unlawful concerted conduct through the testimony of economists who stated that precisely identical bidding will always result in the cement industry without either

---

[408] *Id.* at 696–97.

[409] *See generally* Haddock, *Basing Point Pricing: Competitive vs. Collusive Theories*, 72 Am. Ec. Rev. 289 (1982); G. Stigler, *The Organization of Industry* 147–70 (1968); Kaysen, *Basing Point Pricing and Public Policy*, 63 Q.J. Econ. 289 (1948).

[410] 333 U.S. 683 (1948).

[411] 15 U.S.C. § 45.

[412] 333 U.S. at 693.

express or implied agreements among the bidders. The Commission disagreed and ruled that uniformity of bidding and lack of competition in the industry resulted from understandings or agreements among the defendants. The Supreme Court, upholding the Commission, held that an understanding, express or implied, could be inferred "from evidence that the industry's Institute actively worked, in cooperation with various of its members, to maintain the multiple basing point delivered price system; [and] that this pricing system is calculated to produce, and has produced, uniform prices and terms of sale throughout the country . . . ."[413]

The Court observed the highly concentrated structure of the cement industry and that cement is a fungible, a non–differentiated product. The Court eventually found that multiple basing point delivered pricing was an instrument to effectuate elimination of price competition. There was evidence of "[t]housands of secret sealed bids . . . received by public agencies which corresponded in prices of cement down to a fractional part of a penny."[414] One example showed that eleven separate bidders quoted precisely $3.286854 per barrel of cement in a 1936 sealed bid to the government.[415]

In *Triangle Conduit & Cable Co. v. Federal Trade Commission,*[416] the Seventh Circuit applied the holding of *Cement Institute* to review a Federal Trade Commission cease and desist order issued against fourteen corporate manufacturers of rigid steel conduit that controlled 93% of the conduit industry.[417] The alleged conduct by defendant corporation was the uniform quoting of delivered prices and parallel use of a formula for computing those delivered prices. The formula used a base price at one of only two cites in the United States, regardless of the actual originating point, plus transportation to the actual point of delivery. This scheme resulted in conduit manufacturers "match[ing] their delivered price quotations, and purchasers at or near a place of production could not buy more cheaply from their nearby producer than from producers located at greater distances . . . ."[418]

The court sustained the Federal Trade Commission's cease and desist order, holding that individual use of base point delivery pricing, with knowledge that parallel competitive conduct would yield identical delivered price quotations, constituted an unfair method of competition. The court stated that "price uniformity especially if accompanied by an artificial price level not related to the supply and demand of a given commodity may be evidence from which an agreement or understanding, or some concerted action of sellers operating to restrain commerce, may be inferred."[419] The

---

[413] *Id.* at 716.

[414] *Id.* at 713.

[415] *Id.* n.15.

[416] 168 F.2d 175 (7th Cir. 1948), *aff'd by an equally divided court,* 336 U.S. 956 (1949).

[417] 15 U.S.C. § 45.

[418] 168 F.2d at 180.

[419] *Id.* at 179, *citing Cement Mfrs. Protective Ass'n v. United States,* 268 U.S. 588, 606.

court relied on an earlier Supreme Court case, *Cement Manufacturers Protective Association v. United States*.[420]

In *Cement Manufacturers*, however, the Supreme Court held that information dissemination was not in itself a § 1 violation. The Court reasoned that the evidence in that case "fail[ed] to show any effect on price and production except such as would naturally flow from the dissemination of . . . that information [pertaining to sale and distribution of cement] . . . in the trade and its natural influence on individual action."[421] This, then, suggests that a Sherman Act plaintiff must show something more than "natural" influences on individual action in order to establish an inference of agreement.[422]

Likewise, the Ninth Circuit in *Boise Cascade Corp. v. FTC*,[423] undercut *Triangle Conduit* by holding that evidence of a conspiracy must be present before industry–wide base point pricing is held illegal. "[I]n the absence of evidence of overt agreement to utilize a pricing system to avoid price competition, the Commission must demonstrate that the challenged pricing system has actually had the effect of fixing or stabilizing prices. Without such effect, a mere showing of parallel action will not establish a section 5 violation."

Recently, the District of Columbia Circuit rejected a claim of base point pricing brought by local distribution companies of natural gas against the Federal Energy Regulatory Commission in *United Distribution Companies v. FERC*.[424] The plaintiffs alleged, among other things, that the FERC's act of removing "transportation costs from per unit charges at the supplier level amount[ed] to 'base point pricing,' which. . . 'would be a *per se* violation of the antitrust laws', if done by agreement among private parties to fix the price of transportation added to the price of products."[425] In rejecting the challenge on this theory, the court noted that past base point pricing cases had dealt with "private agreements in otherwise unregulated markets, and commodities such as cement, expensive to transport as contrasted with natural gas. . . ."[426]

[B] Oligopoly Pricing and Facilitating Devices

As discussed in Chapters 2 and 6, an oligopoly is a market characterized by only a few sellers. One theory of antitrust enforcement advances the idea that in oligopoly markets interdependence of action among the competitors

---

[420] 268 U.S. 588 (1925).

[421] *Id*. at 606.

[422] *Id*.

[423] 637 F.2d 573 (9th Cir. 1980). *See also In re Plywood Antitrust Litigation*, 655 F.2d 627, 634 (5th Cir. 1981); *Crouse–Hinds Co.*, 46 F.T.C. 1114 (1950). *See* further discussion in § 6.07, *infra*.

[424] 88 F.3d 1105 (D.C. Cir. 1996).

[425] *Id*. at 1169 (quoting plaintiff's brief).

[426] *Id*. at 577.

characterizes the market. Interdependent action suggests that each seller takes into account the market reactions of the other competitors before price or output decisions are made. Anticipation, reaction and coordination of a competitor's market moves are central to the theory of oligopoly pricing. If one seller were to increase output and lower price in order to capture more sales, other sellers would follow suit and, if the first price change were not concealed, the reaction to lower prices would be swift. A substantial increase in market share would not follow. The price cutter thus would gain little; incentives to price compete are reduced accordingly.

Given the structure of the market, producers are aware of the reaction of competitors to price changes and will take this into account when making price decisions. Common interest and mutual understanding dictate that competitors in concentrated markets forego price competition. The question is whether such market interdependence, known as oligopoly pricing, constitutes an agreement or combination in violation of § 1, or whether the oligopoly behavior is natural and rational in light of the market structure.[427]

One leading commentator, in contrasting oligopoly pricing to conscious parallelism, has opined that:

[C]onscious parallelism is devoid of anything that might reasonably be called agreement when it involves simply the independent responses of a group of competitors to the same set of economic facts—independent in the sense that each would have made the same decision for himself even though his competitors decided otherwise. But the consciously parallel decisions of oligopolists in setting their basic prices, which are interdependent in that they depend on competitors setting the same price, are not nearly so easily disposed of on the ground that no agreement is involved.

. . . .

In this light, several comments may be made. First, there is fair ground for argument that oligopoly price behavior can be described as individual behavior—rational individual decision in the light of relevant economic facts—as well as it can be described as "agreement." It can readily be said that each seller in this situation, in refraining from price competition, is not agreeing with his competitors but simply throwing their probable decisions into his price calculus as impersonal market facts . . . . [E]ach seller has simply decided individually . . . that it is more profitable not to indulge in price competition under any but the most pressing circumstances, appealing as price cutting might appear to be from a less experienced viewpoint.

---

[427] See generally E. Chamberlin, The Theory of Monopolistic Competition (1933); Turner, The Definition of Agreement Under the Sherman Act: Conscious Parallelism and Refusals to Deal, 75 Harv. L. Rev. 655, 663–73 (1962).

Second, it seems questionable to call the behavior of oligopolists in setting their prices unlawful when the behavior in essence is identical to that of sellers in a competitive industry.[428]

Professor Turner concluded that:

Oligopolists who take into account the probable reactions of competitors in setting their basic prices, without more in the way of "agreement" than is found in "conscious parallelism," should not be held unlawful conspirators under the Sherman Act even though . . . they refrain from competing in price. As a legal conclusion, this would be stated in either of two ways: 1) there is no violation because there is no "agreement;" or 2) there is no violation because, although there is "agreement," the agreement cannot properly be called an unlawful agreement.[429]

Professor Areeda has offered three propositions regarding oligopolistic pricing under the Sherman Act.

1) Mere interdependence pricing among oligopolists ought not to be covered by the Sherman Act at all, unless the remedy can be confined to equitable relief, preferably only in government–initiated proceedings.

2) If that condition is satisfied, selective intervention may be warranted under the Sherman Act, but § 1 is less suitable than § 2.

3) If § 1 is nevertheless held applicable, it must be recognized that a very special kind of "conspiracy" is involved and that it calls for different rules of liability as well as different remedies.[430]

To differentiate cartel behavior from interdependent pricing between oligopoly members, consider:

Cartels invite the full range of antitrust remedies; they are easily avoidable and susceptible to simple "stop conspiring" injunctions; they are and should be condemned automatically without proof of power of effect; no complicated, costly, and perhaps unfeasible or inefficient breaking–up or other market restructuring is required. Interdependent pricing is substantially or fundamentally different in each of these respects.[431]

Another approach suggested by Professor (now Judge) Posner argued that while noncompetitive pricing by oligopolists may be facilitated by the structure of the market, it was not inevitably compelled.[432] The voluntary and coordinated action among the sellers was similar to conduct in a

---

[428] Turner, *supra* note 427 at 663–66. Copyright 1962 by the Harvard Law Review Association. Reprinted with permission.

[429] *Id.* at 671 (citation omitted).

[430] VI P.E. Areeda, *Antitrust Law*, ¶ 1432 g (1986).

[431] VI P.E. Areeda, *Antitrust Law*, ¶ 1432 h (1986).

[432] Posner, *Oligopoly and the Antitrust Laws: A Suggested Approach*, 21 Stan. L. Rev. 1562 (1969).

traditional cartel. The only missing link was an explicit agreement but evidence of the structure of the market could bridge this gap by inferring an agreement through price signaling, tacit acceptances, and coordinated pricing decisions.

These economic theories were the bases of federal enforcement actions in the early 1970's. Concentrated industries, characterized by inflated prices and reduced output, were targets of enforcement. Actions brought by the Federal Trade Commission were oriented toward the structure of the industry. They were litigated under a "shared monopoly" theory— a few sellers acting as though they were a single–firm monopoly with output restrictions, higher prices and entry barriers.

The Department of Justice equated shared monopoly actions with oligopoly pricing and advanced enforcement actions when "facilitating devices" were used as a means to further price coordination among firms in an oligopoly. Two preconditions existed: (1) a noncompetitive price structure, and (2) little likelihood that independent action would result in increased profits and market share. The government urged that § 1 of the Sherman Act is violated when there was (1) parallel conduct by firms in a concentrated industry, (2) awareness by each firm that rivals are following lock–step in a parallel fashion, (3) anticompetitive benefits, and (4) actions contradictory to the independent self–interest of each firm.[433] Although its theories of shared monopoly and oligopoly pricing attempted to blend economic theories and traditional cartel agreements into an enforcement theme, the government's litigation successes were minimal.

In re *Ethyl Corp.*,[434] the Federal Trade Commission brought an industry–wide suit directed at oligopoly pricing. The complaint alleged that four companies, with a total market share of 80%, maintained uniform prices for anti–knock gasoline compounds by "signing" future price changes to competitors. In addition, the Commission charged that the scheme was facilitated by defendants (1) using a 30–day price change advance notice clause in all contracts, (2) disclosing advance price changes, (3) selling only on a uniform delivered price basis, and (4) dealing on a most–favored customer arrangement with a customer entitled to the lowest price at which the manufacturer sells to other buyers. The pivotal theory was the price signaling, facilitated by advance price charge announcements in the press, which enabled coordination of prices throughout the industry.

On appeal to the Second Circuit,[435] the FTC's enforcement theory was rejected on the factual record presented. The court held that § 5 of the FTC Act is not violated by "non–collusive, non–predatory, independent conduct."[436] The court held, "The mere existence of an oligopolistic market

---

[433] *See, e.g., In re Ethyl Corp.*, No. 9128 (F.T.C. May 30, 1979) (complaint) [1976– 77 Transfer Binder] Trade Reg. Rep. (CCH) 21,579; *United States v. G.E. Co.*, [1977] 1 Trade Cas. (CCH) 712; *United States v. G.M. Corp.*, [1974] 2 Trade Cas. (CCH) 97,656.

[434] 101 FTC 425 (1983), *rev. sub nom.*, *E.I. DuPont de Nemours & Co. v. F.T.C.*, 729, F.2d 128 (2d Cir. 1984). *See also* discussion in § 6.07, *infra*.

[435] 729 F.2d 128 (2d Cir. 1984).

[436] *Id.* at 137.

structure in which a small group of manufacturers engage in consciously parallel pricing of an identical product does not violate the antitrust laws."[437] The court concluded that in order to find a unfair method of competition under § 5 of the Act, in absence of an agreement, there must be "1) evidence of anticompetitive intent or purpose . . . , or 2) the absence of an independent legitimate business reason for the conduct."[438] Moreover, no § 1 Sherman Act violation occurred because the court refused to find a tacit agreement. To be sure, the court found that the challenged practices were adopted independently and for legitimate business reasons.

It is not clear whether the court in *Ethyl* sounded the death knell for the oligopoly pricing theory *per se*, especially where facilitating devices are present, but the court did order the Commission to first define the conditions under which such practices could be considered "unfair" under § 5 before other suits are brought.

A similar result was reached by the Ninth Circuit in *Boise Cascade Corp. v. FTC*,[439] where the court refused to enforce an FTC order prohibiting a delivered pricing system challenged under conscious parallel conduct theory. *Boise* required a finding of either (1) an overt agreement to avoid price competition or (2) an actual anticompetitive price effect caused by the challenged practice. A mere showing of parallel conduct in a concentrated or oligopoly industry is not enough. "Interdependence is consistent with the existence of a conspiracy but does not itself prove the traditional agreement."[440] One must prove more than the motivation to conspire in order to prove a conspiracy.[441]

[C] The Plurality Requirement & Intra–Enterprise Conspiracy

The "contract, combination, . . . or conspiracy" language of § 1 requires proof of a relationship between at least two legally separate persons. Courts often label such requisite proof as the "plurality requirement." A literal interpretation of § 1 means that any two persons, even officers of the same corporation, could engage in unlawful conduct merely by agreeing to any course of conduct. But logic dictates that no corporation could survive if its officers and employees were not permitted to agree among themselves to engage in otherwise lawful conduct. As the Ninth Circuit has said: "[I]f the Sherman Act forbids such activities it: 'would be socially inconvenient and historically surprising. So long as the business enterprise is regarded as an individual economic unit, it must be permitted to act.'"[442]

---

[437] *Id.* at 139.

[438] *Id.*

[439] 637 F.2d 573 (9th Cir. 1980).

[440] VI P.E. Areeda, *Antitrust Law*, ¶ 1411 (1986).

[441] *Id.* For a detailed discussion of the role of "interdependence" in finding a conspiracy, *see* VI P.E. Areeda *Antitrust Law*, ¶¶ 1411–1415 (1986).

[442] *Knutson v. Daily Review, Inc.*, 548 F.2d 795, 801 (9th Cir. 1976), *quoting* P. Areeda, *Antitrust Analysis* 319 (2d ed. 1974). *See also Nelson Radio & Supply Co. v. Motorola, Inc.*, 200 F.2d 911 (5th Cir. 1952).

A general rule has developed that a single corporation is incapable of conspiring with itself or through its officers, directors, employees, or agents within the meaning of § 1 of the Sherman Act. This general rule, however, does not answer whether the plurality requirement was met in numerous variations in the intra–enterprise structure.

[1] Corporate Parent and Wholly–Owned Incorporated Subsidiary

In *Copperweld Corp. v. Independence Tube Corp.*,[443] the Supreme Court, disapproving the Court's intra–enterprise conspiracy rationale in *Kiefer–Stewart Co. v. Joseph E. Seagram & Sons*,[444] held that as long as the initial parent–subsidiary combination was lawful, a parent and a wholly–owned subsidiary are a single entity incapable of combining or conspiring under § 1 of the Sherman Act.

A parent and its wholly owned subsidiary have a complete unity of interest. Their objectives are common, not disparate; their general corporate actions are guided or determined not by two separate corporate consciousnesses, but one. They are not unlike a multiple team of horses drawing a vehicle under the control of a single driver. With or without a formal "agreement," the subsidiary acts for the benefit of the parent, its sole shareholder. If a parent and a wholly owned subsidiary do "agree" to a course of action, there is no sudden joining of economic resources that had previously served different interests, and there is no justification for § 1 scrutiny.[445]

This idea was extended in *Oksanen v. Page Memorial Hospital*.[446] The court determined that the Board of Trustees and the medical staff of a hospital were not capable of conspiring to exclude the plaintiff through their peer review process. The Court held, "Far from being a competitor with the hospital, the medical staff was in fact a natural component of the hospital's management structure."[447] The court cited *Copperweld*, stating that the Supreme Court cautioned against adopting a rule penalizing coordinated conduct "simply because [such a penalty] might well discourage corporations from creating divisions with their presumed benefits."[448] The plaintiff

---

[443] 467 U.S. 752 (1984).

[444] 340 U.S. 211 (1951). It should be noted that although the Court in *Copperweld* disapproves the reasoning of the *Seagram* Court it nonetheless approves of the ultimate finding of liability "on the ground that the subsidiaries conspired with wholesalers other than the plaintiff." 467 U.S. at 764.

[445] 467 U.S. at 771.

[446] 945 F.2d 696 (4th Cir. 1991). *See also Willman v. Heartland Hosp. E.*, 34 F.3d 605, 611 (1994) ("Corrective action against a physician does not violate the antitrust laws if the peer reviewer had legitimate reasons to believe [it] provided substandard care"); *Mathews v. Lancaster Gen. Hosp.*, 87 F.3d 624, 639–41 (3d Cir. 1996) (evidencing a general intent to not hold peer review committees liable under § 1 unless the evidence is clear and excludes any inference of independent action). *See* § 4.09 *supra* for a discussion of antitrust law's application to other professionals, and § 4.15[c][4] *infra* for a discussion of medical staff as an agent of a hospital and the associated liability under § 1.

[447] *Id.* at 703.

[448] *Id.* (*quoting Copperweld*, 467 U.S. at 771).

then argued that an exception to intra–enterprise immunity existed, since the physicians on the medical staff had personal stakes in the outcome of the peer process. The plaintiff suggested that the doctors' own practices would flourish through the elimination of the plaintiff's practice through an unfavorable peer review. The court declined to accept this argument, cautioning that the "independent personal stake" exception was one which "threaten[ed] to swallow the rule."[449] The court found only one of the physicians was a verifiable competitor to the plaintiff, and he had not taken part in the actions leading to the plaintiff's dismissal from defendant hospital. Any possible economic justifications for the medical staff to discharge the plaintiff were too indirect to be given any serious consideration.[450] Furthermore, "because decisionmaking authority in [the plaintiff's] case was dispersed among a number of individuals, the personal stake exception [was] inapplicable."[451]

The court also denied any inference of a conspiracy within the medical staff itself. "Simply making a peer review recommendation does not prove the existence of a conspiracy; there must be something more such as a conscious commitment by the medical staff to coerce the hospital into accepting its recommendation," it held.[452] Finally, the court found that even if a conspiracy had existed, the plaintiff's claim would still fail because the alleged restraint of trade could not be considered "unreasonable" as required under a rule of reason analysis. Even though the plaintiff was denied staff privileges, "[t]here [was] no evidence that competition as a whole in the relevant market has been harmed."[453] Hence, even setting aside the intraenterprise exception, the plaintiff still failed to prove a punishable violation of § 1.

In contrast, the Tenth Circuit in *Brown v. Presbyterian Healthcare Services*[454] found two defendant doctors who had participated in a peer review committee culminating in the revocation of the plaintiff's obstetrics privileges had conspired in violation of § 1. One of the doctors was a direct competitor of the plaintiff, and, although neither defendant voted in the final decision to exclude Dr. Brown from practicing obstetrics, the evidence showed that each "played an influential role in bringing about the revocation" and that there was not a "reasonable effort to obtain the facts of the matter."[455] The court affirmed the district court's denial of the defendant's motion for judgment as a matter of law on the antitrust claims, and the

---

[449] *Id.* at 705.

[450] *Id.*

[451] *Id.* at 706.

[452] *Id.*

[453] *Id.* at 709. *See also National Ass'n of Review Appraisers & Mortgage Underwriters, Inc. v. Appraisal Found.*, 64 F.3d 1130, 1135 (8th Cir. 1995) (decline in plaintiff's membership because of defendant's refusal to extend association benefits to plaintiff does not "establish harm to overall market").

[454] 101 F.3d 1324 (10th Cir. 1996).

[455] *Id.* at 1333, 1335.

seeming blanket protection previously afforded peer review activities was qualified.

The corporation–subsidiary conspiracy doctrine fell subject to an interesting twist in *International Travel Arrangers v. NWA, Inc.*[456] One of the issues before the court was whether a corporation and its wholly–owned subsidiary which was previously a competitor could conspire after they agreed to merge but before the merger was fully accomplished. The court, relying heavily on its previous decision in *Pink Supply Corp. v. Hiebert, Inc.*,[457] found that "formal consummation of a merger" is not required in affording parent and subsidiary § 1 immunity.[458]

> In *Pink Supply*, this court, applying *Copperweld*, affirmed a district court's grant of summary judgment dismissing a complaint alleging a price–fixing and boycott conspiracy between a manufacturer and its four sales representatives. We conclude[d] that viewed from the perspective of Hiebert's organization, the sales agents were so closely intertwined in economic interest and purpose with Hiebert as to amount to a unified economic consciousness incapable of conspiring with itself. . .In the present case, the district court left it to the jury to determine whether, following the agreement to merge, but before the merger formally was affected, the "economic substance of the relationship" between [defendants] Northwest and Mainline meant they no longer were "separate entities" because they "lacked independent economic consciousness."

The convergence of economic interests between the two defendants overcame the formality regarding the timing of the merger.

Finally, in *Boulware v. State of Nevada, Dept. of HR*,[459] the Ninth Circuit rejected the plaintiff physician's § 1 claim against a hospital and National Care Service Corporation, which was a wholly–owned subsidiary of the hospital. The plaintiff argued that the two entities had violated the Sherman Act by securing a permanent injunction forbidding him from constructing and running a Magnetic Resonance Imaging Unit. The court rejected the claim "at the outset," stating that Humana Hospital and NCSC were incapable of forming the requisite conspiracy to make their activities a violation of § 1.[460]

Note that "wholly–owned" does not necessarily mean 100% ownership. In *Siegel Transfer, Inc. v. Carrier Express, Inc.*,[461] the court held that 99.92% ownership is the same as 100% ownership, and holding 8,993 shares out of 9,000 outstanding shares of stock constitutes complete control of the subsidiary company. If the differences are *de minimus*, courts will apply the "wholly owned" rule and bar a finding of conspiracy.

---

[456] 991 F.2d 1389 (8th Cir. 1993).

[457] 788 F.2d 1313 (8th Cir. 1986).

[458] 991 F.3d at 1398.

[459] 960 F.2d 793 (9th Cir. 1992).

[460] *Id.* at 797.

[461] 54 F.3d 1125, 1133 (3d Cir. 1995).

[2] Corporate Parent and Partially–Owned Incorporated Subsidiary

In *dictum*, the Supreme Court in *Timken Roller Bearing Co. v. United States*,[462] stated that "[t]he fact that there is a common ownership or control of the contracting corporations does not liberate them from the impact of the antitrust laws."[463] This suggests that a parent and partially owned subsidiary may be capable of satisfying the plurality requirement. But in *Timken* other evidence made reliance on the intra–enterprise conspiracy doctrine unnecessary to the result.

In post–*Copperweld* decisions, several circuit courts of appeal have addressed the conspiracy requirement in the context of corporate relationships other than a corporation and its wholly–owned subsidiary. Several cases have held that two corporations which are wholly–owned by the same parent corporation are not capable of conspiring within the meaning of § 1. The Fifth Circuit, in *Hood v. Tenneco Texas Life Insurance Co.*,[464] held that because two corporations which are both wholly–owned by the same parent corporation share a common purpose with their parent corporation, "they cannot conspire with their parent in violation of the Sherman Act. By the same token, neither can they conspire with one another."[465] In *Greenwood Utilities v. Mississippi Power Co.*,[466] another Fifth Circuit case, the court held that two sister corporations wholly–owned by the same corporate parent are incapable of forming a § 1 conspiracy. Moreover, the Third Circuit, in *Weiss v. York Hospital*,[467] held that "[i]f the [two] businesses are controlled at both levels by the same firm, and the divisions at one level of production urge the parent corporation not to deal with their rivals, there is no 'concerted refusal to deal' under § 1."[468]

Second, at least two circuit courts have considered alleged conspiracies between a parent corporation and its less than wholly–owned subsidiary. In *Tunis Bros. Co. v. Ford Motor Co.*,[469] Ford was accused of conspiring with Wenner Ford Tractor, Inc. Ford had established Wenner Ford Tractor and owned 100% of the voting stock, and 79% of the equity stock of Wenner Ford Tractor. Wenner Ford Tractor was an authorized Ford dealer for farm and industrial tractors, machinery, equipment, and parts. The Third Circuit held that *Copperweld* "does not . . . preclude a conspiratorial relationship between Ford and Wenner Ford since Wenner Ford is not wholly–owned

---

[462] 341 U.S. 593 (1951).

[463] *Id.* at 598.

[464] 739 F.2d 1012 (5th Cir. 1984).

[465] *Id.* at 1015.

[466] 751 F.2d 1484, 1496–97, n.8 (5th Cir. 1985), citing *Copperweld Corp. v. Independence Tube Corp.*, 467 U.S. 752 (1984), and *Century Oil Tool, Inc. v. Production Specialties, Inc.*, 737 F.2d 1316 (5th Cir. 1984).

[467] 745 F.2d 786 (3d Cir. 1984).

[468] *Id.* at 819, n.57, *citing Copperweld Corp. v. Independence Tube Corp.*, 467 U.S. 752 (1984).

[469] 763 F.2d 1482 (3d Cir. 1985).

[by Ford]."[470] Thus, even though Ford owned all the voting stock of Wenner Ford Tractor, the fact that a mere 21% of Wenner Ford Tractor's equity stock was owned by other than Ford meant the two corporations were not protected by the reasoning in *Copperweld*.

The First Circuit avoided a direct ruling on whether a corporation and its less than wholly–owned corporation are capable of forming a Sherman § 1 conspiracy when it applied a functional rather than numerical test. In *Computer Identics Corp. v. Southern Pacific Co.*,[471] Southern Pacific and its 80% owned subsidiary, a computer consulting service, were accused of a § 1 conspiracy. The court, citing *Copperweld*, approved a lower court's jury instruction that there can be no conspiracy if "defendants were so closely related that *they were in fact one entity* . . . . [I]t is up to you jurors to decide whether the defendant corporations *acted as a single entity* sharing common management which made decisions controlling all [the defendants] or whether they operated as independent persons."[472] The *Computer Identics* jury found there was no conspiracy, but this does not suggest that the First Circuit would interpret *Copperweld* to mean a parent and less than wholly–owned subsidiary are incapable of conspiring. To the contrary, the fact that the court approved the jury instruction means the jury could have found that Southern Pacific and its 80% owned subsidiary were capable of conspiring. Thus, at least in the First Circuit, *Copperweld* will not necessarily preclude the finding of a conspiracy between a parent and partially owned subsidiary so long as a jury is properly instructed to determine if the two entities were in fact one single entity.

In actual practice, however, it may not be necessary to satisfy the plurality requirement by focusing on the relationship of the parent and the partially owned subsidiary. Partial ownership of the subsidiary means that the subsidiary has at least two owners. It might be argued that plurality is satisfied by the relationship of the two or more owners of the subsidiary, rendering unnecessary a ruling that the parent and subsidiary are not a single entity.

[3] Corporation and its Unincorporated Division

In *Copperweld* the Court left little doubt, when it observed in *dictum*, that "[t]here is . . . general agreement that § 1 is not violated by the internally coordinated conduct of a corporation and one of its unincorporated divisions. Although this Court has not previously addressed the question, there can be little doubt that the operations of a corporate enterprise organized into divisions must be judged as the conduct of a single actor."[473]

---

[470] *Id.* at 1495, n.20.

[471] 756 F.2d 200 (1st Cir. 1985).

[472] *Id.* at 204–05.

[473] 467 U.S. at 770; "A corporate division has no separate legal personality. It is simply a group of employees within the firm. And to say, as everyone does, that a single corporation acting unilaterally cannot conspire with itself is necessarily to say that it cannot conspire with its officers or employees who are its only means of acting." VII P.E. Areeda, *Antitrust Law*, ¶ 1470 (1986).

[4] Corporation and its Agents or Independent Consultants

In *Nelson Radio & Supply Co. v. Motorola, Inc.*,[474] the Fifth Circuit recognized the general rule that a corporation cannot be guilty of conspiring with its officers or agents. However, this rule has been eroded subsequently. Under certain factual conditions, a corporation and its agent or independent contractor are capable of conspiring to form the requisite § 1 plurality.

In *Poller v. CBS, Inc.*,[475] CBS and its independent management consultant were charged with conspiring to cancel the plaintiff's television affiliation with CBS. The Court inferred that CBS and its independent consultant were capable of forming an unlawful agreement if the consultant had a separate interest from that of the corporation. Similarly, in *Greenville Publishing Co. v. Daily Reflector, Inc.*,[476] the Fourth Circuit agreed with the general rule of *Nelson Radio* but concluded that "an exception may be justified when the [corporate] officer has an independent personal stake in achieving the corporation's illegal objective."[477]

The Supreme Court in *Albrecht v. Herald Co.*[478] addressed the question of whether a corporation and its independent consultant were capable of conspiring. In *Albrecht* the plaintiff, a newspaper home delivery carrier had an exclusive delivery territory for defendant's newspaper, the *St. Louis Globe Democrat*. Plaintiff's exclusive territory was subject to termination if the carrier charged prices in excess of a maximum set by defendant Herald Company, a newspaper publisher. Plaintiff's prices exceeded the maximum prices set by defendant, giving defendant the contractual right to make deliveries itself to customers who preferred lower prices. The Herald Company employed Milne Circulation Sales, Inc. to engage in telephone and house–to–house solicitation of newspaper subscriptions in plaintiff's territory.

The *Albrecht* Court held that the combination of the defendant newspaper publisher and Milne, its independent newspaper circulation solicitor, satisfied the conspiracy requirement. This concept of an agreement has been criticized as having "been expanded by some courts to reach what is factually unilateral conduct . . . ."[479] One commentator's concern is "[t]he implication of *Albrecht* . . . that if the motivation is sufficiently anticompetitive, a court may fashion a conspiracy concept to satisfy the concerted action requirements of § 1 even absent any evidence of a contract, combination, or conspiracy."[480]

---

[474] 200 F.2d 911 (5th Cir. 1952).

[475] 368 U.S. 464 (1962).

[476] 496 F.2d 391 (4th Cir. 1974).

[477] *Id.* at 399.

[478] 390 U.S. 145 (1968) *overruled on other grounds by State Oil Co. v. Khan*, 522 U.S. 3 (1997).

[479] Handler, *Reforming the Antitrust Laws*, 82 Colum. L. Rev. 1287, 1301 (1982).

[480] *Id.*

In *Harold Friedman, Inc. v. Kroger Co.*,[481] the Third Circuit suggested that it may be possible for an otherwise unrelated landlord and its corporate tenant, a grocery chain, to constitute concerted activity. In that case, however, the landlord "did everything it could to resist [the tenant] Kroger's attempt to prevent [the plaintiff] from leasing the property . . . [and] successively resisted the attempts of the defendant [Kroger] to force it to go along [with the conspiracy]."[482]

Other courts have focused on the economic realities of the corporate structure, and the relationship of the parties. The Second and Ninth Circuits have both addressed the intra–enterprise conspiracy question by focusing on the economic realities of the relationship between the alleged conspirators. In *Knutson v. Daily Review, Inc.*,[483] the court stated that "whether such [concerted] action has occurred turns on the particular facts" such as the corporate structure.[484] In *Fuchs Sugars & Syrups, Inc. v. Amstar Corp.*,[485] the court, citing and expanding on *Knutson*, reasoned that

> [w]hether two actors constitute distinct economic entities for purposes of the Sherman Act is determined by the economic realities of their relationship . . . . In the context of the principal/agent relationship this analysis requires consideration of a number of elements which include: whether the agent performs a function on behalf of his principal other than securing an offer from a buyer for the principal's product; the degree to which the agent is authorized to exercise his discretion concerning the price and terms under which the principal's product is to be sold; and finally whether use of the agent constitutes a separate step in the vertical distribution of the principal's product.[486]

The Eighth Circuit interpreted the conspiracy requirement in the context of a corporation and its agents in *Pink Supply Corp. v. Heibert, Inc.*[487] The court held that a Sherman Act conspiracy cannot exist between a corporation and its agents, even if the agents are separately incorporated, when the agents' function as an integral part of the corporate entity, do not represent separate steps in the corporation's chain of distribution, do act for the benefit of the corporate principle, and are functionally indistinguishable from the corporation's employees.[488] However, the Eighth Circuit recognized an exception when a corporation's and its agent's interests diverge and the agents act beyond the scope of their authority or for their own benefit. Under these circumstances the corporation and its agents are capable of forming a § 1 conspiracy.[489]

---

[481] 581 F.2d 1068 (3d Cir. 1978).

[482] *Id.* at 1074.

[483] 548 F.2d 795 (9th Cir. 1976).

[484] *Id.* at 802.

[485] 602 F.2d 1025 (2d Cir. 1979).

[486] *Id.* at 1031, n.5.

[487] 788 F.2d 1313 (8th Cir. 1986).

[488] *Id.* at 1317.

[489] *Id.* at 1318. Seven years later, the Eighth Circuit reaffirmed the holding in *Pink Supply* in *International Travel Arrangers v. NWA, Inc.*, 991 F.2d 1389, 1397–98 (8th Cir. 1993).

In *Nurse Midwifery Associates (NMA) v. Hibbett*,[490] two nurse midwives, their supervising obstetrician and three clients alleged that three hospitals, several members of their medical staffs and a mutual insurance company all conspired to deny medical staff privileges for midwifery services at the defendant hospitals. The Sixth Circuit held that the members of the medical staff were acting as agents of the hospitals and that, therefore, the intracorporate conspiracy doctrine immunized their actions. In reaching this decision, however, the court specified that

> When the staff as a group, make decisions or recommendations for the hospital in areas that do not affect the market in which they compete as individuals, there is no reason not to treat them as agents of the hospital. However, when competing physicians are making privilege recommendations concerning another competitor, sufficient anticompetitive concerns are raised to warrant a conclusion that the members of the medical staff are not acting as agents of the hospital for purposes of applying the intracorporate conspiracy doctrine to preclude a conspiracy among staff members.[491]

In general, the agreement requirement may be satisfied if the agent has self–interest involved, is key to the effect on competition, and is an outsider to the corporation.[492]

[5]   Sports League Teams

Generally competing sports league teams are capable of forming a conspiracy, but this rule is subject to statutory and court directed exceptions. In *National Collegiate Athletic Association v. Board of Regents*,[493] the Supreme Court considered an allegation that the NCAA had unreasonably restrained trade in the televising of college football games. The Court's holding, that the NCAA's price and output restrictions were unlawful restraints of trade, implicitly recognizes that an association of sports league

---

[490] 918 F.2d 605 (1990).

[491] *Id.* at 614. *See also Muzquiz v. W.A. Foote Memorial Hospital, Inc.*, 70 F.3d 422, 429–30 (6th Cir. 1995) (affirming *NMA v. Hibbet* in reasoning that, because the hospital was the only defendant and because *NMA* prevents the application of § 1 conspiracy claims to agreements between hospitals and agents or employees, the defendant hospital could not be held liable under a Sherman Act claim).

[492] *See generally* VII P. Areeda, *Antitrust Law* § 1470, at 282–301 (1986). In *Crosby v. Hospital Auth. of Valdosa & Lowndes County*, 93 F.3d 1515 (11th Cir. 1996), the Eleventh Circuit addressed an issue similar to that in *Hibbet*. Specifically, the court considered whether a hospital and its staff can be protected from § 1 as one legal entity incapable of conspiring. The court found that they could not be afforded intra–enterprise immunity, "but the staff physicians may in certain contexts be agents of the hospital for purposes of state action immunity." *Id.* at 1529. *See supra* Chapter 3 § 3.06[A] for further discussion of the state action doctrine.

[493] 468 U.S. 85 (1984). Compare Grauer, *Recognition of the National Football League as a Single Entity Under Sec. 1 of the Sherman Act: Implications of the Consumer Welfare Model*, 82 Mich. L. Rev. 1 (1983) *with* Roberts, *Sports Leagues and the Sherman Act: The Use and Abuse of Section 1 to Regulate Restraints on Intraleague Rivalry*, 32 UCLA L. Rev. 219 (1884).

teams is capable of satisfying § 1. Professional baseball, however, is viewed uniquely in antitrust law.

This implicit holding in *NCAA* recently has been raised in *Chicago Professional Sports Ltd. Partnership v. NBA*,[494] however. Plaintiffs challenged the NBA's ability to cap at thirty the number of games televised on Chicago television station WGN, and the NBA challenged the district court's ruling that the tax it imposed on those games televised nationwide was excessive. In considering the claim, the Court of Appeals held that the NBA bore a greater resemblance to a single firm than an independent group of firms.[495] This is true even though the teams are not subsidiaries of the national organization; they all have separate ownership.[496] The NBA submitted, and the court accepted, that it "functions as a single entity, creating a single product ("NBA Basketball") that competes with other basketball leagues. . . , other sports. . . , and other entertainments. . . ."[497] However, the court conceded that "[t]o say the league is 'more like a single bargaining employer' than a multi–employer unit is not to say that it necessarily is one, for every purpose.[498] Characterization of the league as a "single entity" serves to protect it from any § 1 liability.

Two Supreme Court cases have exempted professional baseball from the antitrust laws. First, *Federal Baseball Club of Baltimore, Inc. v. National League of Professional Baseball Clubs*,[499] found that interstate commerce was not involved in baseball; thus baseball is exempted from the reach of the Sherman Act.[500] Second, *Flood v. Kuhn*,[501] refused to repeal the professional baseball exemption of *Federal Baseball*. In addition, Congress arguably approved implicitly the baseball exemption when it provided that nothing contained in an act relating to telecasting of sporting events "shall be deemed to change, determine, or otherwise affect the applicability or nonapplicability of the antitrust laws to . . . football, baseball, basketball, or hockey."[502] Professional sports other than baseball are not exempt from the antitrust laws.[503]

---

[494] 95 F.3d 593 (7th Cir. 1996).

[495] *Id.* at 600.

[496] *Id.* at 597.

[497] *Id* at 599.

[498] *Id.* "[W]e do not rule out the possibility that an organization such as the NBA is best understood as one firm when selling broadcast rights to a network in competition with a thousand other producers of entertainment, but is best understood as a joint venture when curtailing competition for players who have few other market opportunities."

[499] 259 U.S. 200 (1922).

[500] *Radovich v. National Football League*, 352 U.S. 445, 451 (1957) (restricted the holding in *Federal Baseball* to cases involving only the sport of baseball).

[501] 407 U.S. 258 (1972).

[502] 15 U.S.C. § 1294 (1976).

[503] *See e.g., Brown v Pro Football, Inc.*, 518 U.S. 231 (1996); *Haywood v. National Basketball Ass'n.*, 401 U.S. 1204 (1971); *North Am. Soccer League v. National Football League*, 465 F. Supp. 665 (S.D.N.Y. 1979); *Smith v. Pro Football, Inc.*, 593 F.2d 1173 (D.C. Cir. 1978); *Mackey v. National Football League*, 543 F.2d 606 (8th Cir. 1976); *Denver Rockets v. All–Pro Mgmt., Inc.*, 325 F. Supp. 1049 (C.D. Cal. 1971); *Brown v. Pro Football, Inc.*, 116 S.Ct. 2116 (1996).

[6]   Trade Associations

Several Supreme Court decisions leave little doubt that trade associations are capable of forming a conspiracy. In *Goldfarb v. Virginia State Bar*,[504] the Court considered whether a minimum fee schedule for lawyers, which was enforced by the state bar association, violated the Sherman Act. The Court held that the bar association's rule prescribing minimum fees for legal services did in fact violate § 1. Implicitly the association was capable of forming the requisite conspiracy.[505]

In *National Society of Professional Engineers*,[506] the Court held that the Society's Code of Ethics, which banned competitive bidding by the Society's professional engineer members, was illegal under § 1 of the Sherman Act. As in *Goldfarb*, the Court's holding implies that the Society was capable of conspiring, combining, or agreeing for § 1 purposes. Thus it is not a viable defense for a trade association faced with a § 1 charge to argue that the association is a single entity immune from the Act's coverage.[507] The combination inherent in the association satisfies the plurality requirement.

This idea recently was affirmed in *Alvord–Polk, Inc. v. F. Schumacher & Co.*[508] The Third Circuit held that trade associations are capable of conspiring as long as they are acting like an "entity" and that a full examination of the facts and circumstances would be necessary in such a case.[509]

In addition, an association cannot defeat a § 1 civil antitrust treble damage claim by arguing that it was unaware that one of its agents or employees engaged in the allegedly unlawful conduct. In *American Society of Mechanical Engineers, Inc. v. Hydrolevel Corp.*,[510] the Court held that an association, whether or not it is a nonprofit association, is civilly liable under the Sherman Act for the act of its agent who has apparent authority to act for the association, even when the association is unaware of, and has not ratified, the agent's act.

---

[504] 421 U.S. 773 (1975).

[505] The Court in *Goldfarb* did not discuss directly the question whether the bar association was capable of forming a conspiracy or was merely a single entity incapable of conspiring, combining, or agreeing. The principal questions in the case were whether to apply the "state action" doctrine of *Parker v. Brown*, 317 U.S. 341 (1943), or whether the fact that defendants were members of a "learned profession," exempted them from the Sherman Act. *Goldfarb v. Virginia State Bar*, 421 U.S. 773, 780 (1975). The implicit premise of the Court's holding, however, is that the association was not immune from § 1 of Sherman Act exposure on the basis that it was a single entity incapable of conspiring, agreeing, or combining.

[506] 435 U.S. 679 (1978).

[507] *See also FTC v. Indiana Fed'n of Dentists*, 476 U.S. 447 (1986).

[508] 37 F.3d 996 (3d Cir. 1994).

[509] *Id.* at 1007–08.

[510] 456 U.S. 556 (1982).

[7] Members of Non–Profit Foundations

In *Arizona v. Maricopa County Medical Society*,[511] the Court considered "whether § 1 of the Sherman Act . . . [was] violated by agreements among competing physicians setting, by majority vote, the maximum fees that they may claim in full payment for health services provided to policyholders of specified insurance plans."[512] The physicians were members of foundations which approved certain insurance plans. In considering whether the plurality requirement of § 1 was met, the Court reasoned as follows:

> The foundations are not analogous to partnerships or other joint arrangements in which persons who would otherwise be competitors pool their capital and share the risks of loss as well as the opportunities for profit. In such joint ventures, the partnership is regarded as a single firm competing with other sellers in the market. The agreement under attack is an agreement among hundreds of competing doctors concerning the price at which each will offer his own services to a substantial number of consumers . . . . If a clinic offered complete medical coverage for a flat fee, the cooperating doctors would have the type of partnership arrangement in which a price–fixing agreement among the doctors would be perfectly proper. But the fee agreements disclosed by the record in this case are among independent competing entrepreneurs. They fit squarely into the horizontal price–fixing mode.[513]

Thus, even professional members of a nonprofit foundation are not immunized from § 1 through the argument that the foundation is a single entity incapable of combining or conspiring.

The holding in *Maricopa County* has been accepted with caution. In *DELTA v. Humane Society of the United States, Inc.*,[514] the Ninth Circuit drew a line between non–profit activities amounting to commercial activity and others which did not constitute trade at all. The court found that the Humane Society's practice of mailing letters asking for donations did not constitute a restraint of trade or a "restriction or suppression of commercial competition."[515] The court admitted that charitable organizations do not secure Sherman Act immunity simply because of their form or nonprofit status, but suggested that "it is a leap from the conclusion that charitable activities are subject to the Sherman Act when they do not constitute trade in the sense of the common law."[516] Although DELTA engages in the same activities as the Humane Society in the sense that each seek to prevent cruelty to animals, [t]he division of care between the two animal–loving societies . . . is [not] a division of the market. . . . Not every aspect of life

---

[511] 457 U.S. 332 (1982).

[512] *Id.* at 335–36.

[513] *Id.* at 356–57.

[514] 50 F.3d 710 (9th Cir. 1995).

[515] *Id.* at 713 (*quoting Apex Hosiery Co. v. Leader*, 310 U.S. 469, 550 (1940)).

[516] *Id.*

in the United States is to be reduced to such a single–minded vision of the ubiquity of commerce.[517]

[8] Local Governmental Units

In *Fisher v. City of Berkeley California*,[518] the Supreme Court held that rent controls established by a city ordinance "lack[ed] the element of concerted action needed [to] be characterized as a *per se* violation of § 1 of the Sherman Act . . . ."[519] Plaintiff landlords challenged the constitutionality of an ordinance imposing rent ceilings on residential property. They argued that the ordinance "form[ed] a combination between [the City of Berkeley and its officials], on the one hand, and the property owners on the other" and that it also "create[d] a horizontal combination among the landlords."[520] The Court, however, disagreed:

> A restraint imposed unilaterally by government does not become concerted action . . . simply because it has coercive effect upon parties who must obey the law. The ordinary relationship between the government and those who must obey its regulatory commands whether they wish to or not is not enough to establish a conspiracy . . . . There is no meeting of the minds here.
>
> . . . .
>
> Not all restraints imposed upon private actors by government units necessarily constitute unilateral action outside the purview of § 1. Certain restraints may be characterized as "hybrid," in that nonmarket mechanisms merely enforce private marketing decisions.[521]

The Court then reviewed two earlier "hybrid" decisions. In *Schwegmann Bros. v. Calvert Distillers Corp.*,[522] the Court reasoned that "when a state compels retailers to follow a parallel price policy, it demands private conduct which the Sherman Act forbids."[523] In *Schwegmann*, however, the price selections and power to enforce them were left by the state to the retailers, thus the retailers were capable of conspiring within the meaning of the Sherman Act. Second, in *California Liquor Dealers Ass'n v. Midcal Aluminum, Inc.*[524] the state required that all wine producers, wholesalers, and rectifiers file price schedules with the state, and state licensed wine merchants were required to sell wine to retailers at the scheduled prices. The Court found that the wine producers had the power to prevent price competition by dictating prices and that "the mere existence of legal compulsion did not turn California's scheme into unilateral action by the

---

[517] *Id*. at 714.

[518] 475 U.S. 260 (1986).

[519] *Id*. at 270.

[520] *Id*. at 267 (*quoting* appellants' brief).

[521] *Id*. at 267–68.

[522] 341 U.S. 385 (1951).

[523] *Id*. at 389.

[524] 445 U.S. 97 (1980).

State."[525] "The national policy in favor of competition cannot be thwarted by casting such a cloak of state involvement over what is essentially a private price–fixing arrangement."[526]

The Court in *Fisher* found that the ordinance could not be viewed as a "cloak for any conspiracy among landlords or between the landlords and the municipality."[527] The Court characterized the *Schwegmann* and *Midcal* arrangements as "hybrid" and distinguished them from *Fisher*, where control over rent levels was in the hands of the city's Rent Stabilization Board and not within the landlord's power.

The *Schwegmann, Midcal,* and *Fisher* trilogy suggests that a local governmental entity and those who must obey its laws are not capable of forming a conspiracy unless the ostensibly municipally administered "scheme is really a private . . . conspiracy, concealed under a 'gauzy cloak of state involvement.' "[528]

It should be noted, however, that *Schwegmann, Midcal,* and *Fisher* all dealt with liquor regulations. This has been a distinguishing factor for at least one case. In *Hertz Corp. v. City of New York,*[529] the ordinance at hand prevented the plaintiff from charging different rates or extra fees to people located in certain areas of the city. Hertz previously had introduced a plan which made it more expensive to rent cars in certain boroughs after research showed that renting in these areas led to increased liability for the company. The plaintiff fought the law on an antitrust claim, and the court found that the local government unit defense to conspiracy under § 1 was not applicable.

The Hertz law lacks several features of the "unilateral" Berkeley ordinance. First, the law is not a pure regulatory scheme because it is not a "scheme" at all. . . Second, the law lacks the independent, quasi–judicial board that in *Berkeley* could adjust rates and provide relief in individual circumstances. Finally, the City of Berkeley was operating in an area vital to its municipal authority — housing; less vital is the rental car industry in New York. Nor does the Hertz law easily fit the fact pattern of the cases held to involve "hybrid" restraints. . . The three Supreme Court cases in this category involved the pricing of liquor. . . .

We reject the city's suggestion to apply *Fisher* expansively so as to view Local Law No. 21 as a unilateral action that lacks the degree of private–governmental agreement required to be a contract, combination, or

---

[525] *Fisher v. City of Berkeley California*, 475 U.S. 260, 269 (1986).

[526] *California Liquor Dealers v. Midcal Aluminum*, 445 U.S. 97, 106 (1980).

[527] *Fisher v. City of Berkeley California*, 475 U.S. 260, 269 (1986).

[528] *California Liquor Dealers Ass'n.*, 445 U.S. 97, 106 (1980). *See also 324 Liquor Cor.n v. Duffy*, 479 U.S. 335 (1987), a vertical retail price maintenance case in which the defendant claimed state action exemption to antitrust liability. The Court held New York's statute providing that liquor retailers must charge at least 112% of wholesalers' posted bottle prices violates § 1 of the Sherman Act. The Court's opinion did not specifically address the conspiracy requirement, but did state that "[t]he antitrust violation in this case is essentially similar to the violation in *Midcal*." *Id.* at 724.

[529] 1 F.3d 121 (2d Cir. 1993).

conspiracy in restraint of trade. To do so would remove from the reach of the antitrust laws all local governmental actions not fitting the precise fact pattern of the liquor cases, and would preclude examination of their anticompetitive effects. At the same time, we also reject Hertz's contention that this case, like the "hybrid" liquor cases, presents a straight-forward example of price–fixing that is per se invalid.[530]

The court decided that the law was more like a "hybrid" than a unilateral action, and, thus, it could not be said that a contract, combination, or conspiracy was impossible in that case. Accordingly, *Fisher* did not apply.

[9] Single Entities Created as Instrumentalities for Unlawful Purposes

Occasionally Sherman Act defendants assert that they constitute a single entity and are incapable of conspiring. If, however, the otherwise single entity was formed for a purpose which is determined to be unlawful under the Sherman Act, defendants' single entity argument is not viable. This concept was reiterated most recently in *Copperweld Corp. v. Independence Tube Corp.*,[531] where the Supreme Court held that, so long as the initial parent–subsidiary combination was lawful, a parent and a wholly–owned subsidiary are a single entity incapable of combining or conspiring to satisfy the predicate plurality for a Sherman § 1 cause of action.

In *United States v. Yellow Cab Co.*,[532] the defendants were charged with violating §§ 1 and 2 of the Sherman Act by conspiring to restrain and monopolize trade in the sale of vehicles for use as taxicabs to companies operating in several major metropolitan markets. The corporate defendants were a taxicab manufacturer and the several taxicab operating companies that it had acquired in various cities.

Defendants argued that through merger all of them had been joined as a single entity and as such they were not subject to § 1 scrutiny. The Supreme Court reasoned that "any affiliation or integration flowing from an illegal conspiracy cannot insulate the conspirators from the sanctions which Congress has imposed . . . . [T]he common ownership and control of the various corporate [defendants] are impotent to liberate the alleged combination and conspiracy from the impact of the [Sherman] Act."[533] Because the restraint of trade was the primary object for which the defendants conspired, the combination into an otherwise single entity was no defense to the Sherman allegations.

Copperweld suggests that it may have overruled *Yellow Cab*.[534] However, the Court in *Copperweld* observed that a "corporation's initial acquisition

---

[530] *Id.* at 127. *See also* D. Mandelker, J. Gerard, E.T. Sullivan, *Federal Land Use Law*, ¶ 11.09 (11th ed. 1997).

[531] 467 U.S. 752 (1984).

[532] 332 U.S. 218 (1947).

[533] *Id.* at 227.

[534] 467 U.S. at 777 ("To the extent that prior decisions of this Court are to the contrary, they are disapproved and overruled.").

of control will always be subject to scrutiny under § 1 of the Sherman Act and § 7 of the Clayton Act . . . ."[535]

The Court returned to a similar issue in *United States v. Sealy, Inc.*[536] *Sealy* was a Sherman Act civil action alleging that Sealy, Inc., *inter alia*, unlawfully allocated territories to its licensees. Sealy licensees manufactured and sold mattresses with the Sealy label, and were also the owners of Sealy. All of Sealy, Inc.'s directors were Sealy, Inc. shareholders. The defendant argued that Sealy, Inc. was a single entity incapable of forming a conspiracy. The Court, however, viewed Sealy not as a single entity but rather "as an instrumentality of the individual manufacturers."[537] As such, Sealy, Inc., was a combination of competitors and accordingly capable of conspiring within the meaning of § 1.

Yellow Cab and *Sealy* hold that when an otherwise single entity is either formed for an unlawful purpose or is the instrumentality for several otherwise separate entities, the entity is capable of entering a conspiracy.

Professor Areeda has delineated three prerequisites in finding a conspiracy in such situations.

First, the pawn must have knowledge of the principal's objective to restrain trade. Second, the pawn must not only facilitate the principal's restraint, but must also intend to restrain trade. This usually means that the pawn must have a stake in the restraint, as distinct from merely selling his own services for their usual market price. Third, the pawn must contribute materially to the restraint. Unless these requirements are satisfied, the pawn should be deemed an independent actor pursuing his own lawful business rather than a conspirator with the principal who engages him.[538]

§ 4.16   Criminal Liability

Violations of § 1 of the Sherman Act can result in either civil or criminal liability or both. In *United States v. United States Gypsum Co.*[539] the Supreme Court held that intent is an essential element of a criminal violation under § 1 of the Sherman Act. At issue was the exchange of current price data between competitors. Defendants argued that such an exchange was required in order to establish the "meeting competition" defense to a price discrimination charge under the Robinson–Patman Act.

The district court had instructed the jury that " 'if the effect of the exchanges of pricing information was to raise, fix, maintain, and stabilize prices, then the parties to them are presumed, *as a matter of law*, to have intended that result.' "[540] The Supreme Court rejected this instruction,

---

[535] *Id.*

[536] 388 U.S. 350 (1967).

[537] *Id.* at 356.

[538] VII P.E. Areeda *Antitrust Law*, ¶ 1474 (1986).

[539] 438 U.S. 422 (1978).

[540] *Id.* at 430.

holding that "an effect on prices, without more, will not support a criminal conviction."[541] The requisite intent could be established, the Court concluded, by a showing of "action undertaken with knowledge of its probable consequences [*i.e.*, adverse effects on the market] and having the requisite anticompetitive effects."[542] Thus, a general intent standard is acceptable when anticompetitive effects in fact are demonstrated. This is a lower burden of proof than that of showing "conduct undertaken with the 'conscious object' of producing such [anticompetitive] effects."[543] This specific intent standard, which the Court rejected, is applicable when no anticompetitive effects are established.[544] It requires a specific intent or conscious purpose to bring about the proscribed consequences.[545]

The intent requirement introduced in *Gypsum* usually does not extend to *per se* violations, however. As the Ninth Circuit held in *United States v. Brown*, "[w]here per se conduct is found, a finding of intent to conspire to commit the offence is sufficient; a requirement that intent go further and envision actual anticompetitive results would reopen the very questions of reasonableness which the *per se* rule is designed to avoid."[546]

The Court also stated that, in interpreting the language of criminal statutes, "far more than the simple omission of the appropriate phrase from the statutory definition is necessary to justify dispensing with an intent requirement."[547]

Recently, the First Circuit restated *Gypsum*'s requirement for the plaintiff's burden of proof with regards to intent.[548] The plaintiff must "prove an intent to agree and an intent to effectuate the commission of the substantive offense" on the part of the defendant.[549]

In *United States v. Alston*,[550] the Ninth Circuit clarified the burden of proof requirements for criminal action in antitrust cases. In *Alston*, the Department of Justice initiated a criminal action against three dentists alleging they entered into a price–fixing conspiracy to increase the fee schedules for dental services provided to members of prepaid dental plans. Believing the jury instructions were "technically and legally correct," the Ninth Circuit reversed two motions for acquittal notwithstanding the verdict and a request for a new trial. With respect to the government's burden of proof, the Ninth Circuit commented:

---

[541] *Id.* at 435.

[542] *Id.* at 444.

[543] *Id.*

[544] *Id.*

[545] *Id.* at n.21.

[546] 925 F.2d 1182, 1188 (9th Cir. 1991).

[547] *Id.* at 438. *See also United States v. Gendron*, 18 F.3d 955, 959 (1st Cir. 1994).

[548] *United States v. Piper*, 35 F.3d 611 (1st Cir. 1994).

[549] *Id.* at 615.

[550] 974 F.2d 1206 (9th Cir. 1992).

In order to convict any defendant, the government must prove beyond a reasonable doubt as to that each of the following: First, that the conspiracy charged existed at or about the time stated in the indictment; second, that the defendant knowingly — that is, voluntarily and intentionally — became a member of the conspiracy charged in the indictment, knowing of its goal and intending to help accomplish it; and third, that interstate commerce was involved.[551]

Based upon their review of the record, the Ninth Circuit held that the government presented sufficient evidence to enable the trier of fact to find the dentists guilty beyond a reasonable doubt.

The second element of the *Alston* three–part burden of proof requirement was clarified by the Fourth Circuit in *United States v. Whittington*.[552] The plaintiff need not prove the defendant had knowledge of every detail of the conspiracy in order to prove willful engagement in the conspiracy.[553] Rather, the plaintiff only need show "the defendant knew of the conspiracy's purpose and some action indicating his participation."[554] Circumstantial evidence like the defendant's relationship with other conspirators, the time span of his association, his attitude and behavior, and the nature of the conspiracy all can prove this second prong.[555]

Thus the burden of proof in a criminal case is distinguishable from that in a civil antitrust case.[556] In the criminal case a showing of anticompetitive effect is essential, absent specific intent. The general rule in a civil case is that the plaintiff needs to show either an unlawful purpose or an anticompetitive effect. Admittedly, there are few cases where there may be a finding of unlawful intent and no anticompetitive effects, perhaps because of lack of market power,[557] but it is frequently said that in litigating these cases one can infer effects from intent evidence and vice versa.[558]

---

[551] *Id.* at 1210 (quoting the trial judge's instructions to the jury).

[552] 26 F.3d 456 (4th Cir. 1994).

[553] *Id.* at 465 (*citing United States v. Goldman*, 750 F.2d 1221, 1227 (4th Cir. 1994).

[554] *Id.* (*quoting United States v. Collazo*, 732 F.2d 1200, 1205 (4th Cir. 1984)).

[555] *Id.*

[556] *Id.* For a general discussion on contemporary criminal enforcement under the antitrust laws, *See* First, *Criminal Antitrust Enforcement*, Center for Research in Criminal Justice (1991).

[557] *Id.* at 445–46. *See also United States v. Container Corp.*, 393 U.S. 333, 337 (1969), discussed at § 4.02[B].

[558] *See* Handler, *Antitrust–78*, 78 Colum. L. Rev. 1363, 1402 (1978); *Northwest Power Prods, Inc. v. Omark Indus. Inc.*, 576 F.2d 83, 90 (5th Cir. 1978) ("An evil intent alone is insufficient to establish a violation under the rule of reason, although proof of intent may help a court assess the market impact of defendants' conduct").

Chapter 5

VERTICAL RESTRAINTS

As discussed in Chapter 4, horizontal restraints — agreements between competitors — may be found unlawful under § 1 of the Sherman Act. Vertical restraints — agreements between firms at different levels in the production or distribution chain — also are subject to scrutiny under the antitrust laws. Vertical agreements, however, are less likely to be inherently anticompetitive. Consequently, courts are more tolerant of this type of agreement. It is in this area that antitrust has undergone the greatest change in recent years.

Generally, vertical restraints are limitations placed on retailer activities by the manufacturer or distributor. For purposes of analysis, it is useful to divide vertical restraints into two very broad categories. First are agreements in which a seller attempts to control a factor relating to the eventual resale of the product. The classic example is a manufacturer that only sells to retailers who agree to adhere to a specified resale price. A manufacturer also may control the types of customers to whom the product is sold or the location of the reseller's store.[1] Generally, the direct impact of this category of restraints is on competition between sellers of the same product or intrabrand competition.

The second broad category includes efforts by a seller to limit a buyer's purchases from sellers of competing brands. For example, in the typical tying arrangement, a seller sells one product to a buyer only on the condition that the buyer buy another product from the same seller. Another possibility is that the seller sells the product only on the condition that the buyer purchase all of its needs for that item from that seller. Generally, the impact of these restraints is on competition between brands or on interbrand competition.

§ 5.01 Intrabrand Distributional Restraints

Vertical restraints on distribution can be of the price or nonprice variety. Those in the first category include fixing minimum or maximum resale prices. Nonprice restraints appear in a number of forms, but typically involve the allocation of particular geographic areas or classes of customers to specified resellers. The distinction between fixing minimum resale prices (RPM) and other price and nonprice restraints is crucial. Fixing the minimum price at which a product may be resold is a *per se* violation of

---

[1] In this chapter the terms "manufacturer" and "supplier" will be used to signify the "upstream" firm that is selling a product for resale. The terms "dealer," "retailer" and "reseller" will signify the "downstream" firm that purchases and resells the product.

§ 1 of the Sherman Act. Fixing the maximum resale price and nonprice restraints are examined under the "rule of reason."

Since vertical restraints are analyzed under § 1 of the Sherman Act, the threshold issue is whether an agreement exists. As in the case of horizontal restraints, the agreement issue is especially complex because the question often becomes one of how much circumstantial evidence is necessary to permit the inference of an agreement. The rationale offered for both price and nonprice vertical intrabrand restraints is that they actually enhance interbrand competition. Before examining the law of restraints on distribution, a closer look at this justification is in order.

[A] Intrabrand Restraints and the Free Rider Problem

The difficultly presented by intrabrand restraints is the potential for both procompetitive and anticompetitive effects. As in Chapter 4's discussion of horizontal territorial divisions, a key consideration is the theory of the "free rider." Generally, in economics, the free rider problem occurs whenever an individual or firm is unable to enjoy the full advantage of the fruits of their efforts. For example, without copyright laws, a composer would go uncompensated for the use of his or her works by someone else. The person using the composition would be "free riding" on the efforts of the composer. More technically, the composer would be unable to "internalize" the benefits of his or her efforts.

The argument in the context of vertical restraints is that intrabrand competition can be increased if suppliers are permitted to minimize intra–brand free riding. For example, suppose a distributor of Xenox televisions and stereos locates in a high rent area in the middle of a population center. It also elects to fully train its sales personnel, carry a full line of Xenox brand equipment in stock, maintain a service department and advertise every week in the local newspaper and on television. In contrast, another retailer locates in the low–rent industrial part of town, rarely advertises, carries very little stock and teaches its sales personnel little more than how to operate the cash register.

One would not be surprised to find that the second retailer is able to sell Xenox products for a lower price than the first. Furthermore, it seems likely that many consumers will go to the fully stocked store to see the equipment and to learn about it from the trained personnel. After gathering the information they need they go to the retailer who has lower prices and make their purchases or order the equipment for future delivery. In this case, the free rider is the retailer in the industrial section of town; it benefits from the sales efforts of the downtown retailer.

When the downtown retailer is unable to internalize the benefits of the investment in rent, salesperson training, and maintaining a complete inventory and service department, its motivation to continue making such investments obviously will decline. The manufacturer of Xenox products may find that it is better able to compete with other manufacturers when its products are promoted, not by the lowest possible price, but through advertising, immediate availability and in–store sales efforts. The problem, then, is to shelter retailers who promote Xenox products in a manner that is consistent with the interests of the manufacturer from retailers who free ride on those efforts.

The sheltering can take two basic forms: price and nonprice. The manufacturer could require all retailers to observe a minimum resale price. Buyers then would have little motivation other than to purchase from the full service retailer. In order to compete effectively, other retailers are likely to find they must offer the same services. Another sheltering device is to assign sales territories to retailers or, in some other way, allow them to claim certain groups of potential customers as essentially their own. Again, the full service retailer is able to internalize the benefits of its promotional efforts and will continue to sell in a manner that furthers the interests of the manufacturer.

Does this mean that price and nonprice vertical restraints are only procompetitive? Obviously not. First, such restraints definitely curtail intrabrand competition. Second, there are arguments that the vertical restraints may facilitate anticompetitive arrangements between manufacturers or be instigated by retailers who wish to indirectly engage in horizontal price fixing or territorial division through a dealer cartel. Third, vertical restraints on distribution may be used by a manufacturer to segregate a market in order to effectively practice price discrimination.[2]

[B] Vertical Restraints on Price

[1] Minimum Prices (RPM)

The *per se* prohibition of RPM originated in the 1911 case of *Dr. Miles Medical Co. v John D. Park & Sons*.[3] The case involved efforts by the manufacturer of proprietary medicines to control the price at which the medicines were resold at the wholesale and retail levels. The argument by Dr. Miles was that if it had the right to determine to whom it would sell it should have a right to control the terms of resale. The Court rejected Dr. Miles' argument concluding that a resale price restriction constituted an impermissible restraint upon alienation.[4] The majority offered no economic arguments for or against the arrangement,[5] except to claim that

---

[2] *See* H. Hovenkamp, Federal Antitrust Policy 448–449 (2d ed. 1999).

[3] 220 U.S. 373 (1911). The impact of *Dr. Miles* was substantially abated in 1937 by the Miller–Tydings Fair Trade Amendment, ch. 690, 50 Stat. 693 (1937) (codified as amended at 15 U.S.C. § 1 (1976)), which permitted state legislation to authorize resale price maintenance for branded commodities. "Fair trade" was repealed in 1975 thus returning to *Dr. Miles*. Consumer Goods Pricing Act, Pub. L. No. 94–145. 89 Stat. 801 (codified at 15 U.S.C. § 45 (1976)(amending 15 U.S.C. §§ 1, 45)).

[4] *Id.* at 404.

[5] The Court did, however, consider whether the restraint was ancillary to an otherwise lawful transaction. *Id.* at 407.

the plan enhanced the profits of "favored dealers."[6] Essentially, the Court viewed vertical price fixing as indistinguishable from a horizontal agreement among the dealers reselling Dr. Miles' products.[7] Despite scholarly criticism,[8] the rule established by *Dr. Miles* has not been overruled. Recent interpretations of what constitutes RPM and applications of the antitrust injury requirement, however, have substantially weakened it.[9]

[2] Consignment and the Use of Sales Agents

Since *Dr. Miles* was so firmly based on the concept of restraints on alienation, the decision seemed to open an important avenue for the control of resale prices through the mechanism of consignment or the use of independent sales agents. As long as the consignee or agent did not have title to the product, there was no resale and, therefore, no resale price maintenance. For many years, this avenue appeared to be broad enough to circumvent the *per se* rule. The leading case is *United States v. General Electric Co.*[10] in which G.E. employed "agents" for the wholesale and retail sale of light bulbs at prices determined by the manufacturer. The agents were often wholesalers or retailers in their own business and prior to the consignment they had resold G.E. light bulbs. Under the new arrangement, title passed directly from G.E. to the consumer. The Court found that the agents were not purchasers and not, therefore, within the scope of the prohibitions of *Dr. Miles*.[11]

In *Simpson v. Union Oil*[12] the Court returned to the use of consignment as a means of bypassing *Dr. Miles*. Union Oil leased retail outlets for the sale of its gasoline and entered into a condiment agreement with the lessees through which it controlled retail price. The arrangement was challenged by a retailer who was terminated when it "resold" for less than the price fixed by Union Oil. The Court unconvincingly distinguished *General Electric* as dealing with a patented product[13] and found Union Oil's arrangement to be a violation of § 1.

The Court declined to establish a "wooden formula" for determining when a consignment would be a permissible method of controlling prices. Instead, the Court, through an opinion by Justice Douglas, looked to the substance of the plan and concluded "[w]hen . . . a 'consignment' device is used to

---

[6] *Id.*

[7] *Id.* at 408.

[8] *See, e.g.,* R. Bork, *The Antitrust Paradox* 280–98 (1978); H. Hovenkamp, *supra* note 2, at 465–467; Orstein, *Resale Price Maintenance and Cartels*, 30 Antitrust Bull. 401 (1985); Posner, *The Next Step in the Antitrust Treatment of Restricted Distribution: Per Se Legality*, 48 U.Chi. L. Rev. 6 (1981).

[9] For a more recent case seeming to cut against this trend *see Delong Equipment Co. v. Washington Mills Electro Minerals*, 990 F.2d 1186 (11th Cir. 1993).

[10] 272 U.S. 476 (1926).

[11] *Id.* at 485–87.

[12] 377 U.S. 13 (1964).

[13] *Id.* at 22–24.

cover a vast gasoline distribution system, fixing prices through many retail outlets, the antitrust laws prevent calling the 'consignment' agency for then [the prohibition of price fixing] would be avoided merely by clever manipulation of words, not by differences in substance."[14] In addition to the "vastness" of the distribution scheme involved, the Court seemed influenced by what it perceived to be an imbalance of bargaining power between Union Oil and the retail dealers[15] and the fact that business risks were ultimately borne by the dealers.[16] The critical issue after *Simpson* is not whether a consignment exists but whether the effect of the consignment is to circumvent antitrust policy.

The *Simpson* Court expressly left open the possibility that smaller scale consignments could be legal.[17] This suggestion, along with the particular facts of *Simpson* and the Court's refusal to officially overrule *General Electric*, have left lower courts with sufficient flexibility to hold that consignments often serve legitimate business purposes.[18] A key factor that has been identified as distinguishing legitimate consignments from those designed to bypass the prohibitions of *Dr. Miles* is the allocation of business risks.[19] When most of the risk, unlike *Simpson*, remains with the manufacturer, the consignee is more likely to be a legitimate sales agent as opposed to an independent retailer through whom the manufacturer wishes to control resale prices. This approach makes a great deal of sense from the standpoint of both equity and efficiency; firms bearing the greatest risk in the marketplace probably should be permitted the leeway to make pricing decisions even if a consignment is involved. Another factor the courts have looked to is whether there are nonprice purposes for the consignment. For example, a consignment or the use of a sales agent may be part of a plan to maintain quality standards or simply an efficient method of marketing.[20]

Judge Posner, in a decision by the Seventh Circuit Court of Appeals, pinpointed the characterization problem in sales agent cases by noting that there is no clear line between independent distributors and agents. Accordingly, "distributors are permitted to operate as agents under consignments not intended to circumvent the antitrust laws."[21] Certainly the problem of distinguishing the legitimate use of sales agents from efforts to circumvent the antitrust laws is complicated. No doubt the process is also colored by a factor not addressed by Judge Posner: the *per se* status of resale price

---

[14] *Id.* at 21–22.

[15] *Id.* at 20–21.

[16] *Id.* at 20.

[17] *Id.* at 21.

[18] *See generally* VII P. Areeda, *Antitrust Law* 310–19 (1986).

[19] *Id. See, e g., Mesirow v. Pepperidge Farms, Inc.*, 703 F.2d 339 (9th Cir. 1983), *cert. denied,* 464 U.S. 820 (1983); *Greene v. General Foods*, 517 F.2d 635 (5th Cir), *cert denied*, 424 U.S. 942 (1975).

[20] *See e.g. Illinois Corporate Travel, Inc. v. American Airlines*, 889 F.2d 751 (7th Cir. 1989). *See generally* VII P. Areeda, *supra* note 18, at 313. *See e.g., Pogue v. International Industries, Inc.*, 524 F.2d 342 (6th Cir. 1975).

[21] *Morrison v. Murray Biscuit Co.*, 797 F.2d 1430, 1438 (7th Cir. 1986).

maintenance itself has in recent years been the subject of intense scrutiny. The ambivalence courts and individual judges feel about the *per se* status of RPM may affect their attitudes toward consignments as well as the issue addressed next — when is there sufficient evidence to permit the inference that a vertical agreement exists.

[3] Vertical Agreements: The *Colgate* Doctrine and Dealer Termination

Use of consignment agreements and sales agents are ways for manufacturers to retain control over price as the product works its way through the distribution chain to the ultimate consumer. Another method of controlling resale prices is for the manufacturer to announce "suggested" resale prices and to refuse to deal with retailers who do not adhere to those prices. This possibility is presented by the fact that RPM falls within § 1 of the Sherman Act. Consequently, in order to find liability there must be evidence that a pricing arrangement was the product of a contract, combination or conspiracy.

In the context of vertical restraints, there are at least three intertwined dimensions to the "combination" issue. First, what is sufficient evidence in the absence of an express agreement to permit the inference of an agreement? This is similar to the issue that arises with respect to horizontal restraints and "conscious parallelism." Second, how closely associated with the actual price–fixing effort must the parties to the combination be? Finally, must the combination be designed to fix resale prices or is it sufficient that it has the effect of merely stabilizing prices?

Before examining these issues it is important to note that the question of whether an agreement exists arises in the context of both price and nonprice vertical restraints. It is, however, a crucial determination in the context of RPM because fixing minimum resale prices remains a *per se* violation of § 1 and the proof of an agreement essentially makes the plaintiff's case. Because nonprice vertical restraints are subject to the "rule of reason" the proof of an agreement is only one, and possibly a minor, element of the plaintiff's case.

[a] The *"Colgate* Doctrine"

United States v. Colgate [22] is the beginning point for any analysis of the vertical combination issue. Colgate had engaged in a number of practices designed to influence the resale price of its products including prior announcement of desired resale prices, persistent urging of dealers to adhere to those prices, and the termination of sales to dealers who did not observe the requested resale price. Although some of the practices seemed to involve actual agreements, the Supreme Court confined its analysis to the indictment as interpreted by the trial court. [23]

---

[22] 250 U.S. 300 (1919).

[23] *Id.* at 304–06.

The Court first determined that the trial court had not viewed the indictment as charging that any actual agreements had been made.[24] Instead a retailer could "after buying, if he chose, give away his purchase or sell it at any price that he saw fit . . . affected only by the fact that he might by his action incur the displeasure of the manufacturer who could refuse to make future sales to him . . . ."[25] Thus, the issue became whether the dictates of *Dr. Miles* extended to a seller who announced desired resale prices and refused to deal with those who did not adhere to those prices. According to the Court, the *per se* rule did not apply because, under the Sherman Act, sellers were free to deal with whomever they wished and were similarly free to announce in advance under what circumstances they would refuse to deal.[26]

As a general matter, *Colgate* permits RPM if it can be achieved through unilateral conduct. The problem is, therefore, one of determining when events have gone far enough to permit the reasonable inference that the conduct is no longer unilateral. Again, it is important to remember that the decision of just how far *Colgate* protection can be extended is likely to be a function of the court's view of the *per se* rule against vertical price fixing itself. Thus, any general chronological account of what has become known as the "*Colgate* doctrine" is likely to be an indirect account of the swings in judicial attitudes with respect to vertical price fixing.

Until relatively recently, most of the cases interpreting *Colgate* tended to narrow the protection it offered. For example, in *Frey & Sons, Inc. v. Cudahy Packing Co.*[27] the Court held that proof of a formal written or oral contract was not required. The agreement, according to the Court, "might be implied from a course of dealing or other circumstances."[28] Similar narrowing in subsequent cases suggested that *Colgate* was only available as a defense when a firm had literally done no more than indicate its wishes and refused to deal with those who did not go along.[29] For example, in *United States v. Parke Davis & Co.*,[30] the Court considered an effort by a manufacturer of pharmaceutical products to control the prices charged by retailers by enlisting the aid of wholesalers. Specifically, wholesalers were told that they would be cut off from supplies if they sold for less than suggested wholesale prices or if they sold to retailers who resold for less than the suggested retail prices. The Court found that Parke Davis had gone well beyond *Colgate* in that it used the threat of a refusal to deal as "the vehicle to gain the wholesalers' participation in the program" to maintain retail prices.[31] As for the requirement under § 1 of the Sherman Act

---

[24] *Id.* at 307.

[25] *Id.* at 306.

[26] *Id.* at 307.

[27] 256 U.S. 208 (1921).

[28] *Id.* at 210.

[29] *See United States v. Bausch & Lomb Optical Co.*, 321 U.S. 707, 722–23 (1944).

[30] 362 U.S. 29 (1960).

[31] *Id.* at 46.

that something analogous to an agreement exist, the Court concluded "an unlawful combination is not just as arises from a price maintenance *agreement,* express or implied; such a combination is also organized if the producer secures adherence to his suggested prices by means which go beyond his mere declination to sell to a customer who will not observe his announced policy."[32] In the period immediately after *Parke Davis*, it made sense to echo the concerns of the dissenting Justices in that case and question what was left of *Colgate.*[33]

[b] The Parties Who Can Combine Under § 1

Not only did courts seem willing to find the required "combination" when threatened firms acquiesced in the wishes of the firm demanding adherence to prices, but parties that could come together to form the necessary plurality of actors were not necessarily those with a direct interest in the outcome of the price–fixing effort. The most telling Supreme Court decision with respect the latter point is *Albrecht v. Herald Company*[34] in which the defendant newspaper was charged with fixing the maximum resale price charged by carriers. The case arose when Albrecht, a carrier, charged subscribers a higher price than the suggested maximum. In response, the defendant employed an independent circulation firm to solicit customers away from Albrecht and a new carrier to deliver to those customers.

Although the *per se* prohibition of vertical maximum price fixing found in *Albrecht* has been overturned,[35] its discussion of what constitutes an actionable agreement is still worth noting. The Court found that the necessary combination was formed between the newspaper, the circulation company, and the new carrier.[36] The Court relied on *Parke Davis*, reasoning that if the combination requirement was met in that case by threats to wholesalers, then it was surely met here as the solicitation company and the new carrier knew the purpose was to force Albrecht to observe the maximum price.[37] In addition, the Court suggested in a footnote the possibility of finding a combination between the plaintiff and the defendant "at least as of the day he unwillingly complied with the respondents's advertised price" or between the defendant and other carriers who "acquiesced" in the pricing policy.[38]

---

[32] *Id.* at 43.

[33] *Id.* at 49–57 (Stewart J., dissenting). *See* Pitofsky & Dam, *Is the Colgate Doctrine Dead?,* 37 Antitrust L.J. 772 (1968).

[34] 390 U.S. 145 (1968) *overturned,* 552 U.S. 3 (1997).

[35] *Id.*

[36] *Id.* at 148–50.

[37] *Id.* at 149–50.

[38] *Id.* at 150 n. 6. Justice Harlan dissented noting that there would not have been a combination with the newspaper had it assigned one of its own employees the task of solicitation or delivery. Moreover, neither the solicitation company nor the new carrier had any special interest in the success of the maximum price setting plan. He charged that the majority had removed any significant meaning from the concept of "combination." *Id.* at 160–63 (Harlan, J. dissenting). *See Russell Stover Candies, Inc. v. FTC,* 718 F.2d 256, 260 (8th Cir.

The language in *Albrecht* pertaining to agreements represents the highpoint of the Court's willingness to limit *Colgate* and find the necessary combination in vertical restraint cases. It is not surprising to find that it was decided in a period when both price and nonprice vertical restraints were categorized as *per se* violations. Its liberal view of a § 1 combination, along with a narrow interpretation of *Colgate* and an almost uniform *per se* approach to vertical restraints, made it very easy for any terminated dealer to make a colorable case that the termination was the result of a vertical conspiracy in violation of § 1.

[c] Agreements after *Monsanto*

A change in antitrust philosophy was punctuated a few years later by *Continental T.V. Inc. v. GTE Sylvania*[39] which removed nonprice vertical restraints from the *per se* category. Thereafter the pressing question was whether a combination was formed when competitors of a price–cutting dealer complained to their joint supplier and termination of the dealer resulted. In other words, was evidence of complaints of competing dealers and subsequent termination of the offending dealer sufficient to permit an inference of a combination in violation of § 1. After some conflicting decisions in the circuit courts,[40] the Supreme Court addressed the issue in 1984 in *Monsanto v. Spray–Rite Service Corp.*[41]

In *Monsanto* the Court specifically responded to the rule applied by the Seventh Circuit Court of Appeals that "proof of termination following competitor complaints is sufficient to support an inference of concerted action."[42] Although the Supreme Court held that there was sufficient evidence for an inference of concerted action, it rejected the standard applied by the lower court. In doing so, it emphasized *Colgate* and the manufacturer's freedom to engage in independent action. Proof of complaints from dealers, a common occurrence, was not enough to prove that termination was not the product of independent action allowable under *Colgate*. The evidence must tend "to exclude the possibility that the manufacturer and nonterminated distributors were acting independently."[43] What is required after *Monsanto* is direct or circumstantial evidence

---

1983), where the Eighth Circuit stated: "If Colgate no longer stands for the proposition that a 'simple refusal to sell to customers who will not sell at prices suggested by the seller is permissible under the Sherman Act' . . . it is for the Supreme Court, not this court, to so declare." The court held that acquiescence through coercion did not constitute the requisite agreement.

[39] 433 U.S. 36 (1977). *See* § 5.01[C][3], *infra.*

[40] Compare *Edward J. Sweeney & Sons, Inc. v. Texaco, Inc.*, 637 F.2d 105 (3d Cir. 1980), *cert. denied*, 451 U.S. 911 (1981), with *Spray–Rite Serv. Co. v. Monsanto Co.*, 684 F.2d 1226 (7th Cir. 1982), 465 U.S. 752 (1984), *reh. denied*, 466 U.S. 994 (1984).

[41] 465 U.S. 752 (1984). *See generally*, Hay, *Vertical Restraints After Monsanto*, 66 Cornell. L. Rev. 418 (1985); Floyd, *Vertical Antitrust Conspiracies After Monsanto and Russell Stover*, 33 Kan. L. Rev. 274 (1985).

[42] 465 U.S. at 758, *quoting* 684 F.2d at 1238.

[43] 465 U.S. at 764.

of "a conscious commitment to a common scheme to achieve an unlawful objective."[44] By this the Court meant "that the distributor communicated its acquiescence or agreement, and that this was sought by the manufacturer."[45]

The Court's decision was influenced by the difficulty of distinguishing vertical price restraints, which are *per se* illegal,[46] from nonprice restraints, which are subject to the rule of reason. The Court reasoned that an overly permissive approach to proof of a combination could not only encroach on a manufacturer's rights under *Colgate* but endanger its ability to utilize procompetitive nonprice restraints. The Court recognized that manufacturers may have an interest, independent from complaining dealers, in protecting dealers from free riding discounters.[47] The facts of *Monsanto* serve to illustrate the commingling of price and nonprice restraints about which the *Monsanto* Court was concerned. The plaintiff, Spray–Rite, contended that its price discounts led to its termination. Monsanto, on the other hand, cited Spray–Rite's refusal to hire trained sales staff and promote sales adequately as the factors precipitating termination.[48] Depending on the perspective taken the case could be seen as either concerning a price or a nonprice restraint and, therefore, requiring either a *per se* or rule of reason analysis. The Court, however, chose to treat the case as one involving price restraints.[49]

Monsanto clearly revived *Colgate*. For example, the Court noted that no agreement would arise from a manufacturer's announcement and a dealer's acquiescence[50] — a possibility that the *Albrecht* Court expressly suggested. Moreover, *Monsanto* opened the door to allowing discussions between manufacturers and dealers, even about price, as long as there is no agreement on a price. Indeed, the Court recognized the need for such contacts in order to further lawful nonprice restraints.[51] In essence, by reviving or broadening *Colgate* in the interest of protecting legal nonprice restraints, the Court implicitly discounted the dangers of vertical price

---

[44] *Id. quoting Edward J. Sweeney & Sons*, 637 F.2d at 111.

[45] 465 U.S. at 764 n.9.

[46] At the point *Monsanto* was decided, both vertical maximum and vertical minimum price fixing were *per se* violations.

[47] *Id.* at 762–63. *But see* Note, *A Functional Rule of Reason Analysis for the Law of RPM and its Application to Spray–Rite*, 1984 Wisc. Law. Rev. 1205.

[48] *Id.* at 755–57.

[49] For a criticism of the Court's characterization of the case as involving vertical price restraints *see* Hovenkamp, *Vertical Restrictions and Market Power*, 64 B.U.L. Rev. 521 (1984). For an overview of how a plaintiff after *Monsanto* can make out an antitrust case in order to survive summary judgement, *see* C. Douglas Floyd & E. Thomas Sullivan, Private Antitrust Actions, § 8.3.3. (1996 & 2001 Supp.); Margaret M. Zwisler, *The Susceptibility of Vertical Restraints to Summary Adjudication: Procedural Avenues to Substantive Objectives*, 67 Antitrust L.J. 327 (1999).

[50] 465 U.S. at 761. *See also Russell Stover v. FTC*, 718 F.2d 256 (8th Cir. 1983).

[51] *Id.* at 762–63. *See generally* Faruk, *The Defense of Terminated Dealer Litigation: A Survey of Legal and Strategic Considerations*, 46 Ohio State L.J. 925 (1985).

restraints. Consequently, concerns about vertical price restraints are now subordinate to the interest in promoting nonprice restraints.

The narrow view of what constitutes a vertical agreement on price has carried through to more recent cases. In *Audio Visual Associates, Inc., v. Sharp Electronics Corp.*,[52] the plaintiff, Audio Visual, purchased Sharp's equipment through Douglas Steward Co. Douglas Steward quoted one price and then raised the price, telling Audio Visual that the higher price was fixed by Sharp. The Fourth Circuit Court of Appeals, relying on *Monsanto,* held that this was insufficient to establish an agreement between Sharp and Douglas Stewart.[53] The court indicated that this evidence only showed that Douglas Steward had acquiesced to Sharp's demand but not that it had agreed to fix the resale price.

The view that unilateral action was involved is also found in *Metro Ford Truck Sales, Inc.v. Ford Motor Company,*[54] in which a truck dealer took advantage of Ford's Competitive Price Assistance plan. Under the plan, a dealer could obtain a lower wholesale price when certain conditions were met. Competitors of Metro complained that Metro was circumventing the rules by obtaining concessions on wholesale prices. As a result, Ford threatened to terminate the dealership and to recover the undeserved discounts. This, according to the plaintiff, was a form of fixing resale prices. Again, the court relied on *Monsanto* and reasoned that whatever the impact on resale price, it was the result of unilateral action by Ford.[55]

[d] Price Fixing and Protecting Dealers

The *Monsanto* Court implicitly raised an important issue with which lower courts recently have grappled. The problem flows from the dual approach taken to vertical restraints and the difficulty of distinguishing price and nonprice restraints. Illustrative of the problem is *Business Electronics v. Sharp Electronics Corp.*[56] The plaintiff, Business Electronics, was terminated as a dealer by Sharp after it had repeatedly sold at prices below list and after a competing dealer threatened to drop Sharp products. The complaining dealer testified that it was less concerned about Business Electronics' discounts than it was about the free riding of Business Electronics on its own product promotion efforts. In its instruction to the jury, the trial court indicated that if an agreement existed between Sharp and the complaining dealer to terminate Business Electronics because of price cutting, there was a *per se* violation of the Sherman Act.[57]

---

[52] 210 F.3d 254 (4th Cir. 2000).

[53] *Id.* at 262.

[54] 145 F.3d 320 (5th Cir. 1998).

[55] *Id.* at 325. *But see JTC Petroleum v. Piasa Motor Fuels Co.*, 179 F.3d 1073 (7th Cir. 1999) (finding agreement when competitors in non–compete agreement induce producers of asphalt not to sell to contractor who refused to enter non–compete agreement).

[56] 485 U.S. 717 (1988).

[57] *Id.* at 725.

The issue on appeal concerned this instruction. In particular, was it a *per se* violation to agree to terminate a dealer because of price cutting or was it necessary to find that the that the agreement was part of a scheme to fix an actual resale price. Noting that every vertical restraint could have an impact on price, the Supreme Court reasoned that the *per se* label must be reserved for a very narrow class of cases. To do otherwise, according to Justice Scalia, would "dismantle the doctrine of *GTE Sylvania*."[58] The Court concluded that "economic analysis supports the view, and no precedent opposes it, that a vertical restraint is not illegal *per se* unless it includes some agreement on price or price levels."[59]

The Court emphasized that, without an agreement on the actual resale price, vertical agreements were unlikely to lead to a cartel at either the manufacturer's or retailer's level. It distinguished *Dr. Miles* as based an impermissible restraint on alienation and *Albrecht v. Herald Co.* as involving an express agreement on price.[60] Finally, it rejected the arguments in dissent by Justices Stevens and White that the agreement should be treated as though it were horizontal in nature because it was a naked restraint involving coercion of the manufacturer in order to eliminate price competition.

Lower courts have followed *Business Electronics,* perhaps too closely.[61] For example, when a price cutting dealer was terminated after another dealer charging higher prices demanded that the price cutter raise prices to the higher level prices it was charging, a lower court held that there was still no agreement to sell at prices equal to the higher price.[62] In *Center Video v. United Media,* [63] the court addressed the issue of whether the complaint and termination of *Business Electronics*–type cases could be effective used to facilitate horizontal price fixing at either the manufacturer or reseller's level. In the case of manufacturers, the complain/termination process could be a method of policing and maintaining an agreement among manufacturers. In effect, a price cut by a reseller of a manufacturer's goods would indicate that the manufacturer had cut prices. In the case of reseller's, persistent complaints could be a method of using manufacturers in an effort to stabilize resale prices. Following *Business Electronics*, the court reasoned that neither of these was likely unless there was an agreement to set resale prices with a "certain amount of specificity."[64]

Business Electronics and its interpretations greatly narrow the *per se* rule against prohibiting minimum vertical price fixing thereby decreasing even further the possibility that a terminated dealer could mount a successful action against a manufacturer. Left to a rule of reason standard, the

---

[58] *Id.* at 727.

[59] *Id.* at 735–36.

[60] *Id.* at 731–35.

[61] *See generally*, Phillip E. Areeda & Herbert Hovenkamp, Antitrust Law 319 (2002 Supp.).

[62] *Ben Elfman & Sons v. Criterion Mills*, 774 F.Supp. 683 (D. Mass. 1991).

[63] 995 F.2d 735 (7th Cir. 1993).

[64] *Id.* at 738.

terminated dealer also must be mindful of the Court's skepticism that vertical agreements can be used to foster collusion among manufacturers or among retailers. Finally, as the following suggests, if the terminated dealer were able to prove the existence of an actual agreement on price, the problem of antitrust injury may become an additional hurdle.

[e] Resale Price Maintenance and Antitrust Injury

Lurking in the background of vertical restraints and dealer termination are the enormously important issues of antitrust injury and standing. As discussed in Chapter 3, the Supreme Court has, in recent years, stressed the importance of only recognizing claims of plaintiffs who have suffered the type of injury the antitrust laws are designed to prevent. This concept can have an interesting application in the context of the terminated dealer. *Local Beauty Supply, Inc. v. Lamer, Inc.* [65] is illustrative. Local, a discounting dealer, alleged that it was terminated pursuant to a combination to fix minimum resale prices. It claimed damages based on the lost profits from sales of Lamer products

The Seventh Circuit Court of Appeals reasoned that the discounting plaintiff was actually seeking lost profits that would only have been possible if the defendant's vertical price–fixing efforts were successful. [66] In more general terms, its success as a discounter was due to the anticompetitive conduct of the defendant and its claim was based on its inability to continue to take advantage of this anticompetitive pricing. The court concluded that this loss was not an "antitrust injury." [67]

This case can be contrasted with *Pace Electronics, Inc. v. Canon Computer Systems, Inc.*, [68] in which the Third Circuit Court of Appeals directly addressed the question of whether the termination of a dealer after that dealer's refusal to acquiesce in a minimum resale price resulted in an antitrust injury. Here the court relied on *Simpson v. Union Oil*, and noted that vertical minimum resale maintenance was capable of harming competition by reducing competition both among sellers of the same brand and sellers of different brands. More important in light of the Seventh Circuit's reasoning in *Local Beauty* was the fact that antitrust injury was interpreted to mean a showing that the plaintiff lost profits that it would have made in a market without an illegal arrangement. [69] In short, the terminated dealer in a RPM case is likely to be viewed as having suffered antitrust injury if the theory of damages is that it would have been more profitable if there had not been a vertical price–fixing agreement at all.

The plaintiff, however, must demonstrate some actual harm. In *Lake Hill Motors v. Jim Bennett Yacht Sales, Inc.*, [70] the plaintiff asserted that its

---

[65] 787 F.2d 1197 (7th Cir. 1986).

[66] *Id.* at 1202–03.

[67] *Id.*

[68] 213 F.2d 118 (3d Cir. 2000).

[69] Id. at 122.

[70] 246 F.3d 752 (5th Cir. 2001).

supplier, Yamaha and another dealer conspired to fix minimum resale prices and to terminate the plaintiff for not adhering to those prices. In addition, plaintiff claimed that Yamaha had a policy of reimbursing dealers for advertising only if they did not mention price or only mentioned the suggested retail price. The claim was for damages and for injunctive relief. With respect to the first theory, the court noted that if there were an actual agreement, it would be *per se* unlawful. Here, however, the plaintiff had only been threatened, was not terminated and did not identify any actual harm. This also meant that injunctive relief was unavailable. With respect the cooperative advertising theory, the court ruled that the rule of reason, and not the *per se* standard, should be applied.[71]

[4] The Economics of Resale Price Maintenance

The continued *per se* status of vertical price fixing is an issue of continuing debate. Before looking at the arguments more closely it is important to remember that *per se* status is supposedly reserved for activities that are anticompetitive in the vast majority of instances. The prohibition of an occasional harmless or beneficial arrangement is justified by the fact that the rule almost always reliably identifies conduct that is harmful to competition.

Proponents of the *per se* rule argue that vertical price fixing can be used as a method for retailers to indirectly facilitate their own horizontal restraints by enlisting the aid of the manufacturers and that manufacturers can use vertical price fixing to add stability to a scheme of price fixing at the manufacturing level.[72] Those who oppose the rule discount these possibilities and use the free rider problem as the central pillar in their case for abandoning the *per se* rule.[73]

The argument that retailers may rely on manufacturers to institute or maintain a system of minimum RPM in order to aid their own horizontal price fixing is typically responded to by questioning whether such a plan could work or why a manufacturer would cooperate. In particular, if there are several brands in the market retailers would have to obtain the cooperation of all or most of the manufacturers for the scheme to work. Otherwise consumers would simply switch to brands that are not subject to the dealer--induced RPM.[74] In markets with little or no competition, the question is why a manufacturer would agree to go along.[75] After all, in this

---

[71] Id. at 757.

[72] *See* Pitofsky, *In Defense of Discounters: The No–Frills Case for a Per Se Rule Against Vertical Price Fixing*, 71 Georgetown L. J. 1487, 1490–91 (1983). *See also* Comanor, *Vertical Price Fixing, Vertical Market Restrictions, and the New Antitrust Policy*, 95 Harv. L. Rev. 983 (1985); Flynn, *The "Is" and "Ought" of Vertical Restraints after Monsanto Co. v Spray–Rite Service Corp.*, 71 Cornell L. Rev. 1095 (1986).

[73] *See, e.g.*, R. Bork, *supra* note 8, at 292–295. *See also* Goldberg, *The Free Rider Problem, Imperfect Pricing and Economics of Retailing Services*, 79 Nw. L. Rev. 736 (1984).

[74] *See* H. Hovenkamp, *supra* note 2, at 249–50.

[75] *See Id.* at 250; Easterbrook, *Vertical Restraints and the Rule of Reason*, 53 Antitrust L.J. 135, 142 (1984).

instance, the manufacturer has monopoly power and instituting a RPM scheme for the benefit of retailers would result in a decrease in sales by retailers and, therefore, a decrease in their demand for the manufacturer's product.

It seems clear that RPM would be an attractive way for a manufacturers' cartel to police their own agreement by keeping retailers "in line." The primary problem here again is one of practicality. In all likelihood, to be successful the plan would require multiple manufacturers to supervise hundreds — perhaps thousands — of retailers who may not find that their interests are served by cooperating.[76] The question is not whether it is impossible for RPM to be used by retailers or manufacturers to facilitate horizontal price fixing, but whether it happens often enough to justify making RPM a *per se* offense. Some empirical evidence does not support the argument that RPM is typically used to facilitate horizontal price fixing.[77]

This is not to say that the free rider argument, the mainstay of those favoring removal of the *per se* tag, is not without its inconsistencies. Professor Robert Pitofsky forces us to consider the free rider issue more closely when he reminds us that "it should be clear exactly who these 'free riders' really are. They are the discounters of modern American marketing: low overhead, high volume sellers who aggressively compete as to price."[78] Thus, what precisely is the argument for permitting this competition to be curbed? Figure 5–1 presents the standard justification. Dl is the retail demand for the product in question and MRl is the corresponding marginal revenue curve. If the retailer's marginal cost curve is MC1, the price will be P1 and the quantity sold at that price will be Q1. Now suppose the manufacturer institutes a RPM system and the new retail price is P2. Initially, it appears that the quantity sold will drop to Q2. On the other hand, since retailers can no longer compete on the basis of price they may compete through promotional efforts, more convenient locations, better trained personnel, better services, etc. According to the theory, demand for the product will shift to the right and the quantity sold, Q3, determined by the intersection of the new marginal revenue curve, MR2, and the new marginal cost curve, MC2, will exceed that sold when the price was lower.

Now that output has increased, is anyone better off? Since the manufacturer is in charge of the decision to institute the plan it seems very likely that profits have increased. Are consumers better off? To determine this one must compare consumer surplus before and after RPM. Prior to RPM, it was equal to the area of triangle P1BC on the graph. After RPM, consumer surplus is equal to the area of triangle P2DE. In the diagram, the area P2DE exceeds area P1BC and consumers are, therefore, better off after RPM.[79] Indeed, since consumers and the manufacturer are both better off the outcome can be regarded as efficient.

---

[76] *See* R. Bork, *supra* note 8, at 293–95; H. Hovenkamp, *supra* note 2, at 448.

[77] *See* Ornstein, *supra* note 8.

[78] Pitofsky, *supra* note 72, at 1493.

[79] In Figure 5–1, both legs of the right angle in the triangle P2DE are longer than their counterparts in triangle P1BC. The area of P2DE is, therefore, greater than P1BC. *See* Comanor, *supra* note 72, at 992–98.

FIGURE 5–1

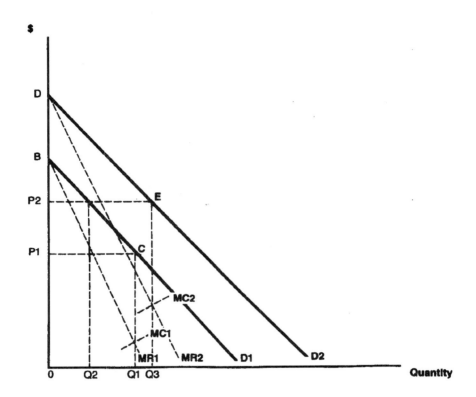

Figure 5–1, however, covers a very special case. In order to understand why, it is important to take a closer look at the concept of demand. From Chapter 2 you know that demand shows the prices and the quantities individuals are willing and able to buy at each price. From a slightly different perspective, however, one can say that demand shows how much people value each unit of output. The shift up and to the right of a demand curve, as occurred in Figure 5–1, indicates that consumers regard each unit as more valuable after dealer services are taken into account. In fact, since the demand curve shifted up by the same amount for all units of output, one can say that it illustrates a case in which all consumers value the new services by the same amount. That is why they are all willing to pay exactly the same amount over what they were willing to pay before services were included.

This is probably an unrealistic assumption.[80] People actually seem more likely to vary in the amount of value they attribute to a carpeted showroom

---

[80] This discussion is based on Comanor, *supra* note 72 and Scherer, *The Economics of Vertical Restraints*, 52 Antitrust L.J. 687 (1983).

or highly trained sales personnel. Thus, the increase in the amount individuals are willing to pay for the service–augmented product will vary. The implications for the demand curve are illustrated in Figure 5–2. As in Figure 5–1, D1, MC1, and MR1 are the initial curves facing the retailer. Price and output are at P1 and Q1, respectively.

Figure 5–2 demonstrates that instituting RPM and a price of P2 means a drop in sales to Q2 until retailers begin promotional efforts. Now, however, under the more realistic assumption that different consumers attribute different values to the services offered, the new demand curve, D2, shifts by different amounts at each level of output. The new quantity sold is Q3 where MR2 and MC2 intersect. One must assume again that the manufacturer is better off, otherwise it would not have placed the plan into operation. On the other hand, are consumers better off? Again the original consumer surplus was P1AB. After the adjustments set off by RPM, it is P2AD. Under the conditions depicted in Figure 5–2, the new consumer surplus is less than that which existed before RPM. The graph here was purposely drawn to produce that result and to illustrate an important point: under more realistic assumptions about the reaction of consumers to "improvements" in quality, there is a distinct possibility that consumers will be harmed by RPM.

This does not necessarily mean that RPM is inefficient. As already noted, it seems safe to assume that there would be no RPM unless the manufacturer thought it would result in increased profits. Even if there is a decrease in consumer surplus, if the manufacturer's increase in profit exceeds this loss then, as a technical matter, the change to RPM is efficient. But there is nothing inherent in RPM to guarantee this outcome. In those instances in which the decrease in consumer surplus is not exceeded by the increase in profit for the manufacturer, RPM is less efficient than a system in which retailers are free to set their own prices.

At this point there is a lack of reliable empirical evidence concerning the economic impact of RPM or even the magnitude of the free rider problem. Indeed, those concerned about free riders may be underestimating the ability of firms to internalize the benefits of services offered simply by charging for them separately. All that can be safely said is that, in some instances, RPM can increase overall efficiency while benefitting both producers and consumers. In others it may increase overall efficiency but leave consumers worse off. Finally, it can decrease overall efficiency even though producers benefit by its use. In sum, though, the present evidence does suggest that it is becoming more difficult to justify continuing the *per se* treatment of RPM, especially if one is reminded of the traditional understanding of the *per se* classification.[81]

---

[81] *See White Motor Co. v. United States*, 372 U.S. 253 (1963) (*per se* treatment reserved for conduct with pernicious effects on competition that lack any redeeming virtue).

FIGURE 5–2

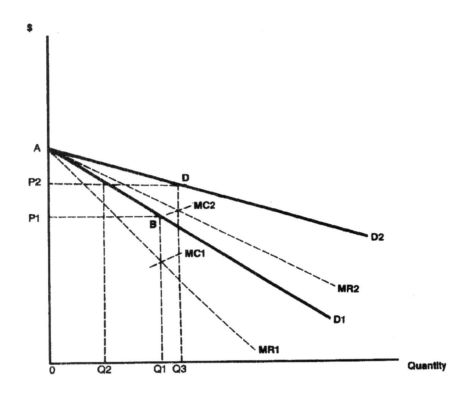

[5]   Maximum Price "Maintenance"

To this point the discussion has focused almost exclusively on vertical price maintenance that governs minimum resale prices. For many years, under the *Albrecht* rule, discussed above, vertical agreements to "maintain" maximum resale prices were also *per se* unlawful. Sellers were not permitted to set the maximum price at which their products may be resold. Finally, in 1997, in *State Oil v. Kahn,* [82] the Supreme Court overturned *Albrecht.*

Even prior to 1997, the continued viability of *Albrecht* came into question in *Atlantic Richfield Co. v. USA Petroleum Co. (ARCO),*[83] a 1990 case in which the Supreme Court addressed the issue of antitrust injury in the context of maximum price fixing. In *ARCO,* USA Petroleum, a retail seller of gasoline, complained that ARCO, an integrated oil company, had conspired with retailers to whom it supplied gasoline, to set retail prices that

---

[82] 522 U.S. 3 (1997).

[83] 495 U.S. 328 (1990).

were "artificially low."[84] The effect of the scheme, according to USA, was to drive independent retailers from the market. USA did not claim that the prices charged were predatory or below cost. The Court noted that the essence of the problem faced by USA Petroleum was that it was unable to *raise* prices.[85] Any loss due to an inability to raise prices, the Court reasoned, could not be viewed properly as a form of antitrust injury. Although the Court seemed to defend the *Albrecht* rule in *ARCO*, the *Albrecht* rule was left toothless.

In *Kahn* the death knell was delivered as the Court unanimously held that vertical maximum price fixing should be assessed under the rule or reason. To some extent the Court's reasoning was a 20 year delayed response to its 1977 decision in *Continental T.V. v. GTE Sylvania.*[86] As will be discussed below, *Sylvania* held that vertical intrabrand restraints on distribution were to be viewed under the rule of reason. This created the possibility that manufacturers could, in effect, grant to distributors or other resellers local monopolies. Under the *Albrecht* rule, however, manufacturers were unable to limit directly the extent to which local monopolists could exploit their power by raising prices. Thus, the *Kahn* Court noted that continued application of *Albrecht* after *Sylvania* could "exacerbate problems related to the unrestrained exercise of market power by monopolist dealers."[87]

Much of the *Kahn* Court's reasoning also reflected doubt about whether any of the original justifications offered in *Albrecht* were well–founded.[88] For example, in *Albrecht* the Court had expressed concern for the freedom of dealers. In *Kahn*, however, the Court noted that one possible industry reaction to *Albrecht* was vertical integration and the elimination of dealers altogether. In addition, *Albrecht* was based on a supposition that maximum prices would be set so low as to make it impossible for the dealer to offer desirable services. The *Kahn* Court questioned this rationale by suggesting that it would be irrational for manufacturers to set prices so low that sales–enhancing services might be sacrificed. Finally, the *Kahn* Court questioned the *Albrecht* reasoning that maximum prices might become minimum prices. The Court conceded that this was a possible result but felt that assessment under the rule of reason would sufficiently recognize and punish those outcomes.[89]

---

[84] *Id.* at 333.

[85] *Id.* at 337–38.

[86] 433 U.S. 36 (1977).

[87] 522 U.S. at 18.

[88] *Id.* at 11–15.

[89] For recent actions involving vertical price fixing since *Kahn, see In re Sony Music Entertainment*, FTC 971–0070, May 10, 2000 (finding agreement between five major music companies and retailers to use minimum advertised price programs to sell and advertise compact discs and end price wars.); *Nine West*, (finding shoe supplier coerced agreements with certain retailers to fix prices at which shoes could be advertised and sold.)

Kahn also has generated significant academic comment. *See, e.g.* Norman W. Hawker, *Maximum Resale Price Maintenance under the Rule of Reason*, 51 Baylor L. Rev. 441 (1999); Benjamin Klein, *Distribution Restrictions Operate By Creating Dealer Profits: Explaining the Use of Maximum Resale Price Maintenance in State Oil v. Kahn*, 7 Sup. Ct. Econ. Rev. 1 (1999).

[C] Territorial and Customer Restraints

Although eroded to a certain extent by *Monsanto*'s expansion of the "*Colgate* doctrine" and by modern applications of the "antitrust injury" requirement, the Supreme Court's position on vertical price restraints has remained relatively firm. The same cannot be said about the Court's approach to nonprice restraints. Over a period of fifteen years, the Court changed course twice. For now, nonprice vertical restraints are evaluated under the "rule of reason." The difference in treatment between price and nonprice restraints continues to be problematic.

First, arguments that the Court has found compelling enough to justify rule of reason treatment for nonprice restraints apply with equal force to price restraints. Second, nonprice restraints can be even more restrictive than price restraints; the retailer who is precluded from competing on the basis of price is still free to compete by other means with other retailers for the same customers. In the case of vertical nonprice restraints, however, retailers may be precluded completely from competing for the business of a specified group of customers.[90]

[1] *White Motor Co. v. United States*

The inconsistent saga of the Supreme Court and nonprice vertical restraints begins with *White Motor Co.*[91] White Motor Company, a manufacturer and seller of trucks and parts, required its dealers to sell only to customers who had places of business within the territory assigned to the dealer. In addition, no sales were to be made to government agencies. The former restriction is a classic example of a territorial clause; the latter is an example of a customer clause. White Motor Company argued that the territorial clause was necessary to develop a system of retail outlets in order to compete effectively with larger manufacturers.[92] The customer clause, in effect, reserved to White Motor the opportunity to make fleet sales. The justification was that large scale buyers, if forced to purchase repair parts from dealers, would lose discounts and become "discontented" with White.[93]

The issue was whether the territorial and customer clauses should be regarded as *per se* violations of § 1 of the Sherman Act. In essence the Court was faced with the question of whether vertical restraints were sufficiently similar to horizontal restraints to be subject to the same standard.[94] By a 5–3 majority, the Court ruled that they were not and declined to apply the *per se* rule. The Court noted that *per se* treatment was reserved for

---

[90] This has been recognized by one lower court which declined to apply the *per se* rule to a requirement that a dealer charge no less than a specified minimum price in sales outside its territory. *Eastern Scientific Co. v. Wild Heerbrugg Instruments*, 572 F.2d 883 (1st Cir.), *cert. denied*, 439 U.S. 833 (1978).

[91] 372 U.S. 253 (1963).

[92] *Id.* at 256–57.

[93] *Id.* at 257–58.

[94] *Id.* at 263.

practices with a "pernicious effect" on competition and a "lack of any redeeming virtue." It reasoned that horizontal territorial limitations were *per se* violations because they fit this description in that they were "naked restraints . . . with no purpose except to stifle competition."[95] On the other hand, it concluded that it did not know "enough of the economic and business stuff out of which [vertical] arrangements emerge"[96] to rule that they too were virtually always anticompetitive in effect.

[2]   *United States v. Arnold, Schwinn & Co.*[97]

Just four years later, in 1967, the Court experienced a change of course. *Schwinn* involved the contractual arrangements of a bicycle manufacturer for the distribution and final sale of its products. The system was three–pronged. Some bicycles were sold by distributors but shipped directly to the retailer by Schwinn with the distributor earning a commission. Others were sold to distributors for resale. Others were consigned to the distributors for sale to retailers. In the latter two cases, the distributors were permitted to sell only to franchised dealers within designated territories. Retailers were permitted only to buy from the distributor in their area and permitted to sell only to consumers.[98]

In a major stroke of judicial activism, since the question of *per se* illegality was not part of the appeal, the Court did what it had declined to do in *White Motor Co;* it announced that vertical territorial and customer restraints were *per se* unlawful.[99] It struck down Schwinn's restrictions on resale as they applied to distributors and retailers who had purchased bicycles. It distinguished, however, sales made on behalf of Schwinn under consignment. The latter restraints remained under the "rule of reason."

Although the Court had indicated in *White Motor Co.* that it would not declare vertical restraints *per se* unlawful without further knowledge of economic factors, the reasoning of the *Schwinn* Court left a great deal — perhaps everything — to be desired in this regard. The Court professed to examine the relevant "economic and business stuff," but its analysis went no further than to focus on the impact on intrabrand competition[100] and to distinguish the case from *White Motor Co.*[101] In large measure, rather than rely on economic analysis at all, the Court reasoned that to permit continued vertical restraints when sales were involved "would violate the ancient rule against restraints on alienation."[102]

It is perhaps too easy to dismiss *Schwinn* as totally inconsistent with the promotion of economic benefits flowing from vertical restraints. Part of the

---

[95] *Id.*

[96] *Id.*

[97] 388 U.S. 365 (1967).

[98] *Id.* at 370–71.

[99] *Id.* at 382.

[100] *Id.* at 374–75.

[101] *Id.* at 373–75.

[102] *Id.* at 380.

rationale for leaving restraints associated with consignments in the "rule of reason" of category was to avoid "hampering smaller enterprises resorting to reasonable means of meeting the competition of giants."[103] In essence, the Court seemed to sense the procompetitive potential of vertical restraints and feel that they could be realized through the preservation of the right of manufacturers to invoke such restraints through consignment sales.

[3] *Continental T.V., Inc. v. GTE Sylvania*

After ten years of nearly uniform scholarly condemnation and judicial efforts at narrowing the reach of *Schwinn*, it was overturned by the Court in *Continental T.V. v. GTE Sylvania*.[104] The case is a landmark in antitrust because it constituted the first absolutely clear signal by the Court that economic analysis was to be the Court's guiding methodology in antitrust matters.[105] The strength of the Court's conviction lies in the fact that it declined to distinguish *Sylvania* from *Schwinn* even though the cases concerned different types of vertical restraints and manufacturers with significantly different market shares.[106]

Sylvania was a struggling manufacturer of television sets with a market share of 1 to 2% in 1962. It then changed its in marketing strategy to one involving the selection of a small group of franchisees. Franchisees could sell any brand of television from their stores and could sell to any class of customer. Under Sylvania's plan, however, they could not sell Sylvania televisions from other than approved locations.[107] The plan was designed to shield Sylvania dealers from competition by other Sylvania dealers in hopes that they would compete aggressively and promote Sylvania televisions. The "location clause" arrangement was eventually challenged by Continental T.V. when it was terminated as a dealer after selling from an unauthorized location.

The Court's analysis consisted of two steps. First it discarded the sale/ consignment distinction of Schwinn as difference with formal but not economic consequence.[108] Thus, whatever the merits or demerits of vertical restraints, the form — sale or consignment — was irrelevant. Having resolved to eliminate this inconsistency, the Court was not then required to upset *Schwinn's* *per se* standards. It could have classified both sales and consignments as *per se* unlawful. Instead it ruled that nonprice restraints associated with consignments and sales would be evaluated under the "rule of reason." The Court specifically cited the possible use of vertical restraints

---

[103] *Id.*

[104] 433 U.S. 36 (1977).

[105] Another clear example came earlier in *United States Steel Corp. v. Fortner Enterprises, Inc.*, 429 U.S. 610 (1977). See § 5.02[B][2][b], *infra*.

[106] Schwinn's market share was over 10% and it used both customer and terriorial restraints. Sylvania's market share eventually reached 5% and its vertical restraint was a "location clause."

[107] 433 U.S. at 38.

[108] *Id.* at 52–54.

as a means of promoting interbrand competition by limiting the free rider effect.[109] Indeed, in this regard, it stated that interbrand competition was the "primary concern of antitrust law,"[110] thereby apparently reducing intrabrand competition to an ancillary concern. Then, reverting to the analysis of *White Motor Co.*, it concluded that there was an absence of evidence generally, and with respect to the case at hand, to decide that vertical restraints had "a 'pernicious effect on competition' or that they 'lack . . . any redeeming virtue.' "[111]

There are several other facets of the opinion that deserve particular note. First, the Court did not rule out "the possibility that particular applications of vertical restraints might justify *per se* prohibition" in the future.[112] Second, in the process of explaining the result in *Sylvania*, it effectively undercut the rationale for *Dr. Miles' per se* treatment of vertical price restraints by reasoning that the notion of "restraints on alienation" had little antitrust significance. Still, it maintained that RPM could be distinguished from nonprice vertical restraints and left intact the *per se* status of RPM.[113]

Finally, and perhaps most importantly, the Court gave very little direction to courts attempting to apply the rule of reason standard to nonprice vertical restraints. As a first step in receding from a *per se* approach, the Court might have suggested presumptions that would guide the lower courts. For example, the Court could have said that proof of the existence of the restraint established a rebuttable presumption of unreasonableness. Or, it could have indicated that the plaintiff's first step in establishing unreasonableness would be a showing that the firm imposing restraints possessed market power. Specific guidance of this variety is, however, not found in the opinion.[114]

The very limited advice offered by the Court came in three general forms. First, was the aforementioned assertion that interbrand competition was the primary concern of the antitrust laws. Thus, although the opinion certainly gives the impression that a balancing of intrabrand and interbrand effects is to take place, the Court's primary objective seemed to be the promotion of interbrand competition. This follows, the Court explained, from the fact that as long as there is aggressive interbrand competition, "it provides a significant check on the exploitation of intrabrand market power."[115]

Second, the Court quoted the general language of the leading rule of reason case, *Chicago Board of Trade v. United States*,[116] and its

---

[109] *Id.* at 54–56.

[110] *Id.* at 52 n.19.

[111] *Id.* at 58 *citing Northern Pacific R.R. v. United States*, 356 U.S. 1, 5 (1958).

[112] 433 U.S. at 58.

[113] *Id.* at 51 n.18.

[114] *See generally* Pitofsky, *The Sylvania Case: Antitrust Analysis of Non–Price Vertical Restraints*, 78 Colum. L. Rev. 1 (1978).

[115] 433 U.S. at 52 n.19.

[116] 246 U.S. 231, 238 (1918), *quoted* at 433 U.S. at 49 n.15.

open–ended list of the factors that can influence a rule of reason analysis. Finally, the Court offered a list of procompetitive reasons for the adoption of vertical restraints. The list includes the use of restrictions during entry into a market in order to induce aggressive marketing by retailers. It also includes the use of vertical restraints as protection from free riders for retailers offering service and repair facilities that might generate good will for the manufacturer. In addition, the Court suggested that vertical restraints could play a role in assuring the safety and quality of the manufacturer's product.[117] This last suggestion, found in a footnote, can be interpreted as an indication that product safety was to have some weight in an antitrust review, a possibility supposedly discarded the following year in *National Society of Professional Engineers v. United States.*[118]

A difficult question left open by *Sylvania* concerns just how one balances a possible decrease in intrabrand competition against an increase in interbrand competition. Presumably, a system without vertical restraints would mean lower prices. If the imposition of restraints does encourage nonprice competition, prices will be higher but the product will be "different" in the sense that it will be accompanied by service and repair opportunities or have enhanced appeal due to promotional activities.[119] Although the problem may not be exactly like the proverbial one of comparing apples and oranges, it is uncomfortably close.

[4] The Aftermath of *Sylvania*

To find the result of the "full" rule of reason approach flowing from *Sylvania*, one need look no further than Professor Robert Pitofsky's prediction issued in 1978, on the heels of the Court's decision:

> A standard under which all circumstances are weighed, and violations found only upon demonstration of specific anticompetitive effects, may sound sober and moderate, but in the real world it has little deterrent effect, produces trials of inordinate length and expense, and often undermines antitrust enforcement. Business practices tested under a full rule of reason, with no presumptions based on any set of facts and with the burden of showing anticompetitive effect on the plaintiff, will usually turn out to be legal.[120]

Professor Pitofsky's prediction of "usual" legality has turned out to be accurate. Antitrust liability based on nonprice vertical restraints on distribution is, in fact, rare.[121] Furthermore, it would be misleading to suggest

---

[117] 433 U.S. at 55 n.23.

[118] 435 U.S. 678 (1978).

[119] *See* Posner, *The Next Step in the Antitrust Treatment of Restricted Distribution: Per Se Legality*, 48 U. Chi. L. Rev. 6, 19 (1981).

[120] Pitofsky, *supra* note 114, at 2. Copyright 1978 by the Directors of the Columbia Law Review Association, Inc. All rights reserved. Reprinted by permission.

[121] Two exceptions are *Graphic Products Distributors, Inc. v. Itek Corp.*, 717 F.2d 1560 (11th Cir. 1983); *Eiberger v. Sony Corp.*, 622 F.2d 1068 (2d Cir. 1980). For a case carrying the *Sylvania* rationale into the analysis of monopolization *see Trans Sport, Inc. v. Starter Sportswear*, 964 F.2d 186 (2d Cir. 1992).

that the courts have arrived at a systematic method of applying the rule of reason to nonprice vertical restraints. Some trends, however, are discernable.

First, perhaps as a result of the *Sylvania* Court's primary interest in interbrand effects, lower courts have tended to emphasize the effect of the restraints on competition between brands.[122] In effect, the notion that the anticompetitive effects of vertical restraints on intrabrand competition would be placed on a scale opposite the procompetitive interbrand effects has given way to an approach that focuses directly on interbrand impact. The logic, which can be gleaned from *Sylvania* itself[123] and which now finds support in most circuits, is that there can be no detrimental intrabrand effects unless the manufacturer has market power.[124] For example, a manufacturer's actions vis–a–vis vertical restraints cannot result in increased prices and restricted output as long as there are aggressive sellers of other brands. The market power of the firm imposing the restraint has become a kind of "threshold issue" because, in the absence of power, a firm "is unlikely to adopt policies that disserve its customers."[125]

Second, and as suggested by *Business Electronics*, the logic of *Sylvania* has found its way into agreements that can be viewed as involving vertical price fixing. For example, in *Wisconsin Music Works v. Muzak Limited Partnership,*[126] Muzak sold to licensees who resold to subscribers. It then negotiated prices directed with subscribers and then terminated a licensee who would not sell at the price agreed upon by Muzak. The court, without citing or seeking to distinguish *Dr. Miles*, applied the rule of reason. Specifically, the court noted the direct negotiation approach used by Muzak made it more competitive with its two national rivals which were vertically integrated. In other words, interbrand competition was likely to be strengthened.[127]

Third, one of the possible interpretations of *Sylvania* is that vertical restraints are lawful when the firm imposing them has little market power and that, when market power is higher, the interbrand and intrabrand effects are to be addressed. In other words there is little utility in addressing the offsetting competitive effects if the firm is unlikely to have the power to have any ultimate anticompetitive impact. The most obvious example is a case in which the restraint shields dealers from free riding and, therefore, encourages their promotional efforts. This would raise little

---

[122] *See, e.g., JBL Enterprises, Inc. v. Jhirmack Enterprises, Inc.,* 698 F.2d 1011 (9th Cir. 1983), *cert. denied,* 464 U.S. 829 (1983); *Valley Liquors, Inc. v. Renfield Importers, Ltd.,* 678 F.2d 742 (7th Cir. 1982); *Daniels v. All Steel Equipment Co.,* 590 F.2d 111 (5th Cir. 1979).

[123] 433 U.S. at 52 n.19.

[124] *See* H. Hovenkamp, *supra* note 2, at 480–481.

[125] *Valley Liquors,* 678 F.2d at 745. See also *Muenster Butane, Inc. v. Stewart Co.,* 651 F.2d 292 (5th Cir. 1980); *Graphic Products Distributors v. Itek Corp.,* 717 F.2d 1560 (11th Cir. 1983), and cases cited in note 111, *supra.*

[126] 5 F.3d 218 (7th Cir. 1992).

[127] *Id.* at 223.

concern if the restraint is employed by a firm with 5% of the market; if the firm has a 60% there would be reason for much greater concern. Thus, in an ideal judicial world one might expect that once the issue of market power is settled the court would move to the issue of procompetitive justifications.[128] In some instances this has been the case[129] In others, courts have approved implicitly of justifications that generally mirror the suggestions in *Sylvania* itself without a detailed market analysis.[130] To date, the issue of how critical a detailed market analysis is required remains unsettled.

[D] Dual Distribution

One of the results of *Sylvania* is that, for the most part, horizontal and vertical restraints are viewed very differently by the courts. Vertical nonprice restraints and vertical maximum price fixing are examined under the rule of reason, while horizontal restraints remain, despite erosion in recent years, basically illegal *per se*. This means that the classification of a restraint as vertical or horizontal can be determinative. Unfortunately, it also can be very difficult. For example, suppose a manufacturer of shoes owns a chain of retail outlets. Plus, it sells shoes to independent retailers who are assigned specific territories in order to decrease intrabrand competition both with each other and with the manufacturer's own outlets. The restraint could be designed to reserve to the manufacturer, and each distributor, an area in which it has monopoly power at the retail level. Or, it could be designed to protect retailers from free riders as means of encouraging promotion of the manufacturer's product. The situation, in either case, has come to be called "dual distribution" because the manufacturer operates on the same level as the firms it supplies. The question is whether the territorial restraint is horizontal or vertical.

In the post–*Sylvania* era, the Supreme Court has yet to indicate the proper treatment to be afforded a system of dual distribution. Lower courts have employed a variety of approaches to the classification problem.[131] One approach, evidently inspired by *Schwinn*, involves ascertaining whether the arrangement is primarily the result of an agreement among competitors or whether it was instituted primarily by the manufacturer.[132] The logic

---

[128] For suggestions in this regard *see* Gellhorn & Tatham, *Making Sense Out of the Rule of Reason*, 35 Case West. Res. L. Rev. 155 (1984); Rill, *Non–Price Vertical Restraints Since Sylvania: Market Conditions and Dual Distribution*, 53 Antitrust L.J. 95 (1983).

[129] *Graphic Products Distributors v. Itek Corp.*, 717 F.2d 1560 (11th Cir. 1983); *Donald B. Rice Tire Co. v. Michelin Tire Corp.*, 438 F. Supp. 750 (D. Md. 1980), *aff'd per curiam*, 638 F.2d 15 (4th Cir.), *cert. denied*, 446 U.S. 965 (1981).

[130] *See, e.g., Mendelovitz v. Aldolph Coors Co.*, 693 F.2d 570, 576 (5th Cir 1982); *Red Diamond Supply, Inc. v. Liquid Carbonic Corp.*, 637 F.2d 1001, 1005 (5th Cir. 1981), *cert. denied*, 454 U.S. 827 (1981).

[131] *See e.g., Donald B. Rice Tire Co. v. Michelin Tire Corp.*, 638 F.2d 15 (4th Cir. 1981); *Krehl v. Baskin–Robbins Ice Cream Co.*, 664 F.2d 1348 (9th Cir. 1982); *Red Diamond Supply, Inc. v. Liquid Carbonic Corp.*, 637 F.2d 1001 (5th Cir. 1981).

[132] *See, e.g. H & B Equipment Co. v. International Harvester Co.*, 577 F.2d 239 (5th Cir. 1978).

is that a restraint imposed by a manufacturer is likely to be driven by the desire to encourage interbrand competition.[133] On the other hand, competitors may enter into the same arrangement for anticompetitive purposes. In a sense, the determination of the source of the restraint is used as a surrogate for an examination of the function of the restraint.[134]

Other courts have been less trusting of a correlation between the source of restraint and its purpose. Thus, rather than a bright line test, a trend toward evaluating dual distribution under the rule of reason has developed.[135] Thus, the Fourth Circuit Court of Appeals has observed, "it is important to distinguish between a conspiracy among dealers and their supplying manufacturer . . . that would benefit the dealers and one involving the same parties but redounding primarily to the benefit of the manufacturer as a result of increased interbrand competition."[136] Implicit in such an approach is the belief that a "vertical" restraint could result from the power wielded by a cartel of dealers. The court admitted in that this substantive analysis is essentially an application of the rule of reason.[137] Similarly, in one of the more influential dual distribution cases, *Krehl v. Baskin–Robbins Ice Cream Co.*,[138] the court observed, "our inquiry focuses not on whether the vertical or horizontal aspects of the system predominate, but rather, on the actual competitive impact."[139] The court essentially skipped the classification step or replaced it with the rule that "in the absence of proof of anti–competitive purpose or effect, dual distribution must be evaluated under the traditional rule of reason standard."[140] Finally, in a Seventh Circuit opinion, Judge Easterbrook reasoned that "[d]ual distribution . . . does not subject to the *per se* ban a practice that would be lawful if the manufacturer were not selling directly to customers; antitrust laws encourage rather than forbid this extra competition."[141]

The trend toward rule of reason treatment of dual distribution finds considerable support in economic theory. The question is whether a manufacturer who institutes dual distribution is after the same types of gains

---

[133] *See Red Diamond Sypply Co. v. Liquid Carbonic Corp.*, 637 F.2d 1001, 1004 n.4 (5th Cir. 1981), *cert. denied*, 454 U.S. 827 (1981).

[134] The Fifth Circuit Court of Appeals, the leading proponent of the "source" approach to classification has altered its course somewhat to one that focuses more on actual impact. *See Abadir & Co. v. First Mississippi Corp.*, 651 F.2d 422 (5th Cir. 1981).

[135] *See e.g. Smalley & Company v. Emerson & Cuming, Inc.*, 13 F.3d 366 (10th Cir. 1993); *Illinois Corporate Travel v. American Airlines*, 889 F.2d.751 (7th Cir. 1989). *See generally, Rill, supra* note 128, at 105–108; *See generally* Note, *Antitrust Treatment of Intrabrand Territorial Restraints Within a Dual Distribution System*, 56 Tex. L. Rev. 1486 (1978).

[136] *Donald B. Rice Tire Co. v. Michelin Tire Corp.*, 638 F.2d 15, 16 (4th Cir. 1981).

[137] *Id.* at 16–17.

[138] 664 F.2d 1348 (9th Cir. 1982).

[139] *Id.* at 1356.

[140] *Id.* at 1357. *Accord Copy–Data Systems, Inc. v. Toshiba America, Inc.*, 663 F.2d 405 (2d Cir. 1981), *cert denied*, 106 S.Ct 80 (1985); *Davis–Watkins Co. v. Service Merchandise Co.*, 686 F.2d 1190 (6th Cir. 1982).

[141] *Illinois Corporate Travel, supra* note 135, at 753.

normally associated with typical horizontal agreements. Some commentators argue that this is extremely unlikely.[142] First, if a manufacturer does not have market power, there is nothing magical about dual distribution that will suddenly enable it to raise prices and restrict output. Second, even if it does have market power, economic theory suggests that the firm can reap the full benefits of that power by its pricing as a manufacturer.[143]

[E] Exclusive Dealerships

A territorial or customer restraint limits the area in which a dealer may compete. This does not necessarily mean that there will not be other dealers sharing that territory. In fact, the manufacturer can "regulate" the amount of intrabrand competition by adjusting the number of sellers sharing a market. Under another type of vertical restraint, the exclusive dealership, the dealer is the exclusive representative of the manufacturer. Franchise agreements are a common form of exclusive dealerships. This does not mean that an exclusive dealer will not compete with other exclusive dealers of the same brand who are willing to transport the product to customers near the first dealer. Thus, the exclusive dealer is protected from intrabrand competition only to the extent that it has an economic advantage over rivals.

Both territorial restraints and exclusive dealership agreements can shield a dealer from intrabrand competition and free rider problems. Thus, either one can be used to promote interbrand competition. A combination of the two means even greater protection. Here the retailer is assigned not only a territory but is the only retailer permitted to sell within that territory. In theory, this completely eliminates intrabrand competition.

Three questions are raised by exclusive dealerships. First, how are they to be treated when unaccompanied by a vertical restraint that makes them "absolute" or "airtight?"[144] Second, does it make a difference how the exclusive dealership is achieved. For example, does it matter whether it comes about by terminating all but one dealer or by the initial appointment of a single dealer and refusals to deal with subsequent applicants. Finally, how is the exclusive dealership to be treated when it is superimposed over a vertical territorial restraint?

With respect to the first question, there is language in *Schwinn*, the case taking the *least* charitable approach to vertical restraints, suggesting that exclusive dealerships are *per se* legal. According to that Court, "a manufacturer of a product other and equivalent brands of which are readily available in the market may select his customers, and for this purpose he may 'franchise' certain dealers to whom, alone he will sell his goods."[145] Although there are interpretations of *Schwinn* that leave open the possibility of successfully challenging exclusive dealerships under § 1,[146] in the

---

[142] *See* H. Hovenkamp, *supra,* note 2, at 484–485.

[143] The argument here is the same one made with respect to the economics of tying, *see infra,* § 5.02[B][1], and vertical integration by a monopolist, *infra* § 6.05[G].

[144] *See generally*, Pitofsky, *supra*, note 114, at 17.

[145] 388 U.S. at 376.

[146] *See* L. Sullivan, *Antitrust* 425 (1977).

aftermath of *Sylvania* and *Monsanto* such a possibility seems remote. For example, in *Paddock Publications v. Chicago Tribune,* [147] a Chicago newspaper sought relief because a rival newspaper had exclusive rights in the Chicago area to the New York Times News Service as a source of stories. The argument by the plaintiff was that this exclusive access rendered the newspaper market less competitive. In finding the exclusivity arrangement lawful, the court did not engage in a detailed market analysis. Instead, it questioned the general anticompetitive potential of the agreement and concluded that the plaintiff had simply lost the "competition–for–the–contract." [148] The same would appear to be true in most instances in which there are exclusive dealers. Although not expressly finding the agreement per se lawful, the court's analysis left seemed to leave little room for a successful attack on this type of exclusivity. [149]

With respect to the second question, a manufacturer that simply appoints an exclusive dealer would fall within the protections of *Colgate* as expanded by *Monsanto*. On the other hand, when an exclusive dealership arises as the result of the insistence of a powerful dealer that a competitor be terminated, the scheme has a horizontal flavor. [150] Indeed, this was addressed in *Klor's Inc. v. Broadway Hale Stores.* [151] If buyers combine to pressure a manufacturer to terminate a cost–cutting competitor, the makings of a horizontal price–fixing case would be especially evident. In the absence of a horizontal agreement, though, the arrangement must be analyzed from the standpoint of a vertical restraint. Two problems for the terminated dealer emerge. First, there must be an agreement, and after *Monsanto*, proof that one or more competitors urged that another be terminated would not be sufficient. [152] Second, even if a vertical agreement to terminate other dealers is shown, procompetitive justifications may allow the agreement to stand. Clearly, at most what would be called for would be a rule of reason analysis, a practical dead end for plaintiff in most of these cases.

Finally, an argument can be made that a scheme of vertical distribution in which a territorial restraint is combined with an exclusive dealership should be scrutinized more closely than either restraint separately. [153] Whatever anticompetitive effects result from either restraint are compounded when they are combined. On the other hand, there is hardly a more

---

[147] 103 F.3d 42 (7th Cir. 1996).

[148] *Id.* at 45.

[149] The court distinguished exclusive dealing arrangements which are discussed in section 5.02[A], *infra*. A comparable analysis is found in *NYNEX Corp., v. Discon, Inc.* 525 U.S. 128 (1998), in which the Supreme Court also ruled out the possibility that a single firm's refusal to deal with more that one buyer or seller is not a *per se* unlawful boycott.

[150] It is possible that the case could be analyzed under § 2 as monopolization or attempt to monopolize.

[151] 359 U.S. 207 (1959). *See* discussion in § 4.13.

[152] Even pre–*Monsanto* cases illustrate the problem the plaintiff faces in this regard. *See, e.g., Valley Liquors, Inc. v. Renfield Importers, Ltd.*, 678 F.2d 742 (7th Cir. 1982); *Packard Motor Car Co. v. Webster Motor Car Co.*, 243 F.2d 418 (D.C. Cir. 1957).

[153] *See* Pitofsky, *supra*, note 114, at 18–25.

effective way to free a dealer from the threat of free rider problems than a territorial restraint combined with an exclusive dealership. Thus, the arrangement may be attractive especially when a manufacturer is attempting to enter a new market or is depending on a dealer to enhance the product's attractiveness through efforts that require a substantial investment. In these instances the dealer may only be willing to take on the risk and expense involved if it is fully protected from intrabrand competition. This means that the rule of reason analysis is more complicated, a happenstance that favors defendants.[154]

§ 5.02 Interbrand Vertical Foreclosure

The vertical restraints considered here — exclusive dealing and tying — are distinguishable from those previously considered because their primary impact is on interbrand competition.[155] Exclusive dealing arrangements are essentially requirements contracts. In the usual case, a manufacturer conditions the sale of a product to a retailer on the purchase by the retailer of all of its requirements for that product. Exclusive dealing is different from the exclusive dealership discussed earlier; the latter does not involve a conditional sale. Under a tying arrangement, a manufacturer sells a product — the tying product — to a buyer only under the condition that the buyer purchase another specified product — the tied product. The chief antitrust concern in the case of exclusive dealing and tying is that the arrangement makes it more difficult for competing manufacturers to find outlets for their products; in effect, they are "foreclosed."

Much of exclusive dealing and tying are prohibited by § 3 of the Clayton Act. Under the Act:

> It shall be unlawful for any person engaged in commerce, in the course of such commerce, to lease or make a sale or contract for sale of good, wares, merchandise, machinery supplies, or other commodities . . . or fix a price charged therefor, or discount from, or rebate upon, such price on the condition, agreement, or understanding that the lessee or purchaser thereof shall not use or deal in the goods, wares, merchandise, machinery, supplies, or other commodities of a competitor or competitors of the lessor or seller, where the effect . . . may be to substantially lessen competition or tend to create a monopoly.[156]

It is important to note some limitations on the application of the Clayton Act. First, the Act only applies to conditions imposed by sellers. Thus, a

---

[154] For a case that deals with an exclusive dealership and a trademarked brand, *see Generac Corp. v. Caterpillar, Inc.* 172 F.3d 971 (7th Cir. 1999) (applying the rule of reason to an agreement between a small generator manufacturer and a trademark holder, in which the manufacturer developed generators that would be marketed under the trademarked name and agreed to restrict sale of the trademarked brand generator to designated dealers and also agreed to restrict sales of its own brand generators to the trademark holder's dealers.)

[155] This is not to say that the overall impact would not be increased interbrand competition at the manufacturing level.

[156] 15 U.S.C. § 14 (1976).

contract under which a buyer agrees to buy the output of a seller only if that seller sells all of its output to him would not fall within the Act. However, it may come under § 1 of the Sherman Act or § 5 of the Federal Trade Commission Act.[157] Second, the Clayton Act refers to goods or commodities, but not services. The Sherman Act or the Federal Trade Commission Act would be the statute applicable for conduct involving services. Finally, the Clayton Act indicates that the arrangements described therein are prohibited when they "may be to lessen competition or tend to create a monopoly." The Sherman Act, on the other hand, does not include comparable language. Thus, the possibility of different treatment for similar activities exists depending upon whether the Sherman Act or Clayton Act is applied.

[A] Exclusive Dealing

[1] Economic Issues

The primary economic concern raised by exclusive dealing is foreclosure of manufacturers because they are unable to find outlets for their products. A related concern is that entry into the industry will become more difficult because, in order to enter, the firm will have to be vertically integrated. That is, it will have to operate at both the manufacturing and retailing level — a prospect that increases the costs of entry. These are, as one would expect, precisely the concerns expressed about vertical mergers.[158] After all, exclusive dealing is essentially a method of vertical integration by contract.

There are two responses to the concerns about anticompetitive effects. The first merely notes that exclusive dealing is not uniformly anticompetitive and that the anticompetitive and procompetitive effects should be weighed. For example, both buyers and sellers may find exclusive dealing attractive. For sellers it will mean an assured outlet and for buyers it means a dependable source of supply. The effect may be to lower transaction costs which could translate into lower prices for consumers. In addition, if the retailer is obligated to purchase only one brand of merchandise, it will be inclined to promote that brand, thus enhancing interbrand competition.[159]

Finally, the use of exclusive dealing may help prevent a type of "free riding" that is different from that already discussed. In the case of RPM, the concern was the free riding of retailers on the efforts of other retailers. The problem is that exclusive dealing is a response to free riding by a retailer on the promotional efforts of a manufacturer from whom it purchases.[160] For example, suppose Xenox is a manufacturer of televisions and advertises its product nationally. If it sells to retailers who sell other

---

[157] 15 U.S.C. § 45 (1976).

[158] *See* § 7.04[B].

[159] *See* R. Blair & D. Kaserman, *Antitrust Economics*, 409–10 (1985).

[160] *Id.* at 411–13.

brands, it may find that consumers go to those retailers because of the advertising by Xenox but, once there, they are sold a different brand of television. In essence, the retailer is the free rider and the manufacturer is unable to "internalize" the benefits of its promotional efforts.[161]

The second response to the anticompetitive concerns about exclusive dealing goes much further and suggests that there are no substantial anticompetitive effects in the first place.[162] For example, if the manufacturer has no market power, the manufacturer will have to offer the retailer something in return for its agreement not to make purchases from others. The likely outcome is that the manufacturer will supply the product at a lower price or perhaps lower the retailer's cost by absorbing promotional expenses.

Accordingly, even if the manufacturer has market power, there is still no real cause for concern. The key is that the market power possessed by the manufacturer which enables it to charge a supracompetitive price is limited. Price can be "charged" as traditionally understood, by simply asking for more money for each unit. Or, the manufacturer can demand something else, such as an exclusive dealing agreement. Therefore, market power can be exploited only to a certain degree. If the manufacturer demands an exclusive dealing agreement, the argument is that it cannot be motivated simply by a desire to charge higher prices since the profit maximizing price can be exacted through the direct use of the firm's market power.[163]

This latter reasoning so undercuts the economic concerns about exclusive dealing that it suggests that exclusive dealing should be *per se* lawful. The first group of procompetitive justifications for exclusive dealing do not suggest *per se* legality, only that exclusive dealing may have procompetitive and anticompetitive effects that must be balanced. As the following discussion indicates, the latter reasoning underlies judicial examination of exclusive dealing.

[2] Exclusive Dealing and the Supreme Court

The two most influential Supreme Court decisions in the area of exclusive dealing are *Standard Oil Co. v. United States (Standard Stations)*[164] and *Tampa Electric Co. v. Nashville Coal Co.*[165] In *Standard Stations*, the Court reviewed the contracts between Standard Oil and independent retailers

---

[161] *See generally H. Hovenkamp, supra*, note 2, at 434.

[162] *See R. Bork, supra*, note 8, at 299–309.

[163] *Id.* at 306–07.

[164] 337 U.S. 293 (1949). *Standard Stations* was preceded by *Standard Fashion Co. v. Magrane–Houston Co.*, 258 U.S. 346 (1922) in which the Court condemned an exclusive dealing arrangement resulting in a 40% foreclosure. It is difficult from the decision, however, to discern a standard for the analysis of exclusive dealing. *See generally* L. Sullivan, *supra*, note 146, at 472.

[165] 365 U.S. 320 (1961).

that required all purchases of gasoline to be from Standard Oil.[166] Standard Oil was the largest seller of gasoline in the "Western Area" which included Arizona, California, Idaho, Nevada, Oregon, Utah and Washington. Sixteen percent of the retail stations in the area were covered by exclusive dealing arrangements with Standard Oil. This accounted for 6.7% of the total taxable gallonage sold in the area.[167]

The issue was whether a showing that a "substantial portion" of the market was affected was enough to satisfy the statutory requirement that the effect of the arrangement "may be to substantially lessen competition."[168] The Court, in short, was faced with the issue of whether the standards then applied to tying agreements should be extended to exclusive dealing.[169] Justice Frankfurter, writing for the majority, reasoned that tying agreements "serve hardly any purpose beyond the suppression of competition."[170] Requirement contracts, on the other hand, could be economically beneficial to both buyers and sellers and, ultimately, to consumers. He observed that this would seem to require an evaluation of competitive effects on a case–by–case basis.

The Court, however, in a five to four decision, opted not to require plaintiffs to show actual anticompetitive effects.[171] Justice Frankfurter noted the difficulty the courts were likely to have in analyzing economic effects. In addition, any error made by prohibiting beneficial agreements could be overcome by legal agreements with similar effects. Finally, he reasoned that a plaintiff would typically find it virtually impossible to show that "but for" the agreement, competition would be more vigorous. However, rather than announce a rigid *per se* standard, he opted for the rule that "§ 3 is satisfied by proof that competition has been foreclosed in a substantial *share* of the line of commerce affected."[172] He concluded that Standard Oil's actions had violated this standard.

Justice Jackson dissented, contending that the majority's announced standard and its application amounted to the establishment of a *per se* rule.[173] He agreed that the requirements contracts, which foreclosed 6.7% of the defined market, did affect a substantial share of commerce. On the other hand, he did not believe that this showing alone met the § 3 requirement of a substantial lessening of competition. Justice Douglas also dissented, arguing that the majority, by closing the door to exclusive dealing

---

[166] 337 U.S. 305–06. Other exclusive dealing contracts extended to products other than gasoline.

[167] *Id.* at 393.

[168] *Id.* at 299.

[169] As will be seen, at the time of *Standard Stations*, tying agreements were treated under a modified *per se* rule. *See* § 5.02[B][2][a], *infra*.

[170] 337 U.S. 293 at 305.

[171] *Id.* at 308–12.

[172] *Id.* at 314 (emphasis added).

[173] *Id.* at 323 (Jackson, J. dissenting).

had, in effect, invited firms to achieve the same result through vertical integration — a more harmful alternative.[174]

In *Tampa Electric*, a utility instituting the use of coal as a boiler fuel, contracted with Nashville Coal Co. for all its coal requirements over a twenty year period.[175] The supplier refused to perform, after which it sought and received a declaratory judgment that the contract violated § 3 of the Clayton Act.[176] The lower courts concentrated on the competitive impact within Florida where the coal was consumed. The Supreme Court rejected this analysis in favor of one focusing on the impact on suppliers who were in competition with Nashville Coal in serving the Tampa area.[177] Under this market definition, the share of commerce affected was .77%.

The Court concluded that the contract plainly did not tend to substantially foreclose competition in the relevant market.[178] Two aspects of the case are important. First, the Court viewed market definition as an indispensable step in its foreclosure analysis. Second, it was willing to review a range of factors regarding the competitive impact of the arrangement. For example, it noted that unlike *Standard Stations* the exclusive dealing here was not industry wide, nor was Nashville Coal a dominate seller. In addition, it suggested that the length of the exclusive dealing contract could be a relevant consideration. In general, the approach taken involved the consideration of a broader range of factors than was the case in *Standard Stations*. The Court, perhaps due to the very limited foreclosure involved, found it unnecessary to give specific indication of the weight to be attributed to these factors.

[3] Exclusive Dealing as an Unfair Method of Competition

Exclusive dealing also has been examined by the Federal Trade Commission under § 5 of the Federal Trade Commission Act. One case, *FTC v. Motion Picture Advertising Service*,[179] is particularly interesting because it dealt with exclusive dealing in the form of an outputs contract. The case involved a producer/distributor of advertisements that were shown in movie theaters. The terms of the contracts required theaters to show only the advertisements made by the producer. In essence, the producer was the exclusive buyer of a theater's advertising display time.[180] The relevant foreclosure took place at the level of buyers. Motion Picture Advertising had exclusive contracts with 40% of the theaters in its area of operation.[181]

---

[174] *Id.* at 320–21 (Douglas, J. dissenting).

[175] 365 U.S. at 322.

[176] *Id.* at 321.

[177] *Id.* at 330–33.

[178] *Id.* at 334.

[179] 344 U.S. 392 (1953).

[180] *Id.* at 393.

[181] *Id.* at 394.

The FTC issued a cease and desist order that limited the duration of the agreements to no more than one year. The Supreme Court generally deferred to the Commission and upheld its order.[182] It seemed influenced, however, by the fact that 75% of the available outlets for exhibiting film advertisements in the United States were foreclosed by similar agreements. The Court seemed unimpressed by the fact that the exclusive arrangements were preferred by both theater owners and advertising film producers.[183]

In *Motion Picture Advertising* the Court noted that the Commission, under § 5 of the Federal Trade Commission Act, could prohibit activities beyond those subject to § 1 of the Sherman Act or § 3 of the Clayton Act.[184] Under the facts of the case and its timing — between *Standard Stations* and *Tampa Electric* — it probably was unnecessary to stretch § 5 that far. The Commission did seem to rely on this extra authority, however, in a post–*Tampa Electric* case, *FTC v. Brown Shoe Co.*[185] The Commission ordered Brown Shoe to cease and desist from entering into exclusive dealing arrangements with 650 retail outlets. The order was challenged as unsupported by sufficient evidence that the effect of the practice may have been to substantially lessen competition.[186] The Court, relying on *Motion Picture Advertising Services*, unanimously recognized the distinction between the requirements of § 3 of the Clayton Act and § 5 of the Federal Trade Commission Act. It upheld the Commission's action, observing that "the Commission has power under § 5 to arrest trade restraints in their incipiency."[187]

Although the Court suggested that the Commission was to be afforded broad leeway in applying § 5 to exclusive dealing, the Commission has not made full use of that power.[188] Indeed, the trend has been for the Commission to apply an analysis similar to that used under the Clayton Act or Sherman Act. The best example of this is *Beltone Electronics Corp.*[189] in which the Commission considered the exclusive dealing arrangement between a manufacturer of hearing aids and its dealer. The Commission went well beyond the analysis suggested in *Tampa Electric* and drew on *Sylvania*. Accordingly, the Commission emphasized the importance of viewing foreclosure in the context of "reasonable justifications" including possible procompetitive effects on interbrand rivalry.[190]

---

[182] *Id.* at 395–97. In so doing it reversed *Motion Pictures Advertising Service v. FTC*, 194 F.2d 633 (D.C. Cir. 1952).

[183] 344 U.S. at 395–96.

[184] *Id.* at 394.

[185] 384 U.S. 316 (1966).

[186] *Id.* at 322–23.

[187] *Id.* at 322; *See generally* Steuer, *Exclusive Dealing in Distribution*, 69 Cornell L. Rev. 101, 106–107 (1983).

[188] *See* Steuer, *supra*, note 187, at 106–16.

[189] 100 F.T.C. 68 (1982). For a complete analysis *see* Steuer, *supra* note 172, at 108–11.

[190] 100 F.T.C. at 204–18.

[4] Exclusive Dealing in the Post–*Tampa Electric* and *Sylvania* Era

Tampa Electric suggested that exclusive dealing should be analyzed under an approach very similar to the rule of reason. *Sylvania* stressed the importance of economic factors in applying the rule of reason and expanded the scope of the analysis. Both cases have influenced lower court evaluations of exclusive dealing. For example, the importance of considering factors beyond statistical evidence of foreclosure was emphasized in *American Motors Inns v. Holiday Inns.*[191] Among other restraints, Holiday Inn precluded franchisees from owning or operating any other hotel or motel which was not a Holiday Inn.[192] The trial court had relied on a foreclosure of 14.7% to find that the exclusive dealing clause violated the Sherman Act.[193] The Court of Appeals reversed, noting the importance of considering percentage foreclosure in light of "economic justification[s]."[194] The justifications offered by defendant and regarded as relevant by the court were ones primarily aimed at strengthening Holiday Inn *vis–a–vis* its competitors. In short, the evaluation of procompetitive justifications for a restraint that might otherwise be unlawful was deemed to be part of a proper analysis of exclusive dealing.[195]

The importance of procompetitive justifications was also underscored in *Joyce Beverages v. Royal Crown Cola.*[196] A soft drink bottler, Joyce Beverages, operated under a licensing agreement with Royal Crown that, in effect, required it to bottle only Royal Crown brand cola.[197] The bottler planned to begin bottling another brand of Cola and Royal Crown threatened to terminate their licensing agreement. Joyce argued that Royal Crown's termination would amount to a breach of contract, and if it did not, the exclusive dealing requirement violated the antitrust laws. In denying a preliminary injunction for Joyce that would bar the termination, the Court relied on the role of exclusive dealing in promoting interbrand competition. In particular, exclusive dealing was a means of assuring that a bottler "devotes undivided loyalty to its particular brand and that it competes vigorously against all competing brands."[198]

Probably the most ambitious attempt to articulate the relevant factors under a modern exclusive dealing analysis is found in a Seventh Circuit

---

[191] 521 F.2d 1230 (3d Cir. 1975).

[192] *Id.* at 1236.

[193] *Id.* at 1252. The practice was analyzed under the Sherman Act because it did not involve the sale of commodities.

[194] *Id.*

[195] As contrasted with vertical nonprice restraints on distribution, the inquiry is whether some anticompetitive interbrand effects are off–set by other procompetitive interbrand effects.

[196] 555 F. Supp. 271 (S.D.N.Y. 1983). *See generally*, Steuer, *Exclusive Dealing After Jefferson Parish*, 54 Antitrust L.J. 1229 (1985).

[197] The actual contract in question included a "best efforts" requirement. 555 F. Supp. at 277.

[198] *Id.* at 278.

decision, *Roland Machinery v. Dresser Industries.*[199] Judge Posner contrasted what he regarded as the current approach to exclusive dealing with that previously applied. Originally the issue was whether the agreement covered "a large fraction of the market."[200] Under Judge Posner's current formulation, the plaintiff must show that (1) the agreement excludes at least one "significant competitor of the defendant from doing business in a relevant market,"[201] and (2) the anticompetitive effects outweigh the procompetitive effects.[202] Whether all circuits will agree with Judge Posner's two–step analysis, it is clear that procompetitive justifications are playing an increasingly important role in the evaluation of exclusive dealing.[203]

An issue that can be important in a exclusive dealing case is whether it arises under the Clayton Act of Sherman Act. Recall that the Clayton Act only applies if the transaction involves the sale of goods. For example, in a recent case, *CDC Technologies v. Idexx Laboratories,* Inc.,[204] the plaintiff complained that the defendant, a competing manufacturer of blood analysis machines, had entered into exclusive dealing arrangements with a network of distributors in violations of § 3 of the Clayton Act. The Clayton Act claim was dismissed since the distributors did not actually buy the equipment. This leaves open a Sherman Act possibility and leads to the question of whether the Sherman Act standard is different. Language in *Tampa Electric* indicates that there is a difference. There the Supreme Court made reference to the Clayton Act's "broader proscription"[205] meaning that, whatever the standard under the Clayton Act, is was less burdensome to plaintiffs than the rule of reason which would be applied under the Sherman Act. Since that time, it is clear that exclusive dealing, even under the Clayton Act, has gravitated to a rule of reason–like analysis but the possibility remains that there could be a difference depending on whether the exclusivity involves good or services.[206]

[B] Tying Arrangements

A "tie–in" or tying arrangement occurs when a seller sells a good to a buyer only on the condition that the buyer buy a second good from the seller. The threshold issue is whether the transaction involves two goods. The product that the purchaser finds more desirable is the tying product. The product that the buyer must purchase in order to buy the tying product is called the tied product. Like exclusive dealing, tying one good to another

---

[199] 749 F.2d 380 (7th Cir. 1984).

[200] *Id.* at 393.

[201] *Id.* at 394.

[202] *Id.*

[203] The same is also true of tying.

[204] 186 F.3d 74 (2d Cir. 1999).

[205] 365 U.S. at 335.

[206] *See CDC Technologies, supra* note 204; *Twin City Sportserive, Inc., v. Charles O. Finley & Co.,* 676 F.2d 1291 (9th Cir. 1982).

is expressly prohibited by § 3 of the Clayton Act.[207] Section 1 of the
Sherman Act comes into play when the tie involves services or goods. Tying
can also be analyzed under § 5 of the Federal Trade Commission Act.
Although historical factors suggest that the analysis of tying may vary
depending upon the statute invoked, today it seems likely that any variation in analysis is likely to be negligible. As in the case of other vertical
restraints, the law of tying has undergone considerable change. Although
tying was once regarded as *per se* illegal, and even today is nominally in
that category, the *per se* rule applied to tying is considerably different than
that applied to horizontal restraints.

The classic tie involves the two product example just described. Tying
arrangements, however, can take a number of more complicated forms. For
example, in the case of a "full line force" the seller permits a dealer to carry
some of its products only if the dealer is willing to carry a complete line
of the seller's products. In other cases, the tie occurs when related products
are only offered as a single–priced package. Some transactions are not
technically ties but have tying–type qualities. For example, the seller may
sell its product only on the condition that the buyer purchase a product
from a designated third party. Finally, in an arrangement labeled "reciprocal dealing," one firm agrees to buy from another only if the second firm
makes purchases from the first. The following pages consider these special
cases along with the general development of tying law and the defenses
that have evolved. First, however, it is important to discuss the economic
consequences of tying.

[1] The Economics of Tying

The changing level of judicial tolerance toward tying can be traced to the
fact that there are a great number of reasons why a firm might wish to
engage in tying and a variety of economic consequences may follow. Some
of the consequences may harm consumers; others are unlikely to produce
anticompetitive effects. The difficult — maybe impossible — task is to segregate those ties that are anticompetitive from those that are not. Much of
the original concern about tying was based on the belief that a firm with
monopoly power in one market would be able to use that power to gain
monopoly power in another market.[208] For example, suppose a firm
manufactures lamps and possesses monopoly power in that market. Suppose further that the market for lampshades is competitive. The question
then becomes: can the firm use its power in the market for lamps as
leverage to gain monopoly power in the lampshade market?

Many economists and antitrust scholars would answer "no." The reasoning, as explained in the context of exclusive dealing, is that the power
associated with the desirability of the tying product enables the monopolist
to collect only a single monopoly profit. For example, suppose the lamp

---

[207] 15 U.S.C. § 14 (1976).

[208] *See* L. Sullivan, *supra* note 146, at 434–35. *See also* Strasser, *Antitrust Policy for Tying
Arrangements*, 34 Emory L. J. 253 (1985).

manufacturer has discovered that the profit maximizing price for its lamps is $50. Lampshades are $10 each in the competitive market. If it packages them together, the total price will be $60. To charge a price that is any higher than $60 when lampshades are available for $10 would be tantamount to charging more than $50 for the lamps.[209] Some consumers would go elsewhere and the firm would no longer maximize profits. To be sure, it sells more lampshades and increases its share of the lampshade market. It does not, however, acquire monopoly power in the lampshade market in the sense that it can now increase its price and restrict output in that market.

As already suggested, the leverage theory has lost substantial favor. Indeed, the idea that monopoly power can be transferred from one market to another whether by exclusive dealing, tying, or even vertical integration is one of the favorite targets of "Chicago School" antitrust scholars. Recently, the theory has experienced a mild revival as some have suggested that it cannot be completely disregarded.[210] Even with this revival, however, the suggestion is not that the theory supports *per se* treatment of tying.

Even if the monopolist is unable to use its power to become a monopolist in another market it may increase its share of sales in the tied product market. In the lamp/lampshade example, this can mean the elimination of sales opportunities for competing manufacturers of lampshades. In other words, if lampshades are sold by the lamp monopolist whenever it sells a lamp, there is less room in the market for a firm that only produces lampshades. The foreclosure of sales or sales opportunities makes it more difficult for firms already in the lampshade market to survive and also raises barriers to the entry of new producers.

One response to this argument is to determine whether consumers are any worse off. Presumably, the lamp manufacturer is producing lampshades at an average cost of $10, the competitive price. The lampshade producers who are foreclosed are those who cannot produce and sell at a lower price. For example, suppose an incumbent or new firm is able to produce lampshades of the same quality for $9.50. There is little reason not to expect the lamp manufacturer to begin purchasing lampshades from that manufacturer and then using the purchased lampshades in the lamp/lampshade package.[211] The point is that greater efficiency is an ideal way to overcome an "entry barrier." Moreover, now that the monopolist's costs of "producing" the package have decreased it will find that its profit maximizing price also will decrease. Thus, consumers, so the argument goes, will be benefitted as well. Of course, much of this rebuttal to the

---

[209] *See* H. Hovenkamp, *supra* note 2, at 416–417; Bowman, *Tying Arrangements and the Leverage Problem*, 67 Yale L. J. 19, 21–23 (1957).

[210] *See, e.g.,* L. Kaplow, *Extension of Monopoly Power Through Leverage*, 85 Colum. L. Rev. 515 (1985); Note, *An Economic Analysis of Tie–In Sales: Re–examination of Leverage Theory*, 39 Stan. L. Rev. 737 (1987).

[211] R. Blair & D. Kaserman, *supra* note 159, at 403–04.

foreclosure argument seems to assume a great deal about the availability of information and the fluidity of resources. Whether it works in the "real world" is another question.

So far the argument has been that tying cannot be successfully employed to collect more than one monopoly profit. It may, however, assist the firm in exploiting the power it has in a single market. One possibility would be when the monopolist is confronted by price regulation and a price ceiling that is below the profit maximizing price for the tying product.[212] For example, suppose that state regulation prohibits hotels from charging more than $100 per night for a room. A hotel in a scenic area may find that it has market power and that its profit maximizing rate is higher than the maximum allowed. It might attempt to bypass the regulation and take greater advantage of its market power by only offering a rate that includes breakfast at a total charge in excess of $100.

Another possibility for increased profit can be illustrated again using the lamp/lampshade example. This time, however, assume lampshades are not sold under competitive conditions.[213] Instead a cartel of lampshade producers is charging $20 per shade even though the cost of production is $10. Since lamps and lampshades are generally purchased together, the price of lampshades will affect the demand for lamps. The higher the price for lampshades, the lower the demand for lamps, and thus the lower the lamp manufacturer's profit maximizing price. By producing lampshades and offering the lamp/lampshade package for $60, the manufacturer is able to bypass the lampshade cartel and effectively raise its price of lamps to a profit maximizing level of $50. In this case the tie increases the profit of the tying firm but consumers are not worse off than before the tie.

In all of the examples so far, it has been assumed that the tying and tied products were used in fixed proportions; that is, one lamp shade is purchased with each lamp. By dropping this assumption, two more functions of tying come into play; one is relatively harmless, while the effect of the other is less clear. Suppose a monopoly manufacturer of commercial ice cream making machines has a policy of only leasing machines at a flat rate per month and only leases on the condition that lessees also buy all their ice cream ingredients from it. One reason for doing this is that the manufacturer's actual costs of serving each customer vary with the intensity with which the machine is used. The life of each machine is, in effect, inversely related to how much it is used. Here the sale of ingredients is a method of "metering" the use of each machine so that each user is charged in proportion to the speed with which the machine they have leased becomes obsolete.[214] The tie can be seen as permitting the manufacturer to collect information that will be useful in legitimate pricing decisions.

---

[212] See generally Bowman, supra note 209, at 22.

[213] See H. Hovenkamp, supra note 2, at 416–418.

[214] For discussion see R. Bork, supra note 8, at 376–78; R. Blair & D. Kaserman, supra note 159, at 384–86; H. Hovenkamp, supra note 2, at 423–424.

On the other hand, suppose the useful life of a machine is unrelated to its intensity of use. Again, tying ingredients to the lease means that high intensity users will pay more than low intensity users. Unless the difference in cost for each lessee precisely reflects the difference in the amount of ingredients purchased, the manufacturer is engaged in price discrimination. In effect, rather than trying to match each lessee with the costs of serving that lessee, the manufacturer charges different prices depending on the lessee's willingness to pay. The key factors in successful price discrimination are identifying groups that will pay different amounts and segregating the groups so that those paying the lower price will not sell to those paying more. Tying can be a method of overcoming both of these obstacles. As discussed at length in Chapter 8, it is not clear that price discrimination always leads to an inefficient result.[215] In fact, price discrimination may lead to higher output and, for some consumers, lower prices. Some forms of price discrimination do, however, violate § 2 of the Clayton Act as amended by the Robinson–Patman Act.

Tying also may be used to aid interbrand competition. For example, a restaurant franchiser may only license franchisees who agree to serve food purchased from the franchiser. The franchiser's argument will be that the tie is necessary to ensure the uniform quality of the product, thereby enhancing the good–will of the franchise and encouraging interbrand competition.[216]

Finally, a transaction that resembles tying may be used to facilitate predatory pricing.[217] As discussed in Chapter 6, predatory pricing involves an effort to eliminate competitors by charging prices below cost.[218] Tying can be useful if the seller wishes to achieve the same result but disguise the effect on prices. Thus, instead of lowering the price of a single product it might offer that item in a package with another item for a total price much less than the price of the two sold separately. While this example suggests a tie–in, it is questionable whether the transaction is a tie in the usual sense of forcing a consumer to buy an unwanted product.

[2]   Tying and the Supreme Court

[a]   Early Interpretations

With this array of reasons for tying, it is not surprising that the Supreme Court has not been entirely consistent in its approach. The wavering of the Court, although far less dramatic than that exhibited with respect to nonprice restraints on distribution, has followed the same basic pattern. One of the first indications of the Court's direction in tying cases came in

---

[215] *See* discussion at § 8.02, *infra.*

[216] *See* § 5.02[B][4], *infra.*

[217] *See* H. Hovenkamp, *supra* note 2, at 423.

[218] Another possible definition would be that predatory pricing occurs whenever a firm prices below its short–run profit maximizing level. *See* discussion in § 6.06, *infra.*

Motion Picture Patents v. Universal Film Co.[219] A holder of a patent for movie projection equipment attempted to preclude licensees from using film other than that produced by the patent holder. It claimed that those licensees who had not acted in accord with this condition were guilty of infringing the patent held on the projection equipment.

The Court held there was no infringement.[220] In so doing, it noted the recent passage of the Clayton Act reflecting legislative intent to prohibit tying arrangements.[221] More importantly, the Court, in *dicta*, reasoned that permitting the restraint would allow the plaintiff to become a monopolist in the motion picture film market.[222] Thus, the Court accepted the "leverage" theory of monopoly power, the primary economic premise for all of its future responses to tying.

The same concerns were reflected in *International Business Machines Corp. v. United States* in 1936.[223] IBM conditioned the lease of its machines on use by lessees of tabulating cards also manufactured by IBM. The Court directly addressed the issue of whether the arrangement "may . . . substantially lessen competition" thereby violating § 3 of the Clayton Act.[224] Although it announced no particular formula for the application of § 3, it focused on the dangers of "monopolistic tying clauses."[225] The clear suggestion was that without monopoly power in the tying product market, this danger would not be present. The Court mentioned the volume of commerce involved but did not, with any degree of clarity, indicate the weight to be afforded this factor.

Eleven years later, the Court took an even less lenient view of tying. In *International Salt Co. v. United States*[226] the defendant, International Salt, leased its patented machines[227] only on the condition that lessees purchase from International Salt all the salt to be used in the machines. In 1944 the defendant had sold $500,000 worth of salt for use in its machines. The Court affirmed the lower court's award of a summary judgment in favor of the plaintiff based on a violation of both § 1 of the Sherman Act and § 3 of the Clayton Act. In so doing, it announced that it was "unreasonable,

---

[219] 243 U.S. 502 (1917). *Motion Picture Patents* was preceded by two pre–Clayton Act cases in which tying was a relevant consideration. In *Henry v. A.B. Dick*, 224 U.S. 1 (1912), the Court felt that a patent gave the holder tying–type powers. In *United States v. Winslow* 227 U.S. 202 (1913), the Court similarly was unresponsive to the dangers of tying again indicating the broad power inherent in the holding of a patent. See generally L. Sullivan, *supra* note 146, at 432–35.

[220] 243 U.S. at 515–19.

[221] *Id.* at 516–17.

[222] *Id.* at 518.

[223] 298 U.S. 131 (1936).

[224] *Id.* at 134.

[225] *Id.* at 140.

[226] 332 U.S. 12 (1947).

[227] *Id.* at 394–95. The "Saltomat" injected salt into canned products. The "Lixator" dissolved rock salt into brine.

per se, to foreclose competitors from any substantial market."[228] The Court made note of the "limited monopoly"[229] held by International Salt but did not expressly indicate that such a finding was necessary for applying the *per se* standard under either the Clayton or Sherman Acts.

In 1953, in *Times–Picayune Publishing Co. v. United States*,[230] the Court considered the requirement of a New Orleans publisher that advertisers buy space in both its morning and evening newspapers. It reviewed the case under § 1 of the Sherman Act. First, however, it interpreted *International Salt* as indicating that the test for tying was different under the Sherman Act than under the Clayton Act. Under the Clayton Act, a tying arrangement was illegal if the tying firm held a "monopolistic" position in the tying good market or "restrained" a substantial volume of commerce in the tied product market.[231] Under the Sherman Act, however, the "rule of *International Salt* [would] only apply only if both conditions are met."[232]

The Court assumed that the "substantiality" test was met and turned its attention to the issue of market dominance, concentrating on the question of whether the publisher had "wielded monopoly leverage."[233] The Court found two flaws in the Government's case. First, it noted that there were three newspapers in New Orleans and that an equal division of the relevant market — advertising in New Orleans dailies — would result in a 33% share for each newspaper. The alleged dominant newspaper, the Times–Picayune, had a market share of only 40% which was insufficient to establish dominance.[234] Second, the Court reasoned that advertisers were purchasing access to readers and that the readers, whether morning or evening, were viewed by advertisers as "fungible customer potential."[235] In essence, there was no tying or use of leverage to gain power in another market because both newspapers were selling the same service and, therefore, occupied the same market.

Next in the line of Supreme Court tying decisions was *Northern Pacific Railway Co. v. United States*.[236] Northern Pacific leased land for various uses on the condition that lessees use Northern Pacific to ship all commodities produced or manufactured on the land as long as Northern Pacific's rates were equal to those of competitors. Like *Times–Picayune*, review was under the Sherman Act and the Court looked to *International Salt* for guidance. The rule the Court devised seemed to be the result of merging the dual approaches announced in *Times–Picayune*: "[tying arrangements]

---

[228] 332 U.S. at 396. The Court cited *Fashion Originators' Guild v. FTC*, 312 U.S. 457 (1941). *See* discussion in § 4.13, *supra*.

[229] 332 U.S. at 395.

[230] 345 U.S. 594 (1953).

[231] *Id.* at 606.

[232] *Id.* at 608–09.

[233] *Id.* at 611.

[234] *Id.* at 611–13.

[235] *Id.* at 613–14.

[236] 356 U.S. 1 (1958).

are unreasonable in and of themselves whenever a party has sufficient economic power with respect to the tying product to appreciably restrain free competition in the market for the tied product and a "not insubstantial' amount of interstate commerce is affected."[237]

The rule is subject to a number of interpretations. The first is that it requires both dominance in the tying product market and the involvement of substantial commerce in the tied product market. This would be consistent with the interpretation of *International Salt* in *Times–Picayune*. This two–step analysis is supported by the Court's observation that the defendant's land holdings had resulted in "substantial economic power" that could be used as leverage.

On the other hand, Justice Black, writing for the majority, observed that a seller without dominance would be unable to have anything but an insignificant effect on trade.[238] The suggestion is that the involvement of a " 'not insubstantial' amount" of commerce indicates that the defendant has the requisite degree of market dominance. The same suggestion is found in the Court's reasoning that "[t]he very existence of this host of tying arrangements is itself . . . evidence of the defendant's great power."[239]

Finally, the same sentiment is found in the *Northern Pacific*'s discussion of *Times–Picayune*. It interpreted the *Time–Picayune* requirement of "dominance" or "monopoly power" in the tying product market to mean "sufficient economic power to impose an appreciable restraint."[240] These observations came very close to suggesting that independent attention to power in the tying product market was unnecessary and that the *per se* standard of *International Salt* would be strictly applied in both Sherman Act and Clayton Act cases. Over the next several years, however, this policy was destined to change.

[b] *Fortner I & II*

In *Fortner Enterprises v. United States Steel, (Fortner I)*[241] the Supreme Court considered a summary judgment that U.S. Steel had not violated § 1 of the Sherman Act when the extension of credit by its wholly–owned credit subsidiary was conditioned on the purchase of prefabricated homes from its Home Division. The tying "product" was credit and the "tied" product was prefabricated homes. The 100% financing offered by U.S. Steel made its credit especially desirable. The trial court ruled that the plaintiff had not shown that the defendant had sufficient power in the credit market or that a "not insubstantial amount of commerce" was involved.

---

237 *Id.* at 6.

238 *Id.* at 6–7.

239 *Id.* at 7–8.

240 *Id.* at 11.

241 394 U.S. 495 (1969). Prior to *Fortner I*, the Court encountered "block booking" in *United States v. Loew's, Inc.* 371 U.S. 38 (1962). It applied a standard that was consistent with that applied in *Northern Pacific*. *See* § 5.02[B][2], *infra*.

In a 5 to 4 decision, the Supreme Court reversed and remanded for trial. It found that the $190,000 involved in sales of the tied product to the defendant was not insubstantial. In addition, the total annual dollar figure for the arrangement when other buyers were included was in the range of $2,000,000 to $4,000,000. The remand, therefore, was on the issue of whether U.S. Steel possessed power in the tying product market. On this issue the Court observed that the lower court had applied too strict a standard. The Supreme Court emphasized that the search was not for dominant market power or monopoly power as traditionally understood.[242] Instead, sufficient power could be found even if that power extended to some buyers, "whether few or many, whether scattered throughout the market or part of some group within the market."[243] Power could be "inferred from the tying product's desirability to consumers or uniqueness in its attributes."[244]

Uniqueness alone, according to the Court, was not determinative. Instead, the uniqueness had to be the product of an economic advantage that U.S. Steel had over competitors. More precisely, it had to flow from barriers that precluded competitors from offering the same product.[245] The Court offered the examples of land and patents and also suggested that the inability of competitors to offer the same product profitably could provide the requisite power. In the case at hand, it suggested that the plaintiff could prevail by showing that local lending institutions would regard such financing as too risky to be profitable or were unable to offer competitive terms because of state or federal regulation.[246] The majority opinion, written by Justice Black, was in many respects as hostile toward tying as any that it followed. On the other hand, it clearly reestablished assessment of economic power in the tying good market as an independent step in tying analysis. On remand, the trial court held for the plaintiff.[247]

Eight years later the case returned to a Supreme Court which now included only four Justices who had participated in *Fortner I*.[248] The issue in *Fortner II*[249] was whether the evidence supported the finding that U.S. Steel did have power in the credit market. This time the Supreme Court engaged in a step–by–step analysis of the factors that had led the trial court to conclude that U.S. Steel did have the requisite power. The first factor cited was that it was one of the nation's largest corporations. Here the Court

---

[242] 394 U.S. at 502–03.

[243] *Id.* at 503.

[244] *Id.* quoting *United States v. Loew's, Inc.*, 371 U.S. 45.

[245] 394 U.S. at 505 n.2.

[246] *Id.* at 505–06.

[247] The case was twice considered by the trial court with its decision eventually being affirmed by the Sixth Circuit Court of Appeals in 1975. *United States Steel Corp. v. Fortner Enterprises, Inc.*, 523 F.2d 961 (6th Cir. 1975).

[248] *See generally* Kramer, *The Supreme Court and Tying Arrangements: Antitrust as History*, 69 Minn. L. Rev. 1013, 1045–50 (1985).

[249] *United States Steel Corp. v. Fortner Enterprises, Inc.*, 429 U.S. 610 (1977).

observed that there was nothing about the affiliation of the credit subsidiary with U.S. Steel that enabled it to borrow funds on more favorable terms than its competitors or to otherwise operate more efficiently.[250]

The Court also was unpersuaded that economic power was shown by the fact that a significant number of customers, in addition to the plaintiff, had entered into the agreement.[251] According to the Court, disproportionately large sales of the tied product in relation to the tying product would be indicative of the type of leverage associated with economic power. Here, though, the plaintiff was only obligated to purchase houses to the extent that it applied for and received financing.[252] The third factor considered by the Court was whether the above–market prices for the tied product meant that U.S. Steel had the requisite power in the credit market. The Court reasoned that higher than market prices were to be expected since the credit terms were unusually attractive. Thus, the above–market prices were not inconsistent with a competitive price for the package.

Finally, the Court responded to the argument that power was inherent in the offering of financing that was unlike that available from other lenders. The Court, recalling its reasoning in *Fortner I*, explained that the power issue was not whether the credit terms were unique but whether the power exercised by U.S. Steel was market power as traditionally defined.[253] The Court, however, went a step further than it had in *Fortner I*. There the Court spoke of power *vis–a–vis* few or scattered buyers. In *Fortner II*, however, the power issue was framed in terms of whether U.S. Steel possessed the type of power in the credit market that would enable it to raise prices and restrict output. In particular, was the price it was exacting from buyers the purchase of homes that otherwise would not be purchased?[254]

The Court held that the evidence did not support a finding that U.S. Steel possessed this type of power. Instead, all that was suggested by the evidence was that U.S. Steel was willing to take a lower profit and accept a greater risk than were competitors when offering credit. Thus, the Court emphatically injected traditional market power analysis into the consideration of tying. Although the *per se* rule survived, it was far from that envisioned in *International Salt* thirty years earlier.[255]

---

[250] *Id.* at 617.

[251] *Id.* at 617–18. This had been a persuasive argument in earlier cases. *See, e.g., United States v. Loew's, Inc.*, 371 U.S. 38 (1962); *Northern Pacific Railway v. United States*, 356 U.S. 1 (1958).

[252] 429 U.S. at 617.

[253] *Id.* at 620.

[254] *Id.*

[255] *See generally* Bauer, *A Simplified Approach to Tying Arrangements: A Legal and Economic Analysis*, 33 Vand. L. Rev. 283, 288–91 (1980); Hovenkamp, *Tying Arrangements and Class Actions*, 36 Vand. L. Rev. 213 (1983); Kramer, *supra* note 248, at 1048–49; Melican, *Tying Arrangements and Related Restrictions After Fortner II*, 51 Antitrust L.J. 157 (1982).

[c] *Jefferson Parish Hospital v. Hyde*

In 1984, the Supreme Court once again considered the standards applicable to tying arrangements. In *Jefferson Parish Hospital v. Hyde*,[256] the defendant, East Jefferson Hospital, contracted with a firm of anesthesiologists to provide all the hospital's anesthesiological services. An excluded anesthesiologist charged the hospital with tying anesthesiological services to hospital services. The plaintiff lost at the trial court level. That decision was reversed by the Court of Appeals for the Fifth Circuit which labeled the arrangement *per se* unlawful.[257]

In arriving at its decision, the appellate court declined to apply the type of analysis that might be involved in more typical markets. It reasoned that the requisite power was present as a result of both the preference of consumers for the closest hospital and the presence of imperfections in the medical care market. In particular, the Court of Appeals believed that the prevalence of third party payers and the relative ignorance of consumers about the quality of medical care increased the power of the hospital to influence consumers' decisions.

The Supreme Court unanimously reversed. There was, however, a 5 to 4 split on the Court, with four Justices arguing that tying should be lifted from the *per se* category.[258] The majority of the Court reaffirmed, at least nominally, the *per se* status of tying. The majority opinion, written by Justice Stevens, focused on whether hospital services and anesthesiological services should be regarded as two products for tying analysis purposes and whether East Jefferson Hospital possessed sufficient power in the tying product market.

With respect to the first issue, the question was whether the hospital's services could be meaningfully separated from anesthesiological services. In effect, if the services were functionally inseparable, the harm to be avoided by prohibiting tying could not occur in the first place;[259] consumers could not be forced to buy something they would not otherwise buy. The hospital argued that it offered "a functionally integrated package of services"[260] — in essence, a single product. The Court viewed the issue as whether hospital services and anesthesiological services were sufficiently distinguished in the eyes of consumers to be subject to separate demands. It concluded the ability of patients to request specific anesthesiologists as well as other factors established that there were two products.

On the issue of market power, the Court began its analysis by invoking the *Fortner II* view that the relevant power was of the type that would ordinarily be used by a firm to raise prices above competitive levels.[261] The

---

[256] 466 U.S. 2 (1984).

[257] *Jefferson Parish v. Jefferson Parish Hospital Dist No. 2*, 686 F.2d 286 (5th Cir. 1982).

[258] The four group included Justices O'Conner, Powell and Rehnquist along with Chief Justice Burger. 466 U.S. at 32–47.

[259] *Id.* at 21–22.

[260] *Id.* at 18–19.

[261] *Id.* at 27 n.46.

Court believed the question was whether the defendant possessed this type of power and used it to coerce the purchase of a tied product that would otherwise not have been purchased.[262] It is this theme of coercion that distinguishes *Jefferson Parish* from *Fortner II*. In the latter case, the Court was most clearly concerned with the simple possession of power. In *Jefferson Parish* the use of this power for coercive purposes is emphasized. Accordingly, the question was whether the hospital's power was used to "force" consumers to purchase an "unwanted product."[263] The Court conceded that the market imperfections the Fifth Circuit had found persuasive would mean that consumers' decisions were less likely to be made on the basis of competitive merit. In effect, third party payers and ignorance insulated consumers from questions of price, value, and quality of service. In this context, the hospital could influence decision making. But, "power" resulting from consumer indifference could hardly be used to force consumers to forego choices that they would have otherwise preferred.[264]

Where the Court stands on the separate issue of what constitutes sufficient power in the tying product market is less clear. The Court seemed to indicate that the 30% market share possessed by East Jefferson Hospital did not constitute sufficient power in the tying product market.[265] If this is the case, the Court was announcing a standard that would be inconsistent with that applied in virtually every prior case in which it has found that the defendant possessed the requisite level of power. On the other hand, the Court cited those earlier cases with approval,[266] suggesting that they could be reconciled with its analysis.

Four of the concurring Justices in *Jefferson Parish* argued for abandoning the *per se* approach to tying. Justice O'Connor's opinion is noteworthy because it reflects an attempt to apply modern economic thought to tying. In particular, she questioned the "leverage" theory as a justification for barring tying.[267] Moreover, she noted the possible beneficial effects of tying. For example, in *Jefferson Parish* the packaging of hospital services and anesthesiological services could increase the efficiency of hospital operations. A rule of reason approach, she concluded, would permit the proper weighing of harmful and beneficial effects.

[d]   *Eastman Kodak Co. v. Image Technical Services*

The issue of market power in a tying context also arose in *Eastman Kodak Co. v. Image Technical Services Co.*,[268] a 1992 case. Kodak manufactured

---

[262] *Id.* at 26.

[263] *Id.* at 18.

[264] *Id.* at 27–28.

[265] Thirty per cent of the patients living in Jefferson Parish entered East Jefferson Parish Hospital. *Id.* at 26.

[266] *Id.* at 13–18. *Cf.* Bern, *Jefferson Parish Hospital District No. 2 v. Jefferson Parish: Return to Reality in Economic Power Analysis in Tying Cases*, 53 UMKC L. Rev. 145, 164–69 (1985).

[267] 466 U.S. at 35–6 (O'Connor, J. concurring). Justices Brennan and Marshall concurred in an opinion that supported continued *per se* treatment of tying.

[268] 112 S. Ct. 2072 (1992). *See also* Hovenkamp, *Market Power in Aftermarkets: Antitrust Policy and the Kodak Case*, 40 UCLA 1447 (1993).

office machinery including photocopiers. It also sold parts for and serviced the machines. In the mid 1980s Kodak instituted a policy of selling parts for its equipment only to buyers who repaired their own machines or used Kodak service. The charge was that Kodak had tied service to Kodak replacement parts thereby foreclosing independent service organizations. Since only Kodak parts could be used in Kodak equipment, the argument was that once purchasers bought Kodak's equipment, they constituted a "captive market" with respect to the aftermarkets in Kodak replacement parts and service.[269]

The Court considered whether it was proper to grant Kodak summary judgment under the theory that, since Kodak did not have market power in the original equipment market, it could not have market power in the market for replacement parts. The logic of Kodak's argument was that forcing purchasers to use Kodak service in order to obtain Kodak replacement parts was comparable to raising the price of the original purchase. Since Kodak did not have market power in the original equipment market, any purchasers who would prefer not to use Kodak service would just shift to competing suppliers of office equipment. Thus, as a matter of law, the absence of market power in the original equipment market would mean that a seller could not have market power in the aftermarket.[270]

The Supreme Court rejected Kodak's reasoning. First, it noted that even if the tie was viewed as comparable to an increase in the price of the original equipment and led to a decrease in original equipment sales, it did not follow that Kodak did not have market power in the aftermarket. The Court explained that all firms, including monopolists, face downward sloping demand curves meaning that higher prices result in fewer sales. This alone did not rule out the presence of market power.[271] Second, the Court noted that Kodak had increased the price of service without incurring decreased equipment sales, a combination that was inconsistent with its theory.[272]

Most important, however, was the Court's response to Kodak's effort to reconcile the phenomenon of higher service prices without a loss in equipment sales with its theory that it did not have market power in the replacement parts market. Kodak attempted the reconciliation by arguing that the cost of its equipment was evaluated by purchasers over the life of the equipment and was composed of the price of the original equipment and anticipated aftermarket purchases of replacement parts and service. Thus, higher service costs would be off–set by lower original equipment prices and the entire cost of the package would be competitively determined.[273]

The Court responded by noting the importance of information and switching costs as sources of market power. With respect to information

---

[269] *Id.* at 2081.

[270] *Id.* at 2088–89.

[271] *Id.* at 2084.

[272] *Id.* at 2085.

[273] *Id.*

costs, the Court explained that the type of "lifecycle pricing" suggested by Kodak required a significant investment by buyers in the acquisition of information about repair costs, breakdown frequency and losses incurred during downtime. If these costs were sufficiently high, or at least high enough that their acquisition was not cost justified, the price of the package could exceed competitive levels.[274] In addition, the Court noted that the cost of switching to a different brand of equipment in response to the tie or higher repair service costs could be high enough that "locked–in" buyers would elect to pay supracompetitive prices.[275] These factors, the Court ruled, meant that the extent of Kodak's market power in the aftermarket was a question of fact.

In adopting the information cost rationale, the Court may have taken a position that is at odds with that stated in *Jefferson Parish*.[276] In *Jefferson Parish*, the indifference of consumers to price due to the presence of third party payers was not viewed as a source of market power. Yet, in *Kodak*, the Court recognized that information costs "could create a less responsive connection between service and parts prices and equipment sales"[277] and viewed that lack of responsiveness as source of market power giving rise to antitrust concerns. The market imperfections in *Jefferson Parish* can be distinguished from those in *Kodak*, but not so completely as to eliminate the possibility that the Court has broadened the scope of factors to be considered in assessing market power.

Another question that remained after *Kodak* was whether it would make a difference if the defendant's policy with respect to the alleged tie was know at the time the sale was made. For example, in *Kodak,* the policy objected to was instituted after many buyers had committed to the original equipment. On the other hand, had the policy been in place at the time of the purchase, so the argument goes, the tying product would more obviously be the original equipment and market power in the original equipment market would be critical. A number of courts have interpreted the holding in *Kodak* as limited to instances in which the seller's policy was not know or was instituted after the sale.[278] In effect, while it is possible that buyers may become "locked–in," they generally may not create market power for tying purposes by volunteering at the outset to forgo buying aftermarket goods from supplier other than the seller of the original equipment.

---

[274] *Id.* at 2085–86.

[275] *Id.* at 2097.

[276] This point was made by Justice Scalia in dissent. *Id.* at 2097–98.

[277] *Id.* at 2085.

[278] *See Queen City Pizza Inc., v. Domino's Pizza, Inc.*, 124 F.3d 430 (3rd Cir. 1997); *PSI Repair Servs v. Honeywell, Inc.* 104 F.3d 811 (6th Cir. 1997); *Digital Equipment Co. v. Uniq Digital Tech.*, 73 F.3d 756 (7th Cir. 1996).

[e] Modern Tying Doctrine and *United States v. Microsoft*[279]

The *Jefferson Parish* Court's emphasis on coercion seemed to resolve an issue surrounding the application of the *per se* rule to tying. Some courts, with support from *International Salt* and *Northern Pacific*, have confined their analyses to the defendant's power in the tying product market and the level of commerce affected in the tied product market.[280] Others have regarded the additional question of whether the tie precluded the buyer from considering the tied product on its competitive merits as a required inquiry.[281] After *Jefferson Parish*, coercion is an independent prerequisite for application of the *per se* rule. This is not to say, however, that coercion can be demonstrated only by direct evidence.[282]

Under the new version of the *"per se* rule" a number of steps are required. First, there must be two products, one of which is the tying product and one of which is the tied product. Second, there must be power in the tying product market. *Kodak* suggests that sufficient market power may result from transaction costs related to the imperfect information. Third, there must be a "not insubstantial" amount of commerce affected in the tied product market. Four, the power in the tying product market must be used to prevent competition on the merits between products in the tied product market. Finally, in cases in which tying firm does not actually sell the tied product, in most jurisdictions the tying firm must have an economic interest in sales of the tied product. Technically, if the plaintiff is unable to establish all of the elements for a *per se* ruling, it may still proceed under the rule of reason. Needless to say, this is not a promising alternative for plaintiffs wishing to pursue a tying claim.[283]

One issue theoretically left open after *Fortner II* was whether the standards to be applied to tying under the Sherman Act and Clayton Act are different. That suggestion, of course, originally appeared in Justice Clark's opinion in *Times–Picayune*. The Supreme Court seemed to foreclose this possibility in *Jefferson Parish* by observing that even though *Jefferson Parish* did not arise under the Clayton Act, "the congressional finding made therein concerning the competitive consequences of tying is illuminating, and must be respected."[284]

---

[279] 253 F.3d 34 (D.C. Cir. 2001).

[280] *See, e.g., Siegel v. Chicken Delight. Inc.*, 448 F.2d 42, 47 (9th Cir. 1971), *cert. denied*, 405 U.S. 905 (1972); *see also, In re Visa Check/Mastermoney Antitrust Litigation*, 280 F.3d 124 (2d Cir. 2001) (upholding certification of class action by 4 million retailers who allege illegal tying of credit card and debit card products due to Visa and Mastercard "honor all cards" requirement.)

[281] *See, e.g., Yentsch v. Texaco, Inc.*, 630 F.2d 46, 56–57 (2d Cir. 1980).

[282] *See, e.g., Tic–X–Press, Inc. v. Omni Promotions Co.*, 815 F.2d 1407, 1418 (11th Cir. 1987).

[283] *See, e.g., Jefferson Parish*, 466 U.S. at 29–32; *Times–Picayune*, 345 U.S. at 614–26; *Digital Equipment Corp. v. Uniq Digital Technologies*, 73 F.3d 756 (7th Cir. 1996).

[284] 466 U.S. 2, 10–11.

Modern tying analysis was put to the test in *United States v. Microsoft Corp.* in which the lower court found several of Microsoft's practices to be *per se* unlawful. These practices included requiring licensees of Windows 95 and 98 also to license Internet Explorer (IE), refusing to allow equipment manufacturers to uninstall from the desktop, designing Windows 98 so that IE could not be removed by use of the add/remove program and designing Windows 98 to override a users efforts to choose a default web browser.[285] The Court of Appeals reversed, indicating that the tying agreements should be assessed under the rule of reason.

The court's concern was not with the issue of market power, or impact on the tied product market but with the wisdom of treating the operating system and the browser as separate products. As noted earlier, for tying to be illegal there must be two products. The court reasoned that the separate demands test of *Jefferson Parish* was essentially a screening mechanism.[286] Ideally, what were screened out of the *per se* category were instances in which significant efficiencies were made available by integrating products. According to the court, an unrefined separate products analysis would mean that even the integration of spell checkers in work processing programs could potentially violate the tying prohibitions. The problem, according to court, is to balance a loss in consumer choice against the gains made possible by integration. The court also recognized the possibility that the *per se* rule could stifle innovation in the sense that producers would be reluctant to experiment with new and possibly beneficial integrations. Given these considerations and others, the court indicated that it was not confident that bundling in computer software markets has sufficiently negligible "redeeming virtue" as to warrant *per se* treatment.[287] The nature of this analysis mirrors that applied in a number of earlier cases in which courts have declined to regard two components as two products when do to so would result in inefficiencies.[288]

[3]   Package Transactions

Tying analysis is relatively simple when the case involves the basic model of a single tying product and a single tied product. The analysis is more complex when the issue itself is one of product separability. One example involves package transactions in which the "product" is actually a group of related components offered at a single price.

The leading case in this regard is *United States v. Loew's, Inc.*[289] in which distributors of motion picture feature films were charged with violating § 1 of the Sherman Act by engaging in block booking. The defendants conditioned the licensing or sales of commercially popular films to television stations on the acceptance of a block of films including movies with limited

---

[285] 253 F.3d at 84–85.

[286] *Id.* at 87.

[287] *Id.* at 94.

[288] *See* cases discussed in section 5.02[B][4], *infra.*

[289] 371 U.S. 38 (1962).

appeal. For example, in order to get "Casablanca" the buyer had to accept a block which also included "Tugboat Annie Sails Again."

The primary issue addressed by the Supreme Court was whether there was sufficient economic power to satisfy the *Northern Pacific* test.[290] The defendants argued that, since films made up only 8% of television programming and were interchangeable with other types of programming, they had no market power. The Court responded that "a copyrighted feature film does not lose its legal or economic uniqueness because it is shown on a television rather than a movie screen."[291] The Court did not prohibit block booking as long as films were also available individually and the price differences between single films and groups of films were cost justified.[292]

Loew's is interesting from a number of perspectives. First, the case was decided in 1962 and the Court's standard for determining the presence of sufficient power in the tying product market is reflective of the then prevailing hostility toward tying. Whether the evidence would be as compelling today is another question. Second, the Court's reasoning is based largely on the potential coercive effect of the arrangement. That is, purchasers would not have the option to accept or reject the less popular films on their individual merit. Even though the Court permitted cost–justified block sales, it noted that price could not be manipulated to have a coercive effect. The notion of coercion has, of course, now under *Jefferson Parish* become central to tying analysis.

Finally, the facts of the case are ideal for raising the issue of how the tie could benefit the seller. In particular, using the "one monopoly profit" theory discussed earlier (*see* § 5.02[B][1]), any distributor would seem to be able to maximize profit by pricing individual films at their profit maximizing level. If this were the case, why would the seller insist on block sales? The suggestion has been made that the block sales actually facilitated a form of price discrimination.[293] For example, suppose a seller has two films, "Star Wars" and "Heaven's Gate." One buyer will pay $1,000 for "Star Wars" and $500 for "Heaven's Gate." Another will pay $1,500 for "Star Wars" and $200 for "Heaven's Gate." If the seller must sell them separately, the maximum revenue it could hope for would be $2,500 — $2,000 for "Star Wars" and $500 for "Heaven's Gate."[294] On the other hand, a package price of $1,500 would result in both buyers buying both films and a total revenue of $3,000.

---

[290] *Id.* at 45.

[291] *Id.* at 47–48.

[292] *Id.* at 53–5. For subsequent interpretations of *Loew's* see *Coniglio v. Hollywood Services, Inc.*, 495 F.2d 1286 (2d Cir. 1974), *cert. denied.*, 419 U.S. 1022 (1974); *American Manufacturers Mutual Insurance Co. v. American Broadcasting–Paramount Theatres, Inc.*, 388 F.2d 272 (2d Cir. 1967).

[293] *See* Stigler, *United States v. Loew's, Inc.: A Note on Block–Booking*, 1963 Sup. Ct. Rev. 152 (P. Kurland ed. 1963).

[294] A price of $1,000 maximizes the possible revenue for "Star Wars" and a price of $500 maximizes the possible revenue for "Heaven's Gate."

[4] Defenses and Justifications

Two arguments have developed that can be employed to justify an arrangement that might otherwise be condemned as a tying agreement. The first focuses on whether the transaction involves one or two products. This issue has been raised repeatedly in the context of franchise agreements. In a technical sense, an argument by a defendant that the exchange involves a single product is not a defense to tying because without two products the plaintiff has not established the *prima facie* elements for a tying claim. In some cases, however, the issue has come to resemble a defense because the question addressed by the court is not so much whether two products are involved but whether the sale should be regarded as involving two products for tying purposes. The second, more traditional, defense seeks to justify an arrangement that clearly involves two products and would otherwise fall within the Sherman or Clayton Act prohibitions against tying.

[a] The Single Product "Defense"

When courts have allowed the single product issue to become an indirect defense, there appear to be two underlying justifications. One is based on the fact that a single product classification may protect the good–will of the seller and enhance interbrand competition. The other suggests that joint sale of two items results in efficiencies in supplying the good that could mean lower prices for consumers.

A leading example of the first type of reasoning is found in *United States v. Jerrold Electronics Corp.*[295] in which the seller of community antenna systems required purchasers to buy the complete system although several components could be sold, and were available, separately. The defendant's unique "head end equipment" provided the necessary economic power for demanding full system sales. The issue for the court was "whether this should be treated as a case of tying the sale of one product to another product or merely as the sale of a single product."[296] One of the factors the court considered was whether there was a "business justification" for complete system sales. Jerrold argued that it was necessary to sell its product as a complete system in order to assure its proper functioning and to protect the good–will of the firm.[297] The court concluded that during the start–up stage of the firm, it was appropriate to classify the system as a single product.[298]

Similar reasoning is found in *Krehl v. Baskin–Robbins Ice Cream Co.*[299] in which the defendant conditioned the grant of a franchise on the purchase

---

[295] 187 F. Supp. 545 (E.D. Pa.), *aff'd per curiam*, 365 U.S. 567 (1961).

[296] 187 F. Supp. at 559.

[297] Jerrold's sales effort included both full system sales and the requirement that all maintenance and installation services be purchased from Jerrold as well.

[298] In an earlier part of the opinion, the court had already accepted Jerrold's justification for tying installation and maintenance service to the equipment. The court regarded the full system requirement as necessary to achieve the beneficial effects of that tie. *Id.* at 560.

[299] 664 F.2d 1348 (9th Cir. 1982).

of ice cream. The issue considered by the Ninth Circuit Court of Appeals was whether the Baskin–Robbins trademark could be treated as a product separate from the ice cream itself. The court distinguished franchises that were "business format systems" from those that were "distribution systems."[300] In the latter case, the franchiser uses the franchised outlet as a "conduit" for final distribution of its products. Baskin–Robbins was in this category because the trademark was merely a means of identifying its product.[301] Control over the ice cream sold was the *sine qua non* of protecting the good–will afforded the trademark itself. In effect, the trademark could not be regarded as having an independent value or an identity separate from the ice cream sold under it. The court distinguished *Siegel v. Chicken Delight*[302] in which it held that the two product requirement was met. The franchise in that case, according to the court, was a "business format system" which served only to conduct business under a common name. The tied items were, in many instances, not likely to have a direct influence on the good–will of the Chicken Delight name.[303]

The second category of single–product issue cases can be seen as being primarily concerned with efficiencies. In essence, they respond to the instances in which the tying of a good that could actually be marketed separately creates efficiencies in production or distribution and lower prices for consumers.[304] For example, automobiles could easily be sold without wheels leaving purchasers to buy wheels from the automobile dealer or from independent wheel producers. Indeed, the near universal tying of wheels to automobiles arguably forecloses an industry of wheel manufacturers. On the other hand, it is probably less costly for a manufacturer of automobiles to produce all its automobiles with wheels intact as opposed to delivering to the dealer automobiles and wheels as separate products. Ultimately, the result could be lower prices for consumers. When faced with these types of cases the courts have often found some basis for avoiding a tying analysis.[305] Most recently in *Microsoft*, the court framed the issue in terms of a trade–off between the economic efficiency of integration and the losses in consumer choice.

Efficiency concerns clearly played a pivotal role in *Principe v. McDonald's Corp.*,[306] one of the most influential franchise cases. McDonald's required

---

[300] *Id.* at 1353.

[301] *Id.* at 1353–54.

[302] *Id.* at 1352–54, distinguishing *Siegel v. Chicken Delight*, 448 F.2d 43 (9th Cir. 1971), *cert. denied*, 405 U.S. 955 (1972).

[303] 664 F.2d at 1352.

[304] *See generally* R. Blair & D. Kaserman, *supra* note 159, at 387–88; H. Hovenkamp, *supra* note 2, at 233–35.

[305] This seems to be the case in "physical ties," in which two components are actually combined, *see, e.g., ILC Peripherals Leasing Corp. v. IBM Corp.*, 448 F.2d 228 (N.D. Cal. 1978), *aff'd*, 636 F.2d 1188 (9th Cir. 1980), *cert. denied*, 452 U.S. 972 (1981); and in cases with products that must be used together because of technological comparability, see, *e.g., Foremost Pro Color v. Eastman Kodak Co.*, 703 F.2d 534 (9th Cir. 1983), *cert. denied*, 465 U.S. 1038 (1984).

[306] 631 F.2d 303 (4th Cir. 1980), *cert. denied*, 451 U.S. 970 (1981). *See also Kypta v. McDonald's Corp.*, 671 F.2d 1282 (11th Cir.), *cert. denied*, 459 U.S. 875 (1982).

licensees to operate their restaurants in premises leased from McDonald's. Both royalties under the license and rent for the premises were calculated as a percentage of gross receipts.[307]

The Fourth Circuit Court of Appeals upheld the decision of the lower court that the license contract and the rental agreement constituted a single product. The court applied the standard that "[w]here the challenged aggregation is an essential ingredient of the franchised system's formula for success, there is but a single product . . . ."[308]

The Court was impressed by the extensive research conducted by McDonald's before deciding on a location and the fact that eventual franchisees were not involved in the process. According to the court, McDonald's system enabled it to (1) obtain superior sites, (2) assure that all the restaurants remained in the system therefore ensuring uniformity and consequent good–will of the system, and (3) select franchisees on the basis of managerial skills rather than financial resources.[309] Moreover, not only did McDonald's train franchisees but it engaged in frequent inspections of each store during operation. What McDonald's offered franchisees was "a complete method of doing business" and virtual guaranteed success.[310] In short, the license/lease aggregation was an essential ingredient of the "formula for success."[311]

A different type of efficiency seemed to play a role in the Seventh Circuit Court of Appeal's decision in *Johnson v. Nationwide Industries, Inc.*[312] Buyers of condominium units were required to assume a proportionate obligation under a pre–existing building management agreement. The court held that a single product was involved as long as the management agreements were of reasonable duration. It noted the difficulty of selling individual units over a period of time without being able to assure purchasers of stability in building management.[313] Without the aggregation,

---

[307] 631 F.2d at 304. The agreement was probably a means of practicing price discrimination since a franchisee's rent increased with its volume of business. As indicated in Chapter 8, the practice of price discrimination may result in higher output — in this case more franchisees — than would be the case if a single price were charged.

[308] 631 F.2d at 309.

[309] *Id.* at 310. The court noted that the arrangement resulted in a "sort of partnership" between McDonald's and the franchisee.

[310] *Id.* at 309.

[311] *Id.* An extensive discussion by Judge Posner of the efficiency justification for finding that an arrangement involves two products is found in *Jack Walters & Sons Corp. v. Morton Building, Inc.*, 737 F.2d 698 (7th Cir. 1984), *cert. denied*, 469 U.S. 1018 (1984). Morton had tied prefabricated building components to the Morton trademark. The actual rationale for finding that there was not a tie seemed to rest on the inherent inseparability of a product and its name, not on Judge Posner's discussion of efficiencies.

[312] 715 F.2d 1233 (7th Cir. 1983).

[313] *Id.* at 1237. The court affirmed denial of the defendant's motion for summary judgment indicating the necessity of determining whether the duration of the management contract was reasonable. One year later, in *Jack Walters v. Morton*, Judge Posner characterized the holding as "a condominium and a contract for the provision of management services to the condominium owner was a single product." 737 F.2d at 703. Judge Posner's interpretation of the *Nationwide Industries* holding attributes to that panel less flexibility on the "one product issue" than is actually reflected in the opinion.

prospective purchasers would have to weigh the risk of not knowing about future building management arrangements and would face the transaction costs resulting from the necessity of combining with other owners and then searching and contracting for management services. By declining to classify the case as one involving two products, the court seemed cognizant of the savings to consumers of combining individual units with building management.

Finally, in *Digital Equipment Corporation v. Uniq Digital Technologies*[314] the Seventh Circuit Court of Appeals responded to a claim that a computer manufacturers was tying its operating system to the computer. Judge Easterbrook focused on the purposes of the antitrust laws and questioned whether it was "useful" to call the practice a tie reasoning that "[a]n operating system is essential to making a bunch of silicon chips a computer."[315] Accordingly, he went on to compare the operating system of the computer to the electrical system of a car. The result of viewing such a combination as a tie, he concluded, would not "help to uncover practices that restrict output, drive up prices, and transfer wealth from consumers to producers."[316]

[b] Good–Will

In case of obviously separate products, some courts have considered directly whether "goodwill" is a defense for what would otherwise be an illegal tie. In *IBM v. United States,*[317] the Supreme Court evaluated the requirement that lessees of IBM's tabulating and other machines use only tabulating cards produced by IBM. The cards had to be manufactured to precise specifications in order to perform properly in the machines. IBM argued that § 3 was not applicable because its goal was to protect good–will by insuring the successful performance of the machines. The Court seemed to leave open the possibility that a good–will defense could be successfully asserted when protection of good will could not be achieved by a less restrictive means.[318] IBM's case was weak on this point since it permitted the Government to make its own cards in exchange for higher rent. In all likelihood, tying cards to the machines was designed to facilitate price discrimination.[319]

In *Jerrold Electronics*, discussed above in the context of the single product issue, the defendant also tied its antenna system to a service contract that covered installation and maintenance.[320] The supplier wanted to avoid do–it–yourself installation and service in order to minimize system failure. Two factors, in particular, seemed to make Jerrold's justification compelling.

---

[314] 73 F.2d 756 (7th Cir. 1996).

[315] *Id.* at 761.

[316] *Id.*

[317] 298 U.S. 131 (1936).

[318] *Id.* at 140.

[319] *See* R. Bork, *supra* note 8, at 376–78.

[320] 187 F. Supp. at 554–58.

First, the industry itself was in a developmental period.[321] Second, the investment was substantial and payment to Jerrold was essentially contingent on successful functioning of the equipment.[322] These factors persuaded the court that, at least at their inception, the restrictions were reasonable.[323] In a statement that seems to sum–up today's judicial attitudes toward application of the *per se* rule to tying cases the court explained that "while the *per se* rule should be followed in almost all cases, the court always must be conscious of the fact that a case might arise in which the facts indicate that an injustice would be done by blindly accepting the *per se* rule."[324]

[5] When the Tying Product is Sold by a Third Party

It is fairly common for sellers to sell goods or services on the condition that the buyer purchase the "tied" good from a third party. As one might expect, however, the firm selling the tying product may receive payment from the seller of the "tied" product. The danger, as in the tying cases, is that the producer of the tying product is using its power in that market to affect competition in the tied product market. The economic concerns of tying — foreclosure, entry barriers, etc. — also are raised by this form of conditional sale. On the other hand, the arguments that tying really is not anticompetitive also are equally applicable.

The leading cases dealing with this type of arrangement concern requirements by major oil companies that their wholesale and retail outlets purchase tires, batteries and accessories from specified major tire manufacturers. The FTC labeled the practice an unfair method of competition under § 5 of the Federal Trade Commission Act. In two cases, *Atlantic Refining Co. v. FTC*[325] and *FTC v. Texaco*[326] the Supreme Court affirmed the position taken by the Commission. The facts of the cases were substantially the same, with the former involving more coercion than the latter.[327]

The Court's approach mirrored that applied to tying during the mid–1960's with particular attention paid to the pervasive control the oil companies had over their outlets.[328] It reasoned that "just as the effect of this plan is similar to that of a tie–in, so is it unnecessary to embark upon a full–scale economic analysis."[329] The Court also indicated that it had been proper for the Commission to refuse to consider economic justifications for the program.[330] Quite obviously the approach taken today to such cases

---

[321] *Id.* at 556.

[322] *Id.*

[323] *Id.* at 558.

[324] *Id.* at 556.

[325] 381 U.S. 357 (1965).

[326] 393 U.S. 223 (1968).

[327] *Id.* at 228.

[328] *Id.* at 228–30.

[329] *Atlantic Refining Co.*, 381 U.S. 357, 371.

[330] *Id.*

would be influenced by the decisions in *Fortner II* and *Jefferson Parish*. In particular, after those cases, proof of market dominance and coercion play a greater role in the analysis of such sales. In addition, possible procompetitive aspects of protecting good–will by such an agreement also would seem to have increased relevance.

One issue lower courts face with increasing frequency is the relevance of the relationship between the sellers of the tying and tied products. For example, in County of *Toulumne v. Sonora Community Hospital*,[331] a hospital required that all caesarian sections be performed by certified obstetricians or specially qualified physicians. The lower court held that the per se standard should not apply since the hospital had no economic interest in the business success of the obstetricians. The appellate court agreed indicating that without a financial interest there was little likelihood that the tying firm would attempt to acquire market power in the tying product market.[332] This extra step does not seem to be one that is required under *Jefferson Parish*; the "economic interest" requirements seems to hold in a majority of jurisdictions.[333]

[6] Reciprocal Dealing

Another arrangement that has a tying–type quality is reciprocal dealing. Here firm A agrees to make purchases from firm B only on the condition that firm B make purchases from firm A. In these instances the "leverage" involved lies in firm A's ability to purchase or withhold its purchases from firm B. In other words, firm A uses its monopsony power — power as a buyer — to coerce firm B to buy its product. The alleged damage occurs to competitors of firm A who will find it more difficult to find outlets for their products. In effect, monopsony leverage is used to promote the sales of A's product on the basis of a factor other than competitive merit. Courts have used tying analysis in such cases.

The principal Supreme Court case regarding reciprocal dealing is *FTC v. Consolidated Foods Corp.*[334] in which the Commission challenged the acquisition of a producer of dehydrated vegetables by a major food processor. The core of the FTC's case was that the acquisition created the threat of reciprocal dealing. More specifically, Consolidated Foods could condition its purchases from other food processors on their purchase of dehydrated onion and garlic from Consolidated's subsidiary. The Court reasoned that, "reciprocity made possible by such an acquisition is one of the congeries of anticompetitive practices at which the antitrust laws are aimed."[335]

---

[331] 236 F.3d 1148 (9th Cir, 2000).

[332] *Id.* at 1158.

[333] *See also, Sports Racing Services, Inc., v. Sports Car Club of America, Inc.*, 131 F.3d 874 (10th Cir. 1997). *But see, Gonzalez v. St. Margaret's Housing Development Fund Corp.*, 880 F.2d 1514 (2d Cir. 1989).

[334] 380 U.S. 592 (1965).

[335] *Id.* at 594–5. One year later *Consolidated Foods* was relied upon to condemn a purely reciprocal dealing arrangement. *United States v. General Dynamics*, 258 F. Supp. 36 (S.D.N.Y.

Accordingly, it upheld the Commission's divestiture order citing *International Salt* and *Northern Pacific*.

The economic issues raised by reciprocal dealing are similar to those that arise in the tying context. The single profit rule can be applied to the firm with monopsony power. Whatever profit producing capabilities the firm has due to monopsony power can be fully realized by making purchases at low prices.[336] In effect, firm A, in the example, may receive its profit by acquiring the goods of firm B at a low price or by selling its own product. In either case, so the argument goes, the total profit is the same. The possibility also exists that reciprocal dealing may promote efficiency.[337] This is likely to be the case when the arrangement, rather than being the result of coercion, is voluntary. Although *Consolidated Foods* did not distinguish between voluntary and involuntary reciprocal dealing and was decided before *Jefferson Parish*, now issues of market power and "forcing" are important in a reciprocal dealing case.

In a recent example of reciprocal dealing case, *Brokerage Concepts Inc., v. United States Healthcare, Inc.*,[338] the court applied all the elements of a modern tying analysis. The practice that was challenged was an arrangement under which an HMO agreed to buy drugs for its members from a group of pharmacists if the pharmacists made use of a third party administrator that was a subsidiary of the HMO.[339] The plaintiff was a competing third party administrator. The court evaluated whether this arrangement should be assessed under the *per se* or rule of reason standard and focused specifically on the market power of the defendant. In this instance, leverage used by the defendant resulted from its ability to steer its membership to a specific group of pharmacists. In a sense, the defendant was seen as "selling" access to its members. Thus the court examined whether there were other reasonable substitutes in the market and reasoned that members of any managed care organization were reasonably interchangeable with those of the defendant. In a properly defined market, the defendant's market share was, at most, 25% which was too small to warrant a *per se* ruling. The court then applied the rule of reason and found that the plaintiff had not demonstrated harm to competition.

1966). *See generally* Note, *A Reevaluation of Reciprocal Dealings, Under the Federal Antitrust Laws: Spartan Grain v. Ayers,"* 11 Loy. U. Chi. L.J. 577 (1980). For more recent discussions of reciprocal dealing *see Betaseed, Inc. v. U and I, Inc.*, 681 F.2d 1203 (9th Cir. 1982); *Spartan Grain & Mill Co. v. Ayers*, 581 F.2d 419 (5th Cir. 1978), *cert. denied*, 444 U.S. 831 (1979).

336 *See generally*, R. Posner & F. Easterbrook, *Antitrust* 855 (2d ed. 1981).

337 *See* H. Hovenkamp, *supra* note 2, at 427–430.

338 140 F.3d 494 (3rd Cir. 1998).

339 The Court viewed the practice as falling somewhere between tying and reciprocal dealing. Id. at 511.

Chapter 6

MONOPOLIZATION AND RELATED OFFENSES

§ 6.01 Introduction

Section 2 of the Sherman Act prohibits monopolization, attempt to monopolize, and conspiracy to monopolize.[1] It has presented a dilemma for the courts because a firm's profits, the spoils of a vigorous competitive process, are frequently accompanied by large market shares and monopoly power. One may ask, how can competition be encouraged if "winning" the competitive game may result in condemnation under the Sherman Act? This dilemma has resulted in a slowly evolving effort by courts to permit the existence of concentrated economic power while devising general guidelines for what is acceptable conduct. The evolutionary process has not been altogether successful. The law of monopoly is still characterized by a lack of consistency and predictability.

This chapter considers three prohibitions of § 2 — monopolization, attempt to monopolize, and conspiracy to monopolize; it also discusses "shared monopoly," — something of a hybrid of §§ 1 and 2 of the Sherman Act. The section that follows is a brief review of the economic concerns raised by the existence of monopoly.

§ 6.02 The Economics of Monopoly

Specific economic concerns about monopoly power depend on one's view of the proper goals of antitrust enforcement. The issue can best be visualized by reviewing the comparison of monopoly and perfect competition in Chapter 2. In Figure 6–1, D is the demand and S is the supply for bagels. From Chapter 2 you know that the supply curve under competitive conditions is actually the horizontal summation of the supply curves of all the manufacturers of bagels. These individual supply curves are the marginal cost curves of the firms. Under competitive conditions, the equilibrium market price will be Pc and output will be Qc. Each firm would sell all it wants at price Pc. By definition, no firm is large enough to affect price by increasing or decreasing the number of bagels it offers for sale. Under competitive conditions, all producers are "price takers" and price will tend to equal marginal cost.

---

[1] 15 U.S.C. § 2 (1983).

FIGURE 6–1

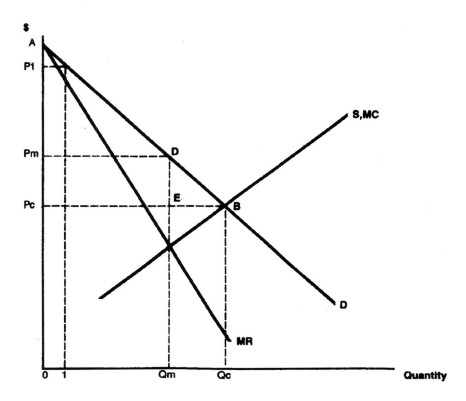

The area of triangle PcAB in Figure 6–1 indicates the total value to consumers of bagels above the amount they are required to pay. This is called "consumer surplus." For example, in Figure 6–1 the first bagel is sold for Pc as are all the others. The demand curve, however, shows that a purchaser would have been willing and able to pay up to price P1 for the bagels. The consumer surplus would be the difference between Pc and P1; it measures the gain to the consumer from the exchange of Pc for a bagel. There must be consumer surplus associated with every bagel sold or the exchange would not take place.

Suppose, through some huge and highly unlikely merger, all the firms producing bagels became a single firm and each plant maintained its own production system. Now the monopolist — the single firm supplier of the product — would face the entire demand curve for the industry, D. Since the monopolist faces a downward sloping demand curve and must lower price in order to sell additional output, its marginal revenue curve becomes an important decision–making tool. Its marginal cost curve (MC) would be what was formerly the industry supply curve.[2] Its profit maximizing level of output is Qm, where the marginal cost and marginal revenue curves intersect. The monopolist then sells the profit maximizing output for Pm, the highest price consistent with selling that quantity. In fact, the primary way the monopolist differs from the competitive firm is in this ability to be a price setter, not a price taker. Consequently, the concept of monopoly power is reduced to "market power," which is a measure of the firm's ability to raise price above what it would be under competitive conditions.

The most important aspect of the change from competition to monopoly is the impact on consumer surplus. The former consumer surplus was PcAB. Under monopoly it has declined to PmAD. What has happened to the remainder? A portion of it, PcPmDE has been transferred to the monopolist. One's reaction to this will depend on whether one feels that antitrust should be guided by distributive goals or should be indifferent to them. Another portion of what was consumer surplus, EDB, is not transferred to the monopolist but simply eliminated. In short, it was a gain to consumers that now does not exist, even in the form of a benefit to the monopolist. This "deadweight" loss, the quantity of which is of some dispute, is most frequently held out as the true social cost of monopoly.

There are two other factors that complicate the evaluation of monopoly. First, although the "deadweight" loss is important, it may not be the only social cost of monopoly. In particular, the lure of capturing some of the consumer surplus resulting from the exchange could be quite tempting to an incumbent and a potential monopolist. Consequently, a monopolist may find it worthwhile to invest a great deal of effort in maintaining or gaining a share of what otherwise would be consumer surplus. In theory, it may use some or nearly all of the surplus it has captured — PcPmDE in Figure 6–1 — in this effort. To the extent that the process involves the use of resources and has no other impact than the transfer of income, the cost may be regarded as an additional form of "deadweight" loss.[3]

Finally, in the simple model examined here, the economies of production for the merged firm are the same as they were for the industry under competitive conditions. However, the larger firm producing bagels may be able to operate at a scale that enables it to produce each unit at a lower per unit cost than several firms operating under competition. The most extreme version of this is called "natural monopoly," a condition under which the lowest per unit cost of production is achieved when one firm serves the market. Thus, production by a monopolist may mean higher prices and lower output and a deadweight loss that would not exist under competition. On the other hand, due to efficiencies in production, the actual cost per unit may be lower; resources may be used more effectively.[4]

---

[2] This assumes that the monopolist does not experience any economies in production over those available when the industry is competitive.

[3] See R. Posner, *Antitrust Law: An Economic Perspective* 11– 14 (1976).

[4] See R. Bork, *The Antitrust Paradox* 107–10 (19780; see *supra* Chapter 2.

The net effect of these complexities is that it is hazardous to condemn monopoly in the abstract. Several questions are especially important. First, is there some reason to protect consumer surplus from capture by the monopolist? The answer may seem simple if one believes that antitrust has a distributive function and that the choice is always between wealthy shareholders and generally helpless consumers. But it is not that simple. The shareholders are not always wealthy individuals. Even large corporate investors like banks and insurance companies may be investing the savings of many individuals of relatively modest means. Moreover, the consumer is often likely to be a corporate giant itself. Additional questions have less to do with personal philosophy and more to do with the difficulty of obtaining economic data. For example, what is the deadweight loss associated with monopoly production? What economies are derived from having a single producer of the good? How does the deadweight loss compare with the possible gains from more efficient production. To what extent do consumers value the presence of a large number of possibly "inefficient" competitors over a relatively efficient monopolist?[5] Only by answering these questions — a practical impossibility — can one be sure about the actual gains or losses due to monopoly.

§ 6.03 The Modern Offense of Monopolization: The Search for Standards

[A] Early Interpretations

[1] Preliminary Issues

Two questions were critical in the early examinations of § 2. To some extent these questions still loom in the background of § 2 cases. First, does the Act condemn the mere possession of monopoly power? In short, is bigness *per se* to be condemned? Second, if there is a separate conduct component of the monopolization offense, what types of behavior are prohibited? Specifically, do the prohibitions of § 2 extend only to behavior that would violate § 1 if engaged in by more than one actor or does it prohibit a broader range of conduct? As a corollary: are otherwise lawful acts prohibited if engaged in by a firm with monopoly power?

The different answers to these questions create a continuum of possible interpretations. At one end lies the possibility that merely being a monopoly is sufficient to bring § 2 into play. At the other extreme is the requirement that the firm possess monopoly power and engage in practices that would otherwise violate § 1. Today we know that courts have opted for a point somewhere between these extremes. Any clarity that has developed, however, is of relatively recent origin.

---

[5] This possibility is suggested by Hovenkamp, *Distributive Justice and the Antitrust Laws*, 51 Geo. Wash. L. Rev. 1, 20 (1982).

[2] *Standard Oil v. United States*

The delay in defining the precise limits of the prohibitions of § 2 can be traced to the factual contexts of its initial interpretations. For example, in the pivotal *Standard Oil* case in 1911, the Court chose to view § 2 as a complement to § 1. Thus, "the 2nd section seeks, if possible, to make the prohibition of the act all the more complete and perfect by embracing all attempts to reach the end prohibited by the 1st section."[6] This "rule of reason," the primary teaching of *Standard Oil*, was to be applied in § 2 as well as § 1 cases.

On the other hand, the defendant in the case obviously possessed monopoly power and had engaged in practices that, from the Court's viewpoint, would fall within the prohibitions of § 1. It, therefore, was unnecessary to consider how crucial each of these elements was for the finding of a § 2 violation. Indeed, although the Court stressed the importance of interpreting §§ 1 and 2 in parallel fashion, it opened the door for an expanded application of § 2 by noting that the evil to be avoided was achievement of monopoly power through other than "normal methods of industrial development."[7] Thus, the decisions in *Standard Oil*, as well as *American Tobacco*,[8] decided the same term, seemed to tie § 2 to § 1 without precluding a broader application.

[3] *United States v. United States Steel Corp.*

The parameters of § 2 became slightly more focused in *United States v. U.S. Steel Corp.*[9] There, all of the Justices agreed that ". . . the law does not make mere size an offense, or the existence of unexercised power an offense. It . . . requires overt acts."[10] Interestingly, as the following discussion of *Alcoa* demonstrates (§ 6.03, *infra*), this did not entirely lay to rest the question of whether § 2 could be a response to bigness *per se*.[11]

Although the Court in *United States Steel* was unanimous in its view that § 2 required both power and conduct, it was deeply divided on the application of this standard to the emergence and practices of U.S. Steel. The majority took the view that U.S. Steel had not achieved power over price, the measure of monopoly power,[12] because various collusive activities engaged in by U.S. Steel would not have been necessary if it had possessed monopoly power. Furthermore, according to the majority, the practices of U.S. Steel could be distinguished from those in *Standard Oil* and *American Tobacco* because the latter cases involved "a persistent and systematic lawbreaker masquerading under legal forms."[13] Finally, the majority was not

---

[6] *Id.* at 61.

[7] *Id.* at 72.

[8] *United States v. American Tobacco*, 221 U.S. 106 (1911).

[9] 251 U.S. 417 (1920).

[10] *Id.* at 451.

[11] *See infra* § 6.03[B].

[12] 251 U.S. at 444–46.

[13] *Id.* at 457.

concerned with practices leading to the accumulation of power because, in their view, the effort to gain control of the market had failed. As a general matter, the majority stressed the need to find wrongdoing by the defendant and suggested a close parallel between the type of conduct condemned by § 1 and the proper scope of § 2.

[B] *United States v. Aluminum Co. of America (Alcoa)*

The 1946 case of *United States v. Aluminum Co. of America*[14] *(Alcoa)* is typically regarded as the landmark monopolization case and the starting point for modern monopolization law. This is ironic because, read as a whole, Judge Hand's opinion would still leave any corporate counsel or antitrust scholar confused about the type of behavior that would lead to antitrust liability. On the other hand, *Alcoa* is critical as a foundation for further development of the monopolization offense.

Alcoa emphasized market power analysis as a component of the monopolization offense. More significantly, it made clear that § 2 would be applied to conduct beyond that condemned for multiple firms under § 1. It is emphasized here for its guidance on the evolution of § 2 standards.[15] A brief note is also in order on whether Judge Hand adhered to his own standards and whether those standards make for a coherent antitrust policy.

[1] **Background**

Alcoa was founded in 1888. It sold virgin "ingot" aluminum and, after 1895, produced aluminum products. Through patents Alcoa effectively possessed a legal monopoly on the production of aluminum until 1909. Alcoa's dominance was bolstered and extended by agreements with foreign competitors limiting competition and with power companies restricting the sale of electricity to potential domestic producers. These activities were enjoined by a consent decree in 1912. After 1912 Alcoa continued to be the only domestic producer of virgin ingot.[16] The Justice Department charged that Alcoa's continued existence as sole domestic producer violated § 2 of the Sherman Act.[17]

[2] **Market Definition**

The market share issue in *Alcoa* centered around the product and geographic markets for aluminum ingot. In addressing the market, Judge Hand saw three choices.[18] The first was a market composed of all the virgin

---

[14] 148 F.2d 416 (2d Cir 1945). *Alcoa* was heard by the Second Circuit Court of Appeals after four members of the Supreme Court disqualified themselves.

[15] *See, e.g.*, III P. Areeda & H. Hovenkamp, 16–28 (2d ed. 2002); Bork, *supra* note 4, at 163–75.

[16] 148 F.2d at 422–23.

[17] The complaint was filed in 1937.

[18] *See generally* 148 F.2d at 424–26.

ingot sold in the United States. This possibility would include all ingot produced by Alcoa including that which it used to produce aluminum products. The result was a 90% market share for Alcoa because only 10% of the ingot sold domestically was produced outside the U.S. The second choice was a market consisting of all virgin ingot plus "secondary" ingot (made from scrap). In this case Aloca's share was 64%. The final possibility was all virgin and secondary ingot sold in the United States excluding Alcoa's own consumption. Here Alcoa's share was 33%.

Judge Hand defined the relevant market as all the virgin ingot sold in the United States resulting in a market share of 90% for Alcoa. In settling on that choice, he recognized that secondary was an acceptable substitute for virgin ingot for many buyers and this could influence Alcoa's power vis–a–vis the sales of virgin ingot. He reasoned, however, that it was inappropriate to include secondary in the market because Alcoa, as the sole producer of virgin ingot, ultimately controlled the amount of secondary that was available.[19] The second step in his analysis was to include Alcoa's internal consumption of virgin ingot as part of the total market although it was not actually sold as ingot. Judge Hand noted that the market analysis was undertaken to determine Alcoa's control over price. Alcoa's use of its own ingot, according to Judge Hand, reduced demand for ingot and affected Alcoa's power.[20] Finally, although he recognized the possible limiting effect of foreign production on Alcoa's pricing, he concluded that this competition was not sufficiently threatening to keep Alcoa from wielding significant power over price.[21]

Judge Hand's market definition was pivotal because he deemed it "doubtful" that 64% would constitute a monopoly. Accordingly, 33% was definitely not a monopoly.[22] Some assumptions used in his market analysis are questionable. For example, the availability of secondary was likely to influence Alcoa's pricing behavior and probably should not have been excluded entirely from the market.[23] Similarly, the limiting effect foreign production had on Alcoa's power was probably not fully reflected by concentrating on actual, as opposed to potential, sales in the United States.[24] The lessons to be drawn, however, from this aspect of the opinion do not lie in questions one may have with Judge Hand's finding that Alcoa was a monopoly. What is instructive is the attention paid to structural detail as a step in § 2 analysis.

---

[19] Id. at 425.

[20] Id. at 424.

[21] Id. at 426.

[22] Id. at 424.

[23] Cf. II P. Areeda & D. Turner, Antitrust Law 391–92 (1978).

[24] See generally, Landes & Posner, Market Power in Antitrust Cases, 94 Harv. L. Rev. 937, 966–68 (1981).

[3] Alcoa's Conduct

Judge Hand's analysis of conduct can be interpreted in a number of ways. All interpretations, however, suggest a broad application of § 2. Much of the opinion is an indictment of bigness *per se*. This follows from his view that "great industrial consolidations are inherently undesirable, regardless of their economic results" and that the antitrust law was designed to preserve an "organization of industry in small units."[25] He reasoned that § 2, at a minimum, prohibits single firms from engaging in acts prohibited under § 1. Since § 1 prohibits a combination of firms from fixing prices, § 2 can be read as applying to the same actions by a monopolist.[26] Merely by operating, a monopolist would seem, therefore, to violate § 2.

Accordingly, "[h]aving proved that 'Alcoa' had a monopoly of the domestic ingot market, the plaintiff had gone far enough; if it was an excuse that 'Alcoa' had not abused its power, it lay on 'Alcoa' to prove that it had not."[27] In some measure, Judge Hand's discussion of abuse left only the narrowest defense for the monopolist since it seemed to require complete competitive passivity. Liability would not attach to a monopolist which had power "thrust upon it,"[28] or which gained its power by "force of accident,"[29] or was a "passive beneficiary."[30]

There is, however, additional language in the opinion that broadens the freedom of monopolists and is more consistent with subsequent development of monopolization law. First, Judge Hand observed that dominance resulting from "skill, foresight and industry"[31] was not to be condemned. Similarly, "[t]he successful competitor, having been urged to compete, must not be turned on when he wins."[32] Moreover, Judge Hand's analysis suggests that complete competitive passivity on behalf of the monopolist is not required. Indeed, in Alcoa's case he saw evidence of "persistent determination to maintain control."[33] Two of Alcoa's practices in particular seemed compelling to Judge Hand. The first was Alcoa's practice of maintaining excess capacity in order to meet increases in demand for ingot, thereby forestalling entry by potential competitors.[34] The second was Aloca's "price squeeze" or the practice of selling ingot to competing fabricators of "sheet" at prices that made it difficult for them to compete with Alcoa in the sale of sheet.[35]

---

[25] 148 F.2d at 429.

[26] *Id.* at 428.

[27] *Id.* at 427.

[28] *Id.* at 429.

[29] *Id.* at 430.

[30] *Id.*

[31] *Id.*

[32] *Id.*

[33] *Id.* at 430.

[34] *Id.* at 431.

[35] *Id.* at 436–37.

Judge Hand also addressed the intent requirement in monopolization cases. He rejected the notion that the intent requirement could be equated with the traditional concept of "specific intent" in criminal law. In Judge Hand's words, "no monopolist monopolizes unconscious of what he is doing."[36]

Judge Hand's opinion ranges from a condemnation of bigness *per se* to a call for an analysis of structure and conduct. His actual analysis of the facts suggests the latter is the proper lesson to be gleaned from the case. Moreover, questions about the maintenance of excess capacity and the "price squeeze" may miss the larger point. Whether Judge Hand applied his elusive standards in a way that would satisfy today's antitrust scholars is in many respects not important. The case stands as a beacon in the world of monopolization law. Its importance lies in its structural analysis and its signal that § 2 and § 1 are separate offenses with differing standards.

Judge Hand's views of monopolization received sweeping Supreme Court approval in 1946 in *American Tobacco Co. v. United States*.[37] The Court addressed the issue of whether actual exclusion was a necessary element of monopolization.[38] It determined that it was not and drew guidance from *Alcoa*.[39] In fact, the court quoted so extensively from Judge Hand's opinion that it can be seen as endorsing either the view that only passive monopoly is permissible or that a more searching examination of actual conduct is required.

[C]   The Search for Standards in the Aftermath of *Alcoa*

[1]   *United States v. Griffith*

The Supreme Court once again had an opportunity to address the issue of monopolization in *United States v. Griffith*.[40] A monopolization charge was leveled at theater owners who were monopolists in some towns but who faced competition in others. Through the mechanism of booking films for the entire chain, defendants were able to force film distributors to make concessions as a condition of having their films shown in the towns where the defendants were the only exhibitors. In essence, the monopoly possessed by the defendants in some towns arguably enabled them to gain an advantage in the towns in which they faced competition.[41]

Unfortunately, Justice Douglas's articulation of the guiding standard was no more enlightening than Judge Hand's in *Alcoa*. At one level he seemed to add credence to the view that § 2 is aimed at bigness alone: "[M]onopoly power, whether lawfully or unlawfully acquired, may itself constitute an

---

[36] *Id.* at 432.

[37] 328 U.S. 781 (1946).

[38] *Id.* at 808–09.

[39] *Id.* at 811–14.

[40] 334 U.S. 100 (1948).

[41] *See* the discussion of monopsony power *supra* at § 2.06[9].

evil and stand condemned under § 2 . . . ."[42] On the other hand, he offered the seemingly inconsistent view that "the existence of power 'to exclude competition when it is desired to do so' is itself a violation of § 2, provided it is coupled with the purpose or intent to exercise that power."[43]

Griffith also raised an issue that has yet to be fully addressed by the Supreme Court. In *Griffith*, the defendants were using power in some markets in order to gain competitive advantage in other markets. The issue left open is whether this use of "leverage" is itself a violation of § 2 of the Sherman Act or is a violation only if the defendant is likely to become a monopolist in the second market.[44]

[2] *United States v. United Shoe Machinery Corp.*

The lack of clarity in monopolization standards was recognized in *United States v. United Shoe Machinery Corp.*[45] Judge Wyzanski reviewed the possible interpretations of § 2 that seemed to be available after *Alcoa* and *Griffith*. First was the "classic" test under which § 2 prohibited single firm conduct that would be deemed illegal under § 1 if undertaken by two or more firms. Judge Wyzanski felt precluded from applying this test due to prior cases involving *United Shoe*.[46] A second approach, which Judge Wyzanski derived from Justice Douglas's *Griffith* opinion, was that monopolization entailed (1) the power to exclude competition and (2) the exercise or purpose to exercise that power.[47] A third choice was that monopolization occurs whenever the monopolist does business, or acts deliberately even if the conduct is not exclusionary. Judge Wyzanski regarded this approach as having been softened by the suggestion in *Alcoa* that a defendant could escape liability by proving that it owes its monopoly solely to superior skill, superior products, natural advantages . . . or technological efficiency."[48] Under the facts of *United Shoe* in which exclusionary conduct was found, Judge Wyanksi reasoned it was unnecessary to choose from the alternatives; nor was he destined to receive guidance from the Supreme Court.[49]

[3] *United States v. Grinnell*

One of the more recent events in the slow evolution of monopolization standards also involved Judge Wyzanski. In his *United States v. Grinnell*[50] opinion, he stated, no doubt hopefully, that since *Alcoa* "most . . . have

---

[42] 334 U.S. at 107.

[43] *Id.*

[44] *See* Hovenkamp, Federal Antitrust Policy 317–318 (2d ed. 1999).

[45] 110 F. Supp. 295 (D. Mass. 1953), *aff'd per curiam*, 347 U.S. 521 (1954).

[46] 110 F. Supp. at 343.

[47] *Id.* at 342.

[48] *Id.*

[49] *Id.* at 343.

[50] 236 F.Supp. 244 (D. R.I. 1964), *affirmed except as to decree*, 384 U.S. 563 (1966). For additional discussion of the facts of *Grinnell see* § 6.04[C][3].

expected that a day would come when the Supreme Court would announce that where one or more persons acting jointly had acquired so clear a dominance in a market as to have the power to exclude competition therefrom, there was a rebuttable presumption that such power was . . . punishable under § 2."[51] The presumption could be rebutted by a showing that the dominant power was attributable to superior skill, foresight and industry. This was, indeed, the approach Judge Wyzanski elected to employ.

The Supreme Court, upon review, acknowledged Judge Wyzanski's request but under the facts of the case felt that it was not required to decide whether a showing of monopoly power resulted in a rebuttable presumption that § 2 had been violated.[52] Although the Court did not settle the issue of the burden of proof it did offer what even today is regarded as the closest thing to a definitive statement of the monopolization offense:

> "The offense of monopoly under § 2 of the Sherman Act has two elements: (1) the possession of monopoly power in the relevant market and (2) the willful acquisition or maintenance of that power as distinguished from growth or development as a consequence of a superior product, business acumen, or historic accident."[53]

This most recent statement seems to be a clear adoption of the middle option outlined by Judge Wyzanski in *United Shoe*. Section 2 has not been interpreted broadly to condemn monopoly *per se*. Nor has it been so narrowly applied to extend only to actions that would violate § 1. The threshold issue is whether the firm has monopoly or market power. The second requirement — monopoly conduct — is far more difficult to articulate. It seems to require conduct that has as its primary purpose the elimination of competition by means that are independent of competitive merit, or that are predatory in nature. The best way to gain insight into the monopolization standard is to look more closely at how courts have reacted to fact patterns with which they have been confronted.

§ 6.04　Markets Under Section 2

The technical economic matters of market definition and assessing market power are the same regardless of the provision of the antitrust laws that is applicable. Most of the judicial discussion of market definition and market power, up until the mid 1970s took place in the context of § 2 cases. After the mid 1970s and the emergence of the rule of reason as the predominant analytical method, market analysis also became a focus of cases arising under § 1. The history of judicial interpretations of market power is discussed in some depth in Chapter 2. Thus, the principal focus throughout the remainder of this Chapter is the conduct component of § 2.

---

[51] 236 F. Supp. at 248.

[52] 384 U.S. at 576 n. 7.

[53] *Id.* at 570–71.

There is, however, a specific market power matter worth further examination. The issue falls under the general topic of matching the market with the alleged anticompetitive conduct. An instructive case is *Aquatherm Industries, Inc., v. Florida Power and Light* (FPL).[54] Aquatherm, a manufacturer of solar–power heating systems for swimming pools, complained that FPL had violated section § 2 by falsely advertising that electric heating was the most cost efficient. The markets affected, according the defendant, were those for pool heating equipment and for electric power. The problem was that FPL did not compete in the market for pool heating equipping and could hardly be said to be monopolizing it or attempting to monopolize it. In addition, FPL already had a 100% market share in the sale of electricity and, thus, could hardly increase its dominance.

A similar problem arose in *Intergraph Corporation v. Intel Corporation*[55] in which Intergraph complained that Intel's refusal to provide certain supplies and information amounted to a violation of § 2. The lower court found that Intel did possess monopoly power on the market for high–end microprocessors and for Intel microprocessors.[56] The problem, as the appellate court pointed out, was that Intergraph did not compete in either of these markets and that Intel did not compete with Intergraph in the market in which it operated. In short, for a monopolization or attempt to monopolize claim to be successful, the market power possessed by the defendant typically must be in the market in which the plaintiff operates. As noted below in the discussion of the "leverage" theory, this may vary in a narrow range of cases but even in those instances it is clear that the defendant must be a powerful participant in the plaintiff's market.[57]

§ 6.05 Monopolizing Conduct

As noted above, the announcement in *Grinnell* that monopolization requires "willful acquisition or maintenance of . . . power as distinguished from growth or development as a consequence of superior product, business acumen or historic accident"[58] is the leading, albeit vague, judicial statement of the conduct component of monopolization. Like so many areas of the law in which only general guidelines are available, monopoly conduct is most likely to be something that a court "knows when it sees it." A systematic analysis is made difficult because of the diversity of conduct arguably characterized as exclusionary.

The problem of classifying conduct properly is exacerbated by the fact that a great deal of conduct that has an exclusionary effect probably should not be condemned under the antitrust laws. For example, if an incumbent monopolist is experiencing economies of scale that a new entrant would be

---

[54] 145 F.3d 1258 (11 Cir. 1998).

[55] 195 F.3d 1346 (Fed Cir. 1999).

[56] *Id.* at 1354.

[57] *See* Section 6.05[D], *infra*.

[58] 384 U.S. at 570–71.

unable to achieve, there is a fairly clear and powerful barrier to entry. If the antitrust laws are efficiency sensitive, though, this is not the type of barrier to be condemned. The problem in each case is one of drawing the distinction between conduct that is competition on the merits, which only incidentally excludes competitors, and conduct that seems aimed primarily at excluding competitors either by preventing their entry or hastening their exit.

The key concept that has emerged in this regard is that of predation. As a general matter, conduct by a firm is predatory when it serves to benefit the firm only by virtue of the harm it does to its competitors. A simple case is useful in grasping this distinction. In a 1997 case, *American Professional Testing Service v. Harcourt, Brace and Jovanovich Legal and Professional Publications*,[59] a bar review service alleged another had engaged in monopolizing conduct by hiring away one of its professors. The court distinguished an instance in which a firm hires a key employee of another but does not use that employee itself from one in which the employee does actually perform services for the new employer. In both case, the expense of the hiring only makes economic sense if the increased revenues are higher than the cost. The problem is that in the first instance the increased profit will not be the result of anything that can be said to make the market more competitive or be of benefit to consumers. In the second case — the firm making use of the professor — the hiring firm can be said to be motivated by the belief that it can make better use of the professor than the first employer.

Of course, as the following cases amply illustrate, not all matters of alleged monopoly conduct are as easily assessed. In addition, predation analysis gets more complicated when a firm, rather than taking steps to injure a competitor, simply avoids taking actions that would assist the competitor. For example, suppose one firm would like access to and is willing to pay for an input over which a monopolist has sole control. By refusing to deal with the firm, the monopolist seems to be passing up an opportunity to increase profits and harming competition at the same time. These types of cases also are discussed below; they tend to be the most difficult to square with a straight–forward predation analysis.

Before turning to the great variety of conduct that has been scrutinized under § 2, two organizational notes are in order. In many monopolization cases, the conduct involved also may be examined to determine if it violates some other provision of the antitrust laws. When the conduct is more directly addressed by some other component of the antitrust laws, it is discussed in the section of this book devoted to that activity. Predatory pricing, currently a frequently discussed form of arguably exclusionary conduct, is reserved for discussion in conjunction with attempts to monopolize because the courts have most often addressed the issue in that context.

---

[59] 108 F.3d 1147 (9th Cir. 1997).

[A] Maintenance of Excess Capacity: *Alcoa*

An illustration of the difficulty of separating predatory conduct from desirable competitive conduct in found in the *Alcoa*'s reasoning that: "we can think of no more effective exclusion than progressively to embrace each new opportunity as it opened, and to face every newcomer with new capacity already geared into a great organization . . . ."[60] Maintenance of excess capacity enabled Alcoa to meet new demands faster and less expensively than competitors and allegedly retarded the entry of new producers. On the other hand, the activity was arguably predatory in nature — perhaps like hiring the law review lecturer but not using him — in that its ultimate profitability was dependent on blocking new entry.

Although it is relatively easy to reconcile Judge Hand's condemnation of Alcoa's conduct with the requirement that monopoly be "thrust upon" the defendant, it is more difficult to see how Alcoa's conduct deviated from his other standard which excused monopoly if it was the result of "skill, foresight, and industry." The problem with Judge Hand's analysis is that the maintenance of excess capacity may be beneficial to consumers. That is, Alcoa may have discouraged entry but did so by being a more attractive supplier in the eyes of buyers than any other firm. Indeed, Alcoa's activity even can be seen as a response to competition, albeit potential. Whether *Alcoa*, at least as far as the excess capacity issue is concerned, would be decided the same way today is open to serious question.

[B] Long Term Leasing: *United Shoe*

United Shoe, notable primarily because of Judge Wyzanski's efforts to articulate the competing conduct standards in monopolization cases, offers additional insight into the question of entry barriers. The defendant, a monopolist in the production of shoe manufacturing equipment leased the equipment for a term of ten years, but would not make the equipment available for purchase. Machines could be returned before the expiration of the lease with the payment of a return charge. This charge was reduced if the lessee replaced the machine with another United Shoe machine. Repair services were included as part of the rental arrangement. In addition, United Shoe evidently charged different prices for different machines depending upon competitive conditions.[61]

The cumulative effect of these practices, as seen by Judge Wyzanski, was retarding the entry of other producers of shoe manufacturing equipment. The long–term lease with reduced return charge possibilities had the effect of tying individual shoe manufacturers to United Shoe. The automatic inclusion of repair service foreclosed the development of an independent repair industry and meant that a new entrant into the shoe machinery industry would have to be integrated to offer machines and service. The leasing–only policy also allegedly retarded the development of a secondary

---

[60] 148 F.2d at 431.

[61] 110 F. Supp. at 314–29.

market in used machines. Judge Wyzanski concluded that the practices, "instead of encouraging competition based on pure merit, further[ed] the dominance of a particular firm."[62] Thus, the lease arrangement created "unnatural barriers."[63]

Contemporary criticism of both *Alcoa* and *United Shoe* are in a sense too easy because those cases were decided when an abstract statement of the conduct element of monopolization was in an embryonic stage. Indeed, at the time of the decisions, the role of efficiency was unclear and there was a possibility that bigness *per se* was the evil to be eliminated. In any case, the result in *United Shoe* is somewhat more comforting than that in *Alcoa*; the practices condemned in the former do seem to be designed to exclude directly competitors without being of great benefit to customers. In fact, if the practices would have been of great benefit to customers, rather than require them, one would have expected United Shoe simply to offer them as a option.

The conduct in *Alcoa*, on the other hand, arguably deterred entry only as an effect incidental to being an effective supplier. Still, Judge Wyzanski's analysis of United Shoe's conduct is vulnerable on a number of points. For example, selling machines with a useful life of 10 years seems as likely to exclude other manufacturers from the new machine market as 10-year leases.[64] The former, though, probably would not be deemed exclusionary. Similarly, the practice of forcing lessees to return machines forecloses competition with secondhand machines only if one assumes that second-hand machines are acceptable substitutes for new ones. Judge Wyzanski did not offer support for his supposition that used machines would compete in significant measure with sales of new machines.

[C]   Product Innovation and Predisclosure: *Berkey Photo Inc. v. Eastman Kodak Co.*[65]

In *Berkey Photo*, Kodak was charged with using its monopoly power in the film market to gain an advantage in the market for cameras by introducing a new film in a new format that could only be used in a camera manufactured by Kodak. The specific question was whether Kodak had monopolized by not disclosing to competing camera manufacturers the upcoming introduction of the new film.[66] In a sense, Kodak possessed unique information without which competitors would be unable to compete effectively. As such, *Berkey* represents one of many cases in which a court must determine whether a firm must share its resources or otherwise deal with competitors.[67]

---

[62] *Id.* at 345.

[63] *Id.*

[64] *See* R. Posner, *supra* note 3, at 203.

[65] 603 F.2d 263 (2d Cir), *cert. denied*, 444 U.S. 1093 (1980).

[66] *Id.* at 279–85. On the issue of leverage *see generally* Kaplow, *Extension of Monopoly Power Through Leverage*, 85 Colum. L Rev. 515 (1985).

[67] *See infra* § 6.05[E]

The Second Circuit Court of Appeals held that Kodak was not subject to a predisclosure duty. First, it disassociated Kodak's introduction of the new film from its market power. It found that even if Kodak had possessed a much smaller share of the market it would have been able to develop and market the new film and camera. Thus, even though Kodak had the requisite power in the film market, nondisclosure was not the use of that power.[68]

The court then considered the argument that predisclosure was required because Kodak had, in the past, excluded competitors by refusing to sell film in certain formats suitable for competing cameras or materials necessary for production of suitable film. In short, the question posited was whether past refusals to deal give rise to a predisclosure obligation. The court noted that refusal to make film available could support a § 2 charge. It found, however, that "the benefits that would flow to Kodak's rivals in the camera market from [predisclosure] bear no relationship to the injury caused them by the monopolist's refusal to sell film."[69] The possible evil inherent in Kodak's past conduct was not sufficiently connected with the current issue of disclosure to warrant a finding that nondisclosure was violative of § 2.

Two facets of *Berkey* are worth noting. First, although it is hard to imagine a case in which the Second Circuit would now require predisclosure, as a technical matter, neither of the lines of reasoning offered by the court rule out that possibility. Second, and far more important, is the *Berkey* court's vision of allowable monopoly conduct:

> So long as we allow a firm to compete in several fields, we must expect it to seek the competitive advantages of its broad based activity — more efficient production, greater ability to develop complementary products, reduced transaction costs and so forth. These are gains that accrue to any integrated firm, regardless of its market share, and they cannot by themselves be considered uses of monopoly power.[70]

This is obviously a very different view than that expressed by Judge Hand for the same court in *Alcoa* 35 years earlier. In his view the only permissible monopolies were essentially passive. The *Berkey* court laid this approach to rest in favor of one that permits the monopolist competitive latitude approaching that of its smallest competitor.[71] Now over twenty years later, it seems clear that the *Berkey* court's view of the competitive latitude allowed monopolists is representative of courts generally.

---

[68] 603 F.2d at 283.

[69] *Id.* at 284.

[70] *Id.* at 276.

[71] *See also Olympia Equip. Leasing v. Western Union Tel.*, 797 F 2d 370, 375 (7th Cir. 1986), *cert. denied*, 480 U.S. 934 (1987); *Foremost Pro Color Inc. v. Eastman Kodak Co.*, 703 F.2d 534, 544 (9th Cir. 1983), *cert. denied*, 465 U.S. 1038 (1984).

[D] Physical and Technological Ties

The facts in *Berkey* also gave rise to another monopolization claim against Kodak founded on a different theory. In *Foremost Pro Color Inc. v. Eastman Kodak Co.*,[72] Kodak was charged with monopolizing the "amateur photographic market" by creating technological incompatibilities. The essence of the complaint was that by producing a desirable film in a format that was only usable in cameras produced by Kodak and which required different paper, chemicals and photofinishing equipment than generally in use, Kodak was able to extend its power by rendering obsolete the cameras and photofinishing services of competitors. Although there was no requirement that a purchaser buy film, cameras, and processing from Kodak, the plaintiff claimed that the incompatibility produced the same result. The Court of Appeals for the Ninth Circuit, while recognizing that in some instances product innovation could violate § 2, ruled that the introduction of incompatible products, without additional abusive conduct, was not violative.[73]

A "tie" that was more physical than technical was addressed by the same court in *California Computer Products Inc. v. IBM Corp.*[74] Manufacturers of disk drives and memory units for computers charged IBM with monopolization when it began to market computers with the disk drives and memory units integrated into the central processing unit. According to the plaintiff, this "technological manipulation" resulted in a competitive disadvantage but did not improve performance. The evidence indicated, however, that the integrated computer was less expensive to produce and priced lower than nonintegrated models.[75] The court reasoned that IBM "had the right to redesign its products to make them more attractive to buyers — whether by reason of lower price or improved performance" and upheld a directed verdict for IBM.[76] *California Computer* as well as *Foremost Pro Color* leave open the possibility that innovations that do not result in superior products or lower prices could fulfill the conduct component of § 2. It seems doubtful, however, that such a strategy would very often make long–term economic sense to a producer.

[E] The Refusal to Supply an Essential Facility or Input

A number of antitrust cases center around one firm's refusal to supply something to another that the second firm needs to be competitive. In some of these cases the issue is whether the "essential facilities" doctrine is applicable. In others the issue is whether the firm has engaged in illegal "refusal to deal." As a practical matter, there is little reason to apply these theories differently. They both address the issue of when a firm is required

---

[72] 703 F.2d 534 (9th Cir. 1983), *cert. denied*, 465 U.S. 1038 (1984).

[73] *Id* at 544–45.

[74] 613 F.2d 727 (9th Cir. 1979).

[75] *Id.* at 744.

[76] *Id.*

to cooperate with a competitor in order to avoid antitrust liability. The refusal to supply can be seen as (1) an effort by the monopolist to protect its dominant position or (2) part of an effort to vertically integrate. Put differently, the practice may enable a firm to solidify its hold in a market in which it already possesses power or it may be part of an effort to extent power into another market. Cases of the second sort are closely related to the technological manipulation and physical ties discussed above, and the price squeeze discussed below. For example, in *California Computer* plaintiff argued that IBM was using its power in the central processing unit market to enhance its power in the disk drive and memory unit markets. In a sense, even *Berkey* can be seen as such a case in that Kodak's refusal to supply a scarce resource (information concerning the technology of its new film) was designed to extend Kodak's power in the market for cameras.

[1]   The "Essential Facilities" Doctrine

The general proposition that monopolists may in certain circumstances be required to cooperate with competitors dates to the 1912 case of *United States v. Terminal Railroad*.[77] A group of railroads acquired control of St. Louis' rail terminal facilities and a bridge crossing the Mississippi River. By controlling this "essential facility" the combination was able to discriminate against competitors and gain an advantage in rail service. The Court held that acquisition and control of the terminal facilities by a group of railroads smaller than the total number dependant on the facilities was a violation of §§ 1 and 2 of the Sherman Act. The Court ordered that any existing or future railroad be allowed to participate in ownership and control.[78]

The implications of *Terminal Railroad* have hovered over the field of antitrust for over 90 years without having a great deal of influence. No doubt, its lack of impact may be due in large measure to its unique factual setting. In addition, the Court's unitary analysis of §§ 1 and 2 of the Sherman Act make it difficult to determine its application.[79] Finally, *Terminal Railroad* raised an antitrust issue with enormous political implications and one that the courts may prefer to avoid: When does a monopolist attain quasi-public utility status?

Terminal Railroad seemed to experience a modest rebirth in *Aspen Skiing Co. v. Aspen Highlands Skiing Corp.*[80] The plaintiff, Aspen Highlands (Highlands), was the operator of a single mountain ski facility in Aspen, Colorado. The defendant, Aspen Skiing (Ski Co.), owned the three remaining ski areas. For a period of time they cooperated in offering an "all-Aspen" ticket which enabled the purchaser to ski on any of the four

---

[77] 224 U.S. 383 (1912); *See generally*, IIIA P. Areeda & H. Hovenkamp, *Antitrust Law* 164–227 (2d ed. 2002).

[78] 224 U.S. at 411.

[79] In *Otter Tail Co. v. United States*, 410 U.S. 366 (1973), the Supreme Court considered the essential facilities issue in the context of a single firm.

[80] 472 U.S. 585 (1985).

areas. The allocation of revenues between the parties was based on the relative use. Eventually Ski Co. offered to continue the all–Aspen pass only if Highlands accepted a fixed percentage of the revenues. Highlands found the percentage offered unacceptable and the all–Aspen ticket was discontinued. Highland's attempts to duplicate the all–Aspen pass by offering a package which included passes for its single mountain and negotiable instruments that could be used to purchase passes from Ski Co. were not successful and its market share fell from 20% to 11% over a four year period.[81]

Highlands claimed that Ski Co. had monopolized by refusing to cooperate in making the multi–area ticket available. A jury verdict for the Highlands was upheld by the Tenth Circuit Court of Appeals which reasoned that (1) under *Terminal Railroad*, Ski Co. was required to cooperate in offering the multi–area pass and (2) there was sufficient evidence to support the finding that Ski Co.'s intent was to "create or maintain a monopoly."[82] On review, the Supreme Court addressed whether the jury's finding was"erroneous as a matter of law because it rests on an assumption that a firm with monopoly power has a duty to cooperate with its smaller rivals . . . ."[83]

The Court began its analysis by observing that there was no general duty for a monopolist to cooperate with a rival and that the trial court unambiguously had instructed the jury to that effect. The right not to cooperate was not, however, unqualified. In this instance, the trial court had instructed the jury that Ski Co. had not violated § 2 if there were valid business reasons for the refusal to cooperate. The jury found that there were no valid business reasons. The Supreme Court reviewed the business justifications offered by Ski Co. and considered whether the change in policy created a gain in efficiency.[84] It held that the jury's finding, that there was an absence of a valid business reason, was not clearly erroneous and therefore must be upheld. The Court suggested that Ski Co.'s conduct was essentially predatory because the change in policy resulted in losses to Ski Co. which it evidently hoped to recoup once the damage to Highlands had been accomplished.[85]

Under *Aspen* it now seems clear that as a firm gains market power its freedom to refuse to deal with another firm is qualified by the need for a valid business justification. The lure of additional profit alone is evidently not such a valid business reason. However, the opportunity for increased profit through greater efficiency does meet this standard. This pronouncement did not deviate from settled § 2 law. The Court supported the notion that acquisition of power through superior efficiency is permissible.

[81] *Id.* at 593–95.

[82] 738 F.2d 1509, 1520–23 (10th Cir. 1984).

[83] 472 U.S. at 587. The approach taken by the Court meant that it was unnecessary to address the relevance of the "essential facilities" doctrine. *Id.* at 611, n. 44.

[84] *Id.* at 605–06.

[85] *Id.* at 610–11.

Aspen can be read as imposing a positive duty on a monopolist to cooperate with competitors as a means of preventing their exclusion when it does not harm its own ability to offer a superior product in the market. Although the Court claimed not to address the issue of essential facilities and it did not directly address the Tenth Circuit's finding that cooperation was required under *Terminal Railroad*, it seemed to breathe new life into the doctrine. After all, Highlands' case was compelling because it probably could not survive without the cooperation of Ski Co. Indeed, it is hard to imagine an instance in which a monopolist would be required to cooperate with a smaller rival unless an essential facility or resource is involved. [86]

Of course, the existence of an antitrust theory like the "essential facilities doctrine" does not assure that its boundaries are defined clearly. In some instances, a facility need not be unique or indispensable in order to be essential. [87] Moreover, the holding in *Aspen* would seem to differ if the defendant merely rejected an initial offer to participate in the joint venture. [88] Here, however, a monopolist with a 75% market share elected to make an important change in the pattern of distribution and access to the product. The change dramatically affected not only a rival's cost of doing business but the availability of a product to consumers. Thus, after *Aspen*, one might have expected a growth in the essential facilities doctrine with the pivotal issues being how much a competitor's costs will increase if access to the facility or product is refused, [89] and how consumer interests are affected. Despite the opening *Aspen* may have created, the essential facilities doctrine remains fairly dormant. [90]

Courts have announced various formulations of the essential facilities doctrine. For example, in *MCI Communications Corp. v. American Telephone and Telegraph*, [91] the Seventh Circuit Court of Appeals indicated that the doctrine would apply when (1) the essential facility is controlled by a monopolist, (2) a competitor cannot reasonably duplicate the facility, (3) the monopolist denies access to the facility and (4) it would be feasible for access to be provided. [92] This later requirement would seem to preclude requiring

---

[86] For an application of the essential facilities doctrine to an arguably natural monopoly market *see Fishman v. Wirtz*, 807 F.2d 520 (7th Cir. 1986). *Aspen* was distinguished in *Olympia Equipment Leasing v. Western Union Telegraph*, 797 F.2d 370 (7th Cir 1986), *cert. denied*, 480 U.S. 934 (1987).

[87] *See Fishman*, 807 F.2d at 533; *MCI Communications Corp. v. AT&T*, 708 F.2d 1081, 1152 (7th Cir.), *cert. denied*, 464 U.S. 891 (1983); *Hecht v. Pro Football Inc.*, 570 F.2d 982, 922 (D.C. Cir 1977), *cert. denied*, 436 U.S. 956 (1978).

[88] This has been the case in subsequent decisions. See *e.g. Simlecare Dental Group v. Delta Dental Plan of California*, 88 F.3d 780 (9th Cir. 1996), *cert denied*, 519 U.S. 1028 (1996).

[89] For a discussion of predatory pricing *see* § 6.06[E], *infra. See also* Krattenmaker & Salop, *Anticompetitive Exclusion: Raising Rival's Costs To Achieve Power Over Price*, 96 Yale L. J. 209 (1986).

[90] *See e.g. Alaska Airlines, Inc. v. United Airlines, Inc.*, 948 F.2d 563 (9th Cir. 1991); *Twin Laboratories, Inc. v. Weider Health and Fitness*, 900 F.2d 566 (2d Cir. 1990); *Olympic Equip. Leasing v. Western Union Tel. Co.*, 797 F.2d 370 (7th Cir. 1986).

[91] 708 F.2d 1081 (7th Cir. 1983).

[92] *Id.* at 1132–33.

a firm to provide access that would lower the quality of its own offering in the market.

An element of this test that was critical recently is the relationship between the firm desiring access and the firm denying access. In *Intergraph Corporation v. Intel Corporation,*[93] the plaintiff complained that the refusal by Intel to continue supplying Advance Chip Samples and design and technical information violated § 2.[94] The Federal Circuit Court of Appeals refused to apply the essential facilities doctrine, reasoning that Intergraph and Intel were not competitors in the market affected by the essential facility. This is a important distinction. The question is not whether the market in which Intergraph operated was likely to become less competitive. Instead it was whether Intel was making an effort to monopolize that market. This is because the concept of "monopolization" must be in reference to a specific market. In this instance, Intel could not be viewed as monopolizing or attempting to monopolize a market in which it did not compete.

An issue that arises when considering essential facilities and the related notion of a refusal to deal is whether the chronology of events makes a difference. For example, in *Aspen*, the plaintiff stopped participating in offering the joint ticket. Suppose instead there had never been a joint ticket and that a new firm operating a single mountain had approached Ski Co. with a proposal for a joint ticket and refused. This would be similar to *Terminal Railroad* in which there had not been a prior profitable relationship. In the case of the firm refusing to cooperate when there had not been a prior arrangement, one could argue that the element of predation is present in the sense that the dominant firm has passed on a possibly competition enhancing opportunity for the purpose of maintaining its monopoly. The element of predation, however, is more likely to be established when a firm discontinues a relationship that it had found to be profitable and which had made the market more competitive. Conversely a firm that has not cooperated is probably more likely to be able to support its preference for the status quo.[95]

[2] Refusals to Deal and Vertical Integration

Closely related to the essential facilities doctrine is the notion of a "refusal to deal." The typical scenario involves a manufacturer, also operating at the retail level, which refuses to sell to independently owned retail competitors.[96] Because a refusal alone could be predatory in nature, courts tend to look for valid justifications for these refusals. *Otter Tail v. United*

---

[93] 195 F.3d 1346 (Fed. Cir. 1999).

[94] *Id.* at 1356.

[95] *See e.g. SmileCare Dental Group v. Delta Dental Plan of California, Inc.*, 88 F.3d 780 (9th Cir. 1996).

[96] *See, e.g., Eastman Kodak Co. of New York v. Southern Photo Materials Co.*, 273 U.S. 359 (1927); *Paschall v. Kansas City Star Co.*, 727 F.2d 692 (8th Cir.) (*en banc*), *cert. denied*, 469 U.S. 872 (1984).

States[97] is a case of a refusal to deal that can also be seen as involving an essential facility. The defendant was a monopolist operator of electric transmission lines and producer of electricity selling electricity directly to retail customers. When Otter Tail's franchise to sell electricity in four municipalities terminated, the municipalities attempted to set up their own retail distribution schemes selling electricity produced or transmitted by Otter Tail. Otter Tail refused to sell electricity to the municipalities or to transmit electricity the municipalities had purchased from other producers.[98]

The Supreme Court held that Otter Tail's refusal to deal violated § 2 because it involved the use of monopoly power in one market as leverage to gain power in another market.[99] Otter Tail's status as a regulated firm possibly influenced the Court's decision.[100] The case indicates, however, that in some instances a monopolist supplier may not refuse to sell when the effect is to destroy competitors. One interpretation is that, while it is not unlawful for a monopolist to integrate forward, the integration must not be fostered through the use of the firm's market power.

Paschall v. Kansas City Star,[101] is representative of the modern view of vertical integration by a monopolist. The case involved a monopoly newspaper publisher that integrated forward by replacing all of its independent carriers with its own delivery agent–employees. Plaintiffs alleged that the newspaper had used its power in the newspaper publishing and wholesale market to displace them in the retail market.

The Eighth Circuit Court of Appeals, sitting *en banc*, determined that the legitimate business purposes put forth by the Star negated a showing of specific intent.[102] It then turned to the question of whether the plaintiff had carried the burden of showing that the integration had an anticompetitive effect. The mainstay of the district court holding for the discharged carriers was the "potential competition" concept typically seen in merger cases. In short, the integration removed the Star as a potential retail competitor thus making the market less competitive.[103] According to the appellate court, the possibility of a dramatic decline in competition in the retail market was off–set by the unlikelihood that a monopolist at one level in the chain of production and distribution can increase its monopoly profit by raising prices and restricting output at a point further down the chain.

---

[97] 410 U.S. 366 (1973).

[98] *Id.* at 368–77.

[99] *Id.* at 377.

[100] Professors Areeda and Hovenkamp suggest that vertical integration by *Otter Tail* may have been motivated by a desire to side–step federal regulation and collect monopoly profits at the retail level. IIA P. Areeda & H. Hovenkamp 355 (2d ed. 2002).

[101] 727 F.2d 692 (8th Cir.) (*en banc*), *cert. denied*, 469 U S. 872, 222 (1984). *See generally* Note, *Application of the Antitrust Laws to Newspaper Distribution Systems: The Sherman Act Turned on Its Head*, 38 U. Fla. L. Rev. 479 (1987).

[102] According to the court, proof of monopolization required either a showing of specific intent or anticompetitive effects. 727 F.2d at 696.

[103] *Id.* at 699–700. *See* discussion *infra* in Chapter 7.

Moreover, under the facts of the case, each independent carrier served an exclusive territory and, therefore, possessed monopoly power within that territory. Thus, a group of monopolists was replaced by another monopolist. Finally, since the newspaper's advertising revenues were tied to circulation, higher retail prices seemed an unlikely goal of the newspaper publisher. The sharply divided court concluded that the plaintiff had not met its burden of proof.

[3]   The Economics of Vertical Integration

Pascall and similar cases may lead to the question of why all refusals to deal leading to vertical integration are not ultimately predatory. Put differently, are all of these cases ones in which competitors are harmed without any improvement in the market? In fact, the question of whether the activity is predatory or not extends to cases involving physical or technological ties and even the "price squeeze," which is discussed below. In order to understand why these refusals and the resulting vertical integration may not be predatory and ultimately harmful to consumers, it is useful to understand the "Chicago School" approach to such matters.[104]

The majority opinion in *Paschall* is unusual in the candor with which the Chicago School approach to antitrust, especially with respect to vertical restraints, is applied. For example, the court cites the oft–stated argument that vertical integration by a monopolist is rarely motivated by the opportunity to raise prices and restrict output at the retail level.[105] The reason for this is that a monopolist manufacturer, selling to those who resell under competitive conditions, can capture all the monopoly profit available by making the right price and output decision at the manufacturing level.

If the resellers are not competitive, there are opportunities for the monopolist to increase profit through vertical integration, but this does not mean higher prices and lower output. For example, if the retail level is characterized by market power due to a cartel or a monopolist, vertical integration can result in lower prices, higher output and increased profit for the monopolist manufacturer.[106] If retailers have monopsony power — market power as buyers — vertical integration may permit the monopolist to transfer to itself some of the profit captured by the retailers. This does not mean, however, that prices to consumers will necessarily increase. In addition, the monopolist may increase its profit if it is a more efficient distributor than the independent retailers. But, this is not a profit attributable to monopoly power as such. Finally, although vertical integration may

---

[104] *See* R. Bork, *supra* note 4, at 225–45, 365–81; IIIA P. Areeda & H. Hovenkamp, *Antitrust Law* 13–19 (2d ed. 2002).

[105] 727 F.2d at 701. Although the court's opinion is marked by candor, it is not similarly marked by clarity. Its discussion of "optimum monopoly price theory" seems to be a defense of vertical integration based on the notion that successive monopoly does not ordinarily mean higher prices and lower output. *See Paschall v. Kansas City Star*, 695 F.2d 322, 328 (8th Cir. 1982).

[106] P. Areeda & H. Hovenkamp. *supra* note 104, at 27–32.

increase the monopolist's ability to practice price discrimination, even this does not mean that there will be higher prices and lower output. Thus, as the argument goes, a refusal to sell to those with whom the firm might end up competing is not always explained by a predatory motivation.

The common argument against vertical integration by a monopolist is that it increases the difficulty of entry by competitors. In particular, a competitor will not be able to enter unless it integrates and this is more costly than entry at one level. Consequently, the monopolist is able to block entry and collect supracompetitive profits. The *Paschall* court disposed of this argument by noting that the Star's carriers were permitted to deliver newspapers for other publishers as well; thus, barriers to entry into newspaper publishing did not increase. [107]

The argument generally offered against the "barriers to entry" justification for limiting vertical integration is that the lure of supracompetitive profits will attract new investors. If any barriers exist, they are, essentially, financial. Financial barriers are, however, the type that can be overcome if investors see an opportunity to produce efficiently enough to undersell the monopolist and earn a return on their investment. Consequently, failure to enter may be an indication that the opportunity for more efficient production is just not present.

When a monopolist controls a unique resource or is a natural monopoly, entry barriers may seem to exist beyond those that are simply financial. It is important to note, however, that the barrier is only to the industry becoming more competitive. This does not mean that a potential entrant who sees the opportunity for gain cannot buy out the "right" that shelters the monopolist from competition. The lure of profit may result, in the absence of prohibitive transaction costs, in the entry of a new monopolist. To the extent greater profit is traceable to lower operating costs, a portion of these savings may be passed on to consumers.

Two final observations are in order on the issue of vertical integration by a monopolist. First, for the most part, the Chicago School argument for a permissive approach to integration by monopolists is based on microeconomic theory and, like most theories, relies on a number of assumptions. For the Chicago School's refutation of the "barriers to entry" objection to vertical integration to work, transaction costs must not be prohibitive. In particular, even though the barriers are essentially financial, potential entrants must identify markets offering opportunities for profit and gauge the magnitude of those opportunities. In addition, entry is more attractive if the incumbent is operating inefficiently. Acquisition of this type of information — especially about possible inefficiencies — may be costly or impossible to obtain. The effect can be to retard entry even when entry would be justified on the basis of the return available.

Second, one's response to the economic arguments in favor of permitting vertical integration by a monopolist depends on one's view of the proper

---

[107] 727 F.2d at 702.

goals of antitrust policy. Without reviewing all the arguments again,[108] it is important to note that the efficiency justification for permitting vertical integration assumes that efficiency is the sole goal of antitrust. Moreover, if there is any "value," for whatever reason, to be attributed to the survival of small competitors, the efficiency measure relied upon is underinclusive.[109] All this being said, it seems clear that simply passing up opportunities to generate revenue by selling to competitors cannot automatically be condemned as predatory.

[F] Price Squeeze

"Price squeeze" is the term used when a manufacturer of a raw material that both fabricates the raw material and sells it to others for fabrication, raises the price of the raw material to competing fabricators while lowering its own price of the finished product in order to make it impossible for independent fabricators to survive. Indeed, in *Alcoa*, Judge Hand found such a practice to be an abuse of Alcoa's power in the ingot market.

More recently, in *Bonjorno v. Kaiser Aluminum & Chemical Corp.*,[110] Kaiser was charged with raising the price of raw materials for one class of fabricators to the same rate it charged for the finished product. The Court of Appeals for the Third Circuit upheld a jury verdict for the plaintiff explaining that "[w]hen a monopolist competes by denying a source of supply to his competitors, raises his competitors' prices for raw materials without affecting his own costs, . . . and threatens his competitor with sustained competition . . . his actions have crossed the shadowy barrier of the Sherman Act."[111] It is not clear that the view of the *Bonjorno* court would be shared by others today. Under a more modern analysis, the issue would seem to be whether the defendant had engaged in predatory pricing with respect to the final product. If it has not, condemnation of the "price squeeze" would amount to basing liability on simply setting the price for the raw material. Unilateral price determination by a monopolist, unless the price is predatory, generally will not satisfy the conduct part of a monopolization claim.[112]

[G] Raising Rivals' Costs

A price squeeze is a direct way of raising the costs of competitors. As suggested earlier, however, the denial of access to "essential facilities" and

---

[108] *See* The Political Economy of the Sherman Act: The First One Hundred Years (E. Thomas Sullivan ed., 1991).

[109] *See* Hovenkamp, *supra* note 5; *see also* Harrison, *Egoism, Altruism, and Market Illusions: The Limits of Law and Economics*, 33 UCLA L. Rev. 1309 (1986).

[110] 752 F.2d 802 (3d. Cir. 1984), *cert. denied*, 477 U.S. 908 (1986).

[111] 752 F.2d at 812.

[112] As the discussion of predatory pricing which follows indicates, antitrust doctrine has, from time to time, addressed the question of whether limit pricing (prices above cost but below short-term profit-maximizing levels) is anticompetitive conduct.

refusals to deal generally also can be viewed as efforts to increase the costs of rivals. A theory of when efforts to raise rivals' costs should run afoul of the antitrust laws is in the development stage. So far, the theory of nonprice predation which focuses on strategic behavior of a competitor designed to raise rival's costs without increasing its own has received considerable attention from commentators,[113] but scant attention from the courts.

The theory posits that a firm may cause the costs, and ultimately the prices, of a competitor to increase. The effect is to create an umbrella under which the firm then has the freedom to raise its own prices above competitive levels. Raising the cost of a rival could either increase the market power of the firm or simply enable it to maintain existing power. Moreover, possession of market power is not required necessarily in order to cause the cost of a rival to increase. Thus, the activity could fulfill the conduct component of a charge of either monopolization or attempted monopolization. The general argument has been advanced that "[r]aising [a] rival's costs is a more credible way to market power than is predatory pricing because it is not necessary to cause the rival to exit, no 'deep pocket' is required, and additional profits are gained immediately."[114]

In order to be effective, the firm must be able to raise substantially its rival's costs. This means that the firm must have considerable direct or indirect control over an input that makes up a not insignificant portion of its rival's total cost of production. The difficulties of establishing this factor and a resulting anticompetitive impact may cause the theory to be difficult to apply in litigation.[115]

The purest example of raising a rival's cost is an instance in which a firm simply refuses to supply an input or causes other firms to refuse to supply an input, thus causing the competitor to rely on a more expensive source.[116] The theory can, however, have much broader applications. For example, *Aspen* could be interpreted as a case in which the defendant engaged in such conduct. Similarly, *Berkey Photo* can be viewed as a case in which product innovation led to increased costs for rivals who would have to engage in extraordinary research efforts in order to compete effectively. Herein lies a major problem with the theory. Many activities that cause the costs of competitors to increase are simply side effects of "competition on the merits." Others may be specifically designed to harm competitors without benefitting consumers. The mere fact that an action raises the costs

---

[113] *See, e.g.* Nonprice Predation Under Section 2 of the Sherman Act (E.T. Sullivan, ed. 1991); Krattenmaker & Salop, *supra* note 110; Hovenkamp, *Antitrust Policy, Restricted Distribution and the Market for Exclusionary Rights*, 71 Minn. L. Rev. 1293 (1987); Salop, *New Economic Theories of Economic Exclusion*, 56 Antitrust L.J. 57 (1967); Salop & Scheffman, *Raising Rival's Costs*, 73 Am. Econ. Rev. 267 (1983); *see also* Calkins, *A Comment on the Presentation of Steven C. Salop*, 56 Antitrust L.J. 65 (1987).

[114] Krattenmaker & Salop, *Competition and Cooperation in the Market for Exclusionary Rights*, 76 Am. Econ Rev 109 (1986). *See also Aspen*, 472 U.S. at 610–11.

[115] *See* Calkins, *supra* note 113, at 66–67; Salop, *supra* note 113 at 59–60.

[116] *Klor's v. Broadway–Hale Stores, Inc.*, discussed in Chapter 4, has been offered as an example. *See* Salop, *New Economic Theories of Economic Exclusion, supra* note 113, at 60–61.

of rivals does not mean one can escape the issue that plagues monopolization law: when is the activity ultimately beneficial and when is its primary purpose the exclusion or hampering of others?

In *Ball Memorial Hospital Inc. v. Mutual Hospital Inc.,*[117] the Seventh Circuit Court of Appeals considered the argument that the low rates paid by a health care insurer to hospitals providing service to its subscribers would force the hospitals to shift costs to patients covered by other insurers, thereby making it more difficult for those insurers to compete. The court declined to apply the theory of raising a rival's costs to find liability, noting that shifting costs was only possible if the insurer possessed market power which, in the case at hand, it did not.

[H] *United States v. Microsoft*[118]

The issue of monopolistic conduct came to the forefront in the much publicized *Microsoft* case. The long term importance of the case, as far as monopolization doctrine is unclear, but the actual practices involved are representative of the types created by new technology.[119] The principal questions with respect to monopoly conduct arose from a series of practices in which Microsoft engaged in order to protect the dominant position of its operating system (Windows). The means of protecting the operating system was to retard development of browsers other than its own Internet Explorer. In order to understand the connection, it is important to understand the chicken and egg like relationship between the operating system and application software. As long as there is one dominant operating system, developers are highly motivated to write software for that operating system. Conversely, as long as software is predominately written for a specific operating system, it is difficult for new operating systems to emerge.

Development of substitute browsers was a threat because browsers can include protocols — Application Programming Interfaces (APIs) — that are widely used in operating systems. If written expansively enough, a browser (or other versions of what is called middleware) could take over many of the functions of an operating system. Software written for a specific operating system would not then be dependent on the user actually using that specific operating system. The lower cost of writing software that could be used on a variety of operating systems would then mean other operating systems could emerge as reasonable substitutes.

Microsoft was alleged to have used numerous tactics to protect its operating system. The court broke these practices into a number of categories. For example, one category concerned Microsoft's relationship with original equipment manufacturers (OMBs). These generally involved packaging its own browser, Internet Explorer (IE), with Windows in order to

---

[117] 784 F.2d 1325 (7th Cir. 1986). *But see Reazin v. Blue Cross & Blue Shield of Kansas, Inc.,* 635 F. Supp. 1287 (D. Kan. 1986) (jury award on theory of raising rival's costs).

[118] 253 F.3d 34 (D.C. Cir. 2002).

[119] For a discussion of the market power issues raised in the *Microsoft* case, *see* Chapter 2.

make it unlikely that a user would substitute another browser. For instance, in its licensing agreements with original equipment manufacturers, OEM, Microsoft required that the start up icons for IE not be removed and that the OEM not create a boot–up sequence that would allow users to choose from a variety of competing browsers.

A second category concerned the actual physical integration of the operating system and the browser. In effect, Microsoft integrated Windows and IE to make it difficult to delete IE. The theory was that OEMs would be unlikely to preinstall another browser if IE could not be removed because that would raise its support costs. Microsoft also did not include IE in the add/remove menu.

Another category concerned the agreements Microsoft had with internet access providers (IAPs), like America On Line. Microsoft offered IE free to the IAPs, offered financial incentives for signing customers up for services using IE, and entered into reciprocal agreements that guaranteed the promotion of IE. Under these later agreements, Microsoft provided easy desktop access to IAPs that promoted the IE browser.[120]

The unanimous appeals court sitting *en banc* held that Microsoft was guilty of monopolization under § 2 for maintaining its monopoly in the operating system. The court largely rejected Microsoft's arguments that it did not possess monopoly power or that there should be an exception for network effects.[121] With respect to conduct, the court found unlawful the licensing and contractual agreements with OEMs and IAPs. Microsoft's licenses had the effect of reducing usage share of Netscape's browser by preventing OEMs from distributing browsers other than Microsoft's IE. In addition, the court held that the contracts with the IAPs were also exclusionary, as were exclusive dealing arrangements with Apple and threats directed to Intel.

The Microsoft litigation has been the subject of a great deal of discussion and debate.[122] Whether the district court or the appellate court reached the "right" answer will no doubt continue to be debated for years. For the purposes here, it is important to note that the analytical approach of the appellate court to monopoly conduct seemed consistent with the idea of determining whether Microsoft's efforts amounted to "competition on the merits," likely to benefit consumers, or were more designed to promote Microsoft's ends by harming competitors. In analyzing each of Microsoft's practices, the court first assessed whether there was an anticompetitive

---

[120] Other categories included (1) Microsoft's dealings with Internet content providers, independent software vendors and Apple Computer and (2) efforts to retard the development of Java.

[121] *See* discussion in Chapter 2, infra. *See also* E. T. Sullivan, *The Jurisprudence of Antitrust Divertiture: The Path Less Traveled*, 86 Minn. L. Rev. 565, 568 (2002).

[122] *See e.g.* David S. Evans (Ed.) *Microsoft, Antitrust and the New Economy: Selected Essays* (2002); Ronald Cass & Keith N. Hylton, *Preserving Competition: Economic Analysis, Legal Standards and Microsoft*, 8 Geo. Mason L. Rev. 1 (1999); Steve C. Salop & Craig Romaine, *Preserving Monopoly: Economic Analysis. Legal Standards and Microsoft,* 8 Geo. Mason L. Rev. 617 (1999).

effect and then whether Microsoft had a procompetitive or valid business purpose.

To take a simple example, as already described, Microsoft required OEMs not to alter the desktop icons. In effect, if an OEM wanted to prepack a browser other than IE, it would have to prepackage and be ready to support two browsers. The anticompetitive effect was that OEMs were unlikely to prepackage two browsers because of increased support costs and the risk of consumer confusion.[123] In effect, by requiring the maintenance of IE, Microsoft was blocking the entry of other browsers. In addition to some copyright justifications that the court rejected,[124] Microsoft argued that the restrictions were designed to prevent OEMs from reducing the value of the operating system by undermining its stability and consistency.[125] Presumably, efforts to prevent OEMs from making the operating system less beneficial to consumers is precisely the type of valid business reason to which a court would be receptive. Microsoft evidently did not substantiate this argument, leaving the appellate court to reason that, since changing the *appearance* of the desktop had no effect on the actual internal codes of the system, it could hardly upset the system's stability and consistency.[126]

[I]   The Exercise of Monopsony Power

To this point in the discussion of monopoly conduct, the emphasis has been only on monopoly conduct. Technically, the concept of monopoly refers to the power of sellers of a good or service. In some instances, however, the "monopoly conduct" is, in reality, power on the buying side or demand side of the market.[127] A buyer having power over price and quantity is said to have monopsony power.[128] Although the abuse of monopsony power is a concept that has not been fully developed by the courts, it does fall within the ambit of § 2 and has been examined by courts in much the same manner as monopoly conduct.

One of the more influential § 2 cases involving monopsony power is *United States v. Griffith*.[129] Defendants operated movie theaters in a number of towns. In some towns (closed towns) they were the only exhibitor. In others, they faced competition. Of course, as an exhibitor–seller in the closed towns

---

[123] 253 F.3d at 61.

[124] *Id.* at 63.

[125] *Id.*

[126] *Id.* at 64.

[127] *See generally*, Blair & Harrison, *Antitrust Policy and Monopsony,* 76 Cornell. L. Rev. 297 (1991).

[128] The issues that arise in determining market power in the case of monopsony mirror those encountered when the market power of sellers is examined. *See* Blair & Harrison, *Cooperative Buying, Monopsony Power, and Antitrust Policy,* 86 NW Univ. L. Rev. 331 (1992).

[129] 334 U.S. 100 (1948). For an application of the concept of monopsony to college sports, see McKenzie & Sullivan, *Does the NCAA Exploit College Athletes: An Economic and Legal Analysis*, 32 Antitrust Bull. 373 (1987).

they possessed some degree of monopoly power. Similarly, as purchasers of films from distributors wishing to have their films shown in those towns, they possessed monopsony power. By linking closed and competitive towns in their negotiations with distributors, the defendants were able to obtain the first run rights to films for exhibition in both closed and competitive towns. The alleged effect was to increase the market power of the exhibitors in competitive towns. The Supreme Court held that a violation of § 2 had been shown. Although it did not discuss expressly the concept of monopsony power, it did so implicitly by condemning the use of "the buying power of the entire circuit" and "[l]arge scale buying."[130]

In *Griffith*, monopsony power was used to increase the exhibitors' market power in towns where it competed with other sellers. Monopsony power also may be used to achieve vertical integration. In the vertical integration cases discussed above, monopolists tended to integrate forward — manufacturing to retailing. In the case of the monopsonist, however, the temptation is to integrate backward. Thus, in the case of the monopsonist exhibitors, the expectation would be that the firm would set up its own distribution scheme and begin to either refuse to deal with or drastically lower the price they offer existing distributors in hopes of excluding them. For the most part, the arguments for and against prohibiting vertical integration by monopolists apply with equal force to vertical integration by monopsonists.

Monopsony power was addressed in a recent decision of the First Circuit Court of Appeals in *Kartell v. Blue Shield of Massachusetts*.[131] Blue Shield provided health insurance for about 74% of the Massachusetts residents who were privately insured. Under the agreement Blue Shield made with physicians, Blue Shield paid for the physicians' services as long as the physicians did not charge subscribers more than the amount paid by Blue Shield. The Blue Shield plan accounted for 14% of all physician practice revenue. The issue was whether Blue Shield's "ban on balance billing" violated §§ 1 or 2 of the Sherman Act.[132] Under the court's analysis, Blue Shield was viewed as a buyer of physicians services. The plaintiffs argued that, as a buyer, Blue Shield possessed market power that forced prices below those that would exist in a "freely competitive market," with the consequence of discouraging the entry of new doctors and the utilization of new medical techniques. Essentially, the complaint was that Blue Shield had used its monopsony power to obtain a low price. The court held that, even if Blue Shield had the power attributed to it, it had not violated the Sherman Act. To hold otherwise, the court noted, would be comparable to extending § 2 to monopoly pricing *per se*,[133] an option long since foreclosed. The court observed:

> Antitrust law rarely stops the buyer of a service from trying to determine the price or characteristics of the product that will be

---

[130] 334 U.S. 100 at 108.

[131] 749 F.2d 922 (1st Cir. 1984), *cert. denied*, 471 U.S. 1029 (1985).

[132] *Id*. at 926.

[133] *Id*. at 927.

sold. Thus, the more closely Blue Shield's activities resemble, in essence, those of a purchaser, the less likely that they are unlawful . . . .

. . . [C]ourts at least should be cautious — reluctant to condemn too speedily — an arrangement that, on its face, appears to bring low price benefits to the consumer.[134]

Although mere price setting by either single buyers or sellers with market power does not violate § 2 of the Sherman Act, it is incorrect as a matter of economic theory to believe that monopsonistically determined prices always will benefit consumers. This is particularly true when the buyer is in the market for inputs and employs monopsony power to obtain lower prices than would exist under competitive conditions. If the buyer offers a lower price, chances are that the seller will sell a lower quantity. Of course, fewer inputs typically mean a lower level of output. And, restrictions in output are generally associated with higher prices for the final good. Thus, the same kinds of welfare losses experienced under monopoly conditions also can be found under conditions of monopsony.[135]

§ 6.06 Attempt to Monopolize

Given the difficulty of arriving at a clear articulation of what constitutes monopolization, it is not comforting to find that § 2 also prohibits an "attempt to monopolize." The attempt offense adds an additional cloud to an already less than bright landscape. The exploration of attempt begins with the oft–quoted passage from Justice Holmes in *Swift & Co. v. United States*:

Where acts are not sufficient in themselves to produce a result which the law seeks to prevent — for instance, the monopoly — but require further acts in addition to the mere forces of nature to bring that result to pass, an intent to bring it to pass is necessary in order to produce a dangerous probability that it will happen. But when that intent and the consequent dangerous probability exist, this statute, like many others and like the common law in some cases, directs itself against that dangerous probability as well as against the completed result.[136]

The passage has been interpreted in a variety of ways. One point of view is that it requires three discrete elements: (1) acts that are to some degree predatory; (2) specific intent; and (3) a dangerous probability of success.[137]

---

[134] *Id.* at 925, 931. This logic may be inconsistent with the Supreme Court's decision in *Maricopa* and *Catalano. See supra* § 4.07. More recently, in a pattern common to professional sports, professional soccer players challenged the use of power on the buying side of the or market when soccer teams acted as a single entity in hiring players. Plaintiffs sought to define the market as Division I professional soccer players in the United States. The market definition was rejected by the jury. *Fraser v. Major League Soccer*, 284 F.3d 47 (1st Cir. 2002).

[135] *See generally,* R. Blair & J. Harrison, *Monopsony: Antitrust Law and Economics* 39–42 (1993).

[136] 196 U.S. 375, 396 (1905) (citation omitted).

[137] *See, e.g., International Distribution Centers v. Walsh Trucking Co.*, 812 F.2d 786 (2d Cir. 1987).

In the vast majority of instances, however, intent will be inferred from conduct, thereby reducing the analysis to two elements: (1) conduct; and (2) dangerous probability of success.

On the other hand, in Justice Holmes' formulation, intent is necessary to create a dangerous probability of success. Thus, through a "double inference," intent is inferred from conduct and a dangerous probability is created by intent. Although the passage can and has been read as suggesting that, in some instances, conduct alone will be sufficient to establish liability, this possibility was expressly rejected by the Supreme Court in a 1993 decision, *Spectrum Sports v. McQuillan*.[138] The Court was clear that in a attempt to monopolize case the plaintiff must prove the dangerous probability element as well as specific intent.

These varying interpretations have been reflected in the ways courts have dealt with attempt to monopolize. For the sake of convenience, the following analysis examines intent, conduct, and dangerous probability separately. The three elements are, however, interrelated. This means that the state of "attempt to monopolize" law remains muddled, perhaps inherently so. This confusing area of antitrust law, however, has become the forum for discussion of the proper definition and the import of predatory pricing, two of the more intriguing antitrust questions facing courts today.

[A] Intent

[1] Intent to Do What?

Although initially in doubt, it is clear now that mere possession of monopoly or market power is not forbidden. Consequently, it would make little sense to read the attempt to monopolize prohibition as encompassing all efforts to acquire market power. Indeed, to do so would mean that new products, advertising, and a great deal of price competition would fall into the scope of § 2 since these acts are literally motivated by the desire to acquire market power. Consequently, a notion of attempt has evolved that parallels monopolization; both structure and conduct are relevant.

The development of attempt "standards" has taken place largely in the context of efforts to define the intent component of the offense. In *Alcoa*, Judge Hand addressed the issue of intent, but did little to clarify the breadth of the activities covered. He noted that the issue was not important in the case of monopolization because, "no monopolist monopolizes unconscious of what he is doing."[139] On the other hand, "conduct falling short of monopoly, is not illegal unless it is part of a plan to monopolize, or to gain such other control of a market as equally forbidden."[140] If one reads Judge Hand's opinion to be a broad condemnation of monopoly power, his concept of attempt can be seen as being expansive enough to include any effort to

---

[138] 506 U.S. 447 (1993).

[139] *United States v. Aluminum Co. of Am.* 148 F.2d 416, 432 (2d Cir. 1943).

[140] *Id.* at 431–32.

gain market power. Conversely, if he is seen as condemning only monopoly power that is unfairly obtained, the notion of attempt is narrower, extending only to efforts to gain power through means that do not reflect "skill, foresight and industry."

A clearer picture of the intent element of attempt was provided by the Court in *Times–Picayune Co. v. United States.*[141] The Court noted that the necessary intent was to "destroy competition or build monopoly."[142] This statement alone would not preclude automatically efforts to gain market power through "competition on the merits" from the attempt label. The Court considered the actions actually taken, however, and found that they were motivated by "legitimate business aims,"[143] thus suggesting that attempt extended to efforts to achieve market power by illegitimate means.

Perhaps the best effort to provide substance to the intent component of attempt is found in *Union Leader Corp. v. Newspapers of New England Inc.*[144] According to Judge Wyzanski, "a person does not necessarily have an exclusionary intent merely because he foresees that a market is only large enough to permit one successful enterprise."[145] Instead, § 2 comes into play only when "the person who foresees a fight to the death intends to use or actually does use unfair weapons."[146] In short, the intent must go further than just a desire to displace competitors. It requires, in the words of the *Spectrum Sports* Court, "something more than an intent to compete vigorously."[147]

[2] Proof of Intent

Proof of "the intention to prevail by improper means" can be established by direct or indirect evidence. The difficulties of relying exclusively on direct evidence have been noted by courts and commentators.[148] A casual comment or memorandum in corporate files may not be a reliable indicator of actual intent and may only show a desire to displace a competitor without using unfair means. For the most part, intent is inferred from the actions of the firm. In *Union Leader* Judge Wyzanski noted the lack of a clear distinction between the "intent to exclude" and the acts themselves. Thus, evidence that shows the use of unfair means is the "very same evidence

---

[141] 345 U.S. 594 (1953).

[142] *Id.* at 626.

[143] *Id.* at 627.

[144] 180 F. Supp 125 (D. Mass. 1959), *modified*, 284 F.2d 582 (1st Cir. 1960), *cert. denied*, 365 U.S. 833 (1961).

[145] 180 F. Supp. at 140.

[146] *Id.*

[147] 506 U.S. at 459. *See generally* Hawk, *Attempts to Monopolize — Specific Intent as Antitrust's Ghost in the Machine*, 58 Cornell L. Rev. 1121 (1973).

[148] *See* H. Hovenkamp, *supra* note 44, at 281–283; R. Posner, *supra* note 3, at 189–90; *Scott Publishing Co. v. Columbia Basin Publishing Inc.*, 293 F.2d 15 (9th Cir. 1961); *cf.* Cooper, *Attempts and Monopolization: A Mildly Expansionary Answer to the Prophylactic Riddle of Section Two*, 72 Mich L. Rev. 375, 396, n.77 (1974).

that shows the existence of an exclusionary intent."[149] In applying the standard, Judge Wyzanski found that evidence that the defendant had organized a group boycott was "conclusive evidence of an intent to exclude competition unlawfully."[150]

Similar in tone is *United States v. Empire Gas Corp.*[151] in which the plaintiff had presented evidence that Empire, a wholesaler and retailer of liquified petroleum gas, had used price cuts or the threat of price cuts to discourage retail competitors from soliciting its customers. The trial court held that the evidence was insufficient to show that the defendant had the requisite specific intent to monopolize. The Eighth Circuit Court of Appeals, while affirming the judgment of the trial court on other grounds, indicated that the evidence of pricing practices was sufficient to establish specific intent.[152]

Union Leader and *Empire Gas* illustrate a primarily objective test for determining intent. The question, in essence, is whether a reasonable person would infer that a firm engaging in these activities intended to eliminate competitors through unfair means. This is not to say that evidence of subjective intent is not relied upon as well. In some instances the courts are receptive to evidence of subjective intent as either part of the plaintiff's case or as a means for the defendant to establish that there was a legitimate business purpose underlying its conduct.[153]

A good example of an approach relying on both subjective as well as objective considerations is found in *William Inglis & Sons v. ITT Continental Baking Co.*,[154] in which the court examined the issue of predatory pricing, discussed in greater detail below. The court established a system of shifting burdens of proof on the issue of whether pricing was actually predatory. If prices were below average total cost but above average variable cost, the plaintiff is charged with the burden of presenting additional evidence that pricing was predatory. In essence, the plaintiff is required to show why pricing in this range by a particular defendant should be indicative of a predatory intent. This follows from the general proposition that, in the short run, pricing below average total cost is often rational and non–predatory. If prices were below average variable cost, the plaintiff's *prima facie* case is established and defendant is required to justify the prices by motivations other than the possible destructive effect on competition. Implicit is the notion that unless its purpose is predatory, it is irrational for a firm to operate if it is unable to charge a price at least equal to average variable cost.[155] Again, the inference of predatory intent can be rebutted by evidence of a non–predatory motivation.

---

[149] 180 F. Supp. at 140.

[150] *Id.*

[151] 537 F.2d 296 (8th Cir. 1976), *cert. denied*, 429 U.S. 1122 (1977).

[152] 537 F.2d at 299–302. Accord, *General Industries Corp. v. Hartz Mountain Corp.*, 810 F.2d 795 (8th Cir. 1987).

[153] *See* Hawk, *supra* note 147, at 1137–42.

[154] 668 F.2d 1014 (9th Cir. 1981), *cert. denied*, 459 U.S. 825 (1982).

[155] 668 F.2d at 1034–36.

[B]　Dangerous Probability of Success

[1]　The Role of Market Analysis

Justice Holmes's description of the elements of attempt mentions a dangerous probability of success but does not literally make it an independent element. Under the *Swift* formulation, the Sherman Act "directs itself against . . . dangerous probability," but it is intent that creates this probability.[156] Despite the implication that a dangerous probability is created by intent which, in turn, is likely to be inferred from conduct, courts nearly uniformly treat "dangerous probability of success" as a separate element.[157] When they do, the analysis typically entails a determination of market power by defining the relevant market and establishing the defendant's market share. The obvious logic seems to be that dangerous probability is in reference to something, and that "something" is market power. Thus, an examination of the current power or market share of the defendant is required.

Although the language of *Swift* is ambiguous, subsequent decisions by the Supreme Court support the proposition that dangerous probability of success is a separate element and that the focus of the inquiry is essentially structural. In *Lorain Journal v. United States*[158] the Court upheld a judgment that a newspaper had attempted to monopolize the sale of advertising by refusing to deal with advertisers who purchased advertising from a radio station. The Court took particular note of the newspaper's market power and the likelihood that the boycott would eventually eliminate the broadcaster/competitor.[159] The same suggestion can be gleaned from *dicta* in *Walker Process Equipment v. Food Machinery and Chemical Corp.*[160] The Court announced that "[w]ithout a definition of [the] market, there is no way to measure [the defendant's] ability to lessen or destroy competition."[161]

Any doubt about the independent importance of market definition and market power as an indicator of dangerous probability was resolved by the Supreme Court in 1993. In *Spectrum Sports, Inc. v. McQuillan*[162] the Court reviewed a long–standing approach of the Ninth Circuit Court of Appeals under which a party could be held to have violated the attempt provisions of § 2 without an inquiry into the relevant market or power in that market. Under the so–called *Lessig* rule,[163] if the conduct was sufficiently predatory or unfair an assessment of market power was unnecessary. The Court

---

[156] *See* quotation at *supra* note 136; *see also* L. Sullivan, *Antitrust Law* 137 (1977).

[157] *See generally Cooper, supra* note 148, at 384–89.

[158] 342 U.S. 143 (1951).

[159] *Id.* at 152–54.

[160] 382 U.S. 172 (1965).

[161] *Id.* at 177.

[162] 506 U.S. 447 (1993).

[163] *See Lessig v. Tidewater Oil Co.*, 327 F.2d 459 (9th Cir.), *cert. denied*, 377 U.S. 993 (1964).

rejected the Ninth Circuit's approach and announced that "demonstrating the dangerous probability of monopolization in an attempt case . . . requires inquiry into the relevant product and geographic market and the defendant's power in that market."[164]

Coleman v. Chrysler Corp.[165] is illustrative of the general approach to market analysis. An independent automobile dealer charged Chrysler with attempting to monopolize retail automobile sales in Allegheny County. The conduct complained of was essentially a price squeeze. The plaintiff contended that Chrysler's granting of more favorable terms to factory affiliated retailers had the effect of excluding independent retailers from the market. The court noted that a definition of the relevant market was critical. In its view, if the proper market was all automobiles in Allegheny County, it was impossible for Chrysler to achieve monopoly status. On the other hand, it was conceivable for Chrysler to become the dominant retailer of Dodge automobiles in the county. The Court of Appeals, citing *Cellophane*, found the jury instructions confusing on what the proper market was and held the evidence insufficient to permit a "reasoned evaluation of the interchangeability of Dodges and other automobiles."[166]

[2] Market Share and "Dangerous Probability"

Although market definition is now expressly required in an attempt case, it is not clear always how the defendant's market share and power are related to dangerous probability. There are two possibilities. First, the market identification process may only be a measure of how close the defendant is to obtaining a dominant market share. Second, market share, as a proxy for market power, can be useful in gauging the firm's actual capacity to achieve market dominance.

The first possibility comes into play when the conduct involved does not depend on the use of power to raise prices above competitive levels.[167] For example, the ability of a firm to increase its market share through below–cost pricing or practices that increase a rival's costs is not a direct function of market power as traditionally understood. Indeed, what the firm hopes to achieve through predation is the power to raise prices, limit output, and deter entry.

Market share, even when utilized only as a measure of proximity to monopoly status, can be misleading. A firm with a market share of 40%, a deep pocket, and excess capacity poses a greater threat of increasing its market share than a financially strapped firm with no excess capacity even if that firm has a higher market share.[168] Overall market structure also

---

[164] 506 U.S. at 459.

[165] 525 F.2d 1338 (3rd Cir. 1975).

[166] *Id.* at 1349.

[167] *See Cooper, supra* note 148, at 439; Hovenkamp, *supra* note 44, at 286; *see also Multistate Legal Services, Inc. v. Harcourt Brace Jovanovich*, 63 F.3d 1540 (10th Cir. 1995), *cert. denied*, 116 S. Ct. 702 (1996).

[168] For a discussion of the rationality of attempting to monopolize through predation, see *infra*, § 6.05[E][1].

can be an important factor. A firm with a market share of 40% in a market with three other firms with 20% shares may be less likely to achieve monopoly status than a firm with a 40% share in a market with 60 competitors each with a 1% market share.[169] The point is that market share alone is a poor indicator of whether a firm is close to attaining market dominance. Rather, market share must be considered in the context of the conduct involved, the overall market structure, changes in market structure, and whether competitors are vulnerable to the efforts of the defendant.

This type of analysis is found in *Springfield Terminal Railway Co. v. Canadian Pacific Limited*,[170] in which the plaintiff claimed that a firm with 10% market share was attempting to monopolize by engaging in predatory pricing. The plaintiff railroad contended that the defendant had submitted a bid for the transportation of paper that was below the plaintiff's average variable cost. This was part of an alleged plan to force the plaintiff out of business at which time the defendant would acquire the plaintiff's assets and raise prices to supracompetitve levels.[171] Part of the court's opinion is devoted to the question of whether a firm with a 10% market share can create a dangerous probability. It reasoned that "[a]n all–powerful outsider with unlimited financing and a record of persistent, unambiguously anti-competitive conduct that has a demonstrably serious adverse impact on its competitor may pass the test."[172] In this instance the "test" was not passed in part because a one–time instance of a below cost bid was not enough to overcome the relatively low market share.

Under the second possibility, market share performs its more typical function of indicating market power. Of course, the firm involved in an attempt is not likely to use its market power to raise prices and restrict output.[173] Instead, market power is used to exact a non–pecuniary "price" from customers that they would not pay if there were alternative sellers. For example, the price exacted in *Lorain Journal* was in the form of a boycott of the broadcaster who was competing in the sales of advertising. The power to raise prices was allegedly used as the leverage necessary to gain a dominant position. The same kind of leverage is important in cases in which the attempt involves a tying arrangement. Of course, in some instances in which the use of market power creates a dangerous probability, the firm may be liable under a theory of monopolization.

[C]　Conduct Generally

The law of attempt has not developed either a class of behavior that automatically fulfills the conduct component of attempt or a category of *per*

---

[169] *See Cooper, supra* note 148, at 400; *see also, e.g., Empire Gas*, 537 F.2d at 305–07.

[170] 133 F. 3d 103 (1st Cir. 1997).

[171] *Id.* at 105–106.

[172] *Id.* at 108.

[173] Of course, a firm that achieves market dominance through predatory pricing will use market power to raise prices in order to recoup its investment in predation.

se attempt practices. The lack of systematic development of the attempt concept follows from the relationship of attempt to monopolize to the offense of monopolization. Conduct by a powerful firm on the verge of becoming a monopoly may be condemned while the same conduct by a less powerful firm may be permissible, at least under § 2. Thus, on a continuum, the more market power a firm possesses the less egregious the conduct must be before § 2 is triggered. Conversely, the less market power, the more offensive the conduct must be.

This is not to say that every activity that may result in the firm becoming a monopoly is prohibited under § 2. The conduct that satisfies attempt must be viewed in the context of the monopolization offense. Consequently, to make any sense within the structure of § 2, the conduct element of attempt must extend only to practices that are outside the scope of "competition on the merits" or "skill, foresight and industry" which are recognized defenses. Otherwise, the attempt component of § 2 can create the same hazards as an expanded notion of monopolization can: socially beneficial practices may be discouraged simply because they result in the attainment of market power. Similarly, consistency within § 2 dictates that the conduct not constitute an attempt simply because it is unfair or anticompetitive. Again the critical issue is whether the activity is likely to carry the firm to the position of monopoly.

This consistency between "attempt" and "monopolization" suggests two general rules. First, the range of activity legally available to the firm charged with attempt should be broader (and more predatory) than that afforded the monopolist.[174] The rationale may best be illustrated by considering the problem of finding a firm with a market share of 10% liable for attempted monopolization if it maintains excess capacity — the questionable conduct in *Alcoa* — or only leases its products — the primary questionable conduct in *United Shoe*. The point is that many of the same actions that may be useful for a monopolist in maintaining power have very little force in the hands of the less powerful firm. Second, activity that is permissible for the monopolist should be permitted similarly for firms possessing less than monopoly power.[175] Thus, if it is "competition on the merits" and not anticompetitive for Kodak to refuse to predisclose news of a new product, it would be illogical to say the same conduct by a less dominant firm constitutes an attempt in that it is an effort to gain power through means not "honestly industrial."

Virtually every conceivable scheme to disadvantage competitors has been considered by the courts under the attempt label. Perhaps too broad, but not particularly useful, categories of behavior can be identified. They follow from the previously discussed uses to which market share data can be put in attempt cases. The first type of conduct involves the actual use of existing market power to exact a non–pecuniary price. The "attempt" may be within the market in which the firm has that power or in some other market.

---

[174] *See* P. Areeda & H. Hovenkamp, *supra* note 104, at 354–356

[175] *Id.* at 321–29.

Lorain Journal is a good example of the former, while *Griffith* and cases involving tying are examples of the latter. A proper consideration of these cases as "attempts" requires a fairly close assessment of the conduct in light of the defendant's market power. There seems little basis for condemning any of these activities as attempts to monopolize unless the requisite market power exists.

The second category is composed of activities that do not depend on market power as traditionally defined to be successful but involve the use of unfair practices. Cases involving threats of physical violence, false advertising, industrial espionage, disparagement of a competitors product, and hiring a competitor's employees fall into this broad category which seems to include every imaginable competitive unkindness.[176] It is tempting to take the view that the conduct in this category is sufficiently offensive so as to be labeled *per se* attempt. The development of a list of activities that would be *per se* attempts is attractive because it would provide bright–line guidance to firms and add some predictability and coherence to an area of antitrust that is in disarray. On the other hand, a *per se* approach is not consistent with the view of attempt as a means of heading off the attainment of monopoly power, and, as a general matter, it is not the direction the courts have taken. The experimentation of the Ninth Circuit with a similar policy suggests the shortcomings of such an approach.

[D] The Use of Leverage

Leverage — the use of power in one market to influence sales in another market — does not fit clearly under either the monopolization or the attempt to monopolization label.[177] The matter was first introduced in *Griffith*, the monopolization case in which a theater chain with monopoly and monopsony power in some towns used that power to gain a competitive advantage in towns in which it had rivals.[178] *Griffith* opened the possibility that a firm could violate § 2 of the Sherman Act by unlawfully maintaining monopoly power in one market or by using that power in another market, regardless of whether monopoly power is achieved or threatened in the second market.

This view was echoed in *Berkey Photo,* in which the Second Circuit announced that "the use of monopoly power attained in one market to gain a competitive advantage in another market is in violation of § 2, even if there has not been an attempt to monopolize in the second market."[179] The Ninth Circuit Court of Appeals took a different tact, rejecting the *Berkey* approach and requiring that the impact in the second market meet the requirements of the attempt to monopolize offense.[180] Although not

---

[176] For a comprehensive listing *see* Cooper, *supra* note 148, at 445–48.

[177] This is, of course, the pattern in tying and similar practices.

[178] *See supra* § 6.05[I].

[179] 603 F.2d at 263. *Berkey* is discussed *supra* at § 6.05[C].

[180] *Alaska Airlines, Inc., v. United Airlines*, 948 F.2d 536 (9th Cir. 1991). *See also Fineman v. Armstrong World Indus.,* 980 F.2d 171 (3d Cir. 1992), *cert. denied,* 507 U.S. 921 (1993).

addressing the issue directly, the Supreme Court in *Spectrum Sports*, noted that "§ 2 makes the conduct of a single firm unlawfully only when it actually monopolizes or dangerously threatens to do so."[181] If followed, this language seemingly ends the simple leverage theory announced in *Berkey*, instead requiring plaintiffs to demonstrate the acquisition of market power in the second market even if the power exercised is a result of monopoly power in another market.[182]

It appears that the leverage theory may still be viable in some circuits albeit with some modification since *Berkey*. Precisely where the leverage theory falls, however, still is not clear. One possibility is that the impact in the leveraged market must rise to the level of an attempt to monopolize. The other is that the impact simply lead to higher prices and lower output without creating a dangerous probability that the firm will monopolize the second market. This is illustrated by *AD/SAT v. Associated Press*[183] in which the plaintiff provided the service of electronically transmitting advertising copy from advertisers to newspapers. In order to do so, it made use of a satellite owned by the Associated Press. The antitrust issue arose when the Associated Press began to offer the same service. The Second Circuit Court of Appeals analyzed the question as an attempt to monopolize and under a theory of monopoly leveraging.[184] The attempt claim was rejected because the market definition offered was AD/SAT — electronic transmission — was deemed too narrow and under the proper definition — the delivery or advertisements to newspaper — the Associated Press did not create a dangerous probability of success.

Under a separate "monopoly leveraging" theory, the court noted the impact of *Spectrum Sports* on leverage theories but stopped short of stating that the leveraging firm must pose a dangerous probability of monopolizing the second market. Accordingly, "a plaintiff alleging monopoly leveraging is not required to demonstrate a substantial market share by the defendant."[185] Instead, "application of the doctrine is limited to those circumstances in which the challenged conduct actually injures competition . . . in the second, non monopolized market."[186] The plaintiff also failed this test but the analysis evidently leaves open the possibility of a theory of monopolization or attempt in instances in which there is not a dangerous probability that the defendant will acquire a dominant position in the market. It seems clear, however, that when the leverage theory is applied the plaintiff will have to demonstrate tangible harm to competition to the market in which it operates.[187]

---

[181] 506 U.S. at 459.

[182] *See Advo, Inc. v. Philadelphia Newspapers, Inc.*, 51 F.3d 1191, 1202–03 (3d Cir. 1995).

[183] 181 F.3d 216 (2d Cir. 1999).

[184] *Id.* at 226–323.

[185] *Id.* at 230.

[186] *Id.*

[187] For an extensive discussion, *see Intergraph Corp. v. Intel Corp.*, 195 F.3d 1346, 1359–1361 (Fed. Cir. 1999).

[E] Predatory Pricing

Predatory pricing involves pricing at levels below profit maximizing levels with the view that weaker competitors will be eventually excluded from the market and the foregone profits can then be recouped by charging higher prices. The foregone profit is a form of investment that must be justified by the income it produces in the future. One of the more intriguing developments in antitrust law is the recent increase in interest in predatory pricing.

Despite this recent flurry of activity, predatory pricing is not an altogether new concern. Originally, the view of predatory pricing was that a firm would increase its prices and profits in markets in which it possessed market power in order to subsidize below–cost pricing in other markets. The practice could be treated as an "attempt to monopolize" under § 2 of the Sherman Act. In addition, because this view of predatory pricing involved two different prices it was treated as price discrimination. Section 2 of the Clayton Act was designed to respond to the supposed dangers.[188]

Today, the notion that a predator uses one market to subsidize another is on the decline.[189] Considerations of predatory pricing, whether in the context of the Clayton Act or the Sherman Act, have taken a decided turn toward examination of objective economic standards in the single market involved. Two general questions predominate:

(1)   Is the danger of predatory pricing sufficient to warrant any real judicial concern? This issue leads to two further inquiries:

- How often will firms decide that they can benefit over the long run by a pricing policy that is successful only if competitors can be eliminated, prices increased, and competitors barred from reentry?

- Even if a firm does view such a strategy as in its long term interest, does it make sense to condemn pricing behavior that is a response to competition and results in lower prices for at least some period of time?

(2)   If the threat of predatory pricing is real, what is the proper standard for distinguishing predatory pricing from competitive pricing?

Before examining these questions, two preliminary points should be made. First, predatory pricing constitutes the conduct portion of the attempt charge. Since intent may be inferred from action, it may also be indicative of specific intent. This still leaves the question of dangerous probability of success. The most suicidal predation is harmless if there is little likelihood that the scheme will work. Second, despite all the discussion

---

[188] *See* discussion *infra* in Chapter 8.

[189] *See generally Kaplow, supra* note 66.

and an outpouring of cases, predatory pricing rarely has been the basis of a successful § 2 claim.[190]

[1] How Likely is Predatory Pricing?

Predatory pricing can be an expensive and risky endeavor. In Figure 6–2, the profit maximizing price is P1 and the profit maximizing quantity is Q1. Suppose the firm lowers price to P2 in hopes of eliminating a competitor or competitors. Note that this necessitates selling quantity Q2. Thus, it is not a matter of simply lowering price to existing customers; it also requires preparation to sell to all those wishing to buy at the new lower price. Two factors influence just how burdensome this undertaking may be. First, the more elastic the industry demand, the more responsive buyers will be to

FIGURE 6–2

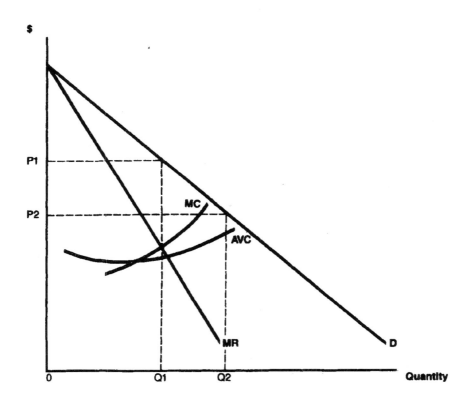

---

[190] For a comprehensive survey of cases decided since 1975, *see* Liebeler, *Whither Predatory Pricing? From Areeda and Turner to Matsushita*, 61 Notre Dame L. Rev. 1052 (1986). *See also* Hurwitz & Kovacic, *Judicial Analysis of Predation: The Emerging Trends*, 35 Vand. L. Rev. 63 (1982); McCall, *Predatory Pricing: An Economic and Legal Analysis*, 32 Antitrust Bull. 1 (1987).

the lower price. Second, if the predator has a relatively small market share it will find that the percentage increase in its own output may have to be quite large to even make a dent in the sales of its competitors.[191]

The problem facing the firm may not be simply one of increased sales at a lower price but one of increased costs as well. For example, as Figure 6–2 illustrates, as the firm begins to exceed its optimal level of output, the average cost of each unit sold (AVC) will increase.[192] A further possibility is that increases in sales may require additions to capacity which, if things go as planned, will not be needed at the eventual profit maximizing price and output.[193]

Another issue is whether, once the firm has eliminated competitors, it can raise price sufficiently and deter entry by old or new competitors long enough to justify the losses incurred during the period of predatory behavior. Again, it is basically an investment decision: current losses or foregone profits must be exceeded by the discounted present value of future increases in profits. Given how heavily the odds are against the predator, most scholars share the view that predatory pricing is a rarity. Some even believe that it is so unlikely that no serious judicial concern is warranted.[194] Those who claim that it may occur, even if only occasionally, believe that the investment can be worthwhile to the predator either because entry can be sufficiently retarded through economic or legal barriers[195] or because predatory pricing can be used as a disciplinary device by a firm to discourage price cutting by competitors.[196]

Over the last several years, the Supreme Court has begun to express its views on predatory pricing as a theory for liability under § 2. In *Matsushita Electric Industry Co. v. Zenith Radio*,[197] Japanese manufacturers of televisions were charged with conspiring to charge predatory prices for televisions sold in the United States. In reversing the court of appeal's refusal to grant the defendant summary judgement, the Court recognized the difficulty of successfully undertaking a scheme of predatory pricing, noting that "predatory pricing schemes are rarely tried, and even more rarely successful."[198] The Court was skeptical about the likelihood that

---

[191] *See generally* R. Bork, *supra* note 4, at 149–52; H. Hovenkamp, *supra* note 44, at 347–348.

[192] *See* R. Bork, *supra* note 4, at 151.

[193] It may, however, serve as a continuing deterrent to competitors considering entering the market. See generally Williamson, *Predatory Pricing: A Strategic and Welfare Analysis*, 87 Yale L. J. 284 (1977).

[194] *See* Bork, *supra* note 4, at 186: Easterbrook, *Predatory Strategies and Counterstrategies*, 48 U. Chi. L. Rev. 263 (1981); Liebeler, *supra* note 190.

[195] *See* H. Hovenkamp, *supra* note 45; Joskow & Klevorick, *A Framework for Analyzing Predatory Pricing Policy*, 89 Yale L. J. 213 (1979).

[196] *See* Posner, *supra* note 3, at 186; *cf.* Williamson, *supra* note 193.

[197] 475 U.S. 574 (1986).

[198] *Id.* at 589. The Court seemed to embrace the views expressed by Judge Bork. *See* Bork, *supra* note 4.

firms engaged in predatory pricing could achieve and maintain monopoly power for a period long enough to recoup the losses sustained during the period of predation. Although the Court was concerned with a conspiracy, it added that its observations applied to single firms as well.[199]

In a similar vein but expressing less skepticism about the theory of predatory pricing is the Court's opinion in *Cargill v. Monfort of Colorado, Inc.*[200] There, a firm challenged the merger of two rivals, claiming that the newly merged firm could engage in predatory practices "by lowering its prices to some level at or slightly above its costs in order to compete . . . for market share . . . . In order to remain competitive [plaintiff] would have to lower its prices; as a result [plaintiff] would suffer a loss in profitability, but would not be driven out of business."[201] The Court held that a competitor does have standing[202] to seek an injunction against threatened injury but found unpersuasive the argument that there was a threat of predatory pricing. The Court reasoned that the record did not support a finding of "antitrust injury"[203] because the threat of less profit was due to increased, not decreased competition. The Court noted, however:

> [P]redatory pricing is an anticompetitive practice forbidden by the antitrust laws. While firms may engage in the practice only infrequently, there is ample evidence suggesting that the practice does occur. It would be novel indeed for a court to deny standing to a party seeking an injunction against threatened injury merely because such injuries rarely occur.[204]

In *Brooke Group Ltd. v. Brown & Williamson Tobacco Co.*,[205] a 1993 case, the Court, repeating many of the reservations it had expressed in *Matsushita*, also seemed reluctant to accept predatory pricing as a legitimate theory for an antitrust claim. Although it ultimately did recognize the legitimacy of the theory, it laid out a framework of analyzing predatory pricing that plaintiffs will find especially burdensome. Plaintiffs are required to show that the defendant (1) charged prices "below an appropriate measure" of the defendant's costs[206] and (2) "had . . . a dangerous probability of recouping its investment in below–cost prices."[207] Since *Brown & Williamson Tobacco*, lower courts have stressed the issue of whether the firm allegedly engaged in predatory pricing can reasonably expect to recoup its

---

[199] 475 U.S. at 590.

[200] 479 U.S. 104 (1986).

[201] *Id.* at 114–15.

[202] *See* discussion *supra* at § 3.02[A].

[203] *See* discussion *supra* § 3.02[B].

[204] 479 U.S. at 121 *citing* Koller, *The Myth of Predatory Pricing: An Empirical Study*, 4 Antitrust L. & Econ. J. 105 (1971); Miller, *Comments on Baumol and Ordover*, 28 J. Law & Econ. 267 (1985)).

[205] 509 U.S. 209 (1993). The case actually dealt with a charge of charge of predatory pricing. For additional discussion *see infra* § 8.04[A][2].

[206] 509 U.S. at 222.

[207] *Id.* at 224.

losses.[208] To a great extent, this emphasis involves an examination of possible entry barriers encountered by firms seeking to compete with the predator once it begins raising prices to supracompetitive levels.

[2] Standards for Predatory Pricing

Although the Court in *Brown & Williamson Tobacco*, provided a framework for the analysis of predatory pricing, it expressly declined to identify what it would regard as the relevant measure of cost in a predatory pricing case.[209] Similarly, it did not indicate the strength of any presumptions about the intent to monopolize that would follow from any particular pricing strategy. Consequently, the search for a more detailed test continues to begin with a look at the proposals of Professors Areeda and Turner in their seminal 1975 article.[210]

The test is actually the application of the logic of elementary economic price theory as a means of identifying a range of prices that a rational nonpredatory competitor might charge and a range that suggests predatory intent. The primary Areeda–Turner guideline is that prices below "reasonably anticipated short run marginal costs" are predatory.[211] Figure 6–3 illustrates the test. The profit maximizing price would be Pl and the profit maximizing quantity would be Q1. Any price at or above marginal cost, even though not profit maximizing, would be regarded as nonpredatory. The general standard has the major exception that prices below short run marginal cost are not predatory if they are equal to or exceed average total cost (ATC).[212] Thus, in Figure 6–3, P2 would be regarded as nonpredatory even though it is below marginal cost. The marginal cost test applies strictly to prices below average total cost. A firm need not earn an economic profit in order to escape the presumption of predatory pricing. The demand and cost curves may be such that the profit maximizing firm is really minimizing losses. As long as price is at or above short run marginal cost, though, the behavior is not predatory.

Because of the difficulties of computing marginal cost, Areeda and Turner propose using average variable cost (AVC) as a surrogate. Thus, "[a] price at or above reasonably anticipated average variable cost should be presumed lawful" and "[a] price below reasonably anticipated average variable cost should be conclusively presumed unlawful."[213] Average variable cost

---

[208] *See, e.g., Israel Travel Advisory Service v. Israel Identity Tours*, 61 F.2d 1250 (7th Cir. 1995), *cert. denied*, 116 S. Ct. 1847 (1996); *Multistate Legal Studies, Inc. v. Harcourt Brace Jovanovich*, 63 F.3d 1540 (10th Cir. 1995), *cert denied*, 116 S.Ct. 702 (1996); *Bathke v. Casey's Central Store*, 64 F.3d 340 (8th Cir 1995); *Advo v. Philadelphia Newspapers*, 51 F.3d 1191 (3d Cir. 1995).

[209] 509 U.S. at 222 n.1.

[210] Areeda & Turner, *Predatory Pricing and Related Practices Under Section 2 of the Sherman Act*, 88 Harv. L. Rev. 687 (1975). Further discussion is found in H. Hovenkamp, *supra* note 44 at 335–368.

[211] III P. Areeda & D. Turner, *Antitrust Law* 153 (1978).

[212] *Id.* at 154.

[213] Areeda & Turner, *supra* note 211, at 154.

FIGURE 6–3

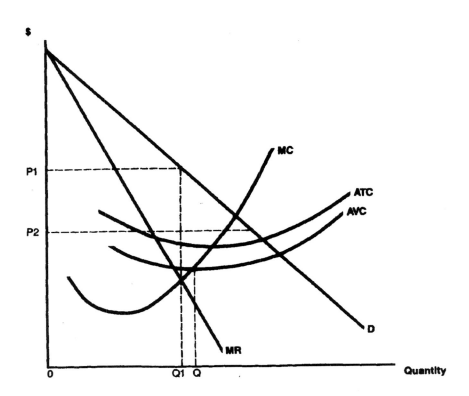

and short run marginal cost may be similar for extended ranges of production. The implications when marginal cost and average variable cost deviate are discussed below.

The Areeda–Turner test has been debated by courts[214] and commentators.[215] The test raises three questions. The first stems from the fact that the firm is permitted to charge a price below the short run profit maximizing level. Yet, any price — even one above marginal cost — other than the short run profit maximizing price signals an effort to exclude competitors.

---

[214] *See, e.g., Barry Wright Corp. v. ITT Grinnell Corp.* 724 F.2d 227 (1st Cir. 1983); *William Inglis & Sons Baking Co. v. ITT Continental Baking Co.*, 668 F.2d 1014 (9th Cir. 1981), *cert. denied*, 459 U.S. 825 (1982); *Pacific Engineering & Prod. Co. v. Kerr McGee Corp.*, 551 F.2d 790 (10th Cir.) *cert. denied*, 434 U.S. 879 (1977).

[215] *See, e.g.,* Posner, *supra* note 3, at 191–93; Joskow & Klevorick, *supra* note 195; Scherer, *Predatory Pricing and the Sherman Act: A Comment*, 89 Harv. L. Rev. 869 (1976); Williamson, *supra* note 193. For an interesting application of these theories *see* Brodly, *The Goals of Antitrust — Pretrial Hearing No. 1: A Verbatim Account of an Imagined Proceeding*, 28 Antitrust Bull. 823 (1983).

The firm could hold price constant at a level below the short run profit maximizing level in order to deter entry[216] or, capacity permitting, increase and decrease prices in this range to discourage potential entrants.[217] These are forms of what is called "limit pricing." Whether either of these activities should be condemned is problematic. If a firm has excess capacity and lowers prices when entry seems likely and raises them to monopoly levels when the threat has passed, the usual efficiency objections to monopoly pricing are applicable. On the other hand, one can argue that such behavior is, in essence, competitive and only injures those firms with higher production costs than the price cutter. Thus, prohibiting above–cost pricing would do little more than shield less efficient firms. For now, the latter view seems to be the one held by the Supreme Court.[218]

A more serious problem with the Areeda–Turner test is presented when the average variable cost surrogate is invoked. Figure 6–3 illustrates the leeway available. Any price at or above average variable cost is presumed nonpredatory. But, at every point to the right of quantity Q on the graph, marginal cost exceeds average variable cost. Thus the test permits a great range of prices to be regarded as nonpredatory even though they are below marginal cost and are irrational unless made up in the future when prices can be increased.[219]

The Areeda–Turner test, and any other cost–based or objective test for predation, encounters problems when the issue is one of precision. For example, when reasonably anticipated average variable cost is substituted for short run marginal cost, the test loses some of its consistency with sound economic theory. The substitution is necessary, though, because average variable cost data are more generally available than marginal cost data. But problems remain of ascertaining what was "reasonably anticipated" and which costs are variable with respect to a particular product of a multiproduct firm. Economists and accountants can provide answers but the estimates depend upon assumptions about the future and cost classifications which are often arbitrary. Thus, an admirable, though fallible, theoretical basis also is subject to practical imprecision.

Other than the predictable issues, there is a fundamental question of how to calculate the cost basis. For example, suppose a seller charges $500 for

---

[216] This is commonly called "limit" pricing. *See generally* Gunther, *Limit Pricing and Predation in the Antitrust Laws: Economic and Legal Aspects.* 35 Ala. L Rev. 211 (1984).

[217] This is a variation of "limit" pricing which involves strategic use of price and capacity to deter entry. *See* Williamson, *supra* note 193; *see also* IIA P. Areeda & H. Hovenkamp, 178–179 (2d ed. 2002; Baumol, *Quasi–Permanence of Price Reductions: A Policy for Prevention of Predatory Pricing,* 89 Yale L.J. 5 (1979).

[218] *See Brook Group Ltd. v. Brown & Williamson Tobacco Corp.,* 509 U.S. 209 (1993); *Atlantic Richfield v. USA Petroleum,* 495 U.S. 328, 340 (1990).

[219] Professors Areeda and Turner have attempted to off–set this difficulty by suggesting that "a monopolist relying on a defense that price was not less than average variable cost should be required to offer proof that his marginal cost . . . did not exceed average variable cost." *See generally* Areeda & Turner, 176 (1978). Professor Hovenkamp points out that the use of average variable cost in the first place was due to the difficulty of ascertaining marginal cost. *See* H. Hovenkamp, *supra* note 45, at 302.

a stereo system and the $500 is above any measure of cost. It then adds to the system a sound filtering device that costs $20 but does not raise the price of the system the average cost of which is still less than $500.[220] In one sense, the firm has just engaged in competition by increasing the quality of the product and not raising the prices. In the other hand, the incremental improvement was provided at a price that as below average marginal cost. At least one court has been interpreted as viewing this activity as predatory pricing.[221]

[3] Predatory Pricing Standards in the Courts

Since 1975 there has been a surge in predatory pricing as a basis for attempted monopolization claims.[222] This interest may now be waning because the *Brown & Williamson Tobacco* two–part, with it emphasis on recoupment, seems to raise the burden for plaintiffs. On the other hand, because *Brown & Williamson Tobacco* leaves questions open as to the details of assessing a predatory pricing claim, lower courts are likely to continue to rely on the Areeda–Turner standard as a starting point.[223] To the extent courts have adopted positions different from that proposed by Professors Areeda and Turner, the direction taken is to move away from the strength of the presumptions of the test.[224] Typically, the focus is on how to regard prices that are above average variable cost.

Perhaps the most discussed and influential lower court predatory pricing case to date is *William Inglis v. ITT Continental Baking Co.*[225] In *Inglis*, the Ninth Circuit, which appeared to endorse the Areeda–Turner test in a prior decision,[226] discussed, among other things, prices in excess of average variable cost but below average total cost. In particular, it reacted to the leeway under the Areeda–Turner formulation afforded firms pricing above average variable cost. It noted that pricing above average variable cost and below average total cost may constitute a rational effort to minimize short term losses but could also signal predatory intent.[227] It,

---

[220] This example is suggested by E.T. Sullivan & H. Hovenkamp, *Antitrust Law, Policy and Procedure* 47 (3d ed. 1997 Supp.).

[221] *See Multistate Legal Services v. Harcourt Brace Jovanovich*, 63 F.3d 1540 (10th Cir. 1995), *cert. denied*, 116 S. Ct. 702 (1996).

[222] For a thorough documentation *see* Liebeler, *supra* note 190.

[223] *See, e.g., D. E. Rogers Assoc., Inc. v. Gardener–Denver Co.*, 718 F.2d 1431 (6th Cir. 1983); *Chillicothe Sand & Gravel v. Martin Marietta Corp.*, 616 F.2d 427 (7th Cir. 1980), and cases cited *supra* in note 218.

[224] *See, e.g, Instructional Systems Development Corp. v. Aetna Casualty and Surety Co.*, 817 F.2d 639 (10th Cir. 1987); *D.E. Rogers Assoc., Inc. v. Gardener–Denver Co.*, 718 F.2d 1431 (6th Cir. 1983), *cert. denied*, 467 U.S. 1242 (1984); *Chillicothe Sand & Gravel v. Martin Marietta Corp.*, 616 F.2d 427 (7th Cir. 1980); *International Air Indus. v. American Excelsior*, 517 F.2d 714 (5th Cir 1975), *cert. denied*, 424 U.S. 943 (1976).

[225] 668 F.2d 1014 (9th Cir. 1981), *cert. denied*, 459 U.S. 825 (1982).

[226] *See Janich Bros., Inc. v. American Distilling Co.*, 570 F.2d 848 (9th Cir. 1977), *cert. denied*, 439 U.S. 829 (1978).

[227] 668 F.2d at 1035.

therefore, constructed a series of presumptions. Prices below average variable cost are presumptively predatory. Prices above average variable cost are presumptively nonpredatory. In both cases the presumptions are rebuttable. Subsequently, in *Transamericana Computer Co. v. IBM Corp.*,[228] the court announced that prices above average total cost were not conclusively nonpredatory but the presumption of legality could only be overcome by "clear and convincing evidence."[229]

A great deal can be gleaned from a close analysis of *Inglis*. First, its position with respect to prices above average total cost seems to open the possibility of a successful challenge to "limit pricing." More generally, it is a case in which the court begins its analysis with the Areeda–Turner test, but does not adopt any of its specific elements. Finally, it may serve as an illustration of a court that became so immersed in describing its economic standards that it did not pay sufficient attention to the standard of dangerous probability.[230]

While *Inglis* is representative of a general trend among the courts to apply less demanding presumptions than those suggested by the Areeda–Turner test, the Ninth Circuit's view of prices above average total cost is probably not representative. In addition, it probably does not survive *Brown & Williamson Tobacco* since the first step in the two–part test announced there is that prices must fall below cost. More in line with the Supreme Court's instructions is *Barry Wright Corp. v. ITT Grinnell Corp.*,[231] in which the First Circuit reacted to the position of the Ninth Circuit that prices above average total cost might be found to be predatory. The court noted the extreme difficulty of determining when a firm pricing above average total cost was acting to discipline competitors as opposed to simply lowering price in order to increase profit in the short run. It also weighed the possibility that a policy of sometimes permitting prices above average total cost to be treated as predatory could " 'chill' highly desirable procompetitive price cutting."[232] Although the "clear and convincing" standard adopted by the Ninth Circuit would protect against this chilling effect, the court reasoned that a standard high enough to avoid the problem was probably not "worth the trouble." It concluded that prices above average and incremental costs were not prohibited under the Sherman Act.[233]

The primary importance of *Brown & Williamson Tobacco* is that it adjusted the focus of predatory pricing analysis by emphasizing the question of whether the firm engaged in predatory pricing will be able to recoup its loses. In order to understand the impact of this, it is useful to recall

---

[228] 698 F.2d 1377 (9th Cir 1983), *cert. denied*, 464 U.S. 955 (1983).

[229] *Id.* at 1388.

[230] See Liebeler, *supra* note 190, at 1057–61.

[231] 724 F.2d 227 (1st Cir. 1983).

[232] *Id.* at 235–36.

[233] 735 F.2d at 235. *Accord Arthur S. Langenderfer v. S.E. Johnson Co.*, 729 F.2d 1050 (6th Cir.), *cert. denied*, 469 U.S. 1036 (1984); *MCI Communications Co v. AT&T*, 708 F.2d 1081 (7th Cir.), *cert. denied*, 464 U.S. 891 (1983).

the role played by pricing behavior in the attempt to monopolize offense. The logic was that a firm pricing below cost would only do so rationally it if *intended* to exclude competitors. Now, because of the recoupment requirement, the analysis has shifted from intent. The question is not so much what the defendant may have intended, but what, given market conditions, the real likelihood was that the effort would have been successful. For example, in *Dial A Car v. Transportation*,[234] the District of Columbia Circuit Court of Appeals denied a predatory pricing claim by the provider of limousine services noting that the plaintiff had failed to allege that the defendant would be able to recoup its losses. Specifically, the court focused on both the ease of entry of new competitors if prices were raised and the presence in the market of other service providers.[235] Similarly, in *Advo v. Philadelphia Newspapers*,[236] a firm engaged in the distribution of advertising circulars claimed that a newspaper was offering the same service on a predatory basis. The court directed its attention to the issue of dangerous probability of success by discussing the problem of recoupment. It noted that, even if the prices charged were predatory, entry barriers into the market were sufficiently low to prevent recoupment.[237] Finally, in *Taylor Publishing Co. v. Jostens, Inc.*,[238] a rival school yearbook publisher claimed that its competitor had sold at prices below average variable cost and, in so doing, had lured away 27 customers per year in the period 1995–1997. As this was out of a total of 6,500 customers, the court reasoned that recoupment could not occur because the likelihood that the plaintiff actually would be forced out of business was extremely remote.[239]

Although the recoupment analysis increases the plaintiff's burden in an attempt case, it does not make it insurmountable. In *Multistate Legal Services v. Harcourt Brace Jonvaovich*,[240] the Tenth Circuit Court of Appeals addressed predatory pricing with respect to bar review courses. In a fairly detained matter, the court discussed the economic determinants of the possibility for successful recoupment. It identified those determinants as the defendant's market share, the defendant's resources, and entry barriers. Plaintiff provided sufficient evidence as to all three to create an issue of fact.[241]

---

[234] 82 F.2d 484 (D.C. Cir. 1996).

[235] *See also Israel Travel Advisory Serv., Inc. v. Israel Identity Tours, Inc.*, 61 F.3d 1250 (7th Cir.), *cert. denied*, 116 S. Ct. 1847 (1996).

[236] 51 F.3d 1191 (3d Cir. 1995).

[237] *Id.* at 119–1200.

[238] 216 F.3d 465 (5th Cir. 2000).

[239] *Id.* at 478.

[240] 63 F.3d 1540 (10th Cir. 1996) *cert. denied*, 116 S. Ct. 702 (1996).

[241] *Id.* at 1554–55.

§ 6.07 Oligopoly and "Shared Monopoly"

Section 2 of the Sherman Act is designed to prevent anticompetitive behavior by a single firm. Section 1 concerns the behavior of more than one firm operating under an agreement. The net result is a gap in antitrust coverage in the case of industries that are characterized by a few large competitors. This gap, which involves what is known as oligopolistic market structure, is not without consequence. Because of their high visibility to each other and their interdependence, the firms may charge supracompetitive prices and restrict output without an express agreement. Without an agreement, though, § 1 is not applicable. And, unless one of the firms approaches a monopoly market share and begins to act in a manner that is not "honestly industrial," § 2 likewise offers no protection for a plaintiff.

[A] Oligopolistic Behavior

The key to oligopolistic behavior[242] is the limited number of competitors and the interdependence it breeds. For instance, consider three airlines all serving the route from Chicago to St. Louis. Any one might consider lowering fares in order to gain a larger share of the market. It must contend, however, with the very real possibility that if it does decrease fares, its competitors will shortly follow suit. As a result the firm will not increase its market share but, quite possibly, it may find that it has lower total revenue.[243] If it raises fares, competitors may or may not follow suit. If they do not, the firm will find itself losing ground and will have to return to the original fare in order to regain its position. On the other hand, the firms may follow the leadership of the airline initially increasing prices with the outcome being higher fares and lower output for the whole industry. As a result of this interdependence, fares are likely to be rigid. When they are not, the outcome will tend to be similar to what one would expect to find under conditions of monopoly. Yet this parallel behavior, which would seem to require some kind of agreement in a less concentrated industrial context, can be the product of independent reaction to market conditions.

[B] "Shared Monopoly"

As a result of this interdependence, oligopolistic industries are characterized by a lack of price competition and may be regarded as "shared" monopolies.[244] A range of approaches designed both to fill the gap between §§ 1 and 2 of the Sherman Act and to respond to the problem of shared monopoly have evolved; however, almost all ultimately have proven unsuccessful. For the most part, these attempts to supplement the Sherman Act

---

[242] For a more detailed discussion *see supra* Chapter 4.

[243] The impact on sales and total revenue will be determined by the elasticity of demand for the entire "industry."

[244] *See generally* Hay, *Oligopoly, Shared Monopoly, and Antitrust Law*, 67 Cornell L. Rev. 439 (1982).

have been made by the Federal Trade Commission through application of § 5 of the Federal Trade Commission Act.[245]

Although all of the theories experimented with by the FTC examine both structure and conduct, there is a difference in emphasis. Those that are conduct oriented seem to respond to the problem presented by the § 1 requirement that an agreement exist. Efforts which emphasize structure on the other hand, can be viewed as attempts to supplement § 2 with the focus on market power possessed collectively by a small group of firms.

Cases in the former category are related to the general issue of when an agreement can be found and how closely § 1 comes to condemning consciously parallel behavior.[246] The recent experience of the Commission with this approach to shared monopoly in *E.I. Du Pont de Nemours & Co. v. FTC*[247] does, however, warrant special note and suggests that the prospects are dim for FTC expansion of the antitrust laws to instances in which there is no agreement and no single dominant firm.

The case involved a challenge in the Second Circuit to an FTC order that Du Pont and Ethyl Corporation, dominant firms in the lead antiknock gasoline additive industry, had engaged in unfair business practices by pursuing practices that facilitated price parallelism at noncompetitive levels. The practices included (1) sales at delivered prices, (2) the giving of advance notice of price increases beyond that contractually provided for, and (3) the use of "most favored nation" clauses under which buyers were promised that they would not be charged a higher price than any other customer.[248] The Commission did not allege that the practices were adopted as the result of an agreement nor did it categorize the practices as predatory or deceitful.[249] The theory was, in effect, that certain practices in a concentrated industry were "unfair" under § 5 because of the probable anticompetitive result. The practices amounted to consciously parallel adoption of practices that facilitated price uniformity or, as it has been labeled, "indirect collusion."[250]

The Second Circuit vacated the Commission's order, noting a lack of standards upon which competitors could depend as to what was acceptable and unacceptable conduct in oligopolistic markets.[251] It announced a general rule that "in the absence of proof of a violation of the antitrust laws or evidence of collusive, predatory, or exclusionary conduct, business practices are not "unfair" in violation of § 5 unless those practices either have an anticompetitive purpose or cannot be supported by an independent legitimate reason."[252] The court found that the FTC's conclusion that the

---

[245] 15 U.S.C. § 45 (1983).

[246] *See supra* § 4.15[A][4].

[247] 729 F.2d 128 (1984).

[248] *Id.* at 133.

[249] *Id.*

[250] *See Hay, supra* note 244, at 468.

[251] 729 F.2d at 138–39.

[252] *Id.* at 140.

practices led to a lessening of competition was not supported by substantial evidence. Moreover, there was overwhelming evidence that the practices were adopted for legitimate independent business reasons. The decision comes very close to rendering the existence of an oligopolistic market structure inconsequential under § 5. Indeed, according to the court "an oligopolistic market structure in which manufacturers engage in consciously parallel pricing" is indicative of a "condition, not a 'method.' "[253]

Undoubtedly, the Commission's most publicized effort at filling the gap between §§ 1 and 2 by way of an extension of § 2 was its prolonged attack on cereal manufacturers during the 1970's.[254] The four cereal manufacturers involved possessed a combined 90% market share and were charged with excluding entry by engaging in the following activities: brand proliferation, misleading advertising, controlling retail shelf space, and acquisition of competitors.[255] At least, initially, there was no claim that there was an actual or tacit horizontal agreement.[256] Instead, the focus was on a "shared monopoly," as opposed to a single–firm monopoly, that engaged in activity that was not competition on the merits. The requested remedy was divestiture and compulsory trademark licensing. The case was eventually dismissed by an administrative law judge.[257] Although it was noted that the Commission, in enforcing § 5 of the Federal Trade Commission Act, was not bound by the limits of § 2 of the Sherman Act, the Judge ruled that there was no showing of monopoly profits in the industry — a condition that would invite entry but for exclusionary conduct. Thus, the cereal manufacturers could not be regarded as responsible for the lack of entry.[258] Nor was there proof that the performance of the industry was consistent with what might be expected under monopoly conditions.[259]

Although the theory of shared monopoly was left alive in the cereal case, the outcome of that litigation read in light of the Second Circuit opinion in *Du Pont* suggests that the FTC's ability to plug the gap between §§ 1 and 2 of the Sherman Act is very limited. The difficulty of determining a workable remedy in such cases may underlie the reluctance to permit Commission expansion of § 5. If an agreement exists it can be enjoined as can predatory practices. When, however, the practice is not predatory and is essentially the result of interdependent behavior, the remedy would have to be one that precludes rational independent profit maximizing behavior. The suggestion has been made that an effective remedy may be to restructure the industry so that sufficient competitors exist to make oligopoly

---

[253] *Id.* at 139.

[254] *In re Kellogg Co.*, 99 F.T.C. 8 (1982). *See generally* Connuck, *"Shared Monopoly," "Conscious Parallelism" and an Approach to Oligopoly Under Section 5 of the FTC Act*, 9 Rut. Computer & Technology L.J. 165 (1982).

[255] 99 F.T.C. at 12–15.

[256] *See* Connuck, *supra* note 254, at 205–06.

[257] 99 F.T.C. at 269.

[258] *Id.* at 267.

[259] *Id.* at 258–61.

behavior difficult or impossible.[260] Of course, this too has efficiency implications if the industry is one in which substantial economics of scale cannot be enjoyed unless each firm serves a substantial share of the market.[261]

§ 6.08 Conspiracy to Monopolize

Section 2 of the Sherman Act expressly prohibits combinations or conspiracies to monopolize. This infrequently invoked portion of § 2 duplicates a great deal of the behavior prohibited by § 1. In fact, in practice, it is commonly attached to a § 1 claim, making difficult an independent analysis of the elements of conspiracy to monopolize. When it is separately considered, it is clear that the essential element of conspiracy to monopolize is 1) specific intent, 2) along with an agreement and 3) at least one overt act in furtherance of the agreement. As with attempted monopolization, specific intent can either be shown through actual agreement or inferred from conduct.[262] It is the specific intent requirement that makes the offense harder to prove than a § 1 charge which does not require intent evidence.

As a general matter, courts have not required a sophisticated market definition or an assessment of the likely impact.[263] It may be that the Supreme Court's emphasis on market definition in *Spectrum Sports* in attempt cases will be extended to conspiracy cases as well. In any case, it is clear that plaintiffs claiming a conspiracy to monopolize who also could have alleged a violation of § 1 should not be able to escape the burdens of § 1 by careful pleading. There appears to be no case in which this has happened.

---

[260] *See* II P. Areeda & D. Turner, *supra* note 211 at 377–78.

[261] There also have been attempts to employ the "shared monopoly" theory by private parties. *See Harkins Amusement Enterprises v. General Cinema*, 850 F.2d 477 (9th Cir. 1988).

[262] *See, e.g., American Tobacco Co. v. United States*, 328 U.S. 781 (1946); *International Distribution Centers v. Walsh Trucking Co.*, 812 F.2d 786 (2d Cir. 1987); *cf. Instructional Systems Development Corp. v. Aetna Casualty Surety Co.*, 817 F.2d 639 (10th Cir. 1987).

[263] *See e.g, Levine v. Central Florida Medical Affiliates, Inc.*, 72 F.3d 1538 (11th Cir. 1996); *Intergraph Corp. v. Intel Corp.*, 195 F.3d 1346 (Fed. Cir. 1999). *See generally*, P. Areeda and H. Hovenkamp, IIIA *Antitrust Law* 390 (2nd Ed. 2002).

Chapter 7

MERGERS AND ACQUISITIONS

§ 7.01 Introduction

In order to expand business, reduce costs or increase market power, firms often seek to merge with or acquire other firms. Generally, mergers occur through either a stock or asset purchase of one firm by another. Mergers may present threats to competition, depending on the type of merger and the size and strength of the companies involved. The entire structure of an industry can be altered by a merger.

§ 7.02 Horizontal Mergers

Horizontal mergers involve firms selling the same or similar products in the same geographical market; these firms compete directly. By merging, firms eliminate competition between themselves. Because of the direct impact on competition within a given market, horizontal mergers receive the most intense scrutiny.

On the other hand, horizontal mergers may serve useful economic purposes. They can result in joint operating efficiencies, economies of scale, and financial economies. Price reductions to consumers may follow. Courts must balance the beneficial effects of horizontal mergers against threats to competition created by the merger. They must determine how much of an effect the merger will have on competition within the defined market. To do this, courts must examine the market size and power of the firms involved and attempt to predict the consequence of the merger. The antitrust concern is whether the resulting firm will result in market power of sufficient size to enable the combined enterprise to act like a monopolist or to facilitate collusion among the remaining competitors. The test under § 7 of the Clayton Act is whether the merger has reasonable probability of lessening competition.[1]

§ 7.03 Non-horizontal Mergers

Non-horizontal mergers do not present the same overt threat to competition. Although horizontal mergers directly remove one competitor from a

---

[1] It should be noted that the government through the FTC or the Department of Justice, or a competitor to the firms proposing a merger, or the very firm targeted for merger, can sue for a preliminary injunction to prevent the merger. *See Anago, Inc. v. Tecnol Medical Products, Inc.*, 976 F.2d 248 (5th Cir. 1992). *See also infra* § 7.10 on private enforcement of § 7. The firms must prove both standing and antitrust injury like any other antitrust plaintiff. *Id.* at 249–50.

market and increase the market share of the merged firm, non–horizontal mergers involve firms that do not compete directly with each other. Because the number of competitors within a given market remains the same, the direct, overt threat of monopoly or oligopolistic collusion apparent in horizontal mergers does not exist. However, non–horizontal mergers may restrain competition in other ways.

The secondary effects of non–horizontal mergers often present a threat to competition. Traditionally, courts define two types of non–horizontal mergers: vertical and conglomerate. Recently, non–horizontal mergers also have been viewed in the context of whether the merger results in a loss of a potential competitor and the effect that will have on the market. In terms of anticompetitive consequences, non–horizontal mergers may create barriers to entry, facilitate collusion or make it possible to evade rate regulation. They may also create transaction cost efficiencies that lead to procompetitive effects. In determining the legality of proposed mergers, courts attempt to balance the harms and benefits of the merger and determine whether there may be a procompetitive effect or a lessening of competition.

[A] Vertical Mergers

Vertical mergers occur when one firm purchases either a customer or a supplier, with the result that the acquiring firm expands into a new market. When a concrete producer purchases a sand plant it then operates in two markets — sand and concrete production. Mergers may be upstream or downstream. Upstream mergers occur when a consumer acquires a supplier — the concrete company purchases the sand operation. Downstream mergers occur when the supplier acquires the purchaser — the sand company acquires the concrete firm.

By merging with a customer or supplier, a firm integrates into different stages of the production process. On its face, this type of merger leaves competitive levels unchanged in each market.[2] To use the above example, both the concrete and sand markets have the same number of competitors as before, only the ownership has changed.

Competition may be affected in other ways by the vertical integration. Two firms in the distribution chain have now become one. Each is assured of a source of supply and demand for its production. The integration may produce advantages over nonintegrated firms, such as economies of scale, distribution efficiencies and reduced transaction costs.[3] To remain competitive, the nonintegrated firms may have to integrate, as well.

Other, less obvious, secondary effects also may occur through vertical integration. One type of threat exists when the downstream firm has

---

[2] *See generally United States v. E.I. Du Pont de Nemours & Co.*, 353 U.S. 586 (1957); *Brown Shoe Co. v. United States*, 370 U.S. 294 (1962); T. Brunner, T. Krattenmaker, R. Skitol & A. Webster, *Mergers In the New Antitrust Era* (1985).

[3] *Paschall v. Kansas City Star Co.*, 727 F.2d 692 (8th Cir. 1984). *See also* discussion of vertical integration in § 7.04[B], *infra*.

monopoly power and is rate regulated on a cost–plus basis. The regulated firm may use the acquisition of a supplier to spread its profits over several transactions. Instead of making all the profits on sales of concrete, a monopolist could transfer some of the profits to the sand company by purchasing at inflated prices. In rate regulated industries, this spreading of profits would look like increased costs incurred by the downstream firm. These increased costs could be presented to the rate–making authority to justify a higher rate. Vertical integration with supply sources for rate–regulated monopolists makes proper rate base computation more complex and allows the monopolist more opportunities to inflate costs.[4]

Vertical integration can result in what courts speak of as "foreclosure." This occurs when the patronage or custom of the acquired firm is no longer available to competitors of the acquiring firm. If the acquiring firm supplies the acquired firm, other suppliers may be deprived of the ability to sell to that firm. Similarly, if the acquiring firm purchases from the acquired firm, competitors of the acquiring firm will be deprived, to a greater or lesser degree, of the ability to obtain needed supplies from the acquired firm. Whether or not this actually occurs, and to what extent this harms consumers by increasing the monopoly power of the firm will be discussed in § 7.04, *infra*, on economic theory in mergers.

[B] Conglomerate Mergers

Conglomerate mergers are those in which the merging firms had no prior relationship. The firms may have been potential competitors but they were not customers or suppliers of each other. "Pure" or "true" conglomerate mergers have no overt effect upon competition or market shares; they merely change the ownership of firms in the markets. We are, nevertheless, concerned with the effects of such a merger in concentrated markets.

Examples of conglomerate mergers include product market extension mergers, involving products closely identified with each other, and geographical market extensions. An example of the first includes when a manufacturer of detergents merges with a bleach producer. The second occurs when a bank in one market decides to enter and compete in another geographical market.[5]

Several theories of prosecution have been used to challenge conglomerate mergers. Reciprocity and entrenchment are two of the traditional theories.[6] Reciprocity may occur when one firm agrees to purchase items from another firm that purchases from it. For example, a silicon chip manufacturer may purchase computers for its office use from a computer firm that purchases

---

[4] *See, e.g., Application of Montana–Dakota Utilities Co. for Authority to Establish Increased Rates for Electric Service*, 278 N.W.2d 189 (S.D. 1979).

[5] *See generally United States v. Continental Can Co.*, 378 U.S. 441 (1964); *United States v. El Paso Natural Gas Co.*, 376 U.S. 651 (1964); *FTC v. Procter & Gamble Co.*, 386 U.S. 568 (1965).

[6] *See* discussion in § 5.02[B][6], *supra*.

silicon chips from it. Courts have feared that certain conglomerate mergers would facilitate these types of actions. A merger between two firms may increase the reciprocal purchasing that exists between those two firms; neither may buy from outside competitors. Those competitors (suppliers) may be foreclosed from supplying products to the two firms. From an antitrust perspective, we are concerned with a firm using its size to influence suppliers or customers to deal with the newly acquired firm in a manner which actually exploits the firm size and structure. The mere possibility of exploitation alone is not enough to warrant a finding of an illegal merger but "a finding of probability of reciprocal buying . . . should [warrant a finding of illegality] if there is substantial evidence to support it."[7]

Another traditional theory used to condemn conglomerate mergers is based on entrenchment. If a firm acquires another firm that already has substantial market share, the resulting acquisition may permit the acquired firm's market position to be further entrenched and reinforce the position of the dominant firm. Generally, however, we are concerned, under this theory, only if a dominant firm in one market is purchased by a large firm in another market. Size alone may discourage competitors from expanding or it may create barriers to entry for new competitors.[8] Certain economies may result, however, because of the vast resources resulting from the merger such as volume discounts, or advertising incentives that permit lower pricing. Cost saving may be passed on to the customer, but other competitors may be injured by this increased competition.

[C] Loss of Potential Competitors

The final theory used to challenge conglomerate mergers centers on diminished competition resulting from a loss of a potential competitor. This is the newest, and currently the most popular theory, for challenging conglomerate mergers. Mergers involving potential competitors are acquisitions between firms that are not in competition with each other but which are "actual potential entrants" in the market of the other or "perceived" as such.

The potential competitor, but for the merger, would have entered the market through some less anticompetitive means than through the challenged merger. This model of analysis is applied to mergers in concentrated industries. Examples include "de novo" entry where entry is without an acquisition of an existing competitor and a "toehold" entry through purchase of a smaller competitor. At the least, the firm is perceived as a potential competitor — one that had the ability to enter the market and would have done so within a reasonable period of time. The argument is that entry through these means, rather than by merger, would have resulted in a more deconcentrated and hence competitive market.[9]

---

[7] *FTC v. Consolidated Foods Corp.*, 380 U.S. 592, 600 (1965).

[8] *FTC v. Procter & Gamble Co.*, 386 U.S. 568, 579 (1967).

[9] *United States v. Marine Bancorporation, Inc.*, 418 U.S. 602 (1974); *United States v. El Paso Natural Gas Co.*, 376 U.S. 651 (1964); *FTC v. Procter & Gamble Co.*, 386 U.S. 568 (1967).

The merger of a potential entrant may be anticompetitive because the potential entrant sitting on the sidelines of a market helps keep prices lower in that market in two ways. The firms in that market may believe that the potential competitor will enter the market if they raise prices. Thus the existence of potential competition creates a restraining effect on prices. Additionally, even if the firms in that market do not believe the outside firm will enter, that firm may enter if the other companies raise their prices. Consequently, the new entrant will increase supply in the market and will help drive prices down.

Many cases that previously would have been decided under the conglomerate mergers theories of reciprocity or entrenchment are today viewed under the potential competitor doctrine.

§ 7.04 Economic Analysis of Mergers

[A] Horizontal Mergers

Horizontal mergers realign competitive relationships within markets. Firms that once competed with each other unite and compete as a single entity. The realignment can have substantial economic impact in the market. For example, it would have been illegal for the two firms to agree on price before a merger. After a merger, coordinated pricing is expected from unified management. The market power of the resulting firm will increase. Increased market power may result in enhanced economic efficiency or it may create a threat of predatory or oligopolistic pricing within the market, either through sheer size, market control or by collusion between the combined firm and other firms within the market.

Market power is the ability to set price without a resulting decrease in consumer demand. A measure of market power is the ability to price above marginal costs. Evidence of market power can be seen when there is price inelasticity of demand — the failure of the quantity demanded to fall commensurate with the price increase. The antitrust concern is that as a firm's market power grows, prices will increase above competitive levels.

Economic benefits may result from horizontal mergers that increase efficiency. Several theories have been advanced in support of mergers. First, mergers permit the movement of assets from lower to higher–valued uses through increased efficiencies and redeployment of assets. Second, mergers serve as a means to replace or discipline ineffective and entrenched corporate management. Third, mergers can produce efficiencies through joint operating agreements, economies of scale, financial economies and economies of scope. Finally, mergers can provide resource and service access for both the acquiring and acquired firms.[10] However, the amount of enhancement may be difficult to determine, even for a trained economist.

---

[10] Pitofsky, *Proposals for Revised United States Merger Enforcement in a Global Economy*, 81 Geo. L.J. 195 (1992); Sullivan, *The Antitrust Division As A Regulatory Agency: An Enforcement Policy In Transition*, 64 Wash. U. L.Q. 997 (1986), and authorities cited therein;

Restraints on competition, if they exist, are similar to those created by contractual agreements between competitors that result in cartels. The underlying theories against a liberal merger policy argue that mergers: (1) force management to operate only on short–term goals and protect against hostile takeovers, thereby diverting management attention away from long/term goals such as technological change; (2) damage management and personnel morale; (3) misallocate financial resources of lending institutions, "crowding out" more productive investments; (4) increase concentration and market power; and (5) permit leveraging to finance the acquisition which increases the debt/equity ratio to unacceptable levels.[11] A reviewing court will attempt to balance the costs of a merger against its benefits and determine whether there is a reasonable probability of the merger creating a substantial lessening of competition.[12]

[B] Vertical Integration Through Merger

Vertical integration usually occurs because a firm believes it can reduce costs by supplying itself a service or product.[13] A television manufacturer builds its own electronic components because it is cheaper than buying them from electronics suppliers. By supplying retail outlets itself, the manufacturer saves mark–up costs added by a wholesale distributor. When a supplier acquires a customer or potential customer, a forward vertical integration has occurred. When a customer acquires a supplier or potential supplier, a backward vertical integration occurs.[14]

Efficiency is one of the expected by–products of vertical integration. Whether done through internal expansion or through the acquisition of an existing firm, a firm is not likely to expand unless there is cost reduction to be gained; otherwise it will be cheaper and more efficient to continue to purchase the product or service from outside suppliers. Cost reductions may occur through technological, transactional, or distributional efficiencies.

Technological efficiencies in the above example would result if the television manufacturer could have the electronic components built into the

---

Cann, *Section 7 of the Clayton Act*, 60 Notre Dame L. Rev. 273 (1985); Fisher & Lande, *Efficiency Consideration In Merger Enforcement*, 71 Calif. L. Rev. 1580, (1983); Fisher, Lande, & Vandaele, *Afterword: Could a Merger Lead to Both a Monopoly and a Lower Price?*, 71 Calif. L. Rev. 1697 (1983). *See also* O. Williamson, *Economies As An Antitrust Defense: The Welfare Tradeoffs*, 58 Am. Econ. Rev. 18 (1968).

[11] Sullivan, *supra* note 10.

[12] For the economic theories outlining these costs and benefits *see* H. Hovenkamp, Federal Antitrust Policy, Chapter 9 (2d ed. 1994); E. Gellhorn, *Antitrust Law and Economics* 334–83 (3d ed. 1986); F.M. Sherer & D. Ross, *Industrial Market Structure and Economic Performance* (3d ed. 1990); Williamson, *supra* note 10.

[13] O. Williamson, *Markets and Hierarchies* (1975); O. Williamson, *The Economic Institutions of Capitalism*, 15–41 (1985); Spiller, *On Vertical Mergers*, 1 J. Law, Econ. & Organ. 285 (1985); Bork, *Vertical Integration and the Sherman Act: The Legal History of An Economic Misconception*, 22 U. Chi. L. Rev. 157 (1954). *See also* § 6.05[G], *supra*.

[14] 1995–2 Trade Reg. Rep. (CCH) ¶ 4330, 8097.

chassis of its sets. This would reduce the cost of placing and anchoring the components onto the chassis at a later time. These efficiencies usually occur when a plant expands internally; the electronics plant would have to be added physically at some point on the chassis assembly line or the electronics components would still have to be manufactured and placed on the chassis in two different steps. Acquiring an existing firm will usually not result in technological efficiencies.

Vertical mergers that do not result in technological efficiencies can still result in transactional efficiencies — costs saved by avoiding contracting in the marketplace.[15] The costs saved are often more substantial than any technological savings. In the above example, the electronics producers include a profit in their prices. These profits represent a cost to the television manufacturer. The profit the electronics company makes does not go into the revenues of the television company, nor does it contribute to the quality of electronics supplies available to the television company. By making its own electronic components, the television company can take the money saved by avoiding a contract with the electronics firms and either improve the quality of its product, or redeploy the savings elsewhere.

Firms can obtain other transactional cost savings through vertical mergers. State and Federal governments may require recordkeeping and payment of taxes for products purchased from other firms. Internal records must be kept of sales or purchases. By incorporating these other levels into its operations, a firm reduces the tax payments, the tax accounting costs and many of the internal accounting costs that result from outside purchases.

Finally, mergers may result in transactional cost savings in one other very significant area — market use costs. When purchasing products on the open market, a firm must expend time and effort obtaining information about, and negotiating with, other firms. Negotiating a contract with another firm involves time and risks that must be included in a firm's costs. One firm wants to produce the least expensive product that another firm will accept at the highest possible price. The other wants the best product at the lowest possible price. Arriving at a compromise between these two conflicting interests involves the costs of transacting. There is also the risk that one or the other may be taken advantage of in the negotiations because of superior bargaining skills or position.

Furthermore, firms want to deal with reliable entities; they want to be assured of adequate future supplies or markets for their products. Obtaining financial information about another firm always involves some risk; no one can be certain of the reliability of another firm's financial records. Checking the information requires increased cost and may not yield correct predictions. The risk created by dealing with other firms must figure into a firm's cost analysis.

Even after a firm begins to deal with another firm, negotiation and information costs can continue to increase. As technology and markets change,

---

[15] *See generally* O. Williamson, *The Economic Institutions of Capitalism* 85–130 (1985).

the firms involved in the original contract may wish revisions of the product. Using the previous television manufacturer example, an improved picture tube may become available. This tube may require higher electrical charges to function efficiently. The television manufacturer may be locked into a contract for electronics that supply lower level electrical charges. Changing the contract specifications will involve additional negotiation costs. For a manufacturer that owned its own electronics plant, an immediate change of electronic specifications may be less costly.

In the past, courts often condemned vertical mergers because increased efficiencies can be used to increase market power. Increases in market power allow firms to charge monopoly prices, to foreclose other rivals by restricting their source of supply, or to erect barriers to entry in either or both levels of the market.

Economists have attacked these theories on several grounds. They point out that increased efficiency most often results in benefits to the consumer. Even a monopolist may decrease prices and increase supply when its costs are reduced.[16]

Economists also point out that in even modestly competitive markets, vertical acquisitions do not really foreclose transactions. Unless both firms involved have substantial market power and the ability to expand production, or supply, a certain amount of readjustment takes place. If a manufacturer has 10% of the market and merges with a purchaser taking 50% of the manufactured market, the purchaser will still need to purchase 40% of its supply from others. Even if the manufacturer originally sold nothing to the purchaser, the 10% it now sells to the purchaser will no longer be available to other purchasers. Unless the manufacturer can significantly expand production, those other purchasers will go to other manufacturers for their supply.

Vertical integration can be anticompetitive in some instances, however. It may facilitate price discrimination, an activity condemned by § 2 of the Clayton Act. Usually, firms must charge approximately the same price to all purchasers. Otherwise, arbitrage takes place; purchasers that buy cheaply sell to other purchasers at a price between what the first purchasers paid and what the other purchasers have to pay. A manufacturer may circumvent arbitrage through a vertical merger. The television manufacturer may sell its products to retail firms for $50.00. However, a manufacturer of entertainment consoles may be able to include the television in the console and sell it for a price that would permit it to pay $100.00 for the television. If the television manufacturer begins to charge $100.00 to the manufacturer of the entertainment consoles, the latter will substitute suppliers and will be supplied by other purchasers of the TV at a price between $50.00 and $100.00.

All price discrimination is not necessarily bad. If the television manufacturer determined that its profit–maximizing price before the merger

---

[16] *But see* Fisher, Lande, & Vandaele, *supra* note 10.

encouraged selling to the entertainment console manufacturer at $100.00, it could make the few sales it could get in the retail market at that price. The television manufacturer may then be able to maximize profits by selling to retail stores at $50.00 and by getting $100.00 for televisions sold to the entertainment console manufacturer. This would increase supply and decrease price to the consumer.

Vertical integration also may foreclose competition in either the supply or the customer markets. It also may erect barriers to entry which chill incentives for potential competitors to enter the market and it may serve as a device to evade a regulatory scheme. Finally, although an entity is not forbidden under § 7 from making a series of small vertical acquisitions, if the combination of the acquisitions becomes large enough to have an adverse effect on trade, a violation may have occurred.[17] A large collection of independent vertical integrations or a pattern of them over time can have the same effect as a single trade–restraining merger in some cases.[18]

§ 7.05 Legal Analysis of § 7: An Overview

Section 7 of the Clayton Act proscribes mergers or acquisitions that have a reasonable probability of substantially lessening competition within a market.[19] This standard allows courts to invalidate mergers only if they threaten to reduce competition in a substantial market by a substantial amount.

In interpreting this standard, courts must estimate what effect a merger will have on competition within the affected market. To accomplish this, courts first determine the relevant market and then estimate the effect the merger will have on that market. In making the first determination, courts must define both the geographical and the product markets.

[A] Geographical Market

The size of the relevant geographical market depends on the type of product sold and the capabilities of firms selling that product. The geographical market includes the area that consumers will look to when satisfying a consumption need: If consumers of televisions located in St. Louis look as far as Chicago to satisfy their needs, then Chicago must be included within the geographical market for televisions sold in the St. Louis area.[20] Likewise, if Chicago suppliers would increase or decrease production because of prices in St. Louis then the geographical market is the same.[21] "The proper definition of a geographic market is determined by a

---

[17] *Chateau De Ville Productions, Inc. v. Tams–Witmark Music Library, Inc.*, 586 F.2d 962 (2d Cir. 1978).

[18] *Id.*

[19] 15 U.S.C. § 18.

[20] *See generally United States v. Grinnell Corp.*, 384 U.S. 563 (1966).

[21] *See generally United States v. Columbia Steel*, 334 U.S. 495 (1948); *Twin City Sportservice Inc. v. Charles O. Finley & Co.*, 512 F.2d 1264 (9th Cir. 1975).

'factual inquiry into the "commercial realities" faced by consumers.' "[22] Presenting evidence concerning only the individual perspectives of certain competitors will not be sufficient in defining the relevant geographic market.[23] Similarly, evidence concerning the present–day habits of consumers of the product or service at hand alone will not suffice to detail the parameters of the market.[24] The main concern is the practicable alternatives of which the consumer is aware.

The relevant geographical area can include distant supply points. If a manufacturer in Los Angeles can supply easily and cheaply the needs of consumers in St. Louis, then Los Angeles becomes an extension of the St. Louis geographical market, even though consumers in St. Louis would not look to Los Angeles to shop for their needs. The price of the product relative to transportation and other market costs significantly affects the supply accessibility to markets. The cheaper the relative costs of selling the product in St. Louis, the more likely Los Angeles manufacturers are to ship that product to St. Louis. Conversely, as the cost of shipping the product to St. Louis rises above what St. Louis manufacturers sell the product for, the more likely it is that the Los Angeles manufacturers will not enter or continue in the St. Louis market.

A study of the marginal, relative movements of firms in two geographical locations often helps determine whether the two are in the same geographical market.

[B] Product Market

In addition to determining the relevant geographical market, courts also must determine the relevant product market.[25] The relevant product market is the smallest market where the hypothetical firm having all the total production of that product could increase price but not lose enough customers to decrease profits. In other words, the product market must be large enough to include all the effective substitutes that buyers would turn to should price increase. "Where an increase in the price of one product leads to an increase in demand for another, both products should be included in the relevant product market."[26] This is a fine distinction, however. Products need not be fungible in order to be part of the same product market, but a minute increase in demand in response to a product's increase in price does not necessarily place the goods in the same product

---

[22] *Bathke v. Casey's General Stores, Inc.*, 64 F.3d 340, 345 (8th Cir. 1995) (citations omitted).

[23] *Id.*

[24] *Id.*

[25] *See generally United States v. E.I. Du Pont de Nemours & Co.*, 351 U.S. 377 (1956); Note, *The Cellophane Fallacy and the Justice Department's Guidelines for Horizontal Mergers*, 94 Yale L.J. 670 (1985). The *Merger Guidelines*, discussed more fully *infra*, use the following terminology when determining who should be included in the market definition: entities that would respond to "a small but significant and nontransitory" price increase (of 5% for the foreseeable future) by beginning to compete in the market by supplying competing products.

[26] *Olin Corp. v. FTC*, 986 F.2d 1295, 1298 (9th Cir. 1993).

market, either.[27] As the court found in *United States v. Bethlehem Steel*,[28] distinct products like iron and steel can be part of the same relevant market when sold in a market that is recognized and has its own competitive standards.

The relevant product market, for example, defined for television sets, would be larger than the market for a certain brand or even a certain type. If price increased for these brands or types, the consumer may switch to others. If the quantity demanded in a product is affected by price changes of other products then the two are defined within the same product market. The relevant market may even be larger than "black and white" or "color" televisions; if color television prices increased, consumers may substitute black and white. The market would not probably include other electronic entertainment devices; radios, for instance, may not be viewed by customers as an adequate substitute for televisions. However, if consumers did substitute or if radio manufacturers could cheaply and easily switch their plants to television production in response to a price change in televisions, then a court might include the production capabilities of radio manufacturers in the relevant product market for televisions.

Finally, courts have held that, in some situations, when the product is truly unique and without adequate substitution, a single product brand can constitute the entire relevant product market.[29] Also, products and their parts do not need to be peculiar to a market in order to be part of it.[30] Thus, even generic products may have enough similarity with the product in question to be "reasonably interchangeable" with it.[31]

[C] Market Power

Once the relevant markets, both product and geographical, have been established, courts examine the percentage of the market, or market shares, controlled by the merging firms. Market share is used frequently as a proxy for market power. Price elasticity of demand and cross–elasticity of demand are also measures of market power. Depending on the relevant product market, other factors also may serve as evidence of market power.

The purpose of antitrust merger law is to deter monopoly and oligopolistic pricing and conditions that facilitate collusion. High concentrations of market shares in the hands of a single monopolist or a few competitors threaten competitive pricing. Courts, therefore, look to the market shares of the merging firms and to the market as a whole. Traditionally, courts used a four–firm concentration ratio to measure market concentration. Under this approach, courts added the shares of the four top competitors

---

[27] *Id.* at 1299.

[28] 168 F. Supp. 579 (S.D.N.Y. 1958).

[29] *See Tarrant Service Agency, Inc. v. American Standard, Inc.*, 12 F.3d 609, 614 (6th Cir. 1993).

[30] *Id.*

[31] *Id.*

in the market. If those firms respectively held 25%, 20%, 15% and 10% of the market, then the concentration ratio was 70%. This would be considered a highly concentrated market, and any merger in that market would fall under close scrutiny.

The original Department of Justice *Merger Guidelines* issued in 1968 considered mergers of two firms with 4% market shares each presumptively illegal in concentrated markets. In less concentrated markets, the shares had to be at least 5% each. Either standard was more lenient than the previous case law suggested. The *Guidelines* were an attempt to identify mergers which would alter market structure towards noncompetitive conduct. [32]

The 1982, 1984 and 1992 *Guidelines* abandoned the use of this traditional four–firm concentration analysis. The *Guidelines* instead use the *Herfindahl–Hirschman Index (HHI)* to determine market concentration. Under the *HHI*, market concentration equals the sum of the squares of the market percentage of every firm in the market. If a market has only four firms, each with 25% of the market, the *HHI* would be 2,500(25^2 x 4). On the other hand, if the market had ten firms each with 10% of the market, the *HHI* would be 1,000. Any market with an *HHI* over 1,800 is considered highly concentrated, between 1,800 and 1,000 moderately concentrated, and below 1,000, unconcentrated.

The *HHI* skews the concentration scale towards one or more large firms with high market shares; a market having one firm with 80% of the market would have a higher *HHI* than would a market with 4 firms having 22% each. Under the old four–firm concentration ratio, if the next three firms in the first market each had 2% of the output, the concentration ratio would be the same in that market as it would be in the market with four firms having 22% each. Markets controlled by one or two very large firms present greater threats of oligopolistic pricing than do markets evenly divided amongst four firms.

By looking at the total market concentration, the *HHI* can be used to determine whether a merger creates a threat to competition in that industry. In markets that have dispersed market power among many competitors, mergers generally will not create significant problems except under unusual circumstances. The *HHI* recognizes this by giving a "safe harbor" status to any merger that results in a post–merger *HHI* of 1,000 or less, "except in extraordinary circumstances." In markets with post–merger *HHI*'s between 1,000 and 1,800 the agency is unlikely to challenge any merger that produces an *HHI* increase of less than 100 points. In

---

[32] *U.S. Department of Justice Merger Guidelines*, 2 Trade Reg. Rep. (CCH) 4510 (May 30, 1968). *See U.S. v. Pabst Brewing Co.*, 384 U.S. 546 (1966). The 1968 *Merger Guidelines* employed the four–firm concentration ratio, while the 1982, 1984 and 1992 *Guidelines* examine the entire market share distribution for all firms. *See generally* Kwoka, *The Effect of Market Share Distribution On Industry Performance*, 61 Rev. Econ. Stat. 101 (1979); Cohen & Sullivan, *The Herfindahl–Hirschman Index and The New Antitrust Merger Guidelines: Concentrating on Concentration*, 62 Texas L. Rev. 453 (1983).

markets with post–merger *HHI*'s above 1,800, the agency is likely to challenge any merger that increases *HHI* by 100 points and is suspect of mergers that increase the *HHI* by 50 points or more.[33]

§ 7.06   Mergers Under The Sherman Act: The Early Years

The history of law governing mergers begins with the railroad merger cases in the early 1900s. In applying the Sherman Act, the Supreme Court originally held that all mergers between competitors violated the law. The Court in *Northern Securities Co. v. United States*[34] reasoned that every time competing firms combined, they lessened competition by eliminating competition between the merging firms.[35] These results bespoke of a rigid test that would condemn any merger and indeed there seemed to be a significant decrease in merger activity after the 1904 decision.[36] In the 1911 decision of *Standard Oil Co. v. United States*[37] the Court struck down a merger under the Sherman Act because the merger resulted in a monopoly in violation of § 2. But in *Standard Oil* the Court announced a broad rule of reason approach which suggested the approval of some mergers.

In *United States v. United States Steel Corp.*,[38] the Court upheld a merger that resulted in a post–merger firm controlling at least 80% of the market, even after finding that the merger occurred with the intent to gain monopoly control of the steel industry. Unless a merger actually resulted in monopoly control, the Court seemed willing to permit it. In *United States v. Columbia Steel Co.*,[39] the Court allowed a merger that brought control of approximately one–quarter of the steel fabrication market into one firm. The Court held that a large market share in and of itself does not constitute unreasonable restraint. Instead, the Court looked to characteristics of the market, including the strength of remaining competition, consumer demands, development in the industry, and most importantly, whether the merger resulted from an intent to monopolize or from business requirements. After these cases, it seemed that the Sherman Act would prevent mergers only where the firms actually intended to, and did, accomplish a monopoly. Congress responded to the Court's permissive treatment in *Standard Oil* with new legislation.

---

[33] 1992 *Justice Department Merger Guidelines*, 57 Fed. Reg. 41, 552–01, § 1.5–1.51 (1992). *See also supra* § 6.04[A][1]–[2], and *infra* § 7.09; T. Brunner, T. Krattenmaker, R. Skitol & A. Webster, *supra* note 2.

[34] 193 U.S. 197 (1904). This approach was similar to that of *Trans Missouri*, discussed *supra*, Chapters 1 & 4.

[35] *Id.* at 327.

[36] *See generally* 221 U.S. 1 (1911). *See Sullivan, supra* note 10.

[37] 221 U.S. 1 (1911).

[38] 251 U.S. 417, 451 (1920) ("the law does not make mere size an offence or the existence of unexerted power an offence").

[39] 334 U.S. 495 (1948).

§ 7.07 The Clayton Act

In 1914, Congress passed § 7 of the Clayton Act in response to the rule of reason standard used by the Supreme Court in *Standard Oil*. The original provision was easily circumvented, though, as many believed that it applied only to stock purchases. If a company acquired the assets of another company rather than its stock, the merger was still tested under the more lenient rule of reason under the Sherman Act.[40]

Furthermore, the Clayton Act only applied to mergers that lessened competition between competing firms. It failed to reach vertical mergers or other nonhorizontal mergers when the merging firms were not in competition with each other. Even if the merger lessened competition between the post merger firm and other businesses in the market, the Clayton Act did not apply.[41]

Concerned with the rising tide of industrial concentration and pushed by a 1948 Federal Trade Commission report concluding that giant corporations were taking over the country,[42] Congress amended § 7 in 1950. The legislative history illustrates that Congress was concerned that large corporations would drive smaller competitors out of the market through predatory conduct, as well as with the threat of monopolistic or oligopolistic pricing. Increased business concentration was the focus of the Act. Congress favored local control over markets and protection for small businesses.[43] The Celler–Kefauver amendments to § 7 were designed to reach both horizontal and vertical acquisitions, to cover mergers in their incipiency when there was a tendency toward a monopoly, and to allow courts to enjoin mergers with only a showing of a reasonable probability of anticompetitive effects.[44]

The first case to embrace the expanded coverage of § 7 was *United States v. E.I. Du Pont de Nemours & Co.*,[45] even though it was decided under the original § 7. In *Du Pont* the Court held that stock acquisitions by Du Pont of 23% of General Motors stock before 1920 had an anticompetitive effect

---

[40] *See, e.g., FTC v. Western Meat Co.*, 272 U.S. 554 (1926).

[41] "Lessening of competition" has been defined broadly to mean having "an effect on competition [which is] injurious to the public." 1995–2 Trade Cas. (CCH) ¶ 4270, 7965. In proving such an effect on competition, it is not necessary to prove intent on the part of the acquiring company or individual. *Id.* at 7966.

[42] FTC, *Report on the Merger Movement: A Summary Report* 68 (1948) ("all forms of economic activity have come under the domination of the Big Four, the Big Six, or in some cases, the leader").

[43] *Brown Shoe Co. v. United States*, 370 U.S. 294, 311–18 (1962); *United States v. E.I. Du Pont de Nemours & Co.*, 353 U.S. 586 (1957). *See also* Bork, *Section 7 of the Clayton Act and the Merging of Law and Economics*, 74 Harv. L. Rev. 226, 233–38 (1960); Lande, *Wealth Transfers as the Original and Primary Concern of Antitrust: The Efficiency Interpretation Challenged*, 34 Hastings L.J. 65 (1982); Fisher & Lande, *Efficiency Considerations in Merger Enforcement*, 72 Calif. L. Rev. 1580 (1983); Hovenkamp, *Antitrust Policy After Chicago*, 84 Mich. L. Rev. 213, 249–50 (1985).

[44] *Id. See also United States v. E.I. Du Pont de Nemours & Co.*, 351 U.S. 377 (1956).

[45] 353 U.S. 586 (1957).

because the merger had the reasonable probability of foreclosing other sellers of automobiles (competitors of General Motors) from dealing with Du Pont and foreclosing Du Pont from selling fabrics and paints to General Motors' competitors. Plaintiff was not required to show an actual restraint as long as there was a reasonable probability of a substantial lessening of competition.

It is interesting to note that the behavior challenged in *du Pont* occurred in 1918–1920, but the suit was not brought until 1949. As explained in *United States v. ITT Continental Baking Company*,[46] the Court in *du Pont* interpreted the words "acquire" and "acquisition" to encompass more than just the original shifting of control of the entity. Rather,

> the Court held that there is a violation 'any time when the acquisition threatens to ripen into a prohibited effect. . .' To accomplish the congressional aim, the Government may proceed at any time that an acquisition may be said with reasonable probability to contain a threat that it may lead to a restraint of commerce or tend to create a monopoly of a line of commerce.[47]

Thus, there can be a violation at some time later even if there was clearly no violation — no realistic threat of restraint of commerce or creation of a monopoly — at the time of the initial acts of acquisition. Clearly, this result can obtain only because "acquisition" under § 7 is not a discrete transaction but a status which continues until the transaction is undone.[48]

[A] Vertical Integration Through Merger

A firm may expand business into new markets by new (*de novo*) entry or through acquisition of an existing firm. The latter is known as vertical integration through merger. It occurs when two firms stand in a buyer–seller relationship. In *United States v. Yellow Cab*,[49] the Supreme Court focused upon the intent of the acquiring firm as well as the anticompetitive effects of foreclosure. The Court held that a civil complaint charging monopolization under § 2 of the Sherman Act should not have been dismissed because defendants were charged with both the intent to restrain interstate commerce and with effectuating that intent. The Court rejected defendant's contention that their common ownership prevented application of the Sherman Act.

---

[46] 420 U.S. 223, 241 (1975). The first paragraph of 15 U.S.C. § 18 provides:

No corporation engaged in commerce shall acquire, directly or indirectly, the whole or any part of the stock or other share capital and no corporation subject to the jurisdiction of the Federal Trade Commission shall acquire the whole or any part of the assets of another corporation engaged also in commerce, where in any line of commerce in any section of the country, the effect of such acquisition may be substantially to lessen competition, or to tend to create a monopoly.

[47] 420 U.S. at 242 (*quoting du Pont* at 597).

[48] *Id.*

[49] 332 U.S. 218 (1947).

In *Yellow Cab*, Checker Cab, a manufacturer of cabs, had acquired several cab companies in several cities. The acquisitions resulted in control of a large portion of the taxicab services available in these cities, including 80% of the market in Chicago. The Court held that if anticompetitive intent could be shown, the acquisition violated the Sherman Act. "[A] conspiracy among those who are affiliated or integrated under common ownership"[50] may violate the Sherman Act if the underlying intent was to foreclose competition.

The acquisition of the cab companies by Checker Cab meant that the cab companies might be forced to purchase their cabs solely from Checker Cab. Competition would be unreasonably affected because other cab suppliers would be "foreclosed" from selling to those cab operators controlled by Checker. Cab companies may have to pay more for the cabs than they would in a competitive market. Higher costs to cab companies would result in higher prices to consumers. The Court concluded that:

> The fact that these restraints occur in . . . a vertically integrated enterprise does not necessarily remove the ban of the Sherman Act . . . . [A] restraint may result as readily from a conspiracy among those who are affiliated or integrated under common ownership as from a conspiracy among those who are otherwise independent . . . . [A]ny affiliation or integration flowing from an illegal conspiracy cannot insulate the conspirators from the sanctions which Congress has imposed.[51]

The Court's analysis has been challenged on the grounds that a vertically integrated firm cannot profit by selling to itself at an inflated price; the selling division's profits would be offset by the purchasing division's losses.[52] More likely is the result that the vertical integration will lead to a reduction of the costs of transacting in the market, thereby permitting cost savings to be passed on to the consumer. Other market factors are relevant, however.

If a manufacturer has a large captive source of sales, which provide sufficient profits, that manufacturer may not be inclined to spend the same amount of research and development money to improve cabs or lower the price. In the case of cab operating companies, the market was limited by local regulation.[53] With Checker Cab controlling so much of the market in major cities, there was little incentive for other cab manufacturers to spend money in research or to lower cab prices. Checker effectively became a price

---

[50] *Id.* at 227. The complaint allegations in *Yellow Cab* were summarized by the Court in *United States v. Columbia Steel Co.* as follows: "there was a plan, an intent, to monopolize the cab business, from manufacture through operation in the four large cities, by acquiring cab operating companies or interests therein; tying those companies into a cab manufacturing company and requiring the operating companies to purchase their cabs from the manufacturer at a price above the prevailing market." 334 U.S. 495, 521 (1948).

[51] 332 U.S. at 227. *But see Copperweld Corp. v. Independence Tube Corp.*, 467 U.S. 752 (1984) (holding that a parent and a wholly owned subsidiary are legally incapable of violating § 1 of the Sherman Act). *See* § 4.15[C].

[52] H. Hovenkamp, *supra* note 11; Bork, *supra* note 13, at 195–201.

[53] Kitch, *The Regulation of Taxicabs in Chicago*, 15 J.L. & Econ. 285, 327 (1972).

leader in the cab manufacturing market by controlling such a large share of the cab purchasing market. The foreclosure theory espoused in *Yellow Cab* has continued, but not without significant challenge.

In another case predating the 1950 amendments to the Clayton Act, the Court, in applying the Sherman Act, permitted a merger between a large steel supplier and a large steel fabricator. In *United States v. Columbia Steel Company*,[54] the Court ruled that an asset merger of the purchaser and supplier did not restrict the market opportunities of other steel suppliers. The *Columbia Steel* Court interpreted *Yellow Cab* as requiring a showing of an unlawful intent to monopolize or a substantial effect on the market in order to sustain a Sherman Act violation.

The Court implied that if a merger results in less than a monopoly it is lawful under the Sherman Act, absent illegal intent. It found that the Government failed to make this showing. "A subsidiary will in all probability deal only with its parent for goods the parent can furnish. That fact, however, does not make the acquisition invalid . . . ."[55] The Court concluded that Consolidated purchases of rolled steel products only accounted for 3% of the relevant product market. The merger produced one firm with a market share of 24% This did not foreclose a great enough percentage of the market to have a substantial effect on competition; 97% of the rolled steel products market was still available to other steel suppliers.

In *United States v. E.I. Du Pont de Nemours & Co.*,[56] the Supreme Court returned to the "foreclosure theory" of *Yellow Cab* and found a violation under the Clayton Act. Du Pont's purchases of 23% of General Motors' stock prior to 1920 were sufficient to support the violation. It was the first time the Supreme Court applied § 7 of the Clayton Act to a vertical merger.

In *Du Pont*, the Court went much further than in *Yellow Cab*. No actual monopoly existed in *Du Pont*. As a matter of fact, General Motors still purchased paint and fabrics from other suppliers when those suppliers were the low bidder. Nonetheless, the Court concentrated on the percentage of the market affected by the purchase of Du Pont products by General Motors. The relevant product market was determined as automotive paint finishes and fabrics, despite a showing that other non–automotive finishes were interchangeable with automotive finishes.

In this limited market, Du Pont's sales to General Motors were seen as foreclosing other suppliers of automotive finishes. Du Pont supplied approximately 67% of General Motors paint finishes. Because General Motors controlled such a large share of the automotive market, approximately one–half, this foreclosed 33% of automotive finish sales from other suppliers.

In *Du Pont*, the Court noted that the two required elements of § 7 had been established: (1) The market affected was substantial, and (2)

---

[54] 334 U.S. 495 (1948). At the time *Yellow Cab* and *Columbia Steel* were decided, courts believed that § 7 of the Clayton Act did not apply to either vertical mergers or asset acquisitions.

[55] *Id.* at 523.

[56] 353 U.S. 586 (1957).

competition would be foreclosed in a substantial share of the relevant market. The automotive fabric and finish markets both were found to be substantial and were substantially affected by General Motors' and Du Pont's market shares. The resulting foreclosure, the Court concluded, also was substantial. The Court held that the standard under § 7 was whether, because of the acquisition, there was a reasonable probability of a substantial lessening of competition or the reasonable likelihood of foreclosure of a substantial share of the market. This "reasonable probability" standard connoted the liberal approach of § 7 — to arrest restraints in their "incipiency."

The Court went even further in the first case decided under the 1950 amendments to the Clayton Act. In *Brown Shoe Co. v. U.S.*,[57] a vertical integration case, the Court invalidated an acquisition of a shoe retailer by a shoe manufacturer when the retailer controlled only 5% of its market and the manufacturer controlled only 1%. Even though the shoe market was unconcentrated and neither party to the merger controlled a substantial share, the Court noted a trend toward acquisitions of retailers by shoe manufacturers with certain manufacturers supplying increasingly large percentages of the captive retailers' needs.[58] Other manufacturers were foreclosed from supplying these captive retailers, the Court opined. It relied upon § 7's expressed intent of halting market concentration in the early stages and the absence of any business justification for the merger. The Court seemed most concerned with the fact that this was a merger between the fourth largest manufacturer and the eighth largest retailer. Said the Court: "Congress was desirous of preventing the formation of further oligopolies with their attendant adverse effects upon local control of industry and upon small business."[59]

In a more recent case, the Second Circuit purported to apply the foreclosure doctrine espoused by the Supreme Court in *Brown Shoe*, but reached a result that seems in conflict with it. In *Fruehauf Corp. v. FTC*,[60] the Second Circuit approved a merger between Fruehauf and Kelsey–Hayes (K–H). Fruehauf was the largest truck manufacturer in the United States; K–H supplied wheels and brakes to truck manufacturers. The FTC found that the merger would lessen competition in both the wheel and brake markets by foreclosing K–H's competitors from selling to Fruehauf, and

---

[57] 370 U.S. 294 (1962).

[58] Others have found contrary evidence, *see* Peterman, *The Federal Trade Commission v. Brown Shoe Company*, 18 J.L. & Econ. 361 (1975). For a discussion of the possible similarities between the industry in *Brown Shoe* and assorted vertical mergers in the entertainment industry, *see* Patrick M. Cox, *What Goes Up Must Come Down: Grounding the Dizzying Height of Vertical Mergers in the Entertainment Industry*, 25 Hofstra L.Rev. 261, (1996). (Cox opines that inquiries into the "real motivations behind the proposed mergers" and "concern regarding motivations and trends in the industry" are potentially successful lines of attack against some vertical mergers in the entertainment field). *Id.* at 309–10, 312.

[59] 370 U.S. at 333. *See also Ford Motor Co. v. United States*, 405 U.S. 562 (1972) (condemning Ford's acquisition of a manufacturer of spark plugs).

[60] 603 F.2d 345 (2d Cir. 1979).

that the merger would give Fruehauf an advantage over other manufacturers in obtaining supply.

The court read *Brown* as requiring a showing of a probable anticompetitive effect on the market, such as "a trend toward integration; reduction in number of potential market competitors; entrenchment of a large supplier or purchaser; [or] increase in barriers to entry."[61]

The Second Circuit found no actual anticompetitive effect. The FTC had alleged that Fruehauf would have "a substantial competitive advantage over other"[62] competitors in times of shortage. The Second Circuit disagreed. It found that K–H was not a significant and substantial supplier to Fruehauf's competitors; it did not sell more than 7% of the supplies purchased by the manufacturers, including Fruehauf. The court also noted that there was no showing that K–H would sell only to Fruehauf in times of shortage; good business practices and the threat of private antitrust actions would prevent such action. Even after accepting the fact that (1) the wheel market was highly concentrated (the top four firms controlled 65–71%, and the top eight firms held 93–95%) and (2) the fact that barriers to entry were substantial (already at $10–20 million), the court found no anticompetitive threat.

The Second Circuit relied most heavily on the fact that no trend existed toward vertical integration. Also, only low market shares were affected and evidence of bad intent was absent. But for the lack of a vertical integration trend in this market, *Brown Shoe* seemed indistinguishable. The Second Circuit decision, therefore, suggests a more hospitable climate for vertical integration through mergers. Other circuits have followed suit in approving vertical integration, largely on the theory that although vertical integration may hurt other competitors, its efficiency–enhancing potential will be a direct benefit to consumers through the pass–on of the cost–savings.[63] For other courts, however, the issues of entry barriers and foreclosure remain problematic.[64]

In sum, courts have focused their attention on the following inquiries when a vertical integration is challenged: (1) whether competitors of the supplier or the buyer will be foreclosed from the market; (2) whether there is a *trend* towards vertical integration in the market; (3) whether there is an intent to foreclose competition; and (4) whether barriers to entry are erected that foreclose equal access to markets.

---

[61] *Id.* at 353.

[62] *Id.* at 354.

[63] *See, e.g., Paschall v. Kansas City Star Co.*, 727 F.2d 692 (8th Cir. 1984). *But see Ash Grove Cement Co. v. FTC*, 577 F.2d 1368 (9th Cir. 1978). Some of the specific efficiencies associated with vertical mergers include design and production coordination and the internalization of incentives for each merger partner to help the other and forego free–riding opportunities. *See* Michael H. Riordan & Steven C. Salop, *Evaluating Vertical Mergers: A Post–Chicago Approach*, 63 Antitrust L.J. 513, 523–25 (1995).

[64] Information exchange and regulation evasion are also of concern. *See* Michael H. Riordan & Steven C. Salop, *Evaluating Vertical Mergers: A Post–Chicago Approach*, 63 Antitrust L.J. 513, 564 (1995).

[B] Horizontal Mergers

As noted previously, horizontal merger law first developed under the Sherman Act. Originally, the Supreme Court held that all mergers between competitors restrained competition and violated § 1 of the Act.[65] By 1948 this *per se* illegality had been extinguished. Subsequent decisions limited the rule to railroad mergers.

In 1948 it became clear that the Supreme Court would only invalidate mergers under the Sherman Act if they verged upon a monopoly.[66] In *Columbia Steel*, the Court sanctioned a merger even though the steel industry was very concentrated, and even though the merger involved concentrated 24% of the market in one firm. The Court looked to other characteristics of the market, including the strength of competitors, the percent of the market controlled, and the intent of the merger. But *Columbia Steel* is distinguishable in several respects from more modern cases under § 7.

Columbia Steel was brought under the Sherman Act because U.S. Steel merely purchased the assets of Consolidated Steel; therefore, the Clayton Act did not apply. The Sherman Act requires a more substantial showing under the rule of reason test than does the amended Clayton Act. Finally, evidence demonstrated that while the two firms both produced fabricated steel products, they were of different types and the two firms rarely bid on the same jobs. This last rationale was undercut by the elasticity of supply that exists among steel products.

The Court's horizontal merger decisions under the Clayton Act also have been somewhat inconsistent. After the 1950 Cellar–Kefauver Amendments to the Clayton Act, the Court began to respond to Congressional fears that larger, merging companies would destroy smaller businesses. In 1962, the Court gave its first response to Congressional concerns. In *Brown Shoe Co. v. United States*,[67] the Court held that the horizontal portion of the merger between Brown Shoe Co. (Brown) and Kinney Shoe Co. (Kinney) violated § 7 of the Clayton Act. In doing so, the Court listed some important factors in judging the validity of a merger in a deconcentrated market under the amended § 7: (1) market share data, (2) concentration percentages, (3) industry trends, and (4) entry barrier evidence.

The Court noted that Congress had plugged the loopholes in the Clayton Act and that § 7 now reached mergers involving acquisitions of assets, as well as stock acquisitions. The amended § 7 also reached vertical and conglomerate mergers, if their effects would tend to lessen competition in any line of commerce in any section of the country.

Most important, the Court noted that § 7 gave courts the authority to stop, in their incipiency, any trends toward a lessening competition. No longer did courts need to find that a substantial lessening of competition

---

[65] *Northern Securities Co. v. United States*, 193 U.S. 197 (1904).

[66] *United States v. Columbia Steel*, 374 U.S. 495 (1948).

[67] 370 U.S. 294 (1962).

would occur as a direct result of the merger; the tendency to do so in the future was enough. Closely coupled to this was the fact that the amended § 7 allowed courts to stop mergers based on reasonable probabilities of anticompetitive effects, rather than certainties.

Brown Shoe, however, did not signal the demise of all mergers. The Court recognized that even under the amended § 7, some mergers were still legal or even commendable. A merger of "small companies . . . [with the purpose] to compete with larger corporations dominating the market" would be permitted, as would mergers involving a failing company that would otherwise be unable to have a viable competitive effect on the market.[68] In short, Congress intended in enacting § 7 to protect "competition, not competitors, and desire[d] to restrain mergers only to the extent that such combinations may tend to lessen competition."[69]

Brown Shoe involved a merger between a retailer and manufacturer of shoes. The merger had horizontal and vertical elements since each competed on two levels. The Court defined as the relative market every city with a population exceeding 10,000 and its surrounding territory in which both Brown and Kinney sold shoes at retail. Within that market, the combined share of Brown and Kinney sales exceeded 20% in most markets, and in some it ran as high as 50%. The Court noted that the merged market share was an important factor to be considered in determining the probable effects of a merger.

The Court, in invalidating the merger, gave effect to the Congressional desire to promote competition by protecting small, locally owned businesses, even if higher prices might occasionally result. In doing so, the Court relied heavily on the fact that the shoe industry had exhibited a trend toward concentration in the years preceding the merger, that a large national chain was involved in the merger, and that it believed that this merger would intensify the existing concentration. These factors resurfaced in significant ways in later decisions.

Brown Shoe established a broad, multifaceted rule of reason under § 7 for evaluating horizontal mergers. A plaintiff need not show monopoly power resulting from the merger or that there is an *actual* lessening of competition. The result in *Brown Shoe* demonstrates an antimerger tone and an inhospitality toward horizontal mergers. The Court feared industry concentration, believed that § 7 was designed to further deconcentration and the dispersion of economic power, and stressed the desirability of protecting small businesses from larger, perhaps more efficient, firms.

In 1963, the Court seemed to move even further toward establishing *prima facie* illegality for horizontal mergers, at least for mergers in concentrated markets. In *United States v. Philadelphia National Bank*,[70] the Court invalidated a merger between two banks, though the merger

---

[68] *Id.* at 331.
[69] *Id.* at 320.
[70] 374 U.S. 321 (1963).

would permit the banks to compete more effectively for loans with larger commercial banks outside the Philadelphia area. The Court reasoned that procompetitive effects in one market did not justify anticompetitive effects in another, and that beneficial economic consequences could not save mergers with anticompetitive tendencies.

The merger between the second and third largest banks in Philadelphia would have created the largest firm in the market, controlling 30% of the banking business in the relevant four county Philadelphia metropolitan area. With this large market share, in an already concentrated market, the Court presumed an inherently anticompetitive tendency that the banks were unable to rebut.[71]

In contrast to *Brown Shoe*'s analysis for mergers in deconcentrated markets, *Philadelphia National Bank* set the standard for mergers in concentrated markets. A presumption of illegality exists for horizontal mergers in concentrated markets when, as a result of the merger, the resulting firm controls an "undue market share" and market concentration significantly increases. Although the Court did not define "undue market share," the 30% challenged there served as the Court's benchmark for invoking the presumption of illegality. The Court noted that even a merger resulting in less than a 30% market share might raise an inference of illegality.

However, the presumption is rebuttable if the defense introduces evidence that the merger is not anticompetitive. The available defenses were not evident. To be sure, the Court seemed to reject as defenses enhanced efficiencies, ease of market entry, economies of scale and increased competition in other markets. The "failing company" defense was approved, however, as an absolute defense. Thus, even if the merger in a concentrated market is not illegal under *Philadelphia National Bank*, the merger may still be examined under the deconcentrated industry test of *Brown Shoe* where the economic effects will be weighed. The next case the Court decided seemed to further the rigidity of the presumption of illegality.

In *United States v. Von's Grocery*,[72] the Court invalidated a merger between the third and sixth largest grocery companies in Los Angeles, even

---

[71] The District Court in the Northern District of Texas in *T&T Geotechnical, Inc. v. Union Pacific Resources Company*, 944 F.Supp. 1317 (N.D. Texas, 1996), recently denied an attempt to define the relevant market narrowly in accord with *Philadelphia National Bank*.

In *Philadelphia Nat'l Bank*, the nature of the banking business at issue required proximity to customers, and the Court relied on this fact in concluding that the relevant market consisted of the immediate four–county area around the banks. In contrast, plaintiffs' business [geologic navigation for horizontal drilling] requires no proximity at all to their customers. Indeed, [one witness] testified that, for efficiency, T&T does all of its work in Fort Worth, communicating with clients by fax. [The witness] further testified that, given this means of operation, T&T could do business anywhere in the world that has good reliable telephone connections.

Id. at 1323–24.

Hence, the type and magnitude of plaintiff's business prevented the defendant from furthering a limited relevant geographic market claim based on the logic of *Philadelphia Nat'l Bank*.

[72] 384 U.S. 270 (1966).

though their combined sales only accounted for 7.5% of total sales in Los Angeles. The merger created the second largest grocery chain in Los Angeles with sales near $200 million. The Court again noted that the applicable product market showed signs of increased concentration. The total number of single store owners had dropped approximately 60%, and the number of chains with two or more stores had increased approximately 60%. "[T]he grocery business was being concentrated into the hands of fewer and fewer owners [and] the small companies were continually being absorbed by the larger firms through mergers."[73] Additionally, acquisitions and mergers in the retail grocery market had occurred rapidly in the Los Angeles area before the litigation began.

The Court felt that this increased concentration (*i.e.*, a decrease in number of single–store retailers) was sufficient to prevent the merger of the third and sixth largest firms in the market. In addition, the Court was concerned that the merger disposed of a substantial competitor. The Court felt that preventing such a merger would further the intent expressed by Congress in its 1950 amendments: to arrest a trend toward increased concentration before that trend developed to the point where the market was left in the grip of a few large companies.[74]

After *Von's Grocery*, it seemed that the Court would invalidate any merger between high ranking market share competitors whenever the relevant industry showed signs of concentration or where an aggressive competitor was acquired. This seemed to further the Congressional intent. But the Court's reasoning can be faulted on several grounds.

Prohibiting all mergers tends to result in harm to both consumers and small business owners. For example, refusing to allow acquisitions of grocery stores by competitors may harm a small grocer who wants to retire. His store is probably more valuable to an existing competitor and that competitor is more likely to be creditworthy than a new entrant. Denying the opportunity to sell to a competitor may lower the sales price of a business or prevent its sale altogether.

The consumer may also be hurt by a refusal to allow acquisitions by competitors. Fewer entrepreneurs are likely to enter a market if they know they will be unable to sell to other established businesses. This will reduce the number of competitors in a market. Additionally, invalidating mergers such as those involved in *Brown Shoe* and *Von's Grocery* may actually prevent increased efficiencies that could result in lower prices to consumers.

Moreover, the Court in *Von's Grocery* seemed to confuse concentration trends with a trend towards a decrease in the number of single–store retailers. Concentration ratios traditionally refer to the market share held by the top four to eight firms, not the total number of firms in the market.

---

[73] *Id.* at 273.

[74] *Id.* at 277. *See also United States v. Pabst Brewing Co.*, 384 U.S. 546 (1966) (combined market share of 4.7% condemned); *United States v. Aluminum Co. of America* (Rome Cable), 377 U.S. 271 (1964); *Marathon Oil Co. v. Mobil Corp.*, 669 F.2d 378 (6th Cir. 1981); *RSR Corp. v. FTC*, 602 F.2d 1317 (9th Cir. 1979).

Similarly, the Court failed to take into account the ease of entry into the market.

It was in light of these two analytical standards that the Court delivered its 1974 opinion in *United States v. General Dynamics Corp.* [75] The Court faced a merger between two of the top ten coal producers in the United States. The merging firms controlled approximately 23% (15% plus 8%) of coal sales in one defined geographic market and 11% (6.5% and 4.4%) in another relevant market. Evidence produced by the Government showed a distinct trend toward increased concentration within the coal production industry. Noting that "[i]n prior decisions involving horizontal mergers between competitors, this Court has found *prima facie* violations of § 7 of the Clayton Act from aggregate statistics of the sort relied on by the United States in this case," [76] the Court nevertheless permitted the merger.

The Court relied on a previously unquoted footnote from *Brown Shoe*, and "cautioned that statistics concerning market share and concentration, while of great significance, were not conclusive indicators of anticompetitive effects." [77] This indicated that the Court would return to a functional approach, where the plaintiff would have to show some actual anticompetitive effects from the merger, rather than relying solely upon statistical evidence of market shares and increasing concentration within the market. The Court concluded that in this market coal *reserves*, rather than market share were a better indicator of future market power. Because defendant had weak reserves, the Court held that the merger did not portend a substantial lessening of competition. [78]

General Dynamics signaled a major shift in § 7 interpretation. It deemphasized market share and concentration ratios as determinative and instead held that such data could be rebutted by evidence that defendant was really an "unpromising or weak competitor." Conversely, such evidence presumably could be used to challenge a merger when the market share and concentration data are low but where the vital competitive factor is substantial. Thus, in *General Dynamics* the Court permitted the government's *prima facie* case to be rebutted by post–acquisition evidence that showed defendant lacked competitive strength and vitality. Accordingly, an analysis of market share data and concentration trends does not end the inquiry. These factors seem to be the primary index for measuring market power and, if left unrebutted, they can be the basis of a § 7 violation. But

---

[75] 415 U.S. 486 (1974).

[76] *Id.* at 496.

[77] *Id.* at 498, *citing Brown Shoe Co. v. United States*, 370 U.S. 294, 322 n.38 (1962).

[78] *See also Olin Corporation v. FTC*, 986 F.2d 1295, 1305–06 (9th Cir. 1993) (refusing to liken the pre–acquisition position of the plaintiff to that of the defendant in *General Dynamics* given the evidence suggesting that Olin's resources were not nearly as limited prior to the acquisition).

industry structural evidence must be an accurate measure of competitive ability; when it is not, nonstructural factors will be considered.[79]

The Court continued the trend away from statistical reliance and towards the functional approach in *United States v. Citizens & Southern National Bank*.[80] In *Citizens & Southern*, the Court permitted a merger between a large Atlanta bank holding company and five of its *de facto* branches. Georgia statutes had prevented the larger bank (Southern) from opening branches. To circumvent this prohibition, the bank sponsored smaller suburban banks, controlled their operations, allowed them to use its logo, and effectuated its policies in controlling those banks. These actions were taken by the bank with an eye towards acquiring those banks as branches when the state law was changed. When Georgia changed its statute to permit ownership by the larger bank, Southern attempted to acquire them. The Government objected.

The Court found that the *de facto* branches set up by Southern to circumvent Georgia law actually had a procompetitive effect; the effective entry of Southern into the geographical areas served by the banks was the same as Southern's *de novo* entry into these areas — competition was increased. Southern had found a means to circumvent Georgia's "compulsory market division" which gave the small rural banks a captive market.

Clearly, the acquisition of these banks would increase Southern's market shares in a highly concentrated market, thereby making a *prima facie* showing of a § 7 violation. But Southern was able to rebut this by showing

---

[79] *See Kaiser Aluminum & Chemical Corp. v. FTC*, 652 F.2d 1324, 1335–37 (7th Cir. 1981). The Eleventh Circuit, in *FTC v. University Health, Inc.*, 938 F.2d 1206 (11th Cir. 1991) rejected an argument based on *General Dynamics'* weak competitor theory. The FTC challenged a proposed merger between two hospitals. The District Court had rejected the FTC's motion for a preliminary injunction, and, upon appeal, the Eleventh Circuit vacated and remanded the decision. The defendant attempted to rebut the FTC's clear evidence of anticompetitive effects by citing *General Dynamics* for the proposition that, because the acquired hospital was a "weak" and "not meaningful" competitor, the increased market share from the merger did not necessarily equal a lessening of competition. *Id.* at 1220. The Court of Appeals rejected the contention.

> We are not prepared, on the strength of [the] language [in *General Dynamics*], to hold that the acquisition of a "weak company" is absolutely immune from § 7 scrutiny. Rather, we view *General Dynamics* as standing for the unremarkable proposition that a defendant may rebut the government's *prima facie* case by showing that the government's market share statistics overstate the acquired firm's ability to compete in the future and that, discounting the acquired firm's market share to take this into account, the merger would not substantially lessen competition. . . The acquired firm's weakness, then, is one of many possible factors that a defendant may introduce to rebut the government's *prima facie* case. It is, however, 'probably the weakest ground of all for justifying a merger.' Therefore, to ensure that competition and consumers are protected, we will credit such a defense only in rare cases, when the defendant makes a substantial showing that the acquired firm's weakness, which cannot be resolved by any competitive means, would cause that firm's market share to reduce to a level that would undermine the government's prima facie case.

Id. at 1221 (citations omitted).

The court determined that the defendant hospital had failed to make such a showing.
[80] 422 U.S. 86 (1975).

that the effect of the *de facto* branching was procompetitive and the proposed acquisition would not alter the effect. In addition, the presence of the *de facto* branches ruled out *de novo* entry.

The newer functional approach is especially helpful in differentiated products markets.[81] In those markets, "products typically appear over a broad and fairly continuous range of prices and attributes."[82] Hence, the defined market is broad and market shares are not as relevant in the antitrust analysis. What is of importance, however, is "how often consumers of the product[s] of either merging firm view a product of the other merging firm as their next–best substitute, and how close other substitutes are in such cases."[83]

A synthesis of the approaches used by the Supreme Court in horizontal mergers follows. *Brown Shoe, Von's Grocery* and *Philadelphia National Bank* show the likelihood of the Court invalidating mergers in markets where the plaintiff makes a statistical showing of increased concentration and a significant increase in market power resulting from the merger. Although statistical evidence is significant under this approach, both *General Dynamics* and *Citizens & Southern* indicate that the importance of market share can be rebutted by showing that either the procompetitive effects outweigh anticompetitive consequences or that no anticompetitive effects exist because other factors indicate that defendant does not lack competitive vigor. A further distinction is that *Philadelphia National Bank* established only a *prima facie* test for a merger in a concentrated market, while *Brown Shoe* chartered a broader–based economic evaluation for mergers in deconcentrated markets. Even if a presumption of illegality exists, *General Dynamics* teaches that it may be rebutted by nonstructural evidence of future market power or lack of it.[84] Under either standard, the Court will weigh the harms and benefits of the merger if rebuttal evidence is produced.

Recent lower federal courts, following *General Dynamics*, have signaled that *Philadelphia National Bank's* presumptive test has been weakened, if not undercut. Consequently, market concentration becomes one, of many, factors for a court to assess. In particular, barriers to entry have become increasingly important in merger analysis. For example, in *United States v. Baker Hughes*,[85] the U.S. Court of Appeals for the District of Columbia

---

[81] Gregory J. Werden, *Simulating Unilateral Competitive Effects from Differentiated Products Mergers*, 11 Antitrust 27 (1997); Carl Shapiro, *Mergers with Differentiated Products*, 10 Antitrust 21 (1996); James A Deyte, *Market Definition & Differentiated Products: The Need for a Workable Standard*, 63 Antitrust L.J. 697 (1995).

[82] Werden at 27.

[83] *Id.*

[84] For a good example of a successful rebuttal to a *prima facie* showing of illegality, *see FTC v. Butterworth Health Corporation*, 946 F. Supp. 1285 (W.D. Mich., 1996).

[85] 908 F.2d 981 (D.C. Cir. 1990). Besides ease of entry, other factors to consider include: product durability, product differentiation, facilitating devices that promote collusion, and the extent of vertical integration in the industry. *See also Olin Corp. v. F.T.C.*, 986 F.2d 1295 (9th Cir. 1993); *Nelson v. Monroe Regional Medical Center*, 925 F.2d 1555 (7th Cir. 1991); *FTC v. University Health, Inc.*, 938 F.2d 1206 (11th Cir. 1991).

Circuit approved a merger with a post–merger HHI over 4000. In support of its holding, the court noted that:

> a defendant seeking to rebut a presumption of anticompetitive effect must show that the *prima facie* case inaccurately predicts the relevant transaction's probable effect on future competition. The more compelling the *prima facie* case, the more evidence the defendant must present to rebut it successfully. A defendant can make the required showing by affirmatively showing why a given transaction is unlikely to substantially lessen competition, or by discrediting the data underlying the initial presumption in the government's favor.

> Imposing a heavy burden of production on a defendant would be particularly anomalous where, as here, it is easy to establish a *prima facie* case. The government, after all, can carry its initial burden of production simply by presenting market concentration statistics. To allow the government virtually to rest its case at that point, leaving the defendant to prove the core of the dispute, would grossly inflate the role of statistics in actions brought under section 7. The Herfindahl–Hirschman Index cannot guarantee litigation victories.[86]

There have been some criticisms of the functional approach, however.

> First, there are often problems with obtaining the necessary underlying data in a form that is of sufficient quality. . . Second, assuming that the data are available and reliable, discussions with the agencies often turn into a battle of the applicable economic assumptions, econometric analysis, and computer simulation models. . . Different answers to these and other technical questions may lead to predictions of either a de minimis or a significant price increase from a merger, so the government's analysis risks being fragile. . . [I]f one can change the analysis substantially by making fair but different assumptions, or if the analysis is based on relatively small differences in statistical estimates, the government's approach is unlikely to be very useful. . . Third, the methodology may be less predictable than traditional market definition analysis. . . [F]aced with a client that wishes to merge with a competitor, a defense lawyer might be in a position of saying 'it depends on the assumptions about the shape of the demand curve.' A fourth drawback is that this new analysis can be time consuming and expensive, especially when the merging parties attempt to challenge the government's analysis or attempt to use these approaches to dissuade the agencies from challenging a merger. It can often cost hundreds of thousands of dollars to do a complete analysis in a particular case, and the analysis moves even more from existing case law to the realm of economists.[87]

Professors Lande and Langenfeld suggest that there needs to be a stricter standard delineating an acceptable maximum post–merger market share,

---

[86] *Id.* at 991–92.

[87] Robert H. Lande and James Langenfeld, *The Evolution of Federal Merger Policy*, 11 Antitrust 5, 7 (1997).

regardless of the functional approach's deemphasis on market share.[88] The agencies also need to set out an acceptable post–merger price increase level, since the new models advanced by economists and antitrust scholars almost always predict some inflated price levels following any merger.[89]

Other commentators have suggested that it is the availability of close alternatives to the merged firm's products, regardless of relative market shares, that will effect prices post–merger.[90] Prices can rise substantially when the buyer is left with no choice but to buy from the merged firm because no other producer of the desired good exists. "The merged firm's negotiating leverage depend[s] upon the attractiveness of the buyer's next best alternative premerger, relative to the next best alternative after the merger, not upon concentration in the market as a whole," in some situations.[91] Hence, although the determination of market shares (one part of the process of market definition) is no longer as important as it once was,[92] identifying viable competitors (another part of the process) is still integral to merger analysis.[93]

Along with the functional approach, another trend places increased attention on properly defining the relevant market when considering horizontal mergers.[94] Two cases illustrate: *FTC v. Freeman Hospital*[95] and *United States v. Mercy Health Services.*[96] The court in *Freeman Hospital* considered a proposed merger between two of three acute care hospitals in Joplin, Missouri. The purpose of the merger was to help one of the hospitals, Oak Hill Hospital, out of its financial difficulties. The FTC challenged the merger, stating that it effectively would lessen competition for acute care hospital services in the Joplin area. The district court disagreed and refused to grant a preliminary injunction.

On appeal, the Court of Appeals stated that determining the relevant market is a "necessary predicate to a finding of a Clayton Act violation."[97] The parties disagreed as to the parameters of the relevant geographical market, with the FTC suggesting that it consisted of a twenty–seven mile area spanning all directions from Joplin, and the hospitals proposing a thirteen county/fifty mile area.[98] The court found for the hospitals, stating

---

[88] *Id.* at 8.

[89] *Id.*

[90] Jonathan B. Baker, *Unilateral Competitive Effects Theories in Merger Analysis*, 11 Antitrust 21, 25 (1997).

[91] *Id.*

[92] *See also Re/Max International, Inc. v. Realty One, Inc.*, 924 F.Supp. 1474, 1489 (N.D. Ohio, 1996) (citing other factors besides market share, such as market competitiveness, trends, and number and viability of competitors, as significant factors in determining market power).

[93] *Id.*

[94] *See also infra* § 7.09.

[95] 69 F.3d 260 (8th Cir. 1995).

[96] 902 F.Supp. 968 (N.D. Iowa 1995).

[97] 69 F.3d at 268 (*quoting U.S. v. EI du Pont de Nemours & Co.*, 365 U.S. 586, 593 (1957)).

[98] *Id.*

that the FTC had failed its burden of "present[ing] evidence addressing the critical question of where consumers of acute care inpatient hospital services could practicably turn for alternative sources of the product should the merger be consummated."[99] The court criticized the evidence presented by the FTC because it dealt only with where acute care patients *currently* seek services as opposed to where they could *practicably* go.[100] The Court of Appeals affirmed the district court's denial of the preliminary injunction motion.

Similarly, in *United States v. Mercy Health Services*,[101] the court found that the geographic market had been too narrowly defined by the government. Again, the proposed merger concerned two hospitals, this time in the Dubuque, Iowa area. Like the court in *Freeman Hospital*, the *Mercy Health Services* court began its analysis by noting that "before a court can determine the effect of a merger on competition, it must first define the relevant market."[102] In defining the relevant market, one must exclude potential suppliers whose product is too substantively different or too geographically distant, as well as those who are not likely to offer a suitable alternative to the defendant's customers.[103]

In its attempt to define the relevant market, the government depended partly on the concepts of patient loyalty and ease of physician transfer between the merging hospitals to conclude that certain rural facilities and outside counties were not included in the relevant market.[104] The court disagreed with this approach.

> This court finds that the government's case rests too heavily on past health care conditions and makes invalid assumptions as to the reactions of third–party payers and patients to price changes. The government's case also fails to undergo a dynamic approach to antitrust analysis, choosing instead to look at the situation as it currently exists within a competitive market.[105]

The court found many of the government's assumptions to be erroneous, including the ideas of an unfaltering doctor–patient loyalty despite potential financial hardships and the government's insisting that no hospitals could challenge a 5% price increase instituted by the merged firms.[106]

> The government asserts that those within twenty–five miles of Dubuque cannot be induced to travel outside of Dubuque for health care; however, the court finds to the contrary for several reasons: (1) a significant portion of the population already chooses to go outside Dubuque for health care,

---

[99] *Id.*

[100] *Id.* at 271 (emphasis added).

[101] 902 F.Supp. 968 (N.D. Iowa 1995).

[102] *Id.* at 975.

[103] *Id.*

[104] *Id.* at 976.

[105] *Id.* at 978.

[106] *Id.* at 978–79, 980–81.

(2) managed care entities have successfully shifted patients in the past, and (3) managed care enrollees are increasingly willing to travel for financial savings.[107]

The government attempted to find precedent in *United States v. Rockford Mem. Corp.*,[108] in which the court found it "ridiculous to conceive of a relevant geographical market area encompassing more than a few counties."[109] The court rejected this argument, however, reiterating the strong evidence of the patients willingness to travel, the lack of a strong doctor–patient bond, and the options outside of the rural facilities should the merged firm raise prices.[110] The Court of Appeals affirmed the denial of the injunction. The merger never occurred, however, as the proposal was abandoned shortly thereafter.[111]

The quest to define the proper market also has occurred in the product market area. In *State of New York v. Kraft General Foods, Inc.*,[112] a vertical merger between the defendant and two ready–to–eat cereal manufacturers was challenged as having an anticompetitive effect on the cereal market. The court looked first to consumer demand in defining the relevant product market and came to the conclusion that "the relevant product market [was] the entire RTE cereal industry, not the more narrowly defined "adult cereal" market proposed by plaintiff."[113] Due to statistics suggesting that there is a high interaction rate between superficially divergent cereals, that many adults eat "kid" cereals, and a high level of consumer fluctuation between different marketing categories of cereals, the plaintiff had defined the relevant product market too narrowly.[114] This finding was reinforced by evidence of supply substitutability through "line extensions of existing brands and switches in production of companion brands."[115]

[C] Conglomerate Mergers

[1] Mergers of Potential Competitors

The loss of a potential competitor has been the central issue in the attack on conglomerate mergers. In these mergers, parties do not compete in the same market before the merger; no direct anticompetitive effects result and there is no change in market structure, market shares, or the level of concentration. Conglomerate mergers have secondary effects on competition and market structure, however. They can reduce future competition by

---

[107] *Id.* at 982.

[108] 898 F.2d 1278 (7th Cir. 1990).

[109] 902 F.Supp. at 986.

[110] *Id.*

[111] *See United States v. Mercy Health Services*, 107 F.3d 632 (8th Cir. 1997).

[112] 926 F.Supp. 321 (S.D.N.Y., 1995).

[113] *Id.* at 360.

[114] *Id.* at 361.

[115] *Id.*

eliminating a potential entrant and they may give the merged firm a decisive edge in financial resources that it can use to erect entry barriers or to engage in predatory conduct. Potential competitors can serve a function similar to that of substitute products — they can increase elasticity of demand facing existing sellers and they can serve as a restraining influence on price increases.[116]

In the first major case involving the merger of potential competitors, *United States v. Sidney W. Winslow*,[117] the Supreme Court permitted a product line extension merger among a firm producing 60% of all shoe lasting machines, a firm producing 70% of all shoe heeling machines, and a firm producing 80% of all shoe welt–sewing machines. These companies had patents for their machines and so entry into the markets was legally restricted. The Court, through Justice Holmes, concluded that the combined control of these companies after the merger was no different than that which existed before the merger. Since the companies did not compete in each others process before the merger, the same proportions of control of each process existed after the merger as before. The Court reasoned that

> [o]n the face of it the combination was simply an effort after greater efficiency . . . . As . . . they did not compete with one another, it is hard to see why the collective business should be any worse than its component parts . . . [w]e can see no greater objection to one corporation manufacturing seventy percent of three noncompeting groups of patented machines collectively used for making a single product than to three corporations making the same proportion of one group each.[118]

The Court ignored, however, the fact each of the three firms may have served as a check or restraining force on the other two firms' pricing practices. If the three could enter each other's market easily, then the combination of three firms reduced potential entrants dramatically and substantially increased the combined firm's market power in each market. The firm producing heeling machines may have controlled 70% of the market but still could have not have any real market power because a slight increase in price would cause the lasting machine manufacturer to enter the market on a large scale. By eliminating this outside source of competition, the merger may have permitted the heeling machine manufacturer to use its full 70% share of market to control supply and prices. At bottom, the Court did not consider the cross–elasticity of supply and the restraining effect on price that a potential competitor can have sitting on the sidelines.

The Court went to the other extreme in 1964 and treated a merger involving potential competitors as if it were a horizontal merger. In *United States v. Continental Can Co.*,[119] the Court faced another product line extension

---

[116] Posner, *An Analysis of the Restricted Distribution, Horizontal Merger and Potential Competition Decisions, Antitrust Policy and the Supreme Court*, 75 Colum. L. Rev. 282, 318 (1975).

[117] 227 U.S. 202 (1913).

[118] *Id.* at 217.

[119] 378 U.S. 441 (1964).

merger between large firms in the can and bottle industries. The second largest maker of metal containers merged with the third largest maker of glass containers. The district court found that the bottle industry did not compete directly with the can industry except in the beer industry; only there did manufacturers use bottles and cans interchangeably.

The Court, however, noted that through extensive sales campaigns, industries using bottles could be tempted to switch to cans and vice–versa. This potential cross–elasticity of demand and supply caused the Court to lump bottles and cans together in some product market in what it termed "inter–industry competition." Once glass and metal containers were classified in the same product market, it followed that the merger was horizontal in nature. The merging firms were thus direct, actual competitors. If they were not grouped in the same market they were only potential competitors. Continental Can controlled 21.9% of industry (glass and metal) sales and Hazel–Atlas Glass controlled 3.1%. The Court concluded that a merger between competitors with such significant market shares would have a detrimental effect on competition. It also was concerned that approval of this merger might trigger a merger wave within the industry.

These two cases point out how firms are viewed as actual competitors, potential competitors, or even non–competitors; it depends on the definition of the relevant market. In turn that will depend on the elasticities of demand and supply. Continental Can and Hazel–Atlas did not compete as much as did the parties in *Brown Shoe*, but they were grouped into the same product market.

This categorization in *Continental Can* may not have been completely unfair, since a glass–using bottler facing a price increase could consider switching to cans and could probably do so at a reasonable price; cross–elasticity of demand would be much higher than in *Winslow*, where a user of shoe lasting machines could not possibly switch to a heeling machine to accomplish the same job. Complementary products, at issue in *Winslow*, are not substitute products as was the case in *Continental Can*.

The "potential competitor" theory first appeared in *United States v. El Paso Natural Gas Co.* [120] In *El Paso*, the Court invalidated a merger between El Paso and Pacific Northwest, two natural gas suppliers. El Paso was the sole out–of–state natural gas supplier in California; it sold a majority of the natural gas consumed in California. Pacific Northwest also was an out–of–state supplier of natural gas that never succeeded in selling in California although it certainly tried. The Court noted that Pacific's attempts to sell to California consumers had resulted in El Paso lowering its price substantially. The Court viewed Pacific Northwest as a potential competitor whose presence on the sideline restrained El Paso's pricing. Actually, Pacific was a direct, if unsuccessful, competitor for sales of natural gas in California. The mistake in nomenclature had little effect on the

---

[120] 376 U.S. 651 (1964). *See* the characterization of *El Paso*'s theory in *United States v. Marine Bancorporation, Inc.*, 418 U.S. 602, 623 n. 24 (1974).

result, however; the Court recognized that the merger would substantially reduce competition for California natural gas markets.

The Court faced a true potential competitor, in *Federal Trade Commission v. Procter & Gamble Co.* [121] Procter & Gamble sought to acquire Clorox, the leading manufacturer of bleach. Even though Procter & Gamble did not manufacture bleach, its ability to do so may have restrained Clorox's pricing. The Court made little effort to analyze whether Procter & Gamble's acquisition of Clorox would lead to unrestrained pricing or even whether it would result in collusion among bleach producers. Instead, the Court condemned the merger largely because Procter & Gamble had an advertising advantage that could injure bleach competitors through advertising discounts. Because all bleaches were chemically the same, advertising played a key role in attempting to distinguish the products and hence in increasing their market share. The Court felt that the huge advertising advantages that would inure to the already dominant Clorox would erect entry barriers that would dissuade new entrants. The merger also would discourage price competition and production increases from existing bleach firms because they would fear retaliation from Procter & Gamble.

In *Procter & Gamble*, the Court also recognized that Procter & Gamble's presence on the sidelines would restrain Clorox's pricing. *De novo* entry into the bleach market was possible for Procter & Gamble and it was found to be a "likely prospective entrant." [122] Clorox probably felt that any use of its market power to increase prices made entry by Procter & Gamble probable. "If Procter had actually entered, Clorox's dominant position would have been eroded and the concentration of the industry reduced . . . ." [123] The Court believed that no other potential competitor could exert this restraining influence once Procter & Gamble had merged with Clorox.

That Procter & Gamble's presence on the edge of the market would restrain Clorox's pricing is an application of the "perceived potential entrant theory" firms in the market fear outside entry and behave competitively. The Court in *Procter & Gamble* accepted that theory as justifying invalidation of the merger between potential competitors. It also rejected the defenses of increased efficiency and economies of scale. "Possible economies cannot be used as a defense to illegality. Congress was aware that some mergers which lessen competition may also result in economies but it struck the balance in favor of protecting competition." [124]

---

[121] 386 U.S. 568 (1967).

[122] *Id.* at 575.

[123] *Id.*

[124] *Id.* at 580, *citing Brown Shoe Co. v. United States*, 370 U.S. 294, 344 (1962). In part this was based on the Court expressed concern over the propensity of mergers to raise entry barriers.The acquisition also may have the tendency of raising the barriers to new entry. The major competitive weapon in the successful marketing of bleach is advertising. Clorox was limited in this area by its relatively small budget and its inability to obtain substantial discounts. By contrast, Procter's budget was much larger; and, although it would not devote its entire budget of advertising Clorox, it could divert a large portion to meet the short–term threat of a new entrant. Procter would be able to use its volume discounts to advantage in advertising Clorox. Thus, a new entrant would be much more reluctant to face the giant Procter than it would have been to face the smaller Clorox. 386 U.S. at 579–80.

The Court has been more reluctant to accept the "actual potential entrant" theory.[125] This theory claims that a merger is illegal if the firm would have entered the market but for the merger and that entry through an alternative means would have been less anticompetitive. The Court has never used this theory to invalidate a merger.

As recently as *United States v. Marine Bancorporation, Inc.*,[126] the Supreme Court refused to adopt the actual potential competitor theory. In *Marine Bancorporation*, a Seattle bank in a geographical market extension merger acquired a bank in Spokane at the opposite end of the state. The merger would have joined the second and ninth largest banks in Washington. The banks were not in direct competition, but the United States claimed that if the merger were prohibited, the Seattle bank would have found an alternative, less anticompetitive method to enter the Spokane market. Specifically, the government contended that the bank would have found a smaller existing firm, developed it through internal expansion, and made it competitive with both the existing banks and the acquired bank in the area.[127]

The Court held that at the very least, the government under the potential competition theory must show the merger is in a concentrated market, that the bank had other alternative means of entering the market and that those means offered a substantial likelihood of producing procompetitive effects. The government failed to carry this burden of proof. Whenever the Government could show the existence of alternative methods of entry and a substantial likelihood of procompetitive effects, then the acquiring firm would be viewed as a perceived potential entrant and the case would be decided on those grounds. If the alternate method of entry and the procompetitive effects were so apparent, surely existing competitors in the market would see them and act accordingly.

But here the ease of entry on the part of the acquiring firm (the Seattle bank) was problematic. Given the entry restrictions on new banks under Washington state law that prohibited *de novo* branches, the Seattle bank could not enter the market without an acquisition of another bank. Thus it is unlikely that the Seattle bank could have been either an actual potential entrant or a perceived potential entrant (with a sideline or "wings" effect on price) since "[r]ational commercial bankers in Spokane, . . . are aware of the regulatory barriers that render [the Seattle bank] an unlikely or an insignificant potential entrant except by merger with [the Spokane bank]."[128]

The Second Circuit has declined to apply the potential entrant theory and approved a merger between the leading manufacturer of automotive shock absorbers and a large manufacturer of auto parts, which did not

---

[125] *See United States v. Falstaff Brewing Corp.*, 410 U.S. 526 (1973).

[126] 418 U.S. 602 (1974).

[127] *Id.* at 615.

[128] *Id.* at 639.

manufacture shock absorbers. In *Tenneco, Inc. v. FTC*,[129] the court found
that Tenneco had actually considered entry into the shock absorber market,
but it had not considered *de novo* or toehold entry because the start up costs
and the level at which economies of scale could be achieved were so high.
The smallest, efficiently sized plant had to produce annually 6,000,000
shock absorbers. This produced barriers to entry so substantial that, the
court held, Tenneco could not be considered an actual potential entrant.
High entry barriers therefore may negate the theory that a firm is an actual
potential competitor. The court held that to establish a § 7 violation under
the actual potential competitor theory

> "[The plaintiff] must show 1) that the relevant market is concen-
> trated; 2) that [but for the acquisition the acquiring firm] would
> likely have entered the market in the near future either *de novo*
> or through toehold acquisition and 3) that such entry. . . carried
> a substantial likelihood of ultimately producing deconcentration of
> the market or other significant procompetitive effects."[130] Although
> the court found that this merger occurred in a highly concentrated
> market, it declined to hold that Tenneco was likely to enter the
> market through other, less anticompetitive means because of the
> high entry barriers.

The court also rejected the perceived potential competition theory,
because, although Tenneco was perceived by other competitors as a potential entrant, there was insufficient evidence to show that Tenneco had
exercised a tempering impact on the conduct of existing firms. Thus, there
was no "wings" effect — the second evidentiary requirement of the theory.[131]

Although the Fifth Circuit has approved the application of the "actual
potential entrant" doctrine,[132] most circuits have not embraced the theory.
For example, the Second Circuit has required a showing that a *de novo* or
toehold entry must be proven to be "sufficiently probable and imminent."[133]

[2]   Potential Competition and Joint Ventures

The Supreme Court has applied the potential entrant doctrine to joint
ventures under a § 7 challenge. In 1964, the Court applied this doctrine
in *United States v. Penn–Olin Chemical Co.*[134] Pennsalt Chemicals and

---

[129] 689 F.2d 346 (2d Cir. 1982).

[130] *Id.* at 352.

[131] *Id.* at 355.

[132] *See Mercantile Texas Corp. v. Board of Governors of the Federal Reserve System*, 638
F.2d 1255 (5th Cir. 1981), where the court approved the principle but remanded to determine
the probable time of entry, the degree of competition within the market, and whether the
potential competition offered was substantial.

[133] *B.O.C. Int'l Limited v. FTC*, 557 F.2d 24, 29 (2d Cir. 1977). *See also* V P. Areeda & D.
Turner, *Antitrust Law* 69–161 (1980).

[134] 378 U.S. 158 (1964).

Olin–Mathieson Corp. had formed jointly Penn–Olin to build a plant to produce sodium chlorate in Kentucky, and to sell the product in the Southeast. Before the joint venture, two firms controlled 90% of the Southeastern market but neither Olin nor Pennsalt sold sodium chlorate in that market; both had considered and rejected the possibility of independently entering the market.

The district court upheld the joint venture on grounds that its effect was procompetitive. The court noted that the joint venture increased the number of competitors in the market by 50%, thus exerting more competitive influence on the market than either Pennsalt, Olin, or both would have done while waiting in the wings.

The Supreme Court disagreed, ruling that if, on remand, the Court found that one firm probably would have entered the market and the other would have remained a potential entrant, then the merger should be invalidated. To make this finding, the district court would have to first find that Pennsalt and Olin were potential competitors in the market, and second that one would enter the market while the other would still provide competitive restraint waiting in the wings. But the district court had found that both firms would not have entered the market and this finding was not disturbed by the Supreme Court. In light of this factual finding, the Court's remand order seemed futile since we know if one would have entered the market the other would not have, thus diminishing the probability that the nonentrant would be perceived as a potential entrant or that it would be in any position to exercise any sideline restraining effect. Nevertheless, *Penn–Olin* is important because the Court applied § 7 to joint ventures and because it set forth a test under the potential competitor theory that only requires a showing of "reasonable probability" of entry.

In sum, the cases teach that in order to strike down a merger under the actual potential competitor theory there must be a showing: (1) of reasonable probability that the acquiring firm, but for this merger, would have entered the market in the near future either through *de novo* entry or a toehold merger, (2) that the entry through other means would have resulted in a deconcentrated market or a procompetitive effect, and (3) that the market under review is concentrated. "Reasonable probability" is defined as to whether the defendant has both the capacity and incentive to enter. Capacity refers to the financial, technological and legal means. On the other hand, the perceived potential entrant theory requires that the firm (1) be perceived by competitors in the market as a potential entrant, (2) that this perception creates a restraining effect on the competitors in the market, and (3) that the market under review is concentrated.

[D] Hart–Scott–Rodino Act

The Hart–Scott–Rodino Improvements Act of 1976[135] has been one of the most controversial pieces of antitrust legislation in recent history, largely due to the huge impact it has had on the level and type of antitrust litigation following its passage. The HSR is broken down into three parts. Title I expands the precomplaint discovery abilities of the Department of Justice in civil investigations of proposed mergers; Title II states the premerger notification requirements for some acquisitions of assets and voting securities, depending on the monetary values associated with the merger; and, Title III allows state attorneys general to bring parens patriae actions.[136] Title II generally has been the most heavily litigated and academically debated part of the Hart–Scott–Rodino Act since its passage twenty years ago.[137]

The notification requirement states that plans for "large mergers" must be presented to either the Department of Justice, the FTC, or both, under § 7a of the Clayton Act.[138] This allows the government to examine the proposed merger for possible anticompetitive effects.[139] The notification requirement applies to mergers "that result in an acquirer holding an aggregate total amount of the voting securities and assets of the acquired party in excess of $200 million . . . no transaction resulting in an acquiring person holding $50 million or less of assets or voting securities of an acquired person need be reported."[140] A tiered filing fee structure is imposed for every notification transaction; once the fee is paid, the standard 30–day waiting period begins to run.[141] This waiting period may be extended by thirty days by either agency should they require more information, and any failure to comply with HSR requirements will lead to fines of as much as $10,000 per day.[142]

The objective of the HSR is to give the government advanced warning of any exceptionally large mergers being planned, and to enjoin illegal

---

[135] 15 U.S.C. § 18a. Subsection (a), the filing requirement section, reads as follows:

(a) Filing

Except as exempted pursuant to subsection (c) of this section, no person shall acquire, directly or indirectly, any voting securities or assets of any other person, unless both persons file notification pursuant to rules under subsection (d)(1) of this section, and the waiting period described in subsection (b)(1) of this section has expired. . .

[136] William Blumenthal, *Symposium: Twenty Years of Hart–Scott–Rodino Merger Enforcement — Introductory Note*, 65 Antitrust L.J. 813, 813 (1997).

[137] *Id.*

[138] 1995–2 Trade Reg. Rep. (CCH) ¶ 4231 at 7927 (Nov. 14, 2001); *see also DOJ's Antitrust Division Unveils Merger Process Review Initiative*, Antitrust & Trade Reg. Daily (BNA)(October 15, 2001).

[139] *Id.*

[140] *Id.* at 7928.

[141] *Id.* at 7928–29. A $45,000 filing fee is required for transactions valued at less than $100 million; a $125,000 filing fee for those valued between $100 million and $500 million; and a $280,000 filing fee is imposed on transactions valued above $500 million. *Id.*

[142] *Id.* A few specific exemptions exist to the HSR requirements, however.

mergers in their inception.[143] Because of the pervasive and sweeping nature of the legislation, its unavoidable consequence is to impede the progress of some harmless mergers in order to prevent the formation of those which violate the Clayton Act.[144] As such, the HSR has been subject to both praise and criticism by many antitrust scholars. Some antitrust lawyers feel that the HSR has helped to decrease the endless litigation associated with merger suits, bringing speedier relief to those potentially or actually harmed by the merger and foregoing the often messy process of dismantling a fully functional merger by preventing its formation altogether.[145] Others criticize the HSR for replacing traditional litigation with far–reaching regulations, saying that the HSR is over–applied and overly costly in both monetary and nonmonetary terms.[146]

Still others have made suggestions for minor improvements in the statute. One proposal is that the government make a conscious effort to treat corporations and partnerships more equally under the HSR.[147] Another suggestion is taking steps toward simplifying the notification form and process.[148] Finally, some suggestion has been made regarding extending the clearance review period until the merging parties have produced evidence of efficiency "ex post."[149] While it is apparent that many antitrust commentators have differing opinions about the HSR, it is also clear that the HSR is one of the most influential pieces of antitrust legislation in the United States.

§ 7.08 Failing Company Defense

Throughout the history of antitrust merger cases, the Court has implied that certain situations, such as acquisitions of undercapitalized or failing

---

[143] William Blumenthal, *Symposium: Twenty Years of Hart–Scott–Rodino Merger Enforcement — Introductory Note*, 65 Antitrust L.J. 813, 814 (1997) (citation omitted).

[144] *Id.* at 818.

[145] William J. Baer, *Reflections on Twenty Years of Merger Enforcement Under the Hart–Scott–Rodino Act*, 65 Antitrust L.J. 825, 826–31 (1997). *See generally* Sullivan, *supra* note 10.

[146] Joe Sims & Deborah P. Herman, *The Effect of Twenty Years of Hart–Scott–Rodino on Merger Practice: A Case Study in the Law of Unintended Consequences Applied to Antitrust Legislation*, 65 Antitrust L.J. 865, 865–66, 877–78, 892 (1997). Much of the authors' criticism revolves around the premise that the HSR has reached proportions unintended by the Congress that passed it.

> Congress plainly did not intend to create a huge new merger regulatory scheme; it did not intend to give the antitrust agencies unilateral power to stop a transaction without ever going to court; and it did not intend to supplant discovery under the Federal Rules or the FTC Rules of Practice with "HSR discovery" or to impose burdensome information production requirements upon merging parties.

Id. at 878.

[147] Malcolm R. Pfunder, *Some Reflections On, and Modest Proposals for Reform of, the Hart–Scott–Rodino Premerger Notification Program*, 65 Antitrust L.J. 905, 917 (1997).

[148] *Id.* at 923.

[149] Joseph F. Brodley, *Proof of Efficiencies in Mergers and Joint Ventures*, 64 Antitrust L.J. 575, 578 (1996).

companies, may justify mergers that otherwise would be invalidated.[150] Although holding this doctrine out as a judicially created defense, the Court has limited its use. The defense will only save acquisitions that were the last resort for the acquired company.[151]

In *Citizen Publishing Co. v. United States*,[152] the Court defined the limitations of the failing company defense. The case involved a merger through a stock acquisition of the Tucson *Star* and the Tucson *Citizen*, the only two newspapers in town. The *Citizen* was losing money and negotiated a joint operating agreement with the *Star*, which placed the management, production and distribution of the two papers in the hands of a jointly held corporation (TNI) and which eliminated any business or commercial competition between the two papers. Relying on *International Shoe Co. v. FTC*,[153] the Court reasoned that the failing company defense would protect the merger only if one company "faced the grave probability of a business failure" and the acquiring company was the only available purchaser.

The Court held that in order to invoke this absolute defense to a § 7 charge, defendant would have to show (1) that the resources of one company were so depleted, and the prospects of rehabilitation were so remote, that it faced the grave probability of a business failure, and (2) that efforts were made before this merger to sell it to a noncompetitor or at least a less threatening competitor, such as a new entrant or a small competitor. Absent evidence on each of these requirements, the defense was unavailable.

The rationale underlying the defense was to protect the interest of the creditors, employees and stockholders, who, without the merger, would suffer substantial loss. From a competitive standpoint, if the acquired firm were going out of business anyway with no possibility of reorganization, this merger will not result in an adverse effect on competition since there will be no increase in concentration. In other words, the failing companies' contribution to the market would have been lost without the acquisition.

Although recognizing the defense, the Court refused to apply it to the facts before it. There was evidence to support the fact that the *Citizen* was failing, but not that it was on the verge of going out of business or that the joint operating agreement was the only salvage prospect. Although the paper had been losing money, it had enough viability as a competitor that the *Star* was willing to share profits with the *Citizen*. Even if the *Citizen* was failing, there was no evidence that a market for its sale to a noncompetitor was not viable; the owners made no effort to sell the paper. The Court noted that even companies forced to reorganize under the Bankruptcy Act often emerged as strong competitive companies. The paper failed to show that no other buyer existed and that prospects of reorganization were nil.

---

[150] For a good survey of the history and application of the Failing Company defense, *see* Edward O. Correia, *Re–examining the Failing Company Defense*, 64 Antitrust L.J. 683 (1996).

[151] *See Dr. Pepper/Seven–Up Cos. v. FTC*, 991 F.2d 859, 865–66 (D.C. Cir. 1993).

[152] 394 U.S. 131 (1969). *See also* Campbell, *The Efficiency of the Failing Company Defense*, 63 Texas L. Rev. 251 (1984).

[153] 280 U.S. 291 (1930).

In response to this judicially created failing company defense, Congress enacted the Newspaper Preservation Act in 1970[154] which permits joint operating agreements between newspapers.[155] To qualify for the exemption, however, one of the papers must, in fact, be a failing newspaper. Under the Act, a "failing newspaper is defined as a newspaper publication which, regardless of its ownership or affiliations, is in probable danger of financial failure."[156] Provided this requisite is satisfied, a joint operating agreement may be appropriate.[157] Today, several large cities have daily newspapers operating under agreements similar to that in *Citizen Publishing*.[158]

§ 7.09   Department of Justice *Merger Guidelines*

In 1982 and later in 1984 the Antitrust Division of the Department of Justice issued revised *Guidelines*,[159] which were first published in 1968. The *Guidelines* state the Department's merger enforcement standards and interpretations, but they are without the force of law since they were not enacted by statute or formal rulemaking. The underlying theme of the *Guidelines* is that mergers should not be condemned unless they facilitate collusion, or increase or enhance market power to proportions of a monopoly or oligopoly — maintaining prices above competitive levels.[160] Accordingly, the *Guidelines* focus on the structure of the market and certain conduct

---

[154] 15 U.S.C. § 1801. *See also* Martel & Haydel, *Judicial Application of the Newspaper Preservation Act: Will Congressional Intent Be Relegated to the Back Pages*, 1984 BYU L. Rev. 123.

[155] In particular, the "Act creates an exemption to the antitrust laws that permits a joint operating arrangement ('JOA') between two newspapers if the Attorney General determines that one of the papers is a 'failing newspaper' and that the arrangement 'will effectuate the policy and purpose' of the Act." *Michigan Citizens for an Independent Press v. Thornburgh*, 868 F.2d 1285, 1287 (D.C. Cir. 1989) (Attorney General's approval of a joint operating arrangement between the Detroit Free Press and Detroit Newspapers was affirmed).

[156] 15 U.S.C. § 1802(5).

[157] Joint operating agreements are appropriate for "printing, time, method and field of publication; allocation of production facilities; distribution; advertising solicitation; circulation solicitation; business department; establishment of advertising rates; establishment of circulation rates and revenue distribution; Provided . . . , that there is no merger, combination, or amalgamation of editorial or reportorial staffs, and that editorial policies can be independently determined." 15 U.S.C. § 1802(2). *See also Hawaii Newspaper Agency v. Bronster*, 103 F.3d 742, 749–50 (9th Cir. 1996) (holding that a Joint Operating Agreement between two Hawaiian newspapers was protected from state challenge by the Newspaper Preservation Act and the doctrine of preemption).

[158] *See Michigan Citizens for an Independent Press v. Thornburgh*, 868 F.2d 1285 (D.C. Dir. 1989); *Committee For An Independent P–I v. Hearst Corp.*, 704 F.2d 467 (9th Cir. 1983) *cert. denied* 464 U.S. 892 (1983). *See also, Reilly v. The Hearst Corp.*, 107 F.Supp. 2d 1192 (N.D. Cal. 2000).

[159] 49 Fed. Reg. 26,823 (1984). *See also* Salop & Simons, *A Practical Guide To Merger Analysis*, 29 Antitrust Bull. 663 (1984); *Symposium: 1982 Merger Guidelines*, 71 Calif. L. Rev. 281 (1983); T. Brunner, T. Krattenmaker, R. Skitol, & A. Webster, *supra* note 2; Cohen & Sullivan, *supra* note 32.

[160] 1984 *Department of Justice Merger Guidelines*, 49 Fed. Reg. 26,823 (1984), § 1. *See also* the 1982 *Guidelines*, § I.

occurring within markets. The *Guidelines* include exhaustive definitions of relevant markets and market power. They begin by defining market power as the ability to maintain price above competitive levels for a significant period of time.[161] Market power also is recognized as the ability of *buyers* to depress prices below competitive levels.

The *Guidelines* analyze market power in terms of the relevant product and geographical markets or service offered by each of the merging firms. For each of these products, the *Guidelines* require the Department of Justice to define the market in which firms could effectively exercise market power through collusion. That market is one in which a hypothetical firm could impose a " 'small but significant and nontransitory increase in price' above current or future competitive levels."[162] The hypothesized price increase that the Department will use is generally 5%.

In analyzing whether a firm could exercise market power, the *Guidelines* evaluate both demand and supply elasticity. The hypothetical firm cannot effectively exercise market power if a price increase would cause: (1) consumers to switch to other products,[163] or (2) consumers to switch to the same product manufactured by other firms in other areas,[164] or (3) producers of other products to shift and produce products in the relevant market,[165] either by modifying the use of present facilities, shifting the production of the present facility or by constructing new facilities. The latter consideration, which affects producers, is known as elasticity of supply.

In 1992, the Department of Justice and the Federal Trade Commission jointly issued the 1992 *Guidelines* concerning horizontal mergers and acquisitions. These *Guidelines* represent the first time that the Department and the Federal Trade Commission have issued jointly such *Guidelines*. Previously, both agencies issued separate *Guidelines* describing the analytical framework and standards used in evaluating a particular merger or acquisition and its effect on commerce.[166] These new *Guidelines*, however, only govern horizontal mergers. Consequently, until the courts specify that non–horizontal mergers will be analyzed under the new *Guidelines*, vertical and conglomerate mergers will be analyzed under the 1984 Guidelines. Presumably, however, each agency may utilize the market definition,[167] barriers to entry[168] and efficiency[169] analysis of the new *Guidelines* in conjunction with the substantive analysis of the 1984 *Guidelines*.[170]

---

[161] *Id.* at § 2.

[162] *Id.*

[163] *Id.* at § 2.11.

[164] *Id.* at § 2.31.

[165] *Id.* at § 2.21.

[166] The 1992 *Merger Guidelines* update the *Merger Guidelines* issued by the U.S. Department of Justice (DOJ) in 1984 and the Statement of the Federal Trade Commission Concerning Horizontal Mergers in 1982. 1992 *Horizontal Merger Guidelines* (hereinafter "1992 *Guidelines*"), § 0.

[167] *Id.* at § 1.

[168] *Id.* at § 3.

[169] *Id.* at § 4.

[170] 1984 *Merger Guidelines* (hereinafter "1984 *Guidelines*").

[A] Product Market[171]

The agency will determine the relevant product market by estimating the group of products that would be controlled by a monopolist in order to maximize profits by imposing a "small but significant and nontransitory" price increase.[172] If an increase in price for all of a products group would cause consumers to shift to substitutes then the increase would not be profitable and the product market is too narrowly defined. The agency will then add the next best substitute to the prevalent product market and continue this process until there is no sufficiently attractive substitute to which consumers could shift. At that point, the product market would be defined.[173]

In making this determination, the agency will use prevailing prices of possible substitutes unless future prices can be predicted based on expected changes in costs or demand or expected changes in regulation that will directly affect price. The agency also will assume that buyers and sellers will immediately become aware of price changes in all the products involved.

The agency will consider both direct and circumstantial evidence of the likely effects of price increases.[174] In determining whether product substitutability exists, the agency will consider as particularly relevant the following factors:

(1) Evidence that buyers have shifted or have considered shifting purchases between products in response to relative changes in price or other competitive variables;

(2) Evidence that sellers base business decisions on the prospect of buyer substitution between products in response to relative changes in price or other competitive variables;

(3) The influence of downstream competition faced by buyers in their output markets; and

(4) The timing and costs of switching products.[175]

---

[171] 1992 *Guidelines supra* note 160 at § 1.1 (*See* § 2.1. in 1984 Guidelines). *See also* § 7.05[B], *supra*.

[172] *Id.* at § 1.0 (*See* § 2.11 in 1984 *Guidelines*).

[173] For a good illustration of how the Department of Justice's product–market analysis is applied to a fact pattern, *see Olin Corporation v. FTC*, 986 F.2d 1295, 1299–1301 (9th Cir. 1993).

[174] *Id.* at § 1.11 (See § 2.12 in 1984 *Guidelines*). The exact wording in the 1984 *Guidelines* is "Although direct evidence . . . may sometimes be available, it usually will be necessary for the Department to infer the likely effects of a price increase from various types of available, circumstantial evidence." This is a change from the 1982 version which reads, "the Department will consider any relevant evidence." 1982 *Merger Guidelines* Section II(A).

[175] *Id.* at § 1.11 1–4. The language used in the 1984 *Guidelines* specified the following elements:

(1) Buyers' perceptions of whether the products involved are substitutes, particularly if buyers have actually considered shifting purchases in response to price increases.

(2) Price movements in the products involved — did they parallel each other or differ?

The agency will include all production of firms currently producing the relevant product as well as all firms that are capable of producing the relevant product and that could easily and economically shift to production of that product within one year in response to a price increase. It will also include production of vertically integrated firms that now consume all their production, if the firms would begin to sell the product in response to a price increase.

The agency's definition of the relevant product market can make or break a merger, as was the case in *FTC v. Staples.*[176] The trial court upheld the Federal Trade Commission's challenge to the merger of two office super-store chains, Staples and Office Depot, who together accounted for only 5.5% of the total consumable office supply sales in North America.[177] The Commission had narrowed the definition of the relevant product market to "the sale of consumable office supplies through office superstores." The defendants countered that the product market was the sale of office products overall. The court issued a preliminary injunction against the merger, finding that the Commission had established likelihood of success on the merits, using the narrower product market of the office superstores, as proposed by the Commission. The court noted that even before the merger, certain geographic markets were highly concentrated, with HHIs between 3,597 and 6,944. After the merger, Staples–Office Depot would have a dominant market share in 42 markets, with a 100% market share in 15 of those.[178]

The court began its analysis by noting the difficulty of "overcom[ing] the first blush or initial gut reaction" that the relevant product market was only the sale of consumable office supplies through office superstores. The products in question — pens, paper, and post–it notes, as opposed to durables such as computers and fax machines — were "the same no matter who sold them."[179] Additionally, these products were sold not only by superstores, but also by other large retailers such as Wal–Mart and Target. However, the court asserted that the broad market definition the defendants advocated was illusory; even though any firm could be a competitor in the overall market, "for antitrust purposes" economically significant submarkets could exist.[180]

Although the 1992 *Guidelines* appear to reject the concept of submarkets because they do not mention them, both the Federal Trade Commission and

(3) Similarities or differences in design and usage of the products.

(4) Sellers' perceptions of the substitutability of the products, particularly if business decisions have been based on those perceptions.

1984 *Guidelines, supra* note 160, at § 2.12 1–4.

[176] 970 F. Supp. 1066 (D.D.C. 1997).

[177] *Id.* at 1073.

[178] *Id.* at 1081.

[179] *Id.* (*citing Brown Shoe Co. v. United States,* 370 U.S. 294 (1962).

[180] *Id.*

the court in *Staples* continued to rely on the concept.[181] Specifically, the court relied on factors iterated in *Brown Shoe* to determine whether the Commission's market definition was correct.[182] It also relied on the Commission's evidence and its own qualitative judgments to assert that office superstores "are, in fact, very different [in terms of] appearance, physical size, format, the number and variety of [products] offered, and the type of customers targeted and served than other sellers of office supplies." Hard pricing evidence indicated that in markets where Staples was the only superstore, it was able to charge prices over 13% higher than where it competed with superstores Office Depot and Office Max, with no significant loss of sales.[183] The court concluded from all of the above factors that there was a low cross–elasticity of demand between consumable office products sold by the superstores and the same products sold by non–superstore retailers. Thus it was likely that the merger would lessen competition substantially in some geographic markets and create a monopoly in others.

Many commentators disavow the concept of submarkets, and courts often find use of the term confusing. In *Staples*, the court asserted that its analysis was guided by the *Brown Shoe* factors, but ultimately it concluded that the sale of office supplies through superstores was the relevant market because absent a superstore competitor, a superstore would be able to sustain a price increase at profitable levels.[184] The court averred that "[w]hatever term is used — market, submarket, relevant product market — the analysis is the same."[185]

[B]　Geographical Markets

The agency will determine the relative geographical market in which firms to the merger produce or sell.[186] The agency will identify the geographical area in which the hypothetical producer of all output could maximize profits by a small but significant nontransitory price increase.[187] If buyers could respond to a price increase by receiving supply from producers outside the immediate area, then the geographical market definition is too narrow and the agency will include the outside locations until it identifies the area in which a hypothetical monopolist could maximize profits by increasing price.[188]

---

[181] The *Brown Shoe* "practical indica" for whether a submarket exists are "industry or public recognition of the submarket as a separate economic entity, the product's peculiar characteristics and uses, unique production facilities, distinct customers, distinct prices, sensitivity to price changes, and specialized vendors." *Brown Shoe*, 370 U.S. 294, 325–26.)

[182] *Staples*, 970 F. Supp. 1066, 1080–1081.

[183] *See infra* § 7.09[C][ii].

[184] *Staples*, 970 F. Supp. 1066, 1080.

[185] *Id.* at n.11.

[186] *Id.* at § 1.2 (*See* § 2.3 in the 1984 *Guidelines*). *See also* § 7.05[A], *supra.*

[187] *Id.* at § 1.2. *See generally* Scheffman & Spiller, *Geographic Market Definition under the U.S. Department of Justice Merger Guidelines*, 30 J.L. & Econ. 123 (1987).

[188] *Id.* at § 1.21 (*See* § 2.31 in 1984 *Guidelines*).

The agency will consider all relevant direct and circumstantial evidence in determining geographic substitutability, but will give particular attention to the following:

(1) Evidence that buyers have shifted or have considered shifting to relative changes in price or other competitive variables;

(2) Evidence that sellers base business decisions on the prospect of buyer substitution between geographic locations in response to relative changes in price or other competitive variables;

(3) The influence of downstream competition faced by buyers in their output markets; and

(4) The timing and costs of switching suppliers.[189]

Finally, if price discrimination is possible after the merger, the Department will narrow its relevant geographical market definition.

[C] Calculating Market Shares

The Department will include the total sales and capacity of all plants determined to be within the relevant product and geographical market.[190] The Department will include only the sales likely to be made, or capacity likely to be used, in response to a price increase. Sales or capacity already committed elsewhere that are not available to respond to a price increase will not be included. Each firm's share of the market will be computed by determining the portion of the market it controls.

[1] Horizontal Mergers[191]

The Department first will focus on the concentration of the market and any increase in concentration caused by a merger. The greater the concentration within the market, the more likely that collusion will exist. Similarly, the greater percentage of the market controlled by a firm, the more likely that an output restriction will be profitable. In determining the concentration that exists and the increased concentration that will result from a merger, the Department will use the *Herfindahl–Hirschman Index (HHI)*.[192] The index is calculated by squaring the percentage market share

---

[189] *Id.* at § 1.21 1–4. The language used in the 1984 *Guidelines* specified the following elements:

(1) Shipment patterns of the merging firm and competitors;

(2) Evidence of buyers shifting to other geographical areas in response to price changes;

(3) Differences or similarities in price movements within different geographical areas;

(4) Transportation and distribution costs; and

(5) Excess capacity of firms outside the location of the merging firm.

1984 *Guidelines*, *supra* note 160, at § 2.32.

[190] *Id.* at § 1.4.

[191] *Id.* at § 1.41 (*See* § 3 in the 1984 *Guidelines*).

[192] *Id.* at § 1.5 (*See* § 3.1 in the 1984 *Guidelines*). *See also supra* at § 7.05[C].

of each firm in the market and summing the squares. This index replaces the traditional four–firm concentration ratio previously used by the Department and by virtually all of the case law prior to 1982.

The Department divides market concentration into three categories: (1) unconcentrated (*HHI* below 1,000); (2) moderately concentrated (*HHI* between 1,000 and 1,800) and; highly concentrated (*HHI* above 1,800). "Safe harbors" are created for unconcentrated markets.

The Department will not challenge horizontal mergers that result in markets with a post–merger *HHI* below 1,000, except in exceptional circumstances. This is so because production in the market is so dispersed that coordination and collusion are unlikely.

In moderately concentrated markets, with a post–merger concentration of between 1,000 and 1,800, the Department will probably not challenge mergers if the increase due to the merger is less than 100 points. The Department is likely to challenge mergers producing increases in the *HHI* of more than 100 points unless factors such as (1) the financial conditions of firms within the relevant market, (2) the relative ease of entry into the market, or (3) the effect of potential competitors, result in a conclusion that the merger is not likely to substantially lessen competition. The Department also will allow some mergers it might otherwise challenge if the parties to the merger establish, by clear and convincing evidence, that the merger is reasonably necessary to achieve available efficiencies. The Department will reject this defense if comparable savings could be achieved by the parties through other means.

The Department is likely to challenge mergers in highly concentrated markets that result in a post–merger *HHI* of 1,800 or more, if those mergers increase the *HHI* by more than 50, unless the above factors "indicate that the merger is not likely substantially to lessen competition."[193] Only in extraordinary cases will the above factors prevent the Department from challenging mergers that increase the *HHI* by more than 100 points in these markets. The Department is unlikely to challenge mergers that produce an increase of less than 50 points in the *HHI*, even in concentrated markets.

Although the 1992 *Guidelines* reaffirm the legal and economic principles contained within the 1984 *Guidelines*, the new *Guidelines* principally expand upon two areas. Perhaps the most significant change is reflected in the "adverse competitive effects of mergers and how particular market factors relate to the analysis of those effects."[194] Furthermore, the new *Guidelines* "sharpen the distinction between the treatment of various supply responses and articulate the framework for analyzing the timeliness, likelihood and sufficiency of entry."[195]

---

[193] *Id.* at § 1.51 (*See* § 3.11(c) in the 1984 *Guidelines*).

[194] U.S. Department of Justice and Federal Trade Commission Statement Accompanying Release of Revised Merger Guidelines (Sept. 10, 1992).

[195] *Id.* at § 1.3 and § 3.

[a] Potential Adverse Competitive Effects of Mergers

"Market share and concentration data provide only the starting point for analyzing the competitive impact of a merger."[196] As such, government agencies will take into account many factors which affect competition when analyzing a merger. In *SBC Communications Inc. v. FCC,*[197] the District of Columbia Circuit upheld the FCC's approach of weighing several potentially competition–altering factors in analyzing the propriety of a merger between a long–distance telephone carrier and a cellular phone carrier.

> When the Commission looked beyond the scope of antitrust law and considered the implications of the merger for the development of the telecommunications industry, technical innovation, international competitiveness, investment in infrastructure, and customer privacy, it found nothing but pro–competitive and otherwise beneficial effects. . .Nothing in the Commission's consideration of the pro–competitive and anti–competitive effects of the merger suggests that it 'manipulated legal standards. . .' BellSouth [plaintiff] gives us no reason to doubt the Commission's conclusion; it argues in effect that the Bell Operating Companies' welfare should have been paramount in the Commission's analysis. The Commission is not at liberty, however, to subordinate the public interest to the interest of 'equalizing competition among competitors.'[198]

Hence, any lessening of competition that may have occurred was deemed to be offset by the positive, competition–enhancing qualities of the merger. Under the new *Guidelines,* the Department and the FTC will scrutinize whether a lessening of competition through either "coordinate interaction" or "unilateral effects" exists. Under the new *Guidelines*, the Department and the FTC will scrutinize whether a lessening of competition through either "coordinated interaction" or "unilateral effects" exist.

[i] Coordinated Interaction

While the 1984 and the 1992 *Guidelines* include substantive provisions governing the facilitation of collusion, the 1992 *Guidelines* are significantly more expansive. Contrary to the 1984 *Guidelines* which principally emphasize collusive price fixing, the new *Guidelines* address "coordinated interaction"[199] among competing firms. "Coordinated effects" essentially are the threat that the merger will introduce collusion between the newly merged entity and its rivals.[200] Since coordinated interaction incorporates parallel or matching conduct by competitors, it includes "both explicit price fixing and tacit oligopoly behavior."[201]

---

[196] *Id.* at § 2.0.

[197] 56 F.3d 1484 (D.C. Cir. 1995).

[198] *Id.* at 1490–91.

[199] "Coordinated interaction is comprised of actions by a group of firms that are profitable for each of them only as a result of the accompanying reactions of the others." *Id.* at § 2.1.

[200] Carl Shapiro, *Mergers with Differentiated Products*, 10 Antitrust 23 (1996).

[201] E. Thomas Sullivan & H. Hovenkamp, *Antitrust Law, Policy and Procedure* 846–853 (4th ed. 1999).

[ii] Unilateral Effects

In addition to analyzing whether "coordinated interaction" among competitors exists, each agency will also determine whether competition is lessened due to unilateral effects.

The logic behind unilateral effects has been described in the following way:

> As the price of Brand A rises, some customers will shift from Brand A to Brand B. Prior to the merger, these customers would be lost to the firm owning Brand A. After the merger, this same firm owns Brand B and thus does not lose these customers. As a result, the price increase is more profitable to the merged entity.[202]

Unilateral effects theory, along with pricing analysis and efficiency considerations, was offered and accepted as valid reasons to enjoin a merger between Staples, Inc. and Office Depot in *FTC v. Staples*.[203] At issue in *Staples* was whether the FTC had produced sufficient evidence to justify granting its motion for a preliminary injunction. The court began by evaluating the FTC's studies comparing the two firms' pricing schedules in markets where one was present and the other was not with markets in which the two office suppliers competed. This was done mainly to determine the relevant product market. The court determined that the evidence showed that the firms' prices were "affected primarily by other superstores and not by non–superstore competitors."[204] Hence, Office Depot and Staples were able to charge higher prices in markets in which they were the only superstore without losing a great deal of business to other competitors like Wal–Mart and Kmart.[205] However, the two superstores pricing schedules did have an effect on each other when occurring in the same market. As such, the court found that the relevant product market entailed "the sale of consumable office supplies through office supply superstores."[206]

> These statistics also had relevance from a unilateral effects standpoint.

> Since prices are significantly lower in markets where Staples and Office Depot compete, eliminating this competition with one another would free the parties to charge higher prices in those markets, especially those in which the combined entity would be the sole office superstore. In addition, allowing the defendants to merge would eliminate significant future competition. Absent the merger, the firms are likely, and in fact have planned, to enter more of each other's markets, leading to a deconcentration of the market and, therefore, increased competition between the superstores. In addition, direct evidence shows that by eliminating Staples' most significant, and in many markets only, rival, this merger

---

[202] Shapiro, *supra* note 200, at 23.

[203] 970 F. Supp. 1066 (D.D.C. 1997).

[204] *Id*. at 1077.

[205] *Id*.

[206] *Id*. at 1080.

would allow Staples to increase prices or otherwise maintain prices at an anticompetitive level.[207]

The court considered the probable effect on competition of a merger between Office Depot and Staples, Inc. through other inquiries, as well. The evidence showed that the firms "would have a document market share in 42 geographic markets across the country" and that the combined shares of the superstores would be 100% of the office superstore market in fifteen metropolitan areas.[208] The post–merger HHI's of the merger ranged from 5.003 to 10,000, depending on the market.[209] These high levels supported the court's decision that the FTC had shown a "reasonable probability" of anticompetitive effects arising from the proposed merger.[210]

According to the new *Guidelines*, "A merger may diminish competition even if it does not lead to increased likelihood of successful coordinated interaction, because merging firms may find it profitable to alter their behavior unilaterally following the acquisition by elevating price and suppressing output."[211] Consequently, analysis of product differentiation[212] and production capacity[213] are necessary.

[b] Efficiencies

The new *Guidelines* reiterate that "the primary benefit of mergers to the economy is their efficiency–enhancing potential, which can increase the competitiveness of firms and result in lower prices to consumers."[214] Under the 1992 *Guidelines*, if a merger does not pose a serious threat to competition, it is unlikely to be challenged. If a substantial threat is present, however, the appropriate agency will exercise prosecutorial discretion to assess whether net efficiencies outweigh the competitive risks.

Initially, efficiencies were not considered a plausible defense by either the Department or the FTC. In the 1982 *Merger Guidelines*, for example, the government specified that "except in extraordinary cases, the Department will not consider a claim of specific efficiencies as a mitigating factor for a merger that would otherwise be challenged."[215] "The 1984 Guidelines, however, removed the "except in ordinary cases" language, but emphasized that efficiencies would have to be demonstrated by 'clear and convincing

---

[207] *Id.* at 1082 (citations omitted).

[208] *Id.* at 1081.

[209] *Id.*

[210] *Id.* at 1093. The court also considered entry barrier and efficiency arguments in its decision to enjoin the merger. *Id.* at 1086–1090. For further discussion of the efficiency defense as offered by the Department of Justice Horizontal Merger Guidelines, *see infra* § 7.09 (C)(1)(b).

[211] 1992 *Guidelines, supra* note 96, at § 2.2.

[212] *Id.* at § 2.21.

[213] *Id.* at § 2.22.

[214] 1992 *Merger Guidelines* at § 4.4.

[215] 1982 *Guidelines*, at § V.A.

evidence'."[216] In the 1992 *Guidelines*, the government removed the "clear and convincing" standard, "but strongly suggested that the party asserting an efficiency claim still would have a burden of persuasion and proof before the government would accept the claim."[217]

Consequently, if a "merger does not present a significant danger to competition,"[218] or otherwise "achieves significant net efficiencies,"[219] it is unlikely to be challenged.

In 1997, the Department of Justice and the FTC clarified their position on the efficiency defense in a revision to § 4 of the 1992 Horizontal Merger Guidelines. The agencies openly admitted the existence of potential benefits associated with efficiencies, such as new or improved products.[220] However, even when efficiencies exist, mergers can still have anticompetitive effects which make them illegal, and "efficiencies are most likely to make a difference in merger analysis when the likely adverse competitive effects, absent the efficiencies, are not great."[221] Efficiencies do not matter when the merger will lead to a monopoly or otherwise restrain trade.[222]

Furthermore, the government agencies will only consider "merger–specific efficiencies," or those efficiencies "unlikely to be accomplished in the absence of either the proposed merger or another means having comparable anticompetitive effects.[223] When giving alternatives to the merger, the government may not present theoretical alternatives; only those which are "practical in the business situation faced by the merging firms" will be considered.[224]

Given the difficulties associated with identifying and proving efficiencies, and the possibility that the proposed efficiencies will never be realized, the merging firms are required to substantiate their efficiency claims to facilitate verification by the government as to the "likelihood and magnitude of each asserted efficiency, how and when each would be achieved, how each would enhance the merged firm's ability and incentive to compete, and why each would be merger–specific."[225] Vague, speculative, or

---

[216] Pitofsky, *Proposals for Revised United States Merger Enforcement In a Global Economy*, 81 Geo. L.J. 195, 206 (1992).

[217] *Id.*

[218] 1992 *Guidelines, supra* note 166, at § 4.

[219] *Id. But see Federal Trade Comm'n v. H.J. Heinz Co.* 246 F.3d 708 (D.C. Cir. 2001) (where the D.C. Circuit ruled that the defendants failed to prove extraordinary merger–specific efficiencies during a hearing for preliminary injunction.)

[220] § 4, ¶ 2 of 1997 Efficiency Revision of Section 4 of Horizontal Merger Guidelines [hereinafter 1997 Guidelines], 72 ANTITRUST & TRADE REG. REP. (BNA) 359, (April 10, 1997).

[221] § 4, ¶¶ 2, 7 of 1997 Guidelines.

[222] § 4 ¶ 7 of 1997 Guidelines.

[223] § 4, ¶ 3 of 1997 Guidelines.

[224] *Id.* at § 4.

[225] § 4, ¶ 4 of 1997 Guidelines.

otherwise unverifiable efficiency claims will not be considered by the government.[226]

Finally, and most importantly, in deciding whether to challenge a merger, the government will consider whether the efficiencies are of such "character and magnitude" that the merger is unlikely to have an anticompetitive effect in any relevant market.[227] The government does not simply compare the relative magnitudes of the efficiency and the potential harm associated with the merger, however; rather, "the Agency considers whether cognizable efficiencies likely would be sufficient to reverse the merger's potential to harm consumers in the relevant market."[228] Certain efficiencies are more likely to be substantial in the relevant market than others, such as efficiencies allowing firms to lower the marginal cost of production, whereas efficiencies dealing with "procurement, management, or capital cost" are less likely to be considered substantial.[229]

These *Guidelines*, while helpful to the firm considering merging in the sense that it shows what the government is looking for when analyzing mergers, have been subject to some criticism. The Guidelines are of little assistance in deciding how efficiencies are squared with the unilateral effects models employed by the government, and there is little guidance in answering the question of exactly how "substantial" the savings must be before they offset any anticompetitive effects.[230] Nonetheless, it should be noted that when the efficiency guidelines were introduced, the Chairman of the FTC admitted that they were not designed to bring about dramatic changes in the FTC's merger enforcement policy, and that, "[a]t most, they [would] make a difference in a few close cases."[231] The purpose of the new Guidelines is to:

1) Explain how efficiencies may affect the analysis of whether a proposed merger may likely lessen competition substantially in a relevant market;

2) Define more precisely which efficiencies are attributable to a proposed merger and which likely could be achieved in other ways without posing as great a cost to competition;

3) Clarify what parties will have to do to demonstrate claimed efficiencies; and

4) Set forth how efficiencies are factored into the analysis of the competitive effects of a merger and indicate how delays in realizing the benefits of efficiencies will be treated.[232]

---

[226] *Id.* at § 4.

[227] § 4, ¶ 6 of 1997 Guidelines.

[228] *Id.* at § 4.

[229] § 4, ¶ 8 of 1997 Guidelines.

[230] Deborah A. Garza, *The New Efficiencies Guidelines: The Same Old Wine in a More Transparent Bottle*, 11 Antitrust 6 (1997).

[231] *Agency Rulings*, 65 U.S.L.W. 2678, (April 22, 1997).

[232] *Id.*

Even before the efficiency guidelines were issued, the Eighth Circuit heard an efficiencies defense in *United States v. Mercy Health Services*.[233] The court found that the defendant had failed to prove that the merger was required to effectuate many of the proposed efficiencies.[234] Also, the implementation of the requisite steps to invoke the efficiencies was quite speculative, and the efficiencies to be achieved were overstated the court reasoned.[235] However, because the plaintiff also failed to show an adverse effect on competition in the relevant market, the weakness of the defendant's affirmative defense was excused.[236]

Although "[c]laims of efficiency can be offered as a relevant factor in the enforcement agencies' exercise of prosecutorial discretion,[237] . . . [they may be inadmissible] when a transaction is examined in court."[238] For example, in *FTC v. Procter & Gamble Co. (P&G)*,[239] the Supreme Court reinstated a district court order requiring P&G, a diversified manufacturer of household products, to divest itself of a liquid bleach company (Clorox) on the ground that the merger might substantially lessen competition or tend to create a monopoly in the production and sale of household liquid bleaches.[240] In reaching this decision, the Court noted that "[p]ossible economies cannot be used as a defense to illegality. Congress was aware that some mergers which lessen competition may also result in economies but it struck the balance in favor of protecting competition."[241] Thus, it remains to be seen whether the Court will affirm the older *P&G* reasoning, or allow efficiencies to be raised as a defense. The clear trend would seem to permit the efficiency defense.

[c]   Entry Analysis

The 1982, 1984 and 1992 *Guidelines* have been influenced by the concept of barriers to entry. Although economists disagree over precise definitional terms, two notions of barriers to entry have been widely acclaimed. The first definition, advanced by economist Joe Bain, specifies that a barrier to entry represents any factor that permits incumbent firms to price above marginal cost, or charge supracompetitive prices, without encouraging new

---

[233] 902 F.Supp. 968 (N.D. Iowa 1995), *vacated on other grounds*, 107 F.3d 632 (8th Cir. 1997).

[234] *Id.* at 987. *See also FTC v. Staples*, 970 F.Supp. 1066 (1997).

[235] *Id.*

[236] *See also Money Station, Inc. v. Bd. of Governors of the Federal Reserve System*, 81 F.3d 1128, 1132 (D.C. Cir. 1996), (holding that the defendant Federal Reserve Board had failed to present evidence of "sufficient public benefits to outweigh the loss of competition" in a merger between the operator of the nation's largest ATM network and a smaller ATM network).

[237] *Id.*

[238] Pitofsky, *supra* note 110, at 206–07.

[239] 386 U.S. 568 (1967).

[240] *Id.* at 604. Prior to the merger, P&G did not produce household liquid bleach. *Id.* at 573.

[241] *Id.* at 580.

entry.[242] The alternative definition, espoused by economist George Stigler and the Chicago School, maintains that an entry barrier "is a cost of producing . . . which must be borne by firms which seek to enter an industry but is not borne by firms already in the industry."[243] Consequently, the two approaches differ in their treatment of economies of scale and pricing practices when either a horizontal merger or toe–hold acquisition occurs.

Under Bain's theory, a merged firm's economies of scale (ability of an established incumbent with high output and lower costs) are a significant barrier to entry for new firms. In particular, potential entrants are faced with significant start–up costs as compared with the merged firm. Namely, lower and more expensive output. Consequently, to minimize the adverse competitive affect(s) of a new entrant, Bain posits that the merged incumbent will charge a price slightly lower than the new entrant's anticipated costs — a pricing level substantially above the merged firm's own costs.

Stigler's theory, by comparison, focuses upon the process of entry rather than the market as an evolving entity. Under Stigler's approach, economies of scale and other start–up costs are not regarded as a barrier to entry because the merged or acquired firm was required to incur these "costs" as a condition of entry. Consequently, Stigler maintains that when the process of entry is similar, no barriers to entry will exist.

Historically, the Department has incorporated Bain's definition into its *Guidelines*, whereas the FTC has emphasized Stigler's approach. Interestingly, the 1992 joint Guidelines principally incorporate a Bainian definition of barriers to entry.

Under the new *Guidelines*, "a merger is not likely to create or enhance market power or to facilitate its exercise, if entry into the market is so easy[244] that market participants, after the merger, either collectively or unilaterally, could not profitably maintain a price increase above premerger levels."[245] To determine whether entry into a market is "easy," the agency will evaluate the likelihood of entry in response to a "small but significant and non–transitory" increase in price. If entry into a market is easy, following a merger, remaining firms are less likely to exercise market power and, therefore, price at supra–competitive levels because ease of market entry deters a price increase.

To assess whether entry into a market is easy, the 1992 *Guidelines* specify that analyses of the timeliness, likelihood and sufficiency of entry are required.

---

[242] *See* J. Bain, Barriers to New Competition 3 (1956).

[243] G. Stigler, The Organization of Industry 67 (1968).

[244] Entry is easy if it "would be timely, likely and sufficient in its magnitude, character and scope to deter or counteract the competitive effects of concern." 1992 *Guidelines, supra* note 166, at § 3.

[245] *Id.*

[i] Timeliness

Under the 1992 *Guidelines*, entry into a market is timely only if, following a merger, "committed entry can be achieved within two years from initial planning to significant market impact on price."[246] Although entry may occur at some point in the future, the *Guidelines* adopt a two year standard for timeliness. Primarily, the Guidelines posit that entry beyond this two year limitation will be insufficient to eliminate the potential for supra–competitive pricing.

[ii] Likelihood

The 1992 *Guidelines* specify that entry into a market is likely "only if a new entrant would be profitable at premerger prices."[247] The *Guidelines* use premerger prices as the relevant criteria since, following a merger, a firm with enhanced market share could, conceivably temporarily reduce prices to significantly discourage new entry, or if entry were to occur to make it considerably more difficult for the new firm to obtain market share. Consequently, if a potential firm is able to acquire market share and profits within the two year period, entry is likely.

[iii] Sufficiency of Entry

Under the new *Guidelines*, entry into a market is sufficient only if a potential competitor would be able to successfully offer a product or service within the two year limitation.[248] For entry to be considered sufficient, a potential entrant must possess the market knowledge and financial ability to introduce a new product or service that will have a significant impact on price to deter supra–competitive pricing by a merged–firm.

[2] Non–horizontal Mergers[249]

[a] Vertical Integration

The *Guidelines* recognize that vertical integration may interfere with competition by creating objectionable barriers to entry or by facilitating collusion. However, the *Guidelines* reveal that the Department is unlikely to challenge most vertical mergers unless certain conditions exist, including the condition that the merger occurred in a concentrated market.

Before the Department will challenge vertical integration on the basis of objectionable entry barriers, three conditions must exist. Each is designed to determine whether the merger will have an effect on the horizontal level. "First, the degree of vertical integration between the two markets

---

[246] *Id.* at § 3.2.

[247] *Id.* at § 3.3.

[248] *Id.* at § 3.4.

[249] 1984 *Guidelines, supra* note 160, at § 4.

must be so extensive that [potential] . . . entrants [of the primary market must also enter the secondary market] . . . . Second, the requirement of entry at the secondary level must make entry at the primary level significantly more difficult and less likely to occur. Finally, the [primary market's] characteristics . . . must be so conducive to non–competitive performance [concentrated market], that the increased difficulty of entry is likely to affect its performance" in an anticompetitive manner.[250] The Department will use the following criteria to determine if these conditions exist:

(1) Whether the secondary market has the unintegrated capacity to supply new entrants to the primary market. If the unintegrated market can supply two firms of the minimally efficient size needed to compete in the market, the Department is unlikely to challenge.[251]

(2) The ease of entry into the secondary market, whatever the difficulty of entry into the primary market, indicates that no additional burden results from the merger. The Department is unlikely to challenge mergers in which firms can easily enter the secondary market.[252]

(3) Degree of concentration in the primary market. Barriers to entry are unlikely to have an anticompetitive effect on the primary market when that market does not have the concentration necessary to facilitate collusion or monopolization. The Department is unlikely to challenge mergers on this ground unless the *HHI* on the primary market is over 1,800 or unless other factors indicate effective collusion is particularly likely.[253]

The Department also is unlikely to challenge vertical mergers on the grounds that they facilitate collusion unless the upstream supply market has enough concentration to make collusion likely.[254] The reduced ability to monitor prices at retail level that results from vertical integration is unlikely to have an effect on the upstream market unless the market is so concentrated that a type of cartelization can occur. The *HHI* of the upstream market must be above 1,800 unless other factors indicate collusion is likely to occur. Additionally, a large portion of the upstream product must be sold through vertically integrated outlets after the merger. Even when these two factors exist, the Department is unlikely to challenge such mergers unless individual evaluation shows a likely anticompetitive effect.

The Department may challenge a merger with a disruptive retail buyer if that buyer had enough market power with the upstream supplier to force the upstream (supply) firm to deviate from a pricing agreement.[255]

The Department is unlikely to challenge these mergers unless the *HHI* of the upstream market is over 1,800 or other factors indicate that effective

---

[250] *Id.* at § 4.21.

[251] *Id.* at § 4.211.

[252] *Id.* at § 4.212 and § 3.3.

[253] *Id.* at § 4.213.

[254] *Id.* at § 4.221 and § 3.4.

[255] *Id.* at § 4.222.

collusion is possible and unless the "disruptive firm differs substantially in volume of purchases or other relevant characteristics from the other firms in its market."[256]

Finally, the Department will consider challenging upstream mergers by rate–regulated monopolists if the merger would allow the monopolist to disguise the costs of supplies from the upstream firm.[257] In mergers with upstream firms that have no independent markets by which to measure the true cost of the supply, monopolists can inflate the prices paid to its upstream subsidiary, and pass inflated prices off to the regulator and on to the consumers as legitimate costs justifing rate increases. The Department will consider the economies of integration that may occur as a result of such a merger and opportunities for abuse when deciding whether to challenge that merger.[258]

[b] Potential Competitors and Conglomerate Mergers[259]

Unlike the case law, the *Guidelines* do not recognize the theories of foreclosure, entrenchment or reciprocity. The Department, however, does recognize that mergers with potential entrants may have an adverse affect on competition even though the firms involved are not competing at the time of the merger. If an outside firm acquires a firm already in the market, and if the merger effectively removes the acquiring firm from a position on the edge of the market, where it exerted a restraining effect on price, the Department may challenge the merger. A procompetitive effect may have been lost by reason of the merger because the outside, acquiring firm was either an actual potential competitor or a perceived potential competitor by firms in the market.[260]

The Department will analyze either actual potential entrants or perceived potential entrants under "a single structural analysis analogous to that applied to horizontal mergers."[261] The factors considered by the Department are as follows:

(1) Market Concentration[262] — The Department is unlikely to challenge mergers unless the *HHI* of the acquired firm's market is above 1,800, unless other factors show that effective collusion is particularly likely.

(2) Ease of Entry[263] — When other firms can reasonably and effectively enter the acquired firm's market, the elimination of one potential entrant

---

[256] *Id.*

[257] *Id.* at § 4.23.

[258] *Id. See* L. Sullivan, *Justice Guidelines On Mergers and Vertical Restraints: A Critique,* 16 Antitrust L. & Econ. Rev. 11 (1984).

[259] 1984 *Guidelines, supra* note 160 at § 4.1.

[260] *See supra* § 7.07[C].

[261] 1984 *Guidelines, supra* note 160, at § 4.13. *See* discussion *supra* at § 7.07[C][1].

[262] *Id.* at § 4.131.

[263] *Id.* at § 4.132.

has less anticompetitive effect. If firms that do not sell the relative product could easily and effectively enter the market by using existing facilities or by constructing new facilities, the Department is unlikely to challenge the merger.

(3) Acquiring Firm's Entry Advantage[264] — If three or more outside firms have a similar entry advantage ascribed to the acquiring firm, their existence will negate the anticompetitive effects of the merger unless the acquiring firm was on the verge of entering the market before the merger. In that case, the Department will analyze the merger as it would a horizontal merger between a firm with the acquiring firm's likely level of entry and the acquired firm. In all other cases, the Department is unlikely to challenge potential entrant mergers when these other firms exist with similar advantages.

(4) Market Share of the Acquired Firm[265] — When the acquired firm has a market share of 5% or less, the Department is unlikely to challenge a merger with that firm; such "toehold" acquisitions have the procompetitive effects of a new entry. The Department is likely to challenge mergers when the acquired firm has a market share of 20% or more, so long as the three previous conditions are met. Similarly, when the above conditions are met, the Department is likely to challenge mergers as the acquired firm's share increases from 5% to 20% of the relevant market.

§ 7.10   Private Enforcement of § 7

Congress provided for private enforcement of § 7. The Clayton Act is included in federal antitrust laws,[266] and § 4 of the Clayton Act creates a private cause of action for treble damages, plus attorney's fees, for injuries caused by anything forbidden in those antitrust laws.[267] Section 16[268] of the Clayton Act also permits private parties to bring an injunction action for violations of § 7.

Section 7 of the Clayton Act specifically provides that "no person engaged in commerce or in any activity affecting commerce shall acquire, directly or indirectly, the stock . . . or . . . assets . . . of another [competitor], where the effect of such acquisition may be substantially to lessen competition, or tend to create a monopoly."[269] When a § 7 violation occurs, a private

---

[264] *Id.* at § 4.133.

[265] *Id.* at § 4.134.

[266] 15 U.S.C. §§ 12, 15.

[267] *See* §§ 3.01 & 3.02 *supra.*

[268] 15 U.S.C. § 26. *See* § 3.01 *supra.* Nothing in the statutory scheme prevents a private plaintiff or state attorney general from challenging a merger or acquisition when the government, through either the Department of Justice or FTC, has approved it. *See generally Chrysler Corp. v. General Motors Corp.*, 589 F. Supp. 1182 (D.D.C. 1984).

[269] 15 U.S.C. § 18.

party may initiate either a treble damages action under § 4 of the Act[270] or seek injunctive relief under § 16.[271]

More specifically, § 16 enables private litigants to seek injunctive relief[272] for antitrust violations which "threaten loss or damage."[273] Provided the alleged harm is "of the type the antitrust harms were designed to prevent and flows from that which makes the defendants' act(s) unlawful,"[274] a claimant may seek equitable relief in the form of: (1) a preliminary injunction, (2) a permanent injunction, or (3) divestiture. Whether an injunction or a realignment of a corporate structure will be ordered, however, depends upon the district court's evaluation of "traditional equitable powers."[275]

In *California v. American Stores, Co.*,[276] the State of California alleged that a merger between American Stores, the fourth largest retail grocery chain in California, and Lucky Stores, the largest supermarket chain in the region, violated Section 7 of the Clayton Act and consequently caused decreased competition and increased prices to consumers in 62 California cities.[277] The district court granted California's request for preliminary

---

[270] 15 U.S.C. § 15.

[271] 15 U.S.C. § 26. "Any person, firm, corporation, or association shall be entitled to sue for and have injunctive relief . . . against threatened loss or damage by a violation of the antitrust laws . . . " *Id. See* § 3.01 *supra*. Nothing in the statutory scheme prevents a private plaintiff or state attorney general from challenging a merger or acquisition when the government, through either the Department of Justice or the FTC, has previously approved it. *See generally Chrysler Corp. v. General Motors Corp.*, 589 F. Supp. 1182 (D.D.C. 1984).

[272] Essentially, an injunction represents an "*in personam* order, directing a party to act, or to refrain from acting in a specified way." Dan B. Dobbs, Remedies, § 2.11 Provisional Injunctions and Other Injunctive Procedures 249 (2d ed. 1993). Injunctions which direct a party to engage in specified conduct are deemed mandatory orders, whereas injunctions which forbid certain conduct are classified as prohibitory. *Id.*

[273] *Zenith Radio Corp. v. Hazeltine Research, Inc.*, 395 U.S. 100, 130 (1969). The burden of proof requirements for injunctive relief under § 16 of the Clayton Act is lower than the actual injury to business or property requisites under § 4 of the Act. Consequently, a claimant may seek recovery for damages, even though no actual injury has transpired. Recovery, however, is dependent upon a claimant demonstrating "a significant threat of injury from an impending violation of the antitrust laws or from a contemporary violation likely to continue or recur." *Id.*

[274] *Cargill Inc. v. Monfort of Colorado, Inc.*, 479 U.S. 104, 113 (1986) *quoting Brunswick Corp. v. Pueblo Bowl–O–Mat, Inc.*, 429 U.S. 477, 489 (1977).

[275] *Zenith Radio Corp.*, 395 U.S. at 130. The Seventh Circuit has enunciated that "appellate review of an equitable award is based upon an abuse of discretion" standard. E. Thomas Sullivan & Herbert Hovenkamp, *Antitrust Law, Policy & Procedure* 917 (4th 1999). However, the Second Circuit has declared that a *de novo* review of the factual findings is warranted. *Id. citing Norlin Corp. v. Rooney, Pace, Inc.*, 744 F.2d 255 (2d Cir. 1985). *See also Miller v. California Pacific Medical Center*, 991 F.2d 536, 540 (9th Cir. 1993) ("[I]njunctions are equitable in nature and should only issue when supported by the equities.") *See generally* E. Thomas Sullivan, *The Jurisprudence of Antitrust Divertiture: The Path Less Traveled*, 86 Minn. L. Rev. 565 (2002).

[276] 495 U.S. 271 (1990).

[277] *Id.* at 274. This suit was commenced after the Federal Trade Commission authorized the merger, provided the merged firm divested itself of several designated supermarkets. *Id.* at 276.

injunction;[278] on appeal, the Ninth Circuit reversed.[279] The Supreme Court granted California's writ of certiorari, to resolve a conflict between the First and Ninth Circuits.[280]

Based upon a review of the legislative history of § 16 and an analysis of each circuit court's reasoning, the Supreme Court declared that a district court is authorized to order divestiture under § 16 of the Clayton Act. Specifically, the Court held that the "statutory language of § 16 indicates Congress' intention that traditional principles of equity govern the grant of injunctive relief."[281] However, for a private litigant to effectively petition a court for such relief, the claimant must prove "threatened loss or damage to [personal] interests."[282] "This limitation [was] not designed to constrict the availability of injunctive remedies against violations that already have begun or occurred, but rather to expand their availability against harms that are as yet realized."[283] In particular, since "Congress endow[ed] the

---

In their complaint, the State of California sought a "preliminary injunction requiring American to operate the acquired stores separately until the case was decided, and then to divest itself of all of the acquired assets located in California." *Id.* at 274.

[278] Noting that "Californians [would] be irreparably harmed if the proposed merger [were] completed," the district court concluded that the "State of California had proved a *prima facie violation* of Section 7 of the Clayton Act." *Id.* at 277.

[279] The Ninth Circuit, relying on the "authority of its earlier decision in *International Telephone & Telegraph Corp. v. General Telephone & Electronics Corp.*, 518 F.2d 913 (9th Cir. 1975), set aside the injunction." *Id.* at 277–78. In particular, the Ninth Circuit "reasoned that divestiture was unavailable as a remedy in private actions under § 16 of the Clayton Act, and that § 16 did not permit indirect divestiture (an injunction which on its face does not order divestiture, but which has the same effect)." *Id.* at 278.

[280] The First Circuit, in *Cia. Petrolera Caribe, Inc. v. Arco Caribbean, Inc.*, 754 F.2d 404 (1st Cir. 1985), held that divestiture was authorized under Section 16 whereas the Ninth Circuit, in *International Telephone & Telegraph Corp. v. General Telephone & Electronics Corp.*, 518 F.2d 913 (9th Cir 1975), held that the legislative history to Section 16 did not indicate the framers intent to authorize dissolution or divestiture as private party remedies. *Id.* at 278–79.

[281] 495 U.S. at 281.

[282] *Id.* at 296 *citing Cargill, Inc. v. Monfort of Colorado, Inc.*, 479 U.S. 104 (1986). An alternative to bringing a private action is to make a third party petition to the FTC or Department of Justice to support or instigate a government challenge to the merger. The "personal threat or injury" requirement may be forgone when the complaining party is not a direct participant in the suit or merger, but, rather, an interested third party. However, the government is more likely to take seriously third party complaints if they come from a party directly or indirectly burdened from the proposed merger. *See* Lawrence R. Fullerton, *How Can I Stop that Merger? The Role of Third Parties in Agency Merger Reviews*, 9 Antitrust 37, 38 (1995). Also, third party complaints from customers may carry more weight than complaints from competitors in some instances. *Id.*

There are threats and possible downsides to this practice for the third party. Presentations can have the opposite of their intended effect, especially if made by competitors, leading the government to abandon challenges. *Id.* at 40. Second, materials submitted to the government by the challenging party may later be used against the third party itself should it attempt to engage in a merger in the future. *Id.* at 41. Finally, third party complainants run the risk of being publicly exposed through the Freedom of Information Act. *Id.*

See also Tefft W. Smith & Hillard M. Sterling, *Challenging Competitor's Mergers: A Real Strategic Option*, 65 Antitrust L.J. 57 (1996).

[283] 495 U.S. at 282, n.8, *citing Zenith Radio Corp. v. Hazeltine Research, Inc.*, 395 U.S. 100, 130 (1969).

federal courts with equitable jurisdiction," absent an express or implicit statutory restriction, "the full scope of that jurisdiction will be recognized and applied."[284]

Consequently, the Court held that the "district court had the power to divest American of any part of its ownership interests in the acquired Lucky Stores, either by forbidding American to integrate operations of the two companies, or by requiring it to sell certain assets located in California." Although not applicable to this case, the Court also commented that equitable defenses are available to block injunctive relief in the form of divestiture. Said the Court: "equitable defenses such as laches or'unclean hands' may protect consummated transactions from belated attacks by private parties when it would not be too late for the Government to vindicate the public interest."[285]

Even though the sweep of these statutes is broad in allowing private injuries to be redressed, the Supreme Court has created limitations on the application of private claims for relief. In both *Brunswick Corp. v. Pueblo Bowl–O–Mat, Inc.*,[286] and *Cargill, Inc. v. Monfort of Colorado, Inc.*,[287] the Court made clear that private plaintiffs, including competitors and targets of mergers, who bring claims under § 7 for either injunctive relief or monetary relief must show standing and antitrust injury — injury caused by a decrease in competition, the cause in fact of which was the merger.

§ 7.11   International Mergers and Acquisitions

Mergers between major firms have the potential for affecting not just United States commerce, but also competition on a multinational or global level.[288] Thus just as the issue of extraterritorial enforcement of United States antitrust laws increasingly has become important in an integrated market,[289] so has international cooperation in merger review and enforcement. Today sixty countries currently have premerger notification requirements; a growing number, specifically the European Community (EC) and the United States, assert jurisdiction over a merger based on its competitive effect, and not the physical presence of the firms.[290] While most commentators agree that procedural convergence on standards for merger review is

---

[284] *Id.* at 295. Sullivan, *supra* note 275

[285] *Id.*

[286] 429 U.S. 477 (1977). *See supra* § 3.02[B].

[287] 479 U.S. 104 (1986). *See supra* § 3.02[B].

[288] Daniel J. Gifford & E. Thomas Sullivan, *Can International Antitrust Be Saved for the Post–Boeing Merger World? A Proposal to Minimize International Conflict and To Rescue Antitrust from Misuse*, 35 Antitrust Bull. 55, 58 (2000).

[289] *See* § 3.03[C], *infra.*

[290] Douglas H. Ginsburg & Scott H. Angstreich, *Multinational Merger Review: Lessons from Our Federalism*, 68 Antitrust L.J. 219, 220–21 (2000). *See generally,* E. Thomas Sullivan, *Harmonizing Global Meger Standards in the Political Economy of International Trade Law* 248–251 (2002).

possible, substantive policy agreement on what constitutes a procompetitive or anticompetitive merger appears to be elusive.[291]

Transnational mergers present unique problems for those firms seeking to merge, both procedurally and substantively. Foreign acquirers seeking to merge with an American firm may be barred altogether from certain industries, or the acquisition may be subject to national security review.[292] With these exceptions, the United States antitrust laws are essentially neutral as to the nationalities of the firms. Transnational firms may merge after meeting the Hart–Scott–Rodino (HSR) filing requirements and passing the substantive merger review by either the Department of Justice or Federal Trade Commission.[293] The 1995 International Enforcement Guidelines delineate the special "foreign commerce" rules of the Hart–Scott Rodino Act; some transactions will be exempt entirely from reporting.[294] The subsequent substantive merger review is identical to that between two domestic firms: the agency will employ the 1992 or 1984 *Merger Guidelines* to assess whether the merger will have the effect of substantially lessening competition in the United States.[295] However, market definition is complicated by inclusion of foreign production.[296] If foreign production is altogether excluded, a prima facie violation of § 7 is likely to occur; if it is over–included, it may reduce the merged firm's market shares and concentration within the United States.[297] Additionally, the relevant geographic market may be narrowed to a few countries, or may be global in scope. However, while these factors are additional variables in the analysis, the structure of the merger evaluation is essentially the same.

The Department of Justice takes further guidance from the 1995 International Operations Guidelines.[298] The 1995 Guidelines analyze the jurisdictional issues that can arise with transnational mergers. If two foreign firms seeking to merge account for a large percentage of United States sales through direct imports, the agency will likely assert jurisdiction over the merger based on the effect on U.S. imports.[299] Conversely, if a proposed merger would have effects on U.S. export commerce, the agencies will also apply the "direct, substantial and reasonably foreseeable" effects test of the FTAIA.[300] The 1995 Guidelines recognize that while the agency may assert

---

[291] *See, e.g;* Ginsburg & Angstreich, *supra* note 290, 222–26. *See also* Daniel J. Gifford & Robert Kudrle, *Alternative Merger Standards and the Prospects for International Cooperation in the Political Economy of International Trade* 208–247 (2002).

[292] *See* Spencer Weber Waller, International Trade and U.S. Antitrust Law, § 8.01 (1992 & 2001 Supp.).

[293] *Id.* at § 8.01; *see also infra* § 7.0.

[294] 1995 *Guidelines* § 2.4; § 4.22.

[295] *See* 1992 *Merger Guidelines* at § 1.0.

[296] Waller, § 8.02.

[297] *Id.*

[298] Waller, § 8.09.

[299] 1995 *Guidelines* at § 3.14.

[300] 1995 *Guidelines* § 3.14; *see also infra* § 3.03.

"technical" jurisdiction over the merger, the principle of "positive comity" may require the DOJ to consult and cooperate with another country's antitrust authorities also reviewing the proposed merger.

Although United States agency may ultimately approve a merger, the parallel enforcement agency of a foreign jurisdiction may consider it anticompetitive. It will thus signal its outright disapproval, effectively killing the merger, as was the case in 2001, when the European Commission quashed a merger between General Electric and Honeywell that the Department of Justice had approved. [301] Even if the parallel agency ultimately clears the merger, it may require the firms to make concessions and compromises in their lines of business. This was the case in 1997, when the EC cleared the McDonnell–Douglas/Boeing merger only after last–minute negotiations.

The McDonnell–Boeing merger threw into dramatic relief the differences in antitrust policy between the United States and the European Community. At issue was the European Commission's finding that the proposed merger, as evaluated under the European Union Merger Regulation, was unlawful. [302] The Federal Trade Commission had approved the merger. Prior to the merger, the market consisted only of three firms: McDonnell–Douglas, Boeing, and Airbus Industrie. The European Commission objected specifically to several exclusive supply contracts that Boeing had negotiated with U.S. airlines, stating that those contracts strengthened Boeing's dominant position. The exclusive supply contracts would have the effect of foreclosing Airbus from the U.S. customer base, and lowering Boeing's cost. When the Commission withdrew its objection to the merger, it did so on the condition that Boeing would not enforce those contracts for ten years, nor seek to enter new exclusive supply contracts during that ten–year period. The reason was to maintain the interfirm rivalry between Boeing and its European counterpart, Airbus, and to protect Airbus from a perceived abuse of dominance by Boeing. [303]

In contrast, the FTC had approved the merger without objection, noting the efficiencies that would result. The conflict in the *Boeing* merger occurred despite the existence of a cooperation agreement between the United States and the EC. The United States and EC enforcement agencies simply differed in the goals each had for their respective antitrust law regimes: while current United States merger review prioritizes the efficiencies that result from a merger, the EC advances a non–economic interest in protecting competitors. [304]

---

[301] *EU Bars Acquisition of Honeywell by General Electric* Antitrust and Trade Reg. Rep. (BNA) (July 5, 2001).

[302] Gifford & Sullivan, *supra* note 288, at 69.

[303] *Id.*

[304] Gifford & Sullivan, *supra* note 288; *see also* A. Douglas Melamed, *International Antitrust in an Age of International Deregulation*, 6 Geo. Mason L.Rev. 437, 444. *But see EU Commissioner Discusses Merger Remedies and Proposals*, Antitrust & Trade Reg. Daily (BNA) (Feb. 4, 2002); Gifford & Kudrle, *supra* note 291.

Currently, the European Community is reevaluating its competition policy, but the problems encountered with the *Boeing* merger are typical, if magnified by the size of the merged firms. As one commentator noted, "[w]hile we live in a global economy. . . we do not live a global state. There is no international antitrust code, nor are there international rules for resolving issues of jurisdiction and enforcement procedure."[305]

§ 7.12   Conclusion

Most merger cases decided under the antitrust laws arise either from the fear (1) that increased size and market power will harm smaller businesses, or (2) that increased concentration in markets will result in supracompetitive profits through higher prices that will harm consumers either by the resulting economic inefficiency or by redistributing wealth from consumers to producers. As a consequence, merger law has developed to prevent mergers and acquisitions from resulting in collusive pricing, monopoly power, exploitation of economies of scale or oligopolistic interdependence. "Bigness" *per se* is no longer the target of § 7. Increased size and concentration also can result from economies of scale that can produce benefits to consumers as long as the savings are passed along. Although almost all antitrust observers agree that mergers that result in higher prices are the core target of § 7, there is much disagreement on why higher prices are suspect: because they are economically inefficient or because they transfer wealth from consumers to producers with market power.

The recent trend away from presumptive illegality, based on statistical showings of increased concentration and market power, and toward a functional approach, based on a showing of actual anticompetitive practices or results, is likely to continue. This will result in increased importance for economic theory, and place greater emphasis on understanding how individual markets are affected by certain market conduct, such as coordinated interaction and ease of entry. This is the essence of the *Guidelines*, with their focus on a detailed quantitative analysis rather than the general, qualitative approach of the case law. The result, under the *Guidelines*, yields fewer merger challenges, less court intervention and more reliance on merger deregulation and market solutions. That resolution, of course, is driven by certain political and economic ideologies. As demonstrated in this chapter, a substantial tension exists between the case law, the present *Guidelines*, and certain economic theories.[306] But enforcement of the laws governing mergers has not been consistent[307] and rarely has there been unanimity in the enforcement of the merger laws.

---

[305] Melamed, *supra* note 304, at 438. *See also* Sullivan, *supra* note 290. *See generally* E. Thomas Sullivan, *Comparing Antitrust Remedies in the U.S. and E.U.: Advancing a Standard of Proportionality* — Antitrust Bull. — (2003).

[306] Cohen & Sullivan, *supra* note 32, at 505.

[307] Sullivan, *supra* note 10, at 1000.

Chapter 8

PRICE DISCRIMINATION

§ 8.01 Introduction

A great deal of controversy has focused on the Robinson–Patman Act. The Act prohibits price and other forms of discrimination. This Depression era Act was passed principally to protect competitors.[1] Arguments based on economic theory suggest that it may actually cause prices to increase and output to decrease.[2] Consequently, the Act is viewed by many as misguided in the context of modern antitrust theory. Just how threatening the Act is to businesses is not entirely clear. Whatever strength the Act had by way of private enforcement has been diminished by two relatively recent Supreme Court decisions.[3] On the other hand, although the interest of the Justice Department and the FTC in enforcing the Act has waned considerably over the years,[4] this could change with the political climate.

[A] The Clayton Act and Robinson–Patman Amendments

For antitrust purposes, the most relevant sections of the Robinson–Patman Act,[5] are §§ 2(a)–(f) which amend § 2 of the Clayton Act.[6] Although both § 2 of the 1914 Clayton Act and the Robinson–Patman Act amendments of 1936 are nominally aimed at prohibiting price discrimination, a comparison of the two reveals the changing nature of the concerns of the drafters in 1914 and their 1936 counterparts. Language in the original version of the Clayton Act and subsequent interpretations indicate that the harm to be prevented was caused by firms, operating in multiple

---

[1] *See* Hansen, *Robinson–Patman Law: A Review and Analysis,* Fordham L. Rev. 1113, 1120–24 (1983). *See generally*, F. Rowe, *Price Discrimination Under the Robinson–Patman Act* (1962).

[2] *See, e.g.*, R. Blair & D. Kaserman. *Antitrust Economics* (1985); R. Bork, *The Antitrust Paradox* (1978); R. Posner, *The Robinson–Patman Act: Federal Regulation of Price Differences* (1976); Schmalensee, *Output and Welfare Implications of Monopolistic Third–Degree Price Discrimination,* 71 Am. Econ. Rev. 242 (1981).

[3] *See Brooke Group Ltd. v. Brown & Williamson Tobacco,* 509 U.S. 209 (1993); *J. Truett Payne Co. v. Chrysler Motors Corp.,* 451 U.S. 557 (1981).

[4] *See* Hansen, *supra* note 1, at 1174–82.

[5] The first section of the Robinson–Patman Act is an amendment to § 2 of the Clayton Act. Section 3 of the Robinson–Patman Act provides for criminal sanctions of up to $5,000, imprisonment not exceeding one year, or both if a person engages or assists in (1) general price discrimination (2) geographical price discrimination, or (3) selling at unreasonably low prices to destroy competition or eliminate competitors. This section is not a subject of private treble damage enforcement. Because the statute is criminal, it generally has been held to require specific intent.

[6] *See generally*, L. Sullivan, *Antitrust*, 472–89 (1977).

markets, who were thought to raise prices in markets in which they possessed market power in order to subsidize price cutting in markets in which they sought to gain power. Consequently, protection extended only to direct competitors of the discriminating firm. This left unprotected competitors of buyers that were able to elicit relatively favorable prices from their suppliers. In response, the 1936 amendments added language so that the Act currently prohibits discrimination:

> [i]n price between different purchasers of commodities of like grade and quality . . . where the effect of such discrimination may be substantially to lessen competition or tend to create a monopoly in any line of commerce, or to injure, destroy, or prevent competition with any person who either grants or knowingly receives the benefit of such discrimination, or with customers of either of them . . . .[7]

Today, Robinson–Patman Act violations are typically categorized as either "primary–line," "secondary–line," or "tertiary–line." Primary–line cases concern discrimination that may result in injury to the seller's competitors. Secondary–line cases, included by the Robinson–Patman amendments, involve discrimination that affects competition among customers of the discriminating seller. Tertiary–line cases involve injury further down the chain of distribution to the customers of the favored and disfavored purchasers.[8]

[B]   Overview: The Components of the Robinson–Patman Act

[1]   Price "Discrimination" and Price "Difference"

Section 2(a) of the Robinson–Patman Act makes it illegal for any person to "discriminate in price." Technically, a seller discriminates when the difference in price charged to different customers does not reflect the difference in the marginal cost of selling to those customers.[9] Thus, even a seller charging the same price to different customers is engaged in price discrimination when the cost of serving those customers is different. Under the Robinson–Patman Act, however, "price discrimination" generally has been held to mean "price difference."[10] Consequently, from the point of view of economic theory, the Act falls considerably short of being a complete bar to price discrimination. To a minor degree this discrepancy between the Act's coverage and the economist's definition of "price discrimination" is cured by the Act's prohibition of "indirect" discrimination[11] and its provision for a "cost justification" defense for different prices.[12]

---

[7] 15 U.S.C. § 13(a)(1976).

[8] *See Perkins v. Standard Oil*, 395 U.S. 642 (1969). *See generally*, F. Rowe, *supra* note 1, at 185–195; H. Shniderman, *Price Discrimination in Perspective* 39–41 (1977).

[9] *See* R. Blair & D. Kaserman, *Antitrust Economics* (1985).

[10] *FTC v. Anheuser–Busch, Inc.*, 363 U.S. 536, 549 (1960).

[11] *See infra* § 8.03[A][3].

[12] *See infra* § 8.05[A].

[2]   Section 2(a) Components

In addition to the "price difference" requirement, § 2(a) contains a number of limiting elements. First, it applies only to *sales* of *commodities* of *like grade and quality*. Additionally, there must be at least two contemporaneous sales to different purchasers and at least one sale must result in the commodity crossing state lines.[13] The primary substantive requirement of the Act is that the discrimination must result in competitive injury. Finally, the Act not only prohibits sellers from discriminatory pricing, but § 2(f) prohibits buyers from inducing such discrimination.

[3]   Defenses

Although their utility to the seller has been limited by judicial interpretation, there are two basic affirmative defenses to a price discrimination claim. First, the Act does not prohibit price differences that reflect "differences in the cost of manufacture, sale or delivery."[14] Second, no violation will be found if the price difference was the product of a good faith attempt to meet the "equally low price of a competitor."[15] An additional and seldomly used defense permits price differences that result from price changes from "time to time" in response to changing market conditions or the "marketability of the goods."[16]

[4]   The *Per Se* Offenses

The Robinson–Patman Act prohibits three forms of discrimination beyond those called price discrimination. They are, in essence, *per se* offenses because, unlike the prohibition of § 2(a), there is no competitive injury requirement. Section 2(c) makes it unlawful for a person "to pay or grant, or receive or accept" brokerage in any form except for "services rendered."[17] Sections 2(d) and (e) prohibit the granting of promotional allowances to the buyer by the seller in the form of payments or the provision of services or facilities unless allowances are available to all customers on "proportionally equal terms."[18]

[5]   Coverage

Some of the more perplexing questions presented by the Robinson–Patman Act arise under § 2(a) and concern the determination of when discrimination occurs, when products are of like grade and quality, and what constitutes "competitive injury." These matters as well as defenses to a price discrimination charge and the *per se* elements of the Act are the

---

[13] *Gulf Oil Corp. v. Copp Paving Co. Inc.*, 419 U.S. 186. 200 (1974).

[14] 15 U.S.C. § 13(a)(1976).

[15] *Id.* at § 13(b). For an example of conduct that goes beyond a "good faith" attempt and implicates § 1 of the Sherman Act, *see United States v. Gypsum Co.*, 438 U.S. 422 (1978).

[16] 15 U.S.C. at § 13(a) (1976).

[17] *Id.* at § 13(c).

[18] *Id.* at §§ 13 (d) and (e).

focus of this Chapter. First, however, a discussion of the economic theory of price discrimination is essential for an understanding of the bases of modern criticism of the Act.

§ 8.02   The Economics of Price Discrimination

Economic theory suggests that the price and output effects of price discrimination cannot be confidently determined without examining demand and supply in the markets involved[19] — a difficult undertaking to say the least. The alarming implication for the Robinson–Patman Act is that price discrimination may, depending on a number of variables, result in lower prices and higher output — goals that the antitrust laws are designed to foster, not hinder.[20] Most of the contemporary criticism of the Act is fueled by uncertainty concerning its economic impact and the likelihood that any of the truly anticompetitive effects of discriminatory pricing can be responded to by enforcing other provisions of the antitrust laws.[21]

[A]   First–Degree Price Discrimination

The fears of economists and antitrust scholars concerning the Robinson–Patman Act can be illustrated by reference to a theoretical construct called "first degree" or "perfect" price discrimination. The concept is best understood by reviewing profit maximizing price and output determination by a monopolist. In Figure 8–1 — a reproduction of Figure 2–8 — profit maximizing output is determined by the intersection of the marginal cost and marginal revenue curves. The profit maximizing price, Pm, is the highest price for which that quantity can be sold. Suppose that quantity Qm is 10. The monopolist would not sell an 11th unit because the marginal cost of that unit would exceed marginal revenue. This is not to say that the price for the 11th unit is not higher than the marginal cost of that unit. In fact, it would be. The problem for the monopolist is that in order to sell unit 11 the price of all units will have to be lowered. The marginal revenue from selling that unit is its selling price minus the revenue lost by lowering the price of all the other units sold. This is, of course, nothing more than an explanation of why the marginal revenue curve lies below the demand curve.

---

[19] *See generally* J. Robinson, *Economics of Imperfect Competition* (1933); Schmalensee, *supra* note 2.

[20] *See* Schmalense, *supra* note 2.

[21] *See e.g.,* R. Posner, *supra* note 2, at 52–53. Most of the contemporary economic analysis of the Robinson–Patman Act is derived from the analysis of A.C. Pigou, *The Economics of Welfare* (4th ed. 1938), and J. Robinson, *supra* note 19.

FIGURE 8–1

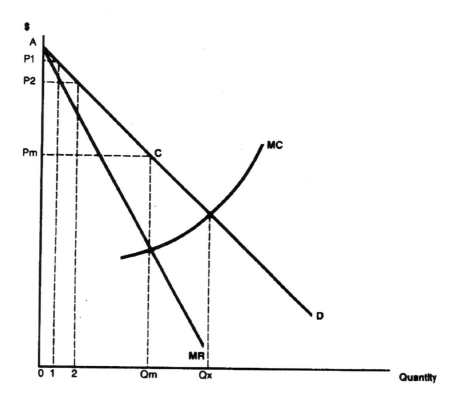

It would be a form of monopolist's heaven if the firm could somehow lower its price to sell additional units and not lower the prices for all units. This is, in fact, the test of the whether it makes sense for the monopolist to discriminate. It must be able to segregate its customers in order to sell to different customers at different prices. To the extent the monopolist can do this, its marginal revenue curve becomes the same as its demand curve. The most extreme example of this possibility holds true under first degree or perfect price discrimination. In this model, the monopolist is able to sell each unit to each customer at that customer's reservation price (the highest amount he or she would be willing to pay). In Figure 8–1, for example, unit 1 would be sold for P1, unit 2 for P2, and so on. Since the monopolist will sell as long as marginal revenue exceeds marginal cost and the demand curve is now the marginal revenue curve, the monopolist will sell a total of Qx units at a series of declining prices.

There are several things to note about this solution. First, the total output — where the demand curve and the marginal cost curves intersect — should look familiar. It's the same output one would expect under perfectly competitive market conditions. Second, the deadweight loss that was discussed as a product of monopoly pricing in Chapters 2 and 6 has also been eliminated. In short, price discrimination has resulted in higher output, lower prices for some (higher for others) and elimination of the deadweight loss.

Other results under first degree discrimination may not be as encouraging. First, there is no longer any consumer surplus. Since the monopolist has sold to each customer at the highest price he or she is willing to pay, the monopolist has transferred all of the area which was consumer surplus (PmAC in Figure 8–1) to itself. One's reaction to this will depend upon whether they feel antitrust law should be concerned with distributive effects.

A second concern is probably less controversial. Obviously, the discriminating monopolist stands to gain a great deal. It must, however, isolate each buyer in order to sell at that buyer's reservation price without lowering the price to others and ensure that each low price buyer does not engage in arbitrage. Indeed, in theory, the attraction of perfect discrimination could be so strong that a monopolist may be tempted to invest a great deal in the buyer segregation effort. These expenditures, to the extent they are only designed to transfer the surplus created by the exchange from consumers to the seller, can be viewed as a new form of deadweight loss.[22]

[B]   Second–Degree Price Discrimination

Perfect or first degree price discrimination is really only a theoretical possibility. In fact, there is little likelihood that a monopolist would expend substantial effort in hopes of achieving perfect market segregation. It is not at all unlikely, however, that a monopolist might perceive an opportunity to segregate the market into two or more parts. This is "second degree" or "imperfect" price discrimination.[23] One possible result is illustrated in Figure 8–2. Here the monopolist has continued to sell to some buyers at Pm, the original profit maximizing price. It has also isolated a group of buyers who are willing and able to pay more, price Ph. In addition, if the monopolist is able to prevent them from reselling to those paying Ph or Pm, it will isolate a third group to which it will sell at price P1. In the graph five units will be sold at Ph, five will be sold at Pm and five will be sold at P1. Here again the monopolist has transferred some of what was consumer surplus to itself. On the other hand, it has increased output and is now selling to a third group that would not have purchased at the non-discriminatory price of Pm. Second degree price discrimination, like first degree, raises the possibility of a deadweight loss arising from efforts to classify buyers into their proper price group and segregate them. And, since second degree price discrimination is a more realistic possibility, the likelihood of experiencing such a loss is greater.

---

[22] R. Posner, *supra* note 2, at 7–10.

[23] *See* A.C. Pigou, *supra* note 21, at 275–79.

FIGURE 8–2

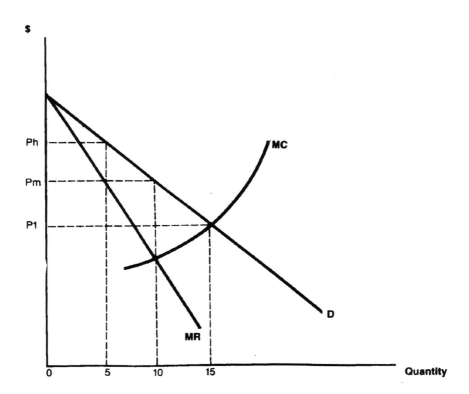

[C] Third–Degree Price Discrimination

Although second degree price discrimination is far more likely than first degree, it involves a simplification that causes it to deviate from what most monopolists are likely to encounter in the real world. Under second degree, the market was divisible so that all buyers willing to pay Ph or more, paid Ph. All buyers willing to pay an amount equal to Pm but less than Ph were charged Pm and only buyers unwilling to pay Pm, but willing to pay at least P1, were charged P1. This degree of market segregation is not likely.

In the more realistic model, "third degree" price discrimination, the problems of market segregation are recognized.[24] For example, by holding to price P1 in one market — say, one that is geographically separate — the seller will not charge as much as it could to those buyers in that market who are willing to pay Pm or Ph. Similarly, adhering to Pm in another market may exclude some individuals who are willing to pay only P1 and permit some buyers who are willing to pay Ph to buy for only Pm. Further

---

[24] *Id. See also* L. Phlips, *The Economics of Price Discrimination* 12–13 (1983).

complications arise because of the investment required to effectively segregate the market to prevent buyers in low price markets from reselling in competition with the monopolist in higher priced markets. Indeed, this investment may be so great that the monopolist may choose not to offer price P1 at all and output will not increase. If so, the only discrimination that would take place would be among those willing to pay at least Pm and output may actually fall.[25]

As a consequence of these more real world considerations, it is difficult to predict whether price discrimination will result in higher output and lower prices or not. The answer depends in large measure on the shape of the demand curves facing the seller.[26] What this means for the Robinson–Patman Act is fairly simple: Even if it were not a drafting nightmare, and even if it were interpreted in a manner that was consistent with the economist's notion of price discrimination, there is no certainty concerning the benefits of its enforcement.

From time to time, in addition to enforcing the Act, courts make efforts to reconcile it with acceptable antitrust goals. One court recently noted the that the Act was designed to curb monopsony power.[27] Thus, it reasoned that "when one or a few large buyers dominate a market in which many sellers compete or sales, these buyers can, if unrestrained, force the suppliers to sell at such low prices as to prevent new buyers from entering the market."[28] Although the court correctly notes the effect on price that the Act was designed to prevent, it is not clear that the impact of enforcing the Act is procompetitive or that the ultimate effect — less competition among buyers — is likely to occur.

§ 8.03 Definitional Issues

As noted earlier, the Robinson–Patman Act is directed at price differences, not price discrimination in a technical sense. The emphasis on price difference means that economic analysis is less important than it would be under a full–blown prohibition of price discrimination. Still, the plaintiff must present evidence that the defendant has made two sales of commodities of like grade and quality at two different prices to two different buyers. The issues of whether there is in fact a price difference and whether the goods are of like grade and quality are intriguing and can be quite complicated.

[A] Two Prices and Two Sales

The importance of the technical requirements of two prices and two sales requirements is illustrated by a recent case, *Lycon, Inc., v. Juneke*.[29] The

---

[25] *See* J. Robinson, *supra* note 19 at 188– 95.

[26] *See Id.* Schmalensee. *supra* note 2.

[27] *Hoover Color Corp. v. Bayer Corp.*, 199 F.3d 160 (4th Cir. 1999).

[28] *Id.* at 163.

[29] 250 F.3d 285 (5th Cir. 2001).

plaintiff was a distributor that purchased equipment from the defendant. It then resold the equipment. The defendant also sold through its own retail stores. The retail prices were lower than the price available to the distributor. The court held that the plaintiff did not fall with the protection of the Act. First, the plaintiff was not a competitor of the supplier, thus, there was no harm at the primary level. Second, although the plaintiff did compete with the retail sales the defendant did not make a sale to its own retail stores. Finally, even though the defendant did make retail sales, these sales were to end users who did not resell in competition with the plaintiff.[30]

The different price issue was also addressed in *Liberty Lincoln–Mercury v. Ford Motor Co.*,[31] in which a Ford dealer used New Jersey law to force Ford to raise its reimbursement rate on parts installed under an automobile's warranty. Other dealers in New Jersey had not sought the same concessions. In reaction, Ford raised the wholesale price of vehicles in order to recoup the lower prices on parts. The court ruled that the plaintiff had failed to demonstrate a price difference. The court reasoned that the surcharge on vehicles actually had the effect of equalizing prices.[32]

[B]   Price Differences

[1]   Discounts

Suppose a seller publishes a price list in which the price per unit declines with the amount purchased. From one point of view, this means that buyers purchasing small quantities will pay a different price per unit than those who purchase larger quantities and § 2(a) would come into play. On the other hand, if the option of purchasing higher amounts for a lower price per unit is available to all, it seems inappropriate to regard the seller as having discriminated in any active fashion. A similar problem is presented when the seller quotes one price but offers a discount from that price for buyers who pay within a stipulated time limit. Again, different buyers are charged different prices but the opportunity for the favorable price would seem to be available to all.

The test of whether such discounts are discriminatory is found in *F.T.C. v. Morton Salt*,[33] perhaps the leading price discrimination case. Morton Salt offered substantial discounts to customers who purchased salt in greater than carload lots. Its defense was that the discounts were available to all purchasers on an equal basis. As a factual matter only five large purchasers qualified for the lowest discount. In finding that the discount amounted to the type of discrimination forbidden by the Robinson–Patman Act, the

---

[30] *Id.* at 289.

[31] 134 F.3d 557 (3d Cir. 1998).

[32] *Id.* at 571. It is noteworthy that the court reasoned that even if there were a price difference it would not have an adverse competitive effect. *Id.* at 571.

[33] 414 U.S. 488 (1942).

Supreme Court noted that "[t]heoretically, these discounts are available to all, but functionally they are not."[34]

A further requirement is illustrated by *Mueller v. FTC*[35] in which a manufacturer offered different discounts to jobbers depending upon whether items purchased were shipped directly to end users or warehoused.[36] The manufacturer contended that the higher discount was available to all jobbers willing to carry an inventory of the items. The Seventh Circuit Court of Appeals sided with the FTC and rejected the argument, noting the lack of *objective* standards to indicate how a jobber became eligible for the more favorable discount.[37]

[2] Base Point Pricing

A potentially troublesome problem in the determination of whether price discrimination exists surfaces when a seller makes use of a uniform delivered price or a basing point pricing system. As noted in the discussion of horizontal restraints in Chapter 4, the use of delivered pricing means that the prices charged to different buyers may deviate in different degrees from the cost of actually serving them. For example, in a uniform delivered price scheme, the marginal cost of serving distant buyers will not be fully reflected in the price. Similarly, in a basing point system, although the delivered prices will vary depending upon the buyer's distance from the seller's basing point, the actual delivered charge will not reflect the seller's costs unless the basing point and point of origin are the same.

The question becomes whether the relevant price for § 2(a) purposes is the delivered price or the "mill–net" return. Certainly the "mill–net" approach would mean that enforcement of the Act would parallel the economist's definition of price discrimination. And, for a period after passage of the Act, the Supreme Court, despite legislative history suggesting the contrary,[38] seemed receptive to a "mill–net" approach and held that basing point pricing violated the Act.[39] In recent years, however, primarily as a result of FTC's enforcement policy,[40] the relevant price has shifted to the delivered price or the price "laid down" by the buyer.[41] The reasoning

---

[34] *Id.* at 42.

[35] 323 F.2d 44 (7th Cir. 1963), *cert. denied,* 377 U.S. 923 (1964). *See also FLM Collision Parts v. Ford Motor Co.,* 543 F.2d 1019 (2d Cir. 1976).

[36] This so–called "functional discount" is discussed in § 8.04 [B][1], *infra.*

[37] 323 F.2d at 46.

[38] *See generally* F. Rowe, *supra* note 1 at 87–89.

[39] *See Corn Products Ref. Co. v. FTC,* 324 U.S. 726 (1945); *FTC v. A.E. Staley Mfg. Co.,* 324 U.S. 746 (1945); *FTC v. Cement Institute,* 333 U.S. 683 (1948). *See generally* P. Areeda, *Antitrust Analysis* 1095–97 (3rd ed.1981); F. Rowe, *supra* note 1, at 88–90.

[40] *See* L. Sullivan, *supra* note 6, at 688, *citing National Lead Co.,* 497 F.T.C. 791 (1953), modified sub. nom., *National Lead Co. v. FTC,* 227 F.2d 825 (7th Cir. 1955), original order aff'd., 352 U.S. 419.

[41] *See e.g., Rose Confections Inc. v. Ambrosia Chocolate Co.,* 52 A & T.R.R. 768 (April 13, 1987). *See generally* P. Areeda, *Antitrust Analysis* 1095–97 (1981); F. Rowe, *supra* note 1, at 92–108. *But see, Chicago Spring Prods. Co. v. United States Steel Corp.,* 254 F. Supp. 83 (N.D. Ill. 1965), *aff'd. per curiam,* 371 F.2d 428 (7th Cir. 1966).

is that the actual price paid is the relevant one in determining the buyer's ability to compete with other buyers in the resale market.[42]

Thus a system of uniform delivered prices probably no longer falls within the purview of § 2(a).[43] On the other hand, a basing point pricing system would result in the requisite price difference.[44] If the basing point were the point of shipment, however, the difference may be excused by the cost justification defense.[45] When the basing point is not the point of actual shipment there exists both the required price difference and the lack of a cost justification defense. Even here, however, one can argue that freight absorption is a form of meeting competition, another defense found in the Act, and the occurrence of phantom freight is simply profit maximizing pricing and not prohibited by the Act.[46]

[3] Indirect Price Discrimination

The Robinson–Patman Act forbids direct as well as "indirect" price discrimination.[47] Applied literally, the concept of "indirect" price discrimination could be broad enough to bring the economist's definition of discrimination into the scope of the Robinson–Patman Act. This has not, however, been the course taken. Indirect discrimination has been reserved for instances in which buyers pay the same nominal price but some are favored by the seller in terms of ancillary services.[48]

For example, in *Corn Products Refining Co. v. FTC*,[49] sellers would announce price increases and then permit buyers a "grace" period during which orders would be filled at the previous price. Some buyers were, however, given a longer period of time during which they could take advantage of the earlier price. The petitioner argued that this was not price discrimination but discrimination in the "terms and condition" of sale.[50] The argument found support in the legislative history of the Act which indicated that Congress specifically had rejected listing discriminatory "terms of sale" as violating the Act.[51] The Court relied on an examination of the "practical effect"[52] of the difference in treatment in order to distinguish differences

---

[42] *See Report of the Attorney General's National Committee to Study the Antitrust Laws* 58 (1955), at 217

[43] *See, e.g., Clay Prods. Ass'n.*, 47 F.T.C. 1256 (1951); *National Lead Co.*, 49 F.T.C. 791 (1953).

[44] *See* P. Areeda, *supra* note 41, at 1095.

[45] *Id.*

[46] This is suggested by Areeda, *supra* note 41, at 1096.

[47] 15 U.S.C. § 13(a) (1976).

[48] *See* F. Rowe, *supra* note 1 at 104–05 *citing Corn Products Refining Co. v. FTC*, 324 U.S. 726 (1945); *National Nut Co. v. Knelling Nut Co.*, 61 F. Supp. 76 (N.D. Ill. 1945); *General Foods Corp.*, 50 F.T.C. 885 (1954). *See also* Hansen. *supra* note 1, at 1127, n. 82.

[49] 324 U.S. 726 (1945).

[50] *Id.* at 740.

[51] *Id.* (citing H. Rep. No. 2951, 74th Cong. 2nd sess., p. 5).

[52] *Id.* at 739.

in "terms of sale" that would constitute an indirect form of price discrimination[53] from those that would not. It held that the petitioner's practice amounted to indirect price discrimination.

[4] Indirect Purchasers

Both the express terms of § 2(a) and any coherent interpretation of the concept of price discrimination require that the different prices be charged to different purchasers. A definitional issue in this regard can arise when a buyer who is unable to purchase directly from the manufacturer, purchases from a middleman to whom the manufacturer has sold. Obviously the resale to this indirect purchaser is likely to be made at a higher price than that paid by those who have purchased directly from the manufacturer.[54] The question is whether the manufacturer is merely exercising its right not to sell to potential purchasers or whether the use of the middleman is a method of practicing price discrimination while attempting to avoid the different purchaser requirement of the Act.[55] Lower court decisions suggest that the dual purchaser requirement of § 2(a) is met when the manufacturer is closely affiliated with or controls the middleman or the manufacturer bargains directly with the eventual indirect purchasers.[56]

Although *FTC v. Fred Meyer, Inc.*, a recent Supreme Court decision interpreting § 2(d) of the Act, reveals an inclination to protect indirect purchasers,[57] the issue must be viewed in light of the notable leeway permitted a seller under the Act. For instance, the Act does not require a manufacturer to sell to anyone who is willing to pay for the product. Moreover, the Act does not require sales at different levels in the chain of distribution to be made at the same price.[58] Finally, the Act permits different discounts to middleman purchasers depending upon the customers to whom the commodity is resold as long as the discount is functionally available to all purchasers at that level of distribution.[59]

[C] Commodities of "Like Grade and Quality"

The proscription of § 2(a) of the Robinson–Patman Act is applicable only if the commodities sold are of "like grade and quality." A difficult problem is presented when two commodities are similar but not the same. The courts have held that a slight physical difference is not enough to escape the

---

[53] *Id.* at 740.

[54] This example is suggested by P. Areeda, *supra* note 41 at 1057.

[55] *See, e.g.* *George Haug Co. v. Rolls Royce Motor Car*, 148 F.3d 136 (2nd Cir. 1998).

[56] *See, e.g., Security Tire & Rubber Co. v. Gates Rubber Co.*, 598 F.2d 962, 965–66 (5th Cir. 1979), *cert. denied*, 444 U.S. 942; *B.B. Walker Co. v. Ashland Chem. Co.*, 474 F. Supp. 651 (M D.N.C 1979); *Snyder v. Howard Johnson's Motor Lodges*, 412 F. Supp. 724, 730–31 (S.D. Ill. 1976).

[57] 390 U.S. 341 (1968).

[58] *See Texaco, Inc. v. Hasbrouck*, 496 U.S. 543 (1990).

[59] *FLM Collision Parts v. Ford Motor Co.*, 543 F.2d. 1019, 1021 (2d Cir. 1976).

coverage of § 2(a) as long as the commodity offers "substantially identical performance."[60]

A related issue arises when the commodities are physically identical but may be perceived by the public to be different due to variations in brand names and labelling. The leading case addressing the problem is *FTC v. Borden Co.*[61] in which the Borden Company sold chemically identical brand name and private label evaporated milk at different prices. The Fifth Circuit Court of Appeals held that different products were involved and set aside a Commission order prohibiting the price difference.[62] The Supreme Court reversed the Fifth Circuit, holding held that a pronounced public preference for a particular name brand, which results in a willingness to pay a higher price for that name brand, does not establish a difference between the products that would render § 2(a) inapplicable.[63] The Court reasoned that the impact of consumer preference should be considered under the competitive injury and cost justification provisions of the Act.[64] Ironically, on remand, the Fifth Circuit found the competitive injury to be insubstantial and once again sanctioned Borden's price differential.[65]

§ 8.04 Injury to Competition

The Clayton Act's pre–1936 ban on price discrimination was intended to prevent injury to competitors of the seller. As indicated earlier, the theory supporting such concerns was that large national firms could eliminate smaller competitors in one market by charging low prices that were subsidized by supracompetitive prices charged by the firm in markets in which it enjoyed significant market power. This is now referred to as primary–line injury. The Robinson–Patman Act amendments to the Clayton Act expanded the protection to "any person."[66] Most importantly, it increased the coverage of the Clayton Act to "secondary–line" cases or the customers of the discriminating firm. In either case, the substantive question is whether the effect of the discrimination "may be to substantially lessen competition or tend to create a monopoly . . . or to injure, destroy or prevent competition."[67]

---

[60] *Bruce's Juices v. American Can Co.*, 87 F. Supp. 985 (S.D. Fla. 1949), *modified*, 190 F.2d 73 (5th Cir. 1951), *cert. dismissed*, 342 U.S. 875.

[61] 383 U.S. 637 (1966).

[62] 339 F.2d 133 (5th Cir. 1964).

[63] 383 U.S. 637, 640 (1966).

[64] *Id.* at 645– 47.

[65] *Id.*

[66] 15 U.S.C. § 13(a) (1976).

[67] 15 U.S.C. § 13(a) (1976).

[A]   Primary–Line Price Discrimination: Reconciling the Robinson–Patman Act with General Antitrust Goals

[1]   *Utah Pie v. Continental Baking*

The most dramatic example of an inconsistency between the Robinson–Patman Act and modern approaches to antitrust policy can be found in the 1967 case, *Utah Pie v. Continental Baking.* [68] The case arose when Utah Pie, a local producer and seller of frozen desert pies with a dominant share of the relevant market, began to experience stiff price competition from national firms. Utah Pie's market share declined from to 66% to 45%. At the same time, though, its total sales increased and it continued to earn a profit. [69] The competitors of Utah Pie were, in fact, selling in the Utah market at prices that were lower than those charged in their other markets. There was some evidence of below cost pricing in Utah. In a suit by Utah Pie against the national producers, a jury found the national producers guilty of violating § 2(a) of the Robinson–Patman Act. The verdict was overturned by the Tenth Circuit Court of Appeals which reasoned that there was insufficient evidence to support a finding of competitive injury. [70]

The Supreme Court reversed, holding that there was sufficient evidence from which a jury could find the necessary injury to competition. [71] The Court explained that the Robinson–Patman Act was not designed to insure that a competitor would survive the forces of price competition but simply that certain rules were observed, one of which was not selling at different prices in different markets. Moreover, it suggested that it was not necessary to find consistent price undercutting or "blatant predatory . . . discrimination." [72]

In a decision that could be regarded as discouraging rather than encouraging competition, [73] the Court found it compelling that there had been a "deteriorating price structure" [74] in the market during the period of competition. The opinion came very close to saying that price differences and resulting increases in competitive pressure in a market are sufficient to satisfy the requirements of § 2(a). The net result is that competitors in the position of the national firms in *Utah Pie* seemed to be faced with the prospect of having to lower prices in all markets in order to engage in competition in any one market. This prospect would have been acceptable if it actually occurred. A more likely prospect, however, is that lower prices in all markets would be too high a price for the national firm to pay in order

---

[68] 386 U.S. 685 (1967).

[69] *Id.* at 689.

[70] *Continental Baking Co. v. Utah Pie*, 349 F.2d 122 (10th Cir. 1965).

[71] 386 U.S. at 700–01.

[72] *Id.* at 702.

[73] *See generally* Bowman, *Restraint of Trade by the Supreme Court: The Utah Pie Case*, 77 Yale L.J. 70 (1967); *See also* R. Blair & D. Kaserman *supra* note 2, at 275–76.

[74] 386 U.S. at 701.

to gain a share of a local market and it would opt to leave the market to a local monopolist.

[2] *Brooke Group Ltd. v. Brown & Williamson Tobacco*

The inconsistency between *Utah Pie* and modern antitrust policy can be boiled down to the issue of whether the antitrust laws are designed to protect competition or competitors. In actuality, both § 2 of the Clayton Act and the Robinson–Patman Act amendments were passed during a period when the protection of small businesses was viewed as a valid independent antitrust concern.[75] Despite this, in a 1993 decision, *Brooke Group Ltd. v. Brown and Williamson Tobacco*,[76] the Supreme Court adopted the view that the Robinson–Patman Act was to be interpreted in a manner that protected competition, not necessarily competitors,[77] and linked the Robinson–Patman Act to § 2 of the Sherman Act.

Brown & Williamson Tobacco arose as the result of a price war between cigarette manufacturers that were attempting to boost sagging sales through the introduction of generic cigarettes. Ligget, the plaintiff, claimed that Brown & Williamson had engaged in a strategy of offering discriminatory volume rebates to wholesalers. Some of the rebates meant that prices were below cost. Ligget claimed that the purpose of the strategy was to force it to raise the price of its generic cigarettes to levels closer to those of branded cigarettes.[78]

The Court distinguished *Utah Pie* by noting that since that decision it had become evident that the injury in primary–line cases "is of the same general character as the injury inflicted by predatory pricing actionable under § 2 of the Sherman Act."[79] The Court noted that the standard in an attempt to monopolize claim under § 2 of the Sherman Act was that the activity create or be accompanied by a dangerous probability of success and that under the Robinson–Patman Act the standard was whether there was " 'a reasonable possibility' of substantial injury to competition." It sought to resolve this distinction by observing that "whatever additional flexibility the Robinson–Patman Act standard may imply, the essence of the claim under either statute is the same . . . ."[80]

Having provided the link between the Robinson–Patman Act and the Sherman Act, the Court then announced a rigorous two–part test for those employing a predatory pricing theory in an attempt to monopolize case and for those claiming primary–line injury under the Robinson–Patman Act. Plaintiffs would be required to show that the defendants had charged below cost prices and that they had either a reasonable prospect, under the

---

[75] *See generally* F. Rowe, *supra* note 1, at 12–23.

[76] 509 U.S. 209 (1993).

[77] *Id.* at 222.

[78] *Id.* at 217.

[79] *Id.* at 221.

[80] *Id.* at 222.

Robinson–Patman Act, or a dangerous probability, under § 2 of the Sherman Act, of "recouping its investment in below–cost prices."[81]

The Court applied its standard to the case at hand by noting that the cigarette industry was a highly concentrated oligopoly. This meant that any efforts by a firm engaged in predatory pricing to recoup its investment was risky. In order to be successful, not only would the price–cutting firm be required to raise its prices to supracompetitive levels, all the firms in the industry would also have to charge recoupment level prices. The Court did not rule out this theory of liability as a matter of law. It did, however, hold that Ligget had not produced sufficient evidence that Brown & Williamson would be able to achieve the market power necessary to raise prices or that coordination among manufacturers was likely to do so.[82]

[B]　Secondary–Line Discrimination

[1]　The Inference of Injury

The victims of secondary–line price discrimination are the customers of the defendant rather than the defendant's competitors. Injury at this level may be inferred from evidence of loss of sales by the disfavored buyer[83] or from substantial price differences. The leading case with respect to the latter possibility is *FTC v. Morton Salt*[84] in which the Supreme Court held evidence of a system of substantial quantity discounts was sufficient to establish a *prima facie* violation of § 2(a). According to the Court, "in a case involving competitive injury between a seller's customers, the Commission need only prove that a seller charged one purchaser a higher price for like goods than he had charged one or more of the purchaser's competitors."[85] The Court thus flatly ruled out the need to show actual injury. Indeed, the inference of injury has been permitted even when the disfavored seller did not raise prices above those charged by favored buyers.[86]

In recent years the Supreme Court seemingly has affirmed its unwillingness to require a detailed analysis of actual effect in order to prevail in a § 2(a) case.[87] Of particular interest is the language of the Court in *Falls City Industries v. Vanco Beverages*[88] in response to the suggestion that recently developed narrower primary–line standards should be extended to secondary line cases:

---

[81] *Id.* at 224.

[82] *Id.* at 234.

[83] *See, e.g. Curtiss Candy*, 44 F.T.C. 237 (1944); *Standard Oil*, 41 F.T.C. 263 (1945), aff'd., 173 F. 2d 270 (7th Cir. 1949), *rev'd on other grounds*, 355 U.S. 396 (1958).

[84] 334 U.S. 37 (1948).

[85] 334 U.S. at 45.

[86] *See, e.g., Standard Motor Products, Inc. v. FTC*, 265 F.2d 674 (2d Cir. 1959); *P. & D. Manufacturing Co. v. FTC*, 245 F.2d 281 (7th Cir. 1957).

[87] *See, e.g., J. Truett Payne Co. v Chrysler Motor Corp.*, 451 U.S. 557. 562 (1981).

[88] 460 U.S. 428 (1983).

[Petitioner] does not, however, suggest any economic reasons why *Morton Salt*'s "self–evident" inference should not apply when the favored competitor is not extraordinarily large. Although concerns about the excessive market power of large purchasers were primarily responsible for passage of the Robinson–Patman Act . . . , the Act "is of general applicability and prohibits discrimination generally," . . . The determination whether to alter the scope of the act must be made by Congress, not this Court . . . .[89]

Although the *Morton Salt* inference is broad, it is important to note that the opinion stressed that the discount was substantial,[90] suggesting that a price difference that was unlikely to be reflected in price may not violate § 2(a). Indeed, even though the *Falls City* Court seems to stand firm on the *Morton Salt* inference, it, too, emphasized the importance of the *Morton Salt* factual context by characterizing *Morton Salt* as permitting the inference of injury to competition when there is "proof of substantial price discrimination between competing purchasers over time . . . ."[91] Moreover, the *Falls City* Court expressly recognized the possibility that the inference may be rebutted by "evidence breaking the causal connection between price difference and lost sales and profits."[92] This *dicta* reflects the outcome in some lower court decisions in which the inference of competitive injury was not permitted because the facts were not sufficiently similar to *Morton Salt*.[93]

The *Morton Salt* inference does not apply automatically when a seller makes a good available to buyers at different prices depending in their position in the chain of distribution. For example, one may take the view that a wholesaler buying from a manufacturer and supplying storage and transportation services in entitled to a lower price than a retailer to whom the manufacturer sells directly. This so–called "functional discount" is a result of the fact that the buyers differ in the marketing functions they provide. According to the Supreme Court in a recent decision, *Texaco v. Hasbrouck*,[94] the presumption of competitive harm is not warranted when the discount does no more than provide "due recognition and reimbursement for actual marketing functions."[95]

One of the issues created by *Morton Salt* is whether defendants in a secondary–line case may overcome the inference of competitive harm by

---

[89] *Id.* at 436.

[90] *Id.* at 437.

[91] *Id.* at 435.

[92] *Id.*

[93] *See, e.g., Minneapolis–Honeywell Regulator Co. v. F.T.C.*, 191 F.2d 786 (7th Cir. 1951), *cert. dismissed*, 344 U.S. 206 (1952).

[94] 496 U.S. 543 (1990). The Court seemed to view the discount as raising a "tertiary–line" issue since the impact was at the retail level and the favored buyers were distributors that purchased from Texaco and sold to retailers.

[95] *Id.* at 562. Interestingly, the defendant, Texaco, was unable to establish the necessary connection between the discounts offered to distributors and the services those distributors provided.

demonstrating that the market itself is has not become less competitive. The issue is fundamental to antitrust and requires a response to the age–old question of whether the antitrust laws protect competitors or competition. In the case of the Robinson–Patman Act there seems to be little debate that the purpose of the Act was to protect small competitors. Still, in an effort to reconcile secondary–line cases with the rest of antitrust, some courts have indicated that defendants may escape liability by showing that the market did not become less competitive[96] while others have rejected this view.[97]

The pressure for this interpretation may have grown after *Brown & Williamson Tobacco*; perhaps price discrimination law generally should be brought into line with the rest of antitrust law. A number of courts have rejected this extension of *Brown & Williams Tobacco*[98] by relying on the fact that the *Brown & Williams Tobacco* Court was only faced with the issue of primary–line price discrimination. More importantly, however, courts have noted the distinct rationale for the passage of the Robinson–Patman Act. Thus, "the Robinson–Patman Act's amendments to the Clayton Act stemmed from dissatisfaction with the original Clayton Act's inability to prevent large retail chains from obtaining volume discounts from suppliers, at the disadvantage of small retailers who competed with chains."[99]

[2] Showing Actual Harm

Although *Falls City* and *Hasbrouck* suggest limitations on the *Morton Salt* inference, the Court's 1981 decision in *J. Truett Payne Co. v. Chrysler Motor Corp.*[100] may be more important in this respect. In *Truett Payne*, the Court, relying primarily on *Brunswick Corp. v. Pueblo Bowl–O–Mat, Inc.*,[101] distinguished the applicable substantive statute, § 2(a) of the Robinson–Patman Act, from § 4 of the Clayton Act, which is the relevant remedial statute when a private plaintiff seeks treble damages. According to the Court, the *Morton Salt* inference is sufficient to establish a *prima facie* substantive violation or that an injury may result. In order to recover treble damages under § 4, though, "a plaintiff must make some showing of actual injury attributable to something the antitrust laws were designed to prevent."[102] Since the antitrust laws protect competition, not

---

[96] *See, e.g., Boise Cascade Corp. v. FTC*, 837 F.2d 1127 (D.C. Cir. 1987).

[97] *See, e.g., J.F. Feeser v. Serv–A–Portion, Inc.*, 909 F.2d 1524 (3d Cir. 1990) *cert. denied* 499 U.S. 921 (1991); *George Haug Co. v. Rolls Royce Motor Co.*, 148 F.2d 136 (2nd Cir. 1998).

[98] *See, e.g., Coastal Fuels of Puerto Rico v. Caribbean Petroleum Corp.*, 79 F.3d 182 (1st Cir. 1996); *Chroma Lighting v. GTE Products Corp.*, 111 F.3d 653 (9th Cir. 1997); *Allied Sales and Service, Inc., v. Global Industrial Technologies*, 2000 U.S. Dist. LEXIS 7774 (S.D. Ala. May 1, 2000). *But see Bob Nicholson Appliance, Inc. v. Maytag Co.* 883 F. Supp. 321 (S.D. Ind. 1994).

[99] *Coastal Fuels*, 79 F.3d at 192.

[100] 451 U.S. 557 (1981).

[101] 429 U.S. 477 (1977).

[102] 451 U.S. at 562.

competitors,[103] it follows that the private plaintiff must demonstrate that the damages were associated with an actual decline in competition.[104] The Court specifically rejected the argument that plaintiff was entitled to "automatic damages" calculated by multiplying the amount of "overcharge" times the number of units purchased.[105]

Truett Payne is consistent with other recent Supreme Court decisions that restrict "private" attorney general enforcement of the antitrust laws.[106] In its wake, *Morton Salt* loses some of its clout. If the plaintiff can meet the requirements of § 4 of the Clayton Act by showing actual harm flowing from a less competitive market, there is far less need to rely on the *Morton Salt* inference of harm. For now, *Morton Salt* appears to be the relevant standard if the FTC or Justice Department were inclined to enforce § 2(a). And, *Morton Salt* also may assist the private plaintiff requesting injunctive relief. After the Court's § 4 decision in *Cargill, Inc. v. Monfort of Colorado*,[107] however, this latter possibility is in doubt.

§ 8.05　Seller's Affirmative Defenses

The Robinson–Patman Act provides two basic defenses. The "cost justification" defense is included as a proviso to § 2(a) and is, therefore, applicable to price differences alone. The "meeting competition defense," on the other hand, is found in § 2(b) and by its terms applies to differences in price, services or facilities. A third defense worth noting, but infrequently invoked, permits price differences associated with "price changes . . . in response to changing conditions affecting the market for or the marketability of the goods concerned . . . ."[108]

[A]　Cost Justification

[1]　The Basic Defense

The cost justification defense permits a seller who has charged different prices to escape liability by showing that the prices reflect "due allowance for cost of manufacture, sale or delivery . . . resulting from the differing methods or quantities in which such commodities are . . . sold or delivered."[109] In theory, the application of a cost–based defense could bring

---

[103] *Brown Shoe v. U.S.*, 370 U.S. 294, 320 (1962).

[104] *See* Chapter 3, § 3.02[B]. *See generally* Blair and Harrison, *Rethinking Antitrust Injury*, 42 Vand. L.R. 1540 (1989).

[105] 451 U.S. at 561.

[106] *See Brunswick Corp. v. Pueblo Bowl–O–Mat Corp.*, 429 U.S. 477 (1977); *Cargill, Inc. v. Monfort of Colorado*, 479 U.S. 104 (1986).

[107] *Cargill, Inc. v. Monfort of Colorado*, 479 U.S. 104 (1986). *See* discussion in Chapter 3.

[108] 15 U.S.C. § 13(a) (1976). *See, e.g., Bargain Car Wash. Inc. v. Standard Oil Co. (Ind.)*, 466 F.2d 1163 (7th Cir. 1972).

[109] 15 U.S.C. § 13(a) (1976). Professor Areeda notes that a policy of marginal cost pricing probably would not satisfy this requirement. P. Areeda, *supra* note 41 at 1104.

enforcement of the Act into conformity with the economist's definition of price discrimination. This has not occurred and the defense, for the most part, has not been of great value to defendants.[110] The problem lies in the fact that the matching of costs and prices required to successfully employ the defense is not always likely to be gleaned from ordinary accounting records.[111] Thus, potentially costly and extensive cost accounting procedures must be developed in anticipation of a possible Robinson–Patman Act charge. Moreover, although the FTC and the courts have permitted the grouping of sales and the use of averages to simplify the defense, a problem arises when members of a classification do not share common characteristics.[112]

[2] *United States v. Borden*

The most important judicial review of the cost justification defense occurred in 1962 in *United States v. Borden*.[113] Two Chicago dairies, Borden and Bowman, were charged with violating the Robinson–Patman Act by granting grocery–store chains discounts in excess of discounts available to independent stores. Buyers were given percentage discounts that increased with volume to a maximum level. The grocery store chains, however, were granted a flat rate discount that was more favorable than the maximum discount available to others and which was not dependent on volume.[114]

Both dairies introduced cost studies to justify the differential. Borden's cost justification study was based on a comparison of its average cost per $100 of sales to the chains with the average cost per $100 of sales to the independents. Bowman based its study on differences in volume and delivery methods. In particular, it noted that deliverymen spent a substantial amount of time on services that benefitted only the independents.[115]

The Court analyzed how accurately the price differences reflected the costs of serving individual buyers. Borden's study was rejected because in many instances buyers were not classified in accordance with the costs of serving them. For example, although the distinction between chains and large independents was based essentially on differences in average volume, there were independents with volumes higher than some chains. In addition, all independents were assigned costs associated with cash collections

---

[110] *See Automatic Canteen Co. of Am. v. FTC*, 346 U.S. 61, 79 (1953); *Sylvania Elec. Prods.*, 51 F.T.C. 282, 290 (1954). *See generally* H. Shniderman, *supra* note 8 at 95–123; Hansen, *supra* note 1, at 1142–45.

[111] *See* F. Rowe, *supra* note 1 at 303–06; Freer, *Accounting Problems Under the Robinson–Patman Act*, 65 J. Acct. 480 (1938).

[112] *See Master Lock Co.*, 27 F.T.C. 982 (1938); *International Salt Co. & E. Salt Co.*, 49 F.T.C. 138 (1952); *American Motors Corp. v. FTC*, 384 F.2d 247 (6th Cir. 1967); *Curtiss Candy Co.*, 44 F.T.C. 237 (1947); *See generally*, Standridge, *An Analysis of the Cost Justification Defense Under Section 2(a) of the Robinson– Patman Act*, 9 Rut. Cam. L.J. 219, 230–33 (1978).

[113] 370 U.S. 460 (1962).

[114] *Id.* at 463.

[115] *Id.* at 470.

but not all independents paid cash.[116] Bowman's customer classification scheme was found to suffer from similar arbitrary divisions and cost assignments.[117]

[3] The "Cost Justification" Standard

In applying its somewhat exacting requirements, the Court announced the standard for reviewing cost classifications:

> A balance is struck by the use of classes for cost justification which are composed of members of such selfsameness as to make the averaging of the cost of dealing with the group a valid and reasonable indicium of the cost of dealing with any specific group member. High on the list of "musts" in the use of the average cost of customer groupings under the proviso of [section] 2(a) is a close resemblance of the individual members of each group on the essential point or points which determine the costs considered.[118]

The general test, as articulated in *Borden*, offers little in the way of certainty with respect to the degree of "selfsameness" required. Nor does the test take into consideration the fact that different sellers may face very different obstacles in determining the costs to be attributed to a particular buyer or group of buyers.[119] Although there are occasional cases that reflect a more receptive attitude toward the cost justification defense, no clear trend has been established.[120]

[B] Meeting Competition

The "meeting competition" defense permits a seller to escape liability by showing that a difference in price, or the availability of services or facilities, was the result of a "good faith" attempt to meet an "equally low price of a competitor, or the services or facilities furnished by a competitor." The defense is limited to attempts to meet, not beat, competition. Although there has been some division of authority on the issue, it now appears that the defense is available whether the action was designed to retain old customers or gain new ones.[121] The defense is available only when the seller is responding to a direct competitor.[122] Discrimination designed to assist a customer in competition with one of it's own competitors has been regarded

---

[116] *Id.*

[117] *Id.*

[118] *Id.* at 469.

[119] *See generally* Standridge, *supra* note 112.

[120] *See, e.g., FTC v. Standard Motor Products*, 371 F.2d 613 (2d Cir. 1967); *American Motors Corp. v. FTC*, 384 F.2d 247 (6th Cir. 1967), *cert. denied, FTC v. American Motors Corp.* 390 U.S. 1012 (1968). *See generally*, F. Rowe. *supra* note 1, at 276–94; H. Shniderman, *supra* note 8 at 15–23.

[121] *See Falls City Indus., Inc. v. Vanco Beverages, Inc.*, 460 U.S. 428 (1983).

[122] *See FTC v. Sun Oil Co.*, 371 U.S. 505 (1963); *see also Exxon Corp. v. Governor of Maryland*, 437 U.S. 117 (1978).

as falling outside the defense.[123] Although it was initially interpreted rather narrowly, the "meeting competition" defense has always offered greater hope to defendants than the "cost justification" defense. Recent decisions strengthen it further.[124]

The "meeting competition" defense is available only to sellers who act in "good faith" when attempting to equal the terms of competitors. This is important because a "good faith" effort that overshoots its goal and actually undercuts competitors still falls within the defense. The issue of what constitutes good faith, however, has been an area of considerable uncertainty and can arise in two contexts.

[1] Good Faith: Verification and Information Exchange

A pivotal issue in the "meeting competition" defense is whether the seller's price differential is based on sufficient information about actions of competitors to be regarded as a good faith response. In *FTC v. A.E. Staley Manufacturing Co.*, the Supreme Court announced that the defendant must show "the existence of facts which would lead a reasonably prudent person to believe"[125] that the discrimination was necessary to meet the offers of competitors. In applying the standard, the Court upheld the Commission's finding that responding to "verbal information received from salesmen, brokers or intending purchasers," in the absence of independent efforts to "investigate or verify" did not satisfy the good faith standard.[126]

The issue of verification can leave defendant in a quandary. On one hand, steps taken to verify the prices charged by competitors may violate § 1 of the Sherman Act.[127] On the other hand, different treatment that is not based on sufficient evidence may leave the seller unable to successfully invoke the "meeting competition" defense. The Supreme Court addressed this dilemma in *U.S. v. United States Gypsum*[128] in which defendants charged with a violation of § 1 of the Sherman Act attempted to justify their price information exchanges as necessary to comply with the terms of the meeting competition defense.[129] The Court noted the dangers inherent in exchanges and the limited reliability of exchanges as a means of verifying prices.[130] It indicated that the "meeting competition" defense did not require direct discussions between competitors.[131] The Court did not go so far as to suggest that the defense was available to a seller who casually

---

[123] *FTC v. Sun Oil Co.*, 371 U.S. 505 (1963).

[124] *See, e.g., Falls City Indus., Inc. v. Vanco Beverage, Inc.*, 460 U.S. 428 (1983).

[125] 324 U.S. 746, 759 (1945).

[126] *Id.* at 758.

[127] *United States v. Container Corp. of America*, 393 U.S. 333 (1969); *United States v. United States Gypsum*, 438 U.S. 422 (1978).

[128] 438 U.S. 422 (1978).

[129] *Id.* at 448.

[130] *Id.* at 456.

[131] *Id.* at 457.

relied on "uncorroborated reports of buyers."[132] It listed, however, independent factors that a seller could rely upon, short of inter–seller verification, to develop a good faith belief that a concession was necessary. These included reports from customers other than those granted the favorable terms, threats of termination, and examination of general market data. It now seems clear that this list includes reports from established customers.[133]

[2] Good Faith: Breadth of Response

The issue of good faith also has arisen when sellers have responded to competitors with a pricing system or area–wide price cuts as opposed to customer–by–customer concessions. The issue is one which, until recently, divided the circuits.[134] The difference between circuits can be traced to *Staley* which rejected the "meeting competition" defense offered for a discriminatory pricing system apparently because the system was not designed to respond to "individual competitive situations."[135] Significantly, the pricing system at issue in *Staley*, a basing point system, was instituted in order to match an illegal basing point system of the defendant's competitor. Thus, the case could stand for the proposition that meeting competition must be on a consumer–specific basis. Alternatively, it suggests that one may not discriminate in order to meet the competition of a rival whose pricing scheme violates the Robinson–Patman Act. *Falls City Industry, Inc. v. Vanco Beverage, Inc.* clarified the issue, indicating that "good faith" did not require consumer–specific pricing. The standard adopted was whether the discriminating seller's area–wide scheme reflected a reasonable belief "that the lower price he charged was generally available from his competitors throughout the territory and throughout the period in which he made the lower price available."[136]

§ 8.06 The *Per Se* Offenses

[A] Section 2(c): Unlawful Brokerage Payments

Three components of the Robinson–Patman Act, — §§ 2(c),(d) and (e) — can be regarded as *per se* in character since they do not require a showing of competitive harm as does § 2(a). Section 2(c) is designed to eliminate price concessions disguised as payments or discounts for brokerage services

---

[132] *Id.* at 453.

[133] *See, e.g., Great Atlantic & Pacific Tea Co. v. FTC*, 440 U.S. 69 (1970).

[134] *See, e.g., Exquisite Form Brassiere. Inc. v. FTC*, 360 F.2d 492 (D.C. Cir. 1965), *cert. denied*, 384 U.S. 459 (1966) (individual customer response required); *William Inglis & Sons Baking Co. v. ITT Continental Baking Co.* 668 F.2d 1014 (9th Cir. 1981), *cert. denied*, 459 U.S. 825 (1982) (market–wide response permissible if reasonable belief of equally low offers available).

[135] 324 U.S. at 753.

[136] 460 U.S. at 451.

"except for services rendered . . . ." Until 1960, three aspects of § 2(c) seemed fairly clear. First, it appeared to cover only payments or discounts that were linked to a claim that the buyer had performed brokerage–type services.[137] Second, the section was distinct from § 2(a) because it did not require more than one transaction. The final area of relative certainty arose from an narrow interpretation of the exception in § 2(c) for instances in which services were actually rendered by the buyer for the benefit of the seller. Courts decided early that any services rendered by the buyer were really for the buyer.[138] Thus, the section worked as a absolute prohibition of payments or discounts based on the brokerage services provided by the buyer.

All three areas of certainty were upset by the Supreme Court's 1960 decision in *FTC v. Henry Broch & Co.*[139] In *Broch*, an independent broker, working on behalf of the seller, lowered his commission from 5% to 3% in order to bring the price of the commodity down to the level acceptable to the buyer. The buyer made no demand for a brokerage allowance and did not know of the agent's agreement to lower his commission. The Court, in a five to four decision, held that the concession violated § 2(c). The rationale of the Court was that the allowance was ultimately the result of the buying power of the buyer and there was no difference between "the seller's broker splitting his brokerage commission with the buyer and his yielding part of the brokerage to the seller to be passed on to the buyer in the form of a lower price."[140]

According to the Court, the primary problem with the defendant's concession was that it was not part of an overall price decrease but was made for the purpose of obtaining a particular sale. Thus, it was discriminatory. Indeed, the Court observed that, "[a] price reduction based upon savings in brokerage expenses is an 'allowance in lieu of brokerage' when given only to favored customers."[141] The key, therefore, was not simply the allowance but the discriminatory result. Although the majority argued otherwise, it seems inescapable that it had somehow combined § 2(a) with § 2(c) or at least blurred the already thin line separating § 2(a) discrimination from § 2(c) "allowances in lieu of brokerage."[142]

A final element of the *Broch* decision is the Court's language concerning the exception for "services rendered." In *dicta* the Court indicated that if there had been a question of whether the buyer had rendered some service to the seller or to the broker, "[w]e would have quite a different case."[143]

---

[137] *See generally*, F. Rowe, *supra* note 1, at 330; L. Sullivan, *supra* note 6, at 69; Hansen, *supra* note 1, at 1155.

[138] *See* L. Sullivan, *supra* note 6 at 698.

[139] 363 U.S. 166 (1960).

[140] *Id.* at 174 (notes omitted).

[141] *Id.* at 176.

[142] *See, e.g., Thomasville Chair Co. v. FTC*, 306 F.2d 541 (5th Cir. 1962). *See generally*, F. Rowe, *supra* note 1, at 343–46.

[143] 363 U.S. at 173.

This statement has had the effect of reviving the dormant "services rendered" exception.[144]

Although § 2(c) generally has been viewed as complementing § 2(a) in the sense of protecting small competitors, it also has been applied to prohibit certain forms of commercial bribery. There is support for this view in a footnote in *Broch*.[145] In general, the connection to the more typical offense is obvious in that a buyer (or seller)who bribes a broker who represents a seller (or buyer) is typically asking for more favorable treatment that a competitor. Moreover, since § 2(c) does not require competitive harm, the section can and has been interpreted broadly to prohibit bribes as long as payment passes ultimately from the buyer to the seller or vice–versa[146] and somewhere in the process there is "corruption of and agency or employment relationship."[147] The difficulty of defining exactly what is required by this second step is illustrated by *Bridges v. MacLean–Stevens Studios, Inc*,[148] in which parents of a students sued a photography studio that the school had selected to take school photos. The school agreed to make the studio the exclusive supplier in return for a twenty percent commission. The parents argued that the commission amounted to a bride and that the school had an obligation to act on their behalf. The court held that section 2(c) did not apply because the parents were not required to buy the photos at all. Because the school had no control over the parents' ultimate decision, the court found that an agency relationship was lacking.[149]

[B] Promotional Allowances

Under § 2(d) payments by a seller to a buyer for services or facilities used by the buyer in "processing, handling, sale or offering for sale" must be available on a "proportionally equal" basis to all customers. Section 2(e) includes the same prohibition with respect to supplying services or facilities. Like § 2(c), §§ 2(d) and 2(e) are designed to prohibit disguised forms of discrimination. Similarly, competitive impact is not at issue.[150] Unlike § 2(c), both sections clearly require more than one transaction. Additionally, the language of the sections suggests substantial differences between §§ (d) and (e) but they have been interpreted in parallel fashion.[151] For

---

[144] *See, e.g., Thomasville Chair Co. v. FTC*, 306 F.2d 541 (5th Cir. 1962); *Central Retailer–Owned Groceries, Inc. v. FTC*, 319 F.2d 410 (7th Cir. 1963).

[145] *Id.* at 166–167, n.6. *See also Motor Transport Co. v. Trucking Unlimited*, 404 U.S. 508, 513)1972).

[146] *See Seaboard Supply Co. v. Congeleum*, 770 F.2d 367 (3d Cir. 1985); *Environmental Tectonics v. W.S. Kirkpatrick, Inc.*, 847 F.2d 1052 (3rd Cir. 1988).

[147] *Stephen Jay Photography, Ltd. v. Olan Mills, Inc.*, 903 F.2d 988, 993 (1st Cir. 1990).

[148] 201 F.3d 6 (1st Cir. 2000).

[149] *Id.* at 11.

[150] *See FTC v. Simplicity Pattern Co.*, 360 U.S. 55 (1959).

[151] *See, e.g., Zwicker v. J.I. Case Co.*, 596 F.2d 305 (8th Cir 1979); *Kirby v. P.R. Mallory & Co.*, 489 F.2d 904 (7th Cir. 1973), *cert. denied*, 417 U.S. 911 (1974); *Vanity Fair Paper Mills, Inc. v. FTC*, 311 F.2d 480 (2d Cir. 1962).

example, since the meeting competition defense of § 2(b) expressly applies to discrimination in price or services, that defense would seem to apply to § 2(e), but not to § 2(d). In fact, the meeting competition defense has been held to apply to both §§ 2(d) and (e).[152]

Another issue is whether the payment or service is properly characterized as an indirect price discrimination under § 2(a) or as an allowance under either § 2(d) or § 2(e). The distinction is crucial because § 2(a) requires proof of competitive injury. The trend that has emerged is to classify assistance that takes place at the original sale as indirect price discrimination. The seller's assistance with his customer's resale, on the other hand, is likely to be examined under §§ 2(d) or 2(e).[153]

Both §§ 2(d) and 2(e) require that allowances be available to all customers or purchasers[154] on proportionally equal terms. In *FTC v. Fred Meyer, Inc.*,[155] suppliers provided allowances to a retail grocery chain. Comparable allowances were not available to wholesalers or to the retailers to whom those wholesalers sold and who ultimately competed with the grocery chain. The action was defended as falling outside the purview of the "any customer" language of § 2(d) because the disfavored wholesalers were not competing with the grocery chain. Moreover, the "disfavored" retailers were not direct customers of the suppliers.[156] The Court, reasoning that a narrower definition of "customer" would frustrate the purposes of the Act, held that the indirect retailers were within the protected class.[157]

The requirement of proportionally equal terms has been defined primarily by the FTC. According to the Commission, "[n]o single way to proportionalize is prescribed by law."[158] On the other hand, it suggests that allowances be available on a dollar volume or quantity of goods purchased basis.[159] In addition, the seller has an affirmative obligation to insure that all competing customers are aware of the allowances.[160]

§ 8.07 Buyer Liability

[A] Generally

The Robinson–Patman amendments to the Clayton Act were primarily aimed at the secondary–line competitive injury resulting from large chain

---

[152] *See, e.g., Allen Pen Co v. Springfield Photo Mount Co.*, 653 F.2d 17 (1st Cir. 1981); *Shulton Inc. v. FTC*, 305 F.2d 36 (7th Cir 1962).

[153] *See generally, F. Rowe, supra* note 1, at 381–85.

[154] 15 U.S.C. §§ 13(d),(e) (1976).

[155] 390 U.S. 341 (1968).

[156] *Id.* at 348–49.

[157] *Id.* at 354.

[158] FTC, *Guides for Advertising Allowances and Other Merchandising Payments and Services*, 16 C.F.R. § 240.7 (1987).

[159] *Id.*

[160] 16 C.F.R. § 240.8 (1987).

stores obtaining more favorable treatment from suppliers than their independent competitors. In this context the buyer's monopsony power is the likely cause of the discrimination. Buyer liability is, therefore, an important component of the regulatory scheme. Section 2(f) imposes liability on buyers that "knowingly . . . induce or receive a discrimination in price."[161] This is, however, a misleadingly narrow account of the buyer's potential liability under the Act in its entirety. For example, buyer liability is also expressly included in the § 2(c) brokerage allowance provisions. Furthermore, although the promotional allowance sections do not seem to extend to buyer liability and do not constitute "discriminations in price," courts have been receptive to the FTC's labeling of buyers' inducement of allowances as an "unfair method of competition" under § 5 of the Federal Trade Commission Act.[162] In addition, allowances in excess of the actual cost of the services provided may be viewed as a form of indirect price discrimination under § 2(a).[163]

Fred Meyer is illustrative of the various routes to buyer liability.[164] It involved both price discrimination and promotional allowances. The buyer was liable under § 2(f) for inducing the seller to discriminate in terms of price and was found to have engaged in an unfair method of competition by inducing the granting of favorable promotional allowances.[165] The substantive analysis of the Court on the latter issue was, however, devoted entirely to § 2(d) of the Robinson–Patman Act.

[B] The Plaintiff's § 2(f) Case

Because § 2(f) refers to "discrimination . . . prohibited by [the Act]," there is no § 2(f) violation unless there is a price difference that is injurious to competition and not excused by any of the defenses in the Act. According to *American Canteen Co. v. FTC*,[166] the leading § 2(f) case, there can be no violation by a buyer "if the lower prices he induces are either within one of the seller's defenses . . . or not known by him not to be within one of those defenses."[167] The plaintiff's burden of establishing a *prima facie* § 2(f) case includes producing evidence of the discrimination and the lack of a reasonable belief by the buyer that a defense was available.[168] This burden is slightly less onerous than it might initially appear due to the

---

[161] 15 U.S.C. § 13(f) (1976). For a discussion of monopsony power *see* Chapter 6.

[162] *See, e.g., Grand Union Co. v. FTC*, 300 F.2d 92 (2d Cir. 1962); *R.H. Macy & Co. v. FTC*, 326 F.2d 445 (2d Cir. 1964).

[163] *American Booksellers Assn., Inc., v. Barnes & Noble, Inc.*, 135 F. Supp. 2d 1031 (N.D. Cal. 2001).

[164] 390 U.S. 341 (1968).

[165] *Id.* at 345–46.

[166] 346 U.S. 61 (1953).

[167] *Id.* at 74.

[168] *Id.* at 62.

inferences courts have permitted regarding reasonable beliefs on behalf of the defendant.[169]

[C] The Circular "Meeting Competition" Defense

American Canteen specifically concerned a cost justification defense. The Court equivocated on where the burden would lie if a meeting competition defense were raised.[170] This question was settled in 1979 by *Great Atlantic & Pacific Tea Co. v. FTC*,[171] a case which produces an interesting twist in the relationship of § 2(f) to buyer's defenses. A & P was charged with violating section 2(f) when, in negotiations with Borden over the sale of "private–brand" milk, it induced Borden to lower its price. Borden's price turned out not simply to meet but actually beat competing sellers.[172] A & P argued that if Borden had a meeting competition defense, then there was no violation of the Act and it had not violated § 2(f). The Commission's position was that the meeting competition defense should be applied from the point of view of the buyer.[173] In this case, even though the seller might have a good faith belief that it had simply met competition, the buyer knew that, in fact, the seller's price exceeded that standard.

The Court held for the buyer relying on a broad view of the derivative nature of § 2(f).[174] In essence, if the seller would have had a meeting competition defense[175] there can be no § 2(f) violation even if the buyer induces the lower price and knows that the seller, in response to that inducement, has gone further than necessary to meet competition. The Court stopped short of saying that the same standard would apply to a buyer who deliberately misled a seller.[176] On the other hand, it did not adopt Justice Marshall's view, in dissent, that sellers charged with violating § 2(f) should be held to the same standard of good faith as buyers who invoke § 2(b).[177]

---

[169] *See, e.g., American Canteen Co. of America v. FTC*, 346 U.S. 61 (1953); *American Motors Specialties v. FTC*, 278 F.2d 225 (2d Cir. 1960), *cert. denied*, 364 U.S. 884 (1960). *See generally* F. Rowe, *supra* note 1, at 442–46.

[170] 346 U.S. at 78.

[171] 440 U.S. 69 (1979).

[172] *Id.* at 73.

[173] *Id.* at 74–75, n. 5.

[174] *Id.* at 81–82.

[175] *Id.*

[176] *Id.*

[177] *Id.* at 89.

Appendix

SELECTED ANTITRUST STATUTES

SHERMAN ACT

Section 1. Every contract, combination in the form of trust or otherwise, or conspiracy, in restraint of trade or commerce among the several States, or with foreign nations, is declared to be illegal. Every person who shall make any contract or engage in any combination or conspiracy hereby declared to be illegal shall be deemed guilty of a felony, and, on conviction thereof, shall be punished by fine not exceeding $10,000,000 if a corporation, or, if any other person, $350,000, or by imprisonment not exceeding three years, or by both said punishments, in the discretion of the court. [15 U.S.C. § 1.]

Section 2. Every person who shall monopolize, or attempt to monopolize, or combine or conspire with any other person or persons, to monopolize any part of the trade or commerce among the several States, or with foreign nations, shall be deemed guilty of a felony, and, on conviction thereof, shall be punished by fine not exceeding $10,000,000 if a corporation, or, if any other person, $350,000, or by imprisonment not exceeding three years, or by both said punishments, in the discretion of the court. [15 U.S.C. § 2.]

Section 3. Every contract, combination in form of trust or otherwise, or conspiracy, in restraint of trade or commerce in any Territory of the United States or of the District of Columbia, or in restraint of trade or commerce between any such Territory and another, or between any such Territory or Territories and any State or States or the District of Columbia, or with foreign nations, or between the District of Columbia and any State or States or foreign nations, is declared illegal. Every person who shall make any such contract or engage in any such combination or conspiracy, shall be deemed guilty of a felony, and, on conviction thereof, shall be punished by fine not exceeding $10,000,000 if a corporation, or, if any other person, $350,000, or by imprisonment not exceeding three years, or both said punishments, in the discretion of the court. [15 U.S.C. § 3.]

Section 4. The several district courts of the United States are invested with jurisdiction to prevent and restrain violations of sections 1 to 7 of this title; and it shall be the duty of the several United States attorneys, in their respective districts, under the direction of the Attorney General, to institute proceedings in equity to prevent and restrain such violations. Such proceedings may be by way of petition setting forth the case and praying that such violation shall be enjoined or otherwise prohibited. When the parties complained of shall have been duly notified of such petition the court shall proceed, as soon as may be, to the hearing and determination of the case;

419

and pending such petition and before final decree, the court may at any time make such temporary restraining order or prohibition as shall be deemed just in the premises. [15 U.S.C. § 4.]

Section 5. Whenever it shall appear to the court before which any proceeding under section 4 of this title may be pending, that the ends of justice require that other parties should be brought before the court, the court may cause them to be summoned, whether they reside in the district in which the court is held or not; and subpoenas to that end may be served in any district by the marshal thereof. [15 U.S.C. § 5.]

Section 6. Any property owned under any contract or by any combination, or pursuant to any conspiracy (and being the subject thereof) mentioned in section 1 of this title, and being in the course of transportation from one State to another, or to a foreign country, shall be forfeited to the United States, and may be seized and condemned by like proceedings as those provided by law for the forfeiture, seizure, and condemnation of property imported into the United States contrary to law. [15 U.S.C. § 6.]

Section 6a. [This Act] shall not apply to conduct involving trade or commerce (other than import trade or import commerce) with foreign nations unless —

(1) such conduct has a direct, substantial, and reasonably foreseeable effect —

(A) on trade or commerce which is not trade or commerce with foreign nations, or on import trade or import commerce with foreign nations; or

(B) on export trade or export commerce with foreign nations, of a person engaged in such trade or commerce in the United States; and

(2) such effect gives rise to a claim under the provisions of this Act, other than this section.

If [this Act] applies to such conduct only because of the operation of paragraph (1)(B), then [this Act] shall apply to such conduct only for injury to export business in the United States. [15 U.S.C. § 6a; added by Foreign Trade Antitrust Improvements Act of 1982, Pub. L. No. 97–290, § 402 96 Stat. 1246.]

Section 7. The word "person," or "persons," wherever used in sections 1 to 7 of this title shall be deemed to include corporations and associations existing under or authorized by the laws of either the United States, the laws of any of the Territories, the laws of any State, or the laws of any foreign country. [15 U.S.C. § 7.]

CLAYTON ACT

Section 1. (a) "Antitrust laws," as used herein, includes the Act entitled "An Act to protect trade and commerce against unlawful restraints and monopolies," approved July second, eighteen hundred and ninety; sections seventy–three to seventy–seven, inclusive, of an Act entitled "An Act to reduce taxation, to provide revenue for the Government, and for other purposes," of August twenty–seventh, eighteen hundred and ninety–four; an Act entitled "An Act to amend sections seventy–three and seventy–six of the Act of August twenty–seventh, eighteen hundred and ninety–four, entitled 'An Act to reduce taxation, to provide revenue for the Government, and for other purposes,' " approved February twelfth, nineteen hundred and thirteen; and also this Act.

"Commerce," as used herein, means trade or commerce among the several States and with foreign nation, or between the District of Columbia or any Territory of the United States and any State, Territory, or foreign nation, or between any insular possessions or other places under the jurisdiction of the United States, or between any such possession or place and any State or Territory of the United States or the District of Columbia or any foreign nation, or within the District of Columbia or any Territory or any insular possession or other place under the jurisdiction of the United States; *Provided,* That nothing in this Act contained shall apply to the Philippine Islands.

The word "person" or "persons" wherever used in this Act shall be deemed to include corporations and associations existing under or authorized by the laws of either the United States, the laws of any of the Territories, the laws of any State, or the laws of any foreign country.

(b) This Act may be cited as the "Clayton Act". [15 U.S.C. § 12.]

Section 2.

[Amended by the Robinson-Patman Act, reprinted *infra.*]

Section 3. It shall be unlawful for any person engaged in commerce, in the course of such commerce, to lease or make a sale or contract for sale of goods, wares, merchandise, machinery, supplies, or other commodities, whether patented or unpatented, for use, consumption, or resale within the United States or any Territory thereof or the District of Columbia or any insular possession or other place under the jurisdiction of the United States, or fix a price charged therefor, or discount from, or rebate upon, such price, on the condition, agreement, or understanding that the lessee or purchaser thereof shall not use or deal in the goods, wares, merchandise, machinery, supplies, or other commodities of a competitor or competitors of the lessor or seller, where the effect of such lease, sale, or contract for sale or such condition, agreement, or understanding may be to substantially lessen competition or tend to create a monopoly in any line of commerce. [15 U.S.C. § 14.]

Section 4. (a) Except as provided in subsection (b), any person who shall be injured in his business or property by reason of anything forbidden in the antitrust laws may sue therefor in any district court of the United States in the district in which the defendant resides or is found or has an agent, without respect to the amount in controversy, and shall recover threefold the damages by him sustained, and the cost of suit, including a reasonable attorney's fee. The court may award under this section, pursuant to a motion by such person promptly made, simple interest on actual damages for the period beginning on the date of service of such person's pleading setting forth a claim under the antitrust laws and ending on the date of judgment, or for any shorter period therein, if the court finds that the award of such interest for such period is just in the circumstances. In determining whether an award of interest under this section for any period is just in the circumstances, the court shall consider only —

(1) whether such person or the opposing party, or either party's representative, made motions or asserted claims or defenses so lacking in merit as to show that such party or representative acted intentionally for delay, or otherwise acted in bad faith;

(2) whether, in the course of the action involved, such person or the opposing party, or either party's representative, violated any applicable rule, status, or court order providing for sanctions for dilatory behavior or otherwise providing for expeditious proceedings; and

(3) whether such person or the opposing party, or either party's representative, engaged in conduct primarily for the purpose of delaying the litigation or increasing the cost thereof.

(b)(1) Except as provided in paragraph (2), any person who is a foreign state may not recover under subsection (a) an amount in excess of the actual damages sustained by it and the cost of suit, including a reasonable attorney's fee.

(2) Paragraph (1) shall not apply to a foreign state if —

(A) such foreign state would be denied, under section 1605(a)(2) of title 28 of the United States Code, immunity in a case in which the action is based upon a commercial activity, or an act, that is the subject matter of its claim under this section;

(B) such foreign state waives all defenses based upon or arising out of its status as a foreign state, to any claims brought against it in the same action;

(C) such foreign state engages primarily in commercial activities; and

(D) such foreign state does not function, with respect to the commercial activity, or the act, that is the subject matter of its claim under this section as a procurement entity for itself or for another foreign state.

(c) For purposes of this section —

(1) the term "commercial activity" shall have the meaning given it in section 1603(d) of title 28, United States Code, and

(2) the term "foreign state" shall have the meaning given it in section 1603(a) of title 28, United States Code. [15 U.S.C. § 15.]

Section 4A. Whenever the United States is hereafter injured in its business or property by reason of anything forbidden in the antitrust laws it may sue therefor in the United States district court for the district in which the defendant resides or is found or has an agent, without respect to the amount in controversy, and shall recover threefold the damages by it sustained and the cost of suit. The court may award under this section, pursuant to a motion by the United States promptly made, simple interest on actual damages for the period beginning on the date of service of the pleading of the United States setting forth a claim under the antitrust laws and ending on the date of judgment, or for any shorter period therein, if the court finds that the award of such interest for such period is just in the circumstances. In determining whether an award of interest under this section for any period is just in the circumstances, the court shall consider only —

(1) whether the United States or the opposing party, or either party's representative, made motions or asserted claims or defenses so lacking in merit as to show that such party or representative acted intentionally for delay or otherwise acted in bad faith;

(2) whether, in the course of the action involved, the United States or the opposing party, or either party's representatives, violated any applicable rule, statute, or court order providing for sanctions for dilatory behavior or otherwise providing for expeditious proceedings;

(3) whether the United States or the opposing party, or either party's representative, engaged in conduct primarily for the purpose of delaying the litigation or increasing the cost thereof; and

(4) whether the award of such interest is necessary to compensate the United States adequately for the injury sustained by the United States. [15 U.S.C. § 15a.]

Section 4B. Any action to enforce any cause of action under sections 15, 15a, or 15c of this title shall be forever barred unless commenced within four years after the cause of action accrued. No cause of action barred under existing law on the effective date of this Act shall be revived by this Act. [15 U.S.C. § 15b.]

Section 4C. (a)(1) Any attorney general of a State may bring a civil action in the name of such State, as parens patriae on behalf of natural persons residing in such State, in any district court of the United States having jurisdiction of the defendant, to secure monetary relief as provided in this section for injury sustained by such natural persons to their property by reason of any violation of sections 1 to 7 of this title. The court shall exclude from the amount of monetary relief awarded in such action any amount of monetary relief (A) which duplicates amounts which have been awarded for the same injury, or (B) which is properly allocable to (i) natural persons who have excluded their claims pursuant to subsection (b)(2) of this section, and (ii) any business entity.

(2) The court shall award the State as monetary relief threefold the total damage sustained as described in paragraph (1) of this subsection, and the cost of suit, including a reasonable attorney's fee. The court may award under this paragraph, pursuant to a motion by such State promptly made, simple interest on the total damage for the period beginning on the date of service of such State's pleading setting forth a claim under the antitrust laws and ending on the date of judgment, or for any shorter period therein, if the court finds that the award of such interest for such period is just in the circumstances. In determining whether an award of interest under this paragraph for any period is just in the circumstances, the court shall consider only —

(A) whether such State or the opposing party, or either party's representative, made motions or asserted claims or defenses so lacking in merit as to show that such party or representative acted intentionally for delay or otherwise acted in bad faith;

(B) whether, in the course of the action involved, such State or the opposing party, or either party's representative, violated any applicable rule, statute, or court order providing for sanctions for dilatory behavior or otherwise providing for expeditious proceedings; and

(C) whether such State or the opposing party, or either party's representative, engaged in conduct primarily for the purpose of delaying the litigation or increasing the cost thereof.

(b)(1) In any action brought under subsection (a)(1) of this section, the State attorney general shall, at such times, in such manner, and with such content as the court may direct, cause notice thereof to be given by publication. If the court finds that notice given solely by publication would deny due process of law to any person or persons, the court may direct further notice to such person or persons according to the circumstances of the case.

(2) Any person on whose behalf an action is brought under subsection (a)(1) of this section may elect to exclude from adjudication the portion of the State claim for monetary relief attributable to him by filing notice of such election with the court within such time as specified in the notice given pursuant to paragraph (1) of this subsection.

(3) The final judgment in an action under subsection (a)(1) of this section shall be res judicata as to any claim under section 15 of this title by any person on behalf of whom such action was brought and who fails to give such notice within the period specified in the notice given pursuant to paragraph (1) of this subsection.

(c) An action under subsection (a)(1) of this section shall not be dismissed or compromised without the approval of the court, and notice of any proposed dismissal or compromise shall be given in such manner as the court directs.

(d) In any action under subsection (a) of this section —

(1) the amount of the plaintiffs' attorney's fee, if any, shall be determined by the court; and

(2) the court may, in its discretion, award a reasonable attorney's fee to a prevailing defendant upon a finding that the State attorney general has acted in bad faith, vexatiously, wantonly, or for oppressive reasons. [15 U.S.C. § 15c.]

Section 4D. In any action under section 15c(a)(1) of this title, in which there has been a determination that a defendant agreed to fix prices in violation of sections 1 to 7 of this title, damages may be proved and assessed in the aggregate by statistical or sampling methods, by the computation of illegal overcharges, or by such other reasonable system of estimating aggregate damages as the court in its discretion may permit without the necessity of separately proving the individual claim of, or amount of damage to, persons on whose behalf the suit was brought. [15 U.S.C. § 15d.]

Section 4E. Monetary relief recovered in an action under section 15c(a)(1) of this title shall —

(1) be distributed in such manner as the district court in its discretion may authorize; or

(2) be deemed a civil penalty by the court and deposited with the State as general revenues;

subject in either case to the requirement that any distribution procedure adopted afford each person a reasonable opportunity to secure his appropriate portion of the net monetary relief. [15 U.S.C. § 15e.]

Section 4F. (a) Whenever the Attorney General of the United States has brought an action under the antitrust laws, and he has reason to believe that any State attorney general would be entitled to bring an action under this Act based substantially on the same alleged violation of the antitrust laws, he shall promptly give written notification thereof to such State attorney general.

(b) To assist a State attorney general in evaluating the notice or in bringing any action under this Act, the Attorney General of the United States shall, upon request by such State attorney general, make available to him, to the extent permitted by law, any investigative files or other materials which are or may be relevant or material to the actual or potential cause of action under this Act. [15 U.S.C. § 15f.]

Section 4G. For the purposes of sections 15c, 15d, 15e, and 15f of this title:

(1) The term "State attorney general" means the chief legal officer of a State, or any other person authorized by State law to bring actions under section 15c of this title, and includes the Corporation Counsel of the District of Columbia, except that such term does not include any person employed or retained on —

(A) a contingency fee based on a percentage of the monetary relief awarded under this section; or

(B) any other contingency fee basis, unless the amount of the award of a reasonable attorney's fee to a prevailing plaintiff is determined by the court under section 15c(d)(1) of this title.

(2) The term "State" means a State, the District of Columbia, the Commonwealth of Puerto Rico, and any other territory or possession of the United States.

(3) The term "natural persons" does not include proprietorships or partnerships. [15 U.S.C. § 15g.]

Section 4H. Sections 15c, 15d, 15e, 15f, and 15g of this title shall apply in any State, unless such State provides by law for its nonapplicability in such State. [15 U.S.C. § 15h.]

Section 5. (a) A final judgment or decree heretofore or hereafter rendered in any civil or criminal proceeding brought by or on behalf of the United States under the antitrust laws to the effect that a defendant has violated said laws shall be prima facie evidence against such defendant in any action or proceeding brought by any other party against such defendant under said laws as to all matters respecting which said judgment or decree would be an estoppel as between the parties thereto: *Provided*, That this section shall not apply to consent judgments or decrees entered before any testimony has been taken. Nothing contained in this section shall be construed to impose any limitation on the application of collateral estoppel, except that, in any action or proceeding brought under the antitrust laws, collateral estoppel effect shall not be given to any finding made by the Federal Trade Commission under the antitrust laws or under section 45 of this title which could give rise to a claim for relief under the antitrust laws. [15 U.S.C. § 16(a).]

* * *

Section 6. The labor of a human being is not a commodity or article of commerce. Nothing contained in the antitrust laws shall be construed to forbid the existence and operation of labor, agricultural, or horticultural organizations, instituted for the purposes of mutual help, and having capital stock or conducted for profit, or to forbid or restrain individual members of such organizations from lawfully carrying out the legitimate objects thereof; nor shall such organizations, or the members thereof, be held or construed to be illegal combinations or conspiracies in restraint of trade, under the antitrust laws. [15 U.S.C. § 17.]

Section 7. No person engaged in commerce or in any activity affecting commerce shall acquire, directly or indirectly, the whole or any part of the stock or other share capital and no person subject to the jurisdiction of the Federal Trade Commission shall acquire the whole or any part of the assets of another person engaged also in commerce or in any activity affecting commerce, where in any line of commerce or in any activity affecting commerce in any section of the country, the effect of such acquisition may be substantially to lessen competition, or to tend to create a monopoly.

No person shall acquire, directly or indirectly, the whole or any part of the stock or other share capital and no person subject to the jurisdiction of the Federal Trade Commission shall acquire the whole or any part of the assets of one or more persons engaged in commerce or in any activity affecting commerce, where in any line of commerce or in any activity affecting commerce in any section of the country, the effect of such acquisition, of such stocks or assets, or of the use of such stock by the voting or granting of proxies or otherwise, may be substantially to lessen competition, or to tend to create a monopoly.

This section shall not apply to persons purchasing such stock solely for investment and not using the same by voting or otherwise to bring about, or in attempting to bring about, the substantial lessening of competition. Nor shall anything contained in this section prevent a corporation engaged in commerce or in any activity affecting commerce from causing the formation of subsidiary corporations for the actual carrying on of their immediate lawful business, or the natural and legitimate branches or extensions thereof, or from owning and holding all or a part of the stock of such subsidiary corporations, when the effect of such formation is not to substantially lessen competition.

Nor shall anything herein contained be construed to prohibit any common carrier subject to the laws to regulate commerce from aiding in the construction of branches or short lines so located so as to become feeders to the main line of the company so aiding in such construction or from acquiring or owning all or any part of the stock of such branch lines, nor to prevent any such common carrier from acquiring and owning all or any part of the stock of a branch or short line constructed by an independent company where there is no substantial competition between the company owning the branch line so constructed and the company owning the main line acquiring the property or an interest therein, nor to prevent such common carrier from extending any of its lines through the medium of the acquisition of stock or otherwise of any other common carrier where there is no substantial competition between the company whose stock, property, or an interest therein is so acquired.

Nothing contained in this section shall be held to affect or impair any right heretofore legally acquired: *Provided,* That nothing in this section shall be held or construed to authorize or make lawful anything heretofore prohibited or made illegal by the antitrust laws, nor to exempt any person from the penal provisions thereof or the civil remedies therein provided.

Nothing contained in this section shall apply to transactions duly consummated pursuant to authority given by the Secretary of Transportation, Federal Power Commission, Surface Transportation Board, the Securities and Exchange Commission in the exercise of its jurisdiction under section 79j of this title, the United States Maritime Commission, or the Secretary of Agriculture under any statutory provision vesting such power in such Commission, Board, or Secretary. [15 U.S.C. § 18.]

Section 7A. (a) Except as exempted pursuant to subsection (c) of this section, no person shall acquire, directly or indirectly, any voting securities or assets of any other person, unless both persons (or in the case of a tender offer, the acquiring person) file notification pursuant to rules under subsection (d)(1) of this section and the waiting period described in subsection (b)(1) of this section has expired, if —

(1) the acquiring person, or the person whose voting securities or assets are being acquired, is engaged in commerce or in any activity affecting commerce;

(2)(A) any voting securities or assets of a person engaged in manufacturing which has annual net sales or total assets of $10,000,000 or more are being acquired by any person which has total assets or annual net sales of $100,000,000 or more;

(B) any voting securities or assets of a person not engaged in manufacturing which has total assets of $10,000,000 or more are being acquired by any person which has total assets or annual net sales of $100,000,000 or more; or

(C) any voting securities or assets of a person with annual net sales or total assets of $100,000,000 or more are being acquired by any person with total assets or annual net sales of $10,000,000 or more; and

(3) as a result of such acquisition, the acquiring person would hold —

(A) 15 per centum or more of the voting securities or assets of the acquired person, or

(B) an aggregate total amount of the voting securities and assets of the acquired person in excess of $15,000,000.

In the case of a tender offer, the person whose voting securities are sought to be acquired by a person required to file notification under this subsection shall file notification pursuant to rules under subsection (d) of this section.

(b)(1) The waiting period required under subsection (a) of this section shall —

(A) begin on the date of the receipt by the Federal Trade Commission and the Assistant Attorney General in charge of the Antitrust Division of the Department of Justice (hereinafter referred to in this section as the "Assistant Attorney General") of —

(i) the completed notification required under subsection (a) of this section, or

(ii) if such notification is not completed, the notification to the extent completed and a statement of the reasons for such noncompliance, from both persons, or, in the case of a tender offer, the acquiring person; and

(B) end of the thirtieth day after the date of such receipt (or in the case of a cash tender offer, the fifteenth day), or on such later date as may be set under subsection (e)(2) or (g)(2) of this section.

(2) The Federal Trade Commission and the Assistant Attorney General may, in individual cases, terminate the waiting period specified in paragraph (1) and allow any person to proceed with any acquisition subject to this section, and promptly shall cause to be published in the Federal Register a notice that neither intends to take any action within such period with respect to such acquisition.

(3) As used in this section —

(A) The term "voting securities" means any securities which at present or upon conversion entitle the owner or holder thereof to vote for the election of directors of the issuer or, with respect to unincorporated issuers, persons exercising similar functions.

(B) The amount or percentage of voting securities or assets of a person which are acquired or held by another person shall be determined by aggregating the amount or percentage of such voting securities or assets held or acquired by such other person and each affiliate thereof.

(c) The following classes of transactions are exempt from the requirements of this section —

(1) acquisitions of goods or realty transferred in the ordinary course of business;

(2) acquisitions of bonds, mortgages, deeds of trust, or other obligations which are not voting securities;

(3) acquisitions of voting securities of an issuer at least 50 per centum of the voting securities of which are owned by the acquiring person prior to such acquisition;

(4) transfers to or from a Federal agency or a State or political subdivision thereof;

(5) transactions specifically exempted from the antitrust laws by Federal statute;

(6) transactions specifically exempted from the antitrust laws by Federal statute if approved by a Federal agency, if copies of all information and documentary material filed with such agency are contemporaneously filed with the Federal Trade Commission and the Assistant Attorney General;

(7) transactions which require agency approval under section 1467a(e) of Title 12, section 1828(c) of Title 12, or section 1842 of Title 12;

(8) transactions which require agency approval under section 1843 of title 12 or section 1464 of title 12, if copies of all information and documentary material filed with any such agency are contemporaneously filed with the Federal Trade Commission and the Assistant Attorney General at least 30 days prior to consummation of the proposed transaction;

(9) acquisitions, solely for the purpose of investment, of voting securities, if, as a result of such acquisition, the securities acquired or held do

not exceed 10 per centum of the outstanding voting securities of the issuer;

(10) acquisitions of voting securities, if, as a result of such acquisition, the voting securities acquired do not increase, directly or indirectly, the acquiring person's per centum share of outstanding voting securities of the issuer;

(11) acquisitions, solely for the purpose of investment, by any bank, banking association, trust company, investment company, or insurance company, of (A) voting securities pursuant to a plan of reorganization or dissolution; or (B) assets in the ordinary course of its business; and

(12) such other acquisitions, transfers or transactions, as may be exempted under subsection (d)(2)(B) of this section.

(d) The Federal Trade Commission, with the concurrence of the Assistant Attorney General and by rule in accordance with section 553 of title 5, consistent with the purposes of this section —

(1) shall require that the notification required under subsection (a) of this section be in such form and contain such documentary material and information relevant to a proposed acquisition as is necessary and appropriate to enable the Federal Trade Commission and the Assistant Attorney General to determine whether such acquisition may, if consummated, violate the antitrust laws; and

(2) may —

(A) define the terms used in this section;

(B) exempt, from the requirements of this section, classes of persons, acquisitions, transfers, or transactions which are not likely to violate the antitrust laws; and

(C) prescribe such other rules as may be necessary and appropriate to carry out the purposes of this section.

(e)(1) The Federal Trade Commission or the Assistant Attorney General may, prior to the expiration of the 30–day waiting period (or in the case of a cash tender offer, the 15–day waiting period) specified in subsection (b)(1) of this section, require the submission of additional information or documentary material relevant to the proposed acquisition, from a person required to file notification with respect to such acquisition under subsection (a) of this section prior to the expiration of the waiting period specified in subsection (b)(1) of this section, or from any officer, director, partner, agent, or employee of such person.

(2) The Federal Trade Commission or the Assistant Attorney General, in its or his discretion, may extend the 30–day waiting period (or in the case of a cash tender offer, the 15–day waiting period) specified in subsection (b)(1) of this section for an additional period of not more than 20 days (or in the case of a cash tender offer, 10 days) after the date on which the Federal Trade Commission or the Assistant Attorney General, as the case may be, receives from any person to whom a request is made

under paragraph (1), or in the case of tender offers, the acquiring person, (A) all the information and documentary material required to be submitted pursuant to such a request, or (B) if such request is not fully complied with, the information and documentary material submitted and a statement of the reasons for such noncompliance. Such additional period may be further extended only by the United States district court, upon an application by the Federal Trade Commission or the Assistant Attorney General pursuant to subsection (g)(2) of this section.

(f) If a proceeding is instituted or an action is filed by the Federal Trade Commission, alleging that a proposed acquisition violates section 18 of this title, or section 45 of this title, or an action is filed by the United States, alleging that a proposed acquisition violates such section 18 of this title, or section 1 or 2 of this title, and the Federal Trade Commission or the Assistant Attorney General (1) files a motion for a preliminary injunction against consummation of such acquisition pendente lite, and (2) certifies to the United States district court for the judicial district within which the respondent resides or carries on business, or in which the action is brought, that it or he believes that the public interest requires relief pendente lite pursuant to this subsection, then upon the filing of such motion and certification, the chief judge of such district court shall immediately notify the chief judge of the United States court of appeals for the circuit in which such district court is located, who shall designate a United States district judge to whom such action shall be assigned for all purposes.

(g)(1) Any person, or any officer, director, or partner thereof, who fails to comply with any provision of this section shall be liable to the United States for a civil penalty of not more than $10,000 for each day during which such person is in violation of this section. Such penalty may be recovered in a civil action brought by the United States. [15 U.S.C. § 18a(a)–(g)(1).]

* * *

Section 8. (a)(1) No person shall, at the same time, serve as a director or officer in any two corporations (other than banks, banking associations, and trust companies) that are —

    (A) engaged in whole or in part in commerce; and

    (B) by virtue of their business and location of operation, competitors, so that the elimination of competition by agreement between them would constitute a violation of any of the antitrust laws;

if each of the corporations has capital, surplus, and undivided profits aggregating more than $10,000,000 as adjusted pursuant to paragraph (5) of this subsection.

    (2) Notwithstanding the provisions of paragraph (1), simultaneous service as a director or officer in any two corporations shall not be prohibited by this section if —

        (A) the competitive sales of either corporation are less than $1,000,000, as adjusted pursuant to paragraph (5) of this subsection;

(B) the competitive sales of either corporation are less than 2 per centum of that corporation's total sales; or

(C) the competitive sales of each corporation are less than 4 per centum of that corporation's total sales.

For purposes of this paragraph, "competitive sales" means the gross revenues for all products and services sold by one corporation in competition with the other, determined on the basis of annual gross revenues for such products and services in that corporation's last completed fiscal year. For the purposes of this paragraph, "total sales" means the gross revenues for all products and services sold by one corporation over that corporation's last completed fiscal year.

(3) The eligibility of a director or officer under the provisions of paragraph (1) shall be determined by the capital, surplus, and undivided profits, exclusive of dividends declared but not paid to stockholders, of each corporation at the end of that corporation's last completed fiscal year.

(4) For purposes of this section, the term "officer" means an officer elected or chosen by the Board of Directors.

(5) For each fiscal year commencing after September 30, 1990, the $10,000,000 and $1,000,000 thresholds in this subsection shall be increased (or decreased) as of October 1 each year by an amount equal to the percentage increase (or decrease) in the gross national product, as determined by the Department of Commerce or its successor, for the year then ended over the level so established for the year ending September 30, 1989. As soon as practicable, but not later than January 31 of each year, the Federal Trade Commission shall publish the adjusted amounts required by this paragraph.

(b) When any person elected or chosen as a director or officer of any corporation subject to the provisions hereof is eligible at the time of his election or selection to act for such corporation in such capacity, his eligibility to act in such capacity shall not be affected by any of the provisions hereof by reason of any change in the capital, surplus, and undivided profits, or affairs of such corporation from whatever cause, until the expiration of one year from the date on which the event causing ineligibility occurred. [15 U.S.C. § 19.]

*   *   *

Section 12. Any suit, action, or proceeding under the antitrust laws against a corporation may be brought not only in the judicial district whereof it is an inhabitant, but also in any district wherein it may be found or transacts business; and all process in such cases may be served in the district of which it is an inhabitant, or wherever it may be found. [15 U.S.C. § 22.]

Section 13. In any suit, action, or proceeding brought by or on behalf of the United States subpoenas for witnesses who are required to attend a court of the United States in any judicial district in any case, civil or criminal, arising under the antitrust laws may run into any other district: *Provided,* That in civil cases no writ of subpoena shall issue for witnesses living out of the district in which the court is held at a greater distance than one hundred miles from the place of holding the same without the permission of the trial court being first had upon proper application and cause shown. [15 U.S.C. § 23.]

Section 14. Whenever a corporation shall violate any of the penal provisions of the antitrust laws, such violation shall be deemed to be also that of the individual directors, officers, or agents of such corporation who shall have authorized, ordered, or done any of the acts constituting in whole or in part such violation, and such violation shall be deemed a misdemeanor, and upon conviction therefor of any such director, officer, or agent he shall be punished by a fine of not exceeding $5,000 or by imprisonment for not exceeding one year, or by both, in the discretion of the court. [15 U.S.C. § 24.]

Section 15. The several district courts of the United States are invested with jurisdiction to prevent and restrain violations of this Act, and it shall be the duty of the several United States attorneys, in their respective districts, under the direction of the Attorney General, to institute proceedings in equity to prevent and restrain such violations. Such proceedings may be by way of petition setting forth the case and praying that such violation shall be enjoined or otherwise prohibited. When the parties complained of shall have been duly notified of such petition, the court shall proceed, as soon as may be, to the hearing and determination of the case; and pending such petition, and before final decree, the court may at any time make such temporary restraining order or prohibition as shall be deemed just in the premises. Whenever it shall appear to the court before which any such proceeding may be pending that the ends of justice require that other parties should be brought before the court, the court may cause them to be summoned whether they reside in the district in which the court is held or not, and subpoenas to that end may be served in any district by the marshal thereof. [15 U.S.C. § 25.]

Section 16. Any person, firm, corporation, or association shall be entitled to sue for and have injunctive relief, in any court of the United States having jurisdiction over the parties, against threatened loss or damage by a violation of the antitrust laws, including sections 13, 14, 18, and 19 of this title, when and under the same conditions and principles as injunctive relief against threatened conduct that will cause loss or damage is granted by courts of equity, under the rules governing such proceedings, and upon the execution of proper bond against damages for an injunction improvidently granted and a showing that the danger of irreparable loss or damage is immediate, a preliminary injunction may issue: *Provided,* That nothing herein contained shall be construed to entitle any person, firm, corporation, or association, except the United States, to bring suit for injunctive relief against any common carrier subject to the jurisdiction of the Surface

Transportation Board under subtitle IV of Title 49. In any action under this section in which the plaintiff substantially prevails, the court shall award the cost of suit, including a reasonable attorney's fee, to such plaintiff. [15 U.S.C. § 26.]

ROBINSON–PATMAN ACT

Section 1. (a) It shall be unlawful for any person engaged in commerce, in the course of such commerce, either directly or indirectly, to discriminate in price between different purchasers of commodities of like grade and quality, where either or any of the purchases involved in such discrimination are in commerce, where such commodities are sold for use, consumption, or resale within the United States or any Territory thereof or the District of Columbia or any insular possession or other place under the jurisdiction of the United States, and where the effect of such discrimination may be substantially to lessen competition or tend to create a monopoly in any line of commerce, or to injure, destroy, or prevent competition with any person who either grants or knowingly receives the benefit of such discrimination, or with customers of either of them: *Provided,* That nothing herein contained shall prevent differentials which make only due allowance for differences in the cost of manufacture, sale, or delivery resulting from the differing methods or quantities in which such commodities are to such purchasers sold or delivered: *Provided, however,* That the Federal Trade Commission may, after due investigation and hearing to all interested parties, fix and establish quantity limits, and revise the same as it finds necessary, as to particular commodities or classes of commodities, where it finds that available purchasers in greater quantities are so few as to render differentials on account thereof unjustly discriminatory or promotive of monopoly in any line of commerce; and the foregoing shall then not be construed to permit differentials based on differences in quantities greater than those so fixed and established: *And provided further,* That nothing herein contained shall prevent persons engaged in selling goods, wares, or merchandise in commerce from selecting their own customers in bona fide transactions and not in restraint of trade: *And provided further,* That nothing herein contained shall prevent price changes from time to time where in response to changing conditions affecting the market for or the marketability of the goods concerned, such as but not limited to actual or imminent deterioration of perishable goods, obsolescence of seasonal goods, distress sales under court process, or sales in good faith in discontinuance of business in the goods concerned.

(b) Upon proof being made, at any hearing on a complaint under this section, that there has been discrimination in price or services or facilities furnished, the burden of rebutting the prima–facie case thus made by showing justification shall be upon the person charged with a violation of this section, and unless justification shall be affirmatively shown, the

Commission is authorized to issue an order terminating the discrimination: *Provided, however,* That nothing herein contained shall prevent a seller rebutting the prima–facie case thus made by showing that his lower price or the furnishing of services or facilities to any purchaser or purchasers was made in good faith to meet an equally low price of a competitor, or the services or facilities furnished by a competitor.

(c) It shall be unlawful for any person engaged in commerce, in the course of such commerce, to pay or grant, or to receive or accept, anything of value as a commission, brokerage, or other compensation, or any allowance or discount in lieu thereof, except for services rendered in connection with the sale or purchase of goods, wares, or merchandise, either to the other party to such transaction or to an agent, representative, or other intermediary therein where such intermediary is acting in fact for or in behalf, or is subject to the direct or indirect control, of any party to such transaction other than the person by whom such compensation is so granted or paid.

(d) It shall be unlawful for any person engaged in commerce to pay or contact for the payment of anything of value to or for the benefit of a customer of such person in the course of such commerce as compensation or in consideration for any services or facilities furnished by or through such customer in connection with the processing, handling, sale, or offering for sale of any products or commodities manufactured, sold, or offered for sale by such person, unless such payment or consideration is available on proportionally equal terms to all other customers competing in the distribution of such products or commodities.

(e) It shall be unlawful for any person to discriminate in favor of one purchaser against another purchaser or purchasers of a commodity bought for resale, with or without processing, by contracting to furnish or furnishing, or by contributing to the furnishing of, any services or facilities connected with the processing, handling, sale, or offering for sale of such commodity so purchased upon terms not accorded to all purchasers on proportionally equal terms.

(f) It shall be unlawful for any person engaged in commerce, in the course of such commerce, knowingly to induce or receive a discrimination in price which is prohibited by this section. [15 U.S.C. § 13.]

Section 2.

[Rights of action prior to June 19, 1936 (15 U.S.C. § 21a); not reproduced.]

Section 3. It shall be unlawful for any person engaged in commerce, in the course of such commerce, to be a party to, or assist in any transaction of sale, or contract to sell, which discriminates to his knowledge against competitors of the purchaser, in that, any discount, rebate, allowance, or advertising service charge is granted to the purchaser over and above any discount, rebate, allowance, or advertising service charge available at the time of such transaction to said competitors in respect of a sale of goods of like grade, quality, and quantity; to sell, or contract to sell, goods in any part of the United States at prices lower than those exacted by said person elsewhere in the United States for the purpose of destroying competition, or eliminating a competitor in such part of the United States; or, to sell, or contract to sell, goods at unreasonably low prices for the purpose of destroying competition or eliminating a competitor.

Any person violating any of the provisions of this section shall, upon conviction thereof, be fined not more than $5,000 or imprisoned not more than one year, or both. [15 U.S.C. § 13a.]

Section 4. Nothing in this Act shall prevent a cooperative association from returning to its members, producers, or consumers the whole, or any part of, the net earnings or surplus resulting from its trading operations, in proportion to their purchases or sales from, to, or through the association. [15 U.S.C. § 13b.]

FEDERAL TRADE COMMISSION ACT
§§ 1, 5

Section 1. A commission is created and established, to be known as the Federal Trade Commission (hereinafter referred to as the Commission), which shall be composed of five Commissioners, who shall be appointed by the President, by and with the advice and consent of the Senate. Not more than three of the Commissioners shall be members of the same political party. The first Commissioners appointed shall continue in office for terms of three, four, five, six, and seven years, respectively, from September 26, 1914, the term of each to be designated by the President, but their successors shall be appointed for terms of seven years, except that any person chosen to fill a vacancy shall be appointed only for the unexpired term of the Commissioner whom he shall succeed: *Provided, however*, That upon the expiration of his term of office a Commissioner shall continue to serve until his successor shall have been appointed and shall have qualified. The President shall choose a chairman from the Commission's membership. No Commissioner shall engage in any other business, vocation, or employment. Any Commissioner may be removed by the President for inefficiency, neglect of duty, or malfeasance in office. A vacancy in the Commission shall not impair the right of the remaining Commissioners to exercise all the powers of the Commission.

The Commission shall have an official seal, which shall be judicially noticed. [15 U.S.C. § 41.]

Section 5. (a) (1) Unfair methods of competition in or affecting commerce, and unfair or deceptive acts or practices in or affecting commerce, are hereby declared unlawful.

(2) The Commission is empowered and directed to prevent persons, partnerships, or corporations, except banks, savings and loan institutions described in section 18(f)(3) of this title, Federal credit unions described in section 18(f)(4) of this title, common carriers subject to the Acts to regulate commerce, air carriers and foreign air carriers subject to part

A of subtitle VII of Title 49, and persons, partnerships, or corporations insofar as they are subject to the Packers and Stockyards Act, 1921, as amended [7 U.S.C. § 181 *et. seq.*], except as provided in section 406(b) of said Act [7 U.S.C. § 227(b)], from using unfair methods of competition in or affecting commerce and unfair or deceptive acts or practices in or affecting commerce.

(3) This subsection shall not apply to unfair methods of competition involving commerce with foreign nations (other than import commerce) unless —

(A) such methods of competition have a direct, substantial, and reasonably foreseeable effect —

(i) on commerce which is not commerce with foreign nations, or on import commerce with foreign nations; or

(ii) on export commerce with foreign nations, of a person engaged in such commerce in the United States; and

(B) such effect gives rise to a claim under the provisions of this subsection, other than this paragraph.

If this subsection applies to such methods of competition only because of the operation of subparagraph (A)(ii), this subsection shall apply to such conduct only for injury to export business in the United States. [Added by Foreign Antitrust Improvements Act of 1982, Pub. L. No. 97–290, § 403.]

(b) Whenever the Commission shall have reason to believe that any such person, partnership, or corporation has been or is using any unfair method of competition or unfair or deceptive act or practice in or affecting commerce, and if it shall appear to the Commission that a proceeding by it in respect thereof would be to the interest of the public, it shall issue and serve upon such person, partnership, or corporation a complaint stating its charges in that respect and containing a notice of a hearing upon a day and at a place therein fixed at least thirty days after the service of said complaint. The person, partnership, or corporation so complained of shall have the right to appear at the place and time so fixed and show cause why an order should not be entered by the Commission requiring such person, partnership, or corporation to cease and desist from the violation of the law so charged in said complaint. Any person, partnership, or corporation may make application, and upon good cause shown may be allowed by the Commission to intervene and appear in said proceeding by counsel or in person. The testimony in any such proceeding shall be reduced to writing and filed in the office of the Commission. If upon such hearing the Commission shall be of the opinion that the method of competition or the act or practice in question is prohibited by this Act, it shall make a report in writing in which it shall state its findings as to the facts and shall issue and cause to be served on such person, partnership, or corporation an order requiring such person, partnership, or corporation to cease and desist from using such method of competition or such act or practice. Until the expiration of the time allowed for filing a petition for review, if no such petition has been duly filed within such time, or, if a petition for review has been filed within such time then until the record in the proceeding has been filed in a court of appeals of the United States, as hereinafter provided, the Commission may at any time, upon such notice and in such manner as it shall deem proper, modify or set aside, in whole or in part, any report or any order made or issued by it under this section. After the expiration of the time allowed for filing a petition for review, if no such petition has been duly filed within such time, the Commission may at any time, after notice and opportunity for hearing, reopen and alter, modify, or set aside, in whole or in part, any report or order made or issued by it under this section, whenever in the opinion of the Commission conditions of fact or of law have so changed as to require such action or if the public interest shall so require, except that (1) the said person, partnership, or corporation may, within sixty days after service upon him or it of said report or order entered after such a reopening, obtain a review thereof in the appropriate court of appeals of the United States, in the manner provided in subsection (c) of this section; and (2) in the case of an order, the Commission shall reopen any such order to consider whether such order (including any affirmative relief provision contained in such order) should be altered, modified, or set aside, in whole or in part, if the person, partnership, or corporation involved files a request with the Commission which makes a satisfactory showing that changed conditions of law or fact require such order to be altered, modified, or set aside, in whole or in part. The Commission shall determine whether to alter, modify, or set aside any order of the Commission in response to a request made by a person, partnership, or corporation under paragraph (2) not later than 120 days after the date of the filing of such request.

(c) Any person, partnership, or corporation required by an order of the Commission to cease and desist from using any method of competition or act or practice may obtain a review of such order in the court of appeals of the United States, within any circuit where the method of competition or the act or practice in question was used or where such person, partnership, or corporation resides or carries on business, by filing in the court, within sixty days from the date of the service of such order, a written petition praying that the order of the Commission be set aside. A copy of such petition shall be forthwith transmitted by the clerk of the court to the Commission, and thereupon the Commission shall file in the court the record in the proceeding, as provided in section 2112 of title 28, United States Code. Upon such filing of the petition the court shall have jurisdiction of the proceeding and of the question determined therein concurrently with the Commission until the filing of the record and shall have power to make and enter a decree affirming, modifying, or setting aside the order of the Commission, and enforcing the same to the extent that such order is affirmed and to issue such writs as are ancillary to its jurisdiction or are necessary in its judgment to prevent injury to the public or to competitors pendente lite. The findings of the Commission as to the facts, if supported by evidence, shall be conclusive. To the extent that the order of the Commission is affirmed, the court shall thereupon issue its own order commanding obedience to the terms of such order of the Commission. If either party shall apply to the court for leave to adduce additional evidence, and shall show to the satisfaction of the court that such additional evidence is material and that there were reasonable grounds for the failure to adduce such evidence in the proceeding before the Commission, the court may order such additional evidence to be taken before the Commission and to be adduced upon the hearing in such manner and upon such terms and conditions as to the court may seem proper. The Commission may modify its findings as to the facts, or make new findings, by reason of the additional evidence so taken, and it shall file such modified or new findings, which, if supported by evidence, shall be conclusive, and its recommendation, if any, for the modification or setting aside of its original order, with the return of such additional evidence. The judgment and decree of the court shall be final, except that the same shall be subject to review by the Supreme Court upon certiorari, as provided in section 1254 of Title 28, United States Code.

(d) Upon the filing of the record with it the jurisdiction of the court of appeals of the United States to affirm, enforce, modify, or set aside orders of the Commission shall be exclusive.

(e) No order of the Commission or judgment of court to enforce the same shall in anywise relieve or absolve any person, partnership, or corporation from any liability under the antitrust acts.

(f) Complaints, orders, and other processes of the Commission under this section may be served by anyone duly authorized by the Commission, either (a) by delivering a copy thereof to the person to be served, or to a member of the partnership to be served, or the president, secretary, or other executive officer or a director of the corporation to be served; or (b) by leaving a copy thereof at the residence or the principal office or place of business of such person, partnership, or corporation; or (c) by mailing a copy thereof by registered mail or by certified mail addressed to such person, partnership, or corporation at his or its residence or principal office or place of business. The verified return by the person so serving said complaint, order, or other process setting forth the manner of said service shall be proof of the same, and the return post office receipt for said complaint, order, or other process mailed by registered mail or by certified mail as aforesaid shall be proof of the service of the same.

(g) An order of the Commission to cease and desist shall become final

—

(1) Upon the expiration of the time allowed for filing a petition for review, if no such petition has been duly filed within such time; but the Commission may thereafter modify or set aside its order to the extent provided in the last sentence of subsection (b) of this section.

(2) Except as to any order provision subject to paragraph (4), upon the sixtieth day after such order is served, if a petition for review has been

duly filed; except that any such order may be stayed, in whole or in part and subject to such conditions as may be appropriate, by —

(A) the Commission;

(B) an appropriate court of appeals of the United States, if (i) a petition for review of such order is pending in such court, and (ii) an application for such a stay was previously submitted to the Commission and the Commission, within the 30–day period beginning on the date the application was received by the Commission, either denied the application or did not grant or deny the application; or

(C) the Supreme Court, if an applicable petition for certiorari is pending.

(3) For purposes of subsection (m)(1)(B) of this section and 57b(a)(2) of this title, if a petition for review of the order of the Commission has been filed —

(A) upon the expiration of the time allowed for filing a petition for certiorari, if the order of the Commission has been affirmed or the petition for review has been dismissed by the court of appeals and no petition for certiorari has been duly filed;

(B) upon the denial of a petition for certiorari, if the order of the Commission has been affirmed or the petition for review has been dismissed by the court of appeals; or

(C) upon the expiration of 30 days from the date of issuance of a mandate of the Supreme Court directing that the order of the Commission be affirmed or the petition for review be dismissed.

(4) In the case of an order provision requiring a person, partnership, or corporation to divest itself of stock, other share capital, or assets, if a petition for review of such order of the Commission has been filed —

(A) upon the expiration of the time allowed for filing a petition for certiorari, if the order of the Commission has been affirmed or the petition for review has been dismissed by the court of appeals and no petition for certiorari has been duly filed;

(B) upon the denial of a petition for certiorari, if the order of the Commission has been affirmed or the petition for review has been dismissed by the court of appeals; or

(C) upon the expiration of 30 days from the date of issuance of a mandate of the Supreme Court directing that the order of the Commission be affirmed or the petition for review be dismissed.

(h) If the Supreme Court directs that the order of the Commission be modified or set aside, the order of the Commission rendered in accordance with the mandate of the Supreme Court shall become final upon the expiration of thirty days from the time it was rendered, unless within such thirty days either party has instituted proceedings to have such order corrected to accord with the mandate, in which event the order of the Commission shall become final when so corrected.

(i) If the order of the Commission is modified or set aside by the court of appeals, and if (1) the time allowed for filing a petition for certiorari has expired and no such petition has been duly filed, or (2) the petition for certiorari has been denied, or (3) the decision of the court has been affirmed by the Supreme Court, then the order of the Commission rendered in accordance with the mandate of the court of appeals shall become final on the expiration of thirty days from the time such order of the Commission was rendered, unless within such thirty days either party has instituted proceedings to have such order corrected so that it will accord with the mandate, in which event the order of the Commission shall become final when so corrected.

(j) If the Supreme Court orders a rehearing; or if the case is remanded by the court of appeals to the Commission for a rehearing, and if (1) the time allowed for filing a petition for certiorari has expired, and no such petition has been duly filed, or (2) the petition for certiorari has been denied, or (3) the decision of the court has been affirmed by the Supreme Court, then the order of the Commission rendered upon such rehearing shall become final in the same manner as though no prior order of the Commission had been rendered.

(k) As used in this section the term "mandate," in case a mandate has been recalled prior to the expiration of thirty days from the date of issuance thereof, means the final mandate.

(l) Any person, partnership, or corporation who violates an order of the Commission after it has become final, and while such order is in effect, shall forfeit and pay to the United States a civil penalty of not more than $10,000 for each violation, which shall accrue to the United States and may be recovered in a civil action brought by the Attorney General of the United States. Each separate violation of such an order shall be a separate offense, except that in the case of a violation through continuing failure to obey or neglect to obey a final order of the Commission, each day of continuance of such failure or neglect shall be deemed a separate offense. In such actions, the United States district courts are empowered to grant mandatory injunctions and such other and further equitable relief as they deem appropriate in the enforcement of such final orders of the Commission.

(m)(1)(A) The Commission may commence a civil action to recover a civil penalty in a district court of the United States against any person, partnership, or corporation which violates any rule under this Act respecting unfair or deceptive acts or practices (other than an interpretive rule or a rule violation of which the Commission has provided is not an unfair or deceptive act or practice in violation of subsection (a)(1)) with actual knowledge fairly implied on the basis of objective circumstances that such act is unfair or deceptive and is prohibited by such rule. In such action, such person, partnership, or corporation shall be liable for a civil penalty of not more than $10,000 for each violation.

(B) If the Commission determines in a proceeding under subsection (b) of this section that any act or practice is unfair or deceptive, and issues a final cease and desist order, other than a consent order, with respect to such act or practice, then the Commission may commence a civil action to obtain a civil penalty in a district court of the United States against any person, partnership, or corporation which engages in such an act or practice —

(i) after such cease and desist order becomes final (whether or not such person, partnership, or corporation was subject to such cease and desist order), and

(ii) with actual knowledge that such act or practice is unfair or deceptive and is unlawful under subsection (a)(1) of this section.

In such action, such person, partnership, or corporation shall be liable for a civil penalty of not more than $10,000 for each violation.

(C) In the case of a violation through continuing failure to comply with a rule or with section 5(a)(1), each day of continuance of such failure shall be treated as a separate violation, for purposes of subparagraphs (A) and (B). In determining the amount of such civil penalty, the court shall take into account the degree of culpability, any history of prior such conduct, ability to pay, effect on ability to continue to do business, and such other matters as justice may require.

(2) If the cease and desist order establishing that the act or practice is unfair or deceptive was not issued against the defendant in a civil penalty action under paragraph (1)(B) the issues of fact in such action against such defendant shall be tried de novo. Upon request of any party to such an action against such defendant, the court shall also review the determination of law made by the Commission in the proceeding under subsection (b) of this section that the act or practice which was the subject of such proceeding constituted an unfair or deceptive act or practice in violation of subsection (a) of this section.

(3) The Commission may compromise or settle any action for a civil penalty if such compromise or settlement is accompanied by a public statement of its reasons and is approved by the court.

(n) The Commission shall have no authority under this section or section 18 of this act to declare unlawful an act or practice on the grounds that such act or practice is unfair unless the act or practice causes or is likely to cause substantial injury to consumers which is not reasonably avoidable by consumers themselves and not outweighed by countervailing benefits to consumers or competition. In determining whether an act or practice is unfair, the Commission may consider established public policies as evidence to be considered with all other evidence. Such public policy considerations may not serve as primary basis for such determination. [15 U.S.C. § 45.]

TABLE OF CASES

[References are to page and footnote numbers. Italic page numbers indicate where a case is discussed in some detail.]

A

[References are to page and footnote numbers. Italic page numbers indicate where a case is discussed in some detail.]

[References are to page and footnote numbers. Italic page numbers indicate where a case is discussed in some detail.]

[References are to page and footnote numbers. Italic page numbers indicate where a case is discussed in some detail.]

[References are to page and footnote numbers. Italic page numbers indicate where a case is discussed in some detail.]

[References are to page and footnote numbers. Italic page numbers indicate where a case is discussed in some detail.]

[References are to page and footnote numbers. Italic page numbers indicate where a case is discussed in some detail.]

[References are to page and footnote numbers. Italic page numbers indicate where a case is discussed in some detail.]

[References are to page and footnote numbers. Italic page numbers indicate where a case is discussed in some detail.]

[References are to page and footnote numbers. Italic page numbers indicate where a case is discussed in some detail.]

[References are to page and footnote numbers. Italic page numbers indicate where a case is discussed in some detail.]

[References are to page and footnote numbers. Italic page numbers indicate where a case is discussed in some detail.]

INDEX

[References are to pages.]

[References are to pages.]

[References are to pages.]

[References are to pages.]

[References are to pages.]

[References are to pages.]